W9-AKV-732

Norway

THE ROUGH GUIDE

written and researched by

Phil Lee

with additional research by

Jules Brown

THE ROUGH GUIDES

THE ROUGH GUIDES

TRAVEL GUIDES • PHRASEBOOKS • MUSIC AND REFERENCE GUIDES

 We set out to do something different when the first Rough Guide was published in 1982. Mark Ellingham, just out of university, was travelling in Greece. He brought along the popular guides of the day, but found they were all lacking in some way. They were either strong on ruins and museums but went on for pages without mentioning a beach or taverna. Or they were so conscious of the need to save money that they lost sight of Greece's cultural and historical significance. Also, none of the books told him anything about Greece's contemporary life – its politics, its culture, its people, and how they lived.

So with no job in prospect, Mark decided to write his own guidebook, one which aimed to provide practical information that was second to none, detailing the best beaches and the hottest clubs and restaurants, while also giving hard-hitting accounts of every sight, both famous and obscure, and providing up-to-the-minute information on contemporary culture. It was a guide that encouraged independent travellers to find the best of Greece, and was a great success, getting shortlisted for the Thomas Cook travel guide award, and encouraging Mark, along with three friends, to expand the series.

The Rough Guide list grew rapidly and the letters flooded in, indicating a much broader readership than had been anticipated, but one which uniformly appreciated the Rough Guide mix of practical detail and humour, irreverence and enthusiasm. Things haven't changed. The same four friends who began the series are still the caretakers of the Rough Guide mission today: to provide the most reliable, up-to-date and entertaining information to independent-minded travellers of all ages, on all budgets.

We now publish more than 150 titles and have offices in London and New York. The travel guides are written and researched by a dedicated team of more than 100 authors, based in Britain, Europe, the USA and Australia. We have also created a unique series of phrasebooks to accompany the travel series, along with an acclaimed series of music guides, and a best-selling pocket guide to the Internet and World Wide Web. We also publish comprehensive travel information on our web site:

www.roughguides.com

HELP US UPDATE

We've gone to a lot of effort to ensure that the second edition of The Rough Guide to Norway is accurate and up-to-date. However, things change – places get "discovered", opening hours are notoriously fickle, restaurants and rooms raise prices or lower standards. If you feel we've got it wrong or left something out, we'd like to know, and if you can remember the address, the price, the time, the phone number, so much the better.

We'll credit all contributions, and send a copy of the next edition (or any other Rough Guide if you prefer) for the best letters. Please mark letters: "Rough Guide Norway Update" and send to:
Rough Guides, 62–70 Shorts Gardens, London WC2H 9AB, or Rough Guides, 375 Hudson St, New York NY 10014.
Or send email to: mail@roughguides.co.uk
Online updates about this book can be found on Rough Guides' Web site at www.roughguides.com

Norway

THE ROUGH GUIDE

There are more than one hundred and fifty Rough Guide titles
covering destinations from Amsterdam to Zimbabwe

Forthcoming titles include

Beijing • Cape Town • Croatia • Ecuador • Switzerland

Rough Guide Reference Series

Classical Music • Drum 'n' Bass • English Football • European Football
House • The Internet • Jazz • Music USA • Opera • Reggae
Rock Music • Techno • World Music

Rough Guide Phrasebooks

Czech • Dutch • Egyptian Arabic • European Languages • French • German
Greek • Hindi & Urdu • Hungarian • Indonesian • Italian • Japanese
Mandarin Chinese • Mexican Spanish • Polish • Portuguese • Russian
Spanish • Swahili • Thai • Turkish • Vietnamese

Rough Guides on the Internet

www.roughguides.com

ROUGH GUIDE CREDITS

Text editor: Richard Lim
Series editor: Mark Ellingham
Editorial: Martin Dunford, Jonathan Buckley, Jo Mead, Kate Berens, Amanda Tomlin, Ann-Marie Shaw, Paul Gray, Helena Smith, Judith Bamber, Orla Duane, Olivia Eccleshall, Ruth Blackmore, Sophie Martin, Geoff Howard, Claire Saunders, Gavin Thomas, Alexander Mark Rogers, Polly Thomas, Joe Staines, Lisa Nellis, Andrew Tomičić, Claire Fogg, Duncan Clark, Peter Buckley (UK); Andrew Rosenberg, Mary Beth Maioli (US)
Production: Susanne Hillen, Andy Hilliard, Link Hall, Helen Ostick, Julia Bovis, Michelle Draycott, Katie Pringle, Robert Evers, Neil Cooper, Niamh Hatton

Cartography: Melissa Baker, Maxine Repath, Nichola Goodliffe, Ed Wright
Picture research: Louise Boulton, Sharon Martins
Online editors: Kelly Cross, Loretta Chilcoat (US)
Finance: John Fisher, Gary Singh, Edward Downey, Mark Hall, Tim Bill
Marketing & Publicity: Richard Trillo, Niki Smith, David Wearn, Jemima Broadbridge (UK); Jean-Marie Kelly, Myra Campolo, Simon Carloss (US)
Administration: Tania Hummel, Charlotte Marriott, Demelza Dallow

ACKNOWLEDGEMENTS

Thanks to Laurence Larroche, for proof-reading; Sam Kirby, for cartography; Silke Kerwick and Robert Mackey, for their help with "Basics"; Helen Ostick, for typesetting; and Sharon Martins, for picture research.

The author's special thanks go to Ruth Rigby, for her careful assistance and cheery company in Oslo – not to mention getting her bag jammed in the lift; Rob Duckett, for his good company also and for hiking round in wet weather bearing a cheerful and determined grin; Tom Ingebrigtsen for helping him with Oslo; Anette Slettbakk for the guided tour of Bergen, and lots of help with the Bergen account; and to Roy Owen for all his detailed checking and advice.

Thanks also to Siri Giil of the Bergen Tourist Board; Alan Doust for hiking hints; and Norvik Press for all their helpful assistance.

Further thanks are also due to all those who wrote in with comments on the first edition, principally: Martin Staniforth; D. Edgar; David Whittaker; Henrietta Dobson; Joan Scott; Jonathan Duke-Evans; Daniel Ross; Eunice Dawson; Carl Levin; Franklin Stephens; Jean White; John McDonald; Andrew Peel; Kevin Osborne; Julia Gessner; Roberto Meliconi; Arthur Bowling; Rolf Luchs; Ralph Hawtrey; Derek Tabor; Alice Brotherton; Esra Bayoglu; Sol Stensland; O. Haugvik; Tim Ryder; and Marlon Tesler.

Finally, last but not least, thanks to my determined and observant editor, Richard Lim, and to Kate Berens for overseeing the whole project.

PUBLISHING INFORMATION

This second edition published March 2000 by Rough Guides Ltd, 62–70 Shorts Gardens, London, WC2H 9AB.

Distributed by the Penguin Group:

Penguin Books Ltd, 27 Wrights Lane, London W8 5TZ

Penguin Books USA Inc., 375 Hudson Street, New York 10014, USA

Penguin Books Australia Ltd, 487 Maroondah Highway, PO Box 257, Ringwood, Victoria 3134, Australia

Penguin Books Canada Ltd, 10 Alcorn Avenue, Toronto, Ontario, Canada M4V 1E4

Penguin Books (NZ) Ltd, 182–190 Wairau Road, Auckland 10, New Zealand

Typeset in Linotron Univers and Century Old Style to an original design by Andrew Oliver.

Printed in England by Clays Ltd, St Ives, PLC.

Illustrations in Part One and Part Three by Edward Briant.

Illustrations on p.1 & p.313 by Henry Iles

© Phil Lee, 2000

No part of this book may be reproduced in any form without permission from the publisher except for the quotation of brief passages in reviews.

384pp – Includes index

A catalogue record for this book is available from the British Library

ISBN 1-85828-524-0

The publishers and authors have done their best to ensure the accuracy and currency of all the information in *The Rough Guide to Norway*, however, they can accept no responsibility for any loss, injury, or inconvenience sustained by any traveller as a result of information or advice contained in the guide.

THE AUTHOR

Phil Lee first experienced Scandinavia as a deckhand on a Danish merchant ship. Subsequent contacts have been less strenuous and have given him an abiding interest in the region. Phil has worked as a freelance author with the Rough Guides for the last twelve years. Previous titles include Mallorca and Menorca, Brussels, Toronto and Canada. He lives in Nottingham, where he was born and raised.

CONTENTS

Introduction ix

• CHAPTER 3: BERGEN AND THE WESTERN FJORDS 155

• CHAPTER 4: TRONDHEIM TO THE LOFOTENS 227

• CHAPTER 5: NORTH NORWAY 278

PART THREE CONTEXTS 313

LIST OF MAPS

MAP SYMBOLS

═══	Major highways	▲	Mountain peak
══	Major road	◉	Accommodation
──	Minor road	⌂	Lodge
▬▬	Pedestrianized streets	ⓘ	Tourist office
- - - - -	Path	✉	Post office
▬·▬·	Railway	⒞	Telephone
— — —	Ferry route	℗	Parking
────	Waterway	★	Bus stop
– – –	Chapter division boundary	▬	Building
▬·▬··	International boundary	⊞	Church (town maps)
▬·· ▬··	County boundary	†₊†	Cemetery
◆	General point of interest		Park
✕	Airport		National park
—Ⓣ—	Tram line		Forest
—Ⓜ—	T-Bane (underground)		Sand/beach
⚓	Church (regional maps)	ᏟᏟᏟ	Glacier

INTRODUCTION

I n a tamed and heavily populated continent, **Norway** remains a wilderness outpost. Everything here is on the grand scale, with some of Europe's finest and wildest land- and seascapes. From the Skagerrak – the choppy channel that separates the country from Denmark – Norway stretches north in a long, narrow band along the Atlantic seaboard, up across the Arctic Circle to the Barents Sea and the Russian border. Behind this rough and rocky coast are great mountain ranges, harsh upland plateaux, plunging river valleys, rippling glaciers, deep forests and, most famously, the mighty fjords which gash deep inland.

The fjords are the apple of the tourist industry's eye, and they are indeed magnificent, but except for the lively capital, Oslo, and perhaps historic Bergen, the rest of the country might as well be blank for all that many visitors know. Few seem aware of the sheer variety of the landscape or the lovely little towns that are sprinkled over it. Neither are the Norwegians given nearly enough credit for their careful construction of one of the most civilized, educated and tolerant societies in the world – one whose even-handed internationalism has set standards that few other European nations can approach. With every justification, the bulk of the population have a deep loyalty for – and pride in – their country, partly at least because independence was so long in coming: after the heady days of the Vikings, Norway was governed by the Danes for four centuries and was then passed to the Swedes, who only left in 1905.

It is the **Vikings** who continue to grab the historical headlines, prompting book after book and film upon film. These formidable warriors burst upon an unsuspecting Europe from the remoteness of Scandinavia in the ninth century. The Norwegian Vikings sailed west, raiding every seaboard from the Shetlands to Sicily, even venturing as far as Greenland and Newfoundland. Wherever they settled, the speed of their assimilation into the indigenous population was extraordinary – William the Conqueror, the archetypal Norman baron, was only a few generations removed from his Viking ancestors – and in the unpopulated Faroes and Iceland, the settlers could begin from scratch, creating societies which then developed in a similar fashion to that of their original homeland.

Norway's so-called "period of greatness" came to an abrupt end: in 1349, an English ship unwittingly brought the Black Death to the country, and in the next two years somewhere between half and two-thirds of the population was wiped out. The enfeebled country was easy meat for the Danes, who took control at the end of the fourteenth century and remained in command until 1814. As colonial powers go, the Danes were comparatively benign, but everything specifically "Norwegian" – from language to dress – became associated with the primitive and uncouth. To redress this state of affairs, Norway's bourgeois nationalists of the mid- and late nineteenth century sought to rediscover – and sometimes to reinvent – a national identity. This ambitious enterprise, enthusiastically undertaken, fuelled a cultural renaissance which formed the backdrop to the work of acclaimed painters, writers and musicians, most notably Munch, Ibsen and Grieg, and the endeavours of explorers like Amundsen and Nansen.

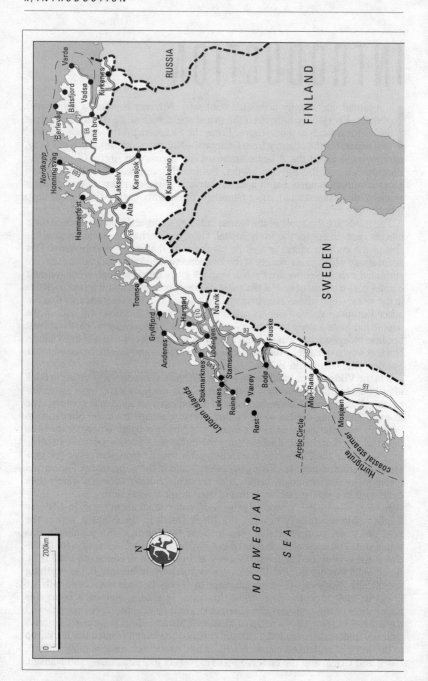

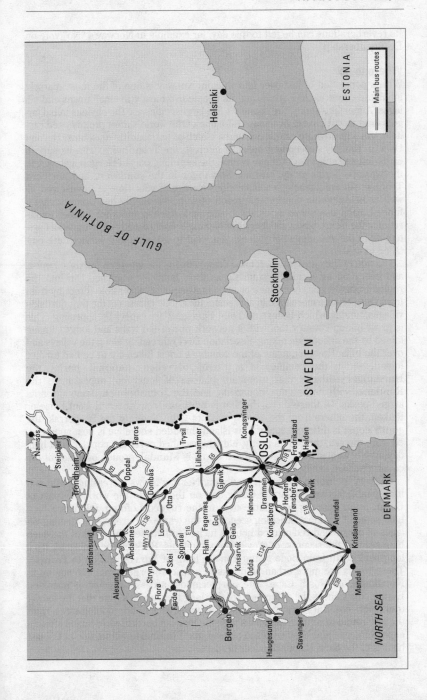

Its reverberations can be felt to this day, for example in Norway's "No" vote on EU membership.

Where to go

With a population of just over four million, Norway is one of the most sparsely inhabited countries in Europe, and its people live mostly in small towns and villages. Almost inevitably, the country's five largest cities are the obvious initial targets for a visit. Urbane, vivacious **Oslo**, one of the world's most prettily sited capitals, has a flourishing café scene and a clutch of outstanding museums. Beyond Oslo, in roughly descending order of interest, are **Trondheim**, with its superb cathedral and charming, antique centre; the beguiling port of **Bergen**, gateway to the western fjords; gritty, bustling **Stavanger** in the southwest; and northern **Tromsø**. All are likeable, walkable cities worthy of your time in themselves, as well as being within comfortable reach of some startlingly handsome scenery. Indeed, each can serve as either a base or a starting point for further explorations: the trains, buses and ferries of Norway's finely tuned public transport system will take you almost anywhere you want to go, although services are curtailed in winter.

Outside of the cities, the perennial draw remains the **western fjords** – a must, and every bit as scenically stunning as their publicity suggests. Dip into the region from Bergen, Åndalsnes or even Stavanger, all accessible direct by train from Oslo, or take more time to appreciate the subtle charms of the tiny, fjordside villages, among which **Balestrand** and **Fjærland** are especially appealing. This is great hiking country too, with a network of cairned trails and lodges (maintained by the nationwide hiking association DNT) threading along the valleys and over the hills. However, many of the country's finest hikes are to be had further inland, within the confines of a trio of marvellous **national parks**: the **Hardangervidda**, a vast mountain plateau of lunar-like appearance; the **Rondane**, with its bulging mountains; and the **Jotunheimen**, famous for its jagged peaks. Of these three, the first is most easily approached from Finse or Rjukan, the others from the comely town of Otta. Nudging the Skagerrak, the **south coast** is different again. This island-shredded shoreline is best appreciated from the sea, though its pretty, old whitewashed ports are popular with holidaying Norwegians; the pick of these towns is **Mandal**, proud possessor of the country's finest sandy beach.

Away to the **north**, beyond Trondheim, Norway grows increasingly wild and inhospitable across the Arctic Circle and on the way to the workaday port of **Bodø**. From here, ferries shuttle over to the rugged **Lofoten Islands**, which hold some of the most ravishing scenery in the whole of Europe – tiny fishing villages of ochre- and red-painted houses tucked in between the swell of the deep blue sea and the severest of grey-green mountains. Back on the mainland, it's a long haul north from Bodø to the iron-ore town of **Narvik**, and on to **Tromsø**. These towns are mere urban pinpricks in a vast wilderness that extends up to **Nordkapp**, or North Cape. The northernmost accessible point of mainland Europe, the Cape is the natural end of this long trek, and it's here that the tourist trail peters out. But Norway continues east for several hundred kilometres, right the way round to remote **Kirkenes** near the Russian border, while inland stretches an immense and hostile upland plateau, the **Finnmarksvidda**, one of the last haunts of the Sami (Lapp) reindeer-herders.

When to go

Choosing when to go to Norway is more complicated than you might expect. The **summer season** – when the midnight sun is visible north of the Arctic Circle – is relatively short, stretching roughly from the beginning of June to the end of August. Visit out of season, and you'll find that tourist offices, museums and other sights have reduced hours, hotels withdraw their generous summer discounts, and buses, ferries and trains run on less frequent schedules. Nevertheless, late May does have its attractions, especially if your visit coincides with the brief Norwegian **spring**, though this is difficult to gauge. Springtime is especially beguiling in the fjords, with myriad cascading waterfalls fed by the melting snow, and wildflowers in abundance. Come before that – from late March to early May – and you're likely to encounter the unprepossessing residue of winter, when the last snow and ice lies soiled on the ground, asphalt dust from studded tyres pollutes city air and the landscape is blankly colourless. **Autumn** is a much better bet, with September often bathed in the soft sunshine of an Indian summer. There are also advantages to travelling during the **winter**, providing you steer well clear of the winter solstice, when the lack of light depresses even the Norwegians, and aim instead for early February up to mid-March. The big incentive to visit at this time of year is the range of **winter sports** – from ice-fishing to dog-sledging and, most popular of all, cross-country and alpine skiing. There are skiing packages to Norway from abroad, but perhaps more appealing – and certainly cheaper – is the ease with which you can arrange a few days' skiing wherever you happen to be. Furthermore, if you are equipped and hardy enough to reach the far north, between November and February there's an above average chance of seeing the phenomenal **northern lights** (Aurora Borealis) beyond the Arctic Circle, and a possibility of glimpsing them as far south as Oslo, too.

Practicalities

From Britain and much of northern Europe, **access** to Norway is easy by plane or ferry, with plenty of scheduled flights and sailings as well as a wide range of complete package deals. There are regular flights from North America and Australasia too, and you can choose to see Norway as part of a wider tour of Europe by train. The majority of visitors arrive at either Oslo or Bergen, each of which is a transport hub, with domestic plane, train, bus and boat services radiating out across the country. Once you're there, you'll also have the opportunity to travel the coast from Bergen to Kirkenes on the Hurtigrute coastal boat, undeniably one of the world's great cruises. Norway's public transport system is punctual and reliable, qualities it shares with an exemplary tourist infrastructure, ensuring that any settlement of any size has a **tourist office** whose employees invariably speak good English. The ease with which information is obtainable helps to keep **costs** down, a useful aid in a country which is, by northern European standards, expensive. However, Norway's high-price reputation is largely based on the cost of consumables – from books to beer – rather than the more substantial items of a traveller's budget like transport and accommodation, for which special deals and discounts are ubiquitous.

Climate

As regards **climate**, the Gulf Stream keeps all of coastal Norway temperate throughout the year, with the warmest months being July and August. Inland, the climate is more extreme – bitterly cold in winter and hot in summer, when temperatures can soar to surprising heights. January and February are normally the coldest months in all regions. Rain is a regular occurrence throughout the year, particularly on the west coast, though there are significant local variations in precipitation.

	Jan	Feb	Mar	Apr	May	June	July	Aug	Sept	Oct	Nov	Dec
AVERAGE DAYTIME TEMPERATURES (°C) AND PRECIPITATION (MM)												
Oslo												
°C	-3.7	-2.8	1.3	6.3	12.6	17.0	18.2	17.2	12.8	7.5	1.5	-2.6
mm	49	36	47	41	53	65	81	89	90	84	73	55
Bergen												
°C	1.5	1.6	3.3	5.9	10.5	13.5	14.5	14.4	11.5	8.7	4.6	1.6
mm	190	152	170	114	106	132	148	190	283	271	259	235
Trondheim												
°C	-3.3	-1.8	1.9	5.4	10.9	13.8	15.1	14.8	11.2	7.0	1.1	-1.8
mm	63	52	54	49	53	68	84	87	113	104	71	84
Tromsø												
°C	-4.7	-4.1	-1.9	1.1	5.6	10.1	12.7	11.8	7.7	2.9	-1.5	-3.7
mm	95	87	72	64	48	59	77	82	102	131	108	106

NORWAY: DISTANCE CHART

DISTANCE IN KM

	Bergen	Bodø	Hamar	Hammerfest	Kirkenes	Kristiansand	Lillehammer	Narvik	Nordkapp	Oslo	Røros	Stavanger	Tromsø	Trondheim	Ålesund
Bergen	0	1380	471	2214	2588	492	439	1561	2283	478	637	170	1844	657	378
Bodø	1380	0	1108	956	1331	1534	1065	304	1025	1217	936	1560	562	723	1010
Hamar	471	1108	0	1942	2316	443	59	1279	2011	123	289	575	1606	385	441
Hammerfest	2214	956	1942	0	494	2368	1899	652	181	2051	1810	2394	549	1567	1844
Kirkenes	2588	1331	2316	494	0	2742	2273	1027	517	2425	2185	2768	944	1931	2218
Kristiansand	492	1534	443	2368	2742	0	471	1715	2437	320	753	245	2054	811	811
Lillehammer	439	1065	59	1899	2273	471	0	1246	1968	167	282	587	1562	342	382
Narvik	1561	304	1279	652	1027	1715	1246	0	721	1398	1123	1741	251	904	1191
Nordkapp	2283	1025	2011	181	517	2437	1968	721	0	2120	1869	2463	609	1626	1913
Oslo	478	1217	123	2051	2425	320	167	1398	2120	0	423	452	1733	494	533
Røros	637	936	289	1810	2185	753	282	1123	1869	423	0	740	1352	166	430
Stavanger	170	1560	575	2394	2768	245	587	1741	2463	452	740	0	1852	837	621
Tromsø	1844	562	1606	549	944	2054	1562	251	609	1733	1352	1852	0	1205	1519
Trondheim	657	723	385	1567	1931	811	342	904	1626	494	166	837	1205	0	287
Ålesund	378	1010	441	1844	2218	811	382	1191	1913	533	430	621	1519	287	0

Ferry crossings not included in distances quoted.

PART ONE

THE
BASICS

GETTING THERE FROM BRITAIN

Getting to Norway by ferry or plane direct from Britain is pretty straightforward, with several options to choose from. If you prefer, you can get there by train or bus via Copenhagen too, though this is much more time-consuming. The details below cover all the major routes to Norway from Great Britain; see p.9 for details of getting there from Ireland. For bus, train and ferry connections to Norway from the rest of Scandinavia, see p.10.

BY PLANE

Although the London–Oslo route bags most of the business, several other **UK airports** have direct services to Oslo too. There are also direct flights from the UK to Stavanger and Bergen, as well as a limited service to Tromsø.

Flying to Norway isn't especially cheap. Low-cost **charter** flights do exist, but they're few and far between, and serve only a few destinations. Special offers are often advertised in many newspapers' weekend travel supplements, or, if you can travel at short notice, Ceefax lists a large number of travel agents touting last-minute discounted tickets. Better still, all major airlines have Web sites giving up-to-the-minute information about timetables and fares and, increasingly, offering on-line booking; there are also a growing number of flight agents' Web sites offering instant access to the best deals. Some of these are listed on p.4; others can be found through the very useful **Cheapflights** (*www.cheapflights. co.uk*), which will signpost you to the booking agent or airline offering the lowest prices. Bear in mind, though, that if you're a student or under 26, it's always worth checking out the student specialist flight agents as well, such as **STA** or **usit CAMPUS** (addresses in the box on p.4).

Standard **fares** vary little between the major scheduled airlines, and you should expect to pay a minimum of £210 plus around £45 tax for a return flight, and at least twice that amount if you're want a fully flexible ticket. If you're able to travel at short notice, however, or pick up a special deal, you can reduce this to between £120 and £150 return. The only **budget airline** operating between the UK and Norway is Ryanair; return flights on its London Stansted–Sandefjord route start at around £80 return plus tax – a real bargain even if Sandefjord is 130km from Oslo (see "Routes", below).

If you're intending to **travel around Norway**, you might also want to consider buying an **airpass**. Widerøe, an SAS partner that flies from Glasgow, does a summertime **Roundtrip Norway** ticket allowing unlimited internal travel (£250) or travel within specified zones (from £140) during a two-week period (with a £75 supplement for an additional week); you must book your flights to and from Norway with them in advance and the cost of these is not included in the price of the pass. Braathens has a similar **Northern Lights Pass**; for details see p.33. SAS also operates various discount schemes, particularly during the summer. It's worth checking out their **Jackpot** and **Get Around Europe** deals.

Finally, package deals may be a viable option, particularly if you're clear about where you want to go and intend to stay for no more than a week; city breaks, especially, can work out very good value.

ROUTES

There's a good choice of **direct flights** from the UK to **Oslo**, with SAS flying **from London** Heathrow up to seven times daily and BA five times daily. From Gatwick, BA operates one or two flights a day and Braathens flies from Stansted twice daily. From elsewhere in the UK, there are flights from **Manchester** run by BA (2 daily) and SAS (1 daily), a daily BA flight from **Aberdeen**, and Braathens flies six times weekly from **Newcastle**. In addition, Ryanair operates

AIRLINES AND ROUTES

Braathens (*www.braathens.no*). Phone enquiries c/o KLM (☎0870/507 4074). London Stansted to Bergen and Oslo, Newcastle to Stavanger and Oslo.

British Airways (☎0345/222111, *www.british-airways.com*). London Heathrow, London Gatwick, Manchester and Aberdeen to Oslo.

British Midland Airways (☎0870/607 0555, *www.britishmidland.com*). Aberdeen to Esbjerg; Edinburgh and Glasgow to Copenhagen; East Midlands and London Heathrow to Amsterdam.

KLM (☎0870/507 4074, *www.klmuk.com*). London Heathrow to Amsterdam; Aberdeen to Bergen and Stavanger.

Maersk Air (☎020/7333 0066, *www.maersk-air.com*). London to Billund and Copenhagen.

Ryanair (☎0870/333 1250 or 0541/569569, *www.ryanair.net/airlines/ryanair*). London Stansted to Oslo (Torp), near Sandefjord.

Scandinavian Airlines (SAS) (☎0845/6072 7727, *www.sas.se*). London Heathrow to Oslo, Stavanger and Tromsø; Manchester to Oslo; Glasgow to Bergen and Stavanger; Aberdeen to Stavanger.

Widerøe Airline (☎0141/887 1381, *www.wideroe.no/english*). Glasgow to Stavanger and Bergen.

two attractively cheap flights daily from London Stansted to **Oslo Torp** airport, near Sandefjord. If you're considering this route, bear in mind that Sandefjord is around 130km south of Oslo, although the airline offers a discounted fare of £12 return on the two-hour bus journey to the capital – ask for details when you book.

The other direct flight destinations from the UK are **Bergen** – reached from **London Stansted** with Braathens (1 daily), from **Aberdeen** with KLM (6 weekly), and from **Glasgow** with Widerøe/SAS (6 weekly) – and **Stavanger**, with flights from **London Heathrow** with SAS (2 daily); from **Aberdeen** with SAS (up to 3 daily), Braathens (up to 2 daily) and KLM (up to 3 daily); from **Glasgow** with SAS/Widerøe (6 weekly); and from **Newcastle** with Braathens (6 weekly). Finally, there's **Tromsø**, reached direct from **London Heathrow** with SAS (twice weekly).

DISCOUNT FLIGHT AGENTS

Alpha Flights (☎020/7609 8188).

APA Travel (☎020/7388 1732).

Benz Travel (☎020/7462 0000).

Dial-a-Flight (☎0870/333 4488, *www.dialaflight.com*). Telephone-only sales of scheduled flights, with an Internet site useful for tracking down bargains.

Flightline (☎01702/715151, *www.flightline.co.uk*). Another telephone-only outfit offering Internet searches for cheap charter and scheduled flights.

North South Travel (☎01245/608291). Friendly, competitive travel agency, offering discounted fares worldwide – profits are used to support projects in the developing world.

STA Travel, 117 Euston Rd, London NW1 2SX, and branches elsewhere in London and in other major cities (☎020/7361 6145, *www.statravel.co.uk*). Worldwide specialists in low-cost flights and tours for students and under-26s.

Trailfinders, 215 Kensington High St, London W8 6BD, and branches elsewhere in London and in other major cities (☎020/7937 5400, *www.trailfinder.com*). One of the best-informed and most efficient agents. Their Web site offers "best buy" information, provides a brochure ordering service and sells travel insurance online.

The Travel Bug, 597 Cheetham Hill Rd, Manchester M8 5EJ (☎0161/721 4000, fax 721 4202); 125 Gloucester Road, London SW7 4SF (☎020/7835 2000, fax 7835 1111). *www.travel-bug.co.uk* Large range of discounted tickets.

Travel CUTS, 295a Regent St, London W1R 7YA (☎020/7255 1944, fax 7528 7532, *www.travel-cuts.co.uk*). British branch of Canada's main youth and student travel specialist.

usit CAMPUS, 52 Grosvenor Gardens, London SW1W 0AG and branches elsewhere in London and in other major cities (☎0870/240 1010, *www.usitcampus.co.uk*). Student/youth travel specialists, with branches also in YHA shops and on university campuses all over Britain.

Flight times range from one hour on the Aberdeen–Stavanger flight to about two hours fifteen minutes from London to Oslo, and four hours fifteen minutes London to Tromsø.

BY TRAIN

Taking a **train** can be a more relaxed, if very long-winded, way of getting to Norway, though it's not a lot cheaper than flying, and is actually more expensive if you're 26 or over. That said, a number of deals and passes make it possible to cut costs, and although some of these are rather more useful if you're touring Scandinavia as a whole, they are still helpful if you're intending to travel round much of Norway by train.

Any rail journey direct from the UK to Norway will take at least 24 hours and you should expect to change trains at least four times. If you're using **Eurostar,** you'll need to aim for Copenhagen following the three-hour trip from London Waterloo to Brussels Midi. Changing as few times as possible, your best bets are via Düsseldorf (around 15hr from Brussels to Copenhagen) or Cologne and possibly Hamburg (a minimum of 12hr). You can then take one of two daily direct trains from Copenhagen through to Oslo S (around 9hr).

Other options include taking the ferry from Hull to Rotterdam, or Harwich to Hook of Holland, but these leave you with an onward journey well in excess of 24 hours. UK to Norway rail **fares** are expensive, starting at about £207 single and £404 return.

RAIL PASSES

One of the most popular deals if you're under 26 is to purchase a **BIJ** ticket, which gives up to forty-percent discount on ordinary fares. Available through Wasteels (see below), these allow as many stopovers as you like and are valid for two

months. Various routes are available, including several Scandinavian destinations. Tickets are direct from the operators (addresses in box below), or from youth and student travel agents. Alternatively, if you're sixty or over, the **Rail Europe Senior Card** gives up to thirty percent discounts on any journeys which cross international frontiers (but not on journeys within countries) in most of Western Europe, including Scandinavia. You can get one if you have a British Senior Citizen Rail Card, available for £18 from any train station.

If you have no clear itinerary, and are under 26, the **InterRail pass** might be a better bet. The pass gives you free travel on all state railways in the countries it covers, though supplements are often payable on the trains you'll most want to use, especially high-speed trains, and there's only a fifty-percent discount in the country where you buy it. This pass also gives discounts on certain ferries between Germany and Scandinavia and on a variety of domestic Norwegian bus and ferry routes (see pp.31–33). Passes are valid in up to seven zones covering most of Europe, the British Isles, Turkey and Morocco, usually for a month – though 22-day passes are also available. To qualify, you have to provide proof that you've been **resident** for at least six months in one of the countries it covers and hold a valid passport. Norway, Sweden and Finland are all in Zone B; Denmark is in Zone C, along with Germany, Switzerland and Austria. Depending on the route you want to take, you may have to buy a pass that covers Zone E (France, Belgium, the Netherlands and Luxembourg) too. A pass covering only one zone and valid for 22 days costs £159, while one-month passes cost £209 for two zones, £229 for three zones, and £259 for four or more zones. The passes are available from many train stations as well as youth and student travel agencies.

RAIL AND COACH TICKET OFFICES

Deutsche Bahn UK, 18 Conduit St, London W1R 9TD (☎020/7317 0919). European rail tickets and passes including Scanrail.

Eurolines, 52 Grosvenor Gardens, London SW1W 0AU (☎0990/808080, www.eurolines.co.uk). European coach operator.

Eurostar, Eurostar House, Waterloo International Station, London SE1 8SE; 102–104 Victoria St, London SW1E 5JL (☎020/7730 8235 or 0990/186 186, www.eurostar.com). Ticket pur-

chasing available at Waterloo International Station, Ashford International and other principal train stations. Channel tunnel services to Paris, or Brussels via Lille.

Rail Europe, 179 Piccadilly, London W1V BA (☎0870/584 8848, www.raileurope.co.uk). European rail tickets and passes.

Wasteels, by platform 2, Victoria Station, London SW1V 1JT (☎020/7834 7066). Youth train and coach ticket specialists.

If you are **26 and over**, you can buy an **InterRail 26-Plus pass** covering some of the countries in the scheme, including Denmark, Norway, Sweden and Finland, as well as the Netherlands and Germany, but not France or Belgium. Current prices are £229 for a single-zone 22-day pass and £279 for a two-zone, one-month pass.

If you're likely to be travelling extensively by train, you would be wise to pick up a copy of the latest monthly *Thomas Cook European Rail Timetable* (the red volume), or its seasonal supplement *Independent Traveller's Edition*, which contains schedules of all major train and ferry routes throughout Europe. For details of discounts and special offers on train travel within Norway, see "Getting Around", p.30.

BY COACH

A **coach** journey to Scandinavia can be an endurance test, but it is often the cheapest way to get from the UK to Norway. That said, savings are generally small and are offset by the additional time spent on the journey as compared with a flight. Only if time is no object and price all-important, or if you specifically do not want to fly, is it really worth taking the bus.

To get to Norway on **Eurolines**, you'll need to change in Copenhagen, from where there are a couple of services a day through to Oslo via Gothenburg (9–10 hrs). There are three direct services a week from London to Copenhagen (20hr 30min), and around six services a week via Amsterdam (total journey time 24–27 hrs). At time of writing, **fares** to all of Eurolines' Norwegian destinations were £115 one-way, £182 return (£108/£172 under-26 or over-60).

Independent operators occasionally offer competition, but at time of writing there are none in the field. Nor are there any through services from anywhere in Britain outside London, so you will either have to go there first, or take a ferry to the Netherlands and a bus from there.

BY CAR FERRY

Two companies – **Fjord Line** and **DFDS Scandinavian Seaways** – operate regular car ferries direct from Newcastle to the west coast of Norway. It's not a short trip, and in rough weather the crossing can seem interminable, but for many Brits (and, heading in the opposite direction, Norwegians) it makes a great way to start a holi-

---

FERRY OPERATORS

Color Line (☎47/81 00 08 11, *www.colorline.com*). Oslo to Kiel (Germany).

DFDS Seaways (☎0990/333000, *www.scansea.com*). Newcastle–Kristiansand–Gothenburg.

Fjord Line (☎0191/296 1313, fax 296 1540). Newcastle to Bergen, Stavanger and Haugesund.

P&O North Sea Ferries (☎01482/377177, *www.ponsf.com*). Hull to Rotterdam and Zeebrugge.

P&O Scottish Ferries (☎01224/572615, *www.poscottishferries.co.uk*). Aberdeen to Lerwick (Shetland), connecting with Smyril crossing (see below).

Smyril Line, *www.smyril-line.fo*, or c/o P&O Scottish Ferries (☎01224/572615). Lerwick (Shetland) to Bergen, mid-May to mid-Sept.

Stena Line (☎0990/707070, *www.stenaline.co.uk*). Harwich to Hook of Holland.

---

day. The Newcastle–Bergen run is especially popular, so book early in summer.

DIRECT ROUTES

Fjord Line sails two or three times a week from **Newcastle to Stavanger and Bergen**, sometimes also calling at **Haugesund**. The Bergen trip takes between 22 and 29 hours and there are sailings all year round, bar a couple of weeks in December and January. DFDS Seaways sails twice weekly between February and December from **Newcastle to Kristiansand**, on Norway's southernmost tip, with an average crossing time of 18 hours.

Fjord Line operates a single-fare-only price structure, with prices starting at around £40 per person one-way, including a berth in a shared cabin in low season. In summer, the equivalent price is £114. From late March to early September, it's cheaper to forego the cabin in favour of a "sleeperette", which reduces the fare to around £50 one-way in mid-season, rising to £90 or £100 in June and July. If you're travelling by car, substantial savings can be made by booking a "car package", allowing up to five people to travel for an inclusive price of £170 one-way in low season, £345 in summer. Note that fifty-percent discounts are available in low and mid-season for travellers with disabilities, people aged over 60, and students. Year-round flat fees apply to the carriage of motorbikes (£30 per trip) and bicycles (£5 per trip).

DFDS Seaways' return fares offer a discount on the standard single, with prices starting at £95 return (£55 one-way) per person in a shared cabin, rising to £180 return (£105 one-way) in high season. If you book at least thirty days in advance, there's an "all in one car" return fare of £315 in low season, £650 throughout July and most of August, covering your car and cabin accommodation for three or four people. Discounts for students (with an ISIC or NUS card) and people over 60 are 25 percent, but apply all year round. Bicycles are carried for free, motorbikes are charged at between £17 and £26 each way.

OTHER FERRY OPTIONS

Clearly, the aforementioned direct ferry services from the UK to Norway are the most convenient options, but there are other, more convoluted possibilities. From mid-May to early September, it's possible to reach Bergen using **P&O Scottish Ferries** from Aberdeen to Lerwick, on Shetland, where you stay overnight, and then **Smyril Line** from Lerwick to Bergen, a seafaring voyage of some proportions. Prices are comparable with direct sailings – a through fare will cost between £90 and £110 one-way, booking a couchette in a two-berth cabin £135–170 – but the total sailing time is considerable. It takes between fourteen to twenty hours for the first leg and twelve hours for the second, plus a hefty

---

SPECIALIST TOUR OPERATORS IN BRITAIN

Aeroscope (☎01608/650103). One- and two-centre city breaks.

Arctic Experience/Discover the World (☎01737/218800, *www.arctic-discover.co.uk*). Excellent specialist adventure tours including whale-watching in Norway, dog-sledging in Lapland and sea voyages around Spitsbergen.

Branta (☎020/7635 5812). Birdwatching tours.

Challenge Adventure Sailing (☎01752/565654, *www.challengebusiness.com/fradsail/*). Seven- to nineteen-day sailing expeditions along the Norwegian coast aboard an ocean-going racing yacht.

DA Study Tours (☎01383/882200). Coach tours for culture vultures.

DFDS Scandinavian Seaways (☎0990/333000, *www.scansea.com*). A broad range of packages on offer, including cottages, resort hotels and camping, as well as short "cruise breaks".

Headwater Holidays (☎01606/813399, *www.headwater.com*). Guided walking holidays in the Rondane National Park.

Huxleys (☎01948/770661). Deluxe coach tours of the fjords.

Inntravel (☎01653/628811). Outdoor holidays in Norway including skiing, walking, fjord cruises, and whale- and reindeer-watching.

Mountain & Wildlife Ventures (☎01539/433285). Vastly experienced company offering walking holidays as well as Nordic skiing and dog-sledging. Agents for Norway's DNT (see p.53), too.

NORSC Holidays (☎01297/560033). Specialists in tailor-made trips to Norway.

Saddle Skedaddle (☎020/8914 7012, *www.skedaddle.demon.co.uk*). Cycling tours of the Lofoten Islands.

Scandinavian Travel Service (☎020/7559 6666). City breaks and resort holidays as well as tours incorporating cruises on the Hurtigrute.

ScanMeridian (☎020/7431 5322). Scandinavia specialists offering city breaks, fly-drive holidays, cottage accommodation, cruises and tailor-made holidays.

Scantours (☎020/7839 2927). Scandinavia specialists with a wide range of packages, including city breaks, and ski packages in Lillehammer, Voss, and Geilo; winter coastal voyages too. Particularly good on train travel.

Specialised Tours (☎01342/712785). City breaks, motoring, cycling and tailor-made holidays.

Sunworld Lakes & Mountains Plus (☎0990/114113). Holidays include self-drive, Hurtigrute cruising and touring by train.

Taber Holidays (☎01274/393480). Their *Norway Only* brochure has dozens of options, including self-catering holidays, fjord cruises, motoring tours and guided coach tours.

Waymark Holidays (☎01753/516477). Cross-country skiing specialists with a broad range of Norwegian holidays to suit novices and the experienced alike. Also offer summer walking packages. Highly recommended.

wait in between. The Smyril Line crossing runs weekly from mid-May to mid-September only (Lerwick to Bergen over Monday/Tuesday night, Bergen to Lerwick over Tuesday/Wednesday night), and P&O sails from Aberdeen to Lerwick five times weekly Monday through Friday; ferries from Lerwick to Aberdeen leave six times weekly Sunday through Friday.

Another possibility is to catch a ferry over to **Holland**, even **Belgium** or **France**, and drive from there. Obviously, these crossings are shorter and less costly, but they mean a much longer drive when you get to the Continent. **DFDS Scandinavian Seaways'** crossings from Harwich or Newcastle to Hamburg and **Stena Line**'s from Harwich to the Hook of Holland are really the only crossings that make much sense, though you might just want to sail with **P&O North Sea Ferries** from Hull to Rotterdam (handy for train connections – see p.5). There are ferry links to Norway from other parts of Scandinavia (see p.10) and from Germany, where **Color Line** operates a once-daily, all-year ferry from Kiel, 84km from Hamburg, to Oslo, with a journey time of around twenty hours.

PACKAGE TOURS

Don't be put off by the idea of an inclusive **package**. In such an expensive part of Europe, it can be the cheapest way to do things, and may also be the only way to reach remote parts at inhospitable times of the year. Apart from the general tour operators, there are also an increasing number of **special-interest** companies, offering everything from ornithological trips to sailing holidays – see the box on p.7. Prices for these specialist holidays are usually steep, but occasionally you'll get the holiday of a lifetime.

In particular, if you just want to see one city and its environs, then **weekend breaks** invariably work out cheaper than arranging the same trip independently. Prices include return travel, usually by plane, and accommodation (including breakfast), with most operators offering a range from hostel to luxury-class hotel. A two-night **city break** to Oslo or Bergen from London will generally cost between £280 and £330 per person. If you prefer to drive and take the ferry, a three-night DFDS Scandinavian Seaways "city cruise break" to Oslo will cost around £220 for two nights on the ferry and one night in an Oslo hotel. There are also a number of weekend and overnight trips to Tromsø to view either the **midnight sun** or the

northern lights: for example, Scantours (see box, p.7) does a three-night weekend in Tromsø, from November to February, to view the northern lights, for around £400 all inclusive.

CRUISE HOLIDAYS

The staggering beauty of the Norwegian coastline attracts **cruise ships** by the shoal. These holidays aren't cheap, starting at around £1500 per person on sailings from the UK, but in terms of comfort and luxury, you almost always get what you pay for. Routes vary tremendously, some concentrating on the fjord coastline, others trawling up to the North Cape (Nordkapp), yet others including Norway on a wider Baltic itinerary. Frequency also varies considerably, with some cruises leaving weekly, but the more exotic weighing anchor only once or twice a year. Among the latter is **Norwegian Cruise Line**'s "Norwegian Highlights", a fourteen-night trip from Southampton, taking in the coastline from Oslo to Trondheim as well as visiting Amsterdam and Ayr. It runs once a year in June, with prices ranging from £1115 to £3591, depending on your choice of cabin. Alternatively, **Fred Olsen Cruises** sail around the Baltic about a dozen times a year, and in July their fourteen-night "North Cape" trip sails from Dover and then along the Norwegian coast from Stavanger to Nordkapp; prices range from £1810 to £3625.

The most celebrated Norwegian sea voyage is, however, the journey up the coast from Bergen to Kirkenes on the **Hurtigrute** coastal ship (see p.32 for details and prices).

CRUISE OPERATORS

Fred. Olsen Cruise Lines (☎01473/292222, *www.gbnet.co.uk/fred.olsen*). Over a dozen Baltic and Norwegian cruises a year.

Norwegian Cruise Line (☎0800/181560, *www.ncl.com*). Among other cruises, this company operates a once-yearly, fourteen-night Norwegian Highlights cruise from Southampton.

P&O Cruises (☎020/7800 2222, *www.pocruises.com*). Eleven mid-price Norwegian cruises a year.

Scandinavian Travel Service (☎020/7559 6666, fax 7371 4070). This tour operator arranges Hurtigrute trips between April and September, with flights or ferry from the UK.

GETTING THERE FROM IRELAND

The only direct **flights** from **Dublin** to Scandinavia are to Copenhagen (twice daily with SAS and once daily with Aer Lingus), from where SAS runs regular flights to several Norwegian destinations. Alternatively, it's easy enough to make the journey changing either within the UK, at London or Manchester, or in Amsterdam. Scheduled fares to Copenhagen start at around IR£240 plus tax for a "Jackpot" or APEX return ticket, although special offers below IR£200 are sometimes available, and a discount agent such as usit NOW (see box, below) may have youth, student or discounted tickets for as little as IR£130. Fares to Oslo from Dublin are generally around IR£280 return, although you'll find the budget airline Ryanair offering frequent flights from **Dublin**, **Cork**, **Knock** and **Kerry** to Oslo Torp, 130km from central Oslo, via London Stansted, at as little as half this price.

AIRLINES

Aer Lingus (reservations ☎01/886 8888 in the Republic, ☎0845/973 7747 in Northern Ireland, *www.aerlingus.ie*). Dublin, Cork and Shannon to London Heathrow; Dublin to London Stansted, Manchester, Edinburgh and Glasgow.

British Airways (reservations ☎1-800/626747 in the Republic, ☎0345/222111 in Northern Ireland, *www.british-airways.com*). Dublin and Cork to London Gatwick and Heathrow, and Shannon to London Heathrow.

British Midland (☎01/283 8833 in the Republic, ☎0870/607 0555 in Northern Ireland). Belfast and Dublin to London Heathrow.

Ryanair (☎01/609 7800 in the Republic, *www.ryanair.ie*). From Dublin, Cork, Knock and Kerry to London Stansted, and London Stansted to Oslo (Torp, 130km from downtown Oslo).

SAS (☎01/844 5888 in the Republic). Dublin to Oslo via Copenhagen.

DISCOUNT AGENTS

Budget Travel, 134 Lower Baggot St, Dublin 2 (☎01/661 1866). General budget fares agent.

Dial A Flight Ireland, 11/12 Warrington Place, Dublin 2 (☎01/662 9933). Flight specialists.

Joe Walsh Tours, 8–11 Baggot St, Dublin (☎01/676 3053, 872 2555 and 021/277 959). General budget fares agent.

Student & Group Travel, 71 Dame St, Dublin 2 (☎01/677 7834). Student specialists.

Thomas Cook, 118 Grafton St, Dublin (☎01/677 1721); 11 Donegal Place, Belfast BT1 5AJ (☎028/9088 3900). Package holiday and flight agent, with occasional discount offers.

usit NOW, O'Connell Bridge, 19–21 Aston Quay, Dublin 2 (☎01/602 1600) and branches elsewhere in the Republic; Fountain Centre, Belfast BT1 6ET (☎028/9032 4073). *www.usitnow.ie* Ireland's main student and youth travel specialists.

FERRY COMPANIES

DFDS Scandinavian Seaways, in the Republic c/o Stena Line (☎01/204 7777) for through fares from Dun Laoghaire to Holyhead and Rosslare to Fishguard; in Belfast c/o SeaCat (☎028/9031 4918) for through fares from Belfast to Stranraer.

Irish Ferries (in the Republic ☎01/638 3333 and 24-hour information 661 0715); *www.irishferries.ie*

TOUR OPERATORS

Crystal Holidays, 38 Dawson St, Dublin 2 (☎01/670 8444). One- and two-centre city breaks, mountain tours and skiing.

Falcon Travel, 19 Lower Camden St, Dublin 2 (☎01/478 0533). City breaks and cruises.

Travelfinders, *www.travelfinders.com* This Irish travel site can email you the latest travel bargains from Ireland weekly, and guide you to the relevant travel agent.

From **Belfast**, there are no direct flights to Scandinavia, and your best bet is probably flying via London with British Airways, British Midland or SAS. Prices to Oslo usually start at about £300 for an APEX return, but special offers can take these as low as £200. Failing that, you should be able to get a reasonable deal through a discount agent, either in Northern Ireland or in Britain.

If you are planning to travel from Ireland by **train**, your best bet by far would be an InterRail pass, details of which are given in the train section of "Getting There from Britain" (p.5). Getting to Scandinavia by **bus** would involve going to London and picking up a connection there. For motorists, combined ferry fares covering Irish Sea and North Sea crossings are generally available through Seacat, Stena Line or Irish Ferries (see box p.9 for details).

Not many operators run **tours** to Norway from Ireland, but a package may well work out to be the cheapest way to get there. In particular, **city breaks** are well worth investigating. British operators are listed on p.7; those based in Ireland are given on p.9.

GETTING THERE FROM THE REST OF SCANDINAVIA

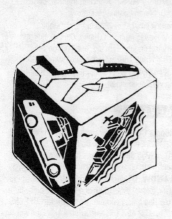

There's no problem in reaching Norway from the rest of **Scandinavia**. There are very regular train services from Sweden, year-round ferry connections from Denmark and flights from both countries as well.

BY TRAIN

By train you can reach **Oslo** from Stockholm (1–3 daily; 6hr) and Copenhagen/Gothenburg (2–4 daily; 4hr/9hr 40min). There are also regular services to **Trondheim** (2 daily; 11hr) and **Narvik** (1 daily; 19hr), again from Stockholm. From Stockholm to Oslo, Trondheim or Narvik, fares are around 650kr one-way. Anyone under 26 can buy a discounted BIJ ticket on these routes and InterRail and Eurail passes are valid – for details see pp.5–6 and pp.14–15.

For train travel within Scandinavia, the best bet is the **ScanRail pass**. These cost £126 (£166 first class) for 5 days of travel within 15 days, £170 for 10 days of travel within 1 month and £191 for 21 consecutive days. **Under 26s** pay £95 for the 5 day pass, £127 for the 10 day pass, and £144 for 21 days. **Seniors** (aged 60 and over) get a discount of about 14 percent on the full price of the pass. There is also an 8-day **Scanrail 'n Drive Pass** which allows 5 days of train travel and 3 days of car rental, with the option of adding extra car days. Note that in all cases a small supplement is charged for certain intercity express trains.

BY CAR FERRY

Of the several **car ferry** services shuttling between **Denmark** and Norway, one of the most useful is DFDS Scandinavian Seaways' once-daily, all-year ferry from **Copenhagen** to Oslo (16hr). Alternatively, Stena Line links **Frederikshavn** with Oslo (1–2 daily; 8hr 30min) and Color Line ferries depart **Hirtshals** for Oslo (6 weekly; 8hr), Kristiansand (2–3 daily; 4hr 30min) and Moss (1–3 daily; 8hr). Details of sailings and costs from any travel agent or local tourist office. Note that **prices** tend to rise sharply in summer, though this is partly offset by all sorts of special deals; rail-pass holders get discounts on some routes. There's also a Color Line ferry service to Norway from **Sweden**, linking Strömstad, north of Gothenburg, with Sandefjord (all year; 2–5 daily; 2hr 30min).

BY PLANE

Norway has international airports at Oslo (Gardermoen), Bergen, Stavanger, Kristiansand, Trondheim and Tromsø; most flights from elsewhere in Scandinavia are with SAS. The **SAS AirPass**, which can only be purchased before you get to Scandinavia, is conditional on you actually flying to Scandinavia with them (and Scandinavians are not eligible). For every return flight to Scandinavia you buy, you're entitled to purchase up to six AirPass vouchers for internal flights within Scandinavia. The vouchers are good for all SAS flights within the region and cost about £50/$80 each (£290/$460 for six); airport taxes are extra.

GETTING THERE FROM NORTH AMERICA

The only airline that flies direct from North America to Norway is **SAS**, which has daily flights from New York to Oslo. There are however numerous non-stop flights, operated both by American and European carriers, to neighbouring countries such as Denmark, Sweden, the Netherlands and Belgium; swift onward connections to Norway are available. (See the section on Airlines in North America on pp.13–14 for more details.)

SHOPPING FOR TICKETS

Special offers aside, the cheapest of the airlines' published fares is usually an **Apex** (Advance Purchase EXcursion) ticket, although this will carry certain restrictions: you have to book – and pay – at least 21 days before departure, spend at least seven days and at most three months abroad, and there tend to be penalties if you change your schedule. On transatlantic routes, there are also winter **Super Apex** tickets, sometimes known as "Eurosavers" – slightly cheaper than an ordinary Apex, but limiting your stay to between 7 and 21 days. Some airlines also issue **Special Apex** tickets to people younger than 24, often extending the maximum stay to a year. Many airlines offer **youth** or **student fares** to under-26s – a passport or driving licence are sufficient proof of age – though these tickets are subject to availability, and can have eccentric booking conditions. It's worth remembering that most cheap return fares involve spending at least one Saturday night away, and that often only a partial refund can be made if you need to cancel or alter your journey, so check the restrictions carefully before buying.

You can normally cut costs further by going through a **specialist flight agent** – either a **consolidator**, who buys up blocks of tickets from the airlines and sells them at a discount, or a **discount agent**, who in addition to dealing with discounted flights may also offer special student and youth fares, and a range of other travel-related services such as travel insurance, rail passes, car rentals, tours and the like. Bear in mind, though, that penalties for changing your bookings can be stiff. Remember too that these companies make their money by dealing in bulk – don't expect them to answer lots of questions. Some agents specialize in **charter flights**, which may be cheaper than scheduled ones, but again departure dates are fixed and withdrawal penalties high – check the refund policy before buying. If you travel a lot, **discount travel clubs** are another option – benefits such as cut-price air tickets and car rental may be worth the annual membership fee.

DISCOUNT TRAVEL COMPANIES IN NORTH AMERICA

Adventure Travel Network (☎1-800/467-4595, *www.atntravel.com*). Discount travel agency.

Air Brokers International (☎1-800/883-3273 or 415/397-1383, *www.airbrokers.com*). Consolidator.

Air Courier Association (☎303/278-8810, *www.aircourier.org*). Courier flight broker.

Airhitch (☎1-800/326-2009 or 212/864-2000, *www.airhitch.org*). Standby-seat broker: for a set price, they guarantee to get you on a flight as close to your preferred destination as possible, and to within a week of your preferred travel date.

Airtech (☎1-800/575-TECH or 212/219-7000, *www.airtech.com*). Stand-by-seat broker; also deals in consolidator fares and courier flights.

Cheap Tickets, Inc., offices nationwide (☎1-800/377-1000 or 212/570-1179, *www.cheaptickets.com*). Consolidator.

Council Travel, 205 E 42nd St, New York, NY 10017 (☎1-800/226-8624 or 212/822-2700, *www.counciltravel.com*), and branches in many other US cities. Student/budget travel agency.

Educational Travel Center (☎1-800/747-5551 or 608/256-5551, *www.edtrav.com*). Student/youth and consolidator fares.

International Student Exchange Flights, 5010 E Shea Blvd, Suite 104A, Scottsdale, AZ 85254 (☎1-800/255-8000 or 480/951-1177, *www.isecards.com*). Student/youth fares, student IDs.

Interworld Travel (☎1-800/468-3796, *www.interworldtravel.com*). Consolidator. Specializes in Scandinavia.

Last Minute Travel Services, offices nationwide (☎1-800/LAST-MIN). Specializes in stand-by flights.

Nouvelles Frontières/New Frontiers, 1001 Sherbrook East, Suite 720, Montreal, H2L 1L3 (☎514/526-8444); in the US 12 E 33rd St, New York, NY 10016 (☎1-800/366-6387); Web site *www.nouvelles-frontieres.com* French discount travel firm.

Now Voyager, 74 Varick St, Suite 307, New York, NY 10013 (☎212/431-1616, *www.nowvoyagertravel.com*). Courier flight broker and consolidator.

Skylink, 265 Madison Ave, 5A, New York, NY 10016 (☎1-800/892-0027 or 212/682-3111, *www.pltravel.com*). Consolidator.

STA Travel, 10 Downing St, New York, NY 10014 (☎1-800/781-4040 or 212/627-3111, *www.statravel.com*), and other branches. Worldwide discount travel firm specializing in student/youth fares.

TFI Tours International (☎1-800/745-8000 or 212/736-1140). Consolidator.

Travac (☎1-800/872-8800 or 212/563-3303, *www.thetravelsite.com*). Consolidator and charter broker. If you have a fax machine you can have a list of fares faxed to you by calling toll-free 1-888/872-8327.

Travel Avenue (☎1-800/333-3335 or 312/876-6866, *www.travelavenue.com*). Full-service travel agent that offers discounts in the form of subsequent rebates.

Travel CUTS, 187 College St, Toronto, ON M5T 1P7 (☎416/979-2406, *www.travelcuts.com*), and other branches all over Canada. Canadian student travel organization specializing in student fares, IDs and other travel services.

Travelers Advantage (☎1-800/548-1116, *www.travelersadvantage.com*). Travel club; annual membership required.

UniTravel (☎1-800/325-2222 or 314/569-2501, *www.flightsforless.com*). Consolidator.

Worldtek Travel (☎1-800/243-1723 or 203/772-0470, *www.worldtek.com*). Discount travel agency.

Worldwide Discount Travel Club (☎305/534-2082). Travel club; annual membership required. Call for membership kit.

Don't automatically assume that tickets purchased through a travel specialist will be the least expensive – once you get a quote, check with the airlines and you may turn up an even better deal. Be advised also that there are sharks out there – exercise caution, and never deal with a company that demands cash upfront or refuses to accept payment by credit card.

Students might be able to find cheaper flights through the major student travel agencies, such as STA Travel, Nouvelles Frontières or, for Canadian students, Travel Cuts (see box for addresses and phone numbers).

If you are travelling to Norway as part of a much longer journey, you might want to consider buying a **round-the-world ticket**. However, as

Oslo is not one of the more obvious destinations, you might need to have a customized round-the-world ticket assembled for you by a travel agent; this costs more than an "off-the-shelf" one and can indeed be quite expensive.

Another option for finding air fares is the **World Wide Web**. In addition to the Web sites of the discount travel firms, there are a number of Web-based companies with sites at which you can look up fares and book tickets. You can search the travel sections of the main web directories, or try Travelocity, *www.travelocity.com*; and FLIFO Cyber Travel Agent, *www.flifo. com*.

FLIGHTS FROM NORTH AMERICA

The only **direct** flight from North America to Norway is the daily service from New York (Newark) to Oslo on SAS. Otherwise, you'll have

---

AIRLINES IN NORTH AMERICA

Air Canada (US ☎1-800/776-3000, Canada 1-800/555-1212 for local toll-free number, *www.aircanada.ca*). Toronto or Vancouver to Oslo via Frankfurt or London, with connections on Lufthansa or British Airways.

Air France (US ☎1-800/237-2747, Canada 1-800/667-2747, *www.airfrance.fr*). Flies daily from many major cities in the USA and Canada to Paris, and can offer connecting flights to Oslo.

American Airlines (☎1-800/433-7300, *www.americanair.com*). Daily flights from Chicago and Miami direct to Stockholm. Offers connections from all major cities in North America and onward connections to Oslo at the other end.

British Airways (US ☎1-800/247-9297, Canada 1-800/668-1059, *www.british-airways.com*). Flies daily from 22 different North American cities to London and has numerous connecting flights to Oslo and Stavanger.

Continental Airlines (☎1-800/231-0856, *www.continental.com*). Flies from New York (Newark) to many major European cities and can offer connecting flights to Norway on another carrier, such as Air France from Paris to Oslo.

Delta Airlines (☎1-800/241-4141, *www.delta-air.com*). Flies daily from many major North American cities via Atlanta and New York (JFK) to Paris and Brussels, with connections to Oslo on Air France or Sabena.

Icelandair (☎1-800/223-5500, *www.icelandair.com*). Flies from New York, Baltimore, Boston, Minneapolis, Orlando, and Halifax in Nova Scotia to Oslo, via Reykjavik. Frequency of flights varies according to season. Can book connections with all major North American cities. Also offers the option of breaking your journey with a stay of one to three nights in Reykjavik.

KLM (☎1-800/374-7747, *www.klm.com*). Flies from major North American cities to Amsterdam, with connections on KLM and Braathens to Oslo and Stavanger.

Lufthansa (☎1-800/645-3880, *www.lufthansa.com*). Flies to Oslo via Frankfurt from many major cities in the USA , and from Toronto and Vancouver in Canada.

Sabena (☎1-800/955-2000, *www.sabena-usa.com*). Flies to Norway via Brussels from all major cities in the USA. If you fly out of New York, Boston, Chicago or Atlanta you will only have to change planes once.

Scandinavian Airlines (SAS) (☎1-800/221-2350, *www.flysas.com*). The largest Scandinavian airline, flying daily from New York (Newark) direct to Oslo. Connections from most major cities in North America via United Airlines. SAS also flies direct from Chicago and Seattle to Copenhagen, Denmark, with a short connecting flight to Oslo or other Norwegian cities.

Swissair (☎1-800/221-4750, *www.swissair.com*). Flies from several US cities to Zürich, with connections to Norway on Swissair or SAS.

TWA (☎1-800/221-2000, *www.twa.com*). Flies to Paris from all major cities in North America, with subsequent connections to Oslo on Air France.

United Airlines (☎1-800/538-2929, *www.ual.com*). Connects most major North American cities with direct SAS flights from New York (Newark) to Oslo.

US Airways (☎1-800/622-1015, *www.usairways.com*). Flies from Philadelphia or Boston hubs to many major European cities, and can offer connecting flights to Norway on other carriers, such as Sabena, Swissair, or Lufthansa.

Virgin Atlantic Airways (☎1-800/862-8621, *www.virgin-atlantic.com*). Flies daily from a number of North American cities to London, connecting to flights to Norway on SAS or British Airways.

to change flights in one of several major European cities – and if you don't live in one of the gateway cities in North America you might have to change planes on that side of the Atlantic as well. Your choice of carrier might be strongly influenced by the city you are departing from.

As always, it is worth shopping around to get the cheapest fares, as prices can vary widely, especially in the low season. The **return fare** to Oslo on a midweek Apex economy-class ticket (excluding taxes and airport fees) from New York can be between US$860–1150 during the high season, and US$400–660 in the low season, with shoulder-season fares anywhere in between. The journey time is 7hr 30min on a direct flight. The fare from Chicago to Oslo (journey time varies between 8hr 30min and 11hr) can be between US$930–1200 during high season and US$550–780 in the low season, with shoulder fares in between. From the West Coast (journey time can be as much as 12hr) fares range between US$1050–1300 during the high season and between US$550–930 in the low season.

From Canada, flying time can vary between 9hr and 12hr 30min from Toronto, and from 13hr to 18hr from Vancouver, depending on connections. From Toronto, fares range between CDN$1000 and CDN$1600 during the high season, and between CDN$750 and CDN$970 in the low season, with shoulder-season fares anywhere in between (as a rule of thumb, from Vancouver add CDN$400 to the fare from Toronto). You might also want to look into cheap flights to New York or Chicago, for onward connections on another carrier.

TRAVEL PASSES FOR NORWAY AND THE REST OF EUROPE

You might want to consider flying to a European city and travelling on from there to Norway by plane, ferry or train. **London** is one of the least expensive European cities to get to; for details of onward routes from the UK to Norway see "Getting there from Britain" (p.3).

Those who travel across the Atlantic with SAS may buy the company's **AirPass**, which takes the form of coupons for flights within Scandinavia. The coupons generally cost $75 each, though they can be as expensive as $135 for a longer flight. If you're visiting Norway as part of a wider tour of Europe by train, consider buying the Eurail pass – available in both youth (under-26) and first-class or adult (26 and over) versions – as this can get you to Norway by train from nearly anywhere in Europe. The **Eurail Youth Pass** costs US$388 for

RAIL CONTACTS IN NORTH AMERICA

Borton Overseas (☎1-800/843-0602, *www.borton.com*). Sells all Eurail and ScanRail passes.

CIT Tours (☎1-800/223-7987, *www.fs-online.com*). Eurail passes only.

DER Tours/German Rail (☎1-800/421-2929 or in Canada ☎416/695-1209, *www.dertravel.com*). Eurail and ScanRail passes.

Rail Europe (US ☎1-800/438-7245, Canada ☎1-800/361-RAIL, *www.raileurope.com*). Official Eurail pass agent in North America; also sells the ScanRail pass.

Rail Pass Express (US & Canada ☎1-800/722 7151, *www.railpass.com*). Eurail pass agent.

ScanTours (☎1-800/223-7226, *www.scantours.com*). Eurail and ScanRail passes.

fifteen days, and there are also one-month and two-month versions; the **first-class Eurail Pass** costs US$554 for the fifteen-day option. You stand a better chance of getting your money's worth out of a **Eurail Flexipass**, which is good for a certain number of travel days, which need not be consecutive, within a two-month period. This, too, comes in under-26/first-class versions: ten days' travel for under-26s costs US$458, for over-26s US$654. The **Eurail Saverpass** and **Saver Flexipass** are group versions of the Eurail pass and Eurail Flexipass respectively, suited for two or more people travelling together. The Saverpass costs US$470 per person for fifteen days, and the Saver Flexipass costs US$556 per person for ten days' travel within a two-month period.

To qualify for a Eurail pass, you must not be resident in Europe, the Commonwealth of Independent States, Turkey, Morocco, Algeria or Tunisia. Though usually purchased before you leave home, the passes can also be obtained from Rail Europe in London (see p.5).

Also worth considering is a pass specifically for travel in Scandinavia (Sweden, Denmark, Finland and Norway) only, called the **ScanRail pass**. These also come in under-26/over-26 versions and are valid for five days of travel within fifteen days (under-26s US$140; over-26s US$187) and ten days within a thirty-day period (US$226; US$301); a 21-day pass is also available. These fares are for the well-regarded second-class ticket; there are also slightly more expensive first-class fares for both under-26 and over-26 passengers. **Seniors** (over 60) get a discount of about fifteen percent on the full price of the pass. There is also an eight-day **Scanrail 'n Drive Pass**, which allows five days of train travel and three days of car rental, with the option of adding additional car days. Note that a small supplement is charged for certain inter-city, express trains.

Finally, the **Norway Rail Pass** allows unlimited travel on the railways of Norway throughout a specified period of three, four or five days within any given month. These can be bought in Norway or from rail agents in North America, with prices for three, four or five days of travel within a thirty-day period of $172/132 (for first/second class); $213/164; or $240/185 respectively.

The companies listed in the box (p.14) specialize in the passes indicated, though the more common European passes can be purchased through most travel agents.

PACKAGES AND ORGANIZED TOURS

There are a number of companies operating **organized tours** of Norway (see box), ranging from cruises to hiking holidays, and from dog-sledge rides to musk-ox safaris. Group tours can be expensive, and quoted prices occasionally do not include the air fare, so check what you are getting for the money. If your visit is centered on Oslo you could simply book a hotel-plus-flight package (which can work out cheaper than booking the two separately). Bennett Tours, Euroseven, Scanam and Passage Tours offer very reasonable weekend deals in the low season. Tour reservations can usually be made through your local travel agent.

NORTH AMERICAN TOUR OPERATORS

Abercrombie & Kent (☎1-800/323-7308, *www.abercrombiekent.com*). Tours of Scandinavia, the Baltic states and Russia by land and sea.

American Express Vacations (☎1-800/446-6234, *www.americanexpress.com/travel*). Flight-plus-hotel packages to Oslo.

Backroads (☎1-800-462-2848, *www.backroads.com*). Offers a six-day bicycling holiday in the Vesterålen and Lofoten Islands and a seven-day hiking tour of Norway's mountains, glaciers and fjords.

Bennett Tours (☎1-800-221-2420, *www.bennett-tours.com*). Scandinavia specialists. Offers inexpensive weekend breaks or fully escorted bus tours throughout Norway.

Bergen Line (☎1-800/323-7436, *www.coastalvoyages.com*). For cruises along the coast and to some of the fjords.

Borton Overseas (☎1-800/843-0602, *www.borton.com*). Company specializing in adventure vacations (hiking, rafting, birdwatching, dog-sledging, cross-country skiing, bicycling) and farm and cabin stays throughout Norway. Agents for Norway's DNT (the Norwegian Mountain Touring Association – see p.53).

Brekke Tours (☎1-800/437-5302, *www.brekketours.com*). Offers escorted tours and cultural tours of Norway.

EuroCruises (☎1-800/688-3876, *www.eurocruises.com*). For fjord cruises.

Euroseven (☎1-800/890-3876, *www.euroseven.com*). Independent hotel-plus-flight pack-ages from New York, Baltimore or Boston to Oslo.

Loma Travel (US ☎604/294-3261, Canada 1-800/665-9899, *www.loma-travel.com*). Scandinavia specialists, offering cheap flights, tours and cruises.

Nordique Tours (☎1-800/995-7997, *www.ptla.com/nordique*). Specializes in package tours, run from mid-May to mid-October, of the Norwegian fjords.

Passage Tours (☎1-800-548-5960, *www.passagetours.com*). Specializes in Scandinavia. Offers escorted and unescorted tours and cheap weekend breaks.

Scanam World Tours (☎1-800/545-2204 or 201/835-7070, *www.scanamtours.com*). Specializes in Scandinavian tours and cruises for groups and individuals. Also cheap weekend breaks.

Scand-America Tours (☎1-800/886-8428, *www.scandamerica.com*). Offers a wide variety of tours – everything from dog-sledging to garden tours – throughout Scandinavia.

Scanditours (☎1-800/432-4176, *www.scanditours.com*). Canadian tour operator specializing in Scandinavia with offices in Toronto and Vancouver.

Scantours (☎1-800/223-7226, *www.scantours.com*). Major Scandinavian holiday specialists offering vacation packages and customized itineraries, including cruises and city sightseeing tours.

Vantage Deluxe World Travel (☎1-800/322-6677). Deluxe group tours and cruises.

GETTING THERE FROM AUSTRALIA & NEW ZEALAND

There are **no direct flights** from Australia or New Zealand to Norway (or any other Scandinavian country); instead you have to fly to either a European or Asian gateway city where you can get a **connecting flight**. If you're on a tight budget or want to take in more of Europe on your trip, it can be worth flying to London (see "Getting there from Britain", p.3), Amsterdam or Frankfurt first and picking up a short-haul flight from there. If you intend to take in a number of other European countries on your trip, it might well be worth buying a **Eurail** pass before you go (further details on p.18).

FLIGHTS AND FARES

Air fares vary significantly with the season. For most major airlines, low season runs from mid-January to the end of February and during October and November; high season runs from mid-May to the end of August and from December to mid-January; the rest of the year is shoulder season. Unless specific routes are mentioned, the fares we list for Australia are for flights from any of the major eastern Australian cities; in comparison, flying from Perth and Darwin via Asia costs between A$100 and A$200 less, or A$200–A$400 more via North America. The fares we give for New Zealand are from Auckland unless otherwise stated; fares from Christchurch and Wellington would cost between NZ$150 and NZ$300 more.

Tickets purchased direct from the airlines tend to be more expensive, with published fares ranging from A$1520/NZ$2199 (low season) and

A$1899/NZ$2399 (shoulder season) to A$2599/NZ$2699 (high season). Travel agents offer better deals on fares and have the latest information on limited special deals, such as free stopovers en route and fly-drive-accommodation packages. Flight Centres and STA (see box on p.18 for addresses) generally offer the best discounts, especially for students and those under 26.

Airlines flying out of Australia and New Zealand often use SAS for connecting services on to Norway. A return ticket to Oslo would cost in the region of A$1375/1750/2050 from Australia or NZ$2099/2299/2599 from New Zealand. For flights to other European cities, the lowest fares are with Airtours and Britannia to London during their limited charter season from November to March, when you can expect to pay A$1100/1450/1760 and NZ$1620/1850/2225. Among scheduled flights, count on paying between A$1350/NZ$1750 and A$1800/NZ$2270 on Garuda, Gulf, Korean or Japan Airlines to London; A$1375/NZ$2100 and A$1875/NZ$2550 on Finnair, Swissair or KLM to Oslo; A$1650/NZ$2150 and A$1850/NZ$2400 on Malaysia Airlines, Thai Airways, Lufthansa or Lauda Air and from A$1800/NZ$2450 to A$2500/NZ$3250 on British Airways, Qantas, Singapore Airlines, Air New Zealand and Canadian Airways depending on the season; see the box opposite for a full list of airlines and routes.

For extended trips taking in several countries, **round-the-world tickets**, valid for up to a year, can be good value. Star Alliance (*www.star-alliance.com*), a grouping of several airlines which includes SAS, issues tickets (A$2699/NZ$3299) that allow six stopovers, including open-jaw travel and limited backtracking. The Qantas-BA "Global Explorer" (A$2399/NZ$2999) and "One World" (A$2999/NZ$3499) tickets offer flexible routings, including Norway, in conjunction with Cathay Pacific, Canadian and American Airlines.

Travellers who want to take a package tour to Norway will find there are very few to choose from. Your best bet is to contact Bentours (see box, p.18), who will put together a package for you, and are about the only agents willing to deal with skiing holidays. Note that the prices given in the list of Australasian tour operators (p.18)

AIRLINES IN AUSTRALIA AND NEW ZEALAND

Air New Zealand (Australia ☎13/2476, NZ 09/366 2424). Several flights weekly to London from Australia, via Auckland and LA; also daily flights to Bangkok (to connect with SAS) from major Australasian cities.

Airtours/Britannia Airways (Australia ☎02/9247 4833). Several charter flights to London each month (Nov–March) from major Australian cities and Auckland, via Singapore and Abu Dhabi/Bahrain.

British Airways (Australia ☎02/8904 8800, NZ 09/356 8690). Daily flights to London from major Australian cities via Asia, and from New Zealand cities via Los Angeles.

Canadian Airlines (Australia ☎1300/655 767, NZ 09/309 0735). Twice weekly to Vancouver and Toronto from Sydney, Melbourne and Auckland; connects with SAS.

Finnair (Australia ☎02/9244 2299, NZ c/o World Aviation, 09/308 3365). Four flights weekly to Helsinki from Sydney via Bangkok and Tokyo, through their links with Qantas, Thai and Gulf, and two flights weekly to Helsinki from Auckland via Singapore, through an arrangement with Singapore Airlines. From Helsinki you can get a connection to Oslo and other major Scandinavian cities.

Garuda (Australia ☎1300/365 330, NZ 09/366 1862). Flies several times weekly to London Gatwick and Amsterdam from major Australian cities, via Jakarta or Denpasar, and from Auckland twice weekly.

Gulf Air (Australia ☎02/9244 2166, NZ 09/308 3366). Several flights weekly to London via Singapore and either Bahrain or Abu Dhabi. Connections on to Oslo with Finnair.

Japan Airlines (Australia ☎02/9272 1111, NZ 09/379 9906). Daily flights to London via Tokyo or Osaka from Brisbane and Sydney, plus several flights weekly from Cairns and Auckland.

Korean Airlines (Australia ☎02/9262 6000, NZ 09/307 3687). Several flights a week to London from Sydney, Brisbane, Auckland and Christchurch, via Seoul.

Lauda Air (Australia ☎02/9251 6155, NZ 09/308 3368). Three flights weekly to Vienna from major Australian cities and Auckland, via Sydney and Singapore.

Lufthansa (Australia ☎02/9367 3888, NZ 09/303 1529). Daily flights to Frankfurt from major Australian cities and Auckland, through arrangements with Singapore Airlines and Thai Airways, connecting with Lufthansa flights in either Singapore or Bangkok.

Malaysia Airlines (Australia ☎13/2627, NZ 09/373 2741). Several flights weekly to London, Amsterdam, Paris and Zurich from major Australian and New Zealand cities via Kuala Lumpur.

Qantas (Australia ☎13/1313, NZ 09/357 8900). Daily to London, Singapore and Bangkok from major cities in Australia and New Zealand, connecting with SAS to destinations in Scandinavia.

Scandinavian Airlines (SAS) (Australia ☎02/9299 9800, NZ c/o Air New Zealand, 09/366 2424). SAS, through a partnership with Qantas and Air New Zealand, have several flights weekly to Oslo and other destinations in Scandinavia from major cities in Australia and New Zealand, via Copenhagen.

Singapore Airlines (Australia ☎13/1011, NZ 09/379 3209 and 0800/808 909). Several flights weekly to London from major Australian cities, via Singapore, and twice weekly from Auckland.

Swissair (Australia ☎02/9232 1744, NZ 09/358 3925). Three flights a week from major cities in Australia and New Zealand to Zürich via Singapore, with daily onward connections to Oslo.

Thai Airlines (Australia ☎1300/651 960, NZ 09/377 3886). Several flights weekly to Stockholm and Copenhagen from major Australian cities and Auckland, via Paris and Bangkok. Connections with Finnair.

exclude air fares. Alternatively, you could wait until you get to Europe, where there's a greater choice of holidays and prices (see "Getting there from Britain", p.3).

PASSES FOR TRAVEL WITHIN EUROPE

There are **air passes** that allow for discounted flights within Europe, such as the SAS **Visit Scandinavia Pass** and the BA-Qantas **Airpass**; these must be purchased before you depart. The passes are coupon-based: each coupon entitles you to a seat on one of the issuing airline's flights within Europe. Coupon prices vary as some are valid for only short-hop flights while others cover longer routes; expect to pay between A\$120/NZ\$150 and A\$180/NZ\$230 per coupon.

DISCOUNT AGENTS

Anywhere Travel, 345 Anzac Parade, Kingsford, Sydney (☎02/9663 0411, *anywhere@ozemail.com.au*).

Budget Travel, 16 Fort St, Auckland (☎09/366 0061, toll-free 0800/808 040).

Destinations Unlimited, 3 Milford Rd, Milford, Auckland (☎09/373 4033).

Flight Centres 82 Elizabeth St, Sydney (☎02/9241 2422; nearest branch ☎13/1600, *www.flightcentre.com.au*), plus branches nationwide; 205–225 Queen St, Auckland (☎09/309 6171), with other branches countrywide.

Passport Travel, Suite 11A, 401 St Kilda Rd, Melbourne (☎03/9867 3888, *www.travelcentre.com.au*).

STA Travel, 702 Harris St, Ultimo, Sydney (nearest branch ☎13/1776, telesales 1300/360 960, *www.statravel.com.au*), and other offices in major cities; Travellers Centre, 10 High St,

Auckland (☎09/309 0458, telesales 366 6673), and other offices in major cities.

Status Travel, 22 Cavenagh St, Darwin (☎08/8941 1843).

Student Uni Travel, 92 Pitt St, Sydney (☎02/9232 8444) plus branches in Brisbane, Cairns, Darwin, Melbourne and Perth.

Thomas Cook, 175 Pitt St, Sydney (local branch ☎13/1771, *www.thomascook.com.au*), plus branches in other state capitals; 159 Queen St, Auckland (☎09/359 5200).

Trailfinders, 8 Spring St, Sydney (☎02/9247 7666).

Travel.com.au, 80 Clarence St, Sydney (☎02/9290 1500, *www.travel.com.au*).

Usit Beyond, corner of Shortland St and Jean Batten Place, Auckland (☎09/379 4224 or toll-free ☎0800/788 336, *www.usitbeyond.co.nz*).

SPECIALIST TOUR OPERATORS IN AUSTRALIA AND NEW ZEALAND

Bentours, Level 11, 2 Bridge St, Sydney (☎02/9241 1353, *scandinavia@bentours.com.au*). Ferry, rail, bus and hotel passes. Also does a host of scenic tours, such as four-day fjord hopping from A\$1350/NZ\$1725 including meals, and the "Norway in a Nutshell" two-day tours from A\$370/NZ\$470.

Explore Holidays, 2nd Floor, 155 Blaxland Rd, Ryde, NSW (☎02/9857 6200). Twenty-one-day adventure tour through coastal Norway from A\$1850/NZ\$2000, including twin share accommodation.

European Travel Office, 122 Rosslyn St, West Melbourne (☎03/9329 8844); 407 Great South Rd, Penrose, Auckland (☎09/525 3074). Oslo hotel accommodation from A\$115 twin share, and sightseeing tours by coach or boat.

Wiltrans/Maupintour, Level 10, 189 Kent Street, Sydney (☎02/9255 0899). Luxury, all-inclusive thirteen-day tours of Scandinavia and the Baltic, travelling by boat, from US\$6250 (when you buy, prices are converted to A\$ at the prevailing exchange rate).

YHA TRAVEL CENTRES

Adelaide 38 Sturt Street (☎08/8231 5583).

Auckland cnr Shortland St and Jean Batten Place (☎09 379 4224).

Brisbane 154 Roma Street (☎07/3236 1680).

Darwin 69 Mitchell Street (☎08/8981 2560).

Hobart 28 Criterion Street (☎03/6234 9617).

Melbourne 205 King Street (☎03/9670 9611).

Perth 236 William Street, Northbridge (☎08/9227 5122).

Sydney 422 Kent Street (☎02/9261 1111).

Web sites: *www.yha.com.au* and *www.yha.co.nz*

The above can arrange budget accommodation in Norway and throughout Scandinavia for YHA members.

If you're planning to travel a lot by train, or to use trains to get to Norway from another European country, consider buying a **train pass**. **Eurail** passes, which come in several versions (see p.14) are available from most travel agents, from CIT, 263 Clarence St, Sydney (☎02/9267 1255; also offices in Melbourne, Brisbane, Adelaide and Perth), or Rail Plus (Australia ☎1300/555 003, NZ ☎09/303 2484, *info@railplus.com.au*). The **Eurail Pass**, available in under-26/first-class versions, costs A\$615/A\$880 for travel within a fifteen-day period. A **Eurail Flexipass** for under-26s costs A$725 for ten days' travel within a two-month period, for over-26s A$1040. The **Eurail Saverpass** and **Saver Flexipass** are group versions of the Eurail Pass and Flexipass respectively, suited for two or more people travelling together. The Saverpass costs A$745 per person for fifteen days, and the Flexipass A$885 per person for ten days' travel within a two-month period.

There's a specific train pass for Scandinavia, the **ScanRail** pass, available in Australia from Bentours. These also come in under-26/over-26 versions. For example, five days of second-class travel within a fifteen-day period costs A$230 for under-26s and A$308 for over-26s; a one-month pass is also available, as are passes for first-class travel. For train travel within Norway alone, consider the **Norway Rail Pass**; see "Rail passes", p.31, for details.

Norway **bus passes** (see p.32) are valid for unlimited travel on consecutive days and cost in the region of A$317 for seven days and A$507 for fourteen. They are usually purchased in Norway, though in Australia you can get them from Bentours (see "Specialist Tour Operators", opposite).

TRAVELLERS WITH DISABILITIES

As you might expect, the Norwegians have adopted a progressive and thoughtful approach to the issues surrounding disability, not least because fully one-third of their own citizens reaching retirement age (67) in 1987 were already in receipt of disability pensions. The upshot, in terms of **travellers with disabilities**, has been a dramatic improvement in facilities in the last decade. An increasing number of hotels, hostels and campsites are equipped for disabled visitors, and are credited as such in the tourist literature by means of the standard wheelchair-in-a-box icon. Furthermore, on most main routes Norwegian State Railways has special carriages with wheelchair space, hydraulic lifts and a disabled toilet; domestic **flights** either cater for or provide assistance to disabled customers; new **ships** on the Hurtigrute coastal sea route have lifts and cabins designed for disabled people; and the newer fjord **ferries** also have lifts from the car deck to the lounge and toilets. In the cities and larger towns, you can also anticipate that many **restaurants** and most **museums** and public places will be wheelchair-accessible, and although facilities are not so advanced in the countryside, matters are improving rapidly. Drivers will find that most motorway **service stations** are wheelchair-accessible and that, if you have a UK-registered vehicle, the orange **car parking disc** is honoured. Note also that several of the larger car rental companies have modified vehicles available. On a less positive note, city pavements can be uneven and difficult to negotiate and, inevitably, winter snow and ice can make things even worse.

Getting to Norway should be relatively straightforward too. You can expect that the various airlines and shipping companies concerned will either provide assistance to disabled travellers or, going one better, have modified their facilities appropriately – for instance, DFDS Scandinavian Seaways' ferries have specially adapted cabins.

CONTACTS FOR TRAVELLERS WITH DISABILITIES

GENERAL

Access Tourism, *www.accesstourism.com* Tourism-business partnership aiming to improve holiday opportunities for disabled people. The Web site includes a useful database of travel agents offering holiday services within Europe for people with disabilities.

Access-Able Travel Source, *www.access-able.com* A useful international database of accessible accommodation, travel tips and other resources.

Euro Booking service, Rådhusgata 17, N-0158 Oslo (☎22 00 77 30, fax 22 00 77 29). Recommended in the Official Travel Guide produced by the tourist office, this organization has information on hotel and car rental discounts as well as on coach tours round Norway especially designed for wheelchair users.

Mobility International, 25 rue de Manchester, 1070 Brussels, Belgium (☎032/2410 6297 or 2410 6874). General international advice and information.

Norges Handikapforbund, Folke Bernadottes vei 2, Oslo, N-0862 (☎22 17 02 55, fax 22 17 61 77). This organization produces an English-language brochure concerning disabled travel in Norway, available through the Oslo tourist office.

UK AND IRELAND

Holiday Care Service, 2nd floor, Imperial Building, Victoria Rd, Horley, Surrey RH6 9HW (☎01293/774535). Information on all aspects of travel.

Irish Wheelchair Association, Blackheath Drive, Clontarf, Dublin 3 (☎01/833 8241). National organization working for people with disabilities; related services for holidaymakers.

RADAR, 12 City Forum, 250 City Rd, London EC1V 8AS (☎020/7250 3222, Minicom ☎7250 0212, *www.radar.org.uk*). An excellent source of advice on holidays and travel abroad.

Tripscope, The Courtyard, Evelyn Rd, London W4 5JL (☎0345/585641, minicom 020/8994 9294). A national telephone information service offering free transport and travel advice.

NORTH AMERICA

Directions Unlimited, 720 N Bedford Rd, Bedford Hills, NY 10507 (☎1-800/533-5343 and 914/241-1700, *cruisesusa@aol.com*). Travel agency specializing in custom tours for people with disabilities.

Mobility International USA, PO Box 10767, Eugene, OR 97440 (☎541/343-1284, *www.miusa.org*). Information and referral services, access guides, tours and exchange programs. Annual membership $25 (includes quarterly newsletter).

MossRehab ResourceNet, MossRehab Hospital, 1200 West Tabor Rd, Philadelphia PA, USA 19141-3099 *(www.mossresourcenet. org/travel.htm)*. Information and resources, including details of travel agents, tourist offices, and airlines, information available on an excellent Web site.

Society for the Advancement of Travel for the Handicapped (SATH), 347 5th Ave, Suite 610, New York, NY 10016 (☎212/447-7284, *www.sath.org*). Non-profit travel-industry referral service that passes queries on to its members as appropriate; allow plenty of time for a response.

Travel Information Service (☎215/456-9600). Telephone information and referral service.

Twin Peaks Press, Box 129, Vancouver, WA 98666-0129 (☎360/694-2462 and 1-800/637-2256, *www.pacifier.com/twinpeak*). Publisher of *Directory of Travel Agencies for the Disabled*, listing more than 370 agencies worldwide; *Travel for the Disabled*; *Directory of Accessible Van Rentals* and *Wheelchair Vagabond*, loaded with personal tips.

Wheels Up! (☎1-888/389-4335, *www.wheelsup.com*). Provides discounted flights, tours and cruises for disabled travelers, publishes a free monthly newsletter and has a comprehensive website.

AUSTRALIA AND NEW ZEALAND

ACROD (Australian Council for Rehabilitation of the Disabled), PO Box 60, Curtin, ACT 2605 (☎02/6282 4333).

Barrier Free Travel, 36 Wheatley St, North Bellingen, NSW 2454 (☎02/6655 1733).

Disabled Persons Assembly, 173-175 Victoria St, Wellington (☎04/801 9100).

RED TAPE AND VISAS

NORWEGIAN EMBASSIES ABROAD

AUSTRALIA 17 Hunter St, Yarralumla, Canberra, ACT 2600 (☎06/273 3444).

CANADA Royal Bank Center, 90 Sparks St, Suite 532, Ottawa, Ontario, K1P 5B4 (☎613/238 6571, fax 238-2765, *ambassade-ottawa@ud.dep.telemax.no*).

IRELAND 34 Molesworth St, Dublin 2 (☎01/662 1800).

UK 25 Belgrave Square, London SW1X 8QD (☎020/7591 5500, fax 7245 6993, *embassy@embassy.norway.org.uk*); 86 George St, Edinburgh EH2 3BU (☎0131/226 5701, fax 220 4976, *no.edinburgh@btinternet.com*).

USA 2720, 34th St NW, Washington, DC 20008 (☎202/333-6000, fax 337-0870), and consular offices in major cities.

The citizens of around ninety countries need only a **valid passport** to enter Norway. US, Canadian, Australian, New Zealand and most European citizens with a valid passport can enter Norway for up to three months. EEA (European Economic Area) nationals, including all EU citizens, are able to stay for up to six months if seeking work and with sufficient money to finance their stay. Other nationals should consult their Norwegian embassy about **visa** requirements.

A **residence permit** is necessary if you want to stay longer than the standard three- or six-month limit. EEA nationals can either apply for the permit within Norway itself, from the local police, or from a Norwegian embassy or consulate before arrival. If the application is successful, the residence permit will normally grant the holder the right to stay in Norway for five years (one year for students). In most cases, it also grants the holder the right to work, to reside anywhere in Norway and is renewable. Particular conditions may be attached: for example, if you apply for a residence permit as a recipient of services (say, as a tourist), you would have to prove that you could both finance yourself and pay for the services you receive.

For non-EEA nationals, the regulations are tighter. Applications must be submitted to a Norwegian embassy or consulate before arrival, and applicants must prove that they can finance themselves. If the application is successful, a residence permit issued to a non-EEA national is rarely for longer than one year, takes time to renew, and does not include the right to work –

for that a work permit is required (see p.57). The applicant is also required to have a fixed address for the period concerned.

Although visa requirements are relatively light, checks are frequently made at the port of entry. If you are young and have a rucksack, be prepared to prove that you have enough money to support yourself during your stay. You may also be asked how long you intend to stay and what you are there for. Be polite and never answer facetiously.

DUTY-FREE RESTRICTIONS

The end of "duty-free" within the EU should not impact on travellers to non-member Norway, except for any legs of the journey taken within the EU. On arrival, visitors to Norway may carry, duty-exempt, a maximum of 200 cigarettes (or 250g of tobacco), one litre of wine, and either one litre of strong spirits or two additional litres of wine per person, for example. (Visitors from North America are permitted the duty-free importation of 400 cigarettes or 500g of tobacco.) Returning home, the limits are generally the same, and there are also restrictions as to the value of other goods/purchases you can take home without paying tax – ask the transport carrier if you're unsure. Remember that the importing of food, plants or animals back into Britain, Ireland, the USA, Canada, Australia or New Zealand is severely restricted.

COSTS, MONEY AND BANKS

Norway has a reputation as one of the most expensive of European holiday destinations. In some ways (but only some) this is entirely justified, as most of what you're likely to buy – a cup of coffee, a roll of film, a book – is costly. On the other hand, certain major items are reasonably priced, beginning with **accommodation** which can be remarkably inexpensive when compared with other north European countries. In particular, Norway's youth hostels, almost all of which have family, double and dormitory rooms, are first rate and exceptionally good value. **Getting around** is good news too. Most travellers use some kind of rail pass, there are a fistful of discounts and internal deals, and the state subsidizes the longer and more remote bus hauls. Furthermore, **concessions** are almost universally applied at attractions and on public transport, with infants (aged under 4) going everywhere free, children and seniors (over 67, or sometimes 60) paying half the standard rate. **Food** is, however, a different matter. With few exceptions – for example tinned fish – it's expensive and the cost of **alcohol** is enough to make even a heavy drinker contemplate abstinence. Consequently, **restaurants** are also pricey, though costs remain manageable if you avoid the extras and concentrate on the main courses, for which around £16/$25 will normally suffice – twice that with a starter and dessert. You can, of course, pay a lot more – prices in top Oslo restaurants can be twice the average level, and then some. More economical are the **café-bars**, but these are largely confined to the bigger towns and cities.

Detailed **costs** for places to stay and eat are given in the guide, and you should consult the box on p.38 for general guidelines on accommodation prices. On average, if you're prepared to buy your own picnic lunch, stay in youth hostels, and stick to the less expensive cafés and restaurants, you could get by on around £25/$40 a day excluding the cost of public transport. Staying in three-star hotels, eating in medium-range restaurants most nights (but avoiding drinking in a bar), you'll get through at least £50/$80 a day – with the main variable being the cost of your room. On £120/$190 a day and upwards, you'll be limited only by your energy reserves – though if you're planning to stay in a five-star hotel and to have a big night out, this figure still won't be enough. As always, if you're travelling alone you'll spend much more on accommodation than in a group of two or more: most hotels do have single rooms, but at between sixty and eighty percent of the price of a double.

CURRENCY AND EXCHANGE RATES

Norwegian **currency** consists of **kroner**, one of which, a **krone** (crown; abbreviated kr or NOK), is divided into 100 **øre**. Coins in circulation are 50 øre, 1kr, 5kr and 10kr; notes are for 50, 100, 200, 500 and 1000kr. You can bring in up to 25,000kr in notes and coins (though there's no limit on travellers' cheques).

At the time of writing the **exchange rate** was around 12.4kr to the pound sterling; 7.8kr or so to the US dollar; 5.3kr to the Canadian dollar; 5.2kr to the Australian dollar; 4.2kr to the New Zealand dollar and 0.118kr to the Euro.

TRAVELLERS' CHEQUES AND CREDIT CARDS

The safest way to carry your funds is in **travellers' cheques**, the usual fee for their purchase being one percent of face value. Keep safe the purchase agreement and a record of cheque serial numbers, separately from the cheques themselves. In the event that cheques are lost or stolen, the issuing company will expect you to report the loss forthwith. Consequently, when you buy your travellers' cheques, ensure you have details of the company's emergency contact numbers or the addresses of their local offices. Most companies claim to replace lost or stolen cheques within 24 hours. American Express cheques are sold through most North American, Australian &

New Zealand and European banks, and are the most widely accepted cheques in Norway. American Express also has a travel office in Oslo – see the relevant chapter for the address. When you cash your cheques, you'll find that almost all banks (as well as post offices) make a small service charge per transaction; if this is waived, double-check the rate to ensure that it hasn't been lowered to compensate the bank. Note also that there is no charge for American Express cheques cashed at their Oslo office.

If you have an ordinary British/EU bank account you can use **Eurocheques** with a Eurocheque card in many banks, and can write out cheques in kroner in shops and hotels. In terms of exchange rates, this works out slightly more expensive than travellers' cheques, but can be more convenient; bear in mind also that you nearly always need to have your passport with you as well as the Eurocheque card. Most Eurocheque cards, many Visa, some Mastercard and British bank cards, as well as US cards supporting the Cirrus or Plus systems, can also be used for withdrawing cash from **ATMs** in Norway. Check with your bank to find out about these reciprocal arrangements – the system is highly sophisticated and can often give instructions in a variety of languages. Make sure you have a personal identification number (PIN) that's designed to work overseas.

Credit cards are pretty much essential for car rental, cash advances (though these incur a high rate of interest from the withdrawal date) and hotel bills. American Express, Visa and Mastercard are all widely accepted. To report lost cards, call American Express (☎80 03 32 44); Diners Club (☎22 83 06 91); Mastercard (☎80 03 02 50); or Visa (☎80 03 02 50).

CHANGING MONEY

All but the tiniest of settlements in Norway have a **bank** or **savings bank**, the vast majority of which will change foreign currency and travellers' cheques. Banks will also handle Eurocheques, and many give cash advances on credit cards. **Banking hours** in Norway are usually Monday to Friday from 8.15am to 3pm, though banks close thirty minutes earlier during the summer (June–Aug) and are open till 5pm on Thursday all year. All major **post offices** change foreign currency and travellers' cheques at rates that are comparable to those of the banks, and have longer opening hours too, generally Monday to Friday 8am to 5pm, and Saturday 9am to 1pm. For changing currency, almost every bank and major post office takes a small commission per transaction.

Outside banking and post office hours, most major hotels, many travel agents and some hostels and campsites will change money at less generous rates and with varying commissions, as will the **exchange facilities** in Oslo (see p.104).

WIRING MONEY

Having **money wired** from home is never convenient or cheap, and should be considered a last resort. One option is to have your own bank send the money through, and for that you need to nominate a receiving bank in Norway. Any local branch will do, but those in the bigger towns will probably be more familiar with the process. Naturally, you need to confirm the co-operation of the local bank before you set the wheels in motion back home. The sending bank's fees are scaled to the amount being transferred and to the urgency of the service you require – the fastest transfers, taking two or three days, start at around £12/$17 for the first £300–400/$420–560.

Money can also be wired via American Express, with funds sent by one office available for collection at the company's Oslo office in within minutes – see "Listings", p.104, in the Oslo chapter for the address. All transactions are done in US dollars and the service is only open to American Express card holders. Again, charges depend on the amount being sent, but as an example, wiring $400 from Britain to Norway will cost $37, $4000 will cost you $130. The maximum that can be sent in one go is $10,000.

TAX-FREE SHOPPING

Taking advantage of their decision not to join the EU, the Norwegians have implemented a **tax-free shopping scheme** that applies to EU and non-EU tourists alike. If you spend more than 308kr at one of 3000 outlets in the scheme you'll get a voucher for the amount of VAT you paid. On departure at an airport, ferry terminal or frontier crossing, present the goods, the voucher and your passport, and – provided you haven't used the item – you'll get an 11–18 percent refund, depending on the price. Note, however, that there isn't a reclaim point at every exit from the country, so pick up a leaflet at any of the participating shops to find out where these are. Note also that many of the smaller reclaim points keep normal shop hours, closing for the weekend at 2pm on Saturday.

INSURANCE AND HEALTH

TRAVEL INSURANCE COMPANIES IN THE UK AND IRELAND

Columbus Travel Insurance (☎020/7375 0011, *www.columbusdirect.co.uk*). Particularly good for long-stay and multi-trip policies.

Endsleigh Insurance (☎020/7436 4451, *www.endsleigh.co.uk*). Student specialists.

Frizzell Insurance (☎01202/292 333).

STA Travel, for contact details see box on UK Discount Flight Agents, p.4. Student specialists.

usit CAMPUS, for contact details see box on UK Discount Flight Agents, p.4.

usit NOW, for contact details see box on Ireland Discount Flight Agents, p.9.

As an EEA (European Economic Area) member, Norway has free reciprocal health agreements with other member states – and that includes all the EU countries. **Treatment** under these arrangements is provided within the Norway public health care system, which generally requires you to make a contribution to the cost of non-hospital treatment: up to a maximum of 330kr towards prescribed medicine, and the full cost of dental treatment.

Taking out your own medical insurance means you won't have to fret about whether a doctor is treating you for free, and will also cover the cost of items not within the EU's scheme, such as dental treatment and repatriation on medical grounds. Usually it will also cover your baggage and tickets in case of theft, as long as you get a crime report from the local police. Non-EEA residents will need to insure themselves for all eventualities, including medical costs. It's a good idea to photocopy your insurance documentation for possible use in emergencies (see p.26 under "medical emergencies"). In terms of local difficulties, the more worthwhile policies promise to sort matters out before you pay (rather than after) in the case of major expense; if you do, however, have to pay up-front, get and keep the receipts.

Note that some **bank and credit cards** have medical or other insurance included, and travel insurance is sometimes covered if you pay for your trip with a credit or charge card.

INSURANCE IN BRITAIN AND IRELAND

In Britain and Ireland, travel insurance schemes (around £20–40 per person for a fortnight, £30–50 for a month) are sold by almost every travel agent and bank, by some supermarkets, and direct by several specialist insurance firms. It's also worth comparing the price of an annual multi-trip policy with single trip cover, as these can start as low as £50 per year. Note that if you're engaging in high-risk outdoor activities (for example, hot air ballooning, skiing), you'll almost certainly have to pay an extra premium; ask your insurers for advice.

To take advantage of health care arrangements within the EEA, British citizens are best advised to get a copy of form E111, a "Certificate of Entitlement to Benefits in Kind", available from main UK post offices; other EU nationalities will need the equivalent documentation. You won't be turned away from a hospital because you don't have an E111, but you will almost certainly have to pay (or contribute towards) the bill; with an E111, hospital treatment is free.

INSURANCE IN NORTH AMERICA

In the USA and Canada, insurance tends to be much more expensive, and may cover medical costs only. Travellers should check their **existing insurance schemes**, including any that may be provided with their bank and credit cards, before taking out specific travel insurance. Canadians are often insured by their provincial health plans, while holders of ISIC cards – and some other student/teacher/youth cards – are entitled to accident coverage and hospital in-patient benefits for

TRAVEL INSURANCE COMPANIES IN NORTH AMERICA

Most travel agents will arrange travel insurance at no extra charge. The following insurance companies can be called directly.

Access America US ☎1-800/284-8300; Canada ☎1-800/654-1908.

Carefree Travel Insurance US & Canada ☎1-800/323-3149.

Desjardins Travel Insurance Canada ☎1-800/463 7830.

International Student Insurance Service (ISIS) – sells STA Travel Insurance. US & Canada ☎1-800/777- 0112.

Travel Guard US ☎1-800/826-1300; Canada ☎715/345-0505.

Travel Insurance Services US ☎1-800/937-1387.

the period during which the card is valid. Furthermore, students will often find that their student health coverage extends during the vacations and for one term beyond the date of last enrolment. Homeowners' or renters' insurance often covers theft or loss of documents, money and valuables while overseas, though conditions and maximum amounts vary from company to company.

Only after exhausting the possibilities above might you want to contact a specialist **travel insurance** company. Policies are quite comprehensive, anticipating everything from charter companies going bankrupt to delayed or lost baggage, and also cover sundry illnesses and accidents. **Premiums** vary widely, so shop around. The best premiums are usually to be had through student/youth travel agencies – ISIS now offers STA Travel Insurance for travellers under the age of 60. The insurance has worldwide validity and comes in packages covering, for example, 7 days ($35), 1 month ($115), and 1 year ($730) – for even longer stays, add an extra $35–50 for each additional month.

Note also that very few insurers will arrange on-the-spot payments in the event of a major expense or loss; you will usually be reimbursed only after returning home. If you're planning on doing any **trekking** or other outdoor activity, you'll need to take out additional cover, thereby adding an extra twenty to fifty percent to the premium.

None of these policies insures against **theft overseas**. North American travel policies apply only to items lost from, or damaged in, the custody of an identifiable, responsible third party – a hotel porter or an airline, for example. Even in these cases, however, you will have to contact the local police and have them file a report so that your insurer can process the claim.

INSURANCE IN AUSTRALIA AND NEW ZEALAND

Travel insurance is put together by the airlines and travel-agent consortia such as UTAG, AFTA, Cover-More and Ready Plan, in conjunction with insurance companies. Schemes are similar in terns of premiums and coverage; however Ready Plan usually gives the best value for money. **Adventure sports** are covered by all the above except for mountaineering with ropes, bungee jumping (only covered by some policies) and unassisted diving without an Open Water licence; check your policy before undertaking any such activities. A typical policy will cost A$190/NZ$240 for one month, A$295/NZ$375 for two months and A$380/NZ$480 for three months.

TRAVEL INSURANCE COMPANIES IN AUSTRALIA AND NEW ZEALAND

AFTA (Australian Federation of Travel Agents) ☎02/9956 4800.

Cover More Australia ☎02/9202 8000 and 1800/251 881, NZ 09/377 5958 or 0800/657 744.

Ready Plan Australia ☎03/9791 5077 and 1800/555 017, NZ ☎09/300 5333.

UTAG (United Travel Agents Group) Australia ☎02/9744 7833 and 1800/809 462.

HEALTH

Health care in Norway is of a very high standard and widely available: even the remotest communities are within relatively easy – or well-organized – reach of medical attention. Neither will English speakers often encounter language problems – if the doctor or nurse can't speak English themselves (which is unlikely) there will almost certainly be someone at hand who can.

If you should fall ill, you can get the address of an **English-speaking doctor** from your local pharmacy, tourist office, hotel or even consulate. If you're seeking free treatment under reciprocal EEA health agreements, double-check that the doctor is working within (and seeing you as) a patient of the public health care system. Even within the EEA agreement, you still have to pay a significant portion of the **prescription** charges (senior citizens and children are exempt). Neither do most private insurance policies help cover prescription charges – their "excesses" are usually greater than the cost of the medicines. Note also that within the terms of the EEA agreement you have to pay a proportion of the costs of any non-hospital treatment you receive, whereas hospital treatment is free. If you do get landed with a bill, get a receipt at the time of payment, and take it and your passport to the local sickness office (Lokale Trygdekontor) of the district where treatment was obtained, or the National Office for Social Insurance Abroad (Folketrygdkontoret for utenlandersaker). EEA citizens will subsequently be reimbursed.

Minor ailments can be dealt with at **pharmacies** (*Apotek*). Most are open Monday to Friday 9am–5pm and Saturday mornings, and in the cities a rota system keeps at least one open 24 hours a day. The rota should be displayed in the window of every pharmacy; the tourist offices also have the rota details, and so do some of the better hotels. Outside the cities, you'll find a pharmacy in every town and in some of the larger villages, but the smaller the place, the less likelihood there is of late-night opening.

In medical **emergencies**, telephone ☎113. If you're reliant on free treatment within the EEA health scheme, try to remember to make this clear to the ambulance staff and, if you're whisked off to hospital, to the medic you subsequently encounter. To ensure your non-private status is clearly understood, it's a good idea to have your E111 or equivalent documentation with you always.

INFORMATION AND MAPS

Before you leave home, there's a wealth of information which you can pick up on the Internet (see box opposite) and from the Norwegian Tourist Board offices (see box). Once inside the country all the major towns and most of the larger villages have tourist information offices too. Maps are widely available in Norwegian bookshops and sometimes at the tourist offices as well, but buying one before you go helps in planning – and if

you're driving you will, of course, need a good road map.

TOURIST OFFICES

With offices in half a dozen countries worldwide, the **Norwegian Tourist Board** offers an effi-

---

NORWEGIAN TOURIST BOARD OFFICES

AUSTRALIA No tourist office, but the embassy handles tourist information: 17 Hunter St, Yarralumla, Canberra ACT 2600 (☎062/733 444).

CANADA All travel enquiries dealt with by the US office (see below).

IRELAND No tourist office, but the embassy handles tourist information: 34 Molesworth St, Dublin 2 (☎01/662 1800).

NEW ZEALAND No tourist office or consulate – refer to Australia.

UK Charles House, 5 Lower Regent St, London SW1Y 4LR (☎020/7839 6255, *greatbritain@nortra.no*).

USA 655 Third Ave, Suite 1810, New York, NY 10017 (☎212/855 9700, *usa@nortra.no*).

NORWAY WEB SITES

www.norway.org.uk The Norwegian government's official UK Web site allows you to access embassy and consular information as well as contact the country's tourist board. It's well presented and easy to navigate, but is most useful for its links to other sites. The equivalent US site is at *www.norway.org*

www.tourist.no Norwegian Tourist Board's site, in English.

odin.dep.no/html/english/ ODIN – Official Documentation and Information from Norway. A Norwegian government site, as its name suggests, and despite the plain presentation it has everything you ever wanted to know about Norway and maybe more. Its opening page has links to key information sources, including *Norway Daily*, a digest of news and comment from the Norwegian press. The search engine page is in Norwegian but it works fine with English terms.

www.oslopro.no This official guide to Oslo provides a wealth of information on accommodation, transport, restaurants, entertainment, shopping etc, but the structure of the site is rather confusing.

www.unginfo.oslo.no/streetwise An English guide to Oslo specifically designed for young people. Apart from comprehensive practical information, including a list of public toilets, it contains well-observed and carefully presented guides to cheap eating places, the club scene, outdoor bathing, and a gay guide.

www.bergen-travel.com Bergen tourist board's Web site. Standard transport, accommodation and events information, in Norwegian, English, German, and French. You may prefer **www.bergen-guide.com**, an English-only site with much more detailed, and more current, information.

www.vandrerhjem.no The official site of Norwegian Youth Hostelling, providing clear and detailed information in Norwegian and English. You can make a reservation, order brochures and other publications, and there's a useful news section too.

www.museumsnett.no This Norwegian and English site provides comprehensive information on the country's museums and current exhibitions, incorporating the Web sites of some – such as the National Gallery – with links to others. It's not designed for tourists, so only information about major exhibitions is in English, but it's a pleasure to browse.

www.bike-norway.com Perhaps the best of the English-language cycling sites, it suggests around a dozen routes around the country from around 100km up to 400km, providing you with useful practical information about road conditions, traffic, cycle repair facilities and places of interest en route. Also in German and Norwegian.

www.turistforeningen.no The Norwegian Mountain Touring Association's rather confusing site outlines many of the country's most popular hiking routes, region by region, and gives details of the best maps to buy, as well as selling its own hiking gear. In Norwegian, German and English.

cient service, stocking a wide range of glossy, free booklets. One of their most useful brochures is the official travel guide, currently called *Where on Earth: Norway* in the UK, and *Norway All-Year Travel Directory* in the US. This has touring suggestions and all sorts of background information. There's also the free *NRI Guide to Transport and Accommodation*, a comprehensive and classified listing of all the country's hotels and most guest houses, and including a digest of the main public transport routes. There are also brochures tailored to meet specific interests, for example *Camping*, which lists and grades several hundred major campsites. Furthermore, the Norwegian Tourist Board has a substantial collection of local material – mainly regional guides – and more specific material in the case of the more popular tourist destinations like the fjords, Oslo and Bergen.

The tourist board works in conjunction with **NORTRA**, a commercial foundation jointly funded by the government and the private sector. Among other functions, NORTRA publishes about ten titles on specific aspects of holidaying in Norway, including encyclopaedic information on angling, motoring, mountain hiking, guest harbours and the Hurtigrute coastal ship. The tourist board has the complete list of NORTRA publications.

Inside Norway, **tourist offices** are ten-a-penny. In the smaller towns and larger villages, you can pretty much guarantee you'll get a free map and a list of local sights and hotels. The

MAP OUTLETS IN THE UK

BRISTOL

Stanfords, 29 Corn Street, Bristol BS1 1HT
(☎0117/929 9966).

CAMBRIDGE

Heffers Map and Travel, 3rd Floor, 19 Sidney
St, Cambridge, CB2 3HL (☎01223/568467,
www.heffers.co.uk).

GLASGOW

John Smith and Sons, 57–61 St Vincent St,
Glasgow, G2 5TB (☎0141/221 7472, fax
0141/248 4412, www.johnsmith.co.uk).

LONDON

Daunt Books, 83 Marylebone High St, W1M
3DE (☎020/7224 2295, fax 020/7224 6893); 193
Haverstock Hill, NW3 4QL (☎020/7794 4006).

National Map Centre, 22–24 Caxton St, SW1H
0QU (☎020/7222 2466, www.mapsworld.com).

Stanfords, 12–14 Long Acre, WC2E 9LP
(☎020/7836 1321, sales@stanfords.co.uk).

The Travel Bookshop, 13–15 Blenheim
Crescent, W11 2EE (☎020/7229 5260,
www.thetravelbookshop.co.uk).

NEWCASTLE-UPON-TYNE

Newcastle Map Centre, 55 Grey St,
Newcastle-upon-Tyne, NE1 6EF (☎0191/261
5622, nmc@enterprise.net).

OXFORD

Blackwell's Map and Travel Shop, 53 Broad
St, Oxford OX1 3BQ (☎01865/792792, book-
shop.blackwell.co.uk).

MANCHESTER

Waterstone's, 91 Deansgate, Manchester, M3
2BW (☎0161/837 3000, fax 0161/835 1534,
www.waterstones-manchester-deansgate.co.uk).

MAP OUTLETS IN NORTH AMERICA

CHICAGO

Rand McNally, 444 North Michigan Ave, IL
60611 (☎312/321-1751).

LOS ANGELES

Map Link Inc, 30 S LaPatera Lane, Suite 5,
Santa Barbara, CA 93117 (☎805/692-6777).

same applies in the larger towns and cities, but
here the tourist offices often rent bikes, sell local
discount cards, change money and have access to
a small supply of rooms in private houses. They
will book these on your behalf (either free or for a
minimal charge of around 20–30kr) as part of
their accommodation service, which also includes
the booking of hotel rooms, again for a minimal
charge. Note, however, that you'll usually need to
stump up a refundable deposit of about 200kr in
addition to paying the booking fee. **Opening
hours** vary considerably, but the larger urban
offices are open all year, sometimes every day of
the week, while the smaller concerns operate
from April or May to September, from Monday to
Friday and often during the weekend. Throughout

the summer, the majority are open well into the
evening. We've specified individual opening
hours throughout the guide.

MAPS

The Norwegian Tourist Board's official travel
guide contains several general **maps** of the country and, once you've got to Norway, you'll find it
easy to pick up free city, town and regional maps
from the various tourist offices; we've printed
around thirty maps in the guide to help too. In
popular **cycling** areas, some tourist offices also
sell maps marking local cycle routes; for more on
cycling see p.36.

Drivers will need to invest in proper **road
maps**, the best being the Cappelens series, wide-

MONTRÉAL
Ulysses Travel Bookshop, 4176 St-Denis (☎514/843-9447).

NEW YORK
The Complete Traveler Bookstore, 199 Madison Ave, NY 10016 (☎212/685-9007).
Rand McNally, 150 East 52nd St, NY 10022 (☎212/758-7488).
Traveler's Choice Bookstore, 22 West 52nd St, NY 10019 (☎212/941-1535).

SAN FRANCISCO
The Complete Traveler Bookstore, 3207 Filmore St, CA 92123 (☎415/923-1511).
Rand McNally, 595 Market St, CA 94105 (☎415/777-3131).
Phileas Fogg's Books & Maps, Stanford

Shopping Center, Suite 87, Palo Alto, CA 94304 (☎1-800/233-FOGG in California; ☎1-800/533-FOGG elsewhere in US).

SEATTLE
Elliot Bay Book Company, 101 South Main St, WA 98104 (☎206/624-6600).

TORONTO
Open Air Books and Maps, 25 Toronto St, M5C 2R1 (☎416/363-0719).

VANCOUVER
World Wide Books and Maps, 736 Granville St, BC V6Z 1E4 (☎604/687-3320).

WASHINGTON, DC
Rand McNally, 7988 Tysons Corner Center, McLean, VA 22102 (☎703/556-8688).

MAP OUTLETS IN AUSTRALIA AND NEW ZEALAND

ADELAIDE
The Map Shop, 16a Peel St (☎08/8231 2033).

AUCKLAND
Specialty Maps, 58 Albert St (☎09/307 2217).

MELBOURNE
Mapland, 372 Little Bourke St (☎03/9670 4383).

PERTH
Perth Map Centre, 891 Hay St (☎08/9322 5733).

SYDNEY
Travel Bookshop, Shop 3, 175 Liverpool St (☎02/9261 8200).

ly available in Norway, less so elsewhere. The only drawbacks are that they don't have place-name indexes and that, at their usual scale of 1:325,000, it takes six maps (each retailing at around 85kr) to cover the whole country. Hallwag's 1:1000,000 *Norge* map has an index and a sliding distance guide on the back cover, but the scale is a tad too large. Look out for a new, updated edition of Roger Lascelles' first-rate map of Norway (1:800,000), which also has an index. Alternatively, several companies produce all-in-one maps of Norway and/or Scandinavia. For general touring, the optimum scale is 1:800,000 as is used in the *Euro Country Map of Norway, Denmark and Sweden*, published by Euromap. This is particularly clear and easy to fol-

low, and has a helpful place-name index, but its inclusion of Denmark and Sweden makes it a little unwieldy.

Authoritative **hiking maps** at the 1:50,000 scale are produced to a very high standard by the government's highways department. They cover every part of the country and carry the trademark *Statens Kartverk*. They are available abroad (see specialist map shops in the box above), but note there's usually a twenty percent mark-up on the domestic price of 50–60kr. For more information, see "Planning a Hike", p.53.

Finally, if you intend getting to know **Oslo** well, the fold-out *Falkplan* is the best on the market and is easy to get hold of both in Norway and abroad.

GETTING AROUND

Norway's **public transport system** – a huge mesh of trains, buses, car ferries and passenger express ferries – is comprehensive and reliable. In the winter services can be cut back severely (especially in the north), but no part of the country is unreachable for long. Bear in mind, however, that Norwegian villages and towns usually spread over a large distance, so don't be surprised if you end up having to walk a kilometre or two from the station to where you want to go. It's this sprawling nature of the country's towns, and more especially the remoteness of many of the sights, that encourages visitors to rent a car (see p.34).

With regard to **public transport timetables**, most of the principal air, train, bus and ferry services are detailed in the *NRI Guide to Transport and Accommodation*, a free and easy-to-use booklet available in advance from Norwegian Tourist Board offices (see p.26). Once you get to the country, you'll find that almost every tourist office carries a comprehensive range of free local and regional public transport timetables. In addition, all major train stations carry *NSB Togruter*, a free brochure detailing all Norway's train timetables, while long-distance bus routes operated by the national carrier, Nor-Way Bussekspress, are listed in a twice-yearly free *Rutehefte* (timetable), available at principal bus stations. However, for complex itineraries you might want to invest in the hefty *Rutebok for Norge*. Published five times a year, and costing around 200kr, this contains every schedule in the country as well as prices and lists of all government-approved accommo-

dation. The book also gives the fixed-price taxi tariffs that apply to all town-to-town journeys – though expensive, these can be a real life-saver in remote regions – and a very useful route-planning section with maps. An English section helps you navigate round the book, available from leading bookshops, many travel agents and some tourist offices.

TRAINS

Train services are operated by NSB – Norges Statsbaner (Norwegian State Railways, ☎81 50 08 88, *www.nsb.no*) – and run, apart from a sprinkling of branch lines, on three main routes, linking Oslo to Stavanger in the southwest, to Bergen in the west, and to Trondheim and on to Bodø in the north. In places, the rail system is extended by a TogBuss (literally "train-bus") service, with connecting coaches continuing on from the train terminal. The nature of the country means most of the routes are engineering feats of some magnitude, and worth a trip in their own right – the tiny **Flåm line** and sweeping **Rauma line** from Dombås to Åndalsnes are exciting examples.

Prices are bearable, the popular Oslo–Bergen run, for example, costing around 580kr one-way, Oslo–Trondheim 670kr. Both journeys take around six and a half hours, sometimes longer. Costs can be reduced by purchasing a **rail pass** (see opposite). NSB also offers a variety of special **discount fares**. There are two main discount schemes: with **Minipris** tickets, you can shave up to fifty percent off the price of long-distance journeys, the main restrictions being that they must be purchased at least one day in advance, are not available on peak periods and on certain trains, and do not permit stopovers. The trains you *can* take are indicated with a green dot on timetables. In general terms, the further you travel, the more economic they become with, for instance, the Minipris ticket from Oslo to Bodø costing 565kr as compared to the regular fare of 1060kr. Alternatively, NSB's **Customer Card** offers a fifty-percent reduction on the normal second-class fare on these same "green-dot" departures and a twenty-percent reduction on all other trains. The cards cost around 420kr, are valid for one year and are sold at all staffed train stations. In addition, NSB offer a variety of special deals

DISCOUNT FARES WITH RAIL PASSES ON BOATS AND BUSES

The following list is not comprehensive – it's always worth showing a rail pass to see if there are any special discounts on bus and boat trips – but it does give details of some of the more important discounts. InterRail and ScanRail passes entitle holders to a discount of fifty percent on the price of a ticket on the following **bus routes**: the Møreekspressen (Oslo–Otta–Ålesund); Nordfjordekspressen (Oslo–Otta–Stryn); Øst-Vestxpressen (Lillehammer–Sogndal–Bergen); Sogn og Fjordane ekspressen (Oslo–Sogndal–Florø); Vestlandsbussen (Bergen–Ålesund); Vestlandsekspressen (Ålesund–Kristiansund); Bergen–Trondheim; Bodø–Fauske–Narvik; Fauske–Lofotens; Fauske–Harstad; Narvik–Lofotens; Narvik–Tromsø; and Tromsø–Alta. Certain Hurtigbåt (Ekspressbåt) **passenger express boats** also offer fifty-percent discounts to these same rail pass holders, principally on the Bergen–Haugesund–Stavanger, Narvik–Svolvaer and Bergen–Flåm and Flåm–Gudvangen routes.

and discounts – enquire locally (and ahead of time) for details on any specific route.

Concessionary fares include group and family reductions, while children aged 3 and under travel free provided they don't take up a seat; those under 16 pay half fare and so do senior citizens. It's worth noting that inter-city trains and all overnight and international services require an advance **seat reservation** (25kr) whether you have a rail pass or not. In high season it's wise to make a seat reservation on main routes anyway, as trains can be packed. **Sleepers** are reasonably priced if you consider you'll save a night's hotel accommodation: a bed in a three-berth cabin costs around 110kr, in a two-berth cabin from 220kr, and a one-berth cabin about 600kr.

Train travel is offered in two classes, referred to as **standard** and **economy** (NSB markets "first-class" rail tickets and passes abroad only, on the reasonable assumption that the term "standard class" might be misunderstood). NSB **timetables** are available for free at every train station. The general timetable, the *NSB Togruter*, is supplemented by individual timetables on each of the lines and, in the case of the more scenic routes, by leaflets describing the sights as you go.

For further advance advice about passes, discounts and tickets, either contact the specialist agents listed in the "Getting There" section (pp.3–19) or NSB direct.

RAIL PASSES

The **Norway Rail Pass** allows unlimited travel on the railways of Norway on a specified number of days within a given period. Three days of economy-class travel in a one-month period costs about 1000kr, four days 1270kr, five days 1430kr. These passes can be bought both inside Norway

and abroad from specialist rail-ticket agents. Children aged 3 and under travel free, 4- to 16-year-olds get a fifty percent discount and seniors (aged 60 and over) twenty percent. Both the **InterRail** and **Eurail** passes (for more details of which see pp.5–6 and pp.14–15) are valid for the Norwegian railway system, as is the **ScanRail** pass covering Norway, Sweden, Denmark and Finland (see p.14).

All rail pass holders have to shell out a small additional **surcharge** on certain trains on certain routes, and also have to pay the 25kr seat reservation fee that is compulsory on most Inter-City trains and all overnight and international services. On the plus side, rail passes are good for travel on the TogBuss (see opposite), and both ScanRail and InterRail provide a fifty-percent discount on specified bus and boat routes (see box above).

BUSES

Where the train network won't take you, **buses** will – and at no great cost, either: a substantial fjord journey, like the Sogndal–Florø trip, costs 228kr, while the ten-hour bus ride between Ålesund and Bergen is a reasonable 470kr. All tolls and ferry costs are included in the price of a ticket, which can represent a significant saving. Though the express bus network connects major towns throughout Norway, you'll need to use buses principally in the western fjords and the far north. Most long-distance buses are operated by the national carrier, **Nor-Way Bussekspress**, whose head office is at Karl Johans gate 2, N-0154 Oslo (national enquiry number ☎23 00 24 40, *www.nor-way.no*, *ruteinformasjon@nor-way.no*). Their services are supplemented by a dense network of local buses, whose timetables are available at most tourist offices and bus stations. In general terms, most longer routes tend to operate once daily, usually early, while shorter hauls, although more frequent, often tail off in the late afternoon. **Tickets** are usually bought on board, but travel agents sell advance tickets on the more popular long-distance routes; be sure to keep your ticket till the journey is completed. Whenever the bus crosses on a ferry, the price of the bus ticket includes that cost. (On those rare occasions when the bus drops you on one jetty with another waiting on the other side, then passengers have to fork out for the ferry ride.)

Rail pass and student card holders should always ask about **discounts** when purchasing a ticket. Nor-Way Bussekspress offers InterRail and ScanRail pass holders a fifty-percent reduction on certain bus services (see box on p.31), and some local bus companies have comparable discount deals. Other **concessionary fares** include group and family reductions; children aged 3 and under travel free provided they don't take up a seat, and youngsters under 16 pay half fare, as do senior citizens (over 67).

If you are going to travel by bus to any degree, then Nor-Way Bussekspress' **NOR-WAY BusPass** is excellent value. Valid on all their services, the pass covers travel and guarantees a seat without any advance booking (except for groups of more than eight) – the idea being that if one bus gets full, then they will lay on another. It is not, however, valid on the majority of local bus services. There are seven-day (1375kr) and fourteen-day (2200kr) passes, and any toll and ferry costs are covered. Infants under three travel free and a pass for a child (aged 4 to 15) costs 75 percent of the adult rate. The pass can be purchased at any of the larger bus stations in Norway, and at the company's head office, Karl Johans gate 2, Oslo; at the time of its issue you're given a complimentary timetable detailing all Nor-Way Bussekspress services.

FERRIES

Using a **ferry** in Norway is one of the highlights of any visit – and indeed among the western fjords and around the Lofotens they are all but impossible to avoid. The majority are roll-on, roll-off **car-ferries** and represent an economical means of transport, with prices fixed on a nationwide sliding scale: short journeys (of ten to fifteen minutes) cost foot passengers 15–20kr, whereas a car and driver (who are always lumped togeth-

er) would pay in the region of 80kr. Ferry **procedures** are straightforward: foot passengers walk on and pay the conductor, drivers wait in line with their vehicles on the jetty till the conductor comes to the car window to collect the money. However, some busier routes have a drive-by ticket office. One or two of the longer car ferry journeys (in particular Bodø–Moskenes) take advance reservations, but the rest operate on a first-come first-served basis. Off-season, there's no real need to arrive more than twenty minutes before departure – with the possible exception of the Lofoten Island ferries – but in the summer allow two to three hours to be safe.

HURTIGBÅT PASSENGER EXPRESS BOATS

Called either Hurtigbåt or simply Ekspressbåt, Norway's **passenger express boats** are catamarans which make up in speed what they lack in enjoyment – unlike the ordinary ferries, you're cooped up and view the passing landscape through a window. In choppy seas, the ride can be very bumpy too. Nonetheless, they are a very convenient way of saving time: for instance, the Hurtigbåt service from Harstad to Tromsø takes merely two-and-a-half hours, compared with six and a half by Hurtigrute (see below). Hurtigbåt services are concentrated on the west coast around Bergen and the neighbouring fjords; the majority operate all year. Fares are significantly more expensive per kilometre than on the car ferries, and there's no fixed tariff table, so rates also vary considerably. For example, the Hurtigbåt from Bergen to Stavanger, a four-hour trip, costs 510kr, whereas the Oslo to Arendal service takes almost seven hours and costs 440kr. There are **concessionary fares** on all routes, with infants up to the age of 3 travelling free, children (aged 4 to 15) and senior citizens getting a fifty-percent discount. In addition, rail pass holders and students are often eligible for a fifty-percent reduction on the full adult rate – ask the boat operator.

HURTIGRUTE COASTAL FERRIES

Norway's most celebrated ferry journey is the long and beautiful haul up the coast from Bergen to Kirkenes on the **Hurtigrute** (the word literally means "rapid route") **coastal ship** – or "coastal steamer" in honour of its past rather than present means of locomotion. The service began in 1893, earning its nickname by completing the journey in a fraction of the time it took to travel overland. To many the Hurtigrute remains the quintessential

Norwegian experience and it certainly is the best way to observe the rigours of this extraordinary coastline. Until fairly recently, the ferry was a vital supply line to the remote towns of northern Norway, but the extension of the road system has taken away much of its earlier importance. Nonetheless, it continues to act as a delivery service, its survival assured by its popularity with tourists – and you may find the lounges full of elderly British and American travellers.

Although the Hurtigrute fleet comprises cruise ships, you don't need to have a cabin as sleeping in the lounges or on deck is allowed. Also note that the older ships are the more interesting vessels to travel on, even if the showering arrangements are a little less extensive. That apart, the new ships are more appropriate for cars as the old ones only have room for five or six vehicles, which have to be winched – expensively – on and off. Bikes travel free. Each ship has a first-rate restaurant and a 24-hour cafeteria.

There is one service daily in each direction, stopping off at over thirty ports along the way. **Tickets** for the whole return trip, which lasts eleven days and includes all meals, go for anything from 8000kr to 24,000kr depending on whether you're sailing on one of the old or new vessels, where your cabin is on the boat and when you sail – October to March departures are around forty percent cheaper than those in the summer. There are also **concessionary fares** offering fifty-percent discounts for senior citizens (over 67), families, groups of ten or more, students, and children (aged 4 to 15). Infants up to 3 years old travel free providing they do not occupy a separate berth. Note that these discounts are only valid for a limited number of cabins in the summer, which makes pre-booking pretty much essential. If you're over 16 and under 26 and travelling between September and April, another option is a **coastal pass**, which costs 1750kr for 21 days' unlimited travel. Further details are available from many travel agencies outside Norway, and they can also make bookings. Making a booking once you've got to Norway is easy too, either through a travel agency or with the shippers themselves: **OVDS** (☎76 96 76 96, fax 76 96 76 11) and **TFDS** (☎77 64 82 00, fax 77 64 82 40). Most travel agents and local tourist offices have copies of the sailing schedule and there is an informative Web site – *www.hurtigruten.com/uk* – giving details of the ships and timetables.

If you have neither the time nor money nor inclination to embark upon an extended voyage with the Hurtigrute, a **short hop** along the coast is well worth considering. Fares are not particularly cheap, especially in comparison with the bus: for example a standard, high-season, one-way passenger fare from Kristiansund to Trondheim costs 452kr (7hr), Stamsund to Bodø 278kr (4hr 30min). But last-minute bargains can bring the rates right down to amazingly low levels, with or without car transport. All the tourist offices in the Hurtigrute ports have the latest details and should be willing to telephone the nearest ship to make a reservation on your behalf.

PLANES

Internal flights can prove a surprisingly inexpensive way of hopping about the country and are especially useful if you're short on time and want to reach, say, the far north. Tromsø to Kirkenes takes the best part of two days by bus, but it's just an hour by plane. Domestic air routes are served by several companies, but the two big players are **Braathens** (part of the KLM group) and **SAS**. Both operate a variety of **discount** schemes. For instance, Braathens offer a special youth fare for under-25s which knocks between 50 and 75 percent off the full price, though you have to pay in full at the time you make your booking. The same airline also has special **excursion fares** bookable no fewer than seven days prior to departure and including a Saturday night away: Trondheim–Tromsø in this scheme costs 1330kr return. Otherwise, always check out Braathens' special offers, which often provide some great bargains. In terms of **concessionary fares**, both SAS and Braathens permit infants aged 2 and under to travel free, while seniors, and children under 16 pay half-price when travelling in a family group with at least one full-fare-paying adult.

The details of these various discounts vary year to year, so it's always worth shopping around. But as a baseline, one can expect a discount of around forty percent off the standard fares.

Braathens, SAS and the Norwegian company Widerøe have excellent-value **air passes**. Braathens' **Northern Lights Pass** is valid on all the company's routes from May to September, the only restriction being that you're not eligible if you are resident in Scandinavia. Under the terms of the pass, one-way flights within southern or northern Norway cost around 500kr, one-way flights between south and north are about 1000kr. The dividing line between north and south is drawn through Trondheim, which is counted as belonging to both zones. The pass can be bought before or after you get to Norway. Further details direct from Braathens either in Britain (for addresses see p.4) or in Norway, where they operate one nationwide central reservation number (☎67 58 60 00). Widerøe's **Summerpass** (June–August) offers cheap flights within four designated zones (£40 within a zone, or £80 across two), but there are a number of conditions, the most important being that you must buy your pass *before* travelling to Norway. For details of SAS' **AirPass**, valid on flights within Scandinavia, see p.14.

DRIVING AND CAR RENTAL

Norway's main roads are excellent, especially when you consider the vagaries of the climate, and now that most of the more hazardous sections have been ironed out or bypassed by tunnelling, driving them is comparatively straightforward. That said, you still have to be careful on some of the higher sections and in the enormous tunnels, and once you leave the main roads for the narrow byroads that wind across the mountains, you'll be in for some nail-biting experiences – and that's in the summertime. In winter the Norwegians close many roads to concentrate their efforts on keeping the main highways open, but obviously blizzards and ice can make driving anywhere difficult, even dangerous, winter tyres, studs and chains notwithstanding. Always seek local advice especially if you're venturing onto minor roads; in the north you can't assume that even the E6 Arctic Highway will be driveable. At any time of the year, the more adventurous the drive, the better equipped you need to be: on remote drives you should pack provisions, have proper hiking gear, check the car thoroughly before departure and carry a spare can of petrol.

Norway's main highways have an E prefix – E6, E18 etc; all the country's other significant roads (*riksvei*, or *rv*) are assigned a number and, as a general rule, the lower the number, the busier the road. In our guide, we've used the E prefix, but designated the other roads as Highways (followed by their numbers). Don't be too amazed if a road number given in the guide is wrong – the Norwegians are forever changing the numbers.

Tolls are imposed on certain roads to pay for construction projects such as bridges and tunnels. Once the costs are covered the toll is removed. The older building projects levy a fee of around 20–30kr, but the toll for some of the newer works (like the tunnel near Fjaerland) runs to well over 100kr per vehicle. There's also a modest toll (5–15kr) on entering the country's larger cities, but whether this is an environmental measure or a means of boosting city coffers is debatable. To avoid getting flustered at a toll booth, Norwegian drivers carry a supply of coins.

Fuel is readily available, even in the north, though here the settlements are so far from one another that you'll need to keep your tank pretty full; if you're using the byroads extensively, remember to carry an extra can. Current fuel prices are around 8–10kr a litre and there are four

ACCESS TO MAJOR MOUNTAIN PASSES

Obviously enough, there's no preordained date for opening mountain roads in the springtime – it depends on the weather, and the threat of avalanches is often much more of a limitation than actual snowfall. The dates below should therefore be treated with caution, and you should seek advice from a local tourist office if in doubt. If you should head along a mountain road that's closed, sooner or later you'll come to a barrier and have to turn round.

E6: Oslo–Trondheim via the **Dovrefjell**. Usually open all year.

E69: Skarsvåg–Nordkapp. Closed late Oct to early April.

E134: Oslo–Bergen–Stavanger, via **Haukelifjell**. Usually open all year.

Highway 7: Oslo–Bergen via the **Hardangervidda**. Usually open all year.

Highway 51: Otta–Fagernes. Closed mid-Dec to early May.

Highway 55: Lom–Sogndal via the **Sognefjellet**. Closed early Dec to early May.

Highway 63: Grotli–Geiranger–Linge via the **Trollstigen**. Closed mid-Oct to late May.

main grades – Unleaded (*blyfri*) 95 octane; Unleaded 98 octane; Super 98 octane; and diesel. It's worth remembering that many petrol stations don't accept credit cards, so make sure you have enough cash before filling up.

DOCUMENTATION AND RULES OF THE ROAD

EU **driving licences** are honoured in Norway, but other nationals will need an **International Driver's Licence** (available at minimal cost from your home motoring organization). Any sort of provisional licence is, however, not acceptable. If you're bringing your own car, you must have vehicle registration papers, adequate insurance, a first-aid kit, a warning triangle and a green card (available from your insurer or motoring organization). Extra insurance coverage for unforeseen legal costs is also well worth having, as is an appropriate **breakdown policy** from a motoring organization. In Britain, for example, the RAC and AA charge members and non-members about £95 for a month's Europe-wide breakdown cover, with all the appropriate documentation, including green card, provided.

Rules of the road are strict: you drive on the right, with dipped headlights required at all times and seatbelts compulsory for drivers and front-seat passengers (back-seat passengers too, if fitted). There's a speed limit of 30kph in residential areas, 50kph in built-up areas, 80kph on open roads and 90kph on motorways and some main roads. Cameras monitor hundreds of kilometres of main road – watch for the *Automatisk Trafikk Kontroll* warning signs – and speeding fines are so heavy that local drivers stick religiously within the speed limit. If you are filmed speeding in a rental car, expect your credit card to be stung by the rental company to the tune of at least 700kr. If you're stopped for **speeding**, note that there are large spot fines (700–3000kr) payable and rarely is any leniency shown to unwitting foreigners. **Drunken driving** is also severely frowned upon. You can be asked to take a breath test during a routine traffic-check; if over the limit, you will have your licence confiscated and may face 28 days in prison.

If you **break down** in a rental car, you'll get roadside assistance from the particular repair company the car hire firm has contracted. The same principle applies to your own vehicle and its insurance/breakdown policy. Two major **breakdown companies** in Norway are Norges Automobil-Forbund (NAF; 24hr assistance on ☎81 00 05 05) and Viking Redningstjeneste (24hr assistance on ☎80 03 29 00). There are emergency telephones along some motorways, and NAF patrols all mountain passes between mid-June and mid-August.

CAR RENTAL

All the major international **car rental** companies are represented in Norway, and details are given

---

CAR RENTAL AGENCIES

BRITAIN
Avis ☎0990/900 500
Budget ☎0541/56 56 56
Europcar ☎0870/607 5000
Hertz ☎0990/99 66 99
Holiday Autos ☎0990/300 400
Thrifty ☎0990/168 238

NORTH AMERICA
Auto Europe ☎1-800/223-5555,
www.autoeurope.com
Avis ☎1-800/331-1084, *www.avis.com*
Budget ☎1-800/527-0700,
www.drivebudget.com
Europe by Car ☎1-800/223-1516,
www.europebycar.com

Hertz ☎1-800/654-3001, *www.hertz.com*
Holiday Autos ☎1-800/422-7737,
www.kemwel.com
National ☎1-800/227-7368,
www.nationalcar.com

AUSTRALIA
Avis ☎1800/225 533
Budget ☎1300/362 848
Hertz ☎1800/550 067

NEW ZEALAND
Avis ☎09/526 2847 and ☎0800/655 111
Budget ☎09/375 2222
Hertz ☎09/309 0989 and ☎0800/655 955

in the guide's "Listings" sections for the larger cities. To rent a car, you'll have to be 21 or over (and have been driving for at least a year), and you'll need a credit card – though occasionally an agency will accept a hefty cash deposit. Rental **charges** are fairly high, beginning around 3600kr per week for unlimited mileage in the smallest vehicle, but include collision damage waiver and vehicle (but not personal) insurance. To cut costs, watch for special deals offered by the bigger companies – a Friday to Monday weekend rental might, for example, cost you as little as 1000kr. If you go to a smaller, local company (of which there are many, listed in the telephone directory under *Bilutleie*), you should proceed with care. In particular, check the policy – it will usually be in Norwegian and in English – for the excess applied to claims and ensure that it includes collision damage waiver (applicable if an accident is your fault) as well as adequate levels of financial cover. Bear in mind, too, that it's almost always less expensive to make your rental arrangements before you leave home and pick the car up at the airport on arrival (see box p.35).

CYCLING

Cycling in Norway is not as ludicrous as it sounds, and is a great way of taking in the scenery – just be sure to wrap up warm and dry, and don't be over-ambitious in the distances you expect to cover. Dedicated cycle tracks are few and far between, and mainly confined to the larger towns, but there's precious little traffic on most of the minor roads and cycling them is a popular pastime. Furthermore, whenever a road is improved or re-routed, the old highway is usually redesigned as a cycle route. At almost every place you're likely to stay in, you can anticipate that someone – the tourist office, a sports shop, youth hostel or campsite – will **rent bikes**. Costs are pretty uniform; reckon on paying between 120kr and 200kr a day for a 7-speed bike plus a refund-

able deposit of up to 1000kr; mountain bikes are about thirty percent more. We've given local details of outlets and costs throughout the guide.

A few tourist offices have maps of recommended cycling routes, but this is a rarity. It is, however, important to check your itinerary thoroughly, especially in the more mountainous areas. Cyclists aren't allowed through the longer **tunnels** for their own protection (the fumes can be life-threatening), so discuss your plans with whoever you rent the bike from. You'll also need good lights to ride through those tunnels that aren't prohibited. Bikes mostly go free on car ferries and incur a nominal charge on passenger express boats, but buses vary. The national carrier, Nor-Way Bussekspress, accepts bikes only when there is space and charges the appropriate child fare, while local buses sometimes take them free, sometimes charge and sometimes do not take them at all. There's a fee of between 50kr and 180kr to take bikes on regular, local trains, but in the case of express trains you have to send your bike on ahead at least 24 hours before you yourself set off – the rates are the same.

If you're planning a **cycling holiday**, your first port of call should be the Norwegian Tourist Board (for addresses see p.26). They provide general cycling advice and issue a map that indicates the roads and tunnels inaccessible to cyclists. They also have a list of companies offering all-inclusive cycling **tours**. Among several, Erik & Reidar, Kirkegata 34a, Oslo (☎22 41 23 80, fax 22 41 23 90, *erikogreidar@online.no*), runs tours of the Hardanger plateau, the Lofotens and Geiranger; and *Pedal Nor*, Kløverveien 10, Sandnes (☎51 66 40 60, fax 51 66 48 70, *pedal@robin.no*), has a varied programme including fjord and Lofoten island tours. Tour costs vary enormously, but as a baseline reckon on about 5000kr per week all inclusive. The *Syklistenes Landsforening* (the Norwegian Cyclist Association, Storgata 20c, Oslo; ☎22 41 50 80) has an excellent range of cycling books and maps.

ACCOMMODATION

Inevitably, hotel accommodation is one of the major expenses you will incur on a trip to Norway – indeed, if you're after a degree of comfort, it's going to be the costliest item by far. There are, however, budget alternatives, principally private rooms (arranged via the local tourist office), campsites and cabins, and last but certainly not least, an abundance of HI-registered youth hostels. Also bear in mind that most hotels offer 25–40 percent **discounts** in summer and often give all-year weekend discounts too.

HOTELS

Norwegian **hotels** are almost universally of a high standard: neat, clean and efficient.

LEADING HOTEL DISCOUNT AND PASS SCHEMES

Best Western Summer Pass Costing about 60kr, this ensures you get the best bed-and-breakfast rates at any of Best Western's fifty-odd Norwegian hotels during high summer (mid-June to late August) and at the less popular hotels from May to September. Discounted prices start at around 590kr per night for a double room. Advance reservations are required to guarantee a bed – either via any hotel in the chain or through the central reservations office, Cort Adelers gate 16, PO Box 2773 Solli, N-0204 Oslo. Reservations can be made in the UK (☎0800/393130).

Fjord Pass Over 200 hotels and guesthouses across most of Norway participate in this scheme, with prices for bed and breakfast ranging from 200kr to 500kr per person per night. The only initial outlay is for the pass itself, which costs 75kr; it's valid for two adults and their children under the age of 15. Savings are generally around ten percent on summer prices. The pass is valid from May to September, but many of the hotels only participate for a part of the period. Several different chains take part and so do some family-run guesthouses, and you can make advance bookings direct with the participants. In Norway, the pass is available at some travel agents and tourist offices or direct from Fjord Tours, PO Box 1752, N-5024 Bergen (☎55 32 65 50, fax 55 31 20 60, *fjordpass@ru-gruppen.no*).

The Oslo Package If you're spending time in Oslo, this package offers you discounted bed-and-breakfast rates at over forty hotels in the city, and provides an **Oslo Card** (see p.67) too. The offer is available from mid-June to mid-August, over Christmas, Easter, and weekends all year. Prices start at 399kr per person in a double room, with up to two children under 16, sharing with adults, staying for free. The package can be arranged at Oslo tourist information offices or, in the UK, from Norsc Holidays (☎01297/560033).

Rica Summer Hotel Pass (Sommerdager Feriepass) Around forty Rica-chain establishments and affiliated hotels participate in this scheme. Valid from mid-June to early August, the hotel pass entitles you to discounts of up to fifty percent on standard tariffs. Under its terms, double rooms cost between 325kr and 520kr per person, with infants under five staying free of charge. Passes can be obtained at Rica hotels (PO Box 453, N-1301 Sandvika, ☎67 80 72 00, fax 67 80 72 50, *www.rica.no*) and most major tourist offices.

Scan + Hotel Pass Offering discounts of up to fifty percent in over 200 hotels throughout Scandinavia, with around a third of these scattered the length of Norway. The pass costs about 100kr and is valid at a number of different hotel chains in Norway, including the mid-price *Rainbow* and *Norlandia* hotels. It's valid at weekends and throughout the summer, and can be purchased from PO Box 6615, St Olavs plass, 0129 Oslo (☎22 01 07 00, fax 22 83 22 23, *service@rainbowhotel.com*).

ACCOMMODATION PRICE CODES

All the accommodation listed in this guide has been graded according to the following categories. These are primarily intended as a guide to price; the description of the level of facilities in each category given below is a rough outline of what you might reasonably expect, not a hard-and-fast rule. Note that the price categories are for the **least expensive double room** – for example without private bath, etc – during high season, excluding special deals. We also give price codes with some chalets and cabin-style accommodation; these buildings are nominally for two people but many can take up to six comfortably. With youth hostels, the price codes are based on rates that apply to HI members (non-members pay a surcharge of 25kr a night); additionally we give the krone rates for dorm beds.

Over the summer period, many hotels offer fixed discounts, and such discounted rates are denoted by s/r throughout the guide. Note also that many hotels have a wide range of rooms, and sometimes the only rooms available will be a grade higher than we have given. Finally, mitigating the cost is the buffet breakfast that's usually included with the price – for more on food see p.41.

① **Under 500kr.** This category covers the bulk of hostel accommodation, where the charge for a bunk in a dormitory will normally be around 120kr per person per night. Most dormitories have four bunks, some six, but few are larger. Showers and toilets are often shared between dormitories, though almost never to excess, but many have their own. Most Norwegian hostels also have some form of private accommodation – single- and double-bedded rooms – costing in the region of 320kr per room; some are en suite. Rooms in private houses – private rooms – are arranged through the local tourist office and normally cost in the region of 300–400kr per room.

② **500–700kr** In this category are the more expensive private rooms and the majority of guesthouses. The rooms are normally without private facilities except for washbasins or, sometimes, showers. Expect the rooms to be fairly simple, particularly in the cities. Also in this grade are the most expensive family rooms in hostels; many of these rooms are en suite.

③ **700–900kr** In wintertime, this category covers only the least expensive Norwegian hotels, most of which are fairly modern, with functional, en-suite bedrooms. In summer, however, discounts bring into this price category some excellent rooms in better hotels, from plush and commodious doubles to attractive period rooms in the older establishments.

④ **900–1200kr** In winter, this grade covers most of the country's better hotels, from modern high-rises with all mod cons to the majority of older, period places. A substantial proportion of them drop their prices to a less expensive category in the summer. Rooms are always en suite and mostly equipped with phone, TV, perhaps a mini-bar, and occasionally room service.

⑤ **1200–1500kr** At this price, you can expect every luxury – private bathroom, mini-bar, phone and TV, room service – perhaps a gym, swimming pool and sauna.

⑥ **Over 1500kr** There are surprisingly few hotels – mainly in Oslo and Bergen – in this price band. Every luxury.

Summer prices and more impromptu weekend deals also make many of them, by European standards at least, comparatively economical. Another plus is that the price of a hotel room always includes a buffet breakfast – and especially in middle-ranking hotels and up, breakfasts can be sumptuous banquets. The only negatives are the rooms themselves – they tend to be small, especially singles – and their lack of character: Norway abounds in mundane concrete and glass high-rise hotels, though to be fair there is a fair smattering of original and often antique places too.

In summer you can take advantage of one of several **hotel discount and pass schemes** in operation throughout Norway (see box, p.37). There are five main ones to choose from and each serves to cut costs, but often at the expense of a flexible, or rather spontaneous, itinerary – advance booking is the norm – and diversity: you might prefer to mix hotel and hostel accommodation rather than staying in a hotel every night. Most Norwegian hotels are members of one discount/pass scheme or another. All Norwegian hotels, their room rates, summer discounts and facilities, are listed in the free booklet *Transport og Overnatting*, available from Norwegian tourist offices.

PENSIONS AND GUESTHOUSES

For something a little more informal and less anonymous than the average hotel, **pensions** – *pensjonater* or *hospits* – are your best bet, small, intimate guesthouses usually available in the larger cities and more touristy towns, which go for about 350–450kr single, 450–550kr double; breakfast is generally extra. A *gjestgiveri* is a **guesthouse** or **inn**, charging the same sort of price and sometimes occupying fine old premises. Facilities in all are usually adequate and homely without being overwhelmingly comfortable; more often than not bathrooms are communal. Some pensions and guesthouses have kitchens available for the use of guests; ask at the local tourist office. A main advantage of this type of accommodation is that you're very likely to meet other residents – a real boon (perhaps) if you're travelling alone.

YOUTH HOSTELS

For many budget travellers as well as hikers, climbers and skiers, the country's **youth hostels** (*Vandrerjhem*) provide the accommodation mainstay: almost one hundred in all, spread right across the country, with handy concentrations in the western fjords, the central hiking and skiing regions and around Oslo. The hostels are invariably excellent and the Norwegian hostelling association, **Norske Vandrerhjem**, Dronningens gate 26, Oslo (☎23 13 93 00, fax 23 13 93 50, *hostels@online.no*), puts out a free booklet, *Norske Vandrerhjem*, which details locations, opening dates, prices and telephone numbers. There's just one quibble: those hostels that occupy school buildings do tend to be rather drab and institutional.

Prices vary, anything from 100kr to 180kr, although the more expensive ones nearly always include a good breakfast. On average, reckon on paying 120kr a night for a bed, 50kr for breakfast and 80–100kr for a hot meal. Bear in mind also that almost all hostels have a few regular double and family rooms on offer: these are, at 250–450kr a double a night, among the cheapest rooms you'll find in Norway. Incidentally, non-members can use the hostels, too, for an extra 25kr a night – which can soon mount up, so join HI before you leave home. If you don't have your

own sheet sleeping bag, you'll have to rent one for around 40–50kr a time.

It cannot be stressed too strongly that **calling ahead** to reserve a hostel bed in peak season, summer or winter, will save you lots of unnecessary legwork. Many hostels are only open from mid-June to mid-August and most close between 11am and 4pm. There's sometimes an 11pm or midnight curfew, though this is not much of a drawback in a country where carousing is so expensive. Evening meals in hostels are of variable quality, but the breakfasts are usually very good; where breakfast is included, ask for a breakfast packet if you have to leave early to catch transport. Most hostels have small **kitchens**, but often no pots, pans, cutlery or crockery, so self-caterers should bring their own.

PRIVATE ROOMS

Tourist offices in the larger towns and among the more touristy settlements of the fjords can often fix you up with a **private room** in someone's house, which may include kitchen facilities. Prices are competitive – between 180–230kr single, 300–350kr double – though there's usually a

YOUTH HOSTEL ASSOCIATIONS

Australia Australian Youth Hostels Association, Level 3, 10 Mallet St, Camperdown, Sydney (☎02/9565 1699).

Canada Hostelling International – Canada, 205 Catherine St, Suite 400, Ottawa, Ontario K2P 1C3 (☎613/237-7884).

England and Wales Youth Hostel Association (YHA), Trevelyan House, 8 St Stephen's Hill, St Albans, Herts AL1 2DY (☎01727/845 047). London information office: 14 Southampton St, London WC2 7HY (☎020/7373 3400).

Ireland Hostelling International – Northern Ireland, 22 Donegall Rd, Belfast BT12 5JN (☎028/9031 5435); *An Óige*, 61 Mountjoy St, Dublin 7 (☎01/830 4555).

New Zealand Youth Hostel Association of New Zealand, PO Box 436, Christchurch (☎03/379 9970).

Scotland Scottish Youth Hostel Association, 7 Glebe Crescent, Stirling, FK8 2JA (☎01786/891 400).

USA American Youth Hostels Inc, 733 15th St NW, Suite 840, Washington, DC 20005 (☎202/783-6161).

booking fee (20–30kr) on top, and the rooms themselves are typically some way out of the centre. Nonetheless, they're frequently the best bargain available and, in certain instances, an improvement on the local youth hostel. Where this is the case, we've said so. If you don't have a sleeping bag, check that the room comes with bedding – not all of them do; and if you're cooking for yourself, a few basic utensils wouldn't go amiss either.

CABINS AND MOUNTAIN HUTS

The Norwegian countryside is dotted with thousands of timber **cabins/chalets** (called *hytter*), ranging from simple wooden huts through to comfortable lodges. They are usually two- or four-bedded affairs with full kitchen facilities and sometimes a bathroom, even TV. Some hostels have them in their grounds, and there are at least a handful of *hytter* at most campsites. In the Lofoten islands they are the most popular form of accommodation, many occupying refurbished fishermen's huts called *rorbuer*. Costs vary enormously, depending on the location, size and amenities of the *hytter*, and there are significant seasonal variations too. However, a one-night stay in a four-bedded *hytter* will rarely cost more than 500kr – a more usual price would be about 300kr – and most of the larger versions fall within the 500kr to 700kr price band. If you're travelling in a group, they are easily the cheapest way to see the countryside – and in some comfort. Hundreds of *hytter* are also hired out by the week as holiday cottages. There are two main agencies and they produce lavish, detailed brochures of the *hytter* on offer. For further details contact either Den Norske Hytteformidling, PO Box 309, Sentrum, N-0105 Oslo (☎22 35 62 70, fax 23 35 62 75, *www.hytte.com*) – street address Nedre Vollgate 3; or Fjordhytter Den Norske Hytteformidling, PO Box 103, Lille Markevei 13, N-5005 Bergen (☎55 23 20 80, fax 55 23 24 04), which specializes in western Norway.

One further option for hikers is the chain of **mountain huts** (again called *hytter*) on hiking routes countrywide. Some are privately run, but the majority are operated by the Norwegian Mountain Hiking Association, and its affiliated regional hiking organizations. For further details see p.52.

CAMPSITES

Camping is a popular pastime in Norway, and there are literally hundreds of campsites to choose from, anything from a field with a few spaces for tents through to extensive complexes with all mod cons. The Norwegian tourist authorities detail around four hundred campsites in their free *Camping* brochure, giving them one to five stars based purely on the facilities offered (and not on the aesthetics of the location). Most sites are situated with the motorist in mind and a good few occupy key locations beside the main roads. The majority are two- and three-star establishments, where prices are usually per tent, plus a small charge per person; on average expect to pay around 120kr per night for two people using a tent, with four- and five-star sites on average twenty percent more. During peak season it can be a good idea to **reserve ahead** if you have a car and large tent or trailer; phone numbers are listed in the *Camping* booklet and throughout the guide. The **Norwegian Camping Card** brings faster registration at many campsites and occasionally entitles the bearer to special local camping rates. It is valid for one year, costs 60kr and can be purchased from participating campsites.

Camping rough in Norway is more than tolerated; indeed, as in Sweden, it is a tradition enshrined in law. You can camp anywhere in open areas as long as you are at least 150m away from any houses or cabins. As a courtesy, ask farmers for permission to use their land – it is rarely refused. Between April 15 and September 15 fires are not permitted in woodland areas nor in fields, and throughout the year camper vans are not allowed to be stationed overnight in lay-bys. For other countryside restrictions, see "Hiking" (p.52). A good sleeping bag is, not surprisingly, essential, since even in summer it can get very cold, and, in the north at least, mosquito repellent and sun-protection cream can be vital.

FOOD AND DRINK

Norwegian food can, at its best, be excellent: fish is plentiful, and carnivores can have a field day trying meats like reindeer steak, elk, or even – conscience permitting – seal. Admittedly it's not inexpensive, and those on a tight budget may have problems varying their diet, but by exercising a little prudence in the face of the average menu (which is almost always in Norwegian and English), you can keep costs down to reasonable levels. Vegetarians, however, will have slim pickings, except in big-city Oslo, and drinkers will have to dig very deep into their pockets to maintain much of an intake. Indeed, most drinkers end up visiting the supermarkets and state off-licences so that they can imbibe at home (in true Norwegian style) before setting out for the evening.

FOOD

Many travellers exist almost entirely on a mixture of picnic food and hot meals that they rustle up themselves, with the odd café meal thrown in to boost morale. Frankly, this isn't really necessary (except on the tightest of budgets) as there are a number of ways to eat out inexpensively. To begin with, a satisfying buffet breakfast, served in almost every hostel and hotel, is an affordable way to vary your diet, whilst special lunch deals will get you a tasty, hot meal for around 60–70kr. Finally, alongside the regular restaurants – which are expensive – there's the usual array of budget pizzerias and cafeterias in most towns.

BREAKFAST, PICNICS AND SNACKS

Breakfast (*frokost*) in Norway is a substantial self-service affair of bread, crackers, cheese, eggs, preserves, cold meat and fish, washed down by unlimited tea and coffee. It's usually first-rate at youth hostels, and often truly memorable in hotels, filling you up for the day for around 50–70kr where it's not included with the price of your room (a rare event).

If you're buying your own **picnic food**, bread, cheese, yoghurt and local fruit are all relatively good value, but other staple foodstuffs – rice, pasta, meat, cereals and vegetables – can cost up to around twice what they would at home. Anything tinned is particularly dear, with the exception of tinned fish, but coffee and tea are quite reasonably priced. Beware of a sandwich spread called *Kaviar* – bright pink, sold in tubes and full of additives. Real caviar, on the other hand – from lump-fish rather than sturgeon – is widely available and relatively inexpensive (around 45–50kr for a small jar). **Supermarkets** are ten-a-penny – Rimi and Rema 2000 are the two biggest chains.

Fast food offers the best chance of a hot take-away snack. The indigenous Norwegian stuff, served up from **gatekjøkken** – street kiosks or stalls – in every town, consists mainly of rubbery hot dogs (*varm pølse*), while pizza slices and chicken pieces and chips are much in evidence too. American-style burger bars are also creeping in – both at motorway service stations and in the towns and cities, with McDonald's and Burger King particularly well represented.

A better choice, and usually not much more expensive, is simply to get a sandwich, normally a huge open affair called a **smørbrød** (pronounced "smurrbrur"), heaped with a variety of garnishes. You'll see *smørbrød* groaning under meat or shrimps, salad and mayonnaise, in the windows of bakeries and cafés, or in the newer, trendier sandwich bars in the cities. **Cakes** and **biscuits** are good, too: watch for doughnuts, Danish pastries (*wienerbrød*), butter biscuits (*kjeks*) and waffles (*vafler*).

Good **coffee** is available everywhere, served black or with cream, rich, strong, and, in some places, free after the first cup, particularly at breakfast. **Tea**, too, is ubiquitous, but the local preference is for lemon tea or a variety of

GLOSSARY OF NORWEGIAN FOOD TERMS

Basics and snacks

appelsin-marmelade	marmalade	kaviar	caviar	pommes-frites	chips (French fries)
brød	bread	kjeks	biscuits	ris	rice
eddik	vinegar	krem	whipped cream	rundstykker	bread roll
egg	egg	melk	milk	salat	salad
eggerøre	scrambled eggs	mineralvann	mineral water	salt	salt
flatbrød	crispbread	nøtter	nuts	sennep	mustard
fløte	cream	olje	oil	smør	butter
grøt	porridge	omelett	omelette	smørbrød	open sandwich
iskrem	ice cream	ost	cheese	sukker	sugar
kaffefløte	single cream for coffee	pannekake	pancakes	suppe	soup
		pepper	pepper	syltetøy	jam
		potetchips	crisps (potato chips)	varm pølse	hot dog
kake	cake			yoghurt	yoghurt

Meat (*kjøtt*) and game (*vilt*)

dyrestek	venison	lammekjøtt	lamb	ribbe	pork rib
elg	elk	lever	liver	skinke	ham
kalkun	turkey	oksekjøtt	beef	spekemat	dried meat
kjøttboller	meatballs	postei	pâté	stek	steak
kjøttkaker	rissoles	pølser	sausages	svinekjøtt	pork
kylling	chicken	reinsdyr	reindeer	varm pølse	frankfurter/hot-dog

Fish (*fisk*) and shellfish (*skalldyr*)

ansjos	anchovies (brisling)	laks	salmon	sjøtunge	sole
		makrell	mackerel	småfisk	whitebait
blåskjell	mussels	piggvar	turbot	steinbit	catfish
brisling	sprats	reker	shrimps	torsk	cod
hummer	lobster	rødspette	plaice	tunfisk	tuna
hvitting	whiting	røkelaks	smoked salmon	ørret	trout
kaviar	caviar	sardiner	sardines (brisling)	ål	eel
krabbe	crab	sei	coalfish		
kreps	crayfish	sild	herring		

Vegetables (*grønsaker*)

agurk	cucumber/gherkin/pickle	hvitløk	garlic	poteter	potatoes
		kål	cabbage	rosenkål	Brussels sprouts
blomkål	cauliflower	linser	lentils		
bønner	beans	løk	onion	selleri	celery
erter	peas	mais	sweetcorn	sopp	mushrooms
gulrøtter	carrots	nepe	turnip	spinat	spinach
hodesalat	lettuce	paprika	peppers	tomater	tomatoes

Fruit (*frukt*)

ananas	pineapple	eple	apple	plommer	plums
appelsin	orange	fersken	peach	pærer	pears
aprikos	apricot	fruktsalat	fruit salad	sitron	lemon
banan	banana	grapefrukt	grapefruit	solbær	blackcurrants
blåbær	blueberries	jordbær	strawberries	tyttbær	cranberries
druer	grapes	multer	cloudberries		

Cooking terms

blodig	rare, underdone	*marinert*	marinated	*sur*	sour, pickled
godt stekt	well done	*ovnstekt*	baked/roasted	*syltet*	pickled
grillet	grilled	*røkt*	smoked	*saltet*	cured
grytestekt	braised	*stekt*	fried		
kokt	boiled	*stuet*	stewed		

Norwegian specialities

brun saus	gravy served with most meats, rissoles, fishcakes and sausages		in the south and east, using salted or fresh meat, or leftovers, in a thick brown gravy
fenalår	marinaded mutton, smoked, sliced, salted, dried and served with crispbread, scrambled egg and beer	*lutefisk*	fish (usually cod) preserved in an alkali solution and seasoned; an acquired taste
fiskeboller	fish balls, served under a white sauce or on open sandwiches	*multer (med krem)*	cloudberries – wild berries mostly found north of the Arctic Circle and served with cream
fiskekabaret	shrimps, fish and vegetables in aspic		
fiskesuppe	fish soup	*mysost*	brown whey cheese, made from cow's milk
flatbrød	a flat unleavened cracker, half barley, half wheat	*nedlagtsild*	marinaded herring
gammelost	a hard, strong smelling, yellow-brown cheese with veins	*pinnekjøtt*	western Norwegian Christmas dish of smoked mutton steamed over shredded birch bark, served with cabbage; or accompanied by boiled potatoes and mashed swedes (*kålrabistappe*)
geitost/gjetost	goat's cheese, slightly sweet and fudge-coloured. Similar cheeses have different ratios of goat's milk to cow's milk		
gravetlaks	salmon marinaded in salt, sugar, dill and brandy	*reinsdyrstek*	reindeer steak, usually served with boiled potatoes and cranberry sauce
juleskinke	marinaded boiled ham, served at Christmas	*rekesalat*	shrimp salad in mayonnaise
kjøttkaker med surkål	homemade burgers with cabbage and a sweet and sour sauce	*ribbe, julepølse, medisterkake*	eastern Norwegian Christmas dish of pork ribs, sausage and dumplings
koldtbord	a midday buffet with cold meats, herrings, salads, bread and perhaps soup, eggs or hot meats	*spekemat*	various types of smoked, dried meat
lapskaus	pork, venison (or other meats) and vegetable stew, common	*Trondhjemsuppea*	kind of milk broth with raisins, rice, cinnamon and sugar

Bread, cake and desserts

bløtkake	cream cake with fruit		served with *frukt saus*, a slighly thickened fruit sauce
fløtelapper	pancakes made with cream, served with sugar and jam		
havrekjeks	oatmeal biscuits, eaten with goat's cheese	*tilslørtbondepiker*	stewed apples and breadcrumbs, served with cream
knekkebrød	crispbread	*trollkrem*	beaten egg whites (or whipped cream) and sugar mixed with cloudberries (or cranberries)
kransekake	cake made from almonds, sugar and eggs, served at celebrations		
lomper	potato scones-cum-tortillas	*vafle*	waffles
riskrem	rice pudding with whipped cream and sugar, usually		

GLOSSARY OF NORWEGIAN DRINK TERMS

akevitt	aquavit	*te med melk/*	tea with milk
appelsin	orange squash/	*sitron*	/lemon
saft/juice	juice	*vann*	water
brus	fizzy soft drink	*varm sjokolade*	hot chocolate
eplesider	cider	*vin*	wine
fruktsaft	sweetened fruit juice	*søt*	sweet
kaffe	coffee	*tørr*	dry
melk	milk	*rød*	red
mineralvann	mineral water	*hvit*	white
øl	beer	*rosé*	rosé
sitronbrus	lemonade	*skål*	cheers

flavoured infusions. All the familiar **soft drinks** are also available.

LUNCH AND DINNER

For the best deals, you're going to have to have your main meal of the day at lunchtime (*lunsj*), when **kafeterias** (often self-service restaurants) lay on **daily specials**, the *dagens rett*, for around 70–80kr. This is a fish or meat dish served with potatoes and a vegetable or salad, often including a drink, sometimes bread, and occasionally coffee, too. Dipping into the menu is more expensive, but not cripplingly so if you stick to omelettes and suchlike. Many department stores – including the Domus chain – have *kafeterias*, as does every large train station. You'll also find them hidden above shops and offices, and next to hotels in larger towns, where they might be called *Kaffistovas*. Most close at around 6pm and many don't open at all on Sunday. As a general rule, the food these places serve is plain, verging on the ordinary (though there are some excellent exceptions), but the same cannot be said of the continental-style **café-bars** which abound in Oslo and, increasingly, in all of Norway's larger towns and cities. These eminently affordable establishments offer much tastier and more adventurous meals like pasta dishes, salads and vegetarian options.

In all of the cities, but especially in Oslo, there are first-class **restaurants**, serving dinner (*middag*) in quite formal surroundings. Apart from exotica such as reindeer and elk, the one real speciality is the seafood, characteristically simple in preparation and wonderfully fresh: whatever you do, don't go home without treating yourself to it at least once. In the smaller towns and villages, gourmets will be harder pressed – many of the restaurants are pretty mundane, though the general standard is improving rapidly. In all but the most exclusive places, main courses begin at around 150kr, starters and desserts start around 60kr each. If in doubt, smoked salmon comes highly recommended, and so does the catfish and monkfish. Again, the best deals are at lunchtime, when a few restaurants put out a **koldtbord** (the Norwegian version of *smörgåsbord*), where for a fixed price of around 150–200kr you can get through as much as possible during the three or four hours it's served. Highlights include vast arrays of pickled herring, salmon (*laks*), cold cuts of meat, dried reindeer, a feast of breads and crackers, and usually a few hot dishes too – meatballs, soup and scrambled eggs.

In the towns, and especially in Oslo, there is also a sprinkling of **ethnic restaurants**, mostly Italian with a good helping of Chinese and Indian places. Other cuisines pop up here and there too – Japanese, Moroccan and Mongolian to name but three. The most affordable are the Chinese restaurants and the pizza joints.

VEGETARIANS

Vegetarians are in for a hard time. Apart from a couple of specialist restaurants in Oslo, you can do little except make do with salads, look out for egg dishes in *kafeterias* and supplement your diet from supermarkets. If you are a **vegan** the problem is greater: when the Norwegians are not eating meat and fish, they are attacking a fantastic selection of milks, cheeses and yoghurts. At least you'll know what's in every dish you eat, since everyone speaks English. If you're self-catering, look for **health food shops** (*helsekost*), found in some of the larger towns and cities.

DRINK

One of the less savoury sights in Norway is the fall-over drunk. For reasons that remain obscure – or at least culturally complex – many Norwegians can't just have a drink or two, but have to get absolutely wasted. The majority of their compatriots deplore such behaviour and have consequently imposed what amounts to alcoholic rationing: thus, although booze is readily available in the bars and restaurants, it's taxed up to the eyeballs (half a litre of beer costs 35kr or more) and the distribution of wines and spirits is strictly controlled by a state-run monopoly, **Vinmonopolet**. Whether this type of paternalistic control makes matters better or worse is debatable, but the majority of Norwegians support it.

WHAT TO DRINK

If you decide to lash out on a few drinks, you'll find Norwegian **beer** is lager-like and comes in three strengths (class I, II or III), of which the strongest and most expensive is class III. Brands to look out for include Hansa and Ringsnes. There's hardly any domestically produced **wine** and most **spirits** are imported too, but one local brew worth experimenting with at least once is **aquavit**, served ice-cold in little glasses. At forty percent proof, it's real headache material, though more palatable with beer chasers: Linie aquavit is one of the more popular brands.

RETAIL OUTLETS FOR DRINK

Beer is sold in supermarkets and shops all over Norway, though some local communities, particularly in the west, have their own rules and restrictions. It's about half the price you'd pay in a bar. The strongest beer, along with wines and spirits, can only be purchased from the state-controlled Vinmonopolet shops. There's generally one in each medium-size town, though there are more branches in the cities (twenty in Oslo). Opening hours are generally Monday–Wednesday 10am to 4/5pm, Thursday 10am to 5/6pm, Friday 9am to 4/6pm, Saturday 9am to 1pm, though these times can vary depending on the area, and all stores close the day before a public holiday. At these stores wine is quite a bargain, from around 55kr a bottle, and there's generally a fairly bizarre choice of vintages from various South American countries.

WHERE TO DRINK

Wherever you **go for a drink**, a half-litre of beer costs between 35kr and 45kr and a glass of wine from 30kr. You can get a drink at most outdoor cafés, in restaurants, and in bars, pubs and cocktail bars. That said, only in the towns and cities is there any kind of bar life and in many places you'll be limited to a drink in the local hotel bar or restaurant. However, in Oslo, Bergen, Stavanger, Trondheim and Tromsø you will be able to keep drinking in bars until at least 1am – until 4am in some places.

Norwegians are not as a general rule social drinkers, and **buying a round** is virtually unheard of: people normally pay for their own drink, something which, considering the prices, is worth remembering. Incidentally, a small number of people make their own brews in illegal **stills**. If you are invited over "for a drink", be very careful about what you think you are drinking. Swigging something akin to aviation fuel in any sort of quantity can leave you, quite literally, speechless.

POST AND TELEPHONES

INTERNATIONAL DIALLING CODES

Country code for Norway: 47
From Norway to:

Australia	☎0061
Ireland	☎00353
New Zealand	☎0064
UK	☎0044
USA and Canada	☎001

In Norway both the post and phone services are very efficient, and things are made even easier by the fact that the staff nearly all speak good English.

POSTAL SERVICES

Post offices in Norway are plentiful and the usual opening hours are Monday to Friday 8am or 8.30am to 4pm, and Saturday 8am or 9am to 1pm. Some urban post offices open longer hours, notably the one inside Oslo S station (Mon–Fri 7am–6pm, Sat 9am–3pm). At the time of writing, **postage** costs 5.5kr for a postcard or letter under 20g sent within Europe (3,80kr within Scandinavia), and 6kr to countries outside. Mail to the USA takes 7–10 days, within Europe 2–3 days. You can receive letters at any main city post office by having them addressed "Poste Restante" followed by the surname of the addressee (preferably underlined and in capitals), and then the name of the town and country. When collecting, take along your passport or identity card. If you're expecting post and your initial enquiry produces nothing, ask the clerk to check under all of your names and initials as letters often get misfiled. Alternatively, American Express, which has an office in Oslo, will hold incoming mail (but not parcels or registered mail) for a month on behalf of card and travellers' cheque holders.

TELEPHONES

Norway has a reliable telephone system, run by Telenor, and you can make domestic and interna-

tional **telephone calls** with ease from public phones. Phone booths are plentiful and almost invariably work, but if you can't find one, some bars have pay phones you can use. All the more expensive hotel rooms have phones too, but note that using these always incurs an exorbitant surcharge.

Public telephones are of the usual western European kind, where you deposit the money before you make your call – they take 1kr, 5kr, 10kr and 20kr coins. Coin-operated public phones are gradually being phased out in favour of those that only take **telecards** (*TeleKort*), sold at newsstands, post offices, major train stations and some supermarkets. These cost 35kr, 98kr and 210kr. An increasing number of public phones also accept major credit cards.

Most phone booths have English instructions displayed inside. To make a direct call to the UK, dial the code listed in the box, wait for the tone and then dial the number, omitting the initial 0. To make a direct call to North America, dial the code in the box, wait for the tone and then dial 1 followed by the area code and number. All Norwegian telephone numbers have eight digits

USEFUL NUMBERS

Directory enquiries (Scandinavia)	☎180
Directory enquiries (international)	☎181
Emergencies (Fire)	☎110
Emergencies (Police)	☎112
Emergencies (Ambulance)	☎113
International operator assistance (inc. collect & reverse-charge calls)	☎115
Domestic operator assistance (inc. collect & reverse-charge calls)	☎117

and there's no area code. Local telephone calls **cost** a minimum of 2kr, while 10kr is enough to start an international telephone call, but not much more. Discount rates (of around 15 percent) on international calls apply from 10pm to 8am.

Finally, note that various telephone companies, including British Telecom, issue phone cards to their subscribers for use abroad. These cards can be used on any phone and the subsequent call is automatically billed to your home telephone number. They are simple to use – you just tap in a code for the country you are dialling from and this accesses your own company's lines. Then you have to tap in your account number and PIN – and you are away. For further details, ask your phone company.

MEDIA

You needn't miss out on English-language TV or newspapers in Norway. It's easy to track down foreign papers, and the television networks carry imported British and American programmes, subtitled for the home audience.

Most British and some American daily **newspapers**, and the odd established foreign periodical, are on sale in most towns at Narvesen kiosks, airports and large train stations. As for the **Norwegian press**, state advertising, loans and subsidized production costs keep a wealth of smaller papers going that would bite the dust elsewhere. Most are closely linked with political parties, although the bigger city-based papers tend to be independent. In Oslo, highest circulations are claimed by the independent *Verdens Gang* and the independent-conservative *Aftenposten*, and in Bergen by the liberal *Bergens Tidende*.

Norway's **television** network has expanded over the last few years, in line with the rest of Europe. Alongside the state channels, NRK and TV2, there are satellite channels like TV Norge, while TV3 is a channel common to Norway, Denmark and Sweden; you can also pick up Swedish TV broadcasts. Many of the programmes are English-language imports, so there is invariably something on that you'll understand – though much of it is pretty unadventurous stuff. Many bars and most hotels are geared up for (at least a couple of) the big pan-European cable and satellite channels, such as MTV, CNN, Sky, Superchannel and Eurosport.

Local **tourist radio** is broadcast during the summer months, giving details of events and festivals; watch for signposts by the roadside advertising these stations. Otherwise, English-language radio broadcasts, featuring news from Norway, are repeated several times daily on FM (93MHz). The BBC World Service is broadcast to all of mainland Scandinavia. Frequencies vary according to area and often change every few months. For the latest details write for the free Programme Guide to BBC World Service, Bush House, Strand, London WC2B 4PH (☎020/7240 3456, *www.bbc.co.uk/worldservice*).

OPENING HOURS, PUBLIC HOLIDAYS AND FESTIVALS

Although there's recently been some movement towards greater flexibility, **opening hours** for shops and businesses remain fairly restrictive. On the other hand, **tourist attractions** and leisure amenities tend to have extended opening hours in the summer, but close down early (or completely) in winter. On **public holidays**, most things close – though not, of course, restaurants, bars and hotels – and public transport is reduced to a limited (Sunday) timetable.

OPENING HOURS

Normal **shopping hours** are Monday through Friday 9am to 4pm or 5pm, with late opening on Thursdays till 6pm or 8pm, plus Saturdays 9am to 1pm or 3pm. Some supermarkets stay open much longer – until 8pm in the week and 6pm on Saturdays. In addition, the majority of kiosks-cum-newsstands stay open till 9pm or 10pm every night of the week (including Sundays), but much more so in the cities and towns than in the villages. Many petrol stations sell a basic range of groceries and stay open till 11pm daily; Vinmonopolet, the state-run liquor store chain, has limited opening hours – see p.45. **Office hours** are normally Monday to Friday 8.30am or 9am to 5pm or 5.30pm.

Almost every Norwegian town and most of the larger villages have a **museum** of some description. Specific opening times are given in this guide, but in general they are open from 10am to 6pm from May to September, and to around 4pm the rest of the year. Monday is a common closing day. However, travelling outside the May to September period, expect a lot of the less important and/or less popular museums to be closed. All the major museums and galleries in Norway are described in the guide, but the sheer number of municipal and minor museums, many of which are only of specialist or local interest, means we have had to be selective: the rest you can miss with a clear conscience.

PUBLIC HOLIDAYS

National **public holidays** are a noticeable feature of the Norwegian calendar and act as a further unifying force in what remains an extremely homogeneous society. There are twelve national public holidays per year, most of which are keenly observed, though the tourist industry carries on pretty much regardless. Incidentally, some state-run museums adopt Sunday hours on public holidays, except on Christmas Day and New Year's Day (and often December 26) when they close. Otherwise most businesses and shops close, and the public transport system operates a skeleton or Sunday service. Most Norwegians take their holidays in the summer season, between mid-June and mid-August.

NATIONAL PUBLIC HOLIDAYS

New Year's Day
Maundy Thursday (Thursday before Easter)
Good Friday
Easter Sunday
Easter Monday
Labour Day (May 1)
Ascension Day (mid-May)
National Day (May 17)
Whit Sunday (the seventh Sunday after Easter)
Whit Monday
Christmas Day
Boxing Day (day after Christmas Day)
Note, that when Labour Day or a comparable holiday falls on a Sunday, the next day usually becomes a holiday.

FESTIVALS AND EVENTS

Almost every town in Norway has some sort of summer shindig and there are winter celebrations too. For the most part, these are worth going to if you are already in the area rather than from meriting a special journey. There are two main sorts of **festival**, one being celebrations of historical or folkloric events, the other more contemporary-based jazz and pop music binges and the like. As you might expect, most tourist-oriented events take place in summer and as always national and local tourist offices can supply details of exact dates, which tend to change from year to year. The box (below) lists the more important festivals, some of which are detailed in the guide.

A FESTIVALS CALENDAR

January
The three- to four-day **Northern Lights Festival** of classical and contemporary music takes place in Tromsø.

February
Ski events at Holmenkollen, in Oslo, commence in mid-February and lead up to the **Ski Festival** in mid-March.

March
In late March, Lillehammer stages the **Birkebeinerrennet**, a famous cross-country ski race from Rena to Lillehammer, celebrating the dramatic events of 1206 when the young prince Haakon Håkanson was rushed over the mountains to safety. The race follows what is thought to have been the original route.

May
Constitution or **National Day** sees processions and flag-waving all over the country to celebrate the signing of the Norwegian constitution on May 17, 1814. The **Bergen International**

Festival of contemporary music is held from late May until early June.

July
Held over a five-day period in the middle of the month, the **International Jazz Festival** at Molde is one of the best of its type, attracting big international names as well as Scandinavian artists. At the end of the month, historical pageants and plays are put on over several days at Stiklestad as part of **St Olav's Festival**, honouring Norway's first Christian king who was killed there in battle in 1030.

August
The **Oslo Jazz Festival** is held around the middle of the month, a five-day event attracting some big international names.

October
In early October the week-long **Ultima Contemporary Music Festival** features performances by international and Scandinavian talent at various venues across Oslo.

THE WOMEN'S MOVEMENT

In general, the social and economic position of women in Norway, as in the rest of Scandinavia, is more advanced than in the rest of Europe – something that becomes obvious even during a short visit. Many women are in traditionally male occupations and occupy key managerial positions. A large part of the credit for this state of affairs goes to Norway's well-organized and highly developed **women's movement**, which helped lever into power a series of progressive governments. A key moment was the election of the country's first woman Prime Minister, Dr Gro Harlem Brundtland, in 1981. At the head of a Labour Party administration, Brundtland, who is now head of the World Health Organization, pushed forward a raft of social legislation which improved the position of women and did much to even out parliamentary representation by promoting women into the cabinet. However, some of this progress is now under threat. The current government is a centrist coalition whose equality agenda has switched to the rights of men, and their welfare benefit reforms are seeking to encourage parents to stay at home to care for children, rather than use the state-supported daycare provision. This revisionism has taken many feminists by surprise and there are hints that the movement will return to more active campaigning. Activists can certainly point to the fact that there is still a smaller percentage of women in top executive positions in Norway than in either the UK or US, and a Norwegian woman's average earnings are less than a man's. Contact with the women's movement can be made in Oslo through the Norsk Kvinnessaksforening, Kvinnehuset, Majorstuveien 39, Oslo (☎22 60 42 27); and in Bergen through Zonta, an international women's organization – contact Berit Wollan, St Hanshaugen 56, 5033 Fyllingsdalen (☎55 15 07 95).

GAY NORWAY

Norway was one of the first countries in the world to pass a law (1981) making discrimination against homosexuals and lesbians illegal. In 1993, it became only the second country to pass legislation giving lesbian and gay couples the same rights as married couples, while retaining a bar on church weddings and the right to adopt children. This, however, had more to do with respect for the rights and freedoms of the individual than a positive attitude to homosexuality – Norway remains, in essence at least, very much a (heterosexual) family-oriented society. Nevertheless, the general attitude to gays is so tolerant that few feel the need to disguise their sexuality, and the age of consent is sixteen.

It's commonplace for bars and pubs to have a mixture of straights and gays in their clientele.

There is something of a separate scene in Oslo, Bergen and Trondheim, but it's pretty low-key and barely worth seeking out – and the same applies to the weekly gay and lesbian nights held in some small-town nightclubs. That said, there is the lively Oslo Gay and Lesbian **Pride** Week held in June. Up-to-date infomation about the Oslo scene is available from **Unginfo** (*www.unginfo.oslo.no /streetwise*).

There is a strong and effective nationwide gay organization, **Landsforeningen for Lesbisk og Homofil frigjøing** (LLH; ☎22 36 19 48, fax 22 11 47 45, *www.llh.oslo.no*), with its head office in Oslo at St Olavs plass 2, 2nd floor; the postal address is LLH, Postbox 68, St Olavsplass, 0130 Oslo. LLH has branches throughout the country.

CRIME AND PERSONAL SAFETY

There's little reason why you should ever come into contact with the Norwegian police force. This is one of the least troublesome corners of Europe – in the whole of the country there's an average of only one murder per week. You will find that most public places are well lit and secure, most people genuinely friendly and helpful, and street crime and street hassle have a low profile. Even in Oslo, easily the biggest city, you shouldn't have any problems, though it's obviously advisable to be on your guard against petty theft.

It would be foolish, however, to assume that problems don't exist. Oslo in particular has its share of petty crime, fuelled – as elsewhere – by drug addicts and alcoholics after easy money. But keep tabs on your possessions and you should have little reason to visit the police. If you do, you'll find them courteous, concerned, and usually able to speak English. If you have something stolen, make sure you get a police report – essential if you are to make a claim against your insurance.

As for offences *you* might commit, drinking alcohol in public places is not permitted, and being drunk on the streets can get you arrested. Drinking and driving is treated especially rigorously. Drugs offences, too, are met with as harshly as elsewhere in Europe. Women won't, however, be cautioned for topless sunbathing, which is universally accepted in the resorts (elsewhere there probably won't be anyone around to care), and camping rough is a tradition enshrined in law. Should you be **arrested** on any charge, you have the right to **contact your embassy or consulate** (see p.105 for details). Unfortunately, consular officials are notoriously reluctant to get involved, though most are required to assist you to some degree if you have your passport stolen or lose all your money. If you've been detained for a drugs offence, don't expect any sympathy or help.

AVOIDING TROUBLE

Almost all the problems tourists encounter in Norway are to do with **petty crime** – pickpocketing and bag-snatching – rather than more serious physical confrontations, so it's as well to be on your guard and know where your possessions are at all times. Sensible **precautions** include: carrying bags slung across your neck and not over your shoulder; not carrying anything in pockets that are easy to dip into; having photocopies of your passport, airline ticket and driving licence; leaving passports and tickets in the hotel safe; and noting down the numbers of your travellers' cheques and credit cards. When you're looking for a hotel room, never leave your bags unattended. Vehicle theft is still uncommon, but luggage and valuables left in cars do make a tempting target, so when parking ensure your possessions are not left in view inside. If you're on a **bicycle**, make sure it is well locked up. At **night**, you'd be well advised to avoid walking round the rougher parts of Oslo (to the east of the city centre and especially around the main train and bus station, Oslo S). Also, as general precautions, avoid unlit streets and don't go out loaded with valuables. Using public transport, even late at night, isn't usually a problem, but if in doubt, take a taxi.

Thieves often work in pairs and, although theft is far from rife, you should be aware of certain **ploys** to distract you, such as when a "helpful" person points out "birdshit" (shaving cream or similar) on your coat, while someone else relieves you of your money; being invited in the street to read a card or paper; someone in a café making a move for your drink with one hand and, as you try to prevent your drink being taken, exploring your bag with the other. If you're in a crowd, watch out for people moving in unusually close.

WHAT TO DO IF YOU'RE ROBBED

If you're robbed, you need to **go to the police** (☎112) to report it, not least because your insurance company will require a police report, so remember to make a note of the report number or, better still, ask for a copy of the statement itself. Don't expect a great deal of concern if your loss is relatively small, and don't be surprised if the formalities take ages. In the unlikely event that you're **mugged** or otherwise threatened, *never* resist, and try to reduce your contact with the robber to a minimum. Either just hand over what's wanted, or throw money in one direction and take off in the other. Afterwards, go straight to the police, who will be much more sympathetic and helpful on these occasions.

SEXUAL HARASSMENT

In the normal course of events, **women travellers** in almost any part of Norway are unlikely to feel threatened or attract unwanted attention. The main exception is in the seedier areas of Oslo, where the atmosphere may feel frightening especially late at night, but with common sense and circumspection you shouldn't have anything to worry about. In terms of nightclubs and bars, the men who hang around in them pose no greater or lesser threat than similar operators at home, though the language barrier (where it exists) makes it harder to know who to trust.

OUTDOOR PURSUITS

Norwegians have a love of the great outdoors. They enjoy many kinds of sports – from dogsledging and downhill skiing in winter, through to mountaineering, angling and white-water rafting in the summer – but the two most popular activities are hiking and cross-country skiing.

HIKING

Norway boasts some of the most beautiful mountain landscapes in the world. A sequence of rugged mountain ranges, accentuated by icy glaciers, rocky spires and deep green fjords, traverses the country, creating some of the wildest terrain in Europe. Parts of these mountain ranges have been protected by the creation of a string of **national parks** (see p.54), and these are now the focus for the country's hikers. However, the parks incorporate but a fraction of the mountains and there are still little-known and little-visited areas, particularly in the north where the mountains give way to the vast upland plateau of the Finnmarksvidda.

The more popular hiking areas are usually easily reached by public transport, and are crisscrossed by **trails**. These are often dotted with strategically placed mountain huts and lodges (see below), which provide **meals** and **accommodation**. Each establishment is about a day's walk from its nearest neighbour. The **hiking season** is short and loosely defined by the opening and closing of the mountain lodges. It runs from

early July (mid-June in some areas) through to the middle of September . At this time of the year, the weather is mild and you can anticipate daytime mountain temperatures of between 20°C and 25°C: pleasant, comfortable, and ideal for hiking. And of course it's daylight for most of the time – beyond the Arctic Circle, all the time – so you'll usually not be seeking a mountain lodge after dark.

Visitors attempting **long-distance hiking** tours in the mountains of Norway must have previous experience – the weather is too fickle and conditions too treacherous for novices – and no one, however experienced, should attempt a mountain walk alone. With this in mind, the Norwegian Mountain Touring Association (**DNT**) runs **week-long guided tours** in the more popular hiking areas; contact DNT's main Oslo office (see box opposite) for their English brochure. Many of the participants are Norwegian, but the tours are popular with visitors as well. Prices vary with the itinerary, but average 3000–4000kr for an all-inclusive package. Some specialist tour operators handle hiking tours too – see p.7, p.9, p.15, p.18.

MOUNTAIN LODGES AND CAMPING

The Norwegian Mountain Touring Association (DNT) manages over 300 mountain huts and lodges throughout the country, and its regional affiliates maintain many more. **Charges** for

NORWEGIAN MOUNTAIN TOURING ASSOCIATION (DNT)

Den Norske Turistforening (*www.turistforeningen.no*) plays an active part in managing all aspects of hiking in Norway. It runs mountain lodges throughout the country, takes care of trails and waymarking, sells maps, organizes tours and provides advice on equipment.

PRINCIPAL DNT OUTLETS

Oslo (main office): Postboks 7, Sentrum, 0101 Oslo. Visitors to Storgata 3 (☎22 82 28 05).
Bergen: Tverrgata 4/6, Bergen (☎55 32 22 30).
Bodø: Storgata 44, 3rd Floor (☎75 52 14 13).
Kristiansand: Kristian IV's gate 12 (☎38 02 52 63).

Stavanger: Olav V's gate 18 (☎51 84 02 00).
Tromsø: Grønnegate 32 (☎77 68 51 75).
Trondheim: Munkegata 64 (☎73 92 42 00).
Ålesund: Keiser Wilhelmsgata 22 (☎70 12 58 04).

meals and accommodation are inexpensive. For DNT members staying in staffed huts, a bunk in a dormitory costs 70–100kr, 140kr in a family or double room. Full board and lodging works out at 300–380kr per person. At unstaffed huts, where you leave the money for your stay in a box provided, lodging costs about twenty percent less. Non-members pay about fifty percent more. Membership currently costs just 360kr per annum and can be purchased at any DNT office or staffed mountain lodge.

DNT-staffed mountain lodges, mostly located in the southern part of the country, are often large enough to accommodate over 100 guests, and provide a full service including meals, food, and lodging. Some can be reached by road, others on foot only. They are clean, friendly, and well run. All three meals are available, with lunch taken (and self-prepared) from the breakfast buffet. **Self-service huts**, with twenty to forty beds, are also concentrated in the mountains of southern Norway and offer lodging with bedding. Food can be purchased at the self-service lodges, and kitchen equipment is provided. **Unstaffed DNT huts**, often with less than twenty beds, are found mostly in the north. They provide bedding, stoves for heating and cooking, and all kitchen equipment, but you must bring and prepare your own food.

Reservations are accepted at DNT-staffed (and affiliated) lodges for stays of more than two nights, though the lodges are primarily designed to cater for guests in transit. Otherwise, beds are provided on a first-come, first-served basis. DNT members over 50 years of age are, however, guaranteed a bed. During high season, lodges may sometimes be full, although this is not common. If beds are not available, you are given a mattress and blankets for sleeping in a common area. Norwegians are proud that no one is ever turned away. In walks mentioned in this book, Gjendesheim, Glitterheim, Gjendebu and Rondvassbu are DNT-staffed lodges.

Private lodges, generally resembling the larger staffed DNT lodges, are also found in the mountains of Norway. Prices are somewhat higher than at DNT premises, although DNT members often qualify for a discount. In the walking routes described in this book, Østerbø and Memurubu are privately run and staffed. Private lodges accept reservations, and tourist offices have comprehensive details of those in their locality; many DNT brochures list this information too. Incidentally, lodges on the Finnmarksvidda are owned and operated by the government.

As an alternative to the mountain lodges, note that **rough camping** is allowed freely throughout Norway, although campfires are prohibited from April 15 to September 15. You may camp freely for one night only in any one spot, so long as you are not within 150 metres of a building. In some national parks and other walking areas, these rules have been modified: you must move a bit further away from a hut, or stay near to the hut in a designated camping area. Obviously enough, the main disadvantage of camping, as distinct from staying in a lodge, is the amount of equipment you have to carry; on the other hand, the remoter regions and national parks have few if any lodges.

PLANNING A HIKE

Safety should be a primary concern when walking in any mountain area. You should plan your route before starting out, study the maps, know how much elevation will be gained or lost, and estimate the time you will need to get to your next stopping point. You should not set out without emergency equipment, extra food, and clothing appropriate for cold and wet conditions. Notify someone of your route and dates of travel. In hunting areas (and seasons), it makes sense to wear brightly coloured clothes when walking in countryside and woodland; seek local advice.

The **equipment** you'll need is similar to what you'd use for hiking in other mountainous regions of Europe. If you plan on a day's hike here and there, you should carry warm clothing, including a warm hat, scarf and gloves, waterproofs, a sun-hat, sunglasses, sun cream, food and water or a thermos, a first-aid kit, insect repellent, a map and compass. For long-distance hut-to-hut tours, you will need a sheet sleeping bag (blankets will be provided), extra clothes, thermals, a knife, toiletries and a torch. Up-to-date synthetic materials, such as polyester or fleece, do an excellent job of keeping you warm when wet, since they neither absorb nor retain moisture. Boots, not trainers, are necessary, and although the new lighter-weight boots may suffice for day walking, heavier boots are more comfortable on longer tours. For campers, a plastic survival bag will keep you and your pack dry; note also that Camping Gaz is only available from certain outlets (details at local tourist offices). Always thorough, DNT (see p.53) issues a comprehensive list of what to take, right down to types of underwear.

Hiking trails are typically marked at regular intervals by cairns. Most junctions are marked by signposts, some of which have stood for many years and are on the small side, making them hard to spot. Red T's are also painted on rocks – a welcome route marker when the weather is poor, as they are visible from farther away than the signposts. Although waymarking is quite good, you should purchase area **maps**. These are available at DNT offices (see p.53), many tourist offices, most larger book stores and train stations, and in village shops in some of the more popular hiking areas. The entire country has been mapped by the Norwegian highways department and their *M711 Norge* 1:50,000 series, with red and white covers and carrying the trademark *Statens Kartverk*, are the most detailed. They are extremely accurate and many have recently been updated. Additional maps with a scale of 1:100,000 are available for several popular hiking areas such as Rondane and Jotunheimen.

Guidebooks on mountain hiking in Norway are few and far between: probably the best is

Walking in Norway by Constance Roos, published by Cicerone Press, 2 Police Square, Milnthorpe, Cumbria, LA7 7PY, England (☎015395/62069, fax 63417, *www.cicerone.demon.co.uk*). This outlines an extensive range of mainly long-distance hiking routes. Alternatively, NORTRA publishes *Mountain Hiking in Norway*, a general guide which serves as a good introduction to the various regions – copies can be ordered through the Norwegian Tourist Board (addresses on p.26).

HIKING AREAS AND NATIONAL PARKS

Thirty-six established mountain areas in Norway offer tremendous variety for the walker. From alpine peaks to flat upland plateaux, to green valleys and easy rolling hills, there is walking for everyone. Scramblers will enjoy summits on well-marked routes; older walkers or families with children can easily roam about on gentle slopes; and the energetic travel long distances for days on end. The following is a brief description of the more important hiking areas and national parks, most of which are discussed at greater length in the guide.

Some 300km north of Oslo, Norway's most famous hiking area is the **Jotunheimen National Park** ("Home of the Giants" – see p.128), where pointed summits and undulating glaciers dominate the skyline. Covering only 3900 square kilometres, the park offers an amazing concentration of high peaks, more than two hundred of them rising above 1900 metres. There are no public roads; all visitors to the park's interior either walk or ski in. In Jotunheimen, you will find northern Europe's two highest peaks, Galdhøpiggen (2469m) and Glittertind (2464m). Norway's highest waterfall, Vettisfossen, with a 275-metre drop, is also located here.

About 100km east of Jotunheimen, the **Rondane National Park** (see p.126) has become one of the country's most popular walking areas. The Rondane's 580 square kilometres, one-third of which in the high alpine zone, appeal to walkers of all ages and abilities. Ten peaks exceed the 2000-metre mark; many are accessible to any reasonably fit and eager walker. In the eastern Rondane, the gentle Alvdal Vestfjell appeals to older walkers and families with small children.

Stretching east from the Hardangerfjord to Finse in the north and Rjukan in the east, the **Hardangervidda** (see p.190) is Europe's largest mountain plateau, one third of which – 3430 square kilometres – constitutes the protected Hardangervidda National Park. At one time it was home to 40,000 reindeer, the last wild reindeer in Europe, but overgrazing has reduced their numbers. Five tourist organizations work together here to maintain a network of trails, roads and tourist huts, and the entire plateau, with its distinctive lunar-like appearance, is a favourite haunt of cross-country skiers.

Southeast of Åndalsnes, the mountain ranges of **Tafjord** and **Sunnmøre** are less well-known, incorporating deep fjords, plunging valleys and jagged mountains. Not to be forgotten, either, are the stunning peaks and valleys of the **Trollheimen** ("Home of the Trolls"), which connect to Norway's major climbing centre at Innerdalen. DNT (see p.53) will advise on mountaineering courses.

One of the most accessible of all Norwegian parks, the **Dovrefjell National Park** (see p.132) is bisected by the E6 and the Dombås–Trondheim railway. In Viking times, the park's Dovre mountain range was regarded as dividing the country in two – with "north of the mountains" and "south of the mountains" meaning north and south of the Dovre. In the eastern Dovre undulating mountains predominate, but as you hike west the steep and serrated alpine peaks of the Romsdal come into view. In the eastern Dovrefjell, there are marshes and open moors with rounded ridges. In the west you find the greatest concentration of high peaks outside the Jotunheimen.

East of Trondheim, the **Sylene Mountains** run along the Norwegian–Swedish border for 800km. In spite of hydroelectric development, this popular summer hiking area still feels very remote. With its rolling hills and gentle ascents, the Sylene presents a contrast to the wild and steep areas to the west. It's an ideal area for people who enjoy easy and fairly level walking. A second walking area located along the Norwegian–Swedish border, this time near Røros, is the **Femundsmarka**, where open moorland is broken up by scores of lakes and a few bare peaks.

In the north, it's hard to beat the **Troms Border Trail**. This begins southeast of Tromsø near the Finnish border, and crosses fine mountain scenery in what remains one of Norway's wildest spots. The trail also passes near Treriksrøysa, the point where Norway, Finland and Sweden meet. Cairned routes link up well-appointed unstaffed huts. Walkers seeking isolation will find this area to their liking. The rugged mountains near the northern city of Narvik are equally dramatic and easier to reach.

In the far north, the frozen wastes of Finnmark cover close to 48,000 square kilometres, or fifteen percent of Norway's total surface area. The interior of the region consists of a vast mountain plateau, the **Finnmarksvidda** (see p.290), which holds hundreds of lakes and several thousand kilometres of streams and rivers. At an average height of 300–400m, the plateau's rolling terrain is covered by a carpet of heather turf interspersed with patches of brushwood and birch forest. A handful of lodges (*fjellstuer*) offer accommodation.

SKIING

Norway has as good a claim as anywhere to be regarded as the home of skiing: a 4000-year-old rock carving found in Northern Norway is the oldest-known illustration of a person on skis; the first recorded ski competition was held in Norway in 1767; and Norwegians were the first to introduce skis to North America. One of the oldest cross-country ski races in the world is the 55-km Birkebeinerrennet from Rena to Lillehammer, held annually in late March; about five thousand skiers participate. The race follows the route taken by Norwegian mountain men in 1206 when they rescued the two-year-old Prince Håkon. The rescuers wore birch bark leggings known as Birkebeiners, hence the name of the race.

Downhill skiing and snowboard conditions in Norway are usually excellent from mid-November through to late April, though daylight hours are at a premium around the winter solstice. Temperatures tend to be colder than in the Alps, and in the last few years, Norway has had a more consistent snow record than the Alps. Broadly speaking Norwegian snow is deep, soft and forgiving. Resorts tend to be less crowded, have smaller class sizes and lift queues, and are at a lower altitude than their counterparts further south in Europe. The main centres for downhill skiing are at Geilo, Hemsedal, Oppdal and Voss. In the UK, the Norwegian Tourist Board operates a winter Ski Hotline on ☎020/7321 0666 (Mon–Fri 9am–4.30pm).

Cross-country skiing is a major facet of winter life in Norway. Approximately half the population are active in the sport, and many Norwegians still use skis for the practical purpose of getting to work or school. Norwegian interest in the sport is such that in 1994, thousands waited in the open overnight in temperatures of -25°C to see the final day of racing at the Lillehammer winter Olympics.

In the classic style of cross-country skiing, the whole body is angled forwards and the skis remain parallel except when braking or turning. For forward propulsion the skier transfers all weight to one ski, then straightens that leg while kicking downwards and backwards. At the same time, the arm on the opposite side of the body pushes down and back on the ski pole close to the line of the unweighted ski, which glides forward. At the finish of the kick, weight is transferred to what was the gliding ski, ready for the next kick. An unweighted cross-country ski is arc shaped, with the central section not touching the ground until the skier's down-kick flattens it on to the snow; the ends of the skis glide while the middle grips. Near major ski resorts, sets of parallel ski tracks called *Loipe* are cut in the snow by machine. They provide good gliding conditions and help keep the skis parallel; some *Loipe* are floodlit.

Skis can be waxed or waxless. Waxless skis have a rough tread in the middle called "fish-scales", which grips adequately at temperatures around zero. Waxed skis work better at low temperatures and on new snow. Grip wax is rubbed onto the middle third of the ski's length, but a sticky substance called *klister* is used instead in icy conditions. All skis benefit from hard glide wax applied to the front and back thirds of the base.

In the Telemark region of Southern Norway a technique has been developed to enable skiers to descend steep slopes on free-heel touring skis. "**Telemarking**" provides a stable and effective turning platform in powder snow. Essentially the skier traverses a slope in an upright position, but goes down on a right knee to execute a right turn and vice versa.

For companies specializing in downhill ski packages to Norway see p.7, p.9, p.15, p.18; nearly all of them will also deal with cross-country skiing and other, more obscure winter activities such as frozen waterfall climbing and ice fishing. Several specialist operators organize **cross-country skiing tours** (see p.7, p.9, p.15, p.18), and DNT (see p.53) organize a limited range of guided excursions too. Touring skiers should adopt the precautions taken by winter hill walkers: if going out for more than a couple of hours the skier should have emergency clothing, food and a vacuum flask with a hot drink. Detailed advice about coping with winter conditions is available in the excellent *Welcome to the Norwegian Mountains in Wintertime* booklet available from DNT.

Although you may be tempted to go on a ski package, remember that in most places you should find it easy (and comparatively inexpensive) to make your own arrangements. Even in Oslo, there are downhill ski runs within the city boundaries, and plenty of places from which to rent equipment. Per day, ski rental with boots and poles costs in the region of 150kr, snowboards 250kr, and passes for chair lifts 200kr. Cross-country skiers will have few difficulties in renting skiing tackle by the day (or week). Rental outlets are commonplace in the cities and towns as well as at the ski resorts and costs are similar to those for downhill gear. In terms of preparation, lessons on a dry slope are useful in so far as they develop confidence and balance, but cross-country skiing needs stamina and upper body as well as leg strength.

There's also **summer skiing** on the mountains from May to September – both slalom and cross-country. Lots of places offer this, but the largest and handiest spot for most itineraries is the *Stryn Sommarskisenter*, Stryn (☎57 87 23 33).

FISHING AND RIVER RAFTING

Norway's rivers provide some wonderful opportunities for anglers and river rafters. In particular, the fjord region's rivers offer fabulous freshwater fishing and so do the Arctic rivers further north, with common species including trout, char, pike and perch. Lakselv (see p.304) in Finnmark is one of several places renowned for its salmon fishing – *lakselv* actually means "salmon river" – and there is outstanding sea angling off the Lofoten Islands too (see p.267). To go **freshwater fishing**, you need two licences – a national licence, which costs 90kr a year (45kr a week) and is sold at any post office, and a *fiskekort* (local licence), available from sports shops, a few tourist offices, some hotels and most campsites. The cost of the local licence varies enormously; in the Oslo area it is 165kr. **Seawater fishing** has different rules: there's no local licence and you only need a national one if you go fishing for salmon, trout or sea char. This licence costs 180kr, can be purchased at any post office and also includes the freshwater national licence. If you take your own fishing tackle, you must have it disinfected before use.

NORTRA's *Angling in Norway*, available via the Norwegian Tourist Board, provides a comprehensive account of what you can catch and where. Several tour operators run all-inclusive, tailor-made fishing trips to several parts of Norway.

Details are available from the Norwegian Tourist Board, or start out by contacting Lågendalen Informasjon Brufoss, N-3275 Svarstad (☎33 15 55 55, *www.brufoss.no*), who operate a range of holidays as detailed in their *Fishing and Family Holidays in Norway* brochure.

For a list of operators running **river-rafting trips**, contact the Norwegian Canoe Association (Norges Padleforbund), Hauger Skolevei 1, N-1351 Rud (☎67 15 46 00, *www.nif.idrett.no /padling*); also see under Sjoa in the guide (p.123).

WORK

Like its Scandinavian neighbours, Norway is chary of potential foreign workers, or at least those from non-EEA (European Economic Area) countries, and anyway the chances of finding unskilled casual work are slim to say the least. It's much better to arrive seeking work with a saleable skill, though even then non-EEA nationals stand very little chance of getting a work permit.

THE PAPERWORK

If you're serious about working, though, and an **EEA citizen**, you must apply for a **residence permit** either to a Norwegian embassy or consulate (see p.21), or to the police within Norway itself. The residence permit, if granted, will normally give the holder the right to stay in Norway for five years and (usually) also the right to work. For more details, see "Red Tape and Visas", p.21.

The regulations are tighter for **non-EEA** nationals. For stays of over three months, an application for a residence permit must be submitted to a Norwegian embassy or consulate before you get there. If the application is successful, a residence permit issued to a non-EEA national is rarely for a period of more than one year, takes time to renew, and does not include the right to work – for that a subsequent work permit is required. To grant one, the Norwegians require that you have an offer of employment and apply for the work permit before you arrive in the country – you can't apply once in the country, and if you enter before the permit is granted it will be refused. It can take anything up to three months to process your application, and it's as well to know, anyway, that jobs are very difficult to obtain unless you have a knowledge of the language.

SOME WORK OPTIONS

The best-paid opportunity to live and work for a short period is on a **farm**. You'll live with a farming family, work incredibly hard and receive board and lodging and pocket money in return. Vacancies are usually for the spring and summer although some jobs stay open for a full year. Serious vacancies (ie for young farmers and/or people with experience) are dealt with by the International Farm Experience Programme, YFC Centre, National Agricultural Centre, Stoneleigh Park, Kenilworth, Warwickshire CV8 2LG. For other summer work (no experience necessary), 18- to 30-year-olds should contact the Norwegian Youth Council (*Landsrådet for Norske Ungdomsorgan-sasjoner*), Working Guest Programme, Rolf Hofmos gate 18, 0655 Oslo (*www.lnu.no*).

If you would like to do **voluntary work**, send an SAE to International Voluntary Service (IVS North Office, Castlehill House, 21 Otley Road, Leeds LS6 3AA; IVS South Office, Old Hall, East

Bergholt, Colchester CO7 6TQ; *www.ivsgbn.demon.co.uk*). They organize international workcamps two to three weeks long, with food and accommodation provided. You must be at least 18 and pay your own travel expenses. In the USA, The Council on International Educational Exchange (*www.ciee.org*) can provide you with information on a range of volunteer projects overseas, including Norway.

INFORMATION

For more information about working in Norway – paid or voluntary – consult the series of books published in Britain by the Central Bureau for Educational Visits and Exchanges, 10 Spring Gardens, London SW1A 2BN (☎020/7389 4004). Both *Working Holidays* and *Volunteer Work* are crammed with ideas and contacts.

DIRECTORY

ADDRESSES In Norway addresses are always written with the number after the street-name. In multistorey buildings, the ground floor is referred to as the first floor, and so on (we have numbered floors accordingly in this guide).

ALPHABET The letters Æ, Ø and Å come at the end of the alphabet, after Z (in that order).

BOOKS You'll find English-language books in almost every bookshop, though at twice the price at home. Libraries, too, stock foreign-language books.

BORDERS There is little formality at the Norway–Sweden border, slightly more between Norway and Finland. However, the northern border with Russia is a different story. Despite a recent relaxation of tension in the area following the break-up of the Soviet Union, border patrols (on either side) won't be overjoyed at the prospect of you nosing around. If you have a genuine wish to visit Russia, it's best to sign up for an organized tour from Kirkenes (see p.306).

CHILDREN There are no real problems with taking children to Norway. They travel half-price (infants aged under 3 or 4 free) on all forms of public transport, and the same discount applies to an extra bed in their parents' hotel room. Family rooms are widely available in youth hostels, while many of the summer activities detailed in this book are geared up to cater for kids as well. There are also baby compartments (with their own toilet and changing room) for kids aged 2 and under and their escorts on most trains, and baby-changing rooms at most larger train stations. Many restaurants have children's menus; if not it's always worth asking if there are cheaper, smaller portions.

GLACIERS These slow-moving masses of ice are in constant, if generally imperceptible, motion, and are therefore potentially dangerous. People, often tourists, die on them nearly every year. Never climb a glacier without a guide, never walk beneath one and always heed the instructions at the site. Guided crossings can be terrific – see the relevant accounts in the guide.

LEFT LUGGAGE There are coin-operated lockers in most train and bus stations and at all major ferry terminals.

SMOKING Smoking is prohibited in all public buildings, including train stations, and forbidden on all domestic flights and bus services. Restaurants have to have non-smoking areas by law, and there are supposed to be dividing walls between smoking and non-smoking sections. Hoteliers have by law to designate fifty percent of their rooms as non-smoking.

TIME Norway is one hour ahead of the UK and six to nine hours ahead of continental USA.

TIPPING A service charge is automatically included in hotel and restaurant bills, so no additional tip is expected.

CHAPTER ONE

OSLO AND AROUND

Oslo is a vibrant, self-confident city whose urbane, easy-going air bears comparison with any European capital. This was not always the case, however. Oslo was something of a poor relation until Norway's break with Sweden at the beginning of the century, remaining dourly provincial until the 1950s, but since then the city has developed into a go-ahead and cosmopolitan commercial hub of half a million people. It is also the only major metropolis in a country brimming with small towns and villages; its nearest rival, Bergen, is less than half its size. This gives Oslo a powerful – some say overweening – voice in the political, cultural and economic life of the nation. Inevitably, Norway's big companies are mostly based here, as a rash of concrete and glass tower blocks attests, but fortunately, these monoliths rarely interrupt the stately Neoclassical lines of the late nineteenth-century **town centre**. It's here you should head (at least initially), as Oslo's handsome older quarters contain some excellent museums, are within easy reach of the leafy Bygdøy peninsula – home to the world-famous Viking Ships Museum – and boast a cosmopolitan street life and bar scene that surprises many first-time visitors.

The other surprise is Oslo's size. The centre is compact, but the city's vast boundaries (453 square kilometres) encompass huge areas of forest, sand and water. Almost universally, the inhabitants of Oslo have a deep and abiding affinity for the wide open spaces that surround their city: the waters of the Oslofjord to the south and inland, the forested hills of the Nordmarka to the north, are immensely popular for everything from boating and hiking to skiing. For all but the shortest of stays, there's ample opportunity to join in – the **island beaches** just offshore in the Oslofjord, and the open forest and **ski-jumps** at Holmenkollen, are both easily reached by ferry or underground train.

Oslo curves round the innermost shore of the **Oslofjord**, whose tapered waters extend for some 100km from the Skagerrak, the choppy channel separating Norway and Sweden from Denmark. As Norwegian fjords go, Oslofjord is not spectacularly beautiful – the rocky shores are generally low and unprepossessing – but

---

ACCOMMODATION PRICE CODES

The hotels and guesthouses detailed throughout this guide have been graded according to the price categories listed below. Prices given are for the least expensive double room during the high season, although almost every hotel offers seasonal and/or weekend discounts, which can reduce the rate by one or even two grades. Wherever hotels have an official summer rate we've given it (denoted s/r), but bear in mind that many others will provide impromptu summer and weekend discounts. Single rooms, where available, usually cost between 60 and 80 percent of a double. For a more detailed discussion of accommodation see p.37.

① under 500kr	③ 700–900kr	⑤ 1200–1500kr
② 500–700kr	④ 900–1200kr	⑥ over 1500kr

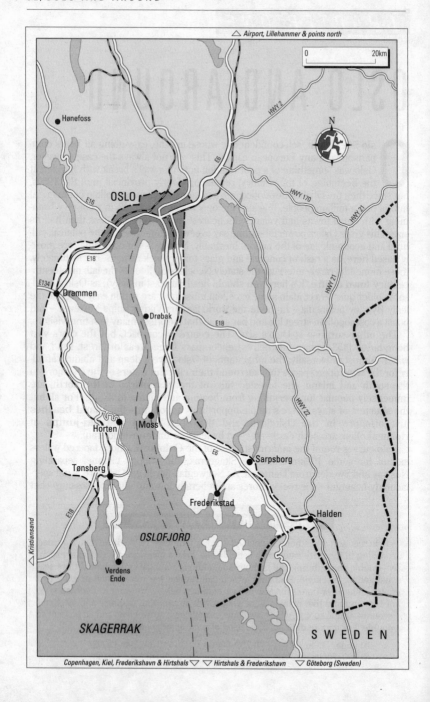

Airport, Lillehammer & points north

0   20km

Hønefoss

HWY 2

E6

OSLO

HWY 170

E16

HWY 21

E18

E134

Drammen

Drøbak

E18

HWY 21

Horten

Moss

HWY 22

Tønsberg

E6

Sarpsborg

E18

Frederikstad

Halden

Kristiansand

OSLOFJORD

Verdens
Ende

SKAGERRAK

SWEDEN

Copenhagen, Kiel, Frederikshavn & Hirtshals ▽   ▽ Hirtshals & Frederikshavn   ▽ Göteborg (Sweden)

scores of islets diversify the seascape. These tiny forested bumps, which once housed the city's seaward defences, now accommodate summer chalets. The towns that trail along the shoreline are less appealing, being for the most part workaday industrial settlements. The main exception is **Fredrikstad**, Norway's only surviving fortified town. Its gridiron streets and angular bastions date from the late sixteenth century, and are best visited as a day-trip by train from the capital.

OSLO

OSLO is the oldest of the Scandinavian capital cities. The name is derived from *Ås*, a Norse word for God, and *Lo*, meaning field. According to the medieval Norse chronicler Snorre Sturlason, the city was founded around 1048 by Harald Hardråda. Harald's son, Olav Kyrre, established a bishopric and built a cathedral (see p.319) here, though the kings of Norway continued to live in Bergen – an oddly inefficient division of state and church, considering the difficulty of communication. At the start of the fourteenth century, Håkon V rectified matters by moving to Oslo, where he built himself the Akershus fortress. The town boomed until 1349, when bubonic plague wiped out almost half the population. The slow decline that followed in the wake of this catastrophe accelerated when Norway came under Danish control in 1397. No longer the seat of power, Oslo became a neglected backwater until its fortunes were eventually revived by the Danish king Christian IV. He moved Oslo lock, stock and barrel, shifting it west to its present site and modestly renaming it Christiania in 1624. The new city prospered, and continued to do so after 1814, when Norway broke away from Denmark and united with Sweden. In the event, this political realignment was a short-lived affair and by the 1880s, Christiania – and the country as a whole – were clamouring for independence. This was eventually achieved in 1905, though the city didn't revert to its original name for another twenty years. Today's city centre is largely the work of the late nineteenth and early twentieth centuries: wide streets, dignified parks and gardens, solid buildings and long Classical vistas combine to lend it a self-satisfied, respectable air. In Oslo you get the feeling the inhabitants are proud of their wealthy city and of the rapid changes that are underway, notably an ambitious construction programme and a fast-growing cultural life.

Oslo's biggest single draw is its **museums**, which cover a hugely varied and stimulating range of topics: the fabulous Viking Ships museum, the Munch Museum showcasing a good chunk of the painter's work, the sculpture park devoted to the bronze and granite works of Gustav Vigeland, and the moving historical documents of the Resistance Museum, are enough to keep even the most weary museum-goer busy for a few days. There's also a decent **outdoor life** – Oslo is enlivened by a good range of parks, pavement cafés, street entertainers and festivals. In summer, when virtually the whole population seems to live outdoors, the city is a real delight. Winter's also a good time to visit, when Oslo's location amid hills and forests makes it a thriving and affordable ski centre.

Arrival and information

Downtown Oslo is at the heart of a superb public transport system, which makes arriving and departing convenient and straightforward. The principal arrival hub

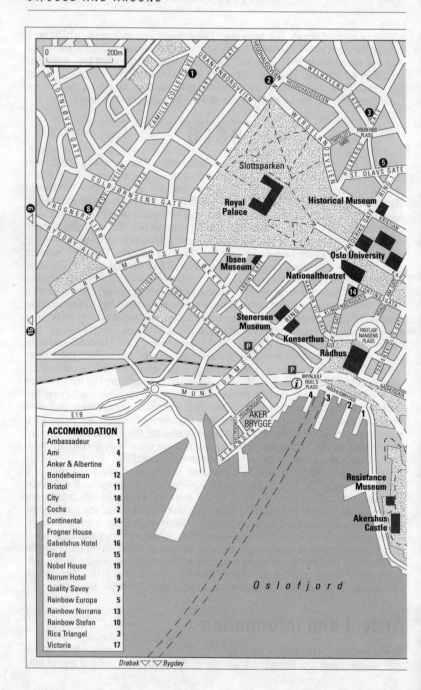

ACCOMMODATION

Ambassadeur	1
Ami	4
Anker & Albertine	6
Bondeheiman	12
Bristol	11
City	18
Cochs	2
Continental	14
Frogner House	8
Gabelshus Hotel	16
Grand	15
Nobel House	19
Norum Hotel	9
Quality Savoy	7
Rainbow Europa	5
Rainbow Norrøna	13
Rainbow Stefan	10
Rica Triangel	3
Victoria	17

Drøbak ▽ ▽ Bygdøy

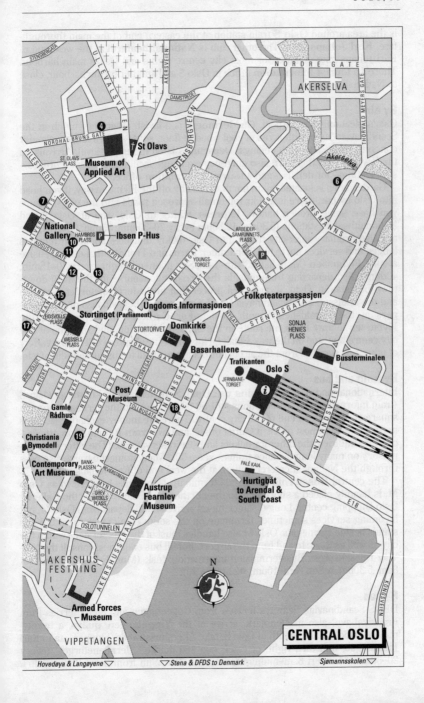

CENTRAL OSLO

Hovedøya & Langøyene ▽   ▽ Stena & DFDS to Denmark   Sjømannsskolen ▽

is the area around **Oslo S** train station at the eastern end of the main thorough-fare, **Karl Johans gate**. The other hub is **Nationaltheateret** at the west end of Karl Johans gate, handier for most city centre sights and Oslo's main harbour. There's a **tourist information** office in Oslo S and another by the harbour, close to Nationaltheateret.

By air

Oslo's gleaming new airport, **Gardermoen**, is a lavish affair very much in the Scandinavian style, with acres of cool wooden floor, softly-spoken angles, slender concrete pillars and high ceilings. Departures is on the upper level, Arrivals on the lower, where there are also currency exchange facilities, car rental offices – see "Listings" for details – and a **tourist information** office.

Gardermoen is located 45km north of the city off the E6 motorway. If you head into Oslo by **car**, there is a 12kr toll on all approach roads into the city – ensure you have some kroner handy. **Express trains** to Oslo stop at Oslo S and Nationaltheatret stations (5.30am–12.30pm every 20–30 min; 35min; 90kr). There are also ordinary inter-city trains into Oslo (60kr) that take about ten minutes longer, and services north to Lillehammer, Røros and Trondheim. Less expensive are the **Flybussen** (Mon–Sat 5.30am–1am, Sun noon–midnight, every 10–15min; 40min; 65kr) departing from outside the Arrivals concourse for the main down-town bus station, Oslo M, and then proceeding on to Jernbanetorget, Grensen and the Radisson SAS Scandinavia Hotel. On request, they will also drop passen-gers at the Haraldsheim youth hostel. For Gardermoen **departures**, the Flybussen follows the same route in the opposite direction, and will stop at any city centre bus stop on the way. Finally, Nor-Way Bussekspress operates a variety of other bus services from the airport direct to the small towns surrounding Oslo.

By train and bus

International and domestic **trains** use **Oslo Sentralstasjon**, known as Oslo S (train information and reservations ☎81 50 08 88), sited in the Jernbanetorget, a square at the eastern end of the city centre. There are money exchange facilities here, as well as a post office, a tourist office, and two **train information** offices – one for enquiries, the other for tickets and seat reservations. (The latter are com-pulsory on many long-distance trains – see p.30). Many domestic trains also pass through the Nationaltheateret station, at the west end of Karl Johans gate.

The central **Bussterminalen** (bus terminal), sometimes referred to as **Oslo M**, is handily placed a short walk to the northeast of Oslo S, under the Galleriet Oslo shopping centre. Long-distance buses arrive at and depart from Oslo M, but incoming services sometimes terminate on the south side of Oslo S, at the bus stands beside Havnegata. Oslo M also handles most of the bus services within the city as well as those to and from the airport. For all bus enquiries, consult the Nor-Way Bussekspress Bussterminalen information desk (Mon–Fri 7am–10pm, Sat 8am–5.30pm & Sun 8am–10pm; ☎23 00 24 40).

By sea

DFDS Scandinavian Seaways **ferries** from Copenhagen and Stena ferries from Fredrikshavn, also in Denmark, arrive at the **Vippetangen quays**, a twenty-minute walk (1300m) south of Oslo S: take Akershusstranda/Skippergata to Karl Johans gate and turn right, or catch bus #60 marked "Jernbanetorget" (every 20–30min Mon–Fri 6am–midnight, Sat from 7am, Sun from 8am; 10min; 20kr).

On Color Line services from Kiel and Denmark's Hirsthals, you'll arrive at the **Hjortneskaia**, some 3km west of the city centre. From here, bus #56 runs into the centre and to Oslo S (every 30min Mon–Fri 6–9.20am & 2.30–5.30pm; 10min; 20kr). Failing that, a taxi to Oslo S will cost about 150kr. Ferry ticket office details are given in "Listings", p.105. Finally, **Hurtigbåt** domestic passenger express ferry boats from Arendal and points on the south coast dock at the Palékaia, a five- to ten-minute walk south from Oslo S.

By car

Eighteen video-controlled toll-points ring the city, and it costs 12kr to enter. Left-hand lanes with blue signs inscribed "Abonnement" are for drivers in possession of toll passes; the "Mynt/Coin" lanes (yellow signs) are for exact cash payments only and frequently have a bucket-shaped receptacle where you throw your money; the "Manuell" lanes (grey) are also used for cash payments, but provide change. Oslo's ring roads encircle and tunnel under the city; if you follow the signs for "Ring 1" you'll be delivered right into the centre and emerge (eventually) at the Ibsen P-Hus, a multistorey car park a short distance from Karl Johans gate.

You won't need your car to sightsee in Oslo, so you'd do best to use a designated **car park**. The Ibsen P-hus at C.J. Hambros Plass 1 (☎22 33 04 80), two blocks from Karl Johans gate, is open 24 hours, as is the Aker Brygge P-hus, Sjøgata 4 (☎22 01 94 94). There are half a dozen other multistorey car parks in the centre, but note that several of them operate restricted hours. Costs begin at 10kr for 25 minutes during the day and evening, mounting up to a maximum charge of 130kr for 24 hours, or 40kr in the evening (6pm–midnight); overnight parking (6pm–9am) costs 80kr. The Ibsen P-hus offers a 20 percent discount to Oslo Card holders (see box below).

Alternatively, you can park in pay-and-display car parks and on-street metered spaces around the city (up to 15kr per hour, 32kr for two hours). Identified by blue "P" signs, these metered spaces are owned and operated by the municipality, and are free of charge from Monday to Friday between 5pm and 8am and over the weekend after 2pm on Saturday. They also provide free parking at any time to Oslo Card holders (make sure to write your registration number, date and time on the card in the space provided).

THE OSLO CARD

The **Oslo Card** is a useful pass that gives free admission to almost every museum and unlimited free travel on the whole municipal transport system, including local trains, plus free on-street parking at metered parking places. It also provides some useful discounts in shops, hotels and restaurants, though in winter, when opening hours for many sights and museums are reduced, you may have to work hard to make the card pay for itself. Valid for either 24, 48 or 72 hours, it costs 150kr, 220kr and 250kr respectively, with children aged four to fifteen charged 50kr, 60kr and 70kr. A 24-hour family card for two adults and two children costs 350kr. It's available at the city's tourist offices, most hotels and campsites in Oslo, the Trafikanten office (see p.68) and downtown Narvesen newsagents. The card is valid for a set number of hours (rather than days) starting from the moment it is first used, at which time it should either be presented and stamped, or (for example, if your first journey is by tram) you should fill in the date and time yourself.

Information

The main tourist information office, the **Norges Informasjonssenter** (Norwegian Information Centre; June–Aug daily 9am–7pm; April, May & Sept Mon–Sat 9am–5pm; Oct–March Mon–Fri 9am–4pm; Mon–Fri on ☎22 83 00 50; *www.oslopro.no*), is housed in what used to be the Oslo Vestbane train station at Brynjulf Bull's plass 1, down by the waterfront at the western end of the city centre. It has some glossy visual displays and an extensive range of brochures relating to Norway as a whole. As regards Oslo, it provides a full range of information, including free city maps, reservations on guided tours and an accommodation booking service. There's also a tourist office inside **Oslo S** (May–Aug daily 8am–11pm, Sept Mon–Sat 8am–11pm, Oct–April Mon–Sat 8am–5pm) with similar services. Both offices sell the Oslo Card and have free copies of various booklets and leaflets, including the excellent and very thorough *Oslo Official Guide* and *What's On in Oslo* – invaluable for listings of events and services. The **Trafikanten** information office (see below) provides information about Oslo's transport system. **Ungdoms Informasjonen**, Møllergata 3, (Mon–Fri 11am–5pm; ☎22 41 51 32; *www.unginfo.oslo.no*), specializes in information for young (ages 16–25) people (see p.106).

City transport

Oslo's public transport system consists of buses, trams, a small underground rail system (the Tunnelbanen) and local ferries. Flat-fare **tickets** (bought on board the bus, tram or ferry, or at T-bane stations) cost 20kr and are valid for unlimited travel within the city boundaries for one hour; children four to sixteen years old travel half price, babies and toddlers free. There are several ways to cut costs. The best is to buy an **Oslo Card** (see p.67), which is valid on the whole network and on certain routes into the surrounding *kommunes* – but not on trains or buses to the airport. If you're not into museums, however, a straight **travel pass** might be a better buy. A Dagskort (24hr pass) valid for unlimited travel within the city limits costs 40kr; or there's the Flexikort (eight rides; 115kr) and other passes for longer stays, available from the Trafikanten office in Jernbanetorget and downtown Narvesen kiosks. On buses, the driver will check your ticket; on trams you're trusted to have one. Flexikort tickets should be cancelled in the machine. Though fare-dodging might seem widespread, bear in mind that it is punished by some hefty spot fines.

The safe and efficient city transport system is operated by AS Oslo Sporveier. Their information office, **Trafikanten**, is in the Jernbanetorget, beneath the high-tech see-through clocktower outside Oslo S (Mon–Fri 7am–8pm, Sat 8am–6pm; ☎22 17 70 30). Apart from selling Oslo Cards and public transport tickets, they give away a useful **transit route map**, the *Sporveiens hovedkart,* as well as a **timetable** booklet called *Rutebok for Oslo*, which details every timetable for every route in the Oslo system.

Buses

Almost all city **bus** services originate at the Bussterminalen beside Oslo S. There are around fifty routes operating strictly within the city limits, and other services out of Oslo. The vast majority of them pass through Jernbanetorget, and another common stop is at the Nationaltheatret. Most buses stop running at around midnight, though at weekends **night buses** (*nattbuss*) take over on certain routes (flat-rate fare 40kr; Oslo Card and other passes not valid) – full details in the timetable, *Rutebok for Oslo*.

Trams

The city's **trams** run on eight routes through the city, crisscrossing the centre from east to west, and sometimes duplicating the bus routes. They are a bit slower than the buses, but are a handy and rather more enjoyable and relaxing way of getting about. Major stops include Jernbanetorget, Nationaltheatret and Aker Brygge. Most operate regularly – every ten or twenty minutes, from 6am to midnight.

Tunnelbanen and trains

The Tunnelbanen – **T-bane** – has eight lines which converge to share a common slice of track crossing the city centre from Majorstuen in the west to Tøyen in the east, with Jernbanetorget, Stortinget and Nationaltheatret stations in between. From this central section, four lines run westbound (*Vest*) and four eastbound (*Øst*). The system mainly serves commuters from the suburbs, but you'll find it useful for trips out to Holmenkollen and Sognsvann – where the trains travel above ground. The system runs from around 6am until 12.30am. A series of **local commuter trains**, run by NSB, links Oslo with Moss, Eidsvoll, Drammen and other outlying towns; departures are from Oslo S, with many also stopping at Nationaltheatret. For details of services to and from the airport, see p.66.

Ferries

Numerous **ferries** shuttle across the northern reaches of the Oslofjord to connect the city centre with its outlying districts and archipelago. To the Bygdøy peninsula and its museums, they leave from the piers behind the Rådhus (late April to Sept), while the all-year services to Hovedøya, Lindøya and the other offshore islets (except Langøyene, June–Aug only) leave from the Vippetangen quay, behind Akershus Castle. To get to the Vippetangen quay, take bus #60 from Jernbanetorget. If you're venturing beyond the city limits, there are also boats to Nesodden (all year), and Drøbak (summer weekends only), leaving from the Aker Brygge piers.

Taxis

The speed and efficiency of Oslo's public transport system means that you should rarely have to resort to a **taxi**, which is probably just as well as they are expensive. Taxi fares are regulated, with the tariff varying according to the time of day. At night you can expect to pay around 130kr for a ten-minute, five-kilometre ride; during the day about 25 percent less. Taxi ranks can be found round the city centre and outside all the big hotels; a convenient one is at the corner of Karl Johans gate and Akersgata. To call a cab ring Oslo Taxi on ☎22 38 80 90.

Bicycles

If you want to get about under your own steam, using a **bicycle** is a pleasant option as the city has a reasonable range of cycle tracks, and roads increasingly have cycle lanes. Oslo's main **bicycle rental** shop is Vestbanen (☎23 11 51 08), just along from the tourist office. Their charges begin at 90kr for a 7-speed bike for 3 hours, rising to 180kr for 24 hours, 600kr for the week. Mountain bikes cost about 30 percent more. Waterproofs and insurance cost extra, as do helmets (25kr per day), and there's a refundable deposit of around 1000kr to pay.

Accommodation

Oslo has the range of hotels you would expect of a capital city, as well as private rooms, a smattering of guesthouses and a quartet of youth hostels. To appreciate the full flavour of the city, you're best off staying on or near the western reaches of Karl Johans gate – between the Stortinget and the Nationaltheatret – though the well-heeled area to the north and west of the Royal Palace (Det Kongelige Slott) is enjoyable too. Many of the least expensive lodgings are, however, to be found in the vicinity of Oslo S, but this somewhat seedy district – along with the grimy suburbs to the north and east of the station – is preferably avoided. That said, if money is tight and you're here in July and August, your choice of location may well be very limited as the scramble for budget beds becomes acute – or at least tight enough to make it well worth phoning ahead to check on space. For peace of mind, it is advisable to make an **advance reservation**, particularly for your first night. A positive way to cut the hassle is to use the **accommodation service** provided by the **tourist office**. Both the Oslo S office and the Norwegian Information Centre (see "Information", p.68) can give you full accommodation lists, or make a booking on your behalf for 20kr per person – a real bargain when you consider that they often get discounted rates. Note also that the Oslo S office is especially good for private rooms.

Hotels

In Oslo, 700–900kr will get you a fairly small and simple en-suite room. You hit the comfort zone at about 900kr, and luxury from around 1000kr. However, special offers and **seasonal deals** often make the smarter hotels more affordable than this. Most offer up to forty percent discounts at weekends, while in July and August – when Norwegians leave town for their holidays – prices everywhere tend to drop radically. Also, most room rates are tempered by the inclusion of a good-to-excellent self-service buffet **breakfast**. The two tourist offices keep regularly updated lists of the best offers.

Ambassadeur, Camilla Colletts vei 15 (☎22 44 18 35, fax 22 44 47 91, *www.bestwestern.com /no/ambassadeur*). One of a long sequence of attractive nineteenth-century town houses graced by wrought-iron balconies. The now slightly grimy pink exterior doesn't do justice to the elegantly furnished interior, where each of the bedrooms has a different theme such as "Shanghai" or "Amsterdam". A great location too, just three blocks west of the Slottsparken. ⑤, s/r ④.

Ami, Nordahl Bruns gate 9 (☎22 11 61 10, fax 22 36 18 01). Resembles a guesthouse as much as a hotel, with modern but frugal rooms and lumpy beds. About ten minutes' walk north of Karl Johans gate, behind the Kunstindustrimuseet at the east end of St Olavs gate. ③, s/r ②.

Anker, Storgata 55 (☎22 99 75 00, fax 22 99 75 20). A large budget hotel in a glum high-rise block beside the murky river at the east end of Storgata. Mainly Norwegian clientele. Facilities are perfectly adequate, if somewhat frugal, but the surrounding area is cheerless. Twenty minutes' walk from Oslo S or five minutes by tram. The *Albertine Hostel* (see p.72) is situated in the same high-rise, as is the *Albert Sommerhotell* (②). ③.

Bondeheimen, Rosenkrantz gate 8 (☎22 42 95 30, fax 22 41 94 37). One of Oslo's most delightful hotels. Both the public areas and the extremely comfortable bedrooms are tastefully decorated in a modern, pan-Scandinavian style, with polished pine everywhere you look. It's handily located just two minutes' walk north of Karl Johans gate, and the inclusive buffet breakfast, served in the *Kaffistova* (see "Cafés", p.97), is excellent. Free coffee, soup and bread in the foyer throughout the evening. The rack rate for a double is 1020kr (single 915kr), but look out for weekend and summer discounts of up to forty percent. ④, s/r ③.

Bristol, Kristian IV's gate 7 (☎22 82 60 00, fax 22 82 60 01, *bristol@online.no*). Plush establishment distinguished by its sumptuous public areas with ornate nineteenth-century chandeliers, columns and fancifully carved arches. ⑥, s/p ④.

City, Skippergaten 19 (☎22 41 36 10, fax 22 42 24 29). This modest but pleasant hotel, a long-time favourite with budget travellers, is located above shops and offices in a typical Oslo apartment block near Oslo S. The surroundings are a little seedy, but the hotel is cheerful enough, with small but perfectly adequate rooms. ②.

Continental, Stortingsgaten 24 (☎22 82 40 00, fax 22 42 96 89). One of Oslo's most prestigious hotels. Sumptuous public areas and amazingly comfortable bedrooms furnished in immaculate modern style. The hotel is ideally located, a stone's throw from Karl Johans gate, and incorporates several bars and restaurants. ⑥, s/r ④.

Frogner House, Skovveien 8 (☎22 56 00 56, fax 22 56 05 00). Located in one of Oslo's ritziest neighbourhoods, this elegant hotel occupies a handsome Victorian townhouse. Each of the comfortable bedrooms is individually decorated in tasteful modern style, with stripped wood and thick carpets throughout. One kilometre west of the centre off Frognerveien – trams #12 or 15. ⑤, s/r ④.

Gabelshus, Gabels gate 16 (☎22 55 22 60, fax 22 44 27 30). This delightful hotel, one of the most intimate in the city, boasts a beautifully maintained interior with ornate fireplaces and antique furnishings. Located in a smart residential area a couple of kilometres west of the city centre, off Drammensveien. Highly recommended. Tram #10 or #13 from the centre. ④, s/r ③.

Grand, Karl Johans gate 31 (☎23 21 20 00, fax 23 21 21 00, *grand.hotel.oslo@rica.no*). Over 100 years of tradition, comfort and style in *the* prime position on Oslo's main street translates into stratospheric room rates. But breakfasts are sumptuous, the lobby opulent and the rooms eminently comfortable. Hefty weekend and summertime discounts make the *Grand* much more affordable. ⑥, s/r ④.

Nobel House, Kongens gate 5 (☎23 10 72 00, fax 23 10 72 10, *anne.aanensen@noblehouse.no*). Deluxe hotel with style – from the smart wooden floors to the cool, modernist decor. Great downtown location too, close to the restaurants and art museums of Bankplassen. ⑥, s/r ④.

Norum, Bygdøy Allé 53 (☎22 44 79 90, fax 22 44 92 39). With its forest of spiky, late nineteenth-century towers, the Norum possesses the most imposing hotel façade in the city. Each room is individually decorated in tasteful modern style. In a busy residential area about 2km west of the centre; to get there use buses #30–33. ④, s/r ③.

Quality Savoy, Universitets gate 11 (☎22 20 26 55, fax 22 11 24 80), at the corner of Universitets gate and Kristian Augusts gate. Attractive choice with pleasant rooms and wood-panelled public areas. Very comfortable. In an interesting area too, with bookshops and bars catering primarily for the city's students. ④.

Rainbow Europa, St Olavs gate 31 (☎22 20 99 90, fax 22 11 27 27). Large, modern chain establishment in dreary surroundings near the west end of Olavs gate. Towards the lower end of its price range. ④, s/r ③.

Rainbow Norrøna, Grensen 19 (☎22 42 64 00, fax 22 33 25 65). Pleasantly modernized hotel with antique flourishes – stained glass windows and heavy brass doors. Occupies part of a nineteenth-century apartment block right in the middle of town, about 400m to the north of the Stortinget. The buffet breakfast is excellent and the breakfast room offers an attractive city view. A bargain at 850kr for doubles, with further summer and weekend discounts of 15 percent. ③, s/r ②.

Rainbow Stefan, Rosenkrantz gate 1 (☎22 42 92 50, fax 22 33 70 22). Unremarkable but spick-and-span modern hotel above the ground floor shops in a five-storey building. Great location, just a couple of minutes' walk north of Karl Johans gate. Near the bottom of its price range, it's one of the city's better deals. ④.

Rica Triangel, Holbergs plass 1 (☎22 20 88 55, fax 22 20 78 25, *rica.triangel.hotel.oslo@rica.no*). Despite its grand nineteenth-century facade, this large chain establishment has an unremarkable modern interior. Overlooks Holbergs plass, a pint-sized square about 500m to the north of the Slottsparken. ④.

Rica Victoria, Rosenkrantz gate 13 (☎22 42 99 40, fax 22 42 99 43, *rica.victoria.hotel.oslo@rica.no*). Verging on the luxurious, this large modern hotel is just south of Karl Johans gate. Spacious rooms with every convenience, and popular with visiting business folk. ⑤.

Hostels, private rooms and guesthouses

There are three HI **hostels** in Oslo, each very popular and open to people of any age, though non-members pay a modest surcharge of 25kr. There is also a fourth hostel, attached to one of the city's budget hotels. Alternatively, the tourist office can book you into a **private room** – the supply rarely dries up. These cost a flat rate of 170kr for a single, and 300kr a double. This is something of a bargain, especially as many also have cooking facilities, but they do tend to be out of the city centre, and there is often a minimum two-night stay. Comparable to hostels and private rooms are the **guesthouses**, which start at around 340kr single, 450kr double. There's only a handful of them, and just one near the city centre. They offer basic but generally adequate accommodation either with or without en-suite facilities; breakfast is, however, not included, and at some places you may need to supply your own sleeping bag.

Albertine Hostel, Storgata 55 (☎22 99 72 00, fax 22 99 72 20). Plain and simple one- (250kr), two- (340kr), four- (560kr) and six-bed (690kr) rooms. Serves an adequate breakfast and has self-catering facilities, but you have to provide your own utensils. Bed linen and towels are for hire, or bring your own. The hostel shares the same glum high-rise block as the *Anker Hotel* – see p.70. ①.

Cochs Pensjonat, Parkveien 25 (☎22 60 48 36, fax 22 46 54 02). No-frills guesthouse occupying the third floor of a drab modern block. Some rooms have a kitchen unit. Singles with shower 420kr (340kr without), doubles 560kr (450kr). In a handy location behind Slottsparken at the foot of Hegdehaugsveien. Triples and quadruples are also available. ②.

Oslo Haraldsheim, Haraldsheimveien 4, Grefsen (☎22 22 29 65, fax 22 22 10 25, *haraldsheim@internet.no*). Best of Oslo's HI youth hostels, 4km northeast of the centre, and open all year except Christmas week. Has 71 rooms, most of which have four beds. The public areas are comfortable and attractively furnished, and the bedrooms clean and frugal, with about forty having their own shower and WC. There are self-catering facilities, a restaurant, and washing machines. The basic 160kr price includes breakfast, while single rooms cost 280kr (350kr with shower), doubles 380kr (460kr). The only drawback can be the presence of parties of noisy schoolkids. It's a very popular spot, so advance booking is essential in summer. To get there, take tram #10 or #11 from the bottom of Storgata, near the Domkirke, to the Sinsenkrysset stop, from where it's a ten-minute signposted walk. Should you somehow miss this stop, the tram's next stop is beside Grefsen station, from where it is a marginally longer walk. Grefsen can also be reached by local train from Oslo S. By road, the hostel is situated close to – and signposted from – Ring 3. ①.

Oslo Ekeberg, Kongsveien 82 (☎22 74 18 90, fax 22 74 75 05). This tiny HI hostel, with just eleven rooms, occupies part of a school complex 4km southeast of Oslo S. Take tram #18 or #19 from the centre and it's 100m from the Holtet tram stop. ①, dorm beds 170kr.

Oslo Holtekilen, Michelets vei 55, 1320 Stabekk, 10km west of the city centre (☎67 51 80 40, fax 67 59 12 30; end of May–mid-Aug). From Oslo M take bus #151, and the hostel is 100m from the Kveldsroveien bus stop. This is another HI Oslo hostel, but much smaller than Haraldsheim. There are kitchen facilities, a restaurant and a laundry. Again, the 160kr price includes breakfast. ①, single rooms 260kr.

Camping and cabins

Camping is a fairly easy proposition in an uncrowded city, and of the sixteen sites dotted within a 50km radius, the nearest to the centre is just 3km away. If you're out of luck with rooms in town, most sites also offer **cabins**, but call ahead to ask about availability.

Bogstad Camping, Ankerveien 117 (☎22 51 08 00, fax 22 51 08 50). Large and well-equipped lakeside campsite, with cabins available for rental. Fifteen kilometres northwest of the centre – take bus #32 from Oslo S or Nationaltheatret. It gets crowded, though, so call ahead first. Open all year. Cabins ①.

Ekeberg Camping, Ekebergveien 65 (☎22 19 85 68, fax 22 67 04 36; Jun–Aug). Large campsite in a rocky, forested piece of parkland just 3km east of the city centre; bus #34 from Jernbanetorget goes past.

Langøyene Camping, Langøyene (☎22 11 53 21; June to mid-Aug). Extremely popular, no-frills campsite on one of the islets just offshore from downtown Oslo. Langøyene has the city's best beaches and an attractive wooded shoreline. To get there, take ferry #94 from the Vippetangen quay.

The City

If Oslo is your first taste of Norway, you'll be struck by the light – soft and brilliantly clear in the summer and broodingly gloomy in winter, each season visited by rafts of rain or chilling blizzards respectively. The grand late nineteenth- and early twentieth-century buildings of central Oslo suit the climate well, providing the sense of security and prosperity that was so important to the emergent nation when they were built, and which is still a feature of the city today. Largely as a result, most of **downtown Oslo** remains easy and pleasant to walk around, a humming, good-natured kind of place whose airy streets and squares accommodate these appealing remnants of the city's early days, as well as a clutch of good museums and dozens of bars, cafés and restaurants.

The city's showpiece museums are located on the **Bygdøy peninsula**, to which ferries shuttle from the jetty behind the **Rådhus** (City Hall); other ferries head south from the Vippetangen quay behind the Akershus to the string of rusticated **islands** that necklace the inner waters of the Oslofjord. Back on the mainland, **east Oslo** is the least prepossessing part of town, a gritty sprawl housing the poorest of the city's inhabitants. You wouldn't come this way were it not for the **Munch Museum**, which boasts a superb collection of the artist's work; afterwards it's mildly tempting to pop along the eastern shore of Oslo's principal harbour for the views over the city and to look at the skimpy remains of the medieval town. **Northwest Oslo** is far more prosperous, with big old houses lining the avenues immediately to the west of the Slottsparken. Beyond is the **Frognerparken**, a chunk of parkland where the stunning open-air sculptures of Gustav Vigeland are displayed in the **Vigelandsparken**. Further west still, there's more prestigious modern art at the **Henie-Onstad Kunstsenter**, beyond the city limits in suburban Høvikodden.

The city's enormous reach becomes apparent only to the north of the centre in the **Nordmarka**. This massive forested wilderness, stretching far inland, is patterned by hiking trails and cross-country ski routes. Two T-bane lines provide ready access, clanking their way up into the rocky hills that herald the region. The more westerly T-bane grinds on past **Holmenkollen**, a ski resort where the

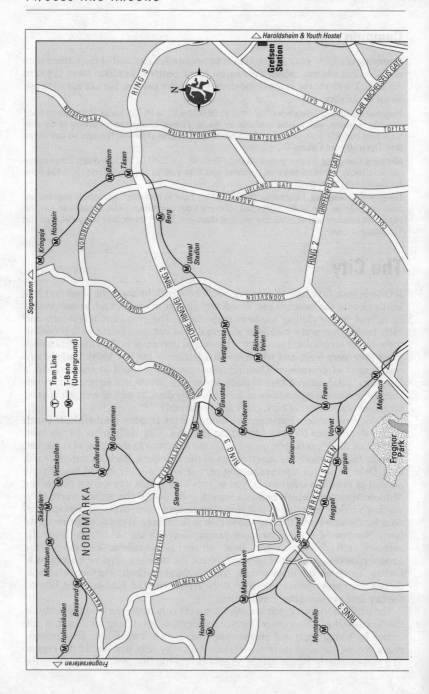

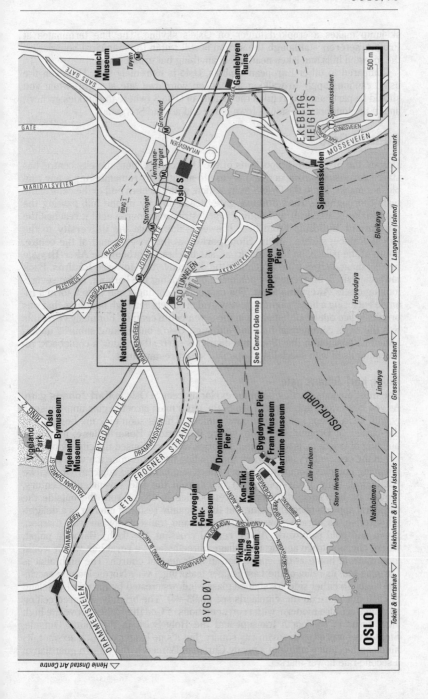

ski-jump makes a crooked finger on Oslo's skyline. The line terminates at **Frognerseteren** – although the station is still within the municipal boundaries, the forested hills and lakes nearby feel anything but urban.

Compared to other European capitals, Oslo is extremely safe. However, the usual cautions apply to walking around on your own late at night, when you should be particularly careful in the vicinity of Oslo S (where the junkies gather), and in the tougher east side of town along and around Storgata.

Central Oslo

Despite the mammoth proportions of the Oslo conurbation, the city centre has stayed surprisingly compact, and is easy to navigate by remembering a few simple landmarks. From the Oslo S train station, at the eastern end of the centre, the main thoroughfare, **Karl Johans gate**, heads directly up the hill, passing the **Domkirke** (Cathedral) and cutting a pedestrianized course until it reaches the **parliament building**. From here it sweeps down past the **university** to the **Royal Palace**, situated in the **Slottsparken** at the western end of the centre. South of the palace, on the waterfront, sits the brash harbourside **Aker Brygge** development, across from which lies the distinctive twin-towered **Rådhus**. Back towards Oslo S, on the lumpy peninsula overlooking the harbour, is the severe-looking castle, **Akershus Slott**. The castle, the Stortinget and Oslo S form a triangle enclosing a tight, slightly gloomy grid of streets and high buildings that was originally laid out by Christian IV in the seventeenth century. For many years this was the city's commercial hub and although Oslo's burgeoning suburbs undermined its position in the 1960s, the district is currently making a comeback, re-inventing itself with specialist **shops** and smart **restaurants**.

Along Karl Johans gate

The most obvious starting point for exploring central Oslo is **Karl Johans gate**. As you head west, uphill from Oslo S, the city's main street begins unpromisingly with tacky shops and hang-around junkies. Things soon pick up, however, at the corner of Dronningens gate, where the curious **Basarhallene**, a circular building of two tiers, is to be found. Its brick cloisters housed the city's food market in the last century, since when the building has undergone a revival as a tiny shopping complex complete with art shops and cafés. The adjacent **Domkirke** (Cathedral; daily 10am–4pm; free) dates from the late seventeenth century, though its heavyweight tower was remodelled in 1850. From the outside the cathedral appears plain and dour, but the elegantly restored interior is a delightful surprise, its homely, low-ceilinged nave and transepts awash with maroon, green and gold paintwork. At the central crossing, the flashy Baroque pulpit, where cherubs frolic among the foliage, directly faces a royal box which would look more at home at the opera than in a Protestant church. The high altar is Baroque too, its relief of the Last Supper featuring a very Nordic-looking sacrificial lamb. To either side are stained-glass windows created by Emanuel Vigeland in 1910 (for more on the Vigelands see pp.93–94). The brightly coloured ceiling paintings are also modern, with representations of God the Father above the high altar, Jesus in the north transept and the Holy Spirit in the south. Outside, **Stortorvet** was once the main city square, but it's no longer of much account, its nineteenth-century statue of a portly Christian IV merely the forlorn guardian of a second-rate flower market.

Returning to Karl Johans gate, it's a brief stroll up to the **Stortinget** (parliament building), an imposing chunk of neo-Romanesque architecture. Completed in 1866, its stolid, sandy-coloured brickwork exudes bourgeois certainty. The Stortinget is open to the public by guided tour only (July to mid-Aug Mon–Sat 10am, 11.30am & 1pm; mid-Sept to mid-June Sat 11am & 12.30pm; free), but the tour shows little more than can be gleaned from the outside. In front of the parliament, a narrow park-piazza runs west to the Nationaltheatret, occupying the gap between Karl Johans gate and Stortingsgata. In summer, the park teems with promenading city folk amidst jewellery hawkers, ice-cream kiosks and street performers, while in winter the park's attraction is its compact and floodlit open-air ice rinks, where skates can be rented at minimal cost.

Lurking at the western end of the park is the Neoclassical **Nationaltheatret**, built in 1899 and flanked by two turgid statues of Henrik Ibsen and Bjørnstjerne Bjørnson. Inside, the red-and-gold main hall, which seats eight hundred, has been restored to its turn-of-the-century glory. Unless you can understand Norwegian, the best way to see the interior is to take one of the occasional **guided tours** (ask for details at the box office or phone ☎22 41 16 40). It's also worth noting that Nationaltheatret is a useful transport interchange. Around the back of the building are two tunnels, the one on the right for the westbound T-bane, the one on the left for local trains and the eastbound T-bane. Many city buses and the Flybussen stop here too, and beside the building on Stortingsgata. (However, these arrangements will undoubtedly be modified when the new Nationaltheatret public transport complex, further west at the end of Drammensveien, comes onstream in the next couple of years.)

The University and its museums

Near the west end of Karl Johans gate, the nineteenth-century buildings of the **University**, all Classical columns and imperial pediments, sit well in this monument-rich end of the city centre. The **Aula** (July Mon–Fri noon–2pm; free), the main hall between the university's two symmetrical wings, has huge interior murals by Edvard Munch. The controversial result of a competition held by the university authorities in 1909, the murals weren't actually unveiled until 1916, after years of heated debate. Munch had just emerged (cured) from a winter in a Copenhagen psychiatric clinic when he started on the murals, and the major parts, *The History*, *Sun*, and *Alma Mater*, reflect a new mood in his work: confident and in tune with the natural world he loved.

Around the corner, the **Historisk Museum** (History Museum; mid-May to mid-Sept Tues–Sun 11am–3pm; mid-Sept to mid-May Tues–Sun noon–3pm; free), at Frederiks gate 2, displays the university's hotch-potch of historical and ethnographical collections. The highlight is the **Viking and early medieval** section, on the first floor: in the rooms to the left of the entrance are several magnificent twelfth- and thirteenth-century stave-church (see p.137) porches and gateposts, alive with dragons and beasts emerging from swirling, intricately carved backgrounds. There are weapons, coins, drinking horns, runic stones, religious bric-a-brac and bits of clothing here too, as well as a superb vaulted room dating from the late thirteenth century and retrieved from the stave church in Ål, near Geilo. The room's brightly coloured wood panels are done in tempera – a technique where each pigment was mixed with glue, egg white and ground chalk – and display a complicated Biblical iconography, beginning at the apex with the Creation, followed by depictions of Christ's childhood and ultimately his death and resurrection. An English-language leaflet, available in the room, gives the full lowdown, but it's the dynamic forcefulness of these naive paintings, as well as the individuality of some of the detail – the nasty-looking Judas at the Last Supper, and the pair of friendly donkeys peeping into the Christ's manger – which really impress.

The rest of the first floor is taken up by a pretty dire sequence of exhibitions on the Stone, Bronze, Iron and Viking ages. Geared towards school parties, the tiny dioramas are downright silly, and detract from the exhibits which (accompanied by long explicatory leaflets) illustrate various aspects of early Norwegian society, from religious beliefs and social structures through to military hardware, trade and craft. Nevertheless, the section entitled *The Love of Art* contains a modest but fascinating sample of early Viking decorative art, starting with the intensely flamboyant, ninth-century Oseberg and Borre styles and continuing into the Jellinge style, where greater emphasis was placed on line and composition. There's also a whole room of precious objects – finger rings, crucifixes, pendants, brooches, buckles and suchlike – illustrating the sustained virtuosity of Norse goldsmiths and silversmiths.

On the second floor, the first part of the **Etnografisk Museum** (same times) is devoted to the Arctic peoples and features an illuminating section on the Sami, who inhabit the northern reaches of Scandinavia. Incongruously, there's a coin collection here as well. The ethnographic displays continue on the upper floors with a large and diverse collection of African and Asiatic art and culture, from samurai suits to African masks and everything in between.

The Slottsparken

Standing on the hill at the west end of Karl Johans gate, **Det Kongelige Slott** (the Royal Palace) is a monument to Norwegian openness. Built between 1825 and 1848, when the monarchs of other European nations were nervously counting their friends, it still stands without railings and walls, its grounds – the **Slottsparken** – freely open to the public. You can't actually go into the palace, but there's a snappy changing of the guard daily at 1.30pm. Right in front of the palace is an equestrian statue of **Karl XIV Johan** himself. Formerly the French General Bernadotte, he abandoned Napoleon and was subsequently elected king of Sweden. When Norway passed from Denmark to Sweden after the Treaty of Kiel in 1814, he became king of Norway as well. Not content, seemingly, with the terms of his motto (inscribed on the statue), "The people's love is my reward", Karl Johan had this whopping palace built, only to die before it was completed.

The Ibsen and Sternersen museums

The grand old mansions bordering the southern perimeter of the Slottsparken once housed Oslo's social elite. Here, in a fourth floor apartment at Arbins gate 1, **Ibsen** spent the last ten years of his life, strolling down to the *Grand Café* (see p.97) every day to hold court. His old quarters are now maintained as the **Ibsenmuseet** (Tues–Sun noon–3pm; guided tours at noon, 1pm & 2pm; 30kr). Both Ibsen and his wife died here: Ibsen paralyzed in bed, but his wife, unwilling to expire in an undignified pose, dressed herself to die sitting upright in a chair. Only the study looks much like it did in Ibsen's day, but the reverential one-hour tour provides a fascinating background to his work, and helps to explain the importance of the playwright to his emergent nation. For more on Ibsen, see p.147.

East from the Ibsen Museum, it's a couple of minutes' walk to the **Stenersenmuseet**, Munkedamsveien 15 (Tues & Thurs 11am–7pm; Wed, Fri, Sat & Sun 11am–5pm; 30kr), home to an eclectic collection of modern art, the bulk of which was gifted to the city in 1936 by the author and art collector Rolf Stenersen (the same man who gave a second collection to Bergen, p.168). The first-floor entrance, across from the city's main concert hall, leads straight to the museum's pride and joy, its room of Munch paintings – Stenersen was a friend of Munch and bought many of his works. These include early paintings like *The Sick Room* and *Cabaret*, both dating from 1886, and disturbing later works, from the unnerving *Melancholy* to the forceful *Dance of Life*. Adjoining rooms hold an enjoyable sample of early- to mid-twentieth-century Scandinavian paintings, among which look out for Alex Revold's *Small Girl on a Sofa* and Per Krohg's aloof but finely observed *Two Children*, *Actress*, and *Dressmaker*. Other rooms are devoted to Munch sketches, the soft-hued Norwegian landscapes of Amaldus Nielsen (1838–1932), bright burlesques of Oslo life by Ludvig Ravensberg (1871–1958), and two portraits of Stenersen himself. There's also a lively programme of temporary exhibitions.

Nasjonalgalleriet

Returning to Karl Johans gate, head up Universitets gata to get to the **Nasjonalgalleriet**, Universitets gata 13 (National Gallery; Mon, Wed & Fri 10am–6pm, Thurs 10am–8pm, Sat 10am–4pm, Sun 11am–4pm; free), a grand nineteenth-century building housing Norway's largest and best collection of fine art. It may be short on internationally famous painters – the most notable exception being Edvard Munch, of whose work there is a fine selection – but there's compensation in the oodles of Norwegian artists on display, including work by all the leading figures up until the end of World War II. The only irritation is the way it's organized: the works of individual artists are often displayed in several different rooms and although the free plan available at reception sheds some light on matters, it's too skimpy. The text below mentions room numbers where it's helpful, but note that locations are sometimes rotated.

The **first floor** is home to a somewhat garbled and quirky series of collections. The two rooms to the right of the entrance, beyond the gallery's shop, are crammed with plaster casts of Italian Renaissance sculptures (including a massive and militaristic equestrian statue by Donatello) and of a horde of Classical gods and Roman Caesars. To the left of the entrance, one room is devoted to Danish and Norwegian nineteenth-century sculpture; another holds a workaday selection of Norwegian paintings from 1870 to 1900; and yet others are set aside for temporary exhibitions.

Moving on, the wide and gracious stairway – where you'll spot a tortured bronze relief of *Helvete* (Hell) by Gustav Vigeland – leads to the kernel of the gallery's collection on the **second floor**. Broadly speaking, this is divided between Norwegian painting on the right and European art on the left. The latter is particularly strong on **French painting**, with works by **Delacroix** and an enjoyable sample of Impressionist paintings by **Manet**, **Monet** and **Degas**; Post-Impressionism is represented by **Cézanne**, **Gauguin** and a distant, piercing Van Gogh self-portrait, and the early twentieth century by **Picasso**, **Gris** and **Braque**. There's also a set of religious paintings of the medieval Russian Novgorod school and a rather timid selection of **Old Masters**, among which Lucas **Cranach**'s *The Golden Age*, some sketches by **Goya**, and two warm and melodramatic canvases by **El Greco** stand out. Nonetheless, for a national gallery there's very little in the way of older works of significance, reflecting Norway's past poverty and its lack of an earlier royal or aristocratic collection to build upon.

To the right of the staircase, the first room of **Norwegian paintings** (Room 17) features the work of the country's most important nineteenth-century landscape painters, **Johan Christian Dahl** (1788–1857) and his pupil **Thomas Fearnley** (1802–42). The Romantic Naturalism of their finely detailed canvases expressed Norway's growing sense of nationhood after the break-up of the Dano-Norwegian union in 1814. In a clear rejection of Danish lowland civil-servant culture, Dahl and Fearnley asserted the beauty and moral virtue of Norway's wild landscapes, which had previously been seen as uncouth and barbaric. This reassessment was clearly influenced by the ideas of the Swiss-born philosopher Jean Jacques Rousseau (1712–78), who believed that the peoples of mountain regions possessed an intrinsic nobility precisely because they were remote from the corrupting influences of (lowland) civilization. Dahl, who was a professor at the Academy of Art in Dresden for many years, wrote to a friend in 1841: "Like a true Poet, a Painter must not be led by the prevailing, often corrupt Taste, but attempt to create… a landscape [that]… exposes the characteristics of this Country and its Nature – often idyllic, often historical, melancholic – what they have been and are."

Dahl's giant 1842 canvas *Stalheim* is typical of his work, a mountain landscape rendered in soft and dappled hues, dotted with tiny figures and a sleepy village. His *Hjelle in Valdres* (1851) adopts the same approach, although the artifice behind the apparent naturalism is easier to detect. Dahl had completed another painting of Hjelle the year before; returning to the subject here, he widened the valley and heightened the mountains, sprinkling them with snow. Fearnley often lived and worked abroad, but he always returned to Norwegian themes, painting no fewer than five versions of the moody *Labrofossen ved Kongsberg* (The Labro Waterfall at Kongsberg); his 1837 version is displayed here.

At the far end of Room 17, turn right into Room 29 for the work of **Hans Frederik Gude** (1825–1903) and **Adolph Tidemand** (1814–76), not so much for the quality of the painting as for their content. Tidemand's absurdly romantic, folkloric scenes reflect the bourgeois nationalism that swept Norway in the middle of the nineteenth century. The two men were the leading lights of a generation of Norwegian artists, though they actually lived in Düsseldorf, where they lectured at the art academy. They collaborated on the creation of *Spearing Fish by Night* and the *Bridal Voyage on the Hardanger Fjord*, with Gude painting the landscape and Tidemand the figures.

In the 1880s, Norwegian landscape painting took on a mystical and spiritual dimension. Influenced by French painters such as Théodore Rousseau, Norwegian artists abandoned the naturalism of earlier painters for more symbolic representations. **Gerhard Munthe** (1849–1929) dipped into lyrical renditions of the Norwegian countryside, and his cosy, folksy scenes were echoed in the paintings **of Erik Werenskiold** (1855–1938), who is well represented by *Peasant Burial*. There are examples of both artists' work in Room 23. During this period, **Theodor Kittelsen** (1857–1914) defined the Norwegian rendition of trolls, sprites and sirens in his illustrations for Asbjørnsen and Moe's *Norwegian Folk Tales*, published in 1883. Two modest examples of his other work – a self-portrait and a fairy-tale landscape – are in Room 18. **Harald Sohlberg** (1869–1935) clarified the rather hazy vision of many of his Norwegian contemporaries, painting a series of sharply observed Røros streetscapes and expanding into more elemental themes with such stunning works as *A Northern Flower Meadow* and the chilly *Winter Night in the Rondane*. These are exhibited back on the left-hand side of the

Karl Johans gate, Oslo

Vigeland Sculpture Park, Oslo

Replica Viking ship, Oslo

MICHAEL JENNEER

Mural of *The Scream*, Oslo

TRIP/D. SAUNDERS

Stave church detail

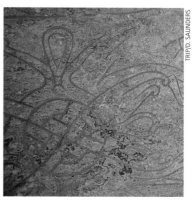

TRIP/D. SAUNDERS

Runic stone, Vang

second floor in Room 31, alongside the comparable *Approaching Storm* by **Halfdan Egedius** (1877–99).

The Nasjonalgalleriet's star turn, however, is the **Munch** collection. Representative works from the 1880s up to 1916 are gathered together in one central room (Room 24), with several lesser pieces displayed elsewhere. His early work is very much in the Naturalist tradition of his mentor Christian Krohg, though by 1885 Munch was already pushing back the boundaries in *The Sick Child*, a heart-wrenching evocation of his sister Sophie's death from tuberculosis. Other works with this same sense of pain include *Mother and Daughter, Moonlight* and one of several versions of *The Scream*. The swirling lines and rhythmic colours of this seminal 1893 canvas were to inspire the Expressionists. The gallery's sample of Munch's work serves as a good introduction to the artist, but those seeking a more comprehensive selection should visit the Munch Museum (p.91).

Aside from the work of Munch, who was always an exceptional figure, Norwegian art was reinvigorated in the 1910s by a new band of artists who had trained in Paris under Henri Matisse. The French painter's emancipation of colour from Naturalist constraints inspired his Norwegian students. The most outstanding of them, **Henrik Sørensen** (1882–1962), summed up his influence thirty years later: "From Matisse, I learned more in fifteen minutes than from all the other teachers I have listened to." Such lessons inspired Sørensen's surging, earthy landscapes of the lowlands of eastern Norway, which he much preferred to the monumental scenery of the west coast. **Axel Revold** (1887–1962) was trained by Matisse too, but he also assimilated Cubist influences in paintings such as *The Fishing Fleet leaves the Harbour*. **Erling Enger** (1899–1990), in contrast, maintained a gently lyrical, slightly tongue-in-cheek approach to the landscape and its seasons. Examples of the work of these and other later artists are concentrated on the **third floor**, where there is also a large collection of paintings from the rest of Scandinavia, mostly dating from the first half of the twentieth century.

Kunstindustrimuseet (Museum of Applied Art)

The **Kunstindustrimuseet** (Tues–Fri 11am–3pm, Sat & Sun noon–4pm; 25kr), St Olavs gate 1, occupies an imposing nineteenth-century building some five minutes' walk from the Nasjonalgalleriet – continue to the far end of Universitets gata, veer to the right and it's at the end of the street. Founded in 1876, it can lay claim to being one of the earliest applied art museums in Europe. Its multifaceted collection is particularly strong on **furniture**, with examples of all the major styles – both domestic and imported – that have been adopted in Norway from the medieval period to the present day.

The museum spreads out over four floors. The **first floor** accommodates temporary exhibitions (which sometimes raise the cost of admission), while one floor up, in the first room to the left of the stairs, there's an engaging hotchpotch of Viking paraphernalia. The museum's top exhibit is here too, the intricate and brightly coloured **Baldishol Tapestry**. Dating from the early thirteenth century, it is one of the finest and earliest examples of woven tapestry in Europe. Next door, the elongated Norwegian Gallery boasts an enjoyable sample of carved wooden furniture, in which the cheerily painted chests from Gudbrandsdal, with their abundance of acanthus leaves, are especially fetching. Alongside is a charming selection of **bedspreads** decorated with religious and folkloric motifs. With skills distantly inherited from Flemish weavers, the Norwegians took to pictorial bedspreads in a big way, their main modification being the elimination of perspective in the attempt to cover the joins. Of ceremonial significance, these bedspreads were brought out on all major occasions – weddings and festivals in particular – to celebrate the event. The bedspreads began as fairly crude affairs at the start of the seventeenth century, but achieved greater precision and detail in the eighteenth, after which the art went into a slow decline. The two most popular subjects were the arrival of the Magi, and the Wise and Foolish Virgins, a suitably didactic subject for any newlyweds.

On the next floor is a sequence of period interiors illustrating foreign fashions from Renaissance and Baroque through to Chippendale, Louis XVI and Art Nouveau. Another floor up are ceramics and glassware from the early nineteenth century onwards, and displays on textiles and fashions. The highlight is the collection of extravagant costumes worn by Norway's royal family at the turn of the twentieth century. Dresses is too prosaic a word for the fairy-tale affairs favoured by Queen Maud, daughter of England's Edward VII and wife of Haakon VII, not to mention Crown Princess Sonja's consecratory robe from the 1930s.

East from the Kunstindustrimuseet

Leaving the museum, walk round the dull, brown-brick pile of **St Olav Domkirke**, built for the city's Catholics in the middle of the nineteenth century, and follow Akersveien as far as the cemetery. There's a choice of routes here. If you keep straight, it's a short stroll up the slope to the **Gamle Aker Kirke** (Mon–Sat noon–2pm; free), a sturdy stone building still in use as a Lutheran parish church. It dates from around 1100, which makes it the oldest stone church in Scandinavia, although most of what you see today is the result of a heavy-handed nineteenth-century refurbishment.

Alternatively, back at the cemetery, hang a right down **Damstredet**, a steep cobbled lane lined with early nineteenth-century clapboard houses built at all kinds of odd angles. Possessing some of the few wooden buildings to have survived Oslo's developers, the street is a picturesque affair, a well-kept reminder of how the city once looked. At the bottom of Damstredet, there's another choice of routes. If you stroll south along Fredensborgveien, you'll thread your way past office blocks and spend about ten minutes regaining the city centre. But if you head east, it's a ten-minute walk across the river to **Akerselva**, the poorest part of the city. It's a drab and dreary district, a long-established working-class area where Edvard Munch lived and worked between 1885 and 1889. Munch didn't have much affection for Oslo, caustically describing the city as a "Siberian town". A blue plaque marks his first-floor flat on the corner of Nordre gate and Thorvald Meyers gate.

To the water: the Rådhus and Aker Brygge

Back in the city centre and a couple of minutes' walk south of the Nationaltheatret, the **Rådhus** (May–Aug Mon–Sat 9am–5pm, Sun noon–5pm; Sept–April Mon–Sat 9am–4pm, Sun noon–4pm) rears high above the waterfront. Oslo's controversial modern City Hall, nearly twenty years in the making, was opened in 1950 to celebrate the city's nine-hundreth anniversary. Designed by Arnstein Arneberg and Manus Poulsson, the Modernist, twin-towered building of dark brown brick was a grandiose statement of civic pride. At first, few people had a good word for what they saw as an ugly and strikingly un-Norwegian addition

MICHAEL JENNER

Downtown Lillehammer

PHIL LEE

Air-dried fish

TRIP/D. SAUNDERS

Gamle Stavanger

PHIL LEE

Viking burial mounds, Borre

CHRIS COE

Waterfall, the Fjords

to the city. But with the passing of time, the obloquy fell on more recent additions to the skyline such as Oslo S, and the Rådhus has become one of the city's more popular buildings.

Initially, the interior was equally contentious. Many leading Norwegian painters and sculptors contributed to the decorations, which were intended to celebrate all things Norwegian. The Rådhushallen (main hall) is decorated with vast, stylized – and for some, completely over-the-top – murals. On the north wall, Per Krohg's *From the Fishing Nets in the West to the Forests of the East* invokes the figures of polar explorer Fridtjof Nansen (on the left) and dramatist Bjørnstjerne Bjørnson (on the right) to symbolize, respectively, the nation's spirit of adventure and its intellectual development. On the south wall is the equally vivid *Work, Administration and Celebration,* which took Henrik Sørensen a decade to complete. The self-congratulatory nationalism of these murals is hardly attractive, although the effect is partly offset by the forceful fresco along the east wall in honour of the Norwegian Resistance of World War II.

At the back of the Rådhus is a line of six muscular bronze figures representing the trades – builders, bricklayers and so on – that worked on the building. Behind them, and beyond the tram lines, stand four massive granite female sculptures surrounding a fountain. Beyond, and shadowed by the bumpy Akershus peninsula, is the central **harbour**, always busy with ferries and boats, Bygdøy and the islands of the Oslofjord filling out the backdrop. This is one of downtown Oslo's prettiest spots, and handy for the **Norges Informasjonssenter,** located in the old, yellow Oslo V train station. A stone's throw away, the old Aker shipyard has been turned into the swish **Aker Brygge** shopping-cum-office complex, a gleaming concoction of walkways, circular staircases and glass lifts, all decked out with neon and plastic; the bars and restaurants here are some of the most popular in town.

Around Rådhusgata

Running east, Rådhusgata cuts off the spur of land on which Akershus Castle is built, and leads down to the other harbour, where most of the ferries from Denmark dock. The gridded street plan on either side is a legacy of Christian IV's seventeenth-century relocation of the city. The layout is just about all that has survived, however; the old timber buildings were almost entirely replaced by grander stone structures in the nineteenth century, when the district flourished as the commercial heart of the city. An exception is the pint-sized **Gamle Rådhus,** Oslo's old town hall, at the corner of Nedre Slotts gate and Rådhusgata. Badly damaged by fire in 1996, the building has recently been restored. In commemoration of the fact that Oslo's first theatrical performance took place here in 1667, its second floor contains the **Teatermuseet** (Theatrical Museum; Wed & Thurs 11am–3pm, Sun noon–4pm; 25kr), stuffed with relics including posters, cartoons and costumes.

If you're into offbeat museums, there's one more close by to the north. The **Postmuseet** (Post Museum; Mon–Fri 10am–5pm, Sat 10am–2pm, Sun noon–4pm; free), Kirkegata 20 at Prinsens gate, outlines the history of the Norwegian postal service and displays hundreds of stamps. It is not, perhaps, essential viewing except for the display on a certain Gunnar Turtveit. A long-distance postman, Turtveit was buried by an avalanche near Odda in 1903. Entombed for 56 hours, he survived thanks to his trusty post horn, which he used to dig a tunnel through the snow.

Museet for Samtidskunst (Contemporary Art Museum)

Arguably the city's most attractive square, **Bankplassen** lies one block south of Rådhusgata, along Kirkegata. Framed by Gothic Revival and Second Empire buildings, the square is a perfect illustration of the grand tastes of the Dano-Norwegian elite who ran the country at the start of the twentieth century. Bankplassen's proudest building, the 1907 Art Nouveau former Norges Bank headquarters at no. 4, has been superbly restored to house the enterprising **Museet for Samtidskunst** (Tues, Wed & Fri 10am–5pm, Thurs 10am–8pm, Sat 11am–4pm, Sun 11am–5pm; free). Based on collections once jumbled together in the Nasjonalgalleriet, the museum owns work by every major post-war Norwegian artist and many leading foreign figures too.

For the most part, the displays take the form of a series of temporary, thematic exhibitions spread over three floors. The works, some of which are massive, are each allowed a generous amount of space and, given that the museum also hosts prestigious international exhibitions, only a fraction of the permanent collection can be shown at any one time. Nonetheless, Norwegian names to look out for include Bjørn Carlsen, Frans Widerberg, Knut Rose and Bjørn Ransve. There are also three permanent installations, including the weird *Inner Room V*, the fifth in a series of angst-rattling rooms made from recycled industrial junk by the Norwegian Per Inge Bjørlo. Tucked away in a room of its own on the top floor, there's also the peculiar – and peculiarly engaging – *The Man Who Never Threw Anything Away*. This is the work of the Russian Ilya Kabakov, who has spent over a decade collecting hundreds of discarded items from the recesses of his house – bits of toenail, string etc, etc – and assembled them here, each precisely labelled and neatly displayed. Kabakov continues turning up to add bits and pieces to his installation, which occupies a sort of parallel reality – originally a retreat from the bureaucratic illogicalities of the Soviet system, but now a tribute to the anally retentive.

Though exhibits hang from every wall and offset every corner and stairwell, it's still difficult not to be more impressed by the building itself, its polished, echoing halls resplendent with gilt and marble, ornamental columns and banisters. Visitors get to leave their bags inside one of the bank's old safes, and you can eke out your time in the museum by stopping off in the first floor *Café Sesam* for cakes and coffee.

Astrup Fearnley Museet

Opened in 1993, the **Astrup Fearnley Museet for Moderne Kunst**, Dronningens gate 4 (Astrup Fearnley Modern Art Museum; Tues, Wed & Fri noon–4pm, Thurs noon–7pm, Sat & Sun noon–5pm; 30kr), about 200m to the east of the Samtidskunst, occupies a sharp modern building of brick and glass, with six-metre-high steel entrance doors. It's meant to impress – a suitably posh setting for the display of several private collections and for prestigious temporary exhibitions, which can take up much of the room. The permanent collection includes examples of the work of most major post-war Norwegian artists, as well as a smattering of foreign works by such celebrated artists as Francis Bacon, Damien Hirst and Anselm Kiefer.

Norway has a well-organized, high-profile body of professional artists whose long-established commitment to encouraging artistic activity throughout the country has brought them respect, not to mention state subsidies. In the 1960s, the scene was dominated by abstract and conceptual artists. At the end of the

1970s, however, there was a renewed interest in older art styles, particularly Expressionism, Surrealism and Cubism, and a new emphasis on technique and materials. To a large degree these opposing impulses fused, or at least overlapped, but by the late 1980s several definable movements had emerged. One of the more popular trends was for artists to use beautifully attractive colours to portray disquieting visions, a dissonance favoured by the likes of **Knut Rose** and **Bjørn Carlsen**. The latter's ghoulish *Searching in a Dead Zebra* has been highly influential, and is now part of the museum's collection. Other artists, the most distinguished of whom is **Tore Hansen**, have developed a naive style. Their paintings, apparently clumsily drawn without thought for composition, are frequently reminiscent of Norwegian folk art, and constitute a highly personal response drawn from the artist's emotions and subconscious experiences.

Both of these trends embody a sincerity of expression which defines the bulk of contemporary Norwegian art. Whereas the prevailing mood in international art circles encourages detached irony, Norway's artists characteristically adhere to the view that their role is to interpret, or at least express, the poignant and personal for their audience. An important exception is **Bjørn Ransve**, who creates sophisticated paintings in constantly changing styles, but always focused on the relationship between art and reality. Another exception is the small group of artists, such as **Bjørn Sigurd Tufta**, who have returned to non-figurative modernism to create works that explore the possibilities of the material, while the content plays no decisive role. An interest in materials has sparked a variety of experiments, particularly among the country's sculptors, whose installations incorporate everyday utensils, natural objects and pictorial art. These have developed their own momentum, pushing back the traditional limits of the visual arts in their use of many different media including photography, video, textiles and furniture. An opposing faction is led by the painter **Odd Nerdrum**, who spearheads the figurative rebellion against the modernists. The most prominent Norwegian sculptor today is **Bård Breivik**, who explores the dialogue between nature and human beings.

Akershus castle, fortress and museums

Though very much part of central Oslo by location, the thumb of land where the castle is sited is quite separate from the city centre in feel. The **Akershus Slott** (May to mid-Sept Mon–Sat 10am–4pm, Sun 12.30–6pm; late April & mid-Sept to Oct Sun only 12.30–4pm; 20kr; free guided tour at 11am, 1pm & 3pm, Sun at 1pm & 3pm), much the most significant memorial to medieval Oslo, was built around 1300 on a rocky knoll overlooking the harbour. The original fort was already the battered veteran of several unsuccessful sieges when Christian IV (1596–1648) took matters in hand. The king had a passion for building cities and a keen interest in Norway – during his reign he visited the country about thirty times, more than all the other kings of the Dano-Norwegian union together. So, when Oslo was badly damaged by fire in 1624, he took his opportunity and simply ordered the town to be moved round the bay from its location at the mouth of the River Alna beneath the Ekeberg heights. He had the town rebuilt in its present position, renamed it Christiania – a name which stuck until 1925 – and modernized the castle as a Renaissance residence. Around the castle he also constructed a new fortress – the **Akershus Festning** – whose thick earth-and-stone walls and protruding bastions were designed to resist artillery bombardment. Refashioned and enlarged on several later occasions, and now bisected by Kongens gate, parts of the fortress have remained in military use until the present day.

There are several entrances to the Akershus complex, but the most interesting is from the west end of Myntgata where there's a choice of two marked footpaths. One leads to the **Christiania Bymodell** (June–Aug Tues–Sun noon–5pm; 20kr), which explains the city's history from 1624 to 1840 by means of an hourly audio-visual performance and a large-scale model of Oslo as it appeared in 1838; drop by to get a better idea of the city's evolution and what the gridded town looked like when it was protected by the fortress. The second footpath leads up to a side gate in the perimeter wall, just beyond which is an uninspired museum-cum-information centre that makes a strange attempt to tie in the history of the castle with modern environmental concerns. There's another choice of signposted routes here, with one path offering heady views over the harbour as it worms its way up to the castle.

In a separate building just outside the castle entrance is the **Hjemmefrontmuseum** (Resistance Museum; mid-April to Sept Mon–Sat 10am–4pm, Sun 11am–4pm; Oct to mid-April Mon–Sat 10am–3pm, Sun 11am–4pm; 20kr); its location is particularly apt as captured Resistance fighters were tortured and sometimes executed in the castle by the Gestapo. Labelled in English and Norwegian, the museum's mostly pictorial displays detail the history of the war in Norway, from defeat and occupation through resistance to final victory. There are tales of extraordinary heroism here – the determined resistance of hundreds of the country's teachers to Nazi instructions, and the story of a certain Petter Moen, who was arrested by the Germans and imprisoned in the Akershus, where he kept a diary by picking out letters on toilet paper with a nail: the diary survived, but he didn't. Another section deals with Norway's Jews, of whom there were 1800 in 1939 – the Germans captured 760, of whom 24 survived. There's also an impressively honest account of Norwegian collaboration: fascism struck a chord with the country's petit bourgeois, and hundreds of volunteers joined the Germany army. The most notorious collaborator was Vidkun Quisling – pressing a button brings up his radio announcement declaring his assumption of power at the start of the German invasion in April 1940.

Next door, the severe stone walls and twin spires of the **Slott** perch on a rocky ridge high above the zigzag fortifications that Christian IV added in the seventeenth century. The castle is approached through a narrow tunnel-gateway, beyond which the stone-flagged courtyard is overlooked by the main gate. The interior is, however, a real disappointment, with a series of bare rooms only enlivened by the tapestries and bedspreads of the Romerike Hall. Also on view are the royal chapel and the royal mausoleum, the last resting place of Norway's current dynasty.

Back outside, a path leads away from the courtyard, running down the side of the castle with the walls pressing in on one side and views out over the harbour on the other. At the foot of the castle, the path continues over a narrow promontory and soon reaches the footbridge over Kongensgate. Cross the footbridge for the Forsvarsmuseet (see below) or keep straight for the string of ochre-coloured barrack blocks that leads back to Myntgata.

Forsvarsmuseet (Armed Forces Museum)

On the far side of the Kongensgate footbridge, among the buildings flanking the parade ground, is the **Forsvarsmuseet** (June–Aug Mon–Fri 10am–6pm, Sat & Sun 11am–4pm; Sept–May Mon–Fri 10am–3pm, Sat & Sun 11am–4pm; free). However, compared to the quiet heroics of the Resistance museum, this is frankly a poor foil, a dreary account of the nation's military history illustrated by an assortment of uniforms, rifles and guns. The only real surprise is the number of wars the Scandinavian countries have waged with each other. From here, it's a short walk to the main entrance of the Akershus at the foot of Kirkegata.

Southwest of the centre: the Bygdøy peninsula

Other than the centre, the place where you're likely to spend most time in Oslo is the **Bygdøy peninsula**, across the bay to the southwest of the city, where five separate **museums** make up an absorbing cultural and historical display. Indeed, it's well worth spending a full day or, less wearyingly, two half-days here. The most enjoyable way to reach Bygdøy is by **ferry**. These leave from the Rådhusbrygge pier 3 behind the Rådhus (daily: May–Aug every 40min 9.05am–9.05pm; late April & Sept every 40min 9.05am–6.25pm), departing and returning to a similar schedule. They have two ports of call on the peninsula – first at the Dronningen (15min from Rådhusbrygge) and then the Bygdøynes piers (20min) – note that they only go in that direction. The two most popular attractions – the Viking Ships and Folk museums – are within easy walking distance of the Dronningen pier; the other three are a stone's throw from Bygdøynes. If you decide to walk between the two groups of museums, allow about fifteen minutes: the route is well signposted but dull. The alternative to the ferry is **bus #30** (every 15min), which runs all year from Jernbanetorget and the Nationaltheatret to the Folk Museum and Viking Ships, and, when the ferry isn't running, to the other three museums as well.

Norsk Folkemuseum (Norwegian Folk Museum)

About 600m uphill from Dronningen pier, the **Norsk Folkemuseum**, at Museumsveien 10 (Jan to mid-May & mid-Sept to Dec Mon–Sat 11am–3pm, Sun 11am–4pm; late May to early June & early Sept daily 10am–5pm; mid-June to Aug daily 10am–6pm; 50kr, concessions 30kr), combines indoor collections on folk art, furniture, dress and customs with an extensive open-air display of reassembled buildings, mostly wooden barns, stables, storehouses and dwellings from the seventeenth to the nineteenth centuries. Look out also for the imaginative temporary exhibitions, for which the museum has a well-deserved reputation.

At the entrance, pick up a free map and English-language guide (10kr) and begin by going upstairs to the Norwegian parliament chamber, a cosy nineteenth-century affair that has been reassembled here, complete with inkwells and quills at the members' seats. The adjoining complex of buildings holds a rather confusing sequence of exhibitions. Some are missable, but the **folk art** section has delightful samples of quilted bedspreads and painted furniture, as well as an intriguing sub-section devoted to **love gifts**, with fancily carved love spoons and mangle boards given by the boys, and mittens and gloves by the girls. In rural Norway, it was considered improper for courting couples to be seen together during the day, but acceptable (or at least tolerated) at night – and to assist the process parents usually moved girls of marrying age into one of the farm's outhouses, where tokens could be swapped without embarrassment. The **folk dress** section is excellent too. Rural customs specified the correct dress for every sort of social gathering; here, it's the extravagant and brightly coloured bridal headdresses that grab the eye. The amount of effort that went into the creation of this folk costume was quite extraordinary, and it perhaps should be remembered that the exhibits were mostly owned by wealthier Norwegians – many others could barely avoid starvation, never mind possess fancy dress.

The open-air collection consists of more than 150 reconstructed buildings, arranged geographically to emphasize their variety and how the architecture evolved. They provide a marvellous sample of Norwegian rural architecture, somewhat marred by inadequate explanation. That said, it's worth tracking down the **stave church** (see p.137), particularly if you don't plan to travel elsewhere in Norway. Dating from the early thirteenth century but extensively restored in the 1880s, when it was moved here from Gol, near Geilo, the church is a good example of its type, with steep, shingle-covered roofs and dragon finials. You can't usually enter the building, but from the outside gallery you can make out the cramped, gloomy nave and the interior, decorated with robust woodcarvings, with a striking *Last Supper* behind the altar. Elsewhere, the cluster of buildings from **Setesdal** in southern Norway holds some especially well-preserved dwellings and storehouses from the seventeenth century, while the **Numedal** section contains one of the museum's oldest buildings, a late thirteenth-century house from Rauland whose door posts are embellished with a Romanesque vine decoration. In summer, many of the buildings are open for viewing, and costumed guides roam the site to explain the vagaries of Norwegian rural life.

Vikingskipshuset (Viking Ships Museum)

A five-minute walk south along the main road is the **Vikingskipshuset** (daily April & Oct 11am–4pm; May–Aug 9am–6pm; Sept 11am–5pm; Nov–March 11am–3pm; 30kr), a large hall specially constructed to house a trio of ninth-century Viking ships, with viewing platforms to enable you to see inside the hulls. The three oak vessels were retrieved from ritual burial mounds in southern Norway around the turn of the twentieth century, each embalmed in a subsoil of clay which accounts for their excellent state of preservation. The size of a Viking burial mound denoted the dead person's rank and wealth, while the possessions buried with the body were designed to make the afterlife as comfortable as possible. Implicit was the assumption that a chieftain in this world would be a chieftain in the next – slaves, for example, were frequently killed and buried with their master or mistress. (This belief gave Christianity, with its alternative, less fatalistic vision, an immediate appeal to those at the bottom of the Viking hierarchy.) Quite how the Vikings saw the transfer to the afterlife taking place is less certain. The evidence is contradictory: sometimes the Vikings stuck the anchor on board the burial ship in preparation for the spiritual journey, but at other times the vessels were moored to large stones before they were buried. Neither was ship burial the only type of Viking funeral – far from it. The Vikings buried their dead in mounds and on level ground, with and without grave goods, in large and small coffins, both with and without boats – and they practised cremation too.

The Vikingskipshuset's star exhibits are the Oseberg and Gokstad ships, named after the places on the west side of the Oslofjord where they were discovered in 1904 and 1880 respectively. The **Oseberg ship**'s ornately carved prow and stern rise high above the hull, where thirty oar-holes indicate the size of the crew. It is thought to be the burial ship of a Viking chieftain's wife; much of the treasure buried with it was retrieved and is on display at the back of the museum. The grave goods reveal an attention to detail and a level of domestic sophistication not usually associated with the Vikings. There are marvellous decorative items like the fierce-looking animal-head posts, exuberantly carved ceremonial sleighs, and a host of smaller, more mundane household items such as agricultural tools and a cooking pot. Here also are finds from another burial mound at Borre in Vestfold (see p.112), most notably a rare dark-blue glass beaker and a fancifully decorated bridle.

The Oseberg ship is 22m long and 5m wide, and probably represents the type of vessel the Vikings would have used to navigate fjords and coastal waters. The **Gokstad ship** is slightly longer and wider, and quite a bit sturdier. Its seaworthiness was demonstrated in 1893 when a copy was sailed across the Atlantic to the USA. Like the Oseberg mound, the Gokstad burial chamber was raided by grave robbers long ago – and to greater effect – but a handful of items were unearthed, and these are exhibited behind the third vessel, the **Tune ship**. Only fragments of this, the smallest of the three vessels, survive; these are displayed unrestored, much as they were discovered in 1867 on the eastern side of the Oslofjord.

The Kon-Tiki, Fram and Maritime museums

A few metres from the Bygdøynes pier, the **Kon-Tiki Museum** (daily April–May & Sept 10.30am–5pm; Oct–March 10.30am–4pm; June–Aug 9.30am–5.45pm; 30kr) is most unusual. On display inside is the balsawood *Kon-Tiki* raft on which, in 1947, **Thor Heyerdahl** made his now legendary journey across the Pacific from Peru to Polynesia. Heyerdahl wanted to prove the trip could be done: he was convinced that the first Polynesian settlers had sailed from pre-Inca Peru, and rejected prevailing opinions that South American balsa rafts were unseaworthy. Looking at the flimsy raft, you could be forgiven for agreeing with Heyerdahl's doubters, and for wondering how the crew didn't murder each other after a week in such a confined space. Heyerdahl's later investigations of Easter Island statues and cave graves gave further weight to his ethnological theory, which has now received a degree of acceptance. The whole saga is outlined here in the museum, and if you're especially interested, the story is also told in his book *The Kon-Tiki Expedition*. Preoccupied with transoceanic contact between prehistoric peoples, Heyerdahl went on to attempt several other voyages, sailing across the Atlantic in a papyrus boat, *Ra II*, in 1970, to prove that there could have been contact between Egypt and South America. *Ra II* is displayed here and the exploit recorded in another of Heyerdahl's books, *The Ra Expeditions*.

In front of the mammoth triangular display hall just over the road is the *Gjøa*, the one-time sealing ship in which **Roald Amundsen** made the first complete sailing of the Northwest Passage in 1906. By any measure, this was a remarkable achievement and the fulfilment of a nautical mission that had preoccupied sailors for several centuries. It took three years, with Amundsen and his crew surviving two ice-bound winters deep in the Arctic, but this epic journey was soon eclipsed when, in 1912, the Norwegian dashed to the South Pole famously just ahead of the ill-starred Captain Scott. The ship that carried Amundsen to within striking distance of the South Pole, the *Fram*, is displayed in the same hall, the **Frammuseet** (March–April & Oct daily 11am–3.45pm; May & Sept daily 10am–4.45pm; June–Aug daily 9am–6.45pm; Nov–Feb Mon–Fri 11am–2.45pm, Sat–Sun 11am–3.45pm; 25kr). Designed by Colin Archer, a Norwegian shipbuilder of Scots ancestry, and launched in 1892, the *Fram*'s design was unique, its sides made smooth to prevent ice from getting a firm grip on the hull, while inside a veritable maze of beams, braces and stanchions held it all together. Inside the ship, the living quarters were necessarily cramped, but – in true Edwardian style

– the Norwegians found space for a piano. Look out also for the assorted knick-knacks the explorers took with them, exhibited in the display cases along the walls. There are playing cards, maps, notebooks, snowshoes and surgical instruments – but this was as nothing to the equipment carted around by Scott, one of the reasons for his failure. (Scott's main mistake, however, was to rely on Siberian ponies to transport his tackle. The animals were useless in Antarctic conditions and Scott and his men ended up pulling the sledges themselves, whereas Amundsen wisely brought a team of huskies.)

The adjacent **Norsk Sjøfartsmuseum** (Norwegian Maritime Museum; Jan to mid-May & Oct–Dec Mon, Wed, Fri, Sat & Sun 10.30am–4pm, Tues & Thurs 10.30am–7pm; mid-May to Sept daily 10am–7pm; 30kr) occupies two buildings, the larger of which is a well-designed brick structure with a pedestrian collection of maritime artefacts. Among the assorted and surprisingly lightweight models, the only real highlight is a display linked by the Internet to the Oslofjord traffic control system, by means of which you can track (but not change!) local shipping movements. There's also the so-called Gibraltar boat, a perilously fragile, canvas-and-board home-made craft on which a bunch of Norwegian sailors fled Morocco for British Gibraltar after their ship had been impounded by the Vichy French authorities. The museum's second building, the **Båthallen** (boat hall) has a mildly diverting selection of wooden boats from all over Norway, mostly inshore sailing and fishing craft from the nineteenth century. Afterwards, the museum's reasonably priced terrace café is a handy vantage point for overlooking the bay.

South of the centre: islands and beaches

The compact archipelago of low-lying, lightly forested **islands** in the inner Oslofjord is the city's summer playground, and makes going to the beach a viable – if unusual – option for a European capital. Jumping on a ferry, attractive enough in the heat of the day, is also one of the more pleasant forms of entertainment during the evenings and, although most of the islets are cluttered with summer homes, the least populated are favourite party venues for the city's preened youth. **Ferries** to the islands (20kr each way, Oslo Card and all other transport passes valid) leave from the Vippetangen quay (see "City transport", p.68).

Conveniently, **Hovedøya** (ferry #92; mid-March to Sept every hour or ninety minutes 7.30am–7pm; Oct to mid-March 3 daily; 10min), the nearest island, is also the most interesting. Its rolling hills contain both farmland and deciduous woods as well as the overgrown ruins of a **Cistercian monastery** built by English monks in the twelfth century. There are also incidental remains from the days when the island was garrisoned and armed to protect Oslo's harbour. A map of the island at the jetty helps with orientation, but on an islet of this size – it's just ten minutes' walk from one end to the other – getting lost is pretty much impossible. There are plenty of footpaths to wander, you can swim at the shingle beaches on the south shore, and there's a seasonal café opposite the monastery ruins. Camping is, however, not permitted as Hovedøya is a protected area – that's why there are no summer homes.

The pick of the other islands is wooded **Langøyene** (ferry #94; June–Aug hourly 10am–6pm; last boat back 7pm; 30min), the most southerly of the archipelago and the one with the best beaches. The H-shaped island has a **campsite**, *Langøyene Camping* (June–Aug; ☎22 11 53 21), and at night the ferries are full of people with sleeping bags and bottles of drink, on their way to join swimming parties.

Northeast of the centre: the Munch Museum

Nearly everyone who visits Oslo makes time for the **Munch-museet** and, if you possibly can, it's worth setting aside a half-day for the experience. In his will, Munch donated all the works in his possession to Oslo city council – a mighty bequest of several thousand paintings, prints, drawings, engravings and photographs, which took nearly twenty years to catalogue and organize for display in this purpose-built gallery.

The **museum** is located to the east of the city centre at Tøyengata 53 (June to early Sept daily 10am–6pm; mid-Sept to May Tues–Sun 10am–4pm, Thurs & Sun until 6pm; 50kr) and is reachable by T-bane – get off at Tøyen and it's a signposted, five-minute walk.

The museum

The collection is huge, and only a small part of it can be shown at any one time – an advantage, since you don't feel overwhelmed by what's on display. Also, visiting exhibitions often limit the Munch paintings to one large gallery, which can appear cluttered, but at least you can reckon on seeing many of the more highly praised works. There's a basement display on Munch's life and times as well, a methodical trawl of which will provide oodles of background information.

In the main gallery, the landscapes and domestic scenes of Munch's **early paintings**, for instance *Tête à Tête* and *At the Coffee Table*, reveal the perceptive if deeply pessimistic realism from which Munch's later work sprang. Even more riveting are the great works of the **1890s**, which form the core of the collection and are considered Munch's finest achievements. Among many, there's *Dagny Juel*, a portrait of the Berlin socialite Ducha Przybyszewska, with whom both Munch and Strindberg were infatuated; the searing representations of *Despair* and *Anxiety*; the chilling *Red Virginia Creeper*, a house being consumed by the plant; and, of course, *The Scream* – of which the museum holds several of a total of fifty versions. Consider Munch's words as you view it:

> *I was walking along a road with two friends. The sun set. I felt a tinge of melancholy. Suddenly the sky became blood red. I stopped and leaned against a railing feeling exhausted, and I looked at the flaming clouds that hung like blood and a sword over the blue-black fjord and the city. My friends walked on. I stood there trembling with fright. And I felt a loud unending scream piercing nature.*

Munch's style was never static, however. **Later paintings** such as *Workers On Their Way Home*, produced after he had recovered from his breakdown and had withdrawn to the tranquillity of the Oslofjord, reflect his renewed interest in nature and physical work. His technique also changed: in works like the *Death of Marat II* he began to use streaks of colour to represent points of light. Later still, his paintings entirely absorb the landscape, himself and people around him. The light *Winter in Kragerø* and *Model by the Wicker Chair*, with skin tones of pink, green and blue, reveal at last a happier, if rather idealized, attitude to his surroundings, most evident in works like *Spring Ploughing*, painted in 1919.

The exhibition is punctuated by **self-portraits**, a graphic illustration of Munch's state of mind at various points in his career. There's a palpable sadness in his *Self-Portrait with Wine Bottle*, along with obvious allusions to his heavy drinking, while the telling perturbation of *In Distress* and *The Night Wanderer* indicates that he remained a tormented, troubled man even in his later years. One of

---

EDVARD MUNCH

Born in 1863, Edvard Munch had a melancholy childhood in what was then Christiana, overshadowed by the early deaths of both his mother and a sister from tuberculosis. After some early works, including several self-portraits, he went on to study in Paris – a city he returned to again and again, and where he fell fleetingly under the sway of the Impressionists. In 1892 he went to Berlin, where his style evolved and he produced some of his best and most famous work, though his first exhibition here was considered so outrageous it was closed after only a week: his paintings were, a critic opined, "an insult to art". Despite the initial criticism, Munch's work was subsequently exhibited in many of the leading galleries of the day. Generally considered the initiator of the Expressionist movement, Munch wandered Europe, creating and exhibiting prolifically. Meanwhile overwork, drink and problematic love affairs were fuelling an instability that culminated, in 1908, in a nervous breakdown. Munch spent six months in a Copenhagen clinic, after which his health was much improved – and his paintings lost the self-destructive edge characteristic of his most celebrated work. However, it wasn't until well into his career that he was fully accepted in his own country, where he was based from 1909 until his death in 1944.

---

his last works, *Self-Portrait By the Window*, shows a glum figure on the borderline between life and death, the strong red of his face and green of his clothing contrasted with the ice-white scene visible through the window.

Munch's **lithographs and woodcuts** are shown in a separate section of the gallery: a dark catalogue of swirls and fogs, technically brilliant pieces of work and often developments of his paintings rather than just simple copies. In these he pioneered a new medium of expression, experimenting with colour schemes and a huge variety of materials, which enhance the works' rawness: wood blocks show a heavy, distinct grain, while there are colours like rust and blue drawn from the Norwegian landscape. As well as the stark woodcuts on display, there are also sensuous, hand-coloured lithographs, many focusing on the theme of love (taking the form of a woman) bringing death.

East of the centre: medieval Oslo and rock carvings

Founded in the middle of the eleventh century by Harald Hardråda, medieval Oslo lay tucked beneath the Ekeberg heights at the mouth of the River Alna, some 3km round the bay to the east of today's city centre. The old town, which had a population of around 3000 by the early fourteenth century, had two palaces – one for the bishop and one for the king – reflecting the uneasy division of responsibility which dogged its history. The settlement was also plagued by fires which ripped through the wooden buildings with depressing regularity. After one such conflagration in 1624, Christian IV moved the city to its modern location, widening the streets to combat the fire danger, and what remained of old Oslo became an insignificant suburb. In successive centuries the traces of the medieval town were almost entirely obliterated, and only recently has there been any attempt to identify the original layout. There are precious few fragments to see, but they're just about worth seeking out when combined with a peek at a group of prehistoric rock carvings and some great views over the Oslofjord from nearby.

From Jernbanetorget, take tram #18 or #19 (direction Ljabru) for the ten-minute ride up to the old **Sjømannsskolen** (Merchant Marine Academy) – now a business school – housed in a large and conspicuous building perched high on a hill. The tram stops opposite the academy, whose fjord-facing terrace offers some of the most extensive views in Oslo, stretching all the way across the inner reaches of the Oslofjord to the Holmenkollen ski-jump. At the back of the academy, a narrow drive – Karlsborgveien – leads downhill into a little dell. Here, on the left-hand side, you'll spot a group of ochre **rock carvings** depicting elk, deer and matchstick people, around 6000 years old and the earliest evidence of settlement along the Oslofjord.

Walking back down from the academy along Kongsveien and then Oslo gate, it takes about ten minutes to reach the junction with Bispegata. On the corner, at Oslo gate 13, is the **Ladegård**, a comely eighteenth-century mansion built on the site of the thirteenth-century Bishop's Palace, whose foundations are underneath. On the other side of Oslo gate, at the heart of the *Gamlebyen* (old town), are the battered, but labelled, ruins of both St Hallvardskatedralen (St Halvard's Cathedral) and St Olavsklosteret (St Olav's Monastery) behind.

Northwest of the centre: Gustav Vigeland Sculpture Park, Bymuseum and the Emanuel Vigeland Museum

The green expanse of **Frognerparken** (Frogner Park) lies to the northwest of the city centre and is reachable by tram #12 from the centre – get off at Vigelandsparken, the stop after Frogner plass. The park incorporates one of Oslo's most celebrated and popular cultural targets, the open-air **Vigelandsparken** which, along with the nearby museum, commemorates a modern Norwegian sculptor of world renown, **Gustav Vigeland** (1869–1943). Between them, park and museum display a good proportion of his work, presented to the city in return for favours received by way of a studio and apartment during the years 1921–30.

Vigeland began his career as a woodcarver but later, heavily influenced by Rodin, turned to stone and bronze as media. He started work on the sculpture park (always open; free) in 1924, and was still working on it when he died in 1943. It's a literally fantastic concoction, medieval in spirit and complexity. Here he had the chance to let his imagination run riot and, when the place was unveiled, many city folk were simply overwhelmed – and no wonder. From the monumental wrought-iron gates, the central path takes you into a world of frowning, fighting and posturing bronze figures, which flank the footbridge over the river. Beyond, the **central fountain**, part of a separate commission begun in 1907, is an enormous bowl representing the burden of life, supported by straining, sinewy bronze Goliaths, while underneath, water tumbles out around figures engaged in play or talk, or simply resting or standing.

But it's the twenty-metre-high **obelisk** up on the stepped embankment, and the granite sculptures grouped around it, which really take the breath away. It's a humanistic work, a writhing mass of sculpture which depicts the cycle of life as Vigeland saw it: a vision of humanity playing, fighting, teaching, loving, eating and sleeping – and clambering on and over each other to reach the top. The granite children scattered around the steps are perfect: little pot-bellied figures who tumble over muscled adults, providing an ideal counterpoint to the real Oslo toddlers who splash around in the fountain, oblivious and undeterred.

A five-minute walk from the obelisk, near the river on the southern edge of the park, the **Vigeland-museet** (Vigeland Museum; May–Sept Tues–Sat 10am–6pm,

Sun noon–7pm; Oct–April Tues–Sat noon–4pm, Sun noon–6pm; 30kr), at the corner of Halvdan Svartes gate and Nobels gate, was the artist's studio and home during the 1920s. It's still stuffed with all sorts of items related to the sculpture park, including photographs of the workforce, discarded or unused sculptures, woodcuts, preparatory drawings, and scores of plaster casts; here and there are scraps of biographical information. Vigeland was obsessed with his creations during his last decades, and you get the feeling that given half a chance he would have had himself cast and exhibited. As it is, his ashes were placed in the museum's tower.

The Oslo Bymuseum

Frogner Park also houses the mildly diverting **Oslo Bymuseum** (City Museum; Jan–May Tues–Fri 10am–4pm, Sat & Sun 11am–4pm; June–Aug Tues–Fri 10am–6pm, Sat & Sun 11am–5pm; Sept–Dec Tues–Fri 10am–6pm, Sat & Sun 11am–4pm; 30kr), housed in the expansive, eighteenth-century Frogner Manor just a couple of hundred metres to the north of the Vigeland-museet. The buildings are actually rather more interesting than the museum: a central courtyard is bounded on one side by the half-timbered Manor House, complete with its appealing clock tower, and by antique agricultural buildings on the other three. Each of the latter has a huge cellar with thick stone walls beneath a rough wooden superstructure, in typical Norwegian country style. The best part of the museum is in the renovated old barn, which holds a sequence of thematic displays exploring the history of the city. Amongst many, there are sections on prisons, kitchens, the fire brigade and the police, but it's the paintings and photos of old Oslo and its people that catch the eye. For once, the labelling is exclusively in Norwegian, so pick up the English brochure at reception, though frankly it's not nearly as detailed as it should be. If you're thirsty, the museum café is all right, but the park's two open-air cafés are more enticing – nurse a beer at either the *Herregårdskroen* or the *Frognerparkens Café*, both between the Bymuseum and the bridge.

The Emanuel Vigeland Museum

Gustav Vigeland enthusiasts may be interested by the work of the sculptor's younger and lesser-known brother, Emanuel, a respected artist in his own right. His stained-glass windows can be seen in Oslo's Domkirke (see p.76), and the **Emanuel Vigeland Museum** (Sun only noon–4pm; 10kr), northwest of the city centre at Grimelundsveien 8 (T-bane #1 to Slemdal), has a collection of his frescoes, sculptures, paintings and drawings.

West of the centre: the Henie-Onstad Art Centre

Overlooking the Oslofjord just beyond the city boundary in Høvikodden, the **Henie-Onstad Kunstsenter** (Mon & Fri–Sun 11am–6pm; Tues–Thurs 10am–9pm, usually 60kr but varies with exhibitions; half-price with Oslo Card; ☎67 54 30 50) is one of Norway's more prestigious modern art centres. There's no false modesty here – it's all about art as an expression of wealth – and the low-slung, modernistic building is a glossy affair on a pretty, wooded headland landscaped to accommodate a smattering of sculptures by the likes of Henry Moore and Arnold Haukeland. The centre was founded by the ice-skater-cum-movie star Sonja Henie (1910–69) and her shipowner-cum-art-collector husband Niels

Onstad in the 1960s. Henie won three Olympic gold medals (1928, 1932 and 1936) and went on to appear in a string of lightweight Hollywood musicals. Her accumulated cups and medals are displayed in a room of their own, and once prompted a critic to remark: "Sonja, you'll never go broke. All you have to do is hock your trophies." In the basement are the autographed photos of many of the leading celebrities of Sonja's day – though the good wishes of a youthful-looking Richard Milhous Nixon hardly inspire empathy.

The wealthy couple accumulated an extensive collection of twentieth-century painting and sculpture. Matisse, Miró and Picasso, postwar French abstract painters, Expressionists and modern Norwegians all figure highly, but these now fight for gallery space with temporary exhibitions by contemporary artists. It is, therefore, impossible to predict what will be on display at any one time, and telephoning ahead is a good idea, especially as the centre also hosts regular concert and theatre performances. After the museum, be sure to spend a little time wandering the surrounding sculpture park – a plan is available at reception.

Getting there is straightforward. By car, the art centre is close to – and signposted from – the E18, just 12km west of Oslo on the way to Drammen. Departing Oslo S – and in most cases from the Nationaltheatret too – buses #151, #161, #162, #251, #252 and #261 all stop on the main road about five minutes' walk from the art centre; make sure to ask the driver to put you off at the Høvikodden stop, or you'll find yourself whizzing along the coast to Sandvika.

North of the centre: the Nordmarka

Crisscrossed by hiking trails and cross-country ski routes, the forested hills and lakes that comprise the **Nordmarka** occupy a tract of land that extends deep inland from downtown Oslo, but is still within the city limits for some 30km. A network of byroads provides dozens of access points to this wilderness, which is extremely popular with the outdoor-minded citizens of Oslo. Den Norske Turistforening (DNT), the Norwegian hiking organization, maintains a handful of staffed and unstaffed huts here. Their Oslo branch, in the city centre at Storgata 3 (Mon–Fri 10am–4pm, Thurs until 6pm, Sat 10am–2pm; ☎22 82 28 00) has detailed maps and will arrange a year's DNT membership for 360kr – a prerequisite if you want to use one of their huts (see p.52 for more on DNT and hiking in general).

For a day trip, one of the easiest and most obvious departure points is **Sognsvann** station, the terminus of T-bane #5, just twenty minutes from the city centre. Maps of the surrounding wilderness are posted at the station and show a network of hiking trails labelled according to season – blue for summer, red for winter and skiing. From the station, it's a signposted five-minute walk to **Sognsvannet**, an attractive loch flanked by forested hills and encircled by an easy 4km-long hiking trail. The lake is iced over until the end of May, after which the hardy can go for a dip, though Norwegian assurances about the water temperature should be treated with caution: their idea of warm may not accord with yours. With the proper equipment (see p.54), it's possible to hike west over the hills to Frognerseteren station (see below), an arduous and not especially rewarding trek of about 5km. Locals mostly shun this route in summer, but – approached from the other direction – it's really popular in winter with parents teaching their children to cross-country ski.

T-bane #1 also delves into the Nordmarka, wriggling up into the hills to the **Frognerseteren** terminus, a thirty-minute ride north of the city centre. From the station, there's a choice of signposted trails across the surrounding countryside. The most popular is the easy but squelchy two-kilometre stroll to the **Tryvannstårnet** TV Tower (daily: May & Sept 10am–5pm; June–Aug 10am–6pm; Oct–April 10am–4pm; 35kr, free with Oslo card), where a lift whisks you up to an observation platform. From here, there are panoramic views over to the Swedish border in the east, Oslo to the south and the forested hills of the Gudbrandsdal, a valley to the north. The weather needs to be clear though, as even a light mist obscures the view. Alternatively, it's just a couple of hundred metres from the T-bane station to the *Frognerseteren Restaurant* (opens 11am; ☎22 92 40 40), a delightful wooden lodge whose terrace offers splendid views out over the Nordmarka. The self-service restaurant is excellent too, if a little pricey – a sandwich and a coffee will set you back around 80kr.

Forest footpaths link Frognerseteren with Sognsvannet, or it's a twenty-minute tramp downhill to the flashy chalets and hotels of the **Holmenkollen ski resort**, whose main claim to fame is its international **ski-jump** – a gargantuan affair that dwarfs its surroundings. At its base, the **Skimuseet** (Ski Museum; daily Jan–April & Oct–Dec 10am–4pm; May & Sept 10am–5pm; June–Aug 9am–8pm; 60kr, including view of ski-jump) exhibits skiing apparel and equipment through the ages, from the latest in competition wear to the seemingly makeshift garb of early Polar explorers like Nansen and Amundsen. The museum also gives access to the mountain of metal steps which leads up the ski-jump for a peek straight down at what is, for most people, a horrifyingly steep, almost vertical, descent: it seems impossible that the tiny bowl at the bottom could pull the skier up in time – or that anyone could possibly want to jump off in the first place. The bowl is also the finishing point for the 8000-strong cross-country skiing race that forms part of the Holmenkollrennene ski festival every March. About 1km downhill from the ski jump lies Holmenkollen T-bane station (line #1), from where it's a 25-minute ride to central Oslo.

Eating and drinking

There was a time when eating out in Oslo hardly set the pulse racing, but things are very different today. At the top end of the market, the city possesses dozens of fine **restaurants**, the pick of which feature Norwegian ingredients, especially fresh North Atlantic fish, but also more exotic dishes of elk, caribou, and salted-and-dried cod – for centuries Norway's staple food. Many of these restaurants have also assimilated the tastes and styles of other cuisines – Mediterranean foods are very much in vogue – and there is a smattering of foreign restaurants too, everything from Italian to Mongolian.

Most of the city's restaurants are fairly formal affairs with prices to burn your fingers, but the city's **cafés** and **café-bars** are much more affordable. These run the gamut from homely family places, offering traditional Norwegian stand-bys, to student haunts and ultra-fashionable hang-outs. Nearly all serve inexpensive lunches, and many offer excellent, competitively priced evening meals as well, though the self-service cafés mostly close at 5 or 6pm. The difference between the city's café-bars and its **bars** is often very blurred. Downtown Oslo's vibrant bar scene is boisterous but generally good-tempered, and at its most frenetic at weekends in summer, when the city is crowded with visitors from all over Norway.

Finally, those carefully counting the kroner will find it easy to buy bread, fruit, snacks and sandwiches from stalls, supermarkets and kiosks across the city centre, while fast-food joints offering hamburgers and *pølser* (hot dogs) are legion.

Restaurants

Dining out at one of Oslo's **restaurants** can make a sizeable dent in most wallets unless you exercise some restraint. In most places, a main course will set you back between 180kr and 220kr – not too steep until you add on a couple of beers (at 50kr a throw) or a bottle of wine (at least 180kr). On a more positive note, Oslo's better restaurants have creative menus marrying Norwegian culinary traditions with those of the Mediterranean – and a lousy meal is a rarity. Restaurant decor is often a real feature too, ranging from the predictable fishing photos and nets to sharp modernist styles, all pastel walls and angular fittings.

Det Gamle Raadhus, Nedre Slotts gate 1 (☎22 42 01 07). This smart, formal restaurant, with its deep leather chairs and neo-baronial fittings, is not to everyone's taste, but there's no quibbling about the quality of the food – Norwegian cuisine at its best. It occupies the first floor of Oslo's seventeenth-century City Hall. Reckon on around 170–250kr for a main course. Reservations advised. Daily from 4pm.

Det Norske Hus, Prinsengate 18 at Kongensgate (☎22 41 12 10). First-rate restaurant serving up traditional Norwegian cuisine, with reindeer at 275kr for a main course, salted cod 175kr. Smart decor here and downstairs in the lunch bar, where meals are very reasonable – 80–100kr. Mon–Sat 11am–midnight.

Engebret Café, Bankplassen 1 (☎22 33 66 94). Smart and intimate restaurant in an attractive old building across from the Museum of Contemporary Art. Specializes in Norwegian delicacies such as reindeer and fish, with mouth-watering main courses in the region of 250kr. Reservations advised. In summer, there's outdoor seating on the pretty cobbled square in front. Mon–Fri 11am–11pm, Sat noon–11pm.

Grand Café, Karl Johans gate 31 (☎22 42 93 90). This is the *Grand Hotel's* café-restaurant where Ibsen once held court – and the murals prove the point. Now popular with pensioner package tourists, the old-fashioned formality of the place, with its chandeliers, bow-tie waiters and glistening cutlery, is its main appeal, plus the reasonably priced set lunches.

Louise, Stranden 3, Aker Brygge (☎22 83 00 60). With great panache, the interior of this large and reasonably priced restaurant has been done up in the style of a steamship, complete with funnels, decks, ships' ledgers, ropes, old nautical photos and – bless them – even a seagull mobile. It's all good fun and the food hits the mark too, the speciality being seafood.

L'Opera, Rosenkrantz gate 13 (☎22 42 67 67). Smart Italian restaurant with stylish modern interior. It divides into two sections – a restaurant where main courses average 200kr, and a "bar-vinothèque", whose three-course set meal at around 300kr is especially delicious – and popular. Imaginative pasta dishes and great desserts too. Mon–Thurs & Sun 4pm–midnight, Fri & Sat 4pm–1am.

Theatercaféen, in the *Hotel Continental*, Stortingsgata 24–26 (☎22 82 40 50). Eat in splendid Art Nouveau surroundings and watch the city's movers and shakers doing their thing. A classy, pricey menu of mixed provenance makes this restaurant a very popular spot. Mon–Sat 11am–11pm, Sun 11am–10pm.

Vegeta Vertshus, Munkedamsveien 3b, at its junction with Stortingsgata (☎22 83 42 32). Near the Nationaltheatret, this unassuming vegetarian restaurant, with its functional décor, has a self-service buffet with fine salads, mixed vegetables, pizza, potatoes and rice. Small platefuls go for around 80kr, while the all-you-can-eat 125kr buffet includes dessert, a drink and coffee; no alcohol is served. Daily 11am–11pm.

Cafés and café-bars

For sit-down food, **cafés** represent the best value in town. Traditional *kafeterias* (often self-service) offer decent portions of Norwegian food, while more

European-style **café-bars** dish up salads, pasta and the like in attractive, often modish surroundings. The most favourable buys are generally at **lunchtime**, when there's usually a dish of the day. Most places listed below are open until about 8 or 9pm, sometimes later. Monday is the most common closing day.

Amsterdam, Universitetsgata 11, entrance on Kristian Augusts gate. Decorated in the style of a traditional Dutch bar, this busy and agreeable café-bar has a moderately priced menu with an international flavour. Offerings include lasagne, satay, and ciabatta with shellfish, and prices are in the 60–80kr range. Kitchen closes around 9pm. Open Mon & Tues 11.30am–12.30am, Wed–Sat 11.30am–2.30am, Sun 1pm–midnight.

Arcimboldo, Wergelandsveien 17. Fashionable but unpretentious self-service café-bar located inside the Kunstnernes Hus, the old art gallery facing onto the Slottsparken from near the foot of Linstows gate. An imaginative menu featuring both Mediterranean-style and Norwegian dishes, with main courses in the region of 140kr. Mon–Wed 11am–midnight, Thurs 11am–1am, Fri & Sat 11am–3am, Sun noon–6pm.

Bacchus, in the Basarhallene behind the Domkirke. Cosy café-bar with period décor and a wrought-iron staircase. Attracts a wide-ranging clientele from day-tripping tourists through to students and city-centre eccentrics. Classical music during the day, all sorts at night when the seediness of the surrounding area is more apparent. Great cakes and pastries plus tasty sandwiches. Mon–Sat 11am–midnight, Sun 12.30pm–midnight.

Celsius, Rådhusgata 19 at Øvre Slottsgate. Hidden away behind a handsome eighteenth-century gateway, this laid-back café-bar occupies one of Oslo's older buildings and offers simply wonderful Mediterranean-inspired food at around 130kr a dish; snacks 40–70kr. It's also a great place for a drink, with plenty of seating, an open courtyard in the summer and log fires in the winter. Tues & Wed 11am–1am, Thurs–Sat 11.30am–2am, Sun 1–10pm.

Clodion Art Café, Bygdøy Allé 63, entrance round the corner on Thomas Heftyes gate. Well to the west of the city centre, not far from Frognerparken, this café-bar, with its second-hand, brightly-painted furniture, hosts regular art displays and has good food: soups at around 40kr, bowls of pasta for 65kr. Food served daily 10am–9pm, drinks until 1am.

Coco Chalet, Øvre Slottsgate 8. Leather booths, heavy drapes and Art Nouveau flourishes characterize this old-fashioned but fashionable café in the city centre. Inexpensive snacks from 25kr. Mon–Fri 8am–5pm, Sat 10am–5pm.

Ett Glass, Karl Johans gate 33, entrance round the corner on Rosenkrantz gate. Trendy, candle-lit café-bar with an imaginative menu focusing on Mediterranean-influenced light meals and lunches. Moderate prices. Mon, Tues & Sun noon–midnight, Wed–Sat noon–2.30am, kitchen till about 10pm.

Falsen, Kongens gate 4. Low-key, genial café favoured by university students. Good Mediterranean-style food with spaghetti at 60kr, moussaka at 65kr. Mon–Fri 11am–6pm, Sat noon–5pm.

Halvorsen's Conditori, Prinsens gate 26. Long-established, traditional café-cum-teashop across from the Stortinget. The cakes and pastries are arguably the best in town – at 25kr to 35kr a slice. Mon–Fri 7am–5pm, Sat 9.30am–4pm.

Harlekin Mat og Vinhus, Hegdehaugsveien 30B. Near the foot of Parkveien. There's something for everyone in this inexpensive rabbit-warren of a place, about twenty minutes' walk northwest from the city centre – with different floors containing a restaurant, bar and café-bar. Filling breakfasts around 60kr, Italian dishes at about 90kr, interesting fondues 170–210kr; also reasonably priced omelettes and baked potatoes. Kitchen closes about 10pm. Mon, Tues & Sun 7.30am–12.30am, Wed–Sat 7.30am–2.30am.

Kaffebrenneriet, 45 Grensen at Akersgata; also at 9 Frognerveien in Skoveien. Great coffee and great cakes in this bright, modern coffee house. Mon–Fri 7.30am–7pm, Sat 9am–5pm, Sun noon–5pm.

Kaffistova, Rosenkrantz gate 8. Part of the *Hotell Bondeheimen*, this spick-and-span self-service café serves tasty, traditional Norwegian cooking at very fair prices. There's usually a vegetarian option, too. Mon–Fri 9.30am–8pm, Sat & Sun 10.30am–5pm.

Paleet, Karl Johans gate 37–43. In the basement of this modern shopping mall is a "Food Street" comprising a dozen bargain places. What's on offer is, to all intents and purposes, fast food, but of a superior standard. Two stalls to look out for are *Italo's*, with its Italian pastas and pizzas, and *Hellas*, a Greek counter selling dishes from 75kr. You order at any of the counters before finding a seat. Mall open Mon–Fri 10am–8pm, Sat 10am–5pm.

Pascal Konditori, Tollbugata 11. Wonderful pastries and tasty coffee in this little café, located in a former bakery, delightfully decorated with ceramic tiles of cherubs and fruit. Mon–Fri 8am–5pm, Sat 10am–5pm, Sun noon–5pm.

Sjakk Matt, Haakon VII's gate 5. Informal, popular and fashionable café-bar near the Rådhus. Offers delicious light meals – broadly Mediterranean-style food at reasonable prices averaging around 60–70kr a plate. Highly recommended. Mon–Thurs 11am–1am, Fri 11am–3pm, Sat noon–3pm, Sun noon–1am.

Bars

The busiest and often flashiest **bars** are concentrated in the side streets near the Rådhus and down along the Aker Brygge, while other popular and less assertively heterosexual bars are clustered around Universitetsgata and on Rosenkrantz gate. Karl Johans gate weighs in with a string of bars too, some of which are staid, others – especially those near Oslo S – a fair bit wilder and less conventional. Many of Oslo's bars stay open until well after midnight – in some cases 3–4am – and a number serve snacks and meals as well. Drinks are expensive, so if you're after a big night out, it's a good idea to follow Norwegian custom and have a few warm-up drinks at home.

Barbeint, Drammensveien 20, close to Parkveien. If you're familiar with Scandinavian bands and films, you may recognize a few faces in this jam-packed, fashionable bar. Loud sounds – everything from rap to rock. About ten minutes' walk west of the Nationaltheatret. Daily 8pm–3.30am.

Beer Palace, Holmensgata 3, Aker Brygge. Cramped bar with old brick walls and a beamed ceiling. Over 50 different brands of beer. Daily noon–3.30am.

Burns Pub, Stortingsgata 28. Deep, dark and busy bar attracting a thirty-something clientele. Occasional live music. Mon–Sat 10am–4am, Sun from noon.

Cruise Kafé, Stranden 3, Aker Brygge. Standard-issue modern bar done out in shades of brown and cream, with photographs of actors on the walls. It's all rather contrived, but the music – rock, and some rock and roll – is excellent, and there are occasional live acts too. Mon, Tues & Sun noon–12.30am, Wed & Thurs noon–2am, Fri & Sat 1pm–2.30am.

Lipp, Olavs gate 2. Part of the *Hotel Continental*, this big and brash bar, all wide windows and wood, is popular with the well-heeled of Oslo. Tues–Sat 3pm–2.30am, Sun & Mon 3pm–1.30am.

Lorry, Parkveien 12. At the corner of Hegdehaugsveien. Popular and enjoyable pub with old-fashioned fittings. Attracts a mixed crowd. Wide choice of beers; outdoor seating in the summer. A ten-minute walk west of the Nationaltheatret. Daily 11am–2.30am.

Nichol & Son, Olav V's gate 1. Crowded, pint-sized bar whose walls are covered with pictures of Jack Nicholson. They do a good line in daytime snacks and sandwiches. In the basement is *Zipper*, an American-style bar with pool table and leather seats. Sun–Wed 10am–1.30am, Thurs–Sat 10am–3.30am.

Palace Grill, Solligata 2. A small American-style bar with Irish beers on draft. Roots, rock and jazz music, plus occasional live acts. Popular with everyone from yuppies to students. A twenty-minute walk west of the Nationaltheatret: follow Drammensveien, turn left down Cort Adelers gate and it's first on the right. Mon–Thurs & Sun 3pm–2am, Fri & Sat 3pm–3am.

Savoy, Universitetsgata 11. With its stained-glass windows and wood-panelled walls, this small, intimate bar is an agreeably low-key spot to nurse a beer. Part of the *Savoy Hotel* on the corner of Kristian Augusts gate. Daily 5pm–2am.

The Scotsman, Karl Johans gate 17 at Nedre Slotts gate. Many visitors to Oslo seek this bar out – though no one is quite sure why. It's an eccentric kind of place: the *Angus Steakhouse* restaurant in the basement serves Scottish pizzas and the regular live music can be unbelievably bad and/or bizarre, but the place is still packed every night. Outdoor seating on the main drag in summer. Mon–Thurs & Sun noon–3.30am, Fri & Sat 11am–3.30am.

Stravinsky, Rosenkrantz gate 17. Extremely popular bar a couple of minutes' walk east of the Rådhus, and one of several on the lower part of Rosenkrantz gate. Early twenties clientele. Sun–Thurs 8pm–1.30am, Fri & Sat 8pm–2.30am.

Studenten, Karl Johans gate 45 at Universitetsgata. A huge copper vat gets centre stage in this bar that brews its own beer. There are views across to the Nationaltheatret from the window seats, and a youthful crowd. Mon, Tues & Sun 11am–1.30am, Wed & Thurs until 2.30am, Fri & Sat until 3.30am.

Entertainment and nightlife

Oslo is good for conveniently located downtown **nightclubs**, which is hardly surprising considering the number of Norwegians who flock to Ibiza every year. Tracking down live music is also straightforward. Though the domestic **rock** scene is far from inspiring, **jazz** fans are well served, with several first-rate venues dotted round the city centre, while **classical music** enthusiasts benefit from an ambitious concert programme. Most **theatre** productions are in Norwegian, but English-language theatre companies visit often, and at the **cinema** films are shown in the original language with Norwegian subtitles.

For **entertainment listings** it's always worth checking out the Norwegian-language weekly listings leaflet *Plakaten*, available free from downtown cafés, bars, shops and tourist offices. More detailed information and reviews are provided by *Natt & Dag*, a free Norwegian-language monthly broadsheet, which is widely distributed downtown. The main alternative is *What's On in Oslo*, a monthly English-language freebie produced by the tourist office. Summer is the best time to be in Oslo for events of almost every description, but winter sees a fair range of happenings too.

For **tickets**, try Ticket Master (☎81 53 31 33), for whom larger Norwegian post offices act as agents, as does the Spektrum performance hall, downtown at Sonja Henies plass 2 (☎22 05 29 29); otherwise, contact the venue direct.

Nightclubs

Oslo's liveliest and trendiest **nightclubs** are bang in the middle of town on and around Karl Johans gate. Entry will set you back in the region of 100kr – though, surprisingly, drink prices are the same as anywhere else. Nothing gets going much before 11pm; closing times are generally around 3am.

Barock, Universitetsgata 26. Brimming with well-heeled thirty-somethings, this smart bar-restaurant is attached to one of Oslo's more popular disco dance floors, kitted out in a sort of modern Baroque, with chandeliers, tall mirrors and frescoes. Just off Karl Johans gate. Opens at 9pm Wed–Sun.

Castro, Kristian IV's gate 7. Busy and big, this is the city's premier gay and lesbian nightspot. 1980s disco sounds plus jungle and house. Tues–Sun 9pm–3am.

The Church, Karl Johans gate 10. Opposite the Domkirke, near Oslo S station, this large club extends over several floors. Ibiza-inspired sounds – everything from deep house to techno. Fri & Sat 10pm–3am.

Head On, Rosenkrantz gate 11. Well-established student favourite where the emphasis is on funk and rap. Mon–Sat 10pm–3am.

Jazid, Pilestredet 17. Great range of music in this brash, youthful dance club – everything from underground house and Latin through to big beat, soul and jungle. A short walk north from the National Gallery. Tues–Sat 10pm–3am.

Mars, Storgata 22 (☎23 16 32 80). Rap and guest deejays. From 8pm.

Rock venues

Big-name **rock** bands often include Oslo in their tours, leavening what would otherwise be a pretty dull scene. The most prestigious annual event is **Norwegian Wood**, a two-day open-air rock festival held in June in the outdoor amphitheatre at Frogner Park, a ten-minute ride from the city centre on tram #12. Previous years have attracted the likes of Bob Dylan, Lou Reed and Van Morrison, and the festival continues to pull in some of the best, supported by a variety of Norwegian acts. The arena holds around six thousand people, but tickets, costing around 350kr per day, sell out long in advance. Tickets are available from the festival Web site (*www.norwegianwood.no*). The following venues host regular gigs – at least once a week.

Blue Monk, St Olavs gate 23 (☎22 20 22 90). Crowded, earthy nightspot noted for its adventurous programme of live music, from blues through to Estonian funk. Below is the equally gritty *Sub Pub*, featuring punk, ska and rock. At the corner of Pilestredet, near the National Gallery. Daily midnight–3am.

Cruise Kafé, Stranden 3, Aker Brygge (☎22 83 64 30). This small modern bar showcases live rock, rock and roll and blues bands, many of whom are American. Mon, Tues & Sun noon–12.30am, Wed & Thurs noon–2am, Fri & Sat 1pm–2.30am.

John Dee Live, Torggata 16 (☎22 20 32 32). Entrance on Henrik Ibsens gate. This club and pub has similar live sounds to the *Rockerfeller* (see below), located in the same building.

Rockerfeller Music Hall, Torggata 16 (☎22 20 32 32). Entrance round the back. Torggata runs north from Stortorvet near the east end of Karl Johans gate. Able to accommodate 1500, this is one of Oslo's grandest nightspots. Hosts well-known and up-and-coming rock groups, with a good sideline in reggae and salsa. Opening times vary.

Oslo Spektrum, Sonja Henies plass 2 (☎22 05 29 00, *www.oslospektrum.no*). Major venue showcasing big international acts, as well as small-fry local bands. See press for details. Opening times vary.

Smuget, Rosenkrantz gate 22 (☎22 42 52 62). Large and popular nightclub with bars, a disco and regular live shows, mostly by home-grown jazz, rock or blues bands. Daily 8pm–3.30am.

Jazz venues

Oslo has a strong **jazz** tradition, and in the middle of August its week-long **Jazz Festival** attracts internationally renowned artists as well as showcasing local talent. Concert tickets cost up to 300kr; there are also many free outdoor performances across the city and its inner suburbs. In October the comparable **Ultima Contemporary Music Festival** gathers together more Scandinavian and international talent: ticket and programme information from tourist offices. At other times of the year, try one of the following for regular jazz acts.

Herr Nilsen, C. J. Hambros plass 5 (☎22 33 54 05). Small and intimate bar whose brick walls are decorated with jazz memorabilia. Live jazz – often traditional and bebop – most nights. Air-conditioned. Daily 1pm–2.30am.

Original Nilsen, Rosenkrantz gate 11. Popular bar featuring regular live jazz. Daily noon–3.30am.

Stortorvets Gjestgiveri, Grensen 1, junction with Grubbegata (☎23 35 63 70). Near the Domkirke, this old rabbit-warren of a place incorporates a jazz café, where there's traditional and modern jazz every Thursday and Friday night, plus Saturday at lunchtime or in the early evening. Daily 3pm–3am.

Classical music and opera

Oslo's major orchestra, the **Oslo Filharmonien** (online bookings *pluto.no/OFO*) gives regular concerts in the city's Konserthus, Munkedamsveien 14 (Concert Hall; box office Mon–Fri 10am–5pm, Sat 11am–2pm; ☎23 11 31 11), under its celebrated principal conductor Mariss Jansons. As you would expect, programmes often include works by Norwegian and other Scandinavian composers. Tickets cost around 350–450kr. In August and September the orchestra traditionally gives a couple of free evening concerts in the Vigeland sculpture park. Watch out also for good classical programmes at a variety of other venues including Oslo Domkirke, Akershus Slott, the Munch Museum and the University Aula.

Den Norske Opera, the country's prolific opera company, offers the popular repertoire – Mozart, R. Strauss and the Italians – but also undertakes a number of contemporary works each year. Ticket prices range between 180kr and 490kr and performances are usually held at the Folketeaterpassasjen, Storgata 23 (information ☎22 42 94 75, booking office ☎81 54 44 88, *pluto.no/norskopera*).

Cinema

The facility with which the Norwegians tackle other languages is best demonstrated at the **cinema**, where films are shown in their original language with Norwegian subtitles. Given that American (and British) films are the most popular, this has obvious advantages for visiting English speakers. Oslo has its share of mainstream multi-screens, as well as a good art house cinema. Prices are surprisingly reasonable: tickets average around 60kr and there are reductions of around twenty percent for some matinee and early evening showings. From May to July, Oslo Card holders get a similar discount on any film at any cinema.

Cinema listings – including details of late-night screenings – appear daily in the local press and the tourist office has programme times too. Following is a selection of central screens.

Eldorado, Torggata 9 (☎82 03 00 00). Mainstream.

Felix, Aker Brygge (☎82 03 00 00). Mainstream.

Filmens Hus, Dronningens gate 16 (☎22 47 45 00). Art house.

Klingenberg, Olav V's gate 4, close to the Rådhus (☎82 03 00 00). Mainstream.

Saga, Stortingsgata 28, at Olav V's gate (☎82 03 00 00). Mainstream.

Theatre

Nearly all **theatre** productions are in Norwegian, making them of limited interest to tourists. There's a full list of theatres, mainstream and fringe, in the tourist office's *Oslo Guide*. The **Nationaltheatret**, Stortingsgata 15 (☎22 41 27 10), stages an annual **Ibsen Festival** and this sometimes includes performances by visiting English-language theatre companies, who may also appear at the more adventurous **Det Norske Teatret**, Kristian IV's gate 8 (☎22 42 43 44, *www.detnorsketeatret.no*).

Sports

Surrounded by forest and fjord, Oslo is very much an outdoor city, offering a wide range of sports and active pastimes. In summer, locals take to the hills to walk the network of trails that lattice the forests and lakes of the Nordmarka (see p.95), where many also fish. Others use the city's open-air swimming pool and tennis courts, or head out to the offshore islets of the Oslofjord (see p.107) to sunbathe and swim. In winter, the cross-country ski routes of the Nordmarka are especially popular, as is downhill skiing at Holmenkollen. Indeed skiing is such an integral part of winter life here that the T-bane carriages all have ski racks. Sleighriding is possible too, and so is ice skating, with the handiest rinks right in the middle of town in front of the Stortinget (see p.70). An indoor option at any time of year is **ten-pin bowling** at Solli Bowlinghall, Drammensveien 40 (Mon–Fri 9am–12.30am, Sat & Sun 10.30am–12.30am; ☎22 44 45 61).

Summer sports

Oslo's main open-air **swimming pool**, Tøyenbadet (Mon & Fri 10am–7pm, Tues & Thurs 7am–7pm, Wed 7am–8am & 11am–7pm, Sat & Sun 10am–2.30pm; 40kr, children 20kr; free with the Oslo Card), is located to the northeast of the city centre, next to the Munch Museum at Helgesens gate 90. To get there, take the T-bane to Tøyen station, from where it's a five-minute walk. Tøyenbadet comprises four unheated swimming pools, a sauna, massage, solarium, diving boards, water chute and keep-fit apparatus. It also has an all-year indoor swimming pool.

Oslo has lots of private **tennis** clubs and one set of municipal courts in Frognerparken, northwest of the centre and reached on tram #12. The courts only cost 40kr per person (20kr for children) and as a result they're very popular, especially at weekends. Hiring a court is done locally at the kiosk.

With regard to **fishing**, the freshwater lakes of the Nordmarka are reasonably well-stocked with such common species as trout, char, pike and perch. The Oslomarkas Fiskeadministrasjon, Kongeveien 5 (☎22 49 07 99), near the Holmenkollen ski-jump, provides information on fishing in the Oslo area. In particular, they can advise about fishing areas and have lists of where local licences can be bought; see p.56 for general information about fishing in Norway.

Winter sports

Skiing is extremely popular throughout Norway; in Oslo, skis and equipment can be rented for 200–300kr a day from Skiservice Tomm Murstad, Tryvannsveien 2 (☎22 13 95 00), at Voksenkollen T-bane station, the penultimate stop on line #1. Both cross-country and downhill enthusiasts should call by the **Skiforeningen** (Ski Society) office, at Kongeveien 5 (☎22 92 32 00), in the ski resort of Holmenkollen, on T-bane #1. They can tell you more about Oslo's floodlit trails, cross-country routes, downhill and slalom slopes, ski schools (including one for children) and organized excursions to the nearest mountain resorts. Guided ski tours are organized by Uten Grenser (☎22 22 77 40, mobile ☎9087 16 21). For spectators, March sees the annual Holmenkollen Ski Festival, which includes the world cross-country and ski-jumping championships – tickets and information from the Skiforeningen.

Three other winter sports are worth noting. **Horsedrawn sleigh rides** in the Nordmarka can be arranged through either Vangen Skistue, PO Box 29, Klemetsrud, N-1212 Oslo (☎64 86 54 81); or Helge Torp, Sørbråten Gård, Maridalen, Oslo (☎22 23 22 21). **Ice fishing** is another Nordmarka option, but follow what the locals do as it can be dangerous (see p.56 for information on fishing licences). Finally, there's a floodlit **skating rink**, Narvisen (Nov–March), in front of the Stortinget beside Karl Johans gate. Admission is free and you can hire skates on the spot at reasonable rates, with a modest discount if you have an Oslo Card.

OSLO WITH CHILDREN

There are several particularly good places to take children, beginning with the open-air **Vigelandsparken** (see p.93). If the weather is good, the **beaches** of the Oslofjord islands (see p.107) are almost bound to appeal, or you can use the city's **swimming pools** – details are given in "Sports", p.103. A winter activity which kids always enjoy is **sleigh riding** in the Oslo forest (see "Winter sports", p.103).

Few children will want to be dragged round Oslo's main museums, except perhaps for the **Frammuseet** (see p.89), but there are several museums geared up for youngsters. The most popular is the **Norsk Teknisk Museum**, at Kjelsåsveien 143 (Technology Museum; mid-June to mid-Aug daily 10am–6pm; late Aug to mid-June Tues–Fri 10am–4pm, Sat & Sun 10am–5pm; 50kr, children 25kr). Out to the north of the city close to Lake Maridal, this is an interactive museum, equipped with working models and a galaxy of things to push and touch, as well as a café and picnic area. To get there from the city centre, take bus #37 to Kjelsås station alongside the museum, or tram #11 or #12 to their Kjelsås terminus from where it's a couple of minutes' walk. Alternatively, there's the rather more creative **Barnekunstmuseet** at Lille Frøens vei 4 (Children's Art Museum; Jan–June Tues–Thurs 9.30am–2pm, Sun 11am–4pm; July to mid-Aug Tues–Thurs 11am–4pm, Sun 11am–4pm; mid-Sept to mid-Dec Tues–Thurs 9.30am–2pm, Sun 11am–4pm; closed mid-Aug to mid-Sept; 40kr, kids and students 20kr; T-bane to Frøen). This has an international collection of children's art – drawings, paintings, sculpture and handicrafts – along with a children's workshop where painting, music and dancing are frequent activities; call ahead for details on ☎22 46 85 73.

The gallant (or foolhardy) can also head off to an **amusement park**, the Tusenfryd (early June to mid-Aug daily 10.30am–7pm, May, late Aug & Sept Sat & Sun only 10.30am–7pm), located about 20km southeast of Oslo along the E18. It has an assortment of over twenty rides, including a roller coaster and a "SpaceShot". Prices vary during the season, peaking at 195kr (160kr for youngsters) in June and early August. The ticket covers entry to the adjacent Vikinglandet (mid-June to mid-Aug daily 1–7pm), a theme park that makes attempts to recreate the Vikings' life and times. In summer, there are special buses here from Oslo M bus station.

Discounts for children are commonplace in Oslo. Almost all sights let babies and toddlers in free, and charge half of the adult tariff for youngsters between 4 and 16 years of age. It's the same on public transport, and hotels are usually very obliging too, adding camp beds of some description to their rooms with the minimum of fuss and expense.

Listings

Airlines Air France, Haakon VII's gate 9 (☎22 83 56 30); Braathens, at the airport (☎67 58 60 00) & Oslo S (☎64 81 07 30); British Airways, at the airport (☎80 03 31 42); Finnair, Jernbanetorget 4a (☎81 00 11 00); KLM, c/o Braathens; Lufthansa, Haakon VII's gate 6 (☎22 83 65 70); SAS, at Radisson SAS Scandinavia Hotel, Holbergs gate 30, and at the airport (one number: ☎81 00 33 00).

American Express Travel Service Offices at Karl Johans gate 33 (☎22 86 13 00) and Fridtjof Nansens plass 6 (☎22 98 37 35). Both Mon–Fri 9am–5pm, Sat 10am–3pm.

Banks and exchange Among many, Den Norske Bank has downtown branches at Stranden 1, Aker Brygge, and Karl Johans gate 2; Sparebanken is at Oslo S, Storgata 1 and Kirkegata

18. Outside normal banking hours (see p.23), the best bet is the exchange office at Oslo S (Mon–Fri 7am–7pm, Sat & Sun 8am–5pm), where there is also a 24hr automatic exchange machine. There are exchange facilities at the airport – machines and offices, both 24hr, in Arrivals (Mon–Fri 8am–10.30pm, Sat 8.30am–7pm & Sun 10am–10.30pm) and Departures (Mon–Fri 5.30am–8pm, Sat 5.30am–6pm & Sun 6.30am–8pm). You can also change money and travellers' cheques at larger post offices, where the rates are especially competitive. There are 24hr credit card cash machines at Oslo S and the airport too.

Bookshops Tanum, at Karl Johans gate 37, has the city's widest selection of travel books and a good stock of Norwegian hiking maps. Aker Libris, Fjordalleèn 10, in the Aker Brygge complex, offers a wide selection of travel guides, hiking maps and English-language books. Tronsmo, Kristian Augusts gate 19, has long been the city's best-stocked leftist bookshop and many of its titles are in English. Norlis Antikvariat, opposite the National Gallery at Universitetsgata 18, sells second-hand and some new English-language books, as does J.W. Cappelens Antikvariat, Universitetsgata 20, which is particularly good on Arctic explorers and their tales of derring-do. The shop of the Norwegian hiking organization, Den Norske Turistforening (DNT), Storgata 3, has a comprehensive collection of Norwegian hiking maps. The Syklistenes Landsforening, Storgata 20c (Norwegian Cyclist Association; ☎22 41 50 80), has specialist cycling books and maps.

Bus Enquiries about long-distance services to Nor-Way Bussekspress, Bussterminalen information desk (☎23 00 24 40). Mon–Fri 7am–10pm, Sat 8am–5.30pm, Sun 8am–10pm.

Car rental Avis, Munkedamsveien 27 (☎66 77 11 11), and at the airport (☎64 81 06 60); Bislet Bilutleie, Bedriftsveien 10 (☎22 16 54 00); Budget, Sonja Henie plass 4 (☎22 17 10 50), and at the airport (☎80 03 02 10); Europcar, at the airport (☎64 81 05 60); Statoil, Statoil service station, Sørkedalsveien (☎22 46 34 40). There are many others – see under *Bilutleie* in the *Yellow Pages*.

Car breakdown For pick-up services, call NAF Alarm (24-hr service; ☎22 34 16 00); Falken Redningskorps (central alarm on ☎22 95 00 00); or Viking Redningstjeneste (24-hr service; ☎80 03 29 00).

Dentist Oslo Kommunale Tannlegevakt, Tøyen Senter, Kolstadgata 18 (☎22 67 30 00). Mon–Fri 7–10pm, plus Sat & Sun 11am–2pm. Otherwise, see under *Tannleger* in the *Yellow Pages*.

Embassies and consulates Australia, use UK embassy; Canada, Wergelandveien 7 (☎22 99 53 00); Germany, Oscars gate 45 (☎22 55 20 10); Ireland, use UK embassy; Netherlands, Oscars gate 29 (☎22 60 21 93); New Zealand, use UK embassy; Poland, Olav Kyrres plass 1 (☎22 55 55 36); *Spain*, Oscars gate 35 (☎22 44 71 22); UK, Thomas Heftyes gate 8 (☎23 13 27 00); USA, Drammensveien 18 (☎22 44 85 50). For others, look under *Ambassadeur og Legasjoner* in the *Yellow Pages*.

Emergencies See p.46 for nationwide emergency numbers. Oslo Kommunale Legevakt, Storgata 40 at Hausmanns gate (☎22 11 70 70), has a 24-hour rape and sexual assault counselling service, as well as casualty and outpatient facilities. For a doctor, refer to the *Yellow Pages* under *Leger*.

Ferry companies DFDS Seaways (to Copenhagen), Vippetangen Utstikker (pier) #2, beside Akershusstranda (☎22 41 90 90); Stena Line (to Frederikshavn in Denmark), Jernbanetorget 2 (☎23 17 90 00); Color Line (to Kiel and Hirtshals, Denmark), Hjortneskaia (☎81 00 08 11). Tickets from the companies direct or travel agents.

Gay Oslo Not much of a scene as such, primarily because Oslo's gays and lesbians are mostly content to share pubs and clubs with heteros. Activities and events are organized by LLH (Landsforeningen for lesbisk og homofil frigjøring), St Olavs plass 2 (☎22 11 05 09, *www.llh.oslo.no*), and they also provide advice.

Hiking Den Norske Turistforening (DNT), Storgata 3 (☎22 82 28 00), sells hiking maps and gives general advice and information on route planning – an invaluable first call before a walking trip in Norway. Join here to use their nationwide network of mountain huts; the subscription fee of 360kr gives a year's membership. Open Mon–Fri 10am–4pm, Thurs until 6pm, Sat 10am–2pm.

Jewellery Juhl's Silver Gallery, Roald Amundsens gate 6 (☎22 42 77 99), is the city outlet for the jewellers and silversmiths of national repute, who established their workshop in remote Kautokeino forty years ago (see p.291). Many of the designs are Sami-inspired.

Laundry Majorstua Myntvaskeri, Vibes gate 15 (Mon–Fri 8am–8pm, Sat 8am–5pm); Mr Clean, Parkveien 6 at Welhavens gate (daily 7am–11pm). The *Haraldsheim* youth hostel has washing and drying facilities.

Left luggage Lockers and luggage office at Oslo S. Mon–Fri 7am–11pm, Sat 7am–3.30pm, Sun 3.30pm–11pm.

Lost property (*hittegods*) Trams, buses and T-bane ☎22 08 40 00; NSB railways ☎23 15 00 00; report losses at *Oslo Politikammer*, a fifteen-minute walk east of the centre at Grønlandsleiret 44 (☎22 66 98 65), near Grønland station on T-bane #1–5.

Markets and supermarkets Oslo's principal open-air market is on Youngstorget (Mon–Sat 7am–2pm), a brief stroll north of the Domkirke along Torggata. There's everything here from second-hand clothes to fresh fruit and veg – and there are several more handily located fresh produce stalls in the Basarhallene, beside Karl Johans gate. Supermarkets are thick on the ground in the suburbs, but rarer in the city centre. The biggest name is Rimi and they have a downtown outlet at Akersgata 45, near the corner with Grensen (Mon–Sat 8am–8pm, Sun 9am–5pm).

Newspapers Many English and American newspapers and magazines are available in downtown Oslo's convenience stores and Narvesen kiosks. There's an especially wide selection at Oslo S.

Pharmacy There is a 24hr service at Jernbanetorgets Apotek, Jernbanetorget 4b (☎22 41 24 82). All pharmacies carry a rota in the window advising of the nearest open shop.

Police In an emergency, ring ☎112.

Post offices Main office, with poste restante, is at Dronningens gate 15 at Prinsens gate (Mon–Fri 8am–6pm, Sat 10am–3pm). There are lots of other post offices dotted across Oslo (usual opening hours Mon–Fri 8am–5pm, Sat 9am–1pm). Downtown locations include Karl Johans gate 22, Universitetsgata 2; Sjøgata 1 in the Aker Brygge; and inside Oslo S (Mon–Fri 7am–6pm & Sat 9am–3pm). All post offices exchange currency and cash travellers' cheques at very reasonable rates.

Ride share For shared lifts out of the city, leave your name, address and contact number at the youth information office, Ungdoms Informasjon, Møllergata 3 (Mon–Fri 11am–5pm; ☎22 41 51 32).

Taxis There are taxi ranks dotted all over the city centre, or you can telephone Oslo Taxi on ☎22 38 80 90.

Trains Enquiries and bookings on ☎81 50 08 88.

Travel agents For discounted flights, train and bus tickets, try either Euro Terra Nova, Dronningens gate 26 (☎22 00 77 30); or KILROY travels, Nedre Slotts gate 23 (☎23 10 23 00). Tourbroker Reisebyrå, Drammensveien 4 (☎22 83 27 15), specializes in tickets for Eurolines. For the full list of Oslo travel agents, see under *Reisebyråer* in the *Yellow Pages*.

Vinmonopolet Off-licences at Klingenberggata 4; Møllergata 10–12; and at the Oslo City shopping complex, Stenersgaten 1.

Women's movement The Norsk Kvinnesaksforening, Majorstuveien 39 (☎22 60 42 27), can put you in touch with women's groups in Oslo and the rest of Norway, and provide information on events and activities.

Youth Hostel Association Norske Vandrerhjem has its main office right in the centre of town, near Oslo S at Dronningens gate 26 (☎23 13 93 00, *www.vandrerhjem.no*). They issue a free and detailed booklet on all the country's hostels.

Youth information Oslo's youth information shop, Ungdoms Informasjonen, Møllergata 3 (☎22 41 51 32, *www.unginfo.oslo.no*), operates an advisory service on everything from sexual health to careers. It's also a good place to find out about live music and events and has a notice board carrying adverts for shared rides out of the city. Open Mon–Fri 11am–5pm.

AROUND OSLO: OSLOFJORD

Around 100km from top to bottom, the narrow straits and podgy basins of the **Oslofjord** link the capital with the open sea. This waterway has long been Norway's busiest, an islet-studded channel whose sheltered waters were once crowded with steamers shuttling passengers along the Norwegian coast. The young Roald Dahl, who spent his summer holidays here from 1920 to 1932, loved the area. In his autobiographical *Boy* he wrote: "Unless you have sailed down the Oslofjord… on a tranquil summer's day, you cannot imagine the sensation of absolute peace and beauty that surrounds you". Even now, though industry has

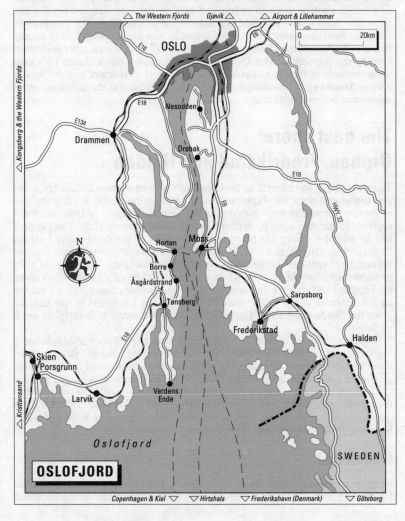

blighted the shoreline and cars have replaced the steamers, the Oslofjord makes for delightful sailing, and on a summer's day you can espy dozens of tiny craft scuttling round its nooks and crannies. The ferry ride from Oslo to **Drøbak**, a pretty village on the fjord's east shore, does provide a pleasant introduction, though it's not quite the same as having your own boat.

Both sides of the fjord are dotted with humdrum industrial towns, and frankly there's not much to tempt you out of Oslo if your time is limited – especially as several of the major city sights are half-day or day excursions in themselves. But if you have more time, there are several places on the train and bus routes out of the city that do warrant a stop. The pick of the bunch is **Fredrikstad**, down the fjord's eastern side on the train route to Sweden. The old part of town is a riverside fortress whose gridiron streets and earthen bastions, dating from the late sixteenth century, have survived in remarkably good condition. The fortress was built to defend the country from the Swedes, as was the imposing hilltop stronghold that rears up above **Halden**, an otherwise innocuous town further southeast, hard by the Swedish border. Oslofjord's western shore has a cluster of Viking burial mounds at **Borre**, just outside the ferry port of **Horten**, and the breezy town of **Tønsberg** is conveniently within striking distance of the shredded archipelago that pokes a rural finger out into the Skagerrak.

The east shore:
Drøbak, Fredrikstad and Halden

The first place of any interest on the Oslofjord's eastern shore is **DRØBAK**, a tiny port that slopes along the shoreline about 40km from the capital. It witnessed one of the few Norwegian successes during the German invasion of 1940, when the cruiser *Blucher* was sunk by artillery as it steamed towards Oslo. The gunners had no way of realizing just how important this was – the delay to the German flotilla gave the Norwegian king, Haakon VII, just enough time to escape the capital and avoid capture. Drøbak today is the sleepiest of spots. The village is at its prettiest round the old harbour, where a cluster of white clapboard houses cover the headland and straggle up towards a handsome timber church dating from the early eighteenth century. The wooden house on the knoll next to the harbour holds the *Skipperstuen* (daily 11am–11pm), a café-restaurant with excellent sandwiches.

Drøbak happens to be at the end of a good **boat trip**. From mid-May to early September, *M/S Prinsessen* departs Oslo's Aker Brygge pier for Drøbak three times weekly, a merry jaunt clipping out across the islet-studded fjord and stopping off at a couple of small islands on the way. The journey takes about an hour (around 50kr one-way), and the boat's timetable makes it possible to complete the return trip on the same day – though this isn't crucial as there's also a fast and frequent bus service between Drøbak and Oslo (#541, Mon–Sat half-hourly, Sun hourly, to Jernbanetorget and several other downtown bus stops).

Fredrikstad

Roughly every two hours, trains leave Oslo to glide down the east side of the Oslofjord, passing through **MOSS**, a grim and grotty port beside the E6, about

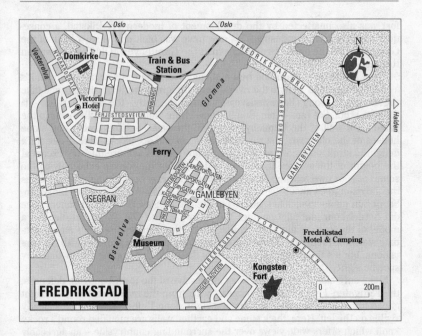

60km from the capital. There's absolutely no reason to visit but for three useful **ferry** connections: one across the Oslofjord to Horten (hourly; 30min); the others with Color Line for Denmark, either to Frederikshavn (1 daily; 11hrs) or to Hirtshals (1 daily; 7hr). Moss ferry port is a short walk from the train station.

It's a half-hour, 33-kilometre train journey south from Moss to **FREDRIK-STAD**, named after the Danish king Frederick II, who had the original fortified town built here at the mouth of the river Glomma in 1567. Norway was ruled by Danish kings from 1387 to 1814 and, with rare exceptions, the country's interests were systematically neglected in favour of Copenhagen. A major consequence was Norway's involvement in the bitter rivalry between the Swedish and Danish monarchies, which prompted a seemingly endless and particularly pointless sequence of wars lasting from the early sixteenth century until 1720. The eastern approaches to Oslo (then Christiania), along the Oslofjord, were especially vulnerable to attack from Sweden, and the area was ravaged by raiding parties on many occasions. Indeed, Frederick II's fortress only lasted three years before it was burnt to the ground, though it didn't take long for a replacement to be constructed – and for the whole process to be repeated again. Finally, in the middle of the seventeenth century, Fredrikstad's fortifications were considerably strengthened. The central gridiron of cobbled streets was encircled on three sides by zigzag bastions which allowed the defenders to fire across and into any attacking force. In turn, these bastions were protected by a moat, concentric earthen banks, and outlying redoubts. Armed with 130 cannon, Fredrikstad was, by 1685, the strongest fortress in all of Norway – and it has remained in military use to this day, which partly accounts for its excellent state of preservation. The fort was also unaffected by the development of modern Fredrikstad, a consequence of the timber industry. This new town was built on the west bank of the Glomma while the old fort – now known as the **Gamlebyen** (Old Town) – was on the east.

From Fredrikstad **train** and **bus** stations, located in the new part of town, it's a couple of minutes' walk to the river – head straight down Jernbanegata and take the first left along Ferjestedsveien. From the jetty, the **ferry** (Mon–Fri 5.30am–11pm, Sat 7am–11pm, Sun 9.30am–11pm; 5min; 6kr) shuttles over to the gated back wall of the Gamlebyen. Inside, the pastel-painted timber and stone houses of the old town, just three blocks deep and six blocks wide, make for a delightful stroll, especially as surprisingly few tourists venture this way except at the height of the season. Indeed, on a drizzly day the streets echo only to the sound of your own footsteps plus the occasional army boot hitting the cobbles as the garrison goes about its duties. A **museum** (May–Aug Mon–Fri 11am–5pm, Sat & Sun noon–5pm; 30kr), housed in the Gamle Slaveri, where prisoners once did hard labour, dutifully outlines the history of the Old Town and displays a model of the fortress in its prime. Elsewhere, the main square holds an unfortunate statue of Frederick II, who appears to have a serious problem with his pantaloons, but it's the general appearance of the place that appeals rather than any specific sight.

Make sure also to take in the most impressive of the town's outlying defences, the **Kongsten Fort**, about ten minutes' walk from the main fortress: go straight ahead from the main gate, take the first right along Heibergsgate and it's clearly visible on the left. Here, thick stone and earthen walls are moulded round a rocky knoll which offers wide views over the surrounding countryside – an agreeably quiet vantage point from where you can take in the lie of the land. When you've finished with the fortifications, drop by the *Cewex Konditori* in the Old Town on Voldportgaten for a **snack**.

Back on the western side of the Glomma, a short walk along Ferjestedsveien away from the river brings you to a small park and the adjacent **Domkirke** (late June to mid-Aug Tues–Sat noon–3pm), a brown, brick building with stained glass by Emanuel Vigeland (see p.94). Beyond the church is the centre of modern Fredrikstad, an uninteresting place on a bend in the river.

Although it's preferable to visit Fredrikstad as a day trip, there are a handful of **hotels**, including the *Victoria*, Turngaten 3 (☎69 31 11 65, fax 69 31 87 55; ⑤), a comfortable *Best Western* chain establishment in an Art Nouveau building overlooking the park next to the Domkirke. Alternatively, the bargain basement *Fredrikstad Motel & Camping*, Torsnesveien 16 (☎69 32 05 32, fax 69 32 36 66; ①), is located about 300m straight ahead outside the main gate of the Old Town; it provides tent space as well as inexpensive rooms.

Halden

Just 2km from the Swedish border and 35km from Fredrikstad, the workaday wood-processing town of **HALDEN** is bisected by the River Tista and hemmed in by steep forested hills, the closest of which is crowned by the commanding **Fredriksten fortress**. Work began on the stronghold in 1661 at the instigation of Frederick III, during a lull in the fighting between Sweden and Denmark. The stakes were high: the Swedes were determined to annihilate the Dano-

Norwegian monarchy and had only just failed in their attempt to capture Oslo and Copenhagen. Consequently, Frederick was keen to build a fortress of immense strength to secure his northerly possessions. He called in Dutch engineers to design it and, after a decade, the result was a labyrinthine citadel whose thick perimeter walls, heavily protected gates, bastions and outlying forts were brilliantly designed for the contours of the two steep, parallel ridges on which they were built. The proof of the pudding was in the eating. The Swedes besieged Fredriksten on several occasions, but without success, though the town itself suffered badly. In 1716, the Norwegians razed it to the ground, a scorched earth policy that later prompted some nationalistic poppycock from the writer Bjørnstjerne Bjørnson: "We chose to burn our nation, ere we let it fall."

Halden **train** station abuts the south bank of the Tista, and the **bus** station is a couple of minutes' walk away to the south on Tollbugata. The fortress is on this side of the river too, its forested slopes climbed by several steep footpaths, the most enjoyable of which begins on Peder Colbjørnsens gate and leads up to the main gatehouse. Allow at least an hour for a thorough exploration of the fort, whose ingenuity and impregnability are its salient features. The citadel is still in use by the army, so although many of the buildings are labelled, only one or two are open to the public, including the **War History Museum** in the old prison in the eastern curtain wall (mid-May to late Aug daily 10am–5pm; 30kr). There are also one-hour **guided tours** (late June to mid-Aug 3 daily; 40kr), but you shouldn't require any help to absorb the obvious and powerful atmosphere. On the far side of the fortress the terrain is nowhere near as steep, and here you'll find a café-restaurant, and a monument to the Swedish king Karl XII, who was killed by a bullet in the temple as he besieged the fort in 1718. A compulsive warmonger, Karl had exhausted the loyalty of his troops, and whether the bullet came from the fortress or one of his own men has been a matter of considerable Scandinavian speculation.

Despite its fortress, Halden is too dull a place to spend the night. If you're marooned, however, head for the 35-bed **youth hostel** (late June to mid-Aug; ☎69 18 00 77, fax 69 18 40 05; ①, dorm beds 90kr), sited in a chalet-like school building on Flintveien, in the suburb of Gimle, 3km north of the train station and readily reached by any of several local buses. The pick of the handful of **hotels** is the *Park Hotel*, Marcus Tranes gate 30 (☎69 18 40 44, fax 69 18 45 53; ④, s/r ③), on the northwest edge of the town centre just off Highway 21. It's a smart, modern place with an outside swimming pool. As well as tent space, *Fredriksten Camping* (☎69 18 40 32), behind the fort, also has cabins and rents bikes.

The west shore: Drammen, Horten and Tønsberg

West of the city centre, Oslo's rangy suburbs curve round the final basin of the Oslofjord before bubbling up over the hills almost as far as **DRAMMEN**, a substantial industrial settlement some forty kilometres southwest of the capital. Built on an arm of the Oslofjord and astride the Drammenselva, a fast-flowing river, the town handles most of the vehicles imported into Norway. This is hardly a reason to visit, however, and nor do the modern office blocks and stuffy late nineteenth-century buildings of its centre conjure up much interest. From here, there's a choice of routes, with the E134 wriggling west through Kongsberg and on to the western fjords (see p.176), while the E18 presses on south down the Oslofjord. The latter bypasses **HORTEN**, a small port and naval base from where a car ferry shuttles across the Oslofjord to Moss (hourly; 30min). Appropriately enough, Horten is home to one of the region's better seafaring museums, the **Marinemuseet**, in part of the naval complex, a short drive to the north of the town centre on Karljohansvern (Mon–Fri 10am–3pm, Sat & Sun noon–4pm; Sept–May closed Sat; free). The museum bounces smartly through the history of the Norwegian navy with the assistance of scale models and a hotchpotch of maritime artefacts – ships' bells, figureheads and suchlike.

Borre's Viking burial mounds

Heading south from Horten on Highway 19, it's about 4km along the fjord to **BORRE**, a scattered hamlet that boasts the largest collection of extant **Viking burial mounds** in all of Scandinavia. There are seven large and twenty-one small mounds in total; the best preserved are clustered together in the woods by the water's edge – follow the "*borrehaugene*" sign. These grassy bumps date from the seventh to the tenth century, when Borre was a royal burial ground and one of the wealthiest districts in southern Norway. The mounds are quite interesting and well worth a wander, but the setting is even better – in springtime wild flowers carpet the woods and the sea gently laps the shoreline, making this a perfect spot for a picnic. The area has been designated a national park, and a visitor centre giving the historical lowdown is nearing completion.

From Borre, it's just 17km south on Highway 19 to Tønsberg. On the way, you can detour east along Highway 311 to the seaside village of **ÅSGÅRDSTRAND**, where Munch's old summer home and studio have survived as a particularly dull attraction – the two timber buildings overlooking the fjord hold just a few Munch prints and bits and bobs of period furniture.

Tønsberg and around

The last town of any size on the Oslofjord's western shore, **TØNSBERG**, some 100km from Oslo, was allegedly founded by Harald Hårfagre in the ninth century, and rose to prominence in the Middle Ages as a major ecclesiastical and trading centre. The sheltered sound made a safe harbour, the plain was ideal for settlement, and once built, the town's palace and fortress assured it the patronage of successive monarchs. All of which sounds exciting, and you might expect Tønsberg to be one of the country's more important historical attractions. Sadly though, there's little of the period left, the best of a poor hand being the renovated, nineteenth-century warehouses of the **Tønsberg Brygge**, a pedestrianized area whose narrow lanes cluster in the middle of town by the waterfront.

As for the castle, the **Slottsfjellet**, only the foundations have survived, fragmentary ruins perched on a wooded hill immediately to the north of the centre, though it takes little imagination to appreciate the castle's strategic and defensive position. The Swedes burned it down in 1503 and the place was never rebuilt – today's watchtower, the inelegant **Slottsfjelltårnet** (mid-May to late June Mon–Fri 10am–3pm, Sat & Sun noon–5pm; late June to mid-Aug daily 11am–6pm; late Aug to mid-Sept Sat & Sun noon–5pm; late Sept Sun noon–3pm; 10kr), was plonked on top in the nineteenth century.

Its medieval importance aside, Tønsberg was known for whaling, an industry common to the whole coast, and the **Vestfold Fylkesmuseum** (Vestfold County Museum; mid-May to mid-Sept Mon–Sat 10am–5pm, Sun noon–5pm; 20kr), on Farmannsveien – turn right out of the train station – has a rather sad array of whale skeletons on show. Rather more cheery are displays devoted to the town's history and the evolution of Vestfold shipping, while outside, on the slopes of the Slottsfjellet, the grazing livestock is actually part of the "Farming" section.

Practicalities

From Tønsberg **train station**, it's a five- to ten-minute walk south to the town centre, where the waterfront Tønsberg Brygge, at the foot of Rådhusgaten, holds the **tourist office** (July daily 10am–8pm; Aug–June Mon–Fri 8.30am–4pm; ☎33 31 02 20). Among several central **hotels**, the waterfront *Rica Klubben*, Nedre Lang gate 49 (☎33 35 97 00, fax 33 35 97 97; ⑤, s/r ③), though something of a brick-and-concrete monstrosity, offers comfortable rooms and fine views out over the harbour. The **youth hostel**, Dronning Blancasgate 22 (☎33 31 28 48; ①, dorm beds 160kr; closed Christmas week), is located on a side street beneath the Slottsfjellet – turn right out of the train station and follow the signs for the five-minute walk. The rooms here are frugal but neat and cared for, and you get a first-rate Norwegian breakfast. The nearest **campsite**, *Furustrand Camping* (☎33 32 44 03, fax 33 32 74 03), overlooks the Oslofjord 5.5km east of town. For **food**, there are several café-bars and restaurants in the Tønsberg Brygge: try the popular, harbourside *Esmeralda*, where the seafood is tasty, or the nearby *Brygga Restaurant*, which has a pleasant outside terrace.

Around Tønsberg

The low-lying islands and skerries that nudge out into the Skagerrak to the south of Tønsberg are a popular holiday destination. By and large, people come here for the peace and quiet, with a bit of fishing and swimming thrown in, and the whole coast is dotted with summer homes. To the outsider, this is not especially stimulating, but there is one wonderfully scenic spot, **Verdens Ende** – "World's End" – about thirty minutes' drive from Tønsberg, right at the southernmost tip of the southernmost island, Tjøme. In this blustery spot, rickety fishing jetties straggle across a cove whose blue-black waters are surrounded by bare, sea-smoothened rocks and islets. It would be nice to think a wandering Viking gave the place its name, but in fact this was a romantic gesture by visiting Victorians. To wet your whistle, pop along to the seashore restaurant.

Verdens Ende apart, the most enjoyable way to see the archipelago is by **boat**, and the Tønsberg tourist office has information about archipelago cruises. These include the *D/S Kysten I*, a 1909 tramp steamer that chugs round these waters in July (1 daily; 4hr; 110kr), departing from Honnørbryggen, the jetty just to the north of the tourist office.

travel details

Trains

Oslo to: Bergen (4–5 daily; 6hr 30min); Dombås (3–4 daily; 4hr 20min); Drammen (4–5 daily; 40min); Fredrikstad (8 daily; 1hr 15min); Geilo (4–5 daily; 3hr 20min); Halden (8 daily; 1hr 45min); Hamar (7 daily; 1hr 40min); Hjerkinn (3 daily; 4hr 45min); Kongsberg (4–5 daily; 1hr 20min); Kristiansand (4–5 daily; 5hr); Larvik (2–7 daily; 2hr 15min); Lillehammer (7 daily; 2hr 30min); Moss (8 daily; 50min); Myrdal (4–5 daily; 4hr 30min); Otta (4–5 daily; 4hr 10min); Røros (2–3 daily; 6hr); Stavanger (3 daily; 9hr); Trondheim (3–4 daily; 8hr 15min); Tønsberg (2–7 daily; 1hr 40min); Voss (4–5 daily; 5hr 40min); Åndalsnes (2–3 daily; 6hr 30min).

Buses

Oslo to: Alta via Sweden (3 weekly; 27hr; reservations obligatory); Arendal (1 daily; 4hr 15min); Balestrand (3 daily; 8hr 15min); Bergen (1 daily; 11hr 40min); Drøbak (hourly; 40min); Fagernes (3 daily; 3hr 20min); Fjaerland (3 daily; 7hr 50min); Grimstad (1 daily; 4hr 40min); Hamar (1 daily; 2hr); Hammerfest via Sweden (3 weekly; 30hr; reservations obligatory); Haugesund (1 daily; 10hr); Kongsberg (1 daily; 2hr); Kristiansand (1 daily; 5hr 40min); Lillehammer (1 daily; 3hr); Lillesand (1 daily; 5hr); Odda (1 daily; 8hr); Otta (2 daily; 5hr); Sogndal (3 daily; 7hr); Stavanger (1 daily; 10hr); Stryn (1 daily; 8hr); Voss (1 daily; 10hr 30min).

Ferries

Oslo to: Dronningen/Bygdøynes (May–Aug every 40min 9.05am–9.05pm; late April & Sept every 40min 9.05am–6.25pm; 10min/15min); Hovedøya (mid-March to Sept every hour or 90min; Oct to mid-March 3 daily; 10min); Langøyene (June–Aug hourly 10am–6pm; 30min).

Horten

Horten to: Moss (every hour, daily 6am–1am; 30min).

Domestic flights

Oslo to: Bergen (hourly; 1 hr); Bodø (6 daily; 1 hr); Harstad/Narvik (5 daily; 1hr 40min); Tromsø (8 daily; 2 hr); Trondheim (10 daily; 1 hr).

Hurtigbåt services

Oslo to: Arendal (July to mid-Aug 4 weekly; 6hr 45min); Kragerø (July to mid-Aug 4 weekly; 4hr 30min); Stavern (July to mid-Aug 4 weekly; 3hr 15min).

International trains

Oslo to: Hamburg (1 daily; 14hrs) for connections on to London and Paris; Copenhagen via Gothenburg (2 daily; 8hr 20min); Stockholm (1–2 daily; 6hr).

International buses

Oslo to: Amsterdam (2–3 weekly; 22hr); Copenhagen (2–3 daily; 9hr 15min); Gothenburg (2–3 daily; 4hr 45min); London (3–5 weekly; 35hr); Stockholm (3–4 daily; 10hr). Also services to Austria, Belgium, Germany, Greece, Hungary, Italy and Russia. Further information from Nor-Way Bussekspress (☎23 00 24 40) – offices inside the Oslo M bus station, and at Karl Johans gate 2.

International ferries

Moss to: Frederikshavn (1 daily; 11 hr); Hirtshals (1–3 daily; 8hr).

Oslo to: Copenhagen (1 daily; 16hr); Frederikshavn (1–2 daily; 8hr 30min); Hirtshals (6 weekly; 8hr); Kiel (1 daily; 19hr).

CHAPTER TWO

SOUTHERN AND CENTRAL NORWAY

Preoccupied by the fjords and the long road to the Nordkapp, few tourists have any interest in exploring **southern and central Norway**. The Norwegians know better. Trapped between Sweden and the fjords, this great chunk of land boasts some of the country's finest scenery, with the forested dales that trail north and west from Oslo heralding the rearing peaks that extend down towards the coast. The country's principal **train** line and the **E6** run through here – historically this route was the main line of communication linking Oslo, Trondheim and the north – and conveniently serve three of Norway's prime **hiking areas**. These are a trio of mountain ranges, each partly lying within the **Jotunheimen**, **Rondane** and the **Dovrefjell** national parks respectively. Each park is equipped with well-maintained walking trails and DNT huts, and **Otta** and **Kongsvoll** are particularly good starting points for hiking expeditions.

Entirely different from the mountainous interior, but just as popular with the Norwegians, is the **south coast**. Countless islets, beaches and coves shred a shoreline in the shape of a giant "V" that extends west from the Oslofjord, backed by forested valleys, fells and flatlands. Along the prettiest stretch, in the east, are a handful of old timber ports – **Arendal**, **Lillesand** and **Mandal** – where bright white, antique clapboard houses string out along the harbourfronts. **Kristiansand**, easily the largest town on the coast, is different again, a brisk modern place that successfully combines its role as a resort with being a major ferry port for connections to Denmark.

Despite its rural aspects, it's not difficult to think of the whole region as a **transport corridor**. The E6 not only links the capital with the north, but is also the starting point for Highway 15 and the E136, two wonderful roads which thread through the mountains to the fjords – the first to Lom (see p.206) and Geiranger (see p.216), the second to Åndalsnes (see p.218). To the west of Oslo, the **E18** – and its continuation the E39 – ramble round the south coast to link Oslo with Kristiansand and ultimately Stavanger. Branching off this arterial highway are three more main roads to the fjords – the speedy and comparatively tedious **E16**, the more interesting **Highway 7** and, further south, the long-winded **E134**. The railway follows the route of the E6 and the E18/E39, but the finest train journeys are elsewhere – over the windswept mountain plateaux of the interior on the Oslo to Bergen route and on the sweeping branch line that shadows the E136 to Åndalsnes. That said, whichever way you're heading, it would be a great pity if you didn't allow at least a couple of days for the south coast and/or the national parks to the north of Oslo.

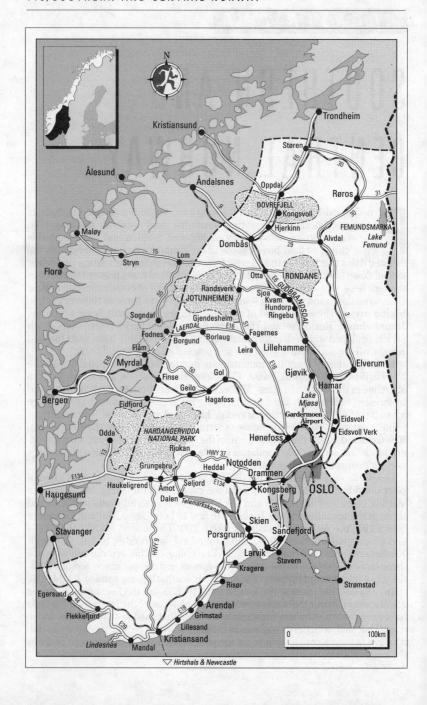

ACCOMMODATION PRICE CODES

The hotels and guesthouses detailed throughout this guide have been graded according to the price categories listed below. Prices given are for the least expensive double room during the high season, although almost every hotel offers seasonal and/or weekend discounts, which can reduce the rate by one or even two grades. Wherever hotels have an official summer rate we've given it (denoted s/r), but bear in mind that many others will provide impromptu summer and weekend discounts. Single rooms, where available, usually cost between 60 and 80 percent of a double. For a more detailed discussion of accommodation see p.37.

① under 500kr   ③ 700–900kr   ⑤ 1200–1500kr
② 500–700kr   ④ 900–1200kr   ⑥ over 1500kr

As you might expect, **bus** services along these main highways are excellent, and **trains** are fast and frequent too. Leave the arterial highways, however, and the bus system thins out, so much so that the most practical thing may be to rent a car locally. **Accommodation** is not a problem, though: roadside campgrounds are commonplace, there's a reasonable supply of youth hostels, and every town and village has at least one hotel or guesthouse.

From Oslo: North to Kongsvoll and Røros

The **E6**, linking Oslo to Trondheim and points north, remains the most important highway in Norway, and is consequently kept in excellent condition – and sometimes has the road works to prove it. Unsurprisingly, the road is used by many of the region's long-distance **buses** and for much of its length – as far as Trondheim and beyond – it's also shadowed by Norway's principal **train** line. Leaving Oslo, both the E6 and the railway connect with the spanking new international airport at Gardermoen before following the north bank of Lake Mjøsa en route to **Lillehammer**, where the 1994 Winter Olympic Games were staged, and home to one of the best of Norway's open-air folk museums. Thereafter, road and rail sweep on up the **Gudbrandsbal** river valley, within sight of a string of modest little towns and villages; the first significant attraction here is **Ringebu stave church**. The Gudbrandsbal witnessed some of the fiercest fighting of World War II when the Norwegians and their British allies tried to stem the northward German advance, a campaign remembered at the war museum in **Kvam**. Pushing on, it's just a few kilometres more to **Sjoa**, a centre for white-water rafting, and a little further north, **Otta**, an undistinguished town but within easy reach by bus of the magnificent mountains and uplands of the **Jotunheimen** and **Rondane national parks**; staying in the mountain lodges here is the best way to take it all in. Further north still is the beautiful **Dovrefjell** range and equally beautiful national park, most pleasingly approached from tiny **Kongsvoll**. All three parks are famous for their hiking, and are networked by an extensive and well-planned system of **hiking trails**. From Kongsvoll, Trondheim is within easy striking distance; alternatively, you can detour east via either Highway 29 or 30 to **Røros** (see p.132), a fascinating old iron-mining town on the mountain plateau which stretches across to Sweden.

Eidsvoll-bygningen

Some 80km from Oslo and clearly signposted off the E6, **Eidsvoll-bygningen** (mid-May to mid-June & mid-Aug to mid-Sept daily 10am–3pm; mid-June to mid-Aug daily 10am–5pm; mid-Sept to mid-May Sat & Sun 11am–2pm; 30kr) is a handsome and spacious old manor hall that gives a real insight into the tastes of Norway's early nineteenth-century upper class. This two-storey timber house has just over thirty rooms, with what would have been the owners' living areas on the first floor, beneath the servants' quarters and above the basement kitchens. The main entrance hall is in the Neoclassical style favoured by the Dano-Norwegian elite, its columns a suitably formal introduction to the spacious suites which lie beyond. The library is well stocked, there's a billiard room and smoking room, and a string of elegant dining rooms and bedrooms. Oriental knick-knacks and English furniture appear throughout, and the occasional mural depicts Greek mythological figures. The house was owned by the Ankers family, who made their money from the local iron works – hence the splendid cast-iron stoves.

It's a delightful ensemble, but the house owes its preservation to its historical significance rather than aesthetics. One of the Ankers, Carsten, was a close friend and ally of the Danish crown prince **Christian Frederik**, and this connection has given the house national importance. Towards the end of the Napoleonic Wars, the Russians and British insisted the Danes be punished for their alliance with the French, and proposed taking Norway from Denmark and handing it over to Sweden. In an attempt to forestall these territorial shenanigans, the Danes dispatched Christian Frederik to Norway, where he set up home in Carsten Ankers' house in 1813, and proceeded to lobby for Norwegian support. In April of the following year more than a hundred of the country's leading citizens gathered here at Eidsvoll manor house to decide whether to accept union with Sweden or go for independence with Christian Frederik on the throne. The majority of this National Assembly chose independence, and set about drafting a liberal constitution based on that of the United States. Predictably, the Swedes would have none of this. Four years earlier, the Swedes had picked one of Napoleon's marshals, Jean-Baptiste Bernadotte, to succeed their previous king who had died without an heir. As King Karl Johan, Bernadotte was keen to flex his military muscles and, irritated by these developments, invaded Norway in July 1814. Frederik was soon forced to abdicate and the Norwegians were pressed into union, though Karl Johan did head off much of the opposition by guaranteeing the Norwegians' new constitution and parliament, the Storting.

Carsten Ankers converted the upper storey of his home into premises for the National Assembly, comprising a handful of administrative offices plus the **Room for the Constitutional Committee**, where the original wooden benches have survived along with various landscape paintings. There's a rusticated modesty to it all which is really rather charming. A statue of Venus has been put back in the room after years of being shunted up and down the adjoining corridors: it had originally been removed, after prolonged discussion, because the representatives considered it an erotic distraction.

Eidsvoll-bygningen is a little over 4km east of the E6 on the edge of the sprawling town of **Eidsvoll Verk** – which should not be confused with Eidsvoll village itself, 8km further to the northeast along Highway 181. It's possible to get to the manor house by public transport from Oslo – take train #450 to Eidsvoll (every 1–2hr; 50min) and continue by local bus to Eidsvoll Verk – but it's a long-winded and tedious journey.

Hamar

Just beyond Eidsvoll Verk, the E6 curves round the eastern shore of Norway's largest lake, **Lake Mjøsa**. Its 360-odd square kilometres are a favourite haunt of Norwegian families who own second homes here, set amid fertile farmland, woods and pastures. Before the railway arrived in the 1880s, the lake was a major transport route, used by boats in summer and by horse and sleigh across its frozen surface in winter. It's also halfway country: the quiet settlements around the lake give a taste of small-town southern Norway, while further north the E6 plunges on into much wilder regions.

Midway along the lake's eastern shore, some 130km from Oslo, lies **HAMAR**. Though hardly an essential stop, it's an easy-going, relaxed little place of 25,000 souls, and its marinas and waterside cafés make a gallant attempt to sustain a nautical flavour. However humdrum it may seem today, Hamar was the seat of an important medieval bishopric and the scant remains of its **Domkirke** (cathedral) – not much more than a chunk of wall with four Gothic arches – are stuck out on the Domkirkeodden (cathedral point), a low, grassy headland towards the west end of town. The cathedral is thought to have been built by the "English pope" Nicholas Breakspear, who spent a couple of years in Norway as the papal legate before becoming Adrian IV in 1154. During the Reformation, the building, along with the surrounding episcopal complex, was ransacked and local road-builders subsequently helped themselves to the stone. The ruins have now been incorporated into the **Hedmarksmuseet** (mid-May to mid-June daily 10am–4pm; mid-June to mid-Aug daily 10am–6pm; mid-Aug to mid-Sept daily 10am–4pm; 30kr), which comprises an archeological museum and an open-air folk museum. The latter contains fifty buildings brought here from all over the region and, although it's not as comprehensive as the one in Lillehammer (see p.121), it does contain one or two particularly fine buildings, including the parsonage of Bolstad with its beautifully decorated log walls. The most scenic approach to the headland is along a pleasant lakeshore footpath, which extends the 2km north from the train station.

Hamar is also as good a place as any to pick up the 130-year-old **paddle steamer**, the *Skibladner*, which shuttles up and down Lake Mjøsa between late June and late August: on Tuesdays, Thursdays and Saturdays the boat makes the return trip across the lake from Hamar to Gjøvik and on up to Lillehammer, while on Mondays, Wednesdays and Fridays it chugs down to Eidsvoll and back; there's no Sunday service. Departure details are available at any local tourist office and from the *Skibladner* office, next door to the tourist office in Hamar on Parkgata (☎62 52 70 85, *www.skibladner.no*). Tickets are bought on board: return trips from Hamar to Eidsvoll cost 200kr and last two and a half hours, those to Lillehammer cost 250kr and last eight hours. One-way fares cost a little over half these rates. Travellers heading north may find the trip to Lillehammer tempting at first sight, but the lake is not particularly scenic, and the tedium of spending eight hours on the boat will make you feel like jumping overboard. The best bet is to take a short ride instead.

Practicalities

Hamar's **train station** is in the town centre beside the lake; **buses** stop outside. It's here that some trains from Oslo pause before heading up the secondary branch line to Røros (see p.132), a fine three-and-a-half-hour ride over hills and through huge forests. Some 100m from the train station – turn left out of the terminal building along Stangevegen – is the **tourist office**, at Parkgata 2 (mid-June to mid-Aug Mon–Fri 8am–8pm, Sat & Sun noon–6pm; mid-Aug to mid-June Mon–Fri 8am–3.30pm; ☎62 51 02 26), and next door is the booking office for the *Skibladner* paddle steamer (see p.119). The jetty for the *Skibladner* ferry is 500m further north.

There's a fair choice of central hotel **accommodation**. The most attractive option is the lakeshore *First Hotel Victoria*, Strandgata 21 (☎62 53 05 00, fax 62 53 32 23; ⑤), which has a bar and a reasonably good restaurant serving Norwegian favourites. Sharing premises with a motel (②), the **youth hostel**, Åkersvikavegen 10 (☎62 52 60 60, fax 62 53 24 60; ①, dorm beds 125kr), occupies smart modern buildings about 2km south along the lakeshore from the train station, just across from the massive skating arena built in the shape of an upturned Viking ship for the 1994 Winter Olympics.

Lillehammer

LILLEHAMMER (literally "Little Hammer"), 50km north of Hamar and 180km from Oslo, is Lake Mjøsa's most worthwhile destination. In **winter**, it's *the* Norwegian ski centre, a young and vibrant place whose rural lakeshore setting and extensive cross-country ski trails contributed to its selection as host to the 1994 Olympic Winter Games. In preparation for the games, the Norwegian government spent a massive two billion kroner on the town's **sporting facilities**, which are now the best in the country, including a ski-jumping tower, an ice hockey arena, a bobsleigh track and a cross-country skiing stadium which gives access to about 30km of trails. Several local companies, including Saga Arrangement, Gudbrandsdalsvegen 203 (☎61 26 92 44, fax 61 26 24 22), offer all-inclusive winter sports and activity holiday packages, though if this is what you have in mind, you may as well book your holiday with an agent back home. As you would expect, most Norwegians arriving here in winter come fully equipped, but it's possible to rent or buy equipment here – the tourist office (see p.122) will advise.

Lillehammer remains a popular holiday spot in **summer** too. Hundreds of Norwegians hunker down in their second homes in the hills, popping into the town centre for drinks or meals. Cycling, walking, fishing and canoeing are popular pastimes at this time of year, with all sorts of possibilities for guided tours. But however appealing the area may be to Norwegians, the countryside round here has little of the wonderful wildness of other parts of Norway and frankly, unless you're part of a group, you'll probably feel rather out on a limb. That said, Lillehammer is not a bad place to break your journey, and there are a couple of attractions to keep you busy.

Lillehammer's briskly efficient centre, just 600m across, is tucked into the hillside above the lake, the E6 and the railway. It has just one really notable attraction, the **Kunstmuseum** at Stortorget 2 (municipal art museum; mid-June to mid-Aug daily 10am–5pm; mid-Aug to mid-June Tues–Sun 11am–4pm; 40kr; free English guided tours at 2pm: daily in July, rest of the year Sat & Sun only). Housed in a flashy modern edifice, the gallery specializes in temporary exhibitions of contemporary art (which attract an extra admission charge), but the small permanent collection is also very worthwhile, comprising a representative sample of the works of most major Norwegian painters, from Johan Dahl and

Christian Krohg to Munch and Erik Werenskiold. In particular, look out for the striking landscapes by one of the less familiar Norwegian artists, **Axel Revold** (1887–1962). A student of Matisse and an admirer of Cézanne, Revold spent years working abroad before returning home and applying the techniques he had learnt to his favourite subject, northern Norway: his beautifully composed and brightly coloured *Nordland* is typical.

The much-vaunted **Maihaugen open-air folk museum** (late May & late Aug to Sept daily 10am–5pm; June to mid-Aug daily 9am–6pm; Oct to mid-May Tues–Sun 11am–4pm; 70kr including free 40min guided tour in English every other hour, on the hour, until 2hr before closing, mid-May to Sept only; bus #7 hourly from the Skysstasjon), a twenty-minute walk southeast from the town centre along Anders Sandvigsgate, is the largest of its type in northern Europe. Incredibly, the whole collection represents the lifetime's work of one man with a propensity for hoarding, a dentist by the name of Anders Sandvig. The Maihaugen contains around 140 relocated buildings, moved here from all over the region, including a charming seventeenth-century presbytery (*prestegårdshagen*), a thirteenth-century stave church from Garmo, a thick-log storehouse and smokehouses, summer grazing huts and various workshops.

The key exhibits, however, are the two **farms** from Bjørnstad and Øygarden, dating from the late seventeenth century. Complete with their various outhouses and living areas, the two farms between them comprise 36 buildings. Each building had a specific function, with separate structures serving as, for example, food-store, sheep-shed, hay barn, stable and bathhouse. This setup may have worked, and it certainly looks quaint today, but it was, in fact, forced upon farmers by their tried-and-tested method of construction, **laft**. Based on the use of pine logs notched together at right angles, the technique strictly limited the dimensions of every building, as the usable part of the pine tree was rarely more than eight metres long. Indeed, it seems likely that many farmers would have preferred to keep their winter supplies in the main farmhouse rather than in a separate store, as the latter might have given rise to confrontations as implied by a draconian medieval law: "When a man discovers another in his storehouse... then he may kill the man if he so wishes." Outside there are farmyard animals, and costumed guides give the lowdown on traditional rural life; in the summertime there's often the chance to have a go at domestic activities such as spinning, baking, weaving and pottery – good, wholesome fun. You can spend time too in the main museum building, which features temporary exhibitions on folkloric themes. Allow a good half-day for a visit and take advantage of the free guided tour (every other hour, on the hour), though these are not as informative as perhaps they might be.

You might also be tempted by the **Norges Olympiske Museum**, in Håkons Hall (Norwegian Olympic Museum; mid-May to mid-Sept daily 10am–6pm; 50kr, combined ticket with Maihaugen 100kr), part of Olympic Park, about 1km to the northeast of the centre via Nordsetervegen. Housed in one of the arenas built for the 1994 Olympics, the museum offers a jaunty run-through of the history of the games.

Practicalities

The E6 runs along the lakeshore about 500m below the centre of Lillehammer, where the ultra-modern **Skysstasjon**, on Jernbanetorget, incorporates both the **train station** and the **bus terminal**. The **information kiosk** here (Mon–Fri 7.30am–4.30pm, Sat 10am–2pm; ☎61 26 41 99) has public transport timetables and some tourist material, but the main **tourist office** is a five-minute walk away up the hill and off the main street, Storgata, at Elvegata 19 (late June to mid-Aug Mon–Sat 9am–7pm, Sun 11am–6pm; mid-Aug to late June Mon–Fri 9am–4pm, Sat 10am–2pm; ☎61 25 92 99 or 81 54 81 70). **Orientation** couldn't be easier, with all activity focused on the pedestrianized part of Storgata which runs north from Bankgata, across Jernbanegata to the tumbling River Mesnaelva; Anders Sandvigsgate and Kirkegata run parallel on either side to the east and west respectively.

The tourist office will help with finding **accommodation**, but note that there are no private rooms available. You might as well use the popular **youth hostel** (☎61 26 25 66, fax 61 26 25 77; ➀, dorm beds 170kr), which is perfect for an overnight visit. It occupies part of the Skysstasjon, and the thirty or so four-bunk rooms are kitted out with smoked-glass windows and smart modern furnishings. If you're around for longer, you may want something rather more cosy: a recommended **guesthouse** is *Gjestehuset Ersgaard*, Nordseterveien 201 (☎ 61 25 06 84, fax 61 25 31 09; ➀), a couple of kilometres above the town (towards Nordseter), which serves excellent breakfasts in its dining room and offers good views. For **hotel** accommodation in the centre, the *First Hotell Breiseth*, Jernbanegata 3 (☎61 26 95 00, fax 61 26 95 05), across from the Skysstasjon, is a large chain hotel with comfortable rooms.

Lillehammer has a good supply of downtown **restaurants** and **cafés**. The busy *Bøndernes Hus Kafeteria*, at Kirkegata 68 (Mon–Fri 8.30am–7pm, Sat 8.30am–4pm, Sun noon–6pm), is a big, old-fashioned sort of place with cheap and filling self-service meals. Moving up a rung, the *Vertshuset Solveig*, down an alley off the pedestrianized part of Storgata, is cafeteria-style too, but the meals are first-rate with main courses averaging around 100kr. For something entirely different, the *Teppanyaki*, Storgata 73 (☎61 25 74 44), is a very good and moderately priced Japanese restaurant. In sunny weather, head for the *Terrassen*, a large and moderately priced outdoor restaurant by the river at Storgata 84 (☎61 25 00 49), serving all the Norwegian favourites. Lillehammer also has an animated nightlife, with **bars** clustered around the western end of Storgata. Places come and go pretty fast, but *Nikkers* and *Pipas*, both a stone's throw from the main tourist office, are the liveliest spots at time of writing.

For getting out into the surrounding countryside, **bikes** can be rented at the youth hostel, and the antique **Skibladner** paddle steamer shuttles up and down Lake Mjøsa from the jetty about 800m south of the centre – for further details see p.119.

The Gudbrandsdal

Heading north from Lillehammer, the E6 and the railway leave the shores of Lake Mjøsa for the **Gudbrandsdal**, the 160-kilometre-long river valley which extends to Dombås and which was for centuries the main route between Oslo and Trondheim. Enclosed by mountain ranges, the valley has a comparatively dry and mild climate, and its fertile soils have nourished a string of farming villages since Viking times – though there was some light industrialization at the beginning of the twentieth century.

The first part of the Gudbrandsdal is fairly uninspiring, but after 60km the road swings past the distinctive maroon spire that marks **Ringebu stave church** (daily: late May & early Sept 10am–4pm; early June & late Aug 9am–4pm; mid-

June to mid-Aug 9am–6pm; 30kr), standing on a hill 1km off and up above the E6, and a couple of kilometres south of Ringebu village. Dating from the thirteenth century, the original church was modified and enlarged in the 1630s, reflecting both an increase in the local population and new religious practices introduced after the Reformation. At this time, the nave was broadened, the chancel replaced and the over-large tower and spire plonked on top. The exterior is rather glum, but the western entrance portal sports some superb zoomorphic carvings from the original church. Inside, the highlights are mainly eighteenth-century Baroque – from the florid pulpit and altar panel through to the tomb of the Irgens family, complete with trumpeting cherubs and intricate ruffs.

From the church, it's 10km to **HUNDORP**, where a neat little quadrangle of old farm buildings has been tastefully turned into a roadside tourist stop, with a café, art gallery and shop. There has been a farm here since prehistoric times, its most famous owner having been a Viking warrior by the name of Dalegudbrand, who became a bitter enemy of St Olav after his forced baptism in 1021. With a little time to spare, you can head down towards the river from the compound and nose around a couple of Viking burial mounds. Near here too, amongst the orchards overlooking the E6 just 3km further north, is Sygard Grytting (mid-June to mid-Aug; ☎61 29 85 88, fax 61 29 85 10, *www.grytting.com*; ②), an ancient farmstead that provides some of the most wonderful lodgings in the whole of Norway. The eighteenth-century farm buildings are in an almost perfect state of preservation, a beautiful ensemble with the assorted barns, outhouses and main house facing onto a tiny courtyard. One barn actually dates from the fourteenth century, when its upper storey was used to shelter pilgrims on the long haul north to Trondheim and its cathedral (p.229) – and bunk beds are now installed offering inexpensive dormitory accommodation (270kr per person). Most of the rooms are in the main house, which has been superbly renovated to provide extremely comfortable lodgings amidst antique furnishings, fading oil paintings and open fires. Breakfast is splendid too – the bread is baked on the premises – and dinner is available by prior arrangement. The nearest **train station** is Hundorp, 3km away, where long-distance **buses** will drop you too.

Pressing on, the E6 weaves north not following the course of the river to reach, after 25km, **KVAM**, a modest chipboard-producing town that witnessed some of the worst fighting of World War II. Once the Germans had occupied Norway's main towns, they set about extending their control of the main roads and railways, marching up the Gudbrandsdal in quick fashion. At Kvam, they were opposed by a scratch force of Norwegian and British soldiers, who delayed their progress despite being poorly equipped – the captain in charge of the British anti-tank guns had to borrow a bicycle to patrol his defences. The battle for the Gudbrandsdal lasted for two weeks (April 14–30, 1940) and is commemorated at the **Gudbrandsdal Krigsminnesamling** (War Museum; June–Aug daily 10am–5pm; Sept–May Mon–Fri 10am–5pm; 40kr), in the centre of Kvam beside the E6. In the museum, a multilingual series of displays runs through the campaign, supported by a substantial collection of military mementoes and lots of fascinating photographs; an extension is planned to focus on the Kalmar War of 1611–1613. Across the main street from the museum, in the church graveyard, is a Cross of Sacrifice, honouring the 54 British soldiers who died here while trying to halt the German advance in 1940. **Buses** travel through Kvam on the E6 and the town has a **train station**, about 400m south of the museum.

From Kvam, it's 9km further up the valley to **SJOA train station**, sitting beside the E6 at its junction with Highway 257. If you're heading here by train, note that some trains only stop at Sjoa on request – check with the conductor. Sjoa station sits at the start of the **Heidal**, a valley which boasts some of the country's most exciting **white-water rafting** on the River Sjoa. If you want to come to grips with the Sjoa's gorges and rapids, contact Heidal Rafting (☎61 23 60 37, fax 61 23 60 14, *www.heidalrafting.no*), who are based at the Sjoa youth hostel. The season lasts from May to September, and an all-inclusive one-day rafting excursion costs around 700kr; a more strenuous two-day expedition inclusive of meals and lodgings will set you back almost three times that amount. Reservations are recommended, but there's a reasonably good chance of being able to sign up at the last minute.

For **accommodation**, try Sjoa's **youth hostel**, 1300m west of Sjoa train station, near Highway 257 (☎61 23 62 00, fax 61 23 60 14; ①, dorm beds 80kr; May–Sept). To get there on foot from the station, walk south down to the minor road, where you turn right. Proceed underneath the railway bridge and then cross the river on the suspension bridge. On the far side of this, turn left at the T-junction and then follow the signs. Drivers have an easier time – just turn off the E6 along Highway 257 and watch for the sign. The hostel is perched on a wooded hillside high above the river, its main building an old log farmhouse dating from 1747, where meals are now served. Breakfasts are banquet-like, and dinners (by prior arrangement only) are reasonably priced if rather less spectacular. The hostel offers two types of accommodation: there's a no-frills dormitory block at the bottom of the slope (80kr per person) and a handful of spacious and comfortable chalets up above (①). Reservations are advisable for the chalets at weekends.

Beyond the Heidal, Highway 257 continues west and conveniently meets Highway 51, the main access road to the east side of the Jotunheimen National Park at Gjendesheim (see opposite).

Otta

Just 10km beyond Sjoa lies **OTTA**, a thoroughly unexciting little town at the confluence of the rivers Otta and Lågen. It may be dull, but Otta makes an ideal base for hiking in the nearby Rondane and Jotunheimen national parks (see opposite), especially if you're reliant on public transport – that said, staying in one of the parks' mountain lodges is preferable. At least everything you need is within easy reach in Otta: the E6 passes within 200m of the centre, along the east bank of the Lågen, while the **train station**, **bus terminal** and **tourist office** (mid-June to Aug Mon–Fri 8.30am–7.30pm, Sat & Sun 10.30am–6pm; Sept to mid-June Mon–Fri 8.30am–4pm; ☎61 23 66 50, fax 61 23 09 60) are all clumped together on the west bank in the Skysstasjon, itself just 100m from the few gridiron streets that pass for the town centre. There are no sights as such, but the **statue** outside the Skysstasjon commemorates a certain Pillarguri, whose alertness made her an overnight sensation. During the Kalmar War of 1611–13, one of many wars between Sweden and Denmark, a band of Scottish mercenaries hired by the king of Sweden landed in the Romsdalsfjord, in order to head across Norway and join the Swedish army. The Norwegians – Danish subjects at that time – were fearful of the Scots, and when Pillarguri spotted them nearing Otta she dashed to the top of the nearest hill and blew her birch-bark horn to sound the alarm. The locals hastily arranged an ambush at one of the narrowest points of the trail and all but wiped the Scots out – a rare victory for peasants over professionals. One of Pillarguri's rewards was to have the hill named after her and today the stiff hike along the footpath up the forested slopes to the summit, **Pillarguritoppen** (853m), across the Otta river south of the centre, is a popular outing.

Otta's tourist office is exceptionally helpful, providing the usual services; they also have a small supply of **private rooms** (①) which they will reserve on your behalf for a fee of 25kr. Alternatively, the *Grand Gjestegård*, across from the train station at the corner of Ola Dahls gate (☎61 23 12 00, fax 61 23 04 62; ②), is a large pension-cum-hotel with simple but perfectly adequate rooms furnished in brisk modern style. It's the best **hotel** in town, preferable to its main rival the *Norlandia Otta Hotell*, a few metres to the west along Ola Dahls gate (☎61 23 00 33, fax 61 23 15 24; ③), in an unenticing concrete block. Better still is the nearest **campsite**, *Otta Camping*, about 1500km from the town centre on the wooded banks of the River Otta, with cabins and space for tents (☎61 23 03 09; ②). To get there, cross over the bridge on the south side of the centre, turn right and keep going. Otta doesn't have much in the way of **restaurants**, but the *Pillarguri Café* on Storgata musters a range of Norwegian standbys, as does the popular and inexpensive restaurant of the *Grand Gjestegård*; both eateries close between 5pm and 6pm.

For the western fjords (see p.155), **Highway 15** sweeps west from Otta along a wide and fertile river valley, Hjelledal, over to Lom (see p.206), from where there's a choice of wonderful routes. Continuing west, Highway 15 forges ahead to **Stryn** (see p.211), with the nerve-racking Highway 63 (called the **Ørnevegen** or Eagle's Highway) to **Geiranger** (see p.216) branching off northwards about halfway between Lom and Stryn. Alternatively, heading south of Lom, **Highway 55** climbs steeply to travel along the western flank of the Jotunheimen Nasjonalpark, offering breathtaking views of the jagged peaks (see p.128) before leading down to **Sogndal** (see p.203). The Oslo–Måløy NSB **bus** (3 daily) passes through Otta and Lom en route to **Stryn**; from mid-June to August, one of these three buses connects at Grotli with the bus for Geiranger. The bus journey time from Otta to Lom is one hour, from Otta to Stryn three hours. From Lom, there's also a local bus service to Sogndal (mid-June to late Aug; 2 daily; 3hr 30 min).

The Rondane and Jotunheimen national parks

Buses run from Otta to the **Rondane** and **Jotunheimen national parks** nearby. For Rondane, there is one daily summertime service (late June to mid-Aug; 45min) that leaves the Spranghaugen car park (see the Rondane hike box, p.127) in the afternoon for Otta, 25km away; you catch the bus on the subsequent return leg. The afternoon arrival at Spranghausen means you'll almost certainly need to overnight at Rondvassbu (see p.127) if you're after some hiking – not that this is a hardship. There's also a daily morning bus (same dates), but this terminates at Mysuseter, 5km short of Spranghaugen. Getting to the **Jotunheimen national park** is a bit easier. There's a daily summertime bus from Otta to Gjendesheim (see p.129) which leaves early in the morning (late June to Aug Mon–Sat; 2hr) and another leaving around noon (late June to early Sept; 2hr). It's too far from Otta to Gjendesheim (93km) to take a **taxi**, but it's a reasonably economic option for the journey from Otta to the Rondane if you're in a group. Taxis are available at the Skysstasjon from Otta Skysstasjon (☎61 23 05 01) and **cars** can be rented here too, from Otta Auto (☎61 23 64 50).

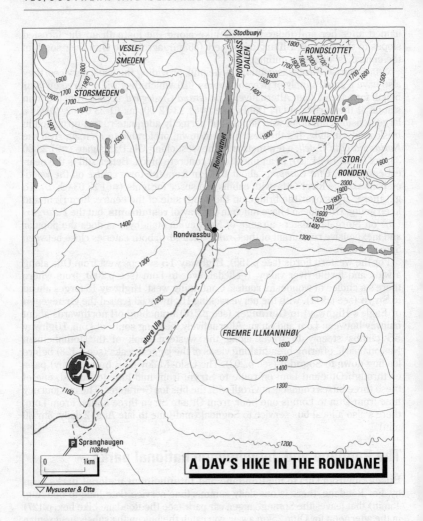

△ Stodbuøyi

VESLE-
SMEDEN

RONDVASS
-DALEN

RONDSLOTTET

STORSMEDEN

VINJERONDEN

STOR-
RONDEN

Rondvatnet

Rondvassbu

store Ula

FREMRE ILLMANNHØI

N

Spranghaugen
(1084m)

0   1km

A DAY'S HIKE IN THE RONDANE

▽ Mysuseter & Otta

Rondane Nasjonalpark

Spreading north and east from Otta towards the Swedish border, the **Rondane Nasjonalpark** was the first park of its kind in Norway, established in 1962. Now one of the country's most popular hiking areas, its 580 square kilometres, one third of which is in the high alpine zone, appeal to walkers of all ages and abilities. The soil is poor, so vegetation is sparse and lichens, especially reindeer moss, predominate, but the views across this bare landscape are serenely beautiful, with a handful of lakes, rivers and patches of dwarf birch forest providing some diversity. Wild mountain peaks divide the Rondane into three distinct areas. To the west of **Rondvatnet**, a centrally located lake, are the wild cirques and jagged peaks of Storsmeden (2017m), Sagtinden (2018m) and Veslesmeden (2015m), while to the

A DAY'S HIKE IN THE RONDANE

Start and finish: Spranghaugen car park (altitude 1084m).
Distance: 17km return.
Time: 8hr.
Highest point: Storronden (2138m).
Maps: 1718 I Rondane (M711); Rondane 1:100,000.
Transport: Bus or taxi from Otta to Spranghaugen car park (see below).
Accommodation: Rondvassbu full-service DNT lodge (late June to mid-Sept; ☎61 23 18 66; ①); or in Otta (see p.124).

Branching off the E6 near Otta, a signposted, 20km-long mountain road wriggles its way up to **Mysuseter**, a sprawling chalet settlement on the edge of the Rondane national park. Beyond the village, a narrow toll road nudges 5km further east to the **Spranghaugen car park**, the starting point of this one-day hike, and no more than a wind-buffeted field with uninterrupted views into the park.

From the car park, it's a ninety-minute level walk along the service road northeast to the lakeshore lodge at **Rondvassbu**, with the bleak and bare peaks of the Rondane slowly revealing themselves – a dozen peaks in all, surrounding the shadowy waters of the **Rondvatnet lake**. The first peak to the right of the lake is **Storronden** (2138m), the target of this hike and a relatively easy five-hour roundtrip climb from Rondvassbu. One of the park's most popular hikes, it makes a fine excursion for the beginner, since except for a short steep and exposed section just below the summit, there is no really difficult terrain to negotiate. Neighbouring peaks involve more arduous mountain hiking with the finest views over the range generally reckoned to be from **Vinjeronden** and nearby **Rondslottet**, both to the north of Storronden. For these longer hikes, you'll need to overnight at the comfortable Rondvassbu **lodge**.

Emerging from the lodge, turn left and after about twenty metres you'll spot a large map of the area. Take your bearings and then follow the signed trail up the hill across the rough, scrabbly terrain to the right of the lake. Initially, the three nearest peaks – Storronden, Vinjeronden and Rondslottet – share a common access path, but after about an hour's hike up across the treeless terrain you reach a signed junction: the trail to Vinjeronden and Rondslottet leads northeast, the trail to Storronden goes east. From the junction, the Storronden track traverses rocky hillsides and modest plateaux, and after about forty minutes you come to a sheltered stone seat where you can take a breather. The summit is another forty minutes' hike from here, a stiff haul with some steep drops where you should be careful. From the summit, there are fine views north to Vinjeronden (2044m) and Rondslottet (2178m), and west across the lake to a circle of peaks, the most imposing of which are Veslesmeden (2015m) and adjacent Storsmeden (2010m).

east of the lake tower Rondslottet (2178m), Vinjeronden (2044m), and Storronden (2138m). Further east still Høgronden (2115m) dominates, linking the mountain lodges of Bjørnhollia and Dørålseter. The mountains, ten of which exceed the 2000-metre mark, are mostly accessible to any reasonably fit and eager walker, thanks to a dense network of trails and hiking huts. For **accommodation**, the **Rondvassbu lodge** (late June to mid-Sept; ☎61 23 18 66; ①) is a typical DNT staffed lodge, with over one hundred beds, filling meals and pleasant service. For all but the briefest of hikes, it is best to arrive at the lodge the day before to have a chance of starting first thing the next morning. If, however, visibility is poor or you don't fancy a climb, there is a charming summer **boat service** (July to late Aug 2–3 daily; 30min each way; 35kr each way, 50kr return) to the far end of Rondvatn, from where it takes about two and a half hours to walk back to Rondvassbu along the lake's steep western shore. In the eastern Rondane, the gentle **Alvdal Vestfjell** appeals to older walkers and families with small children.

Jotunheimen Nasjonalpark

Norway's most celebrated walking area, **Jotunheimen** ("Home of the Giants") **Nasjonalpark** lives up to its name. Pointed summits and undulating glaciers dominate the skyline, soaring high above river valleys and lake-studded plateaux. Covering only 3900 square kilometres, the park offers an amazing concentration of high peaks, more than two hundred of which rise above 1900 metres. In Jotunheimen, you will find Norway's (and Northern Europe's) two highest peaks, Galdhøpiggen (2469m) and Glittertind (2464m), while Norway's highest water-fall, **Vettisfossen**, with a 275-metre drop, is here too, a short walk from the Vetti

---

A DAY'S HIKE IN THE JOTUNHEIM

Start: Memurubu (1008m).

Finish: Gjendesheim (995m).

Distance: 15km.

Time: 6hr.

Highest point: Besseggen Ridge (1743m).

Maps: 1617 IV Gjende (M711); 1618 III Glittertinden (M711); Jotunheimen 1:100,000.

Transport: Bus from Otta to Gjendesheim (see p.125); boat from Gjendesheim to Memurubu (late June to early Sept 1–3 daily; ☎61 23 85 09).

Accommodation: Gjendesheim, full-service DNT hut (late June to mid-Sept; ☎61 23 89 44; ①); Memurubu, full-service private hut (late June to early Sept; ☎61 23 89 99; ②).

Norway's best-known day walk, across the Besseggen Ridge high above Lake Gjende, links the **mountain lodges** of Memurubu and Gjendesheim. **Lake Gjende** is one of Norway's most famous – not least because Ibsen had his character Peer Gynt tumble from the ridge into the lake on the back of a reindeer – and it's certainly one of the country's most beautiful. Eighteen kilometres long and 146m deep, the glacially fed, green-tinted waters (the colour is due to the presence of clay particles) stretch west from Gjendesheim and, if you're reluctant to embark on a hike and/or suffer from vertigo, you can travel the lake's length on a summer boat service (see p.129). The hike east from the lodge at Memurubu to Gjendesheim is easy to complete in a day. If you do the hike in the opposite direction, then you can return by boat to Gjendesheim in the evening if you so wish, but you'll have to calculate your speed accurately to meet the boat at Memurubu – and that isn't easy. Whichever direction you take, be sure to confirm boat departure times before you set out, and check weather conditions too, as snow and ice can linger into July. If you have more time, consider spending another day hiking back from Gjendebu lodge (see p.129), at the western end of Lake Gjende.

Starting at the **Memurubu** jetty, begin by walking behind the lodge along the vehicle access road until – after about two minutes – you encounter a sign to

lodge on the west side of the park. A network of footpaths and mountain lodges lattices the park, but be warned that the weather is very unpredictable and the winds can be bitingly cold – take care and always come well equipped (see p.53).

There are no public roads into the park; visitors usually walk or ski into the interior from Highway 55 in the west (see p.125) or make the slightly easier approach from the east via **Gjendesheim**, 2km off Highway 51 near Otta. Gjendesheim is no more than a couple of buildings, but one of them is the excellent **DNT lodge**, at the eastern tip of long and slender Lake Gjende (late June to mid-Sept; ☎61 23 89 10; ①). **Boats** (late June to early Sept 1–3 daily; ☎61 23 85 09) travel the length of the lake, connecting with mountain trails and dropping by two more **lodges**. These are the privately-owned lodge at **Memurubu** (late June to early Sept; ☎61 23 89 99; ②), halfway along the lake's north shore, and **Gjendebu**'s DNT lodge (late June to mid-Sept; ☎61 23 89 44; ①), right at the western end. A single fare from Gjendesheim to Memurubu costs 55kr, Gjendebu 75kr; returns are twice that unless you make the round trip on the same day, in which case fares are 75kr

Gjendebu. Ignore this and keep to the road as far as the gate. Go through the gate and on the far side you'll see the clearly signposted trail to Besseggen ridge, Gjendesheim and Glitterheim. Follow the trail up towards the first ridge with the Memurubu **lodge** behind. The path, up to 4m wide, is marked by DNT "T"s and worn to a different colour from its surroundings. After about twenty minutes you pass the Glitterheim turn-off, and about thirty minutes after that you reach the first ridge, from where the path offers extravagant views of the lake. Here the path is clearly marked by cairns and DNT "T"s. Some 1hr 30min into the walk, you cross a plateau beside the southern shore of tiny lake **Bjørnbøltjørna** (altitude 1475m). Afterwards, continue to climb up the path across the boulder-strewn terrain until – some two hours from Memurubu – you catch sight of **Bessvatnet**, a lake that's frozen for most of the year but otherwise blue, in contrast with Lake Gjende. After 2hr 30min you arrive at the base of the **Besseggen ridge**. This is a good spot to take a break and enjoy the views over the two lakes before tackling the ridge itself.

The thirty-minute scramble up to the peak of the ridge is very steep, with ledges that are, on occasion, chest high; you need to be moderately fit to negotiate them. In places, the ridge narrows to fifty metres with a sheer drop to either side, but you can avoid straying close to the edge by following the DNT "T"s. The views are superlative, the drops disconcerting – and a head for heights is essential. Beyond the peak of the ridge, the trail crosses a small plateau before meeting rising ground at the start of another, much less demanding thirty-minute scramble up to a wide plateau, where a huge cairn is clearly visible. Hike along the path to the cairn, from where you can readily discern the wide trail that leads across the mountainsides to the lodge at Gjendesheim, a two-hour hike from this point. Beyond the cairn, ignore a second turning to Glitterheim and push on across the wide plateau that leads to the **Veltløyfti gorge**, where a slippery scramble with steep drops requires care. The trail is, however, well-marked and the final destination clearly visible. **Gjendesheim** , with its lodge and ferry dock, has long been a popular base for explorations of the Jotunheimen; the first huts at Gjendesheim and Memurubu were built in the 1870s. Indeed, the original hut at Gjendesheim is still visible, located on the south side of the River Sjoa and accessible by rowboat. The view across Lake Gjende from Gjendesheim is a popular photographic subject, with the north shore flanked by a steep rock rampart which stretches unbroken to Memurubu.

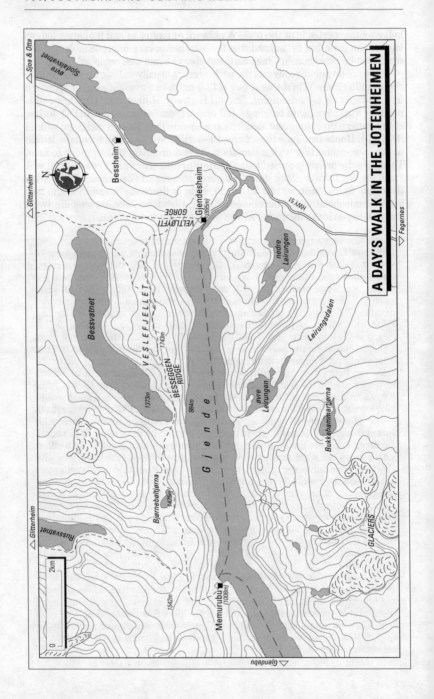

A DAY'S WALK IN THE JOTENHEIMEN

△ Sjoa & Otta

Øvre Sjodalsvatnet

△ Glitterheim

N

Bessheim

Glendesheim
(995m)

VELTLØYFTI GORGE

△ Fagernes

HWY 51

nedre Leirungen

Bessvatnet

VESLEFJELLET

1743m

BESSEGGEN RIDGE

1373m

Leirungsdalen

øvre Leirungen

984m

Gjende

Bukkehammartjørna

△ Glitterheim

Russvatnet

Bjørnebøltjørna

1405m

1542m

GLACIERS

Memurubu
(1008m)

△ Gjendebu

2km

0

and 100kr respectively. It takes the boat twenty minutes to reach Memurubu, 45 minutes for Gjendebu. By boat, you still get to see a slice of the Jotunheimen and sleep at the lodges, and you avoid a hike – not unwise in bad weather.

Dombås, Hjerkinn, Kongsvoll and the Dovrefjell

North of Otta, the E6 and the railway lead on to **DOMBÅS**, 45km north of Otta, a mundane crossroads settlement that's best ignored. Usefully for long-distance drivers, Dombås has a couple of good places to stay. Close to the **train and bus stations** and the E6/E136 junction is the *Dombås Hotell* (☎61 24 10 01, fax 61 24 14 61; ④, s/r ③), whose main building contains a handsome series of long public rooms dating from the turn of the twentieth century, and whose distinctive high gables overlook the Gudbrandsdal. Most of the bedrooms are tucked away in the modern annexe round the back, but the main building has some, a little the worse for wear – the views down the valley more than compensate though. Also offering valley views is Dombås' **youth hostel** (☎61 24 10 45, fax 61 24 13 30; ①, dorm beds 170kr), a comfortable complex of mountain huts way up on the hillside above the E6. To get there, head north out of town along the E6 for around 1km and follow the signs up the hill; if you're heavily laden, consider a taxi as it's a hard slog up from the valley below.

Both routes out of Dombås offer tantalizing prospects: E136 leads west to Åndalsnes and the Romsdalsfjord (see p.217), 110km from Dombås, whilst the E6 plunges north through the mountains towards Trondheim (see p.229). You can complete either journey by rail as well, though the Åndalsnes train only runs a couple of times a day.

Staying on the E6 north from Dombås, it's just 30km to the outpost of **HJERKINN**, stuck out on bare and desolate moorland, its pint-sized military base battened against the wind and snow of winter. The base overlooks the E6/Highway 29 junction, as does the adjacent **train station**. There's been a **mountain inn** here at Hjerkinn since medieval times, a staging post on the long trail to Trondheim, 170km away. The current establishment, the *Hjerkinn Fjellstue* (☎61 24 29 27, fax 61 24 29 49; ③), continues this tradition in a becoming manner, its two expansive wooden buildings featuring big open fires and breezy pine furniture. The restaurant is good, too – try the reindeer culled from local herds – and the stables next door offer a chance to go horse-riding. The inn, a little over 2km from the train station, is set on a hill slope overlooking the moors and beside Highway 29, a turning off the E6. Highway 29 is the shortest route to Røros if you're travelling from the south, but Highway 30 (see p.132) further north is a much more interesting drive.

Beyond Hjerkinn, the E6 slices across the barren uplands before descending into a narrow ravine, the **Drivdal**. Hidden here, just 12km from Hjerkinn, is **KONGSVOLL**, home to a tiny train station and the delightful *Kongsvold Fjeldstue* (☎72 40 43 40, fax 72 40 43 41, *www.kongsvold.no*; ③), which provides some of the most charming accommodation in the whole of Norway. Train passengers should note that only some of the Oslo–Trondheim services stop at Kongsvoll **station**, 500m down the valley from the inn – and then only by prior arrangement with the conductor. As at Hjerkinn, an inn has stood here since medieval times and the present complex, a huddle of tastefully restored old timber buildings with sun-bleached reindeer antlers tacked onto the outside walls, dates back to the eighteenth century. Once a farm as well as an inn, its agricultural days are recalled by several outbuildings such as the little turf-roofed storehouses (*stabbur*), the lodgings for farmhands (*karstuggu*) and the barn (*låve*), atop which is a bell that was rung to summon the hands from the fields. The main building has been beautifully refurbished, retaining many of the original features and now also boasting an eclectic sample of antiques. The bedrooms, dotted round the compound, are of the same high standard – and the old vagabonds' hut (*fantstuggu*), built outside the white picket fence that once defined the physical limits of social respectability, contains the cosiest family rooms imaginable. Dinner is served in the excellent **restaurant**, where prices are reasonable, and the complex also includes a **café** and a Dovrefjell Nasjonalpark **information centre**, making it an ideal base for hiking into the park, which extends to the east and west.

Beyond Drivdal, 35km north of Kongsvoll, **Oppdal** is a crossroads town where the Kristiansund road (Highway 70) meets the E6. Pressing on, **Støren**, a further 70km to the north and just 50km from Trondheim, is the place to turn off for **Røros** (see below) – a lovely 100km drive on Highway 30 along the picturesque Gauldal, though there are other, shorter routes.

Dovrefjell Nasjonalpark

Bisected by the railway and the E6, **Dovrefjell Nasjonalpark** is one of the more accessible of Norway's national parks. A comparative minnow at just 265 square kilometres, it comprises two distinct zones: spreading east from the E6 are the marshes, open moors and rounded peaks that characterize much of eastern Norway, while to the west the mountains become increasingly steep and serrated as they approach the wild peaks of the Romsdal (p.217).

Hiking trails and **huts** are spread throughout the western part of the Dovrefjell. **Kongsvoll** makes an ideal starting point: it's possible to hike all the way from here to the coast at Åndalsnes, but this takes all of nine or ten days; a more feasible expedition for most visitors is the two-day hike to one of the four snow-tipped peaks of mighty **Snøhetta**, at around 2200m. There's accommodation five hours' walk west from Kongsvoll at the unstaffed **Reinheim hut** (mid-Feb to mid-Oct). On the first part of this hike, you're likely to spot **musk ox**, the descendants of animals imported from Greenland in the 1950s. Conventional wisdom is that these chunky beasts will ignore you if you ignore them and keep at a distance of at least 100m. They are, however, not afraid of humans and will charge if irritated – retreat as quickly and quietly as possible if one starts snorting and scraping. Further hiking details and maps are available at the park **information centre** in the *Kongsvold Fjeldstue* (see above).

Røros and around

Located on a treeless mountain plateau, **RØROS** is a blustery place even on a summer's afternoon, when it's full of day-tripping tourists here to survey the old part of town, little changed since its days as a copper-mining centre. Røros is a unique and remarkable survivor, given its history and meagre surroundings: until the mining company went bust a decade or so ago, mining had been the basis of life here since the seventeenth century. This dirty and dangerous work was supplemented by a little farming and hunting, and life for the average villager can't have been anything but hard. Furthermore, Røros' wooden houses, some of them 300 years old, have escaped the fires that have devastated so many of Norway's timber-built towns. Røros is now on UNESCO's World Heritage list, and there are

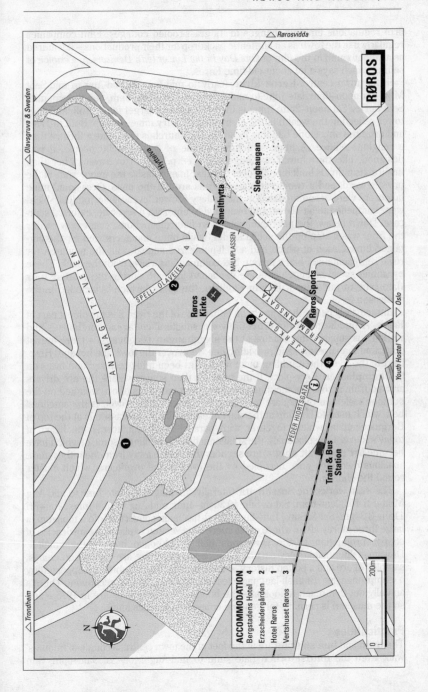

firm regulations limiting changes to its grass-roofed cottages. Film companies regularly use the town as an authentic backdrop for their productions – it featured as a labour camp in the film of *One Day in the Life of Ivan Denisovich*, a choice of setting which says a lot about old-time Røros.

In the town centre, **Røros kirke** (early to mid-June & mid-Aug to mid-Sept Mon–Sat noon–2pm; late June to mid-Aug Mon–Sat 10am–5pm, Sun 2–4pm; mid-Sept to Dec Sat noon–2pm; 15kr) is the most obvious target for a stroll, its heavy tower reflecting the wealth of the eighteenth-century mine owners. Built in 1784, and once the only stone building in Røros, the church is more like a theatre than a religious edifice. A huge structure capable of seating 1600 people, it was designed, like the church at Kongsberg (see p.138), to overawe rather than inspire. Its pulpit is built directly over the altar to emphasize the importance of the priest's word, and a two-tiered gallery runs around the nave. Occasional mine labourers were accommodated in the gallery's lower level, while "undesirables" were compelled to sit above, and even had to enter via a separate, external staircase. Down below, the nave exhibited even finer distinctions: every pew nearer the front was a step up the social ladder, while mine managers vied for the curtained boxes, each of which had a well-publicized annual rent; the monarch (or royal representative) had a private box commanding views from the back. These byzantine social arrangements are explained in depth during the **guided tour** (late June to mid-Aug, 1 daily in English), the cost of which is included in the admission fee.

Immediately below the church, on either side of the river, lies the oldest part of Røros. A huddle of sturdy cross-timbered smelters' cottages, storehouses and workshops squat in the shadow of the **slegghaugan** (slagheaps) – more tourist attraction than eyesore, and providing fine views over the town and beyond. Here, next to the river, the rambling main works has been tidily restored and faces on to **Malmplassen** ("ore-place"), the wide earthen square where the ore drivers arrived from across the mountains to have their cartloads of ore weighed on the outdoor scales. In the square too, hung in a rickety little tower, is the smelters' bell, which used to be rung at the start of each shift. Malmplassen is at the top of Bergmannsgata which, together with parallel Kjerkgata, forms the heart of today's Røros. Conspicuously, the smaller artisans' dwellings, some of which have become **art and craft shops**, are set near the works, away from the rather more spacious dwellings once occupied by the owners and overseers, which cluster round the church.

The main works, the **Smelthytta** (literally "melting hut" ; late June to mid-Aug Mon–Fri 10.30am–6pm, Sat & Sun 10.30am–4pm; mid-Aug to mid-June Mon–Fri 11am–3.30pm, Sat & Sun 11am–2pm; 45kr) has been converted into a museum, a large three-storey affair whose most interesting section explains the intricacies of copper production in the cavernous hall which once housed the smelter. Dioramas illuminate every part of the process, and there are production charts, samples of ore and a potted history of the company – all of which is supported by a comprehensive English-language leaflet available free at reception. There's actually not that much to look at – the building was gutted by fire in 1975 – and so the museum is perhaps for genuine copper enthusiasts only.

Practicalities

The **train** and **bus stations** are at the foot of the town centre, a couple of minutes' walk from the **tourist office** (late June to mid-Aug Mon–Sat 9am–6pm, Sun

10am–4pm; mid-Aug to mid-June Mon–Fri 9am–4pm, Sat 10.30am–12.30pm; ☎72 41 11 65), where you can pick up a comprehensive booklet on Røros and the sur-rounding region. They also have details of local **hikes** out across the uplands that encircle the town, one of the more popular being the five-hour trek east to the self-service DNT hut at Marenvollen. The uplands are also popular with **cross-country skiers** in the winter, and the tourist office has a leaflet mapping out several possible skiing routes. To get around town, pick up one of the free municipal **bicycles** available at the railway station and tourist office, or for those venturing further afield, **mountain bikes** can be rented from *Røros Sports*, on Bergmannsgata (☎72 41 12 18), for around 150kr a day plus a 100kr refundable deposit.

Because of the long drive here and the infrequency of trains to Trondheim and Oslo, you may well want to stay the night in Røros. Fortunately, there's a reason-able range of centrally located **accommodation**. Easily the best deal in town is the *Erzscheidergården* guesthouse, Spell-Olaveien 6 (☎72 41 11 94, fax 72 41 19 00; ②), with some charming, unassuming rooms in its wooden main building. Some rooms also have fine views over town, and there's an attractive subterranean breakfast area and a cosy lounge. Also worth considering are *Hotel Røros*, An-Magritt-veien (☎72 41 10 11, fax 72 41 00 22; ⑤, s/r ③), a big modern place on the northern edge of the centre, and *Vertshuset Røros*, Kjerkgata 34 (☎72 41 24 11, fax 72 41 03 64; ②), a guesthouse with cramped doubles that's bang in the centre of town, and at the bottom end of its price category. Less appealing is *Bergstadens*, Osloveien 2 (☎72 40 60 80, fax 72 41 01 55; ④, s/r ③), conveniently located at the foot of Bergmannsgata, but otherwise a routine, modern hotel with workaday double rooms. There's also a **hostel**, the unappealing *Røros Vandrerhjem*, Øraveien 25 (☎72 41 10 89, fax 72 41 23 77; ①, dorm beds 160kr; open all year), about 800m south of the train station next to the sports ground, in a concrete block shared with the *Idrettsparken Hotell* (same details).

Røros is no gourmet's paradise when it comes to **food**, but there's just enough choice to get by. *Hotel Røros* has a good, if slightly formal, restaurant that's gen-erally reckoned to serve the best meals in town; it's expensive, though, and clos-es at 10pm. In contrast the busy and competent *Papas Pizza*, at the foot of Bergmannsgata in the back of the *Bergstadens Hotel*, is open till late. For sub-stantial meals at fairly reasonable prices there's *Otto's Kro Restaurant*, Peder Hiortsgata 4, just west of the tourist office – try the *entrecôte* at 130kr.

Femundsmarka Nasjonalpark and Olavsgruva copper mine

Tucked in tight between the Swedish border and the elongated Lake Femund some 50km east of Røros, the 385 square kilometres that make up the remote **Femundsmarka Nasjonalpark** encompass a wide variety of terrains. In the north are pine forests, marshes, lakes and rivers, which give way in the south to bare mountains and plateaux. There is no road access into the Femundsmarka, but a minor road leads from Røros to **Sørvika**, on the west side of Lake Femund, from where a **passenger boat**, the *M/S Faemund* (mid-June to mid-Oct 2–4 weekly), shuttles around the lake, stopping at several remote outposts and jetties. Among the latter, several give access to the limited network of unstaffed DNT huts and hiking trails which cross the national park; the jetties at **Røa** and **Haugen** are the handiest. Boat schedules and prices are available from Røros tourist office. Several Røros-based operators run three-day canoeing and fishing expeditions in the park – *Røros Sports* on Bergmannsgata (☎72 41 12 18) is as good as any.

Thirteen kilometres east of Røros off Highway 31, the **Olavsgruva**, one of the old copper mines, has been kept open as a museum, and there are daily guided tours of the workings throughout the summer (early June & late Aug to early Sept Mon–Sat 2 daily, Sun 1 daily; late June to mid-Aug 6 daily; mid-Sept to May Sat 1 daily; 45kr). Special **buses** timed to coincide with the guided tours make the journey once daily from Røros' train station and Smelthytta to the mine in July and early August (60kr return), returning to town afterwards. The temperature down the mine is a constant 5°C, so remember to take something warm to wear – you'll need sturdy shoes too.

From Oslo direct to the western fjords

The western fjords (for detailed coverage see Chapter 3, pp.155–226) are an easy day's drive, bus or train ride from Oslo – which, one could argue, is just as well considering that the forested dales and uplands filling out the interior of southern Norway rarely inspire. In almost any other European country these areas would be attractions in their own right, but in Norway they simply can't compare with the mountains and fjords of the north and west. It doesn't help either that, for the most part, the interior towns and villages hereabouts are dull affairs strung along the roadsides, often accompanied by some small-scale industry blotting the landscape. Almost everywhere, the architecture is modern and routine; most of the old timber buildings that once lined the valleys are long gone, often to the open-air museums that almost every town seems to possess. Three major roads cross the region: the E16, Highway 7 and the E134; there are regular long-distance **buses** along all three.

Of the three major trunk roads crossing the region, the **E16** is the fastest, a quick 350-kilometre haul up from Oslo to the fjord ferry point near Sogndal (see p.203). An enormous bypass tunnel is currently under construction to link the E16 directly to Highway 50 near Flåm, for Bergen. Otherwise, the E16's nearest rival, the slower **Highway 7**, branches off the E16 at Hønefoss and, after a scenic wiggle across the Hardangervidda plateau, finally reaches the coast at Eidfjord near Hardangerfjord, a distance of 334km. For most of its length, Highway 7 is shadowed by the **Oslo–Bergen railway**, though they part company when the train swings north for its spectacular traversal of the coastal mountains.

The E16: Leira, Borgund and Highway 7

It's 180km along the E16 north from Oslo up to ribbon-like **Leira**, where you can break your journey economically – if not exactly thrillingly – at the **youth hostel** (☎61 35 95 00, fax 61 35 95 01; ③, dorm beds 90kr; June to mid-Aug), which occupies part of the high-school complex beside the road. The nearby village, **Fagernes**, is where Highway 51 branches north off the E16 to run along the eastern edge of the Jotunheimen Nasjonalpark. Back along the E16, about 30km west of Fagernes, the scenery improves as you approach the coast; the road dips and weaves from dale to dale until it reaches **Laerdal**. Here, 303km from Oslo, the stepped roofs and angular gables of the **Borgund stave church** (daily May & Sept 10am–5pm; June–Aug 8am–8pm; 50kr) are framed by the forested sides of the valley. One of the best preserved stave churches (see opposite) in Norway, Borgund was built beside what was one of the major pack roads between east and

STAVE CHURCHES

Of the 29 surviving **stave churches** in Norway, all but a handful are in southern and central Norway. Together, these remarkable timber churches represent the country's most original architectural attribute. The key feature of their design is that the timbers are placed vertically into the ground – in contrast to the log-bonding technique used by the Norwegians for everything else. Thus, a stave wall consisted of vertical planks slotted into sills above and below, with the sills connected to upright posts – or **staves**, hence the name – at each corner. Within this general concept, which originated in the twelfth century, there are several variations: in some churches, nave and chancel form a single rectangle; in others the chancel is narrower than, and tacked on to, the nave. External wooden galleries are a common feature, as are shingles and finials. The most distinctive and fetching of these churches are those where the central section of the nave has been raised above the aisles to create – from the outside – an almost pagoda-like effect. In virtually all the stave churches, the **door frames** (where they survive) are decorated from top to bottom with surging, intricate carvings which clearly hark back to Viking design. The dragons in particular are long-limbed creatures, often entwined in vine tendrils.

The **origins** of stave churches have attracted an inordinate amount of academic debate. Some scholars argue that they were originally pagan temples, converted to Christian use by the addition of a chancel, while others are convinced that they were inspired by Russian churches. In the nineteenth century, the stave churches acquired symbolic importance as reminders of the time when Norway was independent. Many had fallen into a dreadful state of repair, and were clumsily renovated – or even remodelled – by enthusiastic medievalists with a nationalist agenda. Undoing this renovation has been a major operation, and one that continues today. For most visitors, sight of one or two stave churches suffices – and two of the finest are those at Heddal (see p.140) and Borgund (see opposite); specialist literature is available for aficionados – see p.338.

west, until bubonic plague wiped out most of the local population in the fourteenth century. Much of the church's medieval appearance has been preserved, its tiered exterior protected by shingles and decorated with dragon and Christian cross finials that culminate in a slender ridge turret. A rickety wooden gallery runs round the outside of the church, and the doors sport an intense swirl of carved animals and foliage. Inside, the dark, pine-scented nave is framed by the upright wooden posts that define this style of church architecture.

Beyond the church, the valley grows wilder as the E16 traverses the 45km down to **Fodnes**, from where the round-the-clock car ferry zips over to **Manheller** (every 30min; 15min; passengers 26kr, car & driver 77kr), some 18km from Sogndal. On the way, you'll pass the entrance to the 24.3km-long tunnel, to be completed in the next couple of years, that will link the E16 with Highway 50 near Flåm.

Highway 7 to Geilo

Highway 7 branches off the E16 about 60km from Oslo at **Hønefoss**, some 180km further on from which the road forks at **Hagafoss**; here Highway 50 begins its descent of the dales to reach the Aurlandsfjord, 100km away, just round the coast from Flåm. En route, Highway 50 passes Østerbø and its lodges, which is at the start of one of our recommended hikes (see p.196). Meanwhile, Highway 7 presses on west to the winter ski resort of **GEILO**, 250km from Oslo, a boring town best avoided out of the skiing season. That said, there are several inexpensive places to stay, including a **youth hostel** (☎32 09 03 00, fax 32 09 18 96; ①, dorm beds 160kr; June–Sept & Nov–April), housed in large barrack-like buildings in the town centre just off the main street. Details of other accommodation are available from the **tourist office** nearby (June & late Aug Mon–Fri 8.30am–6pm, Sat 9am–3pm; July to mid-Aug daily 8.30am–8pm; Sept–May Mon–Fri 8.30am–4pm; ☎32 09 59 00).

Beyond Geilo, the rail line ceases to follow the road, and tunnels off through the mountains to Finse, Myrdal and points to Bergen. Highway 7, on the other hand, continues west for a further 90km, slicing across the upland plateau that is the Hardangervidda. On the far side of the plateau, the road heads down a steep valley to reach the fjords at Eidfjord (see p.190).

The E134 to Kongsberg

The E134 stretches the 418km from Drammen near Oslo to Haugesund, and has the advantage of passing through **Kongsberg**, an attractive town that makes for a pleasant overnight stay. There's an enjoyable detour 60km north off the E134 too, in the shape of **Rjukan**, a small town near which is a museum spotlighting the World War II tale of a German heavy water plant and its Norwegian saboteurs.

Up in the hills 40km west of Drammen on the E134 (and only an hour or two by train or bus from Oslo), **KONGSBERG** is one of the most interesting towns in the region. A local story claims that the silver responsible for its existence was discovered by two goatherds, who stumbled across a vein of the metal laid bare by the scratchings of an ox. True or not, Christian IV was quick to exploit the resource, and with the creation of his mining centre (the town's name means "King's Mountain"), the seventeenth-century **silver rush** began. In the event, it turned out that Kongsberg was the only place in the world where silver was to be found in its pure form, and there was enough of it to sustain the town for a couple of centuries. By the 1750s the town was the largest in Norway, with half of its 8000 inhabitants employed in and around the 300-odd mine shafts that littered the area. The silver works closed in 1805, but by this time Kongsberg was also the site of a royal mint and then an armaments factory, which still employs people to this day.

To appreciate the full economic and political clout of the mine owners, it's necessary to visit the church they funded – **Kongsberg kirke** (mid-May to Aug Mon–Fri 10am–4pm, Sat 10am–1pm; Sept to mid-May Tues–Fri 10am–noon; 15kr), the largest and arguably the most beautiful Baroque church in Norway. It dates from 1761, when the mines were at the peak of their prosperity, and sits impressively in a square surrounded on three sides by period wooden buildings. Inside, too, it's a grand affair, with an enormous and showy mock-marble western wall incorporating altar, pulpit and organ. This arrangement was dictated by political considerations: the pulpit is actually above the altar, to ram home the point that the priest's stern injunctions to work harder on behalf of the mine owners were an expression of God's will. The seating arrangements were rigidly and hierarchically defined, and determined the church's principal fixtures. Facing the pulpit are the King's Box and boxes for the silver-works' managers, while other officials sat in the glass enclosures. The pews on the ground floor were reserved for their womenfolk, while the sweeping balcony was divided into three tiers to accommodate the Kongsberg petits bourgeois, the workers and, squeezing in at the top and the back, the lumpen proletariat.

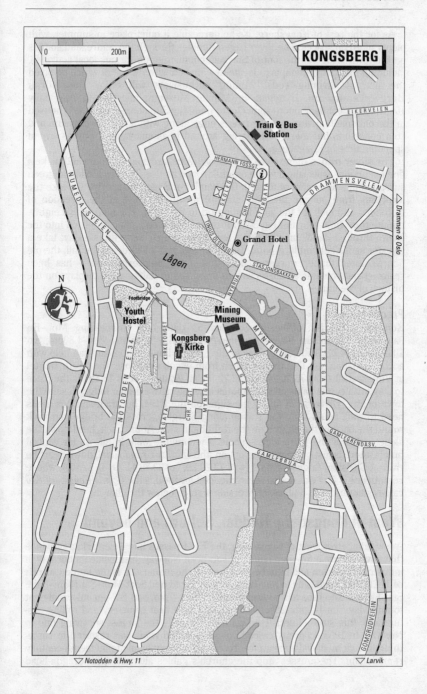

KONGSBERG

0   200m

Train & Bus
Station

EIKERVEIEN

HERMANN FOSSGT

SKOLEGT

CHR. AUG. GT

STORGATA

DRAMMENSVEIEN

▷ Drammen & Oslo

17. MAIG

TINIUS OLSENGT

Grand Hotel

Lågen

STASJONSBAKKEN

NYBRUA

N

Footbridge

Youth
Hostel

Mining
Museum

MYNTBRUA

GITREGATA

KIRKETORGET

Kongsberg
Kirke

NOTODDEN   E134

HYTTEGATA

KIRKEGATA

CHR. V. GT

MYNTGATA

GAMLEGRENDASV.

GAMLEBRUA

NUMEDALSVEIEN

GOMSRUDVEIEN

▽ Notodden & Hwy. 11   ▽ Larvik

As for the rest of Kongsberg, it's an agreeable if quiet place in summer, with plenty of green spaces. The River Lågen tumbles through the centre, and statues on the town bridge at the foot of Storgata commemorate various local activities, including foolhardy attempts to locate new finds of silver – one of which involved the use of divining rods. Mining enthusiasts will enjoy the **Norsk Bergverksmuseum**, Hyttegata 3 (Mining Museum; mid-May to Aug daily 10am–4pm; Sept daily noon–4pm; Oct to mid-May Sun noon–3pm; 30kr), housed in the old smelting works at the river's edge along with a tiny ski museum and coin collection, but merely wandering around is as enjoyable a way as any of spending time in Kongsberg.

The **silver mines** themselves, the Sølvgruvene, are open for tours and make a fine excursion, especially if you have children to amuse. They're hidden in green surroundings 8km west of town in the hamlet of **Saggrenda**; drive (or take the local bus from outside the train station) along the E134 in the direction of Notodden and look for the sign leading off to the right. The informative eighty-minute **tour** (mid-May to Aug; 50kr) includes a ride on a miniature train into the shafts through dark tunnels. There are three or four departures a day; take a sweater as it's cold underground. Back outside, just 350m down the hill, the old ochre-painted timber workers' compound – the **Sakkerhusene** – has been restored and contains a **café** as well as some rather half-hearted displays on the history of the mines.

Practicalities

Kongsberg **tourist office**, at Storgata 53 (late June to mid-Aug Mon–Fri 9am–7pm, Sat & Sun 10am–5pm; mid-Aug to May Mon–Fri 9am–4.30pm, Sat 10am–2pm; ☎32 73 50 00), is close to the train and bus station, and can help with accommodation, not that there's much from which to choose: the **youth hostel** at Vinjesgata 1 (☎32 73 20 24, fax 32 72 05 34; ①, dorm beds 180kr) is the place to stay, with comfortable en-suite rooms in an attractive timber lodge close to the town centre. Drivers can follow the signs on the E134, but train and bus users need to walk south from the station along Storgata, cross the bridge and walk round the back of the church on the right-hand side. At the back, head down the slope and over the footbridge – about a ten-minute walk in all. As for central hotels, there is just one appealing option, the *Quality Grand Hotel*, down near the river at Christian Augusts gate 2 (☎32 73 20 29, fax 32 73 41 29; ④, s/r ③), whose **restaurant** is first class. Also recommended for **food** is the *Gamle Kongsberg Kro* café-restaurant, with a pleasant riverside terrace below the church.

West of Kongsberg: Heddal, Seljord and beyond

A few kilometres west of Kongsberg, the E134 passes into Telemark, a province that covers a great forested chunk of southern Norway. Just inside its borders is industrial **Notoden** and 6km beyond, beside the main road, is the **stave church of HEDDAL** (mid-May to mid-June & mid-Aug to mid-Sept Mon–Sat 10am–5pm, Sun 1–5 pm; late June to mid-Aug Mon–Sat 9am–7pm, Sun 1–7 pm only; mid-Sept to mid-May Sun 1–5pm; 25kr). Surrounded by a neat cemetery and rolling pastureland, this stave church (see p.137) is actually the largest surviving one in Norway. In 1955 its pretty cascade of shingle-clad roofs was restored to something like its medieval appearance, rectifying a heavy-handed nineteenth-century remodelling. The crosses atop the church's gables alternate with dragon-head gargoyles, a characteristic mixture of Christian and pagan symbolism. Inside, the twenty masts of the nave are decorated at the top by masks, and there's some attractive seventeenth-century wall decoration in light blues, browns and whites. Pride of place, however, goes to the ancient **bishop's chair** in the chancel. Dating from around 1250, the chair carries a relief retelling the saga of Sigurd the Dragonslayer, a pagan story that Christians turned to their advantage by recasting the Viking as Jesus and the dragon as the Devil. Across from the church, there's a **café** and a modest **museum** illustrating further aspects of Heddal's history.

There's another fine church around 55km further west, just off the E134 in **SELJORD**, a small industrial town of ancient provenance that spreads out between the forested hills and the lake, Seljordsvatnet. Dating from the twelfth century, the church (open for guided tours Mon–Sat 10am–4pm, Sun 10am–1pm; 20kr) is built of stone and as such is something of a medieval rarity. The town also seems to have attracted more than its fair share of "Believe It or Not" stories: a monstrous serpent is supposed to lurk in the depths of the lake; elves are alleged to gather here for some of their soirées; and the 570kg stone outside the church was, so the story goes, only lifted once, by an eighteenth-century strongman by name of Nils Langedal. Mythical creatures aside, there's nothing much to detain you and you'll soon be ready to move on.

Beyond Seljord

The E134 forges on to the **Åmot crossroads**, 50km west of Seljord. From there, it's a further 30km west along the E134 to the handsome **Grungedal**, a valley that's home to several rustic farmsteads, one of which may soon reopen as the *Grungebru Youth Hostel* – keep your eyes peeled for this eventuality, as it's a convenient place to break your journey. The scenery bordering the E134 becomes wilder and more dramatic as the road slips across the southern edge of the Hardangervidda plateau before tunnelling through the mountains to meet – 120km west of Åmot – the coastal Highway 13. Branching off to the north, Highway 13 passes, 5km on, **Latefossen**, two huge waterfalls that empty into the river with a deafening roar. From here, it's a further 14km to **Odda** (see p.189); try to allow enough time to continue 30km north to the much more appealing hamlet of **Lofthus** (see p.189). Alternatively, if you ignore Highway 13 and keep on the E134, it's 115km from the Highway 13 crossroads to the coast at **Haugesund** (see p.178).

Off the E134 to Dalen and Rjukan

The Åmot crossroads is a possible starting point for two excursions off the E134, south to Dalen and north to Rjukan. If you're heading west from Kongsberg intent on visiting the latter two towns, consider taking Highway 37 which leads straight there (bypassing the Heddal stave church) and then pushes on to the E134 at Åmot.

Some 20km south of Åmot, on Highway 38, is pint-sized **DALEN**, whose main claim to fame is as the starting point for the passenger ferry that wends its way southeast along the **Telemarkskanal** to the coast at **Skien**, a journey that takes ten hours. No less than 105km long, the canal links the lakes and rivers of the district by means of eight locks that negotiate a difference in water levels of 72m. Completed in 1892, the canal was once an important trade route into the interior, but today it's mainly used by pleasure craft and two antique **passenger ferry-boats** which make the trip most days of the week from mid-May to early September. Ferries leave Dalen around 8am in the morning and the one-way fare is 290kr; contact *Telemarkreiser* (☎35 90 00 30, fax 35 90 00 21, *www.telemark-skanalen.com*) for further details and bookings. Dalen also possesses one of the region's more noteworthy country **hotels** in the comfortable *Hotel Dalen*, a sign-posted 1km from Dalen bridge (☎35 07 70 00, fax 35 07 70 11; ④; closed mid-Dec to mid-April). Built two years after the canal in a style influenced by stave church-es, its gables are festooned with dragon heads and gargoyles.

Rjukan and around

Back at Åmot but this time heading north, Highway 37 threads its way up into forested hills on the way to **Vemork** industrial works, 53km from Åmot, and then another 7km to **RJUKAN**, a hydroelectricity-generating town with a fine river valley setting against a backdrop of harsh, rough mountains. Despite this, Rjukan manages to be pretty humdrum, its 3000 inhabitants sharing a modest gridiron town centre originally assembled by the Norsk Hydro power company. The town is however a useful base for visiting Vemork's museum and the **Hardangervidda** (see p.190), the mountain plateau whose southeast corner is above and behind the town.

The prime attraction hereabouts is the **Norsk Industriarbeidermuseum** (Norwegian Industrial Workers' Museum; March & April Sat 11am–4pm; May to mid-June daily 10am–4pm; mid-June to mid-Aug daily 10am–6pm; mid-Aug to Sept Mon–Fri 10am–4pm, Sat & Sun 11am–6pm; 60kr), housed in the old hydroelec-tric station at Vemork. When it was opened in 1911, the power station had the greatest generating capacity in the world – its ten turbines had a combined out-put of 108 megawatts. It is a fine example of industrial architecture pretending to be something else: with its high gables and symmetrical windows it looks more like a country mansion. Inside, the museum explores the effects of industrializa-tion on what was then a profoundly rural country, has displays on hydroelectric power and the development of the trade unions, and features a gallery of propa-gandist paintings about workers and the class struggle by Arne Ekeland.

However, most foreigners come here because of the plant's role in World War II, when it was the Nazis' site for the manufacture of **heavy water** – necessary for regulating nuclear reactions and hence for a nuclear bomb. Aware of the plant's importance, the Americans bombed it on several occasions and the Norwegian resistance mounted a string of guerrilla attacks; as a result, the Nazis decided to move the heavy water they had made to Germany. The only way they could do this was by train, and part of the journey was across Lake Tinnsjø – ingeniously the ferry was fitted with a set of railway tracks. This set the scene for one of the most spectacular escapades of the war, when the Norwegian resistance sunk the whole lot on January 20, 1944. All the heavy water was lost, but so were the fourteen Norwegian passengers – a story recounted in the film *The Heroes of Telemark*, in which Kirk Douglas played the cinematic stereotype of the Norwegian: an earnest man with an honest face, wearing a big pullover. The museum has an excellent exhibition on these wartime escapades, including showing a film entitled *If Hitler had the Bomb*, and does **guided tours** which follow the saboteurs' route. The tours leave from the car park outside the museum (late June to July 3 weekly; 100kr; 2hr), and there are occasional guided trips on the old train ferry along lake Tinnsjø – contact the museum (☎35 09 51 53) for reservations and the schedule.

Long-distance **buses** to Rjukan from Notodden and Kongsberg pull in at the **station** down by the river. From here, cross the bridge and head northeast for about 400m for the **tourist office**, Torget 2 (June–Aug Mon–Fri 9am–7pm, Sat & Sun 10am–4pm; Sept–May Mon–Fri 9am–3.30pm; ☎35 09 12 90). Apart from the usual services, they can also supply useful bus timetables. Rjukan is also a starting point for long-range hikes across the Hardangervidda: a **cable car**, the Krossobanen, carries passengers up to the plateau from a station about 2km from the tourist office, at the west end of town.

For **accommodation**, the **youth hostel** at Birkelands gate 2 (☎35 09 05 27, fax 35 09 09 96; ①, dorm beds 110kr) is the obvious choice, housed in a spruce modern block a short walk across the bridge from the bus station. Another option is the modern *Rica Park Hotell*, at Sam Eydes gate 67 (☎35 09 02 88, fax 35 09 05 05; ③, s/r ②), a stone's throw north of the hostel; it's an efficient, medium-sized chain hotel with friendly staff and commodious rooms. It also has the best **restaurant** in town, serving traditional Norwegian dishes at moderate prices.

The south coast

Arcing out into the Skagerrak, Norway's **south coast** may have little of the imposing grandeur of other, wilder parts of the country, but the fretted coastline that extends from the Oslofjord to Kristiansand is undeniably lovely. Backed by forests and lakes, it's this part of the coast that attracts Norwegians in droves, equipped not so much with bucket and spade as with boat and navigational aids – these waters, with their islands, rocky islets and narrow inlets, make for particularly enjoyable **sailing**. Camping on the offshore islands is easy too, with a few restrictions: that you can't stay in one spot for more than 48 hours, or get close to anyone's home, or light a fire either on bare rock or among vegetation – leaflets detailing further coastal rules and regulations are available at any local tourist office.

If the boats and tents of the coast aren't your thing, the white-painted clapboard houses of tiny towns like **Lillesand**, **Arendal** and – to a lesser degree – **Grimstad** have an appropriately nautical and almost jaunty air. This portion of the coast is also important for Norway's international trade: it's just a short hop to Denmark from here, and several of the larger towns such as Sandefjord, Larvik and Porsgrunn have escaped their former roles as seventeenth-century timber ports to become industrial centres in their own right. Most of the manufacturing towns of the south coast are run-of-the-mill, except for the biggest of them, **Kristiansand**, a lively port and resort some 30km from Lillesand, with enough sights, restaurants, bars and beaches to while away a night, maybe two. Kristiansand is also within easy striking distance of two relics of World War II, the German fortifications on the islet of **Ny Hellesund**, and the Kristiansand **Kanonmuseum**, a former coastal battery. Beyond Kristiansand lies **Mandal**, an especially fetching holiday spot with a great beach, but further west the coast becomes harsher and less absorbing, heralding a sparsely inhabited region with precious little to detain you before Stavanger (see p.179).

There are regular **trains** from Oslo to Kristiansand and Stavanger, but the rail line runs just inland for most of its journey, only dipping down to the coast at the major resorts, which makes for a disappointing ride, the sea views shielded much of the time behind the bony, forested hills. The same applies to the main **road** and bus route – the **E18/E39** – which, though convenient and fast, also sticks stubbornly inland for most of the 300km from Oslo to Kristiansand (E18) and again for the 250km on to Stavanger (E39). Thanks to the E18/E39, only the tiniest of coastal **villages** is bothersome to get to – even if exploring the surrounding area can be awkward without your own vehicle. In the summertime, a further transport option is to take the **Hurtigbåt** from Oslo to Arendal. This zips along the coast, calling at several villages on its six-hour journey, and serves as a good introduction to the south coast – though it's expensive at 440kr per person.

All of the places in this section are easily accessed from the E18/E39 and offer boat trips along the neighbouring coastline. Note that the season is short – running from late June to August – and outside this period many museums are closed and the boat trips curtailed.

South from Oslo to Kragerø

Heading south from Oslo, the E18 skirts Horten and Tønsberg on the Oslofjord (see p.111) before edging round the industrial town of **SANDEFJORD**, from where ferries sail to Strömstad in Sweden. Sandefjord is also the nearest town to Oslo (**Torp**) **airport**, from where there are airport buses direct to Oslo, some 120km away (tickets are bought on the bus; 190kr one-way). There are also two buses daily from the airport to Sandefjord, a ten-minute ride. The town is at its prettiest along the waterfront: here a breezy area of parks and gardens culminates in the old municipal baths, a grandiose complex built in 1899 in the Viking-inspired dragon style. The baths closed at the beginning of World War II and have been turned into a civic centre. Of the town's several **hotels**, easily the most agreeable is the *Rica Park Hotel Sandefjord*, by the harbourfront at Strandpromenaden 9 (☎33 44 74 00, fax 33 44 75 00; ⑤, s/r ③).

Pressing on down the E18, it's 15km from Sandefjord to the turning for **Larvik**, where ferries depart for Frederikshavn in Denmark, and then another 30km to **Porsgrunn**, where there's a rare view of the sea as you cross the massive bridge spanning the fjord. Thereafter, it's an uneventful 20km along the E18 to the turning for Kragerø, a 13km jaunt along Highway 38 to the coast. Meanwhile, the Hurtigbåt has a happier journey; it scoots round rocky coves and myriad islands, calling at the good-looking coastal hamlet of **Stavern**, before pulling into **KRAGERØ**, whose narrow harbour is protected by a pair of bumpy little islets. One of the busiest resorts on the coast, Kragerø's tiny centre, with its cramped lanes and alleys rising steeply from the harbourfront, makes a good living as a supply depot for the surrounding coves and rocky islets, where the Norwegians have built themselves scores of summer cottages. Founded as a timber port in the seventeenth century, Kragerø later boomed as a shipbuilding centre, its past importance recalled by the antique gun battery on the harbour islet of **Gundersholmen**. To take a closer look at this relic of the Napoleonic Wars, walk across the causeway on the south side of town. The port was also a fashionable watering hole in the late nineteenth and early twentieth century. It was here that Edvard Munch produced some of his jollier paintings and where **Theodor Kittelsen** (1857–1914), a native of Kragerø, was a regular summer visitor too. A middling painter but superb illustrator, Kittelsen defined the popular appearance of the country's folkloric creatures – from trolls through to sirens – in his illustrations for Asbjørnsen and Moe's *Norwegian Folk Tales*, published in 1883. The family home is now a museum, the **Kittelsen huset**, Theodor

Kittelsens vei 5, in the town centre above the harbour (late June to Aug Mon–Fri 10am–6pm, Sat 10am–3pm, Sun 11am–3pm; 20kr), celebrating the artist's life and times with a smattering of his paintings and a few family knick-knacks. Also of note is Kragerø's **church**, an imposing brown-brick structure perched on a hill on the north side of the centre. Holidaymakers may shop and eat in Kragerø but few actually stay – and after an hour or two looking round you'll probably do likewise.

Kragerø is on the main Oslo–Kristiansand bus route and NSB railways lay on connecting buses (TogBuss) from the nearest **train station** at Neslandsvatn, a forty-minute journey. The **bus station** is next door to the **tourist office** (June–Aug Mon–Fri 10am–2pm; ☎35 98 23 88), at the northern tip of the harbour and within easy walking distance of all the main sights. The nearest recommendable place to stay is *Kragerø Youth Hostel*, at Lovisenbergveien 20 (☎35 98 33 33, fax 35 98 21 52; ①, dorm beds 195kr; mid-June to mid-Aug), 1700m out of town off Highway 38. The hostel occupies an expansive wooden building beside a pretty cove, rents out bikes and rowing boats, and serves tasty if simple evening **meals** (90kr) as well as breakfasts; buses travelling in to Kragerø on Highway 38 pass right by the hostel.

Arendal

The first place that really merits a stop on the E18 is **ARENDAL**, 260km from Oslo, and one of the most appealing places on the coast. Its sheltered harbour curls right into the town centre, which seems pushed up tight against the forested hills. The town's heyday was in the eighteenth century when its shipyards churned out dozens of the sleek wooden sailing ships that then dominated international trade. There's an attractive reminder of these boom times in the grand **Rådhus** (guided tours, July & Aug, Mon, Tues & Thurs 11am–3pm; 40kr), a four-storey, white timber building from 1812 that faces out over what was once the main city dock. The Rådhus was actually built as a private mansion for a wealthy family of merchants – as the formal rooms inside demonstrate – and there are more elegant old buildings immediately behind it in the oldest part of town, known as **Tyholmen**. You can wander these few blocks and then stroll along the boardwalk flanking the **Pollen**, the short rectangular inner harbour that's bordered by cafés. For the architectural lowdown on the Tyholmen, call in at the tourist office (see p.146) and sign up for one of their city **walking tours** (late June to early Aug Mon, Tues & Thurs at 4pm; 1hr 30min; 40kr). Also available at the tourist office are details of all sorts of **boat trips** which leave the Pollen to explore the surrounding coastline; among the less expensive options are the regular ferries to the offshore islets of **Hisøy** and **Tromøy**, or to tiny **Merdø** (one-way fare 20kr to each islet). At Merdø, you can take a peek at the period interior of the old-fashioned **Merdøgaard Museum** (late June to mid-Aug guided tours only, daily noon–4pm on the hour; 30kr), an eighteenth-century sea captain's house, and have a swim in the Skagerrak. The sheltered channels round Arendal are ideal for boating; **canoes** can be hired at the town train station, where you can also get advice on routes.

Practicalities

From Arendal **train station**, it's a five- to ten-minute walk west to the main square, Torvet – either through the smoky tunnel or up and over the steep hill along Bendiksklev, the latter a distinctly healthier route. Torvet is about 150m north of the inner harbour, Pollen. **Buses** stop in the larger square, west of Pollen across from the huge red-brick church with the copper-green steeple. The Hurtigbåt express passenger ferry (late June to mid-Aug 3 weekly) from Oslo arrives at 3.35pm except on Fridays, when it gets here at 10pm. The journey takes almost seven hours and costs 440kr. The return trip leaves at 4pm, reaching Oslo at 11pm.

Arendal **tourist office** (June to mid-Aug Mon–Sat 9am–7pm, Sun noon–7pm; mid-Aug to May Mon–Fri 8.30am–4pm; ☎37 00 55 44) is at the **bus station**. Easily the nicest **place to stay** is the luxurious *Tyholmen Hotell*, Teaterplassen 2 (☎37 02 68 00, fax 37 02 68 01; ⑤, s/r ④), which occupies a handsome wooden building in the style of an old warehouse on the Tyholmen quayside. The more modest *Scandic Hotel Phönix Arendal*, Friergangen 1 (☎37 02 51 60, fax 37 02 67 07; ⑤, s/r ③), is a straightforward modern hotel just off the west side of Pollen. For **food**, there are a couple of inexpensive cafés on the Torvet and a string of more tempting places along and around Pollen, including *Madam Reiersen*, which offers delicious seafood and fresh pasta dishes from its harbourside premises at Nedre Tyholmsvei 3. Later on, the café-bars lining the Pollen are lively **drinking** haunts till the early hours, especially on a warm summer's night.

Grimstad

From Arendal, it's a short 20km hop south on the E18 to **GRIMSTAD**, where a brisk huddle of white houses with orange-tiled roofs is stacked up behind the harbour. Nowadays scores of yachts are moored in the harbour, but at the beginning of the nineteenth century the town had no fewer than forty shipyards and carried on a lucrative import-export trade with France. It was not particularly surprising, therefore, that when **Henrik Ibsen** left his home in nearby Skien in 1844, aged sixteen, he should come to Grimstad, where he worked as an apprentice pharmacist for the next six years. The ill-judged financial dealings of Ibsen's father had impoverished the family, and Henrik's already jaundiced view of Norway's provincial bourgeoisie was confirmed here in the port, whose worthies Ibsen mocked in poems like *Resignation*, and *The Corpse's Ball*. It was here too that Ibsen picked up first-hand news of the Paris Revolution of 1848, an event that radicalized him and inspired his paean to the insurrectionists of Budapest, *To Hungary*, written in 1849. Nonetheless, Ibsen's stay on the south coast is more usually recalled as providing the setting for some of his better-known plays (see box, opposite), particularly *Pillars of Society*. The pharmacy where Ibsen lived and worked, just up from the harbour in the centre of town on Henrik Ibsens gate, has been turned into the compact **Ibsenhuset og Grimstad bymuseum** (the Ibsen House and Grimstad Town Museum; guided tours: May to mid-Sept Mon–Sat 11am–5pm, Sun 1–5pm; mid-Sept to April Mon–Fri 10am–3pm; 30kr). With its creaking wooden floors and narrow-beamed ceilings, the nineteenth-century appearance of the premises has been maintained. There are various items of Ibsen memorabilia – look out for the glass case displaying the playwright's hat, coat, umbrella and boots as worn on his daily stroll down to Oslo's Grand Café. Also here, courtesy of his son, is the dining-room furniture from Ibsen's apartment in Oslo.

From the museum, it's a couple of minutes' walk south to the pedestrianized part of Storgata, the main drag. Signposted off it as you near the harbourfront is

IBSEN

Henrik Johan Ibsen (1828–1906), Norway's most famous and influential playwright, is generally regarded as one of the greatest dramatists of all time, and certainly his central themes have powerful modern resonances. In essence these concern the alienation of the individual from the ethical bankruptcy of society, loss of religious faith and the yearning of women to transcend the confines of their roles as wives and mothers. Ibsen's central characters often speak evasively, mirroring the repression of their society and their own sense of confusion and guilt. Venomous exchanges – a major characteristic of the playwright's dialogue – start to occur as the underlying tensions break through. Ibsen's protagonists do things which are less than heroic, often incompetent, even malicious. Nevertheless, they aspire to *dåd*, the act of the hero/heroine, arguably a throwback to the old Norse sagas.

These themes run right through Ibsen's plays, the first of which, *Catalina* (1850), was written while he was employed as an apothecary's assistant at Grimstad. The alienation the plays reveal was undoubtedly spawned by his troubled childhood: Ibsen's father had gone bankrupt in 1836, and the disgrace weighed heavily on the whole family. More humiliation followed at Grimstad, where the young and shy Ibsen worked for a pittance and was obliged to share a bed with his boss and two maids; in 1846 one of the women had Ibsen's child.

Ibsen escaped provincial Norway in 1850, settling first in Oslo and then Bergen. But he remained deeply dissatisfied with Norwegian society, which he repeatedly decried as petty, illiberal and small-minded. In 1864, he left the country and spent the next 27 years living in Germany and Italy. It was during his exile that Ibsen established his literary reputation – at first with the rhyming couplets of *Peer Gynt*, featuring the antics of the eponymous hero, a shambolic opportunist in the mould of Don Quixote, and then by a vicious attack on small-town values in *Pillars of Society*. It was, however, *A Doll's House* (1879) which really put him on the map, its controversial protagonist, Nora, making unwise financial decisions before walking out not only on her patronizing husband, Torvald, but also on her loving children – in her desire to control her own destiny. *Ghosts* followed two years later, and its exploration of moral contamination through the metaphor of syphilis created an even greater furore which Ibsen rebutted in his next work, *An Enemy of the People* (1882). Afterwards, Ibsen changed tack (if not theme), firstly with *The Wild Duck* (1884), a mournful tale of the effects of compulsive truth-telling, and then *Hedda Gabler* (1890), where the heroine is denied the ability to make or influence decisions in her adult world, and so becomes perverse, manipulative and ultimately self-destructive.

Ibsen returned to Oslo in 1891. He was treated as a hero, and ironically – considering the length of his exile and his comments on his compatriots – as a symbol of Norwegian virtuosity. Indeed, the daily stroll he took from his apartment to the *Grand Café* in Karl Johans gate became something of a tourist attraction. He was incapacitated by a heart attack in 1901 and died from the effects of another five years later.

---

the **Reimanngården**, an uninspiring collection of four replica eighteenth-century buildings, one of which is a reconstruction of the first pharmacy where Ibsen worked – the original building was demolished in the 1950s – and now home to the town's art society. In the opposite direction from the Ibsen house, it's a short, steep hike north up to **Grimstad Kirke**, a large late nineteenth-century wooden church plonked on a hill above the harbour. Inside, many of the original fittings have survived, including some heavy-duty wrought-iron lamps and candelabras, and there's a tapestry, by the font, of the Resurrection.

Grimstad's **bus station** is at the south end of the harbour, a couple of hundred metres along from the **tourist office** (June–Aug Mon–Fri 10am–6pm, Sat & Sun 11am–5pm; Sept–May Mon–Fri 8.30am–4pm; ☎37 04 40 41), which has the details of the two-hour **boat cruises** that meander round the offshore rocky islets every day throughout the summer. They also issue local maps and directions for the most popular **walk** hereabouts – the seven-kilometre jaunt along the old west road which the E18 bypassed. The hike begins at Landvik Manor, a short drive north of Grimstad, from where the footpath threads its way west to meet the E18 at Kaldvell fjord. Taken at an easy pace, the hike lasts about six hours for the round trip. Grimstad has an attractive and central **hotel**, the *Grimstad Hotell*, Kirkegaten 3 (☎37 25 25 25, fax 37 25 25 35; ④), in an old, cleverly converted clapboard complex amongst the narrow lanes near the Ibsen house; the hotel has the best **restaurant** in town too. Wine buffs can seek out the fruit wines produced by Fuhr, a local firm – with Fuhr Rhubarb and Fuhr Vermouth representing two daunting challenges for the palate.

Lillesand

Bright, cheerful **LILLESAND**, just 20km south of Grimstad, is one of the most popular holiday spots on the coast, the white clapboard houses of its tiny centre draped prettily round the harbourfront. One or two of the buildings, notably the sturdy 1734 **Rådhus**, are especially good-looking, but it's the general appearance of the place which appeals, best appreciated from the terrace of one of the town's waterfront café-restaurants: the *Sjøbua*, midway round the harbour, does nicely.

To investigate Lillesand's architectural nooks and crannies, sign up for one of the hour-long **guided walks** (mid-June to Aug daily at 3pm; 30kr) which leave from the tourist office (see below). They also have information on local **boat trips**, including details of fishing excursions and the timetable of the *badebåten* (bathing boat; July only 4 daily; 15min; 25kr), which shuttles over to a bay on the island of **Skaurøya**, where swimmers don't seem to notice how cold the Skagerrak actually is. South from Lillesand, a narrow channel, the Blindleia, wiggles its way in between the rocky islets and the mainland, and this is the route followed by the *M/S Oya*, a dinky little passenger ferry, as it makes the three-hour summertime cruise to **Kristiansand** (see opposite) (late June to mid-Aug Mon–Sat at 10am; 80kr each way; ☎94 58 33 97). There are other, faster, more prosaic (and slightly more expensive) boats which do the trip too – again, further details from the tourist office.

Lillesand cannot be reached by train, but there are regular **bus** connections up and down the coastal E18, which passes by the edge of town. The bus stops near the south end of the harbour, and the **tourist office**, located in the old waterfront customs house (June–Aug Mon–Fri 10am–6pm, Sat & Sun 11am–5pm; ☎37 27 23 77), is a two-minute walk north along the harbour from the bus stop. Lillesand has one central **hotel**, the first-rate *Hotel Norge*, Strandgaten 3 (☎37 27 01 44, fax 37 27 30 70; ④, s/r ②), which occupies a grand old wooden building near the bus stop. Refurbished in attractive period style, the interior holds some charming stained-glass windows and rooms named after some of the famous people who have stayed here – the novelist Knut Hamsun and the Spanish king Alfonso XIII for starters. Otherwise, the **youth hostel** (☎ & fax 37 27 50 40; ①, dorm beds 100kr; mid-June to mid-Aug) is also located in a dignified timber building, and even has its own garden, but it's an inconvenient 1500m out of town beside

Highway 402. For **food**, the *Hotel Norge* has an excellent restaurant, but it's more expensive and formal than the harbourfront *Sjøbua* (☎37 27 03 66), which serves up excellent fish dishes for around 150kr in a cheesy interior, kitted out like an old sailing ship.

Kristiansand

Norway's fifth largest town, **KRISTIANSAND** is something of a holiday resort, a genial, energetic place which thrives on its ferry connections with Denmark, its busy marinas and passable sandy beaches. In summer, the seafront and adjoining streets are a frenetic bustle of cocktail bars, fast-food joints and flirting holiday-makers, and even in winter Norwegians come here intent on living it up.

Like so many other Scandinavian towns, it was founded by and named after Christian IV, who saw an opportunity to strengthen his coastal defences here. Building started in 1641, and the town has retained the spacious four-quadrant plan that characterized all Christian's projects. There are few specific sights, but it's worth a quick look around – especially when everyone else has gone to the beach and left the central pedestrianized streets relatively empty.

Arrival and information

Trains, **buses** and Color Line **ferries** all arrive close to each other, by Vestre Strandgate, on the edge of the town grid. The main regional **tourist office** is here

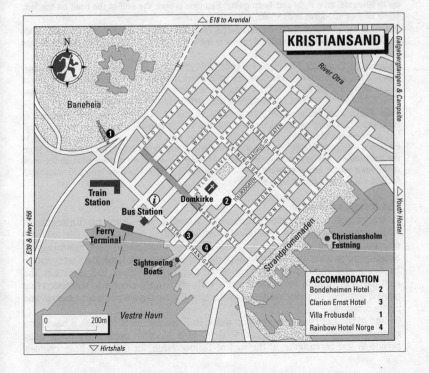

also, at Vestre Strandgate 32 (June–Aug Mon–Fri 8am–8pm, Sat 10am–8pm, Sun noon–8pm; Sept–May Mon–Fri 8.30am–3.30pm; ☎38 12 13 14). As well as providing a handy town map and information on boat sailing times, island bathing and beaches, the office carries a wide range of leaflets on the whole of the south coast. Parking is easy throughout town, with car parks concentrated along Vestre Strandgate. The best way to explore the town centre is on foot – it only takes about ten minutes to walk from one side to the other; there's no bike rental.

Accommodation

Kristiansand has a reasonably good choice of **accommodation** with a fair sprinkling of hotels, a guesthouse or two, a youth hostel and a campsite in or reasonably near the centre.

Bondeheimen, Kirkegata 15 (☎38 02 44 40, fax 38 02 73 21). Located right in the middle of town, near the Domkirke, this hotel offers modern and comfortable if uninspiring rooms in a converted nineteenth-century town house. ③.

Clarion Ernst, Rådhusgaten 2 (☎38 12 86 00, fax 38 02 03 07). Housed in a flashily modernized building, this hotel has large doubles with standard-issue modern furnishings and fittings. The air conditioning can be stuffy, so try to get a room where you can open a window and which doesn't face the interior courtyard. ④, s/r ③.

Kristiansand Vandrerhjem, Skansen 8 (☎38 02 83 10, fax 38 02 75 05). This youth hostel is pricey for what you get – cramped rooms in ugly, prefabricated 1960s boxes in the middle of an industrial estate; there's a kitchen and cafeteria, however. The hostel is about fifteen minutes' walk east of the ferry terminal on the tiny peninsula edging the marina. Take any street up to Elvegata, turn right and keep going: Skansen is near the end of the road on the left. Open all year. ①, dorm beds 160kr.

Rainbow Hotel Norge, Dronningens gate 5 (☎38 02 00 00, fax 38 02 35 30). Pleasant modern hotel with attractively furnished rooms in lively colours. A good downtown choice. ④, s/r ③.

Roligheden Camping, Framnesveien (☎38 09 67 22). Large and fairly formal campsite 3km east of the town centre behind a dusty gravel car park, which edges the yachters' jetty. To get there, drive over the bridge at the end of Dronningens gate, turn right along Marvikveien, then right again at the end, and the site is signposted. Open June to mid-Sept.

Villa Frobusdal, Frobusdalen 2 (☎38 07 05 15, fax 38 07 01 15), near the west end of Kirkegata. This delightful hotel, undoubtedly the best in town, is a family-run affair occupying a shipowner's mansion of 1917. The interior has been sensitively restored and is crammed with period antiques. The only problem is location: it's only five minutes' walk from the train station, but tucked away down a hard-to-find side-street off the ring road on the edge of the town centre. Drivers should head north along three-lane Festningsgata and, at the traffic lights at the end, follow the sign to Evje. ②.

The town and around

Aside from the **Domkirke** (June–Aug Mon–Sat 9am–2pm) on Kirkegata at Rådhusgaten – a modern mock-Gothic edifice seating nearly 2000 – the only significant attraction in town is the squat fortress, **Christiansholm Festning**, on Strandpromenaden (mid-May to Sept daily 9am–9pm; free), whose sturdy circular tower and zigzagging earth-and-stone ramparts overlook the marina in the east harbour. Built in 1672, the tower's walls are five metres thick, a defence that proved unnecessary since it never saw action. These days it plays host to arts and crafts displays.

One of the better moves you can make in Kristiansand is to catch a boat for a **cruise** through the offshore rocky islets. *M/S Maarten* departs from the quay beside Vestre Strandgate, at the foot of Tollbodgaten, for daily two-hour cruises, stopping at several islands which have been designated as public (and free) recreation and camping areas. This means, of course, that you can always stay overnight and catch the boat back the next day – but check first with the tourist office (see p.149) as to the local coastal camping regulations. The boat operates once daily from mid-June to mid-August, and trips cost around 100kr. If you just want a swim without the bother of a boat trip, head for **Galgebergtangen** (Gallows' Point), a pretty, rocky cove with a small sandy beach on the edge of a residential area, 2km east of the town centre; to get there, go over the bridge at the end of Dronningens gate, take the first major right (at the lights) and follow the signs.

Another possibility is the *M/S Maarten's* excursion (late June to early Aug 4 weekly; 3hr 30min; 150kr) to **Ny Hellesund**, the islet site of one of the four hundred coastal defences built by the Germans during the occupation. From the very beginning of World War II, the German admiralty had been trying to persuade Hitler to occupy Norway, largely to avoid their ships being trapped in the Baltic by the British fleet. It seems, however, that Hitler only took the matter seriously after Vidkun Quisling's (see p.326) visit to Berlin in late 1939, when Hitler was no doubt encouraged by the Norwegian's virulent anti-Semitism. Hitler subsequently overestimated both the likelihood of an Allied counter-invasion in the north and Norway's strategic importance, garrisoning the country with nigh on half a million men and building a string of huge coastal artillery batteries.

The cruise to Ny Hellesund makes for an enjoyable trip, but there are much more substantial military remains at the **Kristiansand Kanonmuseum** (May to mid-June Thurs–Sun 11am–6pm; mid-June to Aug daily 11am–6pm; 30min guided tours; 50kr), situated an easy 10km drive south along the coast at **Møvik**: take Highway 456 out of Kristiansand, turning down Highway 457 for the last 3km of the journey. Work began on this coastal artillery battery in 1941, using – like all Nazi sea defences in Norway – the forced labour of POWs. Around 1400 men worked on the project, which involved the construction of protective housings for four big guns at the narrowest part of the Skagerrak. Guns on the Danish shore complemented those here, so that any enemy warship trying to slip through the straits could be shelled. Only a small zone in the middle was out of range, and this the Germans mined. The Møvik complex once covered 220 acres, but today the principal remains hog a narrow ridge, with a massive, empty artillery casement at one end, and a whopping 38cm-calibre **gun** in a concrete well at the other. The gun, which could fire a 500kg shell almost 55km, is in pristine condition, and guided tours include a visit to the loading area, complete with the original ramrods, wedges, trolleys and pulleys. Below, and at the start of the tour, is the underground command post and soldiers' living quarters, again almost exactly as they were in the 1940s – including the odd bit of German graffiti.

Eating and drinking

There are lots of **restaurants** and **cafés** in the centre, but the standard is very variable – we've given a few of the choicer places below. There's also a fairly active nightlife based around several **bars** which stay open until 2am.

FRK Larsen, Markensgate 5. Near the corner of Kongensgate, this laid-back café-bar is an appealing, fashionable place. Also serves meals – salted cod (*bacalao*) for instance is a very reasonable 175kr.

Kick Café Zanzibar, Dronningens gate 8. Arty bar with a terrace at the back, groovy music, and coffee and hot chocolate as well as reasonably cheap beer. Light meals too.

Lille-Dampen, Henrik Wergelandsgate 15 (Mon–Fri 8am–4.30pm). First-rate and inexpensive bakery, where the takeaway baguettes are delicious.

Royal China, Tollbodgaten 7 (☎38 07 02 77). Surprisingly plush Chinese restaurant offering tasty main courses from as little as 90kr.

Sjøhuset, Østre Strandgate 12a (☎38 02 62 60). In an old converted warehouse by the harbour at the east end of Markensgate, this excellent restaurant serves superb fish courses for 170–190kr. Nautical fittings and wooden beams set the scene. Open daily in summer; closed Sun rest of the year.

Moving on from Kristiansand

The obvious route is to push on west to Stavanger (see p.179) by train, or by bus or car along the E39. Both the E39 and the train afford glimpses of the coast, but for the most part they travel through the interior. Some 210km long, it's not a gripping journey, but it's certainly a lot more pleasant than the 240km haul north up **Setesdal** on Highway 9 to join the E134 (for more on which see p.138). Note also that there are summertime cruises northeast along the coast from Kristiansand to Lillesand (late June to mid-Aug, Mon–Sat at 10am; 80kr each way; reservations & information on ☎94 58 33 97 – see p.148).

Mandal and further west

MANDAL, just 40km from Kristiansand along the E39, is Norway's southernmost town. This old timber port reached its heyday in the eighteenth century, when pines and oaks from the surrounding countryside were much sought after by the Dutch to support their canal houses and build their trading fleet. Although it's now bordered by a modern mess, Mandal has preserved its quaint old centre, a narrow strip of white clapboard buildings spread along the north bank of the Mandalselva river just before it enters the sea. It's an attractive spot, well worth a few minutes' walk. You can also drop by the municipal **museum** (July to mid-Aug Mon–Fri 11am–5pm, Sat 11am–2pm, Sun 2–5pm; 20kr), whose rambling collection – from agricultural implements to seafaring tackle – occupies an old merchant's house overlooking the river. Its exhibits also include a small but enjoyable collection of nautical paintings, and outside by the front door is a statue of the town's most famous son, Gustav Vigeland (see p.93). It's not its antiquities that make Mandal a popular tourist spot, however, but its fine beach, **Sjøsanden**. An 800-metre stretch of golden sand backed by pine trees and framed by rocky headlands, it's touted as Norway's best beach – and although this isn't saying a lot, it's a perfectly enjoyable place to unwind for a few hours. The beach is 1500m from the town centre: walk along the harbour, past the tourist office to the end of the road and turn left; keep going until you reach the car park at the beach's eastern end.

If you have your own vehicle, you should also consider an excursion to the windy headland of **Lindesnes** (literally "where the land curves round"), 40km away to the southwest – take the E18 and turn down Highway 460. This is Norway's most southerly point, a bare, lichen-stained promontory topped by a sturdy red-and-white lighthouse that's exposed to extraordinarily ferocious storms when the warm westerly currents of the Skagerrak meet cold easterly winds.

Practicalities

Mandal hasn't got a train station, but there's a fast and frequent **bus** service there from Kristiansand (Mon–Sat hourly, Sun 6 services; 45min; 60kr). Mandal's ugly modern **bus station** is by the bridge on the north bank of the river; from here it's a brief walk west to the old town centre, just beyond which is the **tourist office**, facing the river at Adolf Tidemandsgate 2 (Mon–Fri 9am–4pm; ☎38 27 83 00). There are a couple of good places to **stay**, beginning with the handy and eco-nomical *Kjøbmandsgaarden Hotell*, Store Elvegaten 57 (☎38 26 12 76, fax 38 26 33 02; ②), which occupies a renovated old timber house in a street of such buildings, across from the bus station. They have six rooms with shared bathrooms and six en-suite rooms (costing an extra 260kr). All rooms are spick-and-span and the decor is bright and cheerful. Moving upmarket, the appealing *First Hotel Solborg*, Neseveien 1 (☎38 26 66 66, fax 38 26 48 22; ⑤, s/r ③), is an odd-looking but some-how rather fetching modern structure with every mod con; it's on the west side of the town centre, a good ten-minute walk from the bus station, tight against a wooded escarpment. Alternatively, you can camp or rent a cabin (②) at the Sjøsanden Feriesenter, Sjøsandvei 1 (☎38 26 14 19), a signposted 2km from the town and very close to the western end of the beach.

The *First Hotel Solborg* has the best **restaurant** in town, but for something less pricey and more informal, head into the centre where you'll find several places, including the lively pizzeria-restaurant, *Jonas B Gundersen*. The café-restaurant of the *Kjøbmandsgaarden* comes highly recommended too, offering a tasty range of Norwegian dishes at inexpensive prices.

From Mandal, there are daily **express buses** along the E39 to Flekkefjord (see below) and Stavanger (see p.179), respectively 90km and 210km away to the west. **Train** travellers have to return to Kristiansand (see p.149) to rejoin the rail network.

West of Mandal

Heading west from Mandal on the E39, you'll pass, after 28km, the turning to Lindesnes lighthouse (see opposite) and thereafter the road weaves near but rarely comes in sight of the coast, on its tortuous route to **FLEKKEFJORD**. This humdrum port, which has traditionally depended on its tanneries and lumber, straddles a narrow inlet. The tiny town centre, on the west side of the bridge, com-prises a handful of old timber buildings and has a **tourist office** (mid-June to mid-Aug Mon–Fri 10am–6pm, Sat 10am–4pm, Sun noon–6pm; mid-Aug to mid-June Mon–Fri 9am–3pm; ☎38 32 43 00). There's precious little to detain you, but for a snack head for the harbourside *Selska Pslokaler* café-bar, where the homemade soup (55kr) is a good deal tastier than the pizzas.

At Flekkefjord, the E39 turns inland for the last 125km into Stavanger, but instead you can drive along the more southerly Highway 44 which offers occa-sional glimpses of the sea, especially where it wiggles across the narrow **Jøssingfjord**. It was here that 300 Allied POWs were liberated from the German ship *Altmar* by the Royal Navy destroyer *Cossack* during World War II. This rare British success prompted those opposed to the Germans – the vast majority of the population – to call themselves "Jøssings" for the rest of the war.

After 70km, Highway 44 edges into **EGERSUND**, a desultory port from where it's just 10km back onto E39. Egersund also has a **train station**, where the rail line finally returns to the coast after crossing the interior – an uninspiring journey since the rail line runs (and tunnels) east to west, while the region's valleys run north to south. For the last 80km from Egersund to Stavanger, the E39 stays deep inland, but the train has a final coastal flourish, shuttling across long flat plains with the sea on one side and distant hills away to the east – an enjoyable trip until you hit the industrial estates on the peripheries of Stavanger (see p.179).

travel details

Trains

Dombås to: Oslo (3–4 daily; 4hr 20min).

Geilo to: Oslo (4–5 daily; 3hr 20min).

Hamar to: Oslo (7 daily; 1hr 40min).

Hjerkinn to: Oslo (3 daily; 4hr 45min).

Kongsberg to: Kristiansand (4–5 daily; 3hr 30min); Oslo (5–6 daily; 1hr 30min).

Kristiansand to: Kongsberg (4–5 daily; 3hr 30min); Oslo (4–5 daily; 5hr); Stavanger (3–4 daily; 3hr).

Lillehammer to: Dombås (5 daily; 2hr); Oslo (7 daily; 2hr 30min); Trondheim (4 daily; 4hr 30min).

Oslo to: Kongsvoll (3 daily; 4hr 50min) and Sjoa (2 daily; 4hr 30min) by request only.

Otta to: Oslo (4–5 daily; 4hr 10min).

Røros to: Hamar (1–3 daily; 3hr 50min); Oslo (1–3 daily; 6hr); Trondheim (1–2 daily; 2hr 30min).

Skien to: Larvik (2–7 daily; 45min); Oslo (2–7 daily; 3hr); Sandefjord (2–7 daily; 1hr); Tønsberg (2–7 daily; 1hr 25min).

Stavanger to: Oslo (3 daily; 9hr).

Åndalsnes to: Oslo (2–3 daily; 6hr 30min).

Buses

Arendal to: Lillesand (2–3 daily; 1hr); Oslo (2–3 daily; 4hr 15min).

Grimstad to: Lillesand (2–3 daily; 20min); Oslo (2–3 daily; 4hr 40min).

Fagernes to: Oslo (3 daily; 3hr 20min)

Kongsberg to: Drammen (4 daily; 40min); Haugesund (1 daily; 8hr 30min); Kristiansand (1 daily; 8hr 25min); Oslo (4 daily; 2hr); Rjukan (2 daily; 2hr).

Kristiansand to: Flekkefjord (2 daily; 2hr 20min); Haukeligrend (1–2 daily; 4hr 10min); Mandal

(Mon–Sat hourly, Sun 6 services; 45min); Oslo (2–3 daily; 5hr 45min); Seljord (1–2 daily; 6hr 30min); Stavanger (1 daily except Sun; 4hr 30min); Åmot (1–2 daily; 5hr).

Lillehammer to: Bergen (1 daily; 10hr 25min); Dombås (1–2 daily; 3hr); Fagernes (1 daily; 2hr 15min); Lom (2 daily; 3hr 15min); Oslo (every 1–2 hr; 3 hr); Otta (2 daily; 2hr 20min); Stryn (2 daily; 5hr 30min).

Lillesand to: Arendal (2–3 daily; 1hr); Kristiansand (2–3 daily; 35min); Grimstad (2–3 daily, 20min); Oslo (2–3 daily; 5hr).

Mandal to: Kristiansand (Mon–Sat hourly, 6 on Sun; 45min); Stavanger (1–2 daily; 4hr).

Oppdal to: Kristiansand (1–3 daily; 3hr 30min).

Otta to: Gjendesheim (late June to Aug Mon–Sat 1 daily; 2hr); Lom (3 daily; 1hr); Oslo (2 daily; 5hr).

Rjukan to: Kongsberg (2 daily; 2hr); Oslo (2 daily; 3hr 50min).

Røros to: Trondheim (1–3 daily; 3hr 10min).

Hurtigbåt

Arendal to: Oslo (late June to mid-Aug 4 weekly; 7hr)

Kragerø to: Oslo (late June to mid-Aug 3 weekly; 4hr 30min)

Stavern to: Oslo (late June to mid-Aug 4 weekly; 3hr).

International ferries

Kristianstad to: Hirtshals (5–6 weekly; 4hr 30min).

Larvik to Fredrikshavn (5–6 weekly; 6hr 15min).

Sandefjord to: Strömstad (2 daily; 2hr 30min).

CHAPTER THREE

BERGEN AND THE WESTERN FJORDS

I f there's one familiar and enticing image of Norway it's the **fjords**: huge clefts in the landscape that run from the sea deep into the interior of the country, right up to the Russian border, but which are most easily, and impressively, seen on the west coast near Bergen. Wild, rugged and serene, these huge wedge-shaped inlets are visually stunning; indeed, the entire fjord region elicits inordinate amounts of purple prose from tourist office handouts – for once rarely overstating their case. The fjords are undeniably beautiful, especially around early May, after the brief Norwegian spring has brought colour to the landscape.

In summer, the rolling mountains are roamed by walkers and the fjords cruised by steady flotillas of white ferries, interrupting the peace that prevails for the other nine months of the year. If this smacks of a package-holiday nightmare, don't be put off: even in the most popular regions, it's possible to find many spots not yet penetrated by the coach parties, and what little development there has been is rarely intrusive.

Bergen, Norway's second-largest city, is the self-proclaimed "Capital of the Fjords". It's a welcoming place with an atmospheric old warehouse quarter, a relic of the days when it was the northernmost port of the Hanseatic trade alliance. As

---

GETTING AROUND THE FJORDS

Norway's western fjords are a highly confusing region to tour by **public transport**. This is not down to poor services – bus and ferry connections are excellent – but to the innate difficulty of getting around such a maze of land and water. **Trains** serve only Bergen in the south, the village of Flåm (near the Sognefjord), and Åndalsnes in the north; for everything in between – the Nordfjord, Jostedalsbreen glacier and Sognefjord – you're limited to **buses** and **ferries**, and although they virtually all connect up with each other, it means that there is no set way to navigate the region.

We've covered the fjords region from **south to north** – from Bergen to Åndalsnes via Stavanger, Hardangerfjord, Sognefjord, Nordfjord, Geirangerfjord and Romsdalsfjord. There are certain obvious connections – from Bergen to Flåm, and from Åndalsnes over the Trollstigen to Geiranger, for example – but routes are really a matter of personal choice, and the text details the alternatives. It's a good idea to pick up full bus and ferry **timetables** from the local tourist offices whenever you can. The shorter bus routes are often part of a chain of linked buses and ferries, so you shouldn't get stranded anywhere.

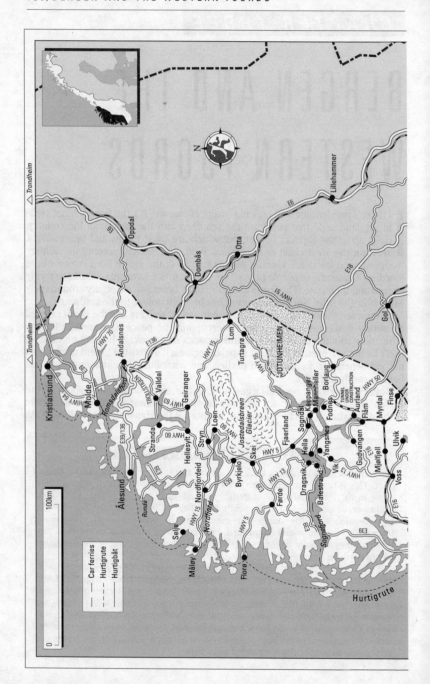

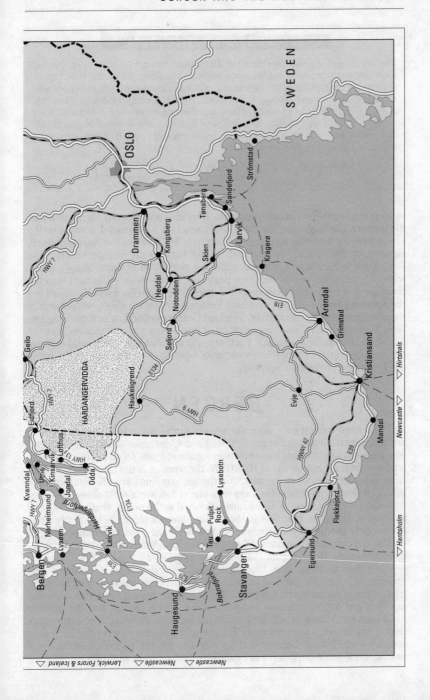

ACCOMMODATION PRICE CODES

The hotels and guesthouses detailed throughout this guide have been graded according to the price categories listed below. Prices given are for the least expensive double room during the high season, although almost every hotel offers seasonal and/or weekend discounts, which can reduce the rate by one or even two grades. Wherever hotels have an official summer rate we've given it (denoted s/r), but bear in mind that many others will provide impromptu summer and weekend discounts. Single rooms, where available, usually cost between 60 and 80 percent of a double. For a more detailed discussion of accommodation see p.37.

| ① under 500kr | ③ 700–900kr | ⑤ 1200–1500kr |
| ② 500–700kr | ④ 900–1200kr | ⑥ over 1500kr |

its aforementioned tourist pitch suggests, Bergen is also a handy springboard for the western fjords. Among the most easily reached is **Flåmsdal**, a valley to the east, where an inspiring mountain railway trundles down to the **Aurlandsfjord**, an arm of the mighty **Sognefjord**. Lined with pretty village resorts, the Sognefjord is the longest, deepest and most celebrated of the country's waterways; it is certainly one of the most beguiling, rather more so, in fact, than the **Nordfjord**, lying parallel to the north. Between the Sognefjord and Nordfjord lies the **Jostedalsbreen** glacier, mainland Europe's largest ice sheet, while north of the Nordfjord there's the narrow, S-shaped **Geirangerfjord**, which contains perhaps the most spectacular concentration of impressive scenery, though here the tourist hordes can be off-putting. Further north still, towards the **Romsdalsfjord**, the landscape becomes more extreme, at its most lonely and isolated in the splendid **Trollstigen** mountain highway.

BERGEN

As it has been raining ever since she arrived in the city, a tourist stops a young boy and asks if it always rains here. "I don't know," he replies, "I'm only thirteen." The joke isn't brilliant, but it does contain a grain of truth. Of all the things to contend with in the western city of **BERGEN**, the weather is the most predictable: it rains relentlessly even in summer, and the surroundings are often shrouded in mist. But despite its dampness, Bergen is one of Norway's most enjoyable cities. Its setting – surrounded by seven hills, sheltered to the north, south and west by a series of straggling islands – is spectacular. There's plenty to see in town too, from sturdy **medieval buildings** to a whole series of good **museums**, and just outside the city limits are Edvard Grieg's home, **Troldhaugen**, and the charming open-air **Gamle Bergen** (Old Bergen) museum.

More than anything else, though, it's the general flavour of the place that appeals. Although Bergen has become a major port and something of an industrial centre in recent years, it remains a laid-back, easy-going town with a nautical air. Fish and fishing continue to underpin the local economy, and the bustling main harbour, **Vågen**, is still very much the focus of attention. If you stay more than a day or two – perhaps using Bergen as a base for viewing the local fjord scenery – you'll soon discover that the city also has the region's best choice of **restaurants**, some impressive **art galleries**, and a decent **nightlife**.

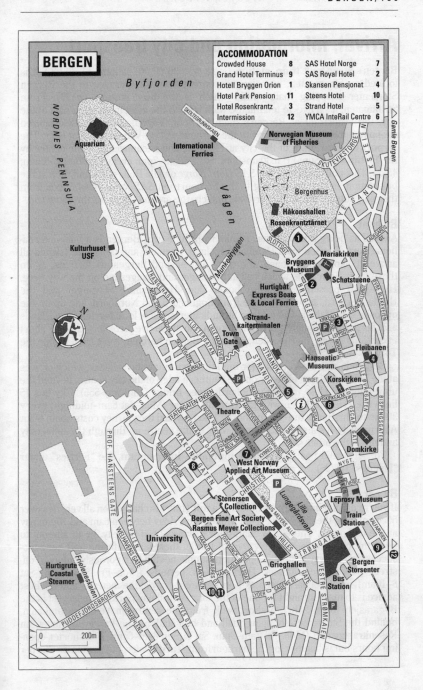

BERGEN

Byfjorden

NORDNES PENINSULA

ACCOMMODATION

Crowded House	8	SAS Hotel Norge	7
Grand Hotel Terminus	9	SAS Royal Hotel	2
Hotell Bryggen Orion	1	Skansen Pensjonat	4
Hotel Park Pension	11	Steens Hotel	10
Hotel Rosenkrantz	3	Strand Hotel	5
Intermission	12	YMCA InteRail Centre	6

△ Gamle Bergen

Aquarium

International Ferries

Norwegian Museum of Fisheries

Bergenhus

Håkonshallen

Rosenkrantztårnet

Kulturhuset USF

Vågen

Munkebryggen

Mariakirken

Bryggens Museum

Schøtstuene

Hurtigbåt Express Boats & Local Ferries

Strand-kaiterminalen

Town Gate

Hanseatic Museum

TORGET

Fløibanen

Korskirken

Theatre

West Norway Applied Art Museum

Domkirke

Stenersen Collection

Bergen Fine Art Society

Rasmus Meyer Collections

Lille Lungegårdsvann

Leprosy Museum

University

Train Station

Hurtigrute Coastal Steamer

Grieghallen

Bergen Storsenter

Bus Station

0   200m

Arrival, information and city transport

Bergen's stone-built **train station** (local ☎55 96 69 00, national 81 50 08 88) is located on Strømgaten, just along the street from the entrance to the Bergen Storsenter shopping mall, within which is the **bus station** (☎177). From Strømgaten, it's a five- to ten-minute walk west to the most interesting part of the city, the waterfront at Bergen's main harbour, **Vågen**, via the pedestrianized shopping street Marken; a taxi to the harbour will set you back about 60kr. The **airport** is 20km south of the city at Flesland, and is connected to the centre by the **Flybussen** (Sun–Fri 5.30am–9pm, Sat 5.30am–7pm; every 20–30min; 40min; 45kr). This pulls in beside the *SAS Hotel Norge* on Ole Bulls plass and then at the bus station, before proceeding to the harbourfront *SAS Royal Hotel*. Taxis from the rank outside the airport arrivals hall charge around 250kr for the same trip.

By boat

As well as being a hub for ferry links with the fjords, Bergen is a busy international port. **Ferries** from Denmark, Iceland, Shetland and the Faroe Islands all arrive at Skoltegrunnskaien, the quay just beyond Bergenhus fortress, as do those from Newcastle, which call at Stavanger and Haugesund on the way here. **Hurtigbåt** passenger express boats from Haugesund, Stavanger and the Hardangerfjord, as well as those from Sognefjord and Nordfjord, line up on the opposite side of the harbour at the Strandkaiterminalen; local **ferries** from islands and fjords immediately north of Bergen mostly arrive here too, though short excursions round the Byforden, adjoining Bergen harbour, leave from beside the Torget.

Bergen is also a port of call for the **Hurtigrute** coastal steamer, which arrives at the Frieleneskaien harbour on the southern edge of the city centre, beyond the university and close to the Puddefjordsbroen bridge (Highway 555). City bus #5 links the Frieleneskaien with the central Torget (Mon–Sat 6am–midnight every 30min to 1hr, Sun 10am–10pm hourly; 17kr); by taxi the journey costs about 60kr. Alternatively, it's a steep 25-minute walk to the centre up through the university and down the other side.

For ferry and boat **ticket and timetable information**, see "Ferries" under "Listings" (p.226).

By car

If you're driving into Bergen, note that a **toll** (10kr) is charged on all vehicles over 50cc entering the city centre from Monday to Friday between 6am and 10pm; pay at the tollbooths. There's no charge for driving out of the city. In an attempt to keep the city centre relatively free of traffic, there's a confusing and none-too-successful one-way system in operation, supplemented by rigorously enforced on-street parking restrictions. During peak periods (Mon–Fri 8am–6pm, Sat 8–10am), on-street parking costs 12kr per hour – pay at the meters – and the best advice is to make straight for one of the four central **car parks**. The largest is the Bygarasjen (open 24hr), a short walk from the centre on Vestre Strømkaien, behind the Storsenter shopping mall and bus station. The Parkeringshuset, on Rosenkrantzgaten (Mon–Fri 7am–9pm, Sat & Sun 8am–6pm), has shorter opening hours but is handier for the harbourfront. **Tariffs** vary, but reckon on 7kr per half-hour up to a maximum of 100kr. Outside of peak periods, on-street parking is relatively easy and free.

Information

The **tourist office** is at Vågsallmenningen 1 (May & Sept daily 9am–8pm; June–Aug daily 8.30am–10pm; Oct–April Mon–Sat 9am–4pm; ☎55 32 14 80; *www.bergen-travel.com*), across the busy road from Torget, at the east end of the main harbour, the Vågen. They give away copies of the *Bergen Guide*, an exhaustive guide to the city, and numerous other free brochures. Here you can also book rooms in private houses, reserve places on guided tours, buy tickets for fjord sightseeing boats, and change foreign currency. In high season, expect long queues. Bergen has two free, bi-monthly **newssheets** containing local news, entertainment listings and reviews – the Bergen edition of the Oslo-based *Natt & Dag* and Bergen's own *Filter*. Naturally enough, both are in Norwegian, but the former has an easy-to-use listings section. Both are widely available across the city centre.

City transport

All of Bergen's main attractions are located in the compact city centre, which is best explored on foot. For outlying attractions and accommodation, however, you'll need to take a city bus. Bergen and its surroundings are served by a dense network of local buses whose hub is the bus station, in the Storsenter shopping mall on Strømgaten (☎177). Flat-fare tickets, available from the driver, cost 17kr and are valid for an hour; if your journey involves more than one bus, ask the driver for a free transfer. Another useful link is the tiny orange ferry (Mon–Fri 7am–4.15pm; 10kr) across Vågen, between Munkebryggen, along Carl Sundts gate, and a point near the *SAS Royal Hotel* on the Bryggen.

Guided tours and sightseeing

The tourist office offers a plethora of **local tours**: bus tours of the city, a mini-train ride around the city environs and fjord sightseeing trips are just a few examples of what's on offer. They're all detailed in the *Bergen Guide*, which gives prices and departure times, so you can make a considered choice. However, it's much cheaper to arrange your own visits than go on an organized tour; details as to how to get around on your own are given throughout this chapter. A couple of tours to be recommended, though, are the guided tours of **Bryggen** (see p.164) and the much-vaunted **Norway in a Nutshell** tour to Flåm (see p.197).

THE BERGEN CARD

The **Bergen Card** is a 24-hour (130kr) or 48-hour (200kr) pass which provides free use of all the city's buses and free or substantially discounted admission to most of the city's sights, and on many sightseeing trips; it comes with a booklet listing all the various concessions. Obviously, the more diligent a sightseer you are, the better value the card becomes, doubly so if you're staying a bus ride from the centre. The card is sold at a wide range of outlets, including the tourist office, major hotels and the train station.

Accommodation

Budget **accommodation** is no great problem in Bergen. There are three hostels, a choice of private rooms and guesthouses, and some of the central hotels are surprisingly good value. Among the better deals here are the **rooms** in private houses that you can book through the tourist office. The vast majority of them provide self-catering facilities and some are fairly central (though most are in the suburbs). Prices are at a fixed nightly rate – at time of writing, 295kr for a double room without en-suite facilities (185kr single), 345kr en suite. There are some apartments too (430kr). Private rooms are very popular, and in summer you'll need to arrive at the tourist office early to secure one for the night.

Camping is also an option, and there are several campsites on the outskirts of the city, but you'll be far from the action at any of them. Most campsites have four-bunk timber **cabins**, and cabin bookings for the whole region are handled by Fjordhytter, in the city centre at Lille Markeveien 13 (☎55 23 20 80).

Hotels

Bryggen Orion, Bradbenken 3 (☎55 31 80 80, fax 55 32 94 14). Deservedly popular mid-range hotel with unassuming but perfectly comfortable modern rooms. Has a handy location, a stone's throw from the Bergenhus fort, and breakfasts are magnificent banquets – with every type of pickled herring. Hard to beat. ④, s/r ③.

Grand Hotel Terminus, Zander Kaaes gate (☎55 31 16 55, fax 55 31 85 76). There was a time when the tweed-jacketed visitors of prewar England headed straight for the *Grand* as soon as they arrived in Bergen – and not just because the hotel is next door to the train station. Those days are long gone, but the hotel has reinvented itself, making the most of its quasi-baronial flourishes, notably its extensive wood panelling, chandeliers and stained glass. Breakfasts are superb and the bedrooms attractive and quiet. ④, s/r ③.

Hotel Park Pension, Harald Hårfagres gate 35 (☎55 54 44 00, fax 55 54 44 44). This excellent, family-run hotel occupies two handsome late nineteenth-century townhouses on the edge of the town centre near the university. The charming interior is painted in soft pastel colours and the public areas are dotted with antiques. The bedrooms are smart, neat and appealing. It's a very popular place, so advance reservations are advised. ③, s/r ②.

Rosenkrantz, Rosenkrantzgaten 7 (☎55 31 50 00, fax 55 31 14 76). Efficient and extremely competent mid-range hotel in an old building just behind the Bryggen. Has everything you'll need and the rooms are tidy and trim – try not to notice the horrid aluminium windows they've stuck in the attractive facade. ④, s/r ③.

SAS Hotel Norge, Ole Bulls plass 4 (☎55 57 30 00, fax 55 57 30 01). Bergen's most central top-class hotel, right in the thick of things and with a full range of facilities from bar to heated swimming pool. ⑥, s/r ⑤.

Steens, Parkveien 22 (☎55 31 40 50, fax 55 32 61 22). One of an attractive terrace of high-gabled townhouses, overlooking a mini-lake on the edge of the town centre near the university, this well-established hotel offers inexpensive lodgings. The interior has lots of late Victorian flourishes, but the overall effect is a tad gloomy. ③, s/r ②.

Strand, Strandkaien 2 (☎55 31 08 15, fax 55 31 00 17). Straightforward but pleasant, modern hotel overlooking the Torget. ④, s/r ③.

Guesthouses

Crowded House, Håkonsgaten 27 (☎55 23 13 10, fax 55 23 13 30). Traditionally, Bergen's guesthouses have been a little dowdy, but this lively, appealing place is the opposite – from the cactuses in the pastel-painted foyer to the bright and airy, if spartan, bedrooms. There are self-catering facilities and breakfast is served for an extra 50kr. Located halfway along traffic-clogged Håkonsgaten, about five minutes' walk from the city centre. ①.

Skansen Pensjonat, Vetrlidsallmenningen 29 (☎55 31 90 80, fax 55 31 15 27). This simple little guesthouse occupies a nineteenth-century stone house of elegant proportions just above – and up the steps from – the terminus of the Fløibanen funicular railway, near Torget. It's a great location, in one of the most beguiling parts of town. The guesthouse has eight perfectly adequate if simple rooms, one of which is en suite. A bargain. ②.

Hostels and campsites

Bergen YMCA InterRail Centre, Nedre Korskirkealmenning 4 (☎55 31 72 52). Close to Torget, a five- to ten-minute walk from the train station. It has 175 dormitory beds but fills quickly. Facilities include showers, kitchen, sauna and laundry, and there's a supermarket nearby. Open mid-June to Aug. ①, dorm beds 100kr including breakfast.

Intermission, Kalfarveien 8 (☎55 31 32 75). Christian-run private hostel close to the train station. Open mid-June to mid-Aug. ①, dorm beds 100kr.

Lone Camping (☎55 39 29 60; fax 55 39 29 79). Bergen's main campsite, 20km east from the centre on Highway 580, is really only practical for those with their own transport. It has a pleasant lakeside location, cabins for rent and a café. Open all year. ①.

Montana Vandrerhjem, Johan Blyttsveien 30, Landås (☎55 20 80 70, fax 55 20 80 75). This large and comfortable hostel occupies lodge-like premises in the hills overlooking the city. Great views and great breakfasts, as well as self-catering facilities. There is dorm accommodation as well as family rooms and doubles, the pick of which are en suite and in a newly added wing. The hostel is 6km east of the centre – 15min on bus #4 (stop Montana) from Nygaten. Popular with school parties, who are housed in a separate wing. ①, dorm beds 170kr.

The City

Founded in 1070 by King Olav Kyrre ("the Peaceful"), **Bergen** was the largest and most important town in medieval Norway and a regular residence of the country's kings and queens. In the fourteenth century Bergen also became a Hanseatic League port, linked to Baltic and other European cities by a vigorous trading life. The prosperity of Bergen made it a religious centre: at the height of its influence the city supported thirty churches and monasteries. However, the League was controlled by German merchants and, after Hansa and local interests started to diverge, the Germans eventually came to dominate the region's economy, reducing the locals to a state of dependency. Neither could the people of Bergen expect help from their kings and queens. Indeed it was the reverse: in return for easily collected taxes from the Hansa merchants, Norway's medieval monarchs compelled west-coast fishermen to sell their catch to the merchants – and at prices the merchants themselves set. As a result, the German trading station that flourished on the Bryggen, Bergen's main wharf, became wealthy and hated in equal measure, a self-regulating trading station with its own laws and an administration that was profoundly indifferent to local sentiment. In the 1550s, with Hansa power evaporating, a local lord – one Kristoffer Valkendorf – finally reasserted Norwegian control, but not out of the goodness of his heart. Valkendorf and his cronies simply took over the monopolies that had enriched their German predecessors, and continued to operate this iniquitous system, which so pauperized the region's fishermen, right up to the nineteenth century.

Very little of medieval Bergen has survived, although parts of the fortress, the **Bergenhus** – which commands the entrance to the harbour – date from the thirteenth century. The rest of the city centre divides into several distinct parts, the most interesting being the wharf area, the **Bryggen**, which accommodates an attractive ensemble of eighteenth- and nineteenth-century merchants' trading houses. The Bryggen ends at the head of the central harbour, **Vågen**, where the **Torget** is home to an open-air fish market. East of here, stretching up towards the train station, is one of the older districts, a mainly nineteenth-century quarter that's at its prettiest along **Lille Øvregaten** and around the narrow lanes that clamber up the adjacent hillside. The main thoroughfare of this quarter, **Kong Oscars gate**, has been roughly treated by the developers, but it does lead to the city's most endearing museum, the **Lepramuseet** (Leprosy Museum). A stone's throw from here, the modern concrete blocks surrounding the central **lake**, Lille Lungegårdsvann, form the cultural focus of the city, containing Bergen's art galleries and main concert hall, while the chief commercial area is a few metres to the west along pedestrianized **Torgalmenningen**. The steep hill to the south of the central lake is crowned by the **university**.

Most of the main sights and museums are concentrated in these areas, but no tour of the city is complete without a stroll out along the **Nordnes peninsula**, where fine timber houses pepper the bumpy terrain and the old USF sardine factory now contains a first-rate arts complex and café.

Torget

Lilian Leland, a nineteenth-century woman traveller and author of *Traveling Alone: A Woman's Journey Around the World,* writing about Bergen in 1890, complained that "Everything is fishy. You eat fish and drink fish and smell fish and breathe fish." Those days are long gone, but now that Bergen is every inch a go-ahead, modern city, tourists in search of things piscine flock to **Torget**, where there is an open-air **fish market** (Mon–Sat 7am–3pm). It's not a patch on the days when scores of fishing vessels moored up against the quayside to empty their bulging holds, but the stalls still display huge mounds of prawns and crab-claws, buckets of herring and a hundred other varieties of marine life on slabs, in tanks and under the knife. Fruit, vegetables and flowers have a place in today's market too, and there's enough variety of produce here for you to be able to pick up the fixings for a picnic lunch. Hang around for a while to assess the comings and goings of the local boats and ferries, and take a peek at the **statue** of Leif Andreas Larsen, nicknamed "Shetland Larsen" for his brave escapades of World War II; for more on the man, see p.242.

Just 200m east of the Torget is the station for the quaint **Fløibanen** funicular railway (May–Aug Mon–Fri 7.30am–midnight, Sat 8am–midnight, Sun 9am–midnight; Sept–April Mon–Fri 7.30am–11pm, Sat 8am–11pm, Sun 9am–11pm; every 30min; return fare 34kr) to the summit of **Mount Fløyen** ("The Vane"). When the weather's fine you get a bird's-eye view of Bergen and its surroundings from the top, 320m above sea level, where there's also a café-restaurant and some colour-coded footpaths heading off through the woods. But the obvious historical and cultural target from Torget is **Bryggen**, a street on the north side of the harbour where the city's old warehouse quarter is to be found.

Bryggen

The site of the original settlement at Bergen, **BRYGGEN** is the city's best-preserved quarter, containing, among other things, the distinctive wooden, gabled trading posts that front the wharf. The area was once known as

Tyskebryggen, or "German Quay", after the Hanseatic merchants who operated their trading station here, but the name was unceremoniously dropped at the end of World War II. Hansa influence dated back to the thirteenth century, and derived from trading grain and beer for fish shipped here from northern Norway. Only later did the Germans come to dominate local affairs, much to the consternation of local landowners. By the middle of the sixteenth century, however, the Hanseatic League was in decline; the last German merchant hung on till 1764 but by then economic power had long since passed to Norwegians.

The medieval buildings of the Bryggen were destroyed by fire in 1702, to be replaced by another set of wooden warehouses. In turn, many of these were later replaced by high-gabled stone warehouses in a style modelled on that of the Hansa period, but a small section of **timber buildings** has survived and now houses shops, restaurants and bars. It's well worth nosing around here, wandering down the passageways in between wherever you can. Interestingly, these eighteenth-century buildings carefully follow the original building line: the governing body of the Hansa trading station stipulated the exact depth and width of each merchant's building, and the width of the passage separating them – a regularity that's actually best observed from Øvregaten (see below). The planning regulations didn't end there: trade had to be carried out in the front section of the building, with storage rooms at the back; above were the merchant's office, bedroom and dining room. Up above those, on the top floor, were the living quarters of the employees, grouped into rooms by rank – junior merchants, journeymen/clerks and foremen, wharf hands and last (and least) errand-boys. Every activity in this rigidly hierarchical, all-male society was tightly controlled – employees were forbidden to fraternize with the locals and stiff fines were imposed for hundreds of "offences" including swearing, waking up the master and singing at work.

At the near end of the Bryggen, just off Torget, the **Hanseatisk Museum** (Hanseatic Museum; June–Aug daily 9am–5pm; Sept–May daily 11am–2pm; 35kr) is the best preserved of the early eighteenth-century merchants' dwellings, kitted out in late Hansa style. Among the assorted bric-a-brac are the possessions and documents of contemporary families, including several fine pieces of furniture, but more than anything else it's the gloomy warren-like layout of the place that impresses, as well as the all-pervading smell of fish which has been absorbed by the wood.

Walking up towards the terminus of the funicular railway (see opposite), you come to **Øvregaten**, which has marked the boundary of the Bryggen for the last 800 years. The Hanseatic warehouses once stretched back from the quayside to this street but no further and, as you stroll northwest along Øvregaten, the old layout of the trading station is still easy to discern – a warren of tiny passages separating warped and crooked buildings. On the upper levels, the eighteenth-century loading bays, staircases and higgledy-piggledy living quarters are still much in evidence, while the overhanging eaves of the passageways were designed to shelter trade goods. Towards the end of the street, at Øvregaten 50, is the **Schøtstuene** (May & Sept daily 11am–2pm; June–Aug daily 9am–5pm; Oct–April Sun 11am–2pm; 35kr), the old Hanseatic assembly rooms, where the merchants would meet to lay down the law or just relax – it was the only building in the trading post whose occupants were allowed to have heating, as the wooden structures were a very real fire hazard. As you explore the comfortable rooms, it's hard not to conclude that the merchants cared not a jot for their employees shivering away nearby.

GUIDED TOURS OF THE BRYGGEN

The English-language **guided tours** of the Bryggen are warmly recommended. They start from the Bryggens Museum daily between June and August at 11am and 1pm, and take roughly an hour and a half. Tickets (60kr) are on sale at the museum, and after the tour you can reuse them to get back into the Bryggens and Hanseatic museums and the Schøtstuene for a longer exploration – but only on the same day.

Just round the corner, the perky twin towers of the **Mariakirken** (St Mary's Church; late May to mid-Sept Mon–Fri 11am–4pm; mid-Sept to late May Tues–Fri noon–1.30pm; 10kr, free in winter) are the most distinguished features of what is Bergen's oldest extant building, a Romanesque-Gothic church dating from the twelfth century. It's still used as a place of worship and was, from 1408 to 1706, the church of the Hanseatic League merchants, who bought it and subsequently installed a fine and ostentatious Baroque pulpit and altar, both of which are well worth close examination. In front of the church, the well-conceived **Bryggens Museum** (May–Aug daily 10am–5pm; Sept–April Mon–Fri 11am–3pm, Sat noon–3pm, Sun noon–4pm; 20kr) features all manner of things dug up in archeological excavations that started on the Bryggen in 1955. A wide range of artefacts – domestic implements, handicrafts, maritime objects and trade goods – forms the basis for a series of lively exhibitions attempting a complete reconstruction of local medieval life. The whole caboodle is put into context by a set of twelfth-century foundations, left *in situ* where they were excavated and now forming the museum's centrepiece.

Bergenhus

Just to the west of the Bryggens Museum lies the **Bergenhus**, a large and roughly star-shaped fortification now used mostly as a park (daily 7am–11pm). Its stone-and-earth walls date from the nineteenth century but enclose the remnants of earlier strongholds. Of the two surviving structures from medieval times (combined guided tour on the hour every hour; mid-May to Aug daily 10am–4pm; Sept to mid-May Sun noon–3pm; 15kr), one is the **Håkonshallen**, a pedestrian reconstruction of the Gothic ceremonial hall built for King Håkon in the mid-thirteenth century and now standing at the back of a cobbled courtyard, flanked by nineteenth-century officers' quarters. Across the courtyard is the rather more diverting **Rosenkrantztårnet**, a tower whose thirteenth-century spiral staircases, medieval rooms and low rough corridors were enlarged in 1565 by the lord of Bergenhus, Erik Rosenkrantz, who used the place as a fortified residence. Both buildings were wrecked by the explosion of a German ammunition ship in 1944, and the newness of the rebuilding shows.

Beyond the Bergenhus, perched on the water's edge, is the **Norges Fiskerimuseum** (Norwegian Museum of Fisheries; June–Aug Mon–Fri 10am–6pm, Sat & Sun noon–4pm; Sept–May Mon–Fri 10am–4pm, Sat & Sun noon–4pm; 20kr), which tells you all you could ever want to know about Norway's fishing industry and then some. There are displays on whaling and sealing, line fishing and trawling, and even on fish farming. It's very popular with school groups.

Strolling back from the Bergenhus along the Bryggen **waterfront**, you'll pass the assorted restaurants, bars and souvenir shops that lure the tourist herds with plastic trolls and the like. Frankly this is not a very appealing prospect, but it only takes a few minutes to regain the relative sanity of the Torget.

Along Lille Øvregaten and Kong Oscars gate

Running east from the Fløibanen terminal (see p.164) is **Lille Øvregaten**, lined with an appealing ensemble of old timber houses, all bright-white clapboard planking and little windows. There's more of the same up the hill in the angle between the Fløibanen terminal and Lille Øvregaten, though if anything these houses are even quainter, pressing in against steep cobbled lanes which steer around occasional hunks of stone that were just too bothersome to move. Meanwhile, Lille Øvregaten curves round to the **Domkirken** (Cathedral; mid-May to Aug Mon–Sat 10am–4pm, Sun 10am–1pm; Sept to mid-May Tues–Fri 11am–2pm, Sat 11am–3pm, Sun 10am–1pm; free), a doughty edifice whose stern exterior has been restored and rebuilt several times since its original construction in the thirteenth century. Neither does the interior set the pulse racing, but the mostly medieval choir has some attractive blind arcading, and there's a noticeable penchant for fancy wooden staircases – two leading to the organ and one to the pulpit – which seems a little flippant given the dour surroundings.

Beyond the cathedral, turn right along Kong Oscars gate and it's a couple of hundred metres to the **Korskirken** (New Church; mid-June to mid-Aug Mon–Fri 10am–2pm; free) in Nedre Korskirkealmenningen. The Korskirken is another austere structure, only partly enlivened by some handsome dogtooth decoration around the archways and by a slender spire. More promising by far is the fascinating **Lepramuseet**, just up from the Domkirke at Kong Oscars gate 59 (Leprosy Museum; late May to Aug daily 11am–3pm; 20kr). Its endearingly anti-quated collection is housed in the eighteenth-century buildings of **St Jørgens Hospital**, ranged around a pretty cobbled courtyard, and tells the tale of the Norwegian fight against leprosy. First appearing in Scandinavia in Viking times, the disease became especially prevalent in the coastal districts of western Norway, with around three percent of the population classified as lepers in the early nineteenth century. The hospital specialized in the care of lepers and assumed a more proactive role from 1830, when a series of Norwegian medics tried to find a cure for the disease. The most successful of them was Armauer Hansen, who in 1873 was the first person to identify the leprosy bacillus. In 1946 the last lepers left the hospital and the building has been left untouched, the small rooms off the central gallery revealing the patients' cramped living quarters. Also on display are medical implements (including cupping glasses for drawing blood) and a few gruesome sketches and paintings of sufferers. Dating from 1702, the adjoining hospital **chapel** is delightful, its rickety, creaking timbers containing a lovely folksy pulpit and altarpiece decorated with cherubs and dainty scrollwork. The two altar paintings are crude but appropriate – *The Ten Lepers* and *Canaanite's Daughter Healed*.

Lille Lungegårdsvann: Bergen's art galleries

Bergen's central lake, **Lille Lungegårdsvann**, is a focus for summertime festivals and events, and its southern side is flanked by the city's four principal art galleries. The most diverting and easternmost of the quartet is the **Bergen Kunstmuseum – Rasmus Meyers Samlinger**, Rasmus Meyers Allé 3 (Bergen

Art Museum – the Rasmus Meyer Collections; mid-May to mid-Sept daily 11am–5pm; mid-Sept to mid-May Tues–Sun 11am–5pm; 35kr, same ticket allows admission to the Kunstforening & Stenersens Samling [see below]), housed in a large building with a pagoda-like roof. Gifted to the city by one of its old merchant families, the collection contains an extensive collection of Norwegian painting from early landscape painters like Dahl and Fearnley (see p.80) through Christian Krohg to later figures such as Alex Revold and Henrik Sørensen. There's a particularly good sample of the work of Erik Werenskiold (1855–1938) and Theodor Kittelsen (1857–1914), who are best known for their illustrations of the folk stories collected by Asbjørnsen and Moe in rural Norway (see p.332). Although the stories had already been through many editions since they were first published in the 1840s, Werenskiold and Kittelsen's illustrations defined the appearance of the various folkloric figures in the popular imagination. It is, however, for its large sample of the work of **Edvard Munch** that the museum is usually visited – if you missed out in Oslo (see p.91), this is the place to make amends. There are examples from all of Munch's major periods, with the disturbing – and disturbed – works of the 1890s stealing the spotlight from the calmer paintings that followed his recovery from the nervous breakdown of 1908. Apart from the paintings, there's also a substantial collection of his woodcuts and lithographs.

Behind the museum is the **Grieghallen** concert hall, a distinctive glass and concrete building that's the main venue for the annual Bergen Festival (see p.174). Just along from the concert hall, the **Bergens Kunstforening** (Bergen Fine Art Society; same times & ticket as the Art Museum) is noted for its temporary exhibitions of contemporary art, whilst the adjacent **Bergen Kunstmuseum – Stenersens Samling** (Bergen Art Museum – the Stenersen Collection; same times & ticket) features the modern art collection of Rolf Stenersen. Something of a Renaissance man, Stenersen (1899–1978) – one-time athlete, financier and chum of Munch – seems to have had a successful stab at almost everything; he even wrote some highly acclaimed short stories in the 1930s. In 1936 he donated his first art collection to his hometown of Oslo (see p.78), and 35 years later he was in a similar giving mood, the beneficiary being his adopted town of Bergen. The collection is especially strong on one of Stenersen's favourites, the Bauhaus painter Paul Klee, and there's a smattering of work by more familiar artists too, featuring the likes of Toulouse-Lautrec, Picasso, Miró, Ernst and Léger. Among the Norwegians, there are several Munch paintings and a selection of watercolours and oils by the versatile Jakob Weidemann (b. 1923), whose work was much influenced by French cubists during the 1940s, though he is now associated with the shimmering, pastel-painted abstracts he churned out in the 1960s.

The westernmost gallery of the four, the **Vestlandske Kunstindustrimuseum** (West Norway Applied Art Museum; mid-May to mid-Sept Tues–Sun 11am–4pm; mid-Sept to mid-May Tues, Wed, Fri & Sat noon–3pm, Thurs noon–6pm, Sun noon–4pm; 30kr), occupies the Permanenten building, a whopping neo-Gothic structure at the corner of Christies gate and Nordahl Bruns gate. A lively exhibition programme with the focus on contemporary craft and design brings in the crowds, and some of the displays are very good indeed – which is more than can be said for the permanent collection and its Chinese marble statues. Fans of Ole Bull (see p.171) will, however, be keen to gawp at one of the great man's violins, made in 1562 by the Italian Salò.

Torgalmenningen and the Nordnes peninsula

The broad sweep of pedestrianized **Torgalmenningen** is a suitable setting for the commercial heart of modern Bergen, lined with shops and department stores and decorated by a vigorous large-scale sculpture celebrating figures from the city's history. Around the corner, **Ole Bulls plass**, also pedestrianized, sports a rock pool and fountain, above which stands a rather jaunty statue of local boy Ole Bull, the nineteenth-century virtuoso violinist and heart-throb – his island villa just outside Bergen is a popular day trip (see p.171). Ole Bulls plass stretches up to the municipal **theatre**, Den Nationale Scene, at the top of the hill, worth the short walk for a look at the fearsome, saucer-eyed statue of Henrik Ibsen that stands in front. Near here too, just down the hill, at the east end of Strandgaten, is the imposing bulk of an old **town gate**, built in 1628 to control access to the city but soon used by the authorities to increase their revenues by the imposition of a toll.

Beyond the theatre, the hilly **Nordnes peninsula** juts out into the fjord, its western tip accommodating the large **Akvariet** (Aquarium; May–Sept daily 9am–8pm, 75kr; Oct–April daily 10am–6pm, 55kr; bus #4) and a pleasant park. It takes about fifteen minutes to walk there from Ole Bulls plass – along Klostergaten/Haugeveien – but the effort is much better spent in choosing a different, more southerly route along the peninsula. This takes you past the charming timber villas of Skottegaten and Nedre Strangehagen before it cuts through the bluff leading to the old, waterside United Sardines Factory, imaginatively converted into an arts complex, the **Kulturhuset USF**, often called Verftet; this incorporates a groovy café-bar, *Kafe Kippers* (see p.173).

Out from the centre

The lochs, fjords and rocky wooded hills surrounding central Bergen have channelled the city's **suburbs** into long ribbons which trail off in every direction. These urban outskirts are not in themselves appealing, though they are extraordinarily handsome when viewed from the highest of the seven hills around town, the 642-metre **Mount Ulriken**. It's reached by the **Ulriksbanen cable car** (June–Aug daily 9am–9pm; Sept–May daily 10am–sunset; 60kr return), whose terminal is behind the Haukeland Sykehus (hospital) and near the *Montana* youth hostel, about 6km east of the Bryggen; there are walks and a café at the hill-top. From mid-May to mid-September, a shuttle bus (daily 9.15am–8.45pm; every 30 min) departs for the Ulriksbanen from outside the tourist office; bus and cable car cost 90kr return. The rest of the year, take city bus #2, #4, or #7 from the main post office.

Tucked away among the city surroundings is a trio of first-rate attractions, each of which could happily occupy you for half a day. Two of them, **Troldhaugen**, Edvard Grieg's home, and **Lysøen**, Ole Bull's island villa, are south of the city, whereas the open-air **Gamle Bergen** (Old Bergen) is just to the north. A trip to the Troldhaugen is usually combined with a quick visit to **Fantoft stave church**, which you pass on the way there. All four attractions are accessible by public transport, though it's a bit of a pain, and there are frequent organized excursions to Troldhaugen and Gamle Bergen, from about 220kr, tickets for which can be booked at Bergen's tourist office.

Fantoft stave church and Troldhaugen

Some 5km south of downtown Bergen, just off the E39 and clearly signposted, **Fantoft stave church** (mid-May to mid-Sept daily 10.30am–2pm & 2.30–6pm; 30kr) was moved here from a tiny village on the Sognefjord in the 1880s. The first owner, a government official, had the structure revamped along the lines of the Borgund stave church (see p.136), complete with dragon finials, high-pitched roofs and an outside gallery. In fact, it's unlikely that the original version looked much like Borgund, though this is somewhat irrelevant considering that the Fantoft church got burnt to the ground in 1992. Extraordinarily, the present owner has had built a replica of the destroyed church, a finely carved affair with

EDVARD GRIEG

Composer of some of the most popular works in the standard orchestral repertoire, **Edvard Grieg** (1843–1907) was born in Bergen, the son of a salt-fish merchant – which, considering the region's historical dependence on the product, was an appropriate background for a man whose romantic compositions have come to epitomize western Norway, or at least an idealized version of it. Certainly, Grieg was quite happy to accept the connection, and as late as 1903 he commented that "I am sure my music has the taste of codfish in it." In part this was sincere, but he had an overt political agenda too. Norway had not been independent since 1380, and after centuries of Danish and Swedish rule its population lacked political and cultural self-confidence – a situation which the Norwegian nationalists of the time, including Ibsen and Grieg, were determined to change. Such was their success that they played a key preparatory role in the build-up to the dissolution of the union with Sweden, and the creation of an independent Norway in 1905.

Musically, it was Grieg's mother, a one-time professional pianist, who egged him on, and at the tender age of 15 he was packed off to the Leipzig Conservatoire to study music, much to the delight of his mentor, **Ole Bull** (see opposite). In 1863, Grieg was on the move again, transferring to Copenhagen for another three-year study stint and ultimately returning to Norway an accomplished performer and composer in 1866. The following year he married the Norwegian soprano Nina Hagerup, helped to found a musical academy in Oslo and produced the first of ten collections of folk-based *Lyric Pieces* for piano. In 1868, Grieg completed his best-known work, the *Piano Concerto in A minor* and, in 1869, his *25 Norwegian Folk Songs and Dances*. Thereafter, the composer's output remained mainly songs and solo piano pieces with a strong folk influence, incorporating snatches of traditional songs.

During the 1870s he collaborated with a number of Norwegian writers, including **Bjørnstjerne Bjørnson** and **Henrik Ibsen**, setting their poetry to music, Grieg also providing incidental music (1876) for Ibsen's *Peer Gynt*, music which he later reworked to create the two popular *Peer Gynt Suites*. In 1884, he composed the *Holberg Suite*, written to commemorate the Dano-Norwegian philosopher and playwright, Ludvig Holberg. It is these orchestral suites, along with the piano concerto, for which he is best remembered today. In 1885, now well-to-do and well-known, Grieg and his family moved into **Troldhaugen** (see opposite), the house they had built for them near Bergen. By that time, Grieg had also established a pattern of composing during the spring and summer, and undertaking extended performance tours around Europe with his wife during the autumn and winter. This gruelling schedule continued until – and contributed to – his death in Bergen in 1907.

disconcertingly fresh timbers, set amongst beech and pine trees just 600m from the main road.

Back on the E39, it's a further 2km south to the prominently-signposted turning that leads to **Troldhaugen** (Hill of the Trolls; late April to Sept daily 9am–6pm; Oct, Nov & early April Mon–Fri 10am–2pm, Sat noon–4pm, Sun 10am–4pm; Jan Mon–Fri 10am–2pm; Feb & March Mon–Fri 10am–2pm, Sun 10am–4pm; 40kr), the lakeside home of **Edvard Grieg** (see box opposite) for the last 22 years of his life – though "home" is something of an exaggeration, as he spent several months every year touring the concert halls of Europe. Norway's only composer of world renown, Grieg has a good share of commemorative monuments in Bergen – the statue in the city park, the *Grieghallen* concert hall – but it's here that you get a sense of the man, an immensely likeable and much-loved figure of leftish opinions and disarming modesty: "I make no pretensions of being in the class with Bach, Mozart and Beethoven," he once wrote. Their works are eternal, while I wrote for my day and generation."

A visit here begins at the **museum**, where Grieg's life and times are exhaustively chronicled, and a short film provides yet further insights. From here, it's a brief walk to the **house**, a pleasant and unassuming villa built in 1885, and still pretty much as Grieg left it, with a jumble of photos, manuscripts and period furniture; if you can bear the hagiographical atmosphere, the obligatory conducted tour is quite entertaining – especially the revelation that Grieg was only 1.52m tall and that he and Einstein bore an uncanny resemblance to each other. Grieg, in fact, didn't compose much in the house, but preferred to walk round to a tiny **hut** he had built just along the shore. The hut has survived, and today it stands beside a modern concert hall, the **Troldsalen**, where there are **recitals** of Grieg's works from late June through to October. Tickets, covering admission and transport, can be bought from Bergen tourist office. The bodies of Grieg and his wife – Nina Hagerup, a singer – are inside a curious **tomb** blasted into a rock face overlooking the lake, and sealed with twin memorial stones; it's only a couple of minutes' walk off from the main footpath but few people venture out to this beautiful, melancholic spot.

Both Fantoft stave church and Grieg's home are reached by regular **buses** (every 20min) from the bus station: take any bus leaving from platforms 19, 20 or 21. For the church, ask to be put off at the Fantoft stop, from where you cross the road, turn right and walk up the hill behind the car park, a ten-minute stroll. For Troldhaugen, get off at the Hopsbroen stop, walk back along the road for about 200m and then turn left up Troldhaugsveien for a stiff and uninteresting twenty-minute (700m) walk.

Ole Bull's villa on Lysøen

Around 25km south of Bergen, the leafy, hilly islet of **Lysøen** boasts the eccentrically ornate summer **villa** of the violinist Ole Bull (1810–1880), which, like Grieg's home, has now been turned into a museum full of personal artefacts. With its onion dome and frilly trelliswork, Bull's villa was supposed to break with what Bull felt to be the dour architectural traditions of Norway, but whether it works or not is hard to say: inside, the arabesque columns and scrollwork of the capacious music hall-cum-main room look muddled rather than inventive. Bull may have chosen to build in a foreign style, but he was a prominent member of that group of nineteenth-century artists and writers, the Norwegian Romanticists, who were determined to revive the country's traditions – his special contribution having been the promulgation of its folk music. He toured America and Europe for several decades, his popularity as a sort of Victorian Mantovani dented neither by his fervent utopian socialism, nor by some of his eccentric remarks: asked who taught him to play the violin, he once replied, "The mountains of Norway". Then again, people were inclined to overlook his faults because of his engaging manner and stunning good looks – smelling salts were kept on hand during his concerts to revive swooning women. The **guided tour** of the house (mid-May to Aug Mon–Sat noon–4pm, Sun 11am–5pm; Sept Sun noon–4pm; 25kr) is a little too reverential for its own good and could do with a bit more pace, but the island's wooded footpaths, laid out by the man himself, make for some energetic walks afterwards. Maps of the island are given away free at the house, from where it's a stiff, steep but short walk over the hill to **Lysevågen**, a sheltered cove where you can go for a dip – but take Norwegian assurances about the water temperature with a pinch of salt.

To reach the villa from Bergen, take the **bus** from the bus station (platform 20, marked "Lysefjordruta"; Mon–Sat only), and after about fifty minutes you'll reach Buena Kai, from where a passenger ferry makes the ten-minute crossing to Lysøen. By **car**, drive south along E39, then take the Fana road (Highway 553) and follow the signs to Lysøen. The **ferry** leaves every hour, on the hour, when the villa is open; the last ferry back from the island is at 4pm (Sun 5pm), and the return fare is 60kr.

Gamle Bergen

From the bus station several local services – including #9, #20, #21, #22 and #50 – travel north along the fjord shore on the E16/E39, passing, after 5km, **Gamle Bergen** (Old Bergen), an open-air complex comprising around forty wooden houses, representative of eighteenth- and nineteenth-century Norwegian architecture. Entry to the site as well as the adjacent park, which stretches down to the water's edge, is free and there's open access, but the **buildings** can only be visited on a guided tour (every hour on the hour; mid-May to Aug daily 10am–4pm; 40kr). Immaculately maintained, the interiors give a real idea of small-town life and although the site, with its careful cobbled paths and trim gardens, is a little too cute, the anecdote-heavy tour is bound to make you grin. The enduring impression is one of social claustrophobia: everyone knew everyone else's business – grim or scandalous, mundane or bizarre. It was this enforced uniformity that Ibsen loathed and William Heinesen explored in *The Black Cauldron* – see "Books", p.336.

Eating, drinking and nightlife

Bergen has a good supply of **restaurants**, the best of which tend to focus on seafood – the city's main gastronomic asset. The pricier tourist haunts are concentrated on the Bryggen, but should not be dismissed out of hand – several are first-rate. Other less expensive places dot the side streets behind the Bryggen and the narrow lanes east of Torget. Generally though, the **cafés** and restaurants to the southwest of Ole Bulls plass serve better food in much more fashionable surroundings. The most appealing **bars** are around here too.

The fish market on the Torget (Mon–Sat from 7am) remains *the* place for **take-away** lunches, offering everything from dressed crab through to smoked-salmon sandwiches and caviar. For a sit-down meal, the town's **cafés** and **café-bars** are easily the most economic option, though you shouldn't leave Bergen without enjoying at least one lavish, seafood **restaurant** meal. The café-bars mentioned below could almost as easily be included in the "Bars" section – the distinction is somewhat arbitrary.

Bergen's **drinkers** have three main choices in terms of ambience and locality: they can plump to join the tourists carousing on the Bryggen; hang around with the high-heeled girls and tattoos on Ole Bulls plass; or seek out the cooler, more studenty places to the southwest of Ole Bulls plass. Several of the more appealing bars offer live music or DJ sounds, and there's a smattering of **clubs** too.

Restaurants

Bryggeloftet & Stuene, Bryggen (☎55 31 06 30). This restaurant may be a tad stuffy, but it serves the widest range of seafood in town – delicious meals featuring every North Atlantic fish you've ever heard of, and some you might not have heard of at all. Main courses around 180kr.

Enhjørningen, Bryggen (☎55 32 79 19). On the second floor of a superbly restored eighteenth-century merchant's house – all low beams and creaking floors – this smart restaurant serves a mouth-watering range of fish and shellfish, with main courses from around 180kr. Worth every *krone* for an indulgent evening out. The daily buffet lunch (Mon–Sat noon–4pm, Sun 1–4pm) is a more affordable alternative here, with heaps of salmon, prawns and herring, along with salads, hot dishes, bread, cheese and desserts.

Den Gode Klode, Fosswinckelsgate 18 (☎55 32 34 32). Near the Grieghallen, this is Bergen's only specialist vegetarian restaurant. A wide range of dishes, pleasantly presented and inexpensive. Mon–Fri 11.30am–7pm, Sat noon–5pm.

Munkestuen Café, Klostergaten 12. Intimate, cosy café-restaurant noted for its excellent Italian dishes and its wine cellar, the best in town. Reckon on 200kr for a main course.

Naboen Pub & Restaurant, Neumannsgate 20 (☎55 90 02 90). Excellent, moderately priced meals at this easy-going restaurant which features Swedish specialities. Snacks and light meals are also available in the downstairs pub.

Pars, Sigurdsgate 5. Very good Persian food at reasonable prices. Main courses from 100kr.

Smauet Mat og Vinhus, Vaskerelvsmuget, off Ole Bulls plass (☎55 23 14 20). This first-rate restaurant offers traditional Norwegian cuisine – including oodles of seafood – and more exotic dishes like ostrich and antelope. Reckon on 180kr for a main course.

To Kokker, Bryggen (☎55 32 28 16). Similar to the *Enhjørningen*, but without the buffet. First-class seafood. Main courses around 200kr, three-course set meals for 500kr. Closed Sun.

Cafés and café-bars

Bergen Chinese Restaurant, Lodin Lepps gate 2b. Behind the Bryggen, this popular spot is, despite the name, more of a café, with customers seated on long benches to savour tasty Chinese, Japanese and vegetarian food. Main courses from 100kr; takeaway also available.

Dromedar Kaffebar, Fosswinkels gate 16. Good coffee, and excellent cheesecake and carrot cake.

Godt Brød, Vestre Torggate 2, also at Nedre Korskirkealmenning 12. More of an eco-bakery than a café, with very good bread and pastries; they also do made-to-order sandwiches.

Kafe Kippers, Kulturhuset USF, Georgernes verft, on the Nordnes peninsula. Part of the city's adventurous contemporary arts complex, this laid-back café-bar serves tasty, inexpensive food, rustles up great barbecues and, with its sea views and terrace, is *the* place to come on a sunny evening – when it's jam-packed. Puts on live music too, notably during its own jazz festival in May.

Kafe Krystall, Kong Oscars gate 16. Swish café-bar offering delicious seafood. Main courses around 170kr. Near the Korskirken.

Det Lille Kaffekompaniet, Christies gate 11 (Mon–Fri 8am–5pm, Sat noon–5pm), branch located one flight of steps above the funicular terminal at Nedre Fjellsmug 2 (Mon–Fri 5–11pm, Sat noon–6pm, Sun noon–11pm). These two coffee bars work in tandem – one opens as the other closes. They're simple, unpretentious places, and locals swear the coffee here is the best in Norway – it was even voted so in a recent national poll.

Café Opera, Engen 24, near Ole Bulls plass. Inside a white wooden building with plant-filled windows and a fashionable crowd drinking beer and good coffee. Tasty, filling snacks from as little as 45kr. DJ sounds at the weekend.

Spisekroken, Klostergaten 8. Economical café-bar with delicious daily specials – the catch of the day is mouth-watering and only costs about 100kr. A fashionable spot.

Zachariasbryggen, Torget. On the quayside, with a few outdoor seats overlooking the fish market, this bakery sells the city's speciality, the *skillingsboller* – a spiral, sugar-coated bun – as well as cakes and coffee. Buy French bread here and some seafood from the market and you've the makings of a good sandwich.

Bars and clubs

Bryggen Tracteursted, Bryggen. Raucous, earthy bar in one of the old wooden merchants' buildings on the Bryggen. Live music on Fridays and Saturdays. Closed Sun.

Dickens, Ole Bulls plass 10. One of the busiest of the downtown bars, with a young clientele spread over two floors, and a glass-walled main bar. Something of a meat market.

Garage, at the corner of Nygårdshgaten and Christies gate. Very busy place with a mixed crowd. They have two bars on the ground floor, and a live music area downstairs. This is one of the places in Bergen that seem to never go out of style, even though the interior definitely has. Crowded at weekends.

Hulen, Olav Ryesvei 48. A club in an old air-raid shelter under Nygårdsparken – on the far side of the university from the city centre, and quite a student hang-out. Live bands and DJ sounds at weekends. Wed & Thurs 10pm–2am, Fri & Sat 10pm–3.30am.

Kafe Permanenten, corner of Christies gate and Nordahl Bruns gate, in the basement of the building housing the West Norway Applied Art Museum. An indifferent café by day, but an excellent club at night, with DJs from all over the world.

Miles Ahead, Torggaten 7 – look for the very small sign on the wall down this alley. Acid jazz and its relatives; the perfect spot to go dancing. Very good DJs. Kind of hip, with a long and well-stocked bar. Wed & Thurs 9pm–1am, Fri & Sat 9pm–4am.

Sjøboden, Bryggen. Sited inside one of the old timber buildings on the Bryggen, this is a lively spot with frequent live music (of very variable quality).

Entertainment

With some justification, Bergen takes pride in its **performing arts** and hosts top-notch events throughout the year. Especially noteworthy is the **Festspillene i Bergen** (Bergen International Festival), held for eleven days at the end of May, which presents a wide-ranging programme of music, ballet, folklore and drama. The principal venue for the festival is the **Grieghallen**, on Lars Hille gate (☎55 21 61 50), where you can pick up programmes, tickets and information (also available at the tourist office). The city's contemporary arts centre, the **Kulturhuset USF** – or Verftet – down on Georgernes Verft on the Nordnes peninsula (☎55 31 55 70), contributes to the main festival with its own **Nattjazz**, an international jazz festival held over the same eleven-day period. The Kulturhuset is a busy place at other times of the year too, putting on an ambitious programme of concerts, art-house films and contemporary plays.

Throughout the summer, Bergen contrives to have an event of some kind almost every day of the week – everything from fishing competitions to chamber music recitals. The tourist office tabulates these summer activities in its *Sommer Bergen* promotional leaflet. Otherwise, **entertainment listings** (in Norwegian) are provided in *Natt & Dag*, a free bi-monthly newssheet widely available across the city centre.

Bergen has one large city-centre **cinema**, Bergen Kino: Konsertpaleet, Neumannsgate 3 (☎55 23 23 15), a five-minute walk south of Ole Bulls plass. Here, as is usual in Norway, films are shown in their original language with Norwegian subtitles if necessary. Predictably, American films rule the roost, so English speakers are at an advantage. The tourist office has full details of all **musical events** held in and around the city. Specific events to watch out for include concerts by the **Bergen Philharmonic**, from September to May in Grieghallen, and **Grieg recitals** at Grieg's home, Troldhaugen, from late June to October. There are **chamber music and organ recitals** at the Mariakirken by the Bryggen in June, July and August. Bergen is big on **folk events** – singing, dancing and costumed goings-on of all kinds. Catch **folk dancing** at the Bryggens Museum (June–Aug, twice weekly at 9pm; 95kr); tickets from the tourist office or on the door. The other main folk event is **Fana Folklore** (☎55 91 52 40), a festival of Norwegian music, food and dancing held on a private estate outside the city. It takes place at 7pm several times a week from June to August and costs 230kr per person, including meal and transport; tickets from hotels and Flø–lo, Torgalmenning 9. Den Nationale Scene, Engen (☎55 54 97 10), is Bergen's main **theatre**, with three stages. Although most performances are in Norwegian, there are occasional performances by English-speaking theatre companies and regular musicals. The theatre is closed in July and most of August.

Listings

Airlines Braathens, Bergen airport (☎55 99 82 50); British Airways enquiries to Braathens; SAS, Bergen airport (☎55 11 43 00).

Bookshop Melvær No 7, Torgalmenningen 7, right in the city centre, is easily the best bookshop in town, with a wide range of English books and French, German and Spanish titles too. The travel section is especially good and the staff extremely helpful. Mon–Fri 9am–8pm, Sat 9am–4pm.

Bus enquiries Timetable information on ☎177.

Car breakdown Viking Redningstjeneste, Inndalsveien 22 (☎55 59 40 70), is a 24-hour breakdown service, as is NAF (☎81 00 05 05).

Car parks Of several multi-storey car parks, Parkeringshuset, on Rosenkrantzgaten (Mon–Fri 7am–9pm, Sat & Sun 8am–6pm), is central and handy for short-stay parking. For longer stays and/or more flexibility, Bygarasjen, on Vestre Strømkaien beside the Storsenter shopping mall and bus station, is open 24hrs.

Car rental All the major international car rental companies have offices in town, including Budget, off the Bryggen at Lodin Lepps gate 1 (☎55 90 26 15) and Avis at Lars Hilles gate 20b (☎55 32 01 30). Statoil Bilutleie has an outlet at the airport (☎55 99 14 90) and so does Budget (☎55 22 75 27).

Consulates UK, Carl Konows gate 34 (☎55 94 47 05).

Exchange The main post office offers competitive exchange rates for foreign currency and travellers' cheques, with longer opening hours (mid-May to Aug Mon–Wed & Fri 8.15am–3pm, Thurs 8.15am–5.30pm; Sept to mid-May Mon–Wed & Fri 8.15am–3.30pm, Thurs 8.15 am–6pm) than those of banks. The tourist office will also change foreign currency and travellers' cheques but their rates are poor, as are rates at the city's big hotels.

Ferries International: Fjord Line, Skoltegrunnskaien (☎81 53 35 00), operate a car ferry service to Haugesund, Stavanger and Newcastle, and another to Egersund and Hantsholm in Denmark; Smyril Line, Slottsgaten 1 (☎55 32 09 70), has car-ferry sailings from the Skoltegrunnskaien to Shetland, the Faroes and Iceland. Domestic: Hurtigbåt operators from the Strandkaiterminalen include HSD (south to Haugesund & Stavanger; north to Hardangerfjord; ☎55 23 87 80); and Fylkesbaatane Reiseservice (Sognefjord & Nordfjord; ☎55 32 40 15). The Hurtigrute sails daily at 10.30pm from the Frieleneskaien on the southern edge of the city centre, about 1500m from the train station. Tickets from local travel agents or the operator.

Gay scene Information on Bergen's low-key scene at the main gay café-bar, *Café Finken*, Nygårdsgaten 2a (☎55 31 21 39), which at weekends is also good for clubbing.

Hiking The DNT-affiliated Bergen Turlag, Tverrgaten 4–6 (Mon–Wed & Fri 10am–4pm, Thurs 10am–6pm; ☎55 32 22 30), will advise on hiking trails in the region, sell hiking maps and arrange guided weekend walks.

Laundry Jarlens Vaskoteque, Lille Øvregate 17, near the funicular (☎55 32 55 64).

Medical emergencies Casualty (24-hr) at Vestre Strømkaien 19 (☎55 32 11 20). Emergency dental care is available here too (Mon–Fri 4–9pm, Sat & Sun 3–9pm; ☎55 32 11 20).

Pharmacy Apoteket Nordstjernen, at the bus station (Mon–Sat 8am–midnight, Sun 9.30am–midnight; ☎55 31 68 84).

Post office Main post office on Olav Kyrres gate at the corner of Rådhusgaten (Mon–Fri 8am–6pm, Sat 9am–3pm). Travellers' cheques and foreign currency exchanged here at competitive rates.

Travel agents Terra Nova Travel, Nygaten 3 (Mon–Fri 8.30am–4pm; ☎55 32 23 77), above Norske Vandrerhjem (the Norwegian Youth Hostel Association), can advise on all aspects of budget travel. The national student travel organization is KILROY Travels, in the Studentsenteret at Parkveien 1 (☎55 30 79 00). Otherwise, central and dependable travel agents include Winge Travel Bureau, Chr. Michelsens gate 1–3 (☎55 55 16 00); Bennett Reisebureau, Strandgaten 197 (☎55 90 07 80); and Reisefeber, Nygårdsgaten 1a (☎55 21 04 00).

Trains National timetable information on ☎81 50 08 88.

Vinmonopolet There is a branch in the Bergen Storsenter, Strømgarten.

THE WESTERN FJORDS

As you head out from Bergen, the western fjords beckon. The main coastal highway jerks its way south across the mouths of several fjords on its way to **Stavanger**, the region's lively second city, but far more people choose to head east to the closest of the major fjords, **Hardangerfjord**. Northeast from Bergen lie **Voss**, a winter sports resort of some renown, and **Flåm**, at the end of one of the most exciting trips of them all, the train down the Flåmsdal to the **Aurlandsfjord**. This is the most popular fjord trip in Norway, and readily done as a day out from Bergen, though it is less expensive from Voss. But scenic as all this is, the fjord region proper only begins to the north of here, where the Aurlandsfjord joins the **Sognefjord**. One of Norway's greatest and most beautiful fjord systems, the Sognefjord cuts eastwards some 180km inland from the coast. Further north, and running parallel, is the **Nordfjord**, smaller at 90km long, but more varied in its scenery, with patches of the **Jostedalsbreen glacier** visible and visitable beyond. Further north again, the **Geirangerfjord** is a marked contrast – narrow, rugged and sheer – while, a short distance to the west of it, the **Hjørundfjord** is remote and beautiful in equal measure. Pushing on to the northernmost of these great inlets, **Romsdalsfjord**, with its many branches, the terrain begins to splinter into the scattered archipelagos that characterize the north Norwegian coast.

This is not a landscape to be hurried – there's little point in dashing from fjord to fjord. Stay put at least for a while, go for at least one hike or cycle ride, and it's then you'll really appreciate the western fjords in all their grandeur. The sheer size of the fjords is breathtaking – but then the geological processes that shaped them were on a grand scale. During the Ice Age, around three million years ago, the whole of Scandinavia was covered in ice, mountainously thick inland but thinner towards the coast. Under the grinding weight of the slow-moving ice, the pre-existing river valleys grew deeper and deeper, leaving basins when the ice retreated that filled with seawater and became the fjords, which the warm Gulf Stream kept ice-free. The pressure of the inland ice actually pushed the fjords down to depths well below that of the ocean: the Sognefjord, for example, reaches depths of 1250m, ten times that of most of the Norwegian Sea.

Visiting the fjords: practicalities

Bergen advertises itself, rather pointedly, as "Capital of the Fjords", and the tourist office does organize a barrage of trips (by bus and ferry) from the city. Most, however, can be done independently much more cheaply. Also, as Bergen is in fact on the western edge of the fjords, most day trips from Bergen involve too much travelling for comfort. This is doubly true as the main road east from Bergen – the E16 – is prone to congestion, and there are over twenty tunnels along the 100km stretch to Voss (see p.192), many of which are horribly noxious. Avoid as much of the E16 east of Bergen as you can, or aim to branch off onto the relatively tunnel-free and much more scenic Highway 7 the first chance you get – about 30km east of the city. For all these reasons, you're much better off using one of the small towns that dot the fjords as a base rather than Bergen, especially as distances within the fjords region are – at least by Norwegian standards – quite modest. In the Hardangerfjord system, **Utne**, **Ulvik** and **Lofthus** are the most appealing bases, Sognefjord has **Fjærland** and **Balestrand**, while further north **Loen**, **Åndalsnes** and **Ålesund** all have their advantages.

The convoluted topography of the western fjords has given rise to a dense and complex **public transport** system designed to take you to all the larger villages and towns at least once every weekday, whether by train, bus, car ferry, Hurtigrute or Hurtigbåt. General travel details for this chapter are given on p.225, and in the text itself we've included local connections where they are especially useful; this information should be used in conjunction with the timetables that are widely available across the region. Bear in mind also that although there may be a transport connection to the place you want to go, many Norwegian settlements are scattered and you may be in for a long walk after you've arrived – a particularly dispiriting experience if it's raining. Check the text and, where appropriate, the maps to find out exact locations.

Throughout the text there are numerous mentions of fjord **car ferries** and **Hurtigbåt** passenger express boats. Hurtigbåt services are usually fairly infrequent – three a day at most – whereas many car ferries shuttle back and forth every hour or two from around 7am in the morning until 10pm at night every day of the week; we've given times of operation where they are either different from the norm or particularly useful. **Hurtigbåt fares** are fixed individually with prices starting at around 70kr for every hour travelled, but rising to well over 120kr: the four-hour trip from Bergen to Stavanger will, for example, cost you around 510kr. Rail pass holders (see p.31) are often entitled to discounts of up to fifty percent and on some routes there are special excursion deals – always ask. **Car ferry fares**, on the other hand, are priced according to a nationally-agreed sliding scale, with ten-minute crossings running at around 16kr per person and 37kr per car and driver, 19kr and 52kr respectively for a twenty-minute trip.

South to Haugesund and Stavanger

The islets which dot the coast **south of Bergen** provide a pleasant introduction to the scenic charms of western Norway – and hint at the sterner beauty of the fjords a few kilometres east. The intricacies of this shoreline, together with the prevailing westerlies, have long made navigation in these parts difficult, while the region's farmers have always struggled to survive on the thin soils that have accumulated in places on the leeward sides of some of the islands.

With great ingenuity, Norway's road builders have in recent years cobbled together the E39 coastal road, the **Kystvegen**, which traverses the coast from Bergen to Haugesund and ultimately Stavanger – with three ferry trips breaking up the journey. Travelling this road by the coastal **bus** service, Kystbussen, takes a little under six hours to Stavanger, and you'll get to see far more of the coast this way than by using the alternative, the **Hurtigbåt**. The Kystbussen leaves Bergen for Haugesund and Stavanger twice or three times daily. Advance booking is recommended – do so at Bergen's bus station – and a one-way Bergen–Haugesund ticket costs around 220kr, though students and rail pass holders qualify for discounts. By **car**, allow four or five hours from Bergen to Haugesund, and a couple more to Stavanger; drivers would be well advised to pick up car ferry timetables at the tourist office before they depart. Altogether, the various ferry crossings will cost around 280kr per driver and car, and 75kr per passenger.

Haugesund

The workaday industrial town of **HAUGESUND**, 110km south of Bergen, is a small and lively port that thrived on the herring fisheries in the nineteenth century and now booms as a major player in the North Sea oil industry. It was here that the first ruler of Norway as one kingdom, Harald Hårfagri (Harald the Fair-Haired), was buried, and a granite obelisk, the **Haraldshaugen**, now marks his supposed resting place, by the seashore about 1500m north of the centre. He gained sovereignty over these coastal districts at a decisive sea battle in 872, an achievement which, according to legend, released him from a ten-year vow not to cut his hair until he became king of all Norway. Haugesund's other claim to fame is as the town from where a local baker, in an attempt to improve his fortunes, emigrated to the USA; his daughter, who later called herself Marilyn Monroe, was born in 1926.

There's no particular reason to tarry after you've had a quick scoot round the grid of streets that constitutes the brisk, modern town centre, though you could check special events with the **tourist office** on the harbourfront (mid-June to Aug Mon–Fri 9am–7pm, Sat 10am–4pm, Sun 11am–3pm; Sept to mid-June Mon–Fri 10am–3.30pm; summer ☎52 72 50 55, out of season ☎52 73 45 25), across from the Hurtigbåt ferry terminal. From here to the **bus station** is about 600m, straight down Torggata. For a **place to stay**, the *Rica Travel Hotel*, Skippergata 11 (☎52 71 11 00, fax 52 72 33 36; ④, s/r ③), has pleasant, comfortable doubles, and is one of several straightforward modern hotels right in the centre of town. Coastal buses continue south for Stavanger (one-way 150kr), or you can also drive there via the Kystvegen, a journey that takes about two hours.

Stavanger and around

STAVANGER is something of a survivor. While other Norwegian coastal towns have fallen foul of the precarious fortunes of fishing, Stavanger has grown and flourished, and is now the proud possessor of a dynamic economy which has swelled the population to around 100,000. It was the herring fishery that first put money into the town, crowding its nineteenth-century wharves with coopers and smiths, net-makers and -menders. When the fishing industry failed the town moved into shipbuilding and ultimately oil: the port builds the rigs for the off-shore oilfields and is a centre for oil refining.

None of which sounds terribly enticing, and certainly no one could describe Stavanger as picturesque. But it's an easy city to adjust to and worthy of spending at least a little time to see the attractive old town before heading onwards. If you stay longer, you can sally out into the surrounding fjords, of which the **Lysefjord** is outstanding, and take advantage of the city's excellent restaurants and lively bars. You'll also hear lots of English spoken – well-paid foreign oil-workers congregate here on furlough.

Arrival, information and city transport

Stavanger **airport** is 14km south of the city at **Sola**. There's a Flybussen into Stavanger (every 20–30min; 40kr), which stops at the major downtown hotels, the ferry terminals and the bus and train stations. The **bus terminal** is on the southern side of the Breiavatnet, a tiny lake that's the most obvious downtown landmark; the **train station** (☎51 56 96 10) is adjacent. The Kystbussen fare from Bergen to Stavanger is 350kr, and there are two or three services daily (5.5hr). Also at the bus station is Ruteservice Rogaland, an agency run collectively by several transport companies (Mon–Fri 8am–5pm, Sat 9am–1.30pm; ☎51 56 71 71), which provides comprehensive details of buses, boats and trains in the city and surrounding area.

Fjord Line **ferries** (☎51 52 45 45) from Newcastle, Haugesund and Bergen berth on the west side of the harbour, beside Strandkaien, a five-minute walk from the main square, Torget, which is itself immediately to the north of the central lake. **Hurtigbåt** services use the terminal at the northern end of Kirkegata, about 1km from the park surrounding Breivatnet. All the **local express boats and ferries**, for the islands and fjords around Stavanger, use either the Hurtigbåt terminal or the Fiskepiren terminal, just a little further to the east along the waterfront. Finally, most pleasure cruises depart from Skagenkaien, on the east side of the main harbour.

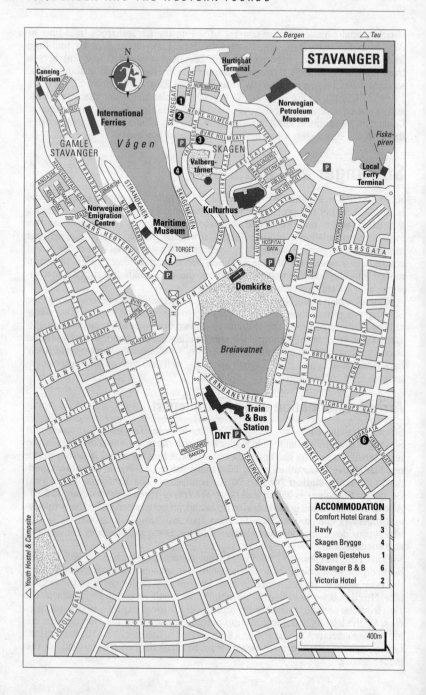

△ Bergen △ Tau

STAVANGER

Canning Museum

International Ferries

GAMLE STAVANGER

Vågen

Hurtigbåt Terminal

Norwegian Petroleum Museum

Fiske-piren

SKAGEN

Valberg-tårnet

Local Ferry Terminal

Norwegian Emigration Centre

Maritime Museum

Kulturhus

TORGET

Domkirke

Breiavatnet

Train & Bus Station

DNT

△ Youth Hostel & Campsite

ACCOMMODATION

Comfort Hotel Grand	5
Havly	3
Skagen Brygge	4
Skagen Gjestehus	1
Stavanger B & B	6
Victoria Hotel	2

0   400m

Driving here takes about two hours from Haugesund, and six or seven hours from Bergen. On-street **parking** is difficult, but not impossible: central car parks include those beside the bus station, the post office and Skagenkaien. See "Listings", p.185, for addresses of car rental agencies.

Information

The **tourist office** overlooks the Torget from its bright and breezy premises at Rosenkildetorget 1 (April & May Mon–Fri 9am–5pm, Sat 9am–2pm; June–Aug daily 9am–8pm; Sept–March Mon–Fri 9am–4pm, Sat 9am–2pm; ☎51 85 92 00; *www.destinasjon-stavanger.no*). They'll give you the free *Stavanger City Guide*, a useful consumer's guide, and *På Gang*, a free monthly brochure detailing up-and-coming cultural events. They also carry a large range of leaflets from elsewhere in Norway, provide local bus and ferry timetables and can arrange guided tours (see below).

City transport

Just about everywhere in Stavanger is walkable, while the town's surroundings can be reached by a variety of local boats and buses that depart from the terminals listed above. For a more formal introduction to the city and surrounding area, consider one of the **guided tours** on offer. There's an enjoyable two-hour walking tour of Stavanger (mid-June to mid-Aug Tues & Thurs at 11am; 105kr), in English and Norwegian, which starts at the tourist office and takes in the historic quarter of Gamle Stavanger. The fjords can be seen from sightseeing boats, which depart regularly throughout the summer from Skagenkaien – tickets are available at the quayside from around 200kr.

Accommodation

There's plenty of choice of **accommodation** in Stavanger. Half a dozen hotels are clustered in Stavanger's compact centre, and each of them offers a substantial summer discount. Alternatively, there are a couple of convenient, no-frills guesthouses and, further afield, the youth hostel and campsites.

Hotels and guesthouses

Comfort Hotel Grand, Klubbgata 3 (☎51 89 58 00, fax 51 89 57 10). A good central choice, close to all the bars and restaurants. The rooms are smart, modern and spacious and the price includes a very good buffet breakfast. ④, s/r ②.

Havly Hotell, Valberggata 1 (☎51 89 67 00, fax 51 89 50 25). Spick-and-span modern hotel in the narrow side streets off Skagenkaien. Comfortable, quiet rooms. ④, s/r ②.

Skagen Gjestehus, Nedre Holmegate 2 (☎51 89 55 85, fax 51 89 55 86). This utilitarian guesthouse occupies an old wooden building on the east side of the harbour. Frugal, basic rooms – not much like being on holiday, but cheap. ②.

Skagen Brygge Hotell, Skagenkaien 30 (☎51 85 00 00, fax 51 85 00 01). A delightful quayside hotel, built in the general style of an old warehouse but with lots of glass, and offering enjoyable views over the harbour. The rooms are modern and tastefully decorated, the buffet breakfast outstanding and delicious mid-afternoon nibbles are on offer, free – cheese, pickled herring etc. The only quibble concerns the noise from outside on summer weekends, when your best bet is probably to get a room at the back or on the top floor. ⑤, s/r ③.

Stavanger Bed & Breakfast, Vikedalsgaten 1a (☎51 56 25 00, fax 51 56 25 01). Straightforward modern place in an unexciting residential area five minutes' walk southeast of the central lake. An inexpensive option. ①.

Victoria Hotel, Skansegata 1 (☎51 86 70 00, fax 51 86 70 10). Part of the *Rica* chain, this large hotel occupies a large old building, with a fancy portico, overlooking the east side of the harbour. The foyer has kept much of its Victorian appearance, complete with wood panelling, leather sofas and ships' models, and the comfortable rooms beyond are in broadly period style, ⑤, s/r ③.

Hostels and camping

Mosvangen Vandrerhjem, Henrik Ibsens gate 21 (☎51 87 29 00, fax 51 87 06 30). This plain HI youth hostel occupies a lakeside setting, a 3km walk from the centre: take Madlaveien west from near the station and turn left just beyond the lake, Mosvatnet, on to Tjensvollveien – Henrik Ibsens gate is its continuation. The hostel is open mid-May to mid-Sept and has self-catering and laundry facilities. Advance reservations are advised. Breakfasts cost 60kr. ①, dorm beds 135kr.

Mosvangen Camping, Tjensvollveien 1 (☎51 53 29 71, fax 51 87 20 55). By the lake, next door to the youth hostel. Has cabins (②) as well as spaces for tents and caravans. Open late May to early September.

The Town

Much of central Stavanger is modern (built with oil money), a flashy and surprisingly likeable ensemble of mini tower-blocks. The only relic of the medieval city is the twelfth-century **Domkirke** (Mon & Tues 11am–2pm, Wed–Sat 10am–3pm; free), up above the Torget, whose pointed-hat towers signify a Romanesque church – one that's suffered from several poorly conceived renovations. The simple interior, originally the work of English craftsmen, has fared badly too, spoilt by ornate seventeenth-century additions including an intricate pulpit and five huge memorial tablets adorning the walls of the aisles – a jumble of richly carved angels, crucifixes, death's-heads, animals and apostles. Organ recitals are held here every Thursday at 11.15am.

A brief stroll away, beyond the stalls of the **Torget** selling fresh fish and flowers, is the **Skagen** area, built on the bumpy protrusion of land that forms the eastern side of the harbour. It's an oddly discordant district, a clumsy mixture of old and new, incorporating the town's main shopping area, whose mazy street plan is the only legacy of the original Viking settlement. The spiky nineteenth-century firewatch, **Valbergtårnet** (Valberg tower), atop the highest point here and guarded by three rusty cannons, is the one specific landmark, the spot offering sweeping views of the city and its industry.

Beside the waterfront on the far side of Skagen, the oil industry celebrates its achievements by way of the gleaming **Norsk Oljemuseum** (Norwegian Petroleum Museum; May–Aug daily 10am–7pm, Sept–April Mon–Wed, Fri & Sat 10am–5pm, Thurs & Sun 10am–7pm; 60kr). Housed in a hangar-like building, the museum has displays on North Sea geology, oil extraction and the like, complete with drill bits and other oil-rig paraphernalia. There are several hands-on exhibits too – including a simulated helicopter ride and a diving bell – plus an honest account of the accidents and occasional disasters that have befallen the industry.

Gamle Stavanger

The town's star turn is **Gamle Stavanger** (Old Stavanger), on the western side of the harbour. Though very different in appearance from the modern structures back in the centre, the buildings here were also the product of a boom. Until around 1870, the herring turned up offshore in their millions. Benefiting from this slice of luck, Stavanger flourished and expanded, and the number of merchants and ship owners in the town increased dramatically. Huge profits were made from the exported fish, which were salted and later, as the technology improved, canned. Today, some of the wooden stores and warehouses flanking the western quayside hint at their nineteenth-century pedigree, but it's the succession of narrow, cobbled lanes behind them that shows Gamle Stavanger to best advantage. Formerly home to local seafarers, craftsmen and cannery workers, the area has been maintained as a residential quarter, mercifully free of tourist tat; the long rows of white-painted, clapboard houses are immaculately maintained, complete with gas lamps, picket fences and tiny terraced gardens. There's little architectural pretension, but here and there flashes of fancy wooden scrollwork must once have raised eyebrows among the Lutheran population.

The **Hermetikkmuséet** at Øvre Strandgate 88 (Canning Museum; early June & late Sept Mon–Thurs 11am–4pm; mid-June to mid-Sept daily 11am–4pm; Oct–May Sun 11am–4pm; 40kr), right in the heart of Gamle Stavanger, occupies an old sardine-canning factory and gives a glimpse of the industry that saved Stavanger from collapse at the end of the nineteenth century. The herring largely disappeared from local waters in the 1870s, but the canning factories managed to keep going on imported fish and kept the economy afloat. They remained Stavanger's main source of employment until as late as 1960: in the 1920s there were seventy canneries in the town, and the last one only closed down in 1983. A visit to an old canning factory may not seem too enticing, but actually the museum is very good, not least because of its collection of sardine tin labels, called *iddis* in these parts from the local pronunciation of *etikett*, the Norwegian for label. Hundreds of labels have survived, in part because they were avidly collected by the town's children. The hobby prompted bouts of adult anxiety – "Label thefts – an unfortunate collection craze", ran a 1915 headline in the *Stavanger Aftenblad*. The variety of design is extraordinary – anything and everything from representations of the Norwegian royal family to surrealistic fish with human qualities. Spare a thought here for a Scottish seaman by the name of William Anderson: it was his face, copied from a photograph, that beamed out from millions of *Skippers'* sardine tins, a celebrity status so frowned upon by shipowners that Anderson couldn't find work. But the story ended happily when Anderson wrote to the cannery and they put him on the payroll for the remainder of his working life. You can watch the museum smoking its own sardines on the first Sunday of every month and every Tuesday and Thursday from mid-June to mid-August, and very tasty they are too.

A five- to ten-minute walk towards the centre, back through the old town, brings you to the **Sjøfartsmuseum** (Maritime Museum; same times as Canning Museum; 40kr) at Nedre Strandgate 17. Sited in a restored warehouse, this gives another insight into the particular history of Stavanger, with the exhibits mostly concerned with the various trades that served the shipping industry. There are some nice touches like the old sailmakers' room, and some reconstructed shop and office interiors.

The Norwegian Emigration Centre

On the west side of the harbour at Strandkaien 31, the **Norwegian Emigration Centre** (Mon–Fri 9am–3pm, Tues till 7pm; ☎51 53 88 60; *www.emigrationcenter. com*) might be of interest if you have Norwegian ancestors. Among a wide portfolio of historical data, they hold parish registers, ship passenger lists and census records covering all of Norway, by means of which they will try to trace your fore-bears on your behalf. To stand a good chance of success, though, you really need to provide the exact name, birthdate and year of emigration. Postal enquiries can be dealt with for a charge of around US$50 for the first three hours of research, US$25 per hour thereafter, and personal enquiries cost three times these rates to process. You can research their archives yourself, for a flat rate of just 35kr, but you'll need to be able to read Danish and Norwegian, often in Gothic script.

Eating, drinking and nightlife

Although prices are marginally inflated by oil-industry expense accounts, Stavanger is a great place to **eat**, with several fine seafood restaurants clustered on the east side of the harbour along Skagenkaien. For something less expensive, the best option is to stick to the more mundane cafés and restaurants near the Kulturhus in the heart of the Skagen shopping area. You can even have salted cod and herring prepared in the traditional way from E. Gundersen, whose little shop (Mon–Fri 9.30am–4pm, Sat 9.30am–1pm) is down a narrow alley off Torget – just beside Burger King.

Stavanger is lively at night, particularly at weekends when a rum assortment of oil workers, sailors, fishermen, executives, tourists and office workers gathers in the **bars and clubs** on and around Skagenkaien to live (or rather drink) it up; most places stay open until 2am or later. For more subdued evenings, check out the programme at the **Stavanger Konserthus** (Concert Hall; ☎51 53 70 00) in Bjergsted park, north of the centre beyond Gamle Stavanger, where there are regular concerts by the Stavanger Symphony Orchestra and visiting artists. There's an eight-screen **cinema**, Stavanger Kinematografer, inside the Kulturhus, on Sølvberggaten (☎51 50 70 30).

Cafés and restaurants

Akropolis, Sølvberggata 14 (☎51 89 14 54). Near the Kulturhus, this is a medium-priced Greek restaurant housed in a white wooden building on a cobbled street. Closed Mon.

Café Sting, Valberget 3. Right next to the Valbergtårnet, this laid-back café-bar is probably the coolest place in town. Tasty, inexpensive food with Mediterranean and Norwegian dishes.

Dolly Dimple's, Kongsgårdsbakken 1, a few metres up from the Torget. Basic pizzeria with a few wooden tables and benches. You can have pizzas by the slice, or whole pizzas which will feed two and are good value at 160–200kr. Eat in or take away.

La Piazza, Rosenkildehuset. Above the tourist office, this smart Italian restaurant serves delicious pizzas, pasta and more, but it's expensive.

Saken er Biff, Skagen 37 (☎51 89 60 80). No self-respecting oil town could do without a steakhouse – and this is it. A couple of stuffed cattle heads remind you what you're eating, and fish dishes, reindeer and ostrich are available too. Around 200kr for a main course.

Sjøhuset Skagen, Skagenkaien 16 (☎51 89 51 80). Fine fish and seafood restaurant on the harbour, with monkfish a speciality. Main dishes are around 200kr.

Skagen Bageri, Skagen 18. This pleasant coffee house, with its finely carved antique door and lintel, occupies the prettiest of the old wooden buildings on Skagen, one block up from the quayside. Great pastries, cakes and snacks at reasonable prices.

Bars and clubs

Hansen Hjørnet, Skagenkaien 18. Whenever the sun pops out, the outside terrace of this bar fills up fast. If it's full, try the comparable *Victoria Terrasse*, along the street at no.37.

Newsman, Skagen 14, one block up from the east side of the harbour. Attractive, busy bar where the newspaper theme means papers to read and a trendy clientele. Open until 2am.

Taket, Strandkaien. The best club in town, across the harbour from most of the bars and metres from the tourist office. Open Mon–Wed & Sun midnight to 4am, Thurs–Sat 10pm–4am; don't be surprised if you have to queue.

Timbuktu, Strandkaien. Flashy café-bar beneath *Taket*. Noted for its imaginative décor and groovy atmosphere.

Yank's, Skagenkaien 24. Popular bar-cum-club, with a gold-painted Statue of Liberty above the door and live bands at the weekend. Open until 4am.

Listings

Airlines Braathens, at the airport (☎51 51 10 00); British Airways, at the airport (☎80 03 00 77); SAS, at the airport (☎81 00 33 00).

Bicycle rental Sykkelhuset, Løkkeveien 33 (☎51 53 99 10).

Car breakdown Viking Redningstjeneste, Madlaveien 26 (24hr helpline ☎51 53 88 88).

Car rental Budget, Lagårdsveien 125 (☎51 52 21 33) and at the airport (☎51 65 07 29); Hertz, Olav V's gate 13 (☎51 52 00 00) and at the airport (☎51 65 10 96); Stavanger Bilutleie, Fritjof Nansensveien 45 (☎51 91 09 70).

Consulates UK, Prinsens gate 12 (☎51 52 97 13).

Exchange Competitive rates at the main post office (see below).

Ferries International: Fjord Line, Strandkaien (☎51 52 45 45). Regional: Ruteservice Rogaland (☎51 56 71 71); Hurtigbåt services to Bergen, Flaggruten (☎51 86 87 80).

Gay scene Information from LLH gay switchboard (☎51 53 14 46).

Hiking The DNT-affiliated Stavanger Turistforening, Olav V's gate 18 (Mon–Fri 10am–4pm; ☎51 84 02 00), will advise on local hiking routes and sells a comprehensive range of hiking maps. They maintain around 900km of hiking trails and run over thirty cabins in the mountains east of Stavanger – as well as organizing ski schools on winter weekends. They also offer general advice about local conditions, weather etc, and you can obtain DNT membership here.

Laundry Sentralvaskeriet, Breibakken 2, by Breiavatnet. Coin-operated machines.

Left luggage In the express boat terminal (Mon–Fri 6.30am–10pm, Sat 6.30am–6pm, Sun 9am–10pm); the train station (daily 6.30am–10pm, Sat until 4pm); and the bus station (daily 7am–midnight).

Medical emergencies Doctor ☎51 53 33 33; dentist, Egil Undem, Kannikbakken 6 (☎51 52 84 52).

Pharmacist Løveapoteket, Olav V's gate 11 (☎51 52 06 07). Daily until 11pm, or 8pm on public holidays.

Post office The main post office is at Haakon VII's gate 9 (Mon–Wed & Fri 8am–5pm, Thurs 8am–6pm, Sat 9am–1pm).

Shops The main shopping centre is Steen & Strøm Arkaden, Klubbgata (Mon–Fri 10am–8pm, Sat 10am–4pm).

Taxis Stavanger Taxisentral, Sjøhagen 10 (☎51 90 90 90).

Vinmonopolet Off-licence at Olav V's gate 13.

Around Stavanger: Lysefjord

Stavanger sits on a narrow promontory just to the south of the wide waters of the **Boknafjord**, a deep indentation in the coast speckled with islets. Behind the town, longer, narrower fjords drill far inland, the most diverting of these is being

Lysefjord. Forming a gash in the mainland and framed by mighty cliffs, Lysefjord's blue-black waters are disturbed by crashing waterfalls and over-looked by occasional homesteads. The fjord is famous for its precipitous cliffs and an especially striking rock formation, the **Preikestolen** (see below), near its mouth. A distinctive 25-metre-square table of rock, Preikestolen offers visitors the chance to peer down a sheer six-hundred-metre drop on three sides to the fjord below.

There are several ways to visit Lysefjord by **boat** from Stavanger. One option is with Clipper Fjord Sightseeing, who run a quick, three-hour circular trip up about half its length, departing from the Skagenkaien (Jan–May, Sept & Oct 5–8 monthly; June 1 daily; July & Aug 2 daily; 205kr). Despite the gushing multilingual commentary, however, the fjord seems disappointingly gloomy when seen from the bottom of its cliffs, and from this angle the Preikestolen hardly makes any impression at all. Rather more worthwhile is the same company's excursion to **Lysebotn**, at the east end of the fjord (May 2 monthly; June–Aug 3 weekly; Sept 1 weekly; 7hr; 290kr), from where a tourist bus tackles the 27 switchbacks up the mountainside to reach the minor road that leads back to Stavanger. The bus ride offers fabulous views back along the fjord, but it's not a frequent service. You can do the same journey independently, and more cheaply, with Rogaland Traffikselskap, which runs ferries to Lysebotn from Stavanger's Fiskepiren between three and five times weekly from mid-June to mid-August. The journey takes four hours and costs 97kr per person, 220kr for car and driver; advance booking is required for vehicles. If you're returning to Stavanger by the tourist bus from Lysebotn, the tourist office will advise which ferries best match the bus times.

Some spectacular views are offered by a demanding **hiking trail** which leads west from the car park of the **Øygardstøl** café and information centre, just above the last hairpin on the road back from Lysebotn road. The trail leads to **Kjerag**, a craggy granite plateau about 1000m above the fjord, where there's a much-photographed boulder – the **Kjeragbolten** – wedged between two rock faces high above the ground. Allow between five and six hours for the round trip – and steel your nerves.

Preikestolen

Lysefjord's celebrated vantage point, **Preikestolen** ("Pulpit"), is a popular spot – indeed on sunny summer weekends it can get fairly crowded – for the views are fabulous. From the middle of June to late August you can get here by public transport: catch the ferry for the forty-minute trip from Fiskepiren in Stavanger to **Tau**, where there's a twice-daily connecting bus running the 20km or so on to the car park at the start of the trail to Preikestolen. Check at Stavanger's tourist office to see which ferries connect with the returning bus service and to confirm bus times. From the car park, it's a four-hour hike there and back to Preikestolen along a clearly marked trail. The first half is along a comparatively easy, stone-flagged path, but the second half is rocky and awkward going. The change in elevation is 350m; take food and water.

Back at the car park, a short sharp hike down leads to **Refsvatn**, a small lake encircled by a footpath which takes three hours to negotiate completely, taking in birch and pine woods, marshes, narrow ridges and bare stretches of rock. It also threads through **Torsnes**, an isolated farm that was inhabited until 1962. The lake footpath connects with a rough path that careers down to the Refsa quay on the Lysefjord.

If you want to **stay**, there's the delightful **Preikestolen youth hostel** (June–Aug; ☎94 53 11 11, off-season ☎51 84 02 00; fax 51 84 02 14, off-season 51 74 91 11; ①, dorm beds 130kr) by the car park. Built on the site of an old mountain farm, the scant remains of which dot the surroundings, the hostel offers great views over the mountains around. It comprises a small complex of turf-roofed lodges, each of which has a spick-and-span pine interior, and reservations are advised as the place is popular with school groups.

The Hardangerfjord

To the east of Bergen, the obvious initial target is the 120-kilometre **Hardangerfjord**, whose wide waters are overlooked by a rough, craggy shoreline and a scattering of tiny settlements. At its eastern end the fjord divides into several lesser fjords, and it's here you'll find the district's most appealing villages, **Utne**, **Lofthus** and **Ulvik**, each of which has an attractive fjordside setting and at least one especially good place to stay. To the east of these tributary fjords rises the **Hardangervidda**, a mountain plateau of remarkable, lunar-like beauty and a favourite with Norwegian hikers. The plateau can be reached from almost any direction, but one favourite starting point is **Kinsarvik**, though this approach does involve a stiff day-long climb up from Sørfjord. Two other primary access points are Finse (see p.195) to the north and Rjukan (see p.142) to the southeast.

There are no trains in the Hardangerfjord area but **buses** are fairly frequent, allowing you to savour the scenery and get to the three recommended villages without any difficulty, except possibly on Sundays when services are reduced.

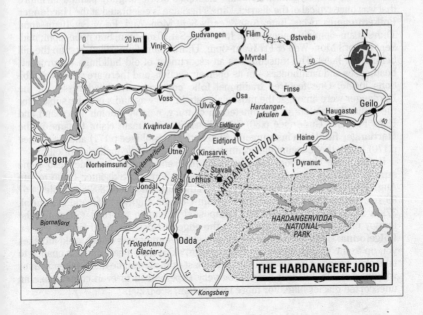

East from Bergen to the Kvanndal ferry

Heading east from Bergen by bus or car to the **Hardangerfjord**, you first have to put behind you the polluted tunnels of the E16, an unpleasant 30km journey, before you can head off down Highway 7. In contrast, this is a rattling trip with the road twisting up the valley past thundering waterfalls and around tight bends before racing down the other side to tiny **Norheimsund**. Sheltered in a bay along the Hardangerfjord, there is precious little to the town – one main street and a pocket-sized harbour – but like many fjord settlements, it's the travel in between that is the real attraction.

From here, **Hurtigbåt** services sail to Utne, Kinsarvik, Lofthus and Ulvik. Leaving Norheimsund by road, Highway 7 sticks to the rugged shoreline as it travels east to the ferry dock at **Kvanndal**, another pleasant ride with every turning bringing fresh mountain and fjord views as the Hardangerfjord begins to split into various subsidiaries. There's a choice of routes from Kvanndal: you can either press on down the northern shore of the Hardangerfjord towards Ulvik and Voss (see pp.190 and 192), or stay with the main, long-distance bus route by taking the Kvanndal **ferry** over to Utne and/or Kinsarvik (every 1–2hr; 20min/50min).

Utne and the Folgefonna glacier

UTNE, the Kvanndal ferry's midway point, is at the tip of the peninsula that divides the Hardangerfjord from the slender Sørfjord. Heading inland, Utne is the first place where you might reasonably consider spending the night; it's small, but the wooden houses huddling the hillside behind the jetty are very pretty. One of these is the appealing *Utne Hotel* (☎53 66 69 83, fax 53 66 69 50; ④), whose twenty-five rooms occupy a cheerful clapboard complex. The older parts of the hotel are stuffed with local bygones, including examples of the brightly painted furniture that was once typical of the district. Utne's heritage is celebrated at the **Hardanger Folkemuseum** (May, June, Aug & early Sept Mon–Wed, Fri & Sat 10am–4pm, Thurs 10am–6pm, Sun noon–4pm; July Mon–Sat 10am–6pm, Sun noon–6pm; mid-Sept to April Mon–Wed & Fri 10am–3pm, Thurs 10am–6pm; 30kr), just up the hill behind the hotel. The museum has an assortment of old buildings – a grocery, boathouses and farmhouses – in its open-air section, and there are several exhibitions inside. One features traditional **folk costume**: the headdresses of the Hardanger were amongst the most elaborate in Norway and a popular subject for the romantic painters of the nineteenth century, notably Adolph Tidemand and Hans Frederik Gude (see p.80). The district's other main claim to fame is the **Hardanger fiddle**, an instrument which both Ole Bull (see p.171) and Grieg (see p.170) loved; the museum has examples, as well as a fiddle-maker's workshop.

If you make Utne your base between June and August, consider also some **summer skiing** on a glacier at the Folgefonn Sommar Skisenter (June to late Aug; daily 10am–4pm; information and weather update ☎53 66 80 28, mobile 94 67 99 70). To get there head southwest from Utne on Highway 550 and at **Jondal**, 37km away, turn east along the signposted mountain toll-road (50kr) for the bumpy nineteen-kilometre ride up to the edge of Norway's third largest glacier, **Folgefonna**. Here, 1200m above sea level at the summer ski centre, a ski lift takes you up to the slopes, and you'll find parking, ski rental, a café and the chance to take ski lessons or go glacier hiking. The last of these can be undertaken with or without a guide, but you have to be very experienced to even contemplate an unescorted glacier hike. For more information, see p.209.

Kinsarvik

From Utne, the car ferry (every 2hr; 30min) bobs over the mouth of the Sørfjord to **KINSARVIK**, a humdrum little town that was once an important Viking marketplace. The Vikings stored their boats in the loft of the town's sturdy stone **church** (May to mid-Sept daily 10am–7pm; free); the building was clumsily restored in the 1880s, leaving only hints of its previous appearance, most notably a series of faint chalk wall paintings dating from the thirteenth century. Kinsarvik also lies at the mouth of the forested **Husedalen valley**, with its four crashing waterfalls. The valley makes an enjoyable hike in itself, though it's mostly used as an access route up to the Hardangervidda plateau. From Kinsarvik, it takes seven hours to reach the nearest DNT hut, the self-service **Stavali**, but be warned that the going is very steep and in rainy conditions intermittently very slippery. Hiking maps can be purchased at Kinsarvik **tourist office** (mid-May to mid-June & late August Mon–Fri 9am–5pm, mid-June to mid-Aug daily 9am–7pm; ☎53 66 31 12). If you decide to stay in Kinsarvik, there's one **hotel** – the *Best Western Kinsarvik Fjord Hotel* (☎53 66 31 00, fax 53 66 33 74; ④), which occupies a large, modern and quite attractive ivy-clad modern block by the ferry dock. An alternative is to stay in nearby Lofthus, 11km to the south along Highway 13.

Lofthus

Draped beside the Sørfjord, with the Folgefonna glacier glinting in the distance, **LOFTHUS** is an idyllic hamlet of narrow lanes and mellow stone walls. Here, a scattering of old grass-roofed houses sits among the orchards which, in spring, are laden with pinky-white blossom. The **church** (May to mid-Sept daily 10am–7pm; free), dating from 1250, is a good-looking stone structure with immensely thick walls and several bright but crude paintings. As at Kinsarvik, a steep **hiking trail** leads up to the Hardangervidda plateau; part of the trail includes stone steps laid by the monks who farmed this remote spot in medieval times. You can also hike up to the Stavali self-service hut, a trek which takes about seven or eight hours from here.

Tumbling down the steep escarpment behind, a stream gushes through the village, bubbling past a delightful **place to stay**, the *Ullensvang Gjesteheim* (☎53 66 12 36, fax 53 66 15 19; ②), a huddle of antique timber buildings with thirteen cosy and unassuming rooms – and great food. Another option is the modern, plush *Hotel Ullensvang* (☎53 66 11 00, fax 53 66 15 20; ⑤, s/r ④), a massive and solitary affair plonked on the water's edge, 1km to the north of Lofthus.

MOVING ON FROM KINSARVIK AND LOFTHUS

Heading north, **Highway 13** runs the 19km from Kinsarvik (and 30km from Lofthus) to Brimnes, where a **car ferry** (every 30min; 10min) shuttles over to Bruravik, for Ulvik (see p.190) and Voss (see p.192). Beyond Brimnes, Highway 13 becomes **Highway 7**, which travels east across the Hardangervidda (see p.190) via Eidfjord for Geilo and ultimately Oslo. Alternatively, if you're planning to travel south down Highway 13 and then east towards Oslo on the E134 – a route covered on p.138 – you certainly shouldn't set out with the intention of overnighting at the next place along the way, **Odda**, an eminently missable zinc-producing and iron-smelting town at the head of the Sørfjord. There are **buses** along all these routes.

The Hardangervidda plateau

The **Hardangervidda** is Europe's largest mountain plateau, occupying a one-hundred-square-kilometre slab of land east of the Hardangerfjord and south of the Oslo–Bergen railway. The plateau is characterized by rolling fells and wide stretches of level ground, its rocky surfaces strewn with pools and connecting rivers. The whole plateau is above the treeline, and at times has an almost lunar look to it. The landscape does have some variation: there are mountains and a glacier, the **Hardangerjøkulen**, in the northwest near Finse, while the west is wetter – and the flora somewhat richer – than the barer moorland to the east. The lichen that covers the rocks is savoured by herds of reindeer, which in the spring leave their winter grazing lands on the east side of the plateau, chewing their way west to their breeding grounds before returning east again after the autumn rutting season.

The reindeer were followed on their migrations by Stone Age hunters, traces of whose presence – arrowheads, pit-traps – have been discovered over much of the plateau. Later, the Hardangervidda became one of the main crossing points between east and west Norway, with horse traders, cattle drivers and Danish dignitaries cutting across the plateau along cairned trails. These are often still in use as part of a dense network of trails and tourist huts that has been developed by several DNT affiliates in recent decades. Roughly one third of the plateau has been incorporated within the **Hardangervidda Nasjonalpark**, but much of the rest is protected too, so hikers won't notice a deal of difference between the park and its immediate surroundings. The entire plateau is also popular for winter cross-country hut-to-hut ski touring. Many hikers and skiers are content with a day on the Hardangervidda, but some find the lichen-dappled scenery, with views down to the very horizon, particularly enchanting, and travel from one end of the plateau to the other, a seven- or eight-day expedition.

For **access** to the plateau, take Highway 7 (see p.137), which runs across the plateau between Eidfjord and Geilo. There's precious little in the way of human habitation on this lonely but handsome one-hundred-kilometre stretch of road, but you can pick up the plateau's hiking trails at several points: **Dyranut** and **Halne** are two such places, respectively 39km and 47km from **EIDFJORD**. A straggling village, Eidfjord has one great place to stay, the *Eidfjord Hotell* (☎53 66 52 64, fax 53 66 52 12; ④, s/r ③), a medium-sized, modern place with tastefully furnished rooms that perches on a knoll high above the fjord. The **restaurant** is very good here too. From Eidfjord, it's 10km to the Brimnes car ferry (see p.189) and 19km more to **Kinsarvik** (see p.189). An alternative approach to the Hardangervidda is by the Oslo–Bergen **train** line, which cuts across the northern edge of the plateau, calling at **Finse** (see p.194), from where hikers and skiers head off across the plateau in all directions. Many hikers prefer to walk eastwards onto the Hardangervidda from Kinsarvik and Lofthus (see p.189) – a journey which involves an arduous day-long trek up to the plateau. Others start from **Rjukan** (see p.142), to the southeast, from where reaching the plateau is partly made easier by a cable-car service.

Ulvik

Tucked away in a snug corner of the Hardangerfjord, the tiny village of **ULVIK** extends prettily along the shoreline with orchards covering the green hills behind. There's nothing specific to see: the town's main claim to fame – as the place where potatoes were first grown in Norway in 1765 – just about sums things up. Nonetheless, it's an excellent place to unwind, a popular little resort with a cluster of good hotels. Hiking trails lattice the rough uplands to the north of Ulvik, with one of the prettiest **hikes** being the seven-hour haul in from Mjølfjell (see p.194). The trail begins by ascending the river valley south of Mjølfjell, then threads past a trio of small upland lakes before descending the lovely Tyssedal to reach the **Sotnos** crossroads, about 1km from Highway 572. The last 5km of the hike are along the road, which zigzags its way back to Ulvik. You can also walk or drive the nine-kilometre-long country road that leads east from Ulvik, over the adjacent promontory and up along the Osafjord, to the smattering of farmsteads that constitute **OSA**. Here, in the forested hills about 1km above the fjord, is one of the region's more unusual sights, the timber and brick *Stream Nest* **sculpture** (May–Sept daily 11am–5pm; 40kr), resembling a gigantic bird's nest and perched on a hillside, above a green river valley lined by stern hills. The work of Takamasa Kuniyasu, the sculpture was built for the 1994 Lillehammer Winter Olympics and moved here afterwards. As you near the site of the sculpture, the road passes the **Hjadlane Gallery** of contemporary art (May–Sept daily noon–6pm; 25kr), which has a programme of temporary exhibitions.

Practicalities

Ulvik is off the main **bus** routes, but there are regular local buses here from Voss, and a sparser service from Kinsarvik and Lofthus, via the Brimnes–Bruravik ferry. There are also **Hurtigbåt** services to Ulvik from Norheimsund via Kinsarvik and Lofthus. Ulvik's jetty is in the centre of the village and buses pull in here too. From the jetty, it's a couple of minutes' walk along the waterfront to the **tourist office** (mid-May to mid-Sept Mon–Sat 8.30am–5pm, Sun 1–5pm; mid-Sept to mid-May Mon–Fri 8.30am–1.30pm; ☎56 52 63 60). They have literature on all the local walks and rent out bikes (150kr per day, 80kr half-day).

Among the **hotels**, the most imposing is the *Rica Brakenes Hotel*, in the centre of the village (☎56 52 61 05, fax 56 52 64 10; ⑤, s/r ③), a large and luxurious modern place with balconied bedrooms that occupies a lovely fjordside location. The *Rica Ulvik* (☎56 52 62 00, fax 56 52 66 41; ④, s/r ③), five minutes' walk away east along the waterfront, is a good deal less overpowering. Again, it's the setting rather than the architecture that appeals, with the fjord stretching out in front of the hotel, overlooked by the balconies of the fifty-odd modern bedrooms. The *Ulvik Fjord Pensjonat* (☎56 52 61 70, fax 56 52 61 60; ③; May to late Sept), situated a ten-minute walk west from the centre along the waterfront, is a well-maintained and appealing **guesthouse**. The rooms in the main building are plain but comfortable, and there's a modern annexe too. Breakfasts are first-rate and evening meals are available by prior arrangement. Otherwise, **eat** at either of the *Rica* hotels – the *Ulvik* edges the other in terms of price and informality.

Voss, Mjølfjell, Ørneberget and Finse

Without a fjord in sight, **Voss** is primarily a winter ski resort, benefiting from the hills that encircle it. It's also the first major station east of Bergen on the Bergen–Oslo rail line, and a handy base for a day trip by train up the scenic Raun Valley to the Hardangervidda (see opposite) beyond. The most popular target on this stretch of the line is the **Myrdal** junction, but only because the railway to

Flåm (see p.195) meets the main line here. You can also disembark at three isolated hiking bases: **Mjølfjell** and **Ørneberget** (served by slow trains only), and
Finse; the last two are ideal for explorations of the Hardangervidda. To savour
the scenery, you're better off catching one of the slow, stop-at-every-station trains,
though it's the fast trains that are timed to connect with services on the Flåm
branch line. Drivers should note that a mountain road heads east from Voss to
Mjølfjell, but no further – leaving Myrdal and Finse beyond reach by car.

Voss

Around 100km east of Bergen on the E16, **VOSS** is the first stop for many heading into the fjord region. Impressions are generally favourable, since it's a lakeside town of just 14,000 people, sporting a thirteenth-century church and surrounded by snow-capped hills. Voss, however, is essentially a winter sports haven,
and despite the tourist office's best efforts to promote the town as a touring centre, in summer it's hard to escape the conclusion that the visiting season is artifi-
cially extended. Consequently, your best bet is to have a quick look round before
moving on, unless, that is, you're here either to ski or to go on the much-touted
"Norway in a Nutshell" tour (see "Practicalities" opposite), for which the town is
much the most convenient base.

With the lake on one side and the river Vosso on the other, Voss has long been
a trading centre on one of the main routes between west and east Norway –
though you'd barely guess this from the modern appearance of the town. In 1023,
King Olav visited to check that the population had all converted to Christianity,
and stuck a big stone cross here to make his point. Two centuries later another
king, Magnus Lagabøte, built a church in Voss to act as the religious focal point
for the region. The church, the **Vangskyrkja** (mid-May to mid-Sept daily
10am–4pm; winter occasional hours; free), still stands, its eccentric octagonal
spire rising above stone walls which are up to two metres thick. The interior is
splendid, a surprisingly flamboyant and colourful affair with a Baroque reredos
and a rood screen showing a crucified Jesus being attended to by two cherubs.
The ceiling is even more unusual, its timbers bearing a 1696 painting of a cotton-
wool cloudy sky inhabited by angels – and the nearer you approach the high altar,
the more angels there are. That's pretty much it as far as specific sights go,
though you could take a stroll by the **lake**, Vangsvatnet, or wander the central
shops and cafés – if you've arrived from the hamlets and villages further north,
shopping might seem something of a treat.

Winter in Voss

Skiing in Voss starts in December and continues until mid-April, and though
there's nothing spectacular here, you should be able to get in a few enjoyable
days' winter sports. From near the train station, a **cable car** – the Hangursbanen
– climbs 700m to give access to several short runs as well as the first of two ski
lifts which, combined, takes you up another 300m. A one-day lift pass costs 200kr,
140kr for half a day, and in January and February some trails are floodlit. There's
a choice of downhill ski routes of international standard, or you can take longer
and gentler downhill routes through the hills above town. Full **equipment** for
both downhill and cross-country skiing can be rented for around 200–300kr per
day from Voss Skiskule & Skiutlege, at the upper Hangursbanen station (☎56 51
00 32). They also offer lessons in skiing and snowboarding techniques.

ONWARDS ROUTES FROM VOSS

From Voss, the **train route east to Oslo** is one of the most impressive rides in the country, taking in a good number of forests, waterfalls, windy mountains and wild valleys. Some of this route's finest scenery is near the beginning, just east of Voss, as the train clambers up the Raun Valley to Myrdal, where you change for the magnificent train journey down to **Flåm** (see p.195). Beyond Myrdal, continuing on the main line, is **Finse** (see p.194), perfectly situated for hiking and skiing on the Hardangervidda (see p.190).

   Express buses run north from Voss along the E16, turning down Highway 13 and reaching the Sognefjord at **Vik** (see p.203). This is another stupendous journey, with the road dramatically traversing the bleak wastes of Vikafjell mountain, snow piled high to either side of the road until at least the end of June. Just beyond Vik, the **Vangsnes** ferry (see p.203) gives ready access to **Balestrand** (see p.200) and the northern shore of the Sognefjord. Also departing Voss is a **local bus** service (4–6 daily; 1hr 10min) straight along the E16 to **Gudvangen**. Primarily this connects with the Hurtigbåt services from Gudvangen to Flåm as well as with car ferries to Kaupanger (2–4 daily; 2hr) – but check connections before you set out. Once daily from late June to mid-September, this bus links with the summertime bus from Gudvangen to Flåm, Østerbø and Geilo. Østerbø is the starting point for the day-long hike in the Aurlandsdal, a valley described on pp.196–197. Incidentally, Flåm and Gudvangen are connected by two of the more spirited pieces of tunnelling in the fjords, with stretches of 5km and 11km bored through the mountainside to link the two villages. However, these are but pipsqueaks compared with the 24-kilometre-long tunnel under construction to link the Aurlandsdal with the E16. This monster is scheduled to open in 2001.

Practicalities

Buses stop outside the **train station** at the western end of the town centre. From the train station, it's five minutes' walk to the **tourist office** (June–Aug Mon–Sat 9am–7pm, Sun 2–7pm; Sept–May Mon–Fri 9am–4pm; ☎56 52 08 00) on the main street, Uttrågata – veer right round the Vangskyrkja church and it's on the right. They largely concern themselves with hiking, skiing and touring in the surrounding area, but can supply handy information and timetables, and the free *Voss Guide*, which has useful listings. If you plan to go to Flåm via Myrdal (see p.195), and don't intend stopping over anywhere on the way, consider buying a "**Norway in a Nutshell**" ticket from Voss tourist office or train station. This is an inclusive train/bus/ferry ticket for the Voss–Myrdal–Flåm–Gudvangen–Voss route. Available all year, it costs just over 350kr and is an excellent way of seeing something of the fjords if time is short.

   A right turn from the train station and a ten-minute walk along the lake, away from the town centre, brings you to the excellent **youth hostel** (☎56 51 20 17, fax 56 51 22 05; ①, dorm beds 175kr; closed April, May & mid-Sept to Jan), overlooking the water and complete with its own sauna. It serves large, cheap evening meals and good breakfasts, though there's no kitchen for guests; you can rent bikes and canoes here, too. The **campsite**, *Voss Camping* (☎56 51 15 97), is by the lake south of the Vangskyrkja church along the Prestegardsalléen footpath – turn left from the train station and take the right fork at the church. It's open all year round and has a few cabins, bicycle and boat rental, and washing machines. As you might expect, there are plenty of cheapish (① and ②) **guesthouses** in Voss and though they'll be fully booked during winter, you should have little trouble in the summer, when special rates apply; ask at the tourist office for the best deals. Easily the best **hotel** is *Fleischer's Hotel* (☎56 52 05 00, fax 56 52 05 01; ⑨, s/r ④), next door to the train station. Dating from the 1880s, the hotel's high-gabled and towered facade overlooks the lake and fronts the original building and a modern wing built in the same style. The place has an air of real luxury: the bedrooms are plush, the **restaurant** is first rate and there's a terrace bar as well. They also offer all-inclusive food-and-lodging deals.

East to Mjølfjell, Ørneberget and Finse

All the trains pulling east out of Voss head up the Raun Valley, but only some of the slower services stop, after about forty minutes, at **Mjølfjell**, the starting point for the day-long hike over the hills to Ulvik (see p.190). Even fewer trains stop just 6km further along the line at **ØRNEBERGET**, from where it's also possible to hike south to Ulvik, though most who disembark at Ørneberget opt instead for the Hardangervidda (see p.190). Ørneberget also boasts the **Mjølfjell youth hostel** (☎56 52 31 50, fax 56 52 31 51; ①, dorm beds 165kr; closed May to mid-June and Oct–Feb), a comfortable mountain lodge in a beautiful, isolated setting beside a rushing river, and with its own heated outdoor pool. The hostel has single, double and family rooms, several of which are en suite; it also offers cycle and canoe rental, has self-catering and laundry facilities and is close to several alpine ski runs. You can drive here too, just about – the hostel is at the end of a narrow minor road that begins in Voss – but you can't drive any further east to either Myrdal or Finse.

Finse

Beyond Ørneberget, the higher reaches of the railway line are desolate even in good weather. All trains stop at **Myrdal**, a remote railway junction where you change for Flåm (see opposite), and then proceed to **FINSE**, the railway's highest point, a solitary lakeside outpost on the northern periphery of the Hardangervidda. Heading southeast from Finse, the train takes 40min to reach **Geilo** (see p.137), three-and-a-half hours more to Oslo.

Finse is nothing more than its station and a few isolated buildings, bunkered down against the howling winds that rip across the plateau in wintertime. Cross-country skiing is particularly enthusiastic here, with locals actually skiing off from the station. You can rent cross-country ski gear in Finse if you want to join in, or, off-season, hike south on the track round the **Hardangerjøkulen** glacier to reach the Hardangervidda with its trails and huts. From Finse, it takes about eleven hours' hike to reach Highway 7 at **Dyranut** (see p.190), so most heading in this direction overnight at the self-service **Kjeldebu** DNT hut (March to mid-Oct), eight hours from Finse. Less energetically, you can visit Finse's **Rallarmuseet** (early Jan to early July daily 10am–8pm; mid-July to Sept daily 10am–10pm; 20kr), a museum that records the planning and building of the Oslo–Bergen railway in the late nineteenth century. The museum is in the building just to the east of the station.

The *Finse 1222* hotel and shop (see opposite) rents **mountain bikes** that have been adapted for the Rallarvegen, the old construction road originally laid to provide access for men and materials during the building of the mountain section of the railway. Surfaced with gravel and sometimes asphalt, the Rallarvegen runs west from Haugastøl to Finse and then continues to Flåm, a total distance of 80km; there's also a 43km extension from Myrdal junction to Mjølfjell and Ørneberget. The most popular stretch of the road leads 38km west from Finse to Myrdal, though you may have to forego the first 21km (to Hallingskeid) as this is the highest part of the route and can be blocked by snow as late as July; check locally as to conditions. You'll need to be reasonably fit to make the journey too. At the end of the cycle ride, NSB railways will transport your bike back to the point of departure for 80kr from any station along the Rallarvegen.

For **accommodation**, DNT operates a fully staffed 150-bed lodge complex at Finse, *Finsehytta* (☎56 52 67 32, fax 56 52 67 60; ①; mid-Feb to mid-May & early July to mid-Sept) and there's also a frugal hotel, *Finse 1222* (☎56 52 67 11, fax 56 52 67 17; ②; Feb–Sept).

Flåm and the Aurlandsfjord

Lonely **Myrdal**, just forty minutes by train from Voss, is the start of one of Europe's most celebrated branch rail lines, the twenty-kilometre-long, nine-hundred-metre plummet down **Flåmsdal**, the valley at whose foot the village of **Flåm** and the **Aurlandsfjord** lie – a fifty-minute **train ride** not to be missed under any circumstances. The track, which took four years to lay in the 1930s, worms down the mountainside, passing through hand-dug tunnels. At one point, the line negotiates an especially steep drop of nearly 300m by doubling back on itself. The line is one of the steepest anywhere in the world, with vistas of the valley below, and as the tiny train screeches its way down the mountain, past cas-

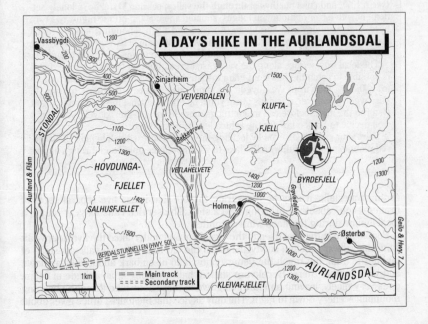

A DAY'S HIKE IN THE AURLANDSDAL

A DAY'S HIKE IN THE AURLANDSDAL

ØSTERBØ TO VASSBYGDI

Start: Østerbø (820m).
Finish: Vassbygdi (94m).
Distance: 21 km.
Time: 6–7hr.
Maps: 1416 I Aurlandsdalen (M711).
Transport: Geilo–Flåm bus to Østerbø (late June to mid-Sept 2 daily; 1hr 40min); or Flåm–Geilo bus to Østerbø (late May to mid-June & late Sept Thurs–Sun 1 daily; late June to mid-Sept 3 daily; 1hr 10min). Taxi (☎94 50 49 31) from Flåm.
Accommodation: In Flåm (see p.198) or in Østerbø, where there are two private-ly-owned mountain lodges, the smart *Østerbø Fjellstove* (mid-May to Sept; ☎57 63 11 77, fax 57 63 11 52; ②), with a first-rate restaurant, and the adjacent *Østerbø Turisthytte* (mid-April to Sept; ☎57 63 11 41, fax 57 63 11 18; ②), run along the same lines but a good deal plainer.

The **trail between Østerbø and Vassbygdi** is justifiably one of Norway's most celebrated one-day hikes. It's actually part of a classic two- or three-day hike from Finse (see p.194), across the northern peripheries of the Hardangervidda and down the Aurlandsdal valley. This longer journey incorporates an extravagant range of scenery, from upland plateau to deep ravines; in the valley, it traces the final miles of an ancient path and cattle drovers' route that once linked eastern and western Norway. Up until the 1970s, hikers would begin at Finse station and get back on the train at Flåm, but then **Highway 50** was rammed through the Aurlandsdal in connection with the development of hydroelectricity generation here. This once-controversial road branches off Highway 7 at Hol, just east of Geilo (see p.137), and runs northwest through the valley, passing **Østerbø**, a lonely set-tlement with a pair of mountain lodges, situated about 800m off the highway. From here, it zigzags down to Vassbygdi, Aurland and Flåm. Though it has improved access to the area, the road has robbed the valley of some of its wild splendour, but that part of the trail between Østerbø and Vassbygdi remains strikingly beautiful.

The local **bus** service along the valley isn't great, but timetables are such that it is possible to catch the bus from Flåm to Østerbø, make the hike and return again to Flåm by bus from Vassbygdi the same day (there's nowhere to stay in Vassbygdi). However, this does mean you'll be hiking against the clock; arriving at Østerbø the night before can make things more leisurely. Alternatively, you might well decide to book a taxi for the return leg from Vassbygdi.

Start your walk in Østerbø by locating the vehicle access track behind the large, red mountain lodge and, with the lake to your rear, hike uphill and through a gate.

cading waterfalls, it may be reassuring to note that it has five separate sets of brakes, each capable of bringing it to a stop. The service runs all year round, a local lifeline during the deep winter months.

People have in the past risen to the challenge and undertaken the five-hour **walk** from the railway junction at Myrdal down the old road into the valley, instead of taking the train, but much the better option is to disembark about halfway down and walk in from there. **Berekvam** station, halfway along at an altitude of 343m, does very nicely, leaving an enthralling two-to three-hour hike through changing mountain scenery down to Flåm. The only advice that the tourist office gives about

A few hundred metres on, cross the bridge you see to your left; it's here you pick up the first DNT sign to Vassbygdi. The path continues downhill towards the lake and eventually passes a small farmhouse. With the Østerbø huts now behind you, the track starts to head steadily uphill. It is etched into the hillside and clearly delineated by worn stones and the occasional red "T".

After 45minutes, you cross over some large slabs of rock to reach a gate. Go through the gate, and almost immediately the track drops down a steep hillside and under a rock overhang, with a marvellous view of the river valley and the **Gravadalen** waterfall. About one hour into the hike you cross the bridge over the Gravadalen river and arrive at a farmhouse with solar panels. Walking alongside the farmhouse, you cross a small meadow to go through another gate, which brings you to a wide stretch of the river. With the river on your left, keep going past the bridge and, half an hour on from the farmhouse, you reach a cairn marked **Grimerodl**. The next bit of the track can get quite boggy as it cuts across numerous streams, but soon you start to climb away from the valley floor, the hillsides dusted with pine and birch trees.

Two hours into the hike, the track reaches a sign marked **Sondrelli**. At this point there is a steep 150-metre descent to the river and the track is cut into the rock. A rope handrail is provided for reassurance, and the track itself is never less than 0.75m wide. About forty-five minutes later, the river disappears from sight to your left and you push on through the trees to a fork in the track – keep to the right. A few minutes later, you're heading down towards the river again and, three hours into the hike, you reach a bridge. Don't cross it, but instead follow the "T"s across the scree and boulder-studded mountainside.

Three-and-a-half hours from the start of your hike, you will come to the sign for **Vetlahelvete** (Little Hell Cave), a sombre and partly water-filled cave with a domed ceiling, a short walk off the trail. The walls are smooth, and there is a narrow open space at the top that lets in a bit of light. Back on the main track, it's another half-hour to the **Bakkegrovi** stream, which you cross, and then there's a further half-hour scramble downwards with the vegetation becoming thicker: wild raspberries, geraniums and ferns all grow freely here.

About five hours into the hike, you cross the spray-splattered bridge over the **Veiverdalselvi** and then head up towards the **Sinjarheim** summer farmhouse. Fifteen minutes' walk after and below the farmhouse, the route – blasted through rock walls – follows the riverside and there are rope handholds to assist hikers. Having traversed this tricky section, scramble down the rocky hillside, crossing several streams by a mixture of stepping stones and bridges, until, nearly six hours' walk from your starting point, you reach the start of a stretch of tree-lined river. An hour on from here and you leave the footpath for a country lane, which brings you down to the car park and bus stop in desultory **Vassbygdi**.

this route is not to walk the other way, *up* to Myrdal, which would take forever, and anyway there's nothing there (apart from the train station) if and when you finally do arrive. If you've come equipped with a decent mountain bike, you could always **cycle** down instead, though the road is too steep to be relaxing.

Flåm

FLÅM village, where the branch railway line from Myrdal ends, lies alongside meadows and orchards on the Aurlandsfjord, a slender branch of the Sognefjord.

However, having made the exciting journey, you could be excused for initially wondering why you bothered. The fjordside complex adjoining the train station is crass
and commercial – on display are souvenir trolls and the like – and on summer days
the tiny village heaves with tourists who pour off the train, have lunch, and then
head out by bus and ferry, having first captured the valley on film. But a brief stroll
is enough to leave the crowds behind at the harbourside, while out of season, or in
the early evening when the day-trippers have all moved on, Flåm is a pleasant spot
– and an especially restful place to spend the night. If you are prepared to risk the
weather, early September is perhaps the best time to visit; the peaks already have a
covering of snow and the vegetation is just turning its autumnal golden brown.

The harbourside complex is ugly but convenient, containing a supermarket, a
train ticket office and the **tourist office** (May & Sept Mon–Fri 10.30am–6.30pm;
June–Aug daily 8.30am–8.30pm; Oct–April Mon–Fri 8am–4pm; ☎57 63 21 06),
where you can buy fjord ferry tickets and pick up local transport timetables, as
well as information on hikes in Flåmsdal. If you do **stay**, neat and trim *Flåm
Camping*, a couple of minutes' signposted walk from the train station, has tent
spaces and cabins (①). It also incorporates a small and well-kept **youth hostel**
(May–Sept; ☎57 63 21 21, fax 57 63 23 80; ①, dorm beds 95kr). Flåm's only **hotel**
is the *Fretheim* (☎57 63 22 00, fax 57 63 23 03; ④, in winter ③), a rambling structure whose attractive older part, with high-pitched roofs and white-painted clapboard, is now flanked by ungainly extensions. The hotel is set back from the water
a couple of hundred metres from the station. The *Heimly Pensjonat* (☎57 63 23 00,
fax 57 63 23 40; ②) provides simple but adequate lodgings in a mundane, modern
block that overlooks the fjord, about 450m east of the train station along the
shore. The only good place to **eat** is the *Fretheim Hotell*.

Moving on from Flåm

From Flåm, there are daily **Hurtigbåt** services up the Aurlandsfjord and then
along the Sognefjord to Bergen; ports of call include Leikanger, Vangsnes,
Balestrand and Vik. The one-way trip to Bergen takes five-and-a-half hours and
costs 420kr, while Balestrand is two hours from Flåm and the ride costs 110kr.
Hurtigbåt ferries from Flåm also serve the Aurlandsfjord's offshoot, **Nærøyfjord**
(June to mid-Sept 4 daily; mid-Sept to May 1 or 2 daily). The Nærøyfjord is the narrowest fjord in Europe, its high rock faces keeping out the sun throughout the
winter, its stern beauty making for a superb trip. At the end of the ride the ferry
pulls into **GUDVANGEN**, a forlorn jetty at the southern tip of Nærøyfjord. From
here, buses head east back to Flåm and south to Voss and Bergen. For the most
part, bus and ferry times are co-ordinated, but confirm connections before you
set out. The one-way ferry fare from Flåm to Gudvangen is 135kr (170kr return),
and the journey takes two hours.

Leaving Flåm by **bus**, there are two to four daily services west to Gudvangen, Voss
and Bergen, and a sparser service (late June to Sept 1–4 daily) east to the
Aurlandsdal hamlets of **Vassbygdi** and **Østerbø** – at either end of the hike described
on pp.196–197. Beyond Østerbø, the bus continues on to Geilo (see p.137).

The Sognefjord and Highway 55 to Lom

Profoundly beautiful, the **Sognefjord** drills inland some 200km from the coast, its
inner recesses splintering into half a dozen subsidiary fjords. None of the villages

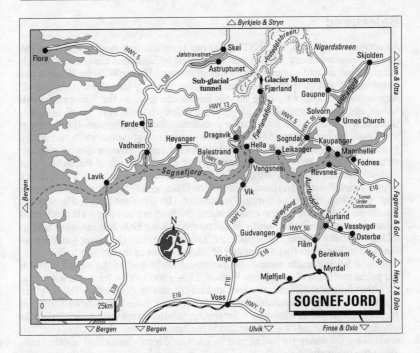

and small towns that dot the fjord quite lives up to the splendid setting, but **Balestrand** and **Fjærland** come close and are easily the best bases. Both are on the north side of the fjord which, given the lack of roads on the south side, is where you want (or pretty much have) to be – unless you're arriving from Flåm (p.197).

The Sognefjord's north bank is hugged by **Highway 55** for almost the whole of its length. At **Sogndal** the highway slices northeast, clipping past the **Lustrafjord** before climbing steeply to run along the western side of the **Jotunheimen mountains**. Even by Norwegian standards, this is an extravagantly beautiful journey, the road eventually heading down to **Lom** (see p.206) on Highway 15. What's more, side roads lead off the highway to a pair of top-notch attractions, **Urnes stave church** and, further north, to the east side of the Jostedalsbreen glacier at **Nigardsbreen**. For more on the glacier, see p.205.

Bus, car ferry and express passenger ferry connections to and around the Sognefjord are excellent. Operating about halfway along the fjord, perhaps the most useful of the **car ferries** links Vangsnes, Hella and Dragsvik (for Balestrand), but in the east of the fjord the 24-hour shuttle between Fodnes and Mannheller is useful too, especially if you're arriving from Oslo on the E16 (see p.136). **Hurtigbåt** services connect Bergen, Balestrand, Vangsnes and Flåm, and long-distance **buses** come up from Bergen via Voss to scuttle along the north shore between Hella and Sogndal, where you change for Balestrand. Here, some services press on east to Oslo, others run up Highway 5 to Fjærland and the Nordfjord (see pp.201 and 207). Along Highway 55, there is only a limited local bus service between Sogndal and Lom; the service runs from the middle of June through to August.

Balestrand

An appealing first stop, **BALESTRAND** has been a tourist destination since the mid-nineteenth century, when it was discovered by European travellers in search of cool, clear air and picturesque mountain scenery. Kaiser Wilhelm II was a frequent visitor, and the British bourgeoisie came regularly too. These days, the village is used as a touring base for the immediate area, as the battery of small hotels and restaurants above the quay testifies. It's still very small in scale, though, and among the 2000-strong population, farming remains the principal livelihood. An hour or so will allow you to take a peek at Balestrand's two attractions. The **English church of St Olav** (free) is a spiky brown-and-beige wooden structure built in 1897 in the general style of a stave church at the behest of a British émigré, a certain Margaret Kvikne. One of those curious relics of Britain's imperial past, the church remains part of the Diocese of Gibraltar, which arranges English-language services during the summer. The Germans have left their mark too. About 400m south of the church along the fjord are two large **Viking burial mounds**, supposedly the tombs of the mythical King Bele and his wife, next to which is a statue of Bele in a heroic pose, plonked there by the kaiser – and across the fjord in Vangsnes there's a statue of his son-in-law to match (see p.203).

Several **hiking trails** ascend the mountains to the west of the village to reach the peaks and lakes of the plateau beyond. This is spectacular territory, with trails for either long and difficult, or short and comparatively easy, hikes. One popular hiking area is the **Saurdalen valley**, 14km from Balestrand: head south on Highway 55 and after 7km watch for the signposted forest road which twists its way up to two car parks – the second is the one you want. From here, one trail leads along the valley, threading past its lakes, and across moorland; another cuts along the ridge above.

Practicalities

There are no **buses** to Balestrand direct from Bergen and Voss; coming from the south the easiest option is to change at Sogndal. Nor are there car ferries to Balestrand – the nearest you'll get is Dragsvik 9km to the north. **Hurtigbåt** services do call at Balestrand, however, docking at the quayside in the town centre. From there it's a couple of minutes' walk uphill to the **tourist office** (mid-June to early Aug Mon–Fri 7.30am–9pm, Sat 7.30am–6.30pm, Sun 8am–5.30pm; mid-Aug to mid-Sept Mon–Fri 7.30am–1pm & 3.30–5.30pm, Sat 7.30am–1pm & 3.30–6.30pm, Sun 8am–12.30pm & 4.30–5.30pm; late Sept Mon–Fri 9am–3pm; ☎57 69 12 55). They have a wide range of fjord leaflets and can supply maps showing hiking routes in the surrounding mountains. Bikes can also be rented here for 100kr a day.

For **accommodation**, try the charming *Midtnes Pensjonat* (☎57 69 11 33, fax 57 69 15 84; ③), about 300m from the dock behind the English church. It's a low-key, pleasantly sedate affair with a few plain but spacious rooms in a modern wing adjoining the original clapboard house; make sure to get a room with a fjord view. Another good choice, just 150m uphill from the dock, is the **youth hostel** (☎57 69 13 03, fax 57 69 16 70; ①, dorm beds 165kr; late June to late Aug), part of the comfortable *Kringsjå Hotel* (same number; ②), whose long verandah overlooks the fjord. The hostel rents bikes and boats and has self-catering facilities.

At the top end here is *Kvikne's Hotel* (☎57 69 11 01, fax 57 69 15 02; ④; May–Sept), whose various buildings dominate much of the waterfront. It's worth popping into the bar to take a look at the fancy furniture and fittings – some of which are in a sort of nineteenth-century version of Viking style. The best rooms here are old and overlook the fjord, but other rooms, some of which also have good views, are round the back in a modern annexe. The town **campsite**, *Sjøtun Camping* (☎57 69 12 23), occupies a treeless field just beyond the burial mounds, a kilometre or so south of the dock. For **food**, both the *Kringsjå* and the *Midtnes* serve tasty, excellent-value dinners; alternatively try the *Kvikne's* restaurant or, more affordably, *Gekkens Café*, upstairs in the pint-sized shopping centre on the quayside.

When it comes to **moving on from Balestrand** you're spoiled for choice. **Buses** travel east along the northern shore of the fjord to Sogndal, the first part of their journey to Oslo. At Sogndal, you can also change for Fjærland and Førde, where you pick up the bus to Stryn (see p.211). **Hurtigbåt** services leave Balestrand for Bergen, Vik, Flåm and Sogndal, and, best of the lot, a local **passenger boat** sails north from Balestrand to Fjærland (June to to mid-September 1 daily; 1hr 25min; 110kr each way). If you drive to Fjærland, be warned that a toll of 130kr is levied on Highway 5 just south of the village. Finally, from Balestrand, it's 9km along the fjord to **Dragsvik**, where **car ferries** operate a triangular service sailing south across the fjord to Vangsnes (20kr passengers; 54kr car and driver) and east to Hella (15kr; 36kr).

North to Fjærland

The most direct route north from Balestrand is a lovely trip by passenger ferry up to the village of Fjærland. The **Fjærlandsfjord** is a wild place, its sides not steep as elsewhere, but blanketed with a thick covering of trees extending down to the water's edge, while vast vertical clefts in the rock sport a succession of tumbling waterfalls. **FJÆRLAND** itself matches its surroundings perfectly – a gentle ribbon of old wooden houses edging the fjord, with the mountains as a backcloth. It's one of the region's most picturesque places, saved from the developers by its isolation: it was one of the last settlements on the Sognefjord to be connected to the road system, with Highway 5 from Sogndal only being completed in 1986. Moreover, it's eschewed the crasser forms of commercialism and become the self-styled "Norwegian Book Town" (Den norske bokbyen), with a dozen old buildings accommodating antiquarian and second-hand bookshops (mid-May to Aug daily 10am–5pm). Naturally enough, most of the books are in Norwegian, but there's a liberal sprinkling of English editions too.

Bookshops aside, the village has two good-looking buildings, the first of which is the **Hotel Mundal** (see p.202), whose nineteenth-century turrets, verandahs and high-pitched roofs overlook the fjord from amongst the handful of buildings that amount to the village centre. Next door, the 1861 **church** may be lacking in ornamentation but is immaculately maintained, and its graveyard hints at the hard but healthy life of the district's farmers – most of them seem to have lived to a ripe old age. Many locals are still farmers, but in summer hardly any of them herd their cattle up to the mountain pastures as was the custom until the 1960s. The disused tracks to these summer farms (*støls*) now provide lots of possible **hiking trails** of varying lengths and difficulties. The tourist office (see p.202) will advise, but one of the easier routes is the two-hour jaunt west along a country lane up **Mundalsdal** to **Heimastølen**, from where a track continues up to the marshy pastures of **Mundalsfjellstølen**.

There are fjordside attractions in Fjærland too. The marshes at the head of the fjord are frequented by a wide range of migratory birds in spring and autumn, enough to have prompted the establishment of the **Bøyaøyri nature reserve**. It's not a large area and there are no hides, but with a pair of binoculars it's easy enough to watch the birds from the road. The reserve is about 2km north of Fjærland, along the quiet byroad that links the village with Highway 5. About 500m further on, metres from the main road, is the **Norsk Bremuseum** (Norwegian Glacier Museum; April, May, Sept & Oct daily 10am–4pm; June–Aug daily 9am–7pm; information and enquiries free but displays 60kr; ☎57 69 32 88), which tells you more than you ever wanted to know about glaciers and then some. It features several lavish hands-on displays – like a simulated walk below a glacier – and screens films about glaciers; package tourists turn up in droves.

The museum is one of the Jostedalsbreen Nasjonalpark's three information centres (see p.209). It therefore has the details of all the various **guided glacier walks** on offer, including those on the nearest hikeable arm, **Supphellebreen** or, to be precise, that part of it called **Flatbreen** (July & Aug). However, this is a challenging part of the glacier and walks here last between six and eight hours – and unlike at Nigardsbreen (see p.205), for example, there are no two-hour or family walks. Hikes start at the car park at **Øygarden**, about 4km off Highway 5 – watch for the sign just 2km north of the Bremuseum. More simply, you can get close to the glacier without breaking sweat just 7km north of the Bremuseum on Highway 5. Here, just before you enter the tunnel, look out for the signposted side road on the right, leading the 200m to the *Brævasshytta* restaurant. This smart, modern place, a tour-package favourite, overlooks the slender glacial lake fed by the **Bøyabreen** arm of the glacier up above. It takes a couple of minutes to stroll down from the restaurant to the lake, close to the sooty shank of the glacier.

Practicalities

The nearest you'll get to Fjærland by regular **bus** is the Norsk Bremuseum on Highway 5, from where it's an easy 2.5-kilometre stroll south along the fjord to the village. **Passenger boats** arriving from Balestrand (and Hella) (June to mid-Sept 1 daily; 1hr 25min) dock in the centre, from where a special bus takes passengers on to the Bremuseum and then, after a stop-off of over an hour, to the glaciers; the return bus fare is 80kr. The **tourist office**, next to the passenger boat dock in the centre (June to mid-Sept daily 9.30am–4pm; ☎57 69 32 33), advises on local hiking routes, sells hiking maps and has bus and ferry timetables. **Cycle rental** is available from the S-laget grocery store close by (Mon–Fri 9am–4.30pm & Sat 9am–2pm; ☎57 69 31 02).

There are two fjordside **hotels** in Fjærland. The obvious choice is the splendid *Hotel Mundal* (☎57 69 31 01, fax 57 69 31 79; ④; late May to mid-Sept), a quirky sort of place, where the public rooms display many original features, from the parquet floors and fancy wooden scrollwork through to the old-fashioned sliding doors of the cavernous dining room. The rooms are frugal and some show their age, but somehow it doesn't matter much. If you do stay, look out for the old photos on the walls of men in plus-fours and hobnail boots clambering round the glaciers – only softies bothered with gloves. Nearby, the *Fjærland Fjordstue Hotell* (☎57 69 32 00, fax 57 69 31 61; ②) is very different – a well-tended family hotel with smart modern furnishings and a conservatory overlooking the fjord. A third option is *Bøyum Camping* (☎57 69 32 52, fax 57 69 31 68) near the Bremuseum; they have huts (①) as well as spaces for tents. Both hotels offer good, wholesome **food**.

Long-distance **buses** travelling along Highway 5 can be picked up close to Fjærland's Bremuseum. There are services south to Sogndal and Oslo along the E16 (see p.136) and north to Skei, Førde (change for Stryn – see p.211) and Florø (see p.213). The road north from Fjærland **tunnels** under the Jostedalsbreen glacier to meet the E39 at Skei near the Astruptunet; this route is covered on p.208. The toll point on Highway 5 is just south of the Fjærland turning; the charge for car and driver is 130kr. Passenger boats from Fjærland to Hella connect with the regular car ferry over the Sognefjord to Vangsnes.

Vangsnes and Vik

From Balestrand, Highway 55 loops for 9km around the Esefjord, an inlet of the Sognefjord, to the quayside at **Dragsvik**, from where car ferries cross the mouth of the Fjærlandsfjord to Hella for the road to Sogndal (see below). They also shuttle across the Sognefjord to **VANGSNES**, where local farmers must have had a real shock when, in 1913, Kaiser Wilhelm erected a twelve-metre high **statue** of the legendary Viking chief Fridtjof the Bold on the hilltop above their jetty. The statue still stands, an eccentric monument to the Kaiser's fascination with Nordic mythology – Fridtjof the Bold was in love with Ingebjorg, daughter of King Bele, whose statue stands back across the fjord at Balestrand. You can walk or drive the 500m up from the jetty to take a closer look at Fridtjof, and though it's hard not to find the underlying Aryan ideology objectionable, it's still worth plodding up there for the fine view.

From Vangsnes, it's a straight 12km south along the water's edge to **VIK**, a rather half-hearted village that sprawls up a wide valley. There would be no point in pausing here were it not for the **Hopperstad stave church** (mid-May to mid-June & mid-Aug to mid-Sept daily 10am–5pm; mid-June to mid-Aug daily 9am–7pm; 40kr), sitting on a hillock off Highway 13 – a signed 1500m from the fjord. In the 1880s the locals were about to knock it down, but a visiting architect and his antiquarian chum persuaded them to change their minds. The pair set about repairing the place and did a good job: today the church is one of the best examples of its type, its angular roofing surmounted by a long and slender tower. The interior has its moments too, with a Gothic side-altar canopy, parts of which may have been swiped from France by the Vikings, and a so-called lepers' window through which the afflicted listened to church services.

Long-distance buses pass through Vik on their way south to Voss (see p.192), a dramatic journey over the barren wastes of the Vikafjell mountain, but the best way of visiting Vangsnes and Vik is by ferry and **bike** from Balestrand – an easy and enjoyable journey.

Sogndal and Kaupanger

From **Hella**, across the fjord from Dragsvik, the eastbound bus from Balestrand continues for 40km along the water's edge to **SOGNDAL** – bigger and livelier than Balestrand, but still hardly a major metropolis, with a population of just 5000. Neither is Sogndal as appealing: it has a pleasant fjord setting in a broad valley, surrounded by low, green hills dotted with apple and pear trees, but its centre is a rash of modern concrete and glass. Frankly, there are other much more agreeable spots within a few kilometres' radius and your best option is to keep going.

Buses drop passengers at the **station** – a major interchange – on the west side of the town centre at the end of Gravensteinsgata, the long main drag. From here, it's about 400m east to the **tourist office** (late June to late Aug Mon–Fri 9am–8pm, Sat 9am–5pm, Sun 3–8pm; Sept to late June Mon–Fri 9am–4pm; ☎57 67 30 83), housed in one of the flashy modern buildings on Gravensteinsgata. They issue bus and ferry timetables, and have a list of local **accommodation**, though pickings are fairly slim. The nicest place to stay – though it's no great shakes – is the *Hofslund Fjord Hotel*, a stone's throw from the tourist office (☎57 67 10 22, fax 57 67 16 30; ③) and comprising an old wooden building and a modern annexe; ask for a room with a fjord view. Another palatable and certainly economical option is the **youth hostel** (☎57 67 20 33, fax 57 67 31 45; ①, dorm beds 95kr; mid-June to mid-Aug), which manages to feel quite homely despite being housed in a *Folkehøgskule* (residential school); it's near the bridge 400m beyond the roundabout at the east end of Gravensteinsgata – just follow the signs. Note also that this same roundabout marks the start of Fjørevegen, the town's other main drag, which cuts through the commercial heart of the town. The choice of **food** is uninspiring, but the restaurant of the *Quality Sogndal Hotell*, Gravensteinsgata 5 (☎57 67 23 11), is reliable and serves tasty Norwegian dishes at reasonable prices.

From Sogndal, there are **Hurtigbåt** services to Balestrand, Bergen, Vik and Flåm. There are also express **buses** northwest to Fjærland and Førde (for Stryn) and east to Oslo via the E16, a route covered on p.136. Far better than these, however, is the stupendous 140-kilometre journey northeast along Highway 55 to Lom. A **local bus** travels this route, but only in summertime (mid-June to late Aug 2 daily; 3hr 30min). Not far out of Sogndal, Highway 55 also runs past the turnings for Solvorn and the Nigardsbreen glacier (see opposite). There are local buses to both: Solvorn (mid-June to late Aug 1–3 daily, intermittent weekday services the rest of the year; 20min) and Nigardsbreen (mid-June to late Aug 2–5 daily, intermittent weekday services the rest of the year; 2hr 40min). Highway 55 is closed by snow from October to late May or so. Heading to Fjærland, there's a toll of 130kr to use Highway 5; the booths are just south of the Fjærland turning. To or from Oslo, the **car ferry** between Manheller (southeast of Kaupanger) and Fodnes operates round the clock (every 30min; 15min; car & driver 77kr, passengers 26kr).

Kaupanger

Driving down towards Oslo from Sogndal, consider a quick detour to **KAUPANGER**, about 11km southeast of Sogndal off Highway 5. Here, the red and white timber houses of the old part of the village slope up from the harbour towards the **stave church** (early June to late Aug daily 9.30am–5.30pm; 30kr), a much modified thirteenth-century structure whose dourness is offset by its situation: the church sits on a hillside amid buttercup meadows with views of the fjord on one side and forested hills on the other. The interior has one or two unusual features, including a musical score painted on one of the walls and a sad portrait of a Danish bailiff and his family with three stillborn babies. Afterwards, if you've the energy, you can pop down to the ferry dock where the **Sognefjord Båtmuseum** (Boat Museum; May & Sept Mon–Fri 10am–3pm, Sat & Sun 10am–6pm; June–Aug daily 10am–6pm; 30kr) has an assortment of mostly nineteenth-century wooden boats, from sturdy inshore fishing boats and ice boats (the latter fitted with runners for use on frozen fjord inlets) to daintier, faster craft used by Danish dignitaries.

Solvorn and the Urnes stave church

Some 15km northeast of Sogndal on Highway 55 is a turning marking the start of a steep three-kilometre-long road that snakes its way down to **SOLVORN**, an attractive little hamlet beneath the mountains on the sheltered foreshore of the **Lustrafjord**. Solvorn is the site of the *Walaker Hotell* (☎57 68 42 07, fax 57 68 45 44; ③), the most conspicuous part of which is an ugly motel-style block; don't let this put you off from lunching – maybe even staying – here, for its old house, a comely pastel-painted building with a lovely garden, has first-rate period bedrooms.

Urnes stave church

From Solvorn, a local **car ferry** (early June to Sept hourly, 8am–5pm; 15min) sails across the Lustrafjord to **Ornes**, from where it's a stiff, ten-minute hike up the hill to **Urnes stave church** (June–Aug guided tours only; daily 10.30am–5.30pm; 40kr). Magnificently sited with the fjord and the snow-dusted mountains as its backdrop, this is the most celebrated stave church in Norway. Parts of it date back to the twelfth century, making it certainly the oldest, though the church is mainly famous for its **carvings**. On the outside, incorporated into the north wall, are two exquisite door panels, the remains of an earlier church dating from around 1070 and alive with a swirling filigree of strange beasts and delicate vegetation. These forceful, superbly crafted panels bear witness to the sophistication of Viking woodcarving, and indeed this distinctively Nordic art form, found in many countries where Viking influence was felt, is generally known as the Urnes style. Most of the interior is seventeenth-century, but there is Viking woodcarving here too, notably the strange-looking figures and beasts on the capitals of the staves and the sacred-heart bench-ends. The distinctive wooden pomegranates, all bulbous and spiky, are, however, seventeenth-century. The guided tour fills in all the details, and a small display in the house-cum-ticket office has photographic enlargements showing carvings that are hard to make out inside the poorly-lit church. If you don't wish to return to Solvorn after seeing the stave church, you can head north along the minor road that follows the east shore of the Lustrafjord, rejoining Highway 55 at **Skjolden**.

Highway 55 northeast to Lom

Solvorn isn't that far from the **Nigardsbreen**, an arm of the Jostedalsbreen glacier (see p.209). Leaving Solvorn, turn north on to Highway 55 and after 15km you come to **Gaupne**, where Highway 604 branches off for the delightful 34-kilometre trip up the wild, forested valley – lined with waterfalls and a turquoise river – leading to the **Breheimsenteret Jostedal information centre** (May to mid-June & late Aug to Sept daily 10am–5pm; mid-June to late Aug daily 9am–7pm; ☎57 68 32 50; displays 50kr). This ultra-modern structure is bleak and spare, which fits in well with the bare peaks that surround it, and as you sip a coffee on the terrace you can admire the glistening glacier dead ahead. From here, it's an easy three-kilometre drive or walk along the toll road to the shores of an icy green lake where a tiny boat shuttles across to the bare rock slope beside the Nigardsbreen, a great rumpled and seamed wall of ice that sweeps between high peaks. There are two- and four-hour **guided glacier walks** (late June to late August) of the Nigardsbreen, most of which start from the car park; further information on glacier walks is on p.209.

Back at Gaupne, Highway 55 continues 26km northeast to **Skjolden**, beyond which the most dramatic part of the road begins. First the highway wriggles up the hillside, twisting and turning until it reaches a mountain plateau which it traverses, providing absolutely stunning views of the jagged, ice-crusted Jotunheimen peaks to the east. This is Norway's highest mountain crossing and if you want to hang around some more, easily the best of a series of roadside lodges is the attractive *Turtagrø Hotel* (☎57 68 61 16, fax 57 68 61 07; ④; Easter–Oct), just 17km beyond Skjolden. There's been a lodge here since 1888 and the present structure is a large and attractive red-timber building with a smart, very Scandinavian pine interior. There are eight en-suite rooms as well as fifty bunk beds in a Swiss-style chalet (②). The food is first-rate too.

The hotel is a favourite haunt for mountaineers, but it also provides ready access to the **hiking** trails that lattice the Jotunheimen Nasjonalpark, and there's summer cross-country skiing in the vicinity as well. However, the terrain is unforgiving and the weather unpredictable, so novice hikers beware. One tough hike from the hotel is the six-hour haul southeast along the well-worn (but not especially well-signed) path up the **Skagastøldalen** to DNT's self-service **Skagastølsbu** hut (mid-Feb to mid-Oct) – though you can of course make the hike shorter (and less strenuous) by only going some of the way. The valley is divided into a number of steps, each preceded by a short, steep ascent; the hotel is 888m above sea level, the hut, surrounded by a staggering confusion of ice caps, mini-glaciers and craggy ridges at 1758m.

Northeast of the *Turtagrø Hotel*, Highway 55 zips down through forested **Leirdal** and **Bøverdal**, the latter valley containing the old farmstead of **ELVESETER**, some 40km from Turtagrø. Elveseter possesses a peculiar, 32-metre-high carved wooden column, the **Sagasøyla**, topped by the figure of the redoubtable Viking Harold Hardråda. He sits on his horse while, down the column below him, a romantic interpretation of Norwegian history unfolds. Dating from the 1830s, the column was brought to this remote place because no one else would have it – not surprising really.

Lom

The crossroads settlement of **LOM**, 23km from Elveseter, has been a trading and transport centre for centuries, benefiting – in a modest sort of way – from the farms which dot the surrounding valleys. Today, with a population of just 700, it's hardly a boom town, but it does make a comfortable living from the passing tourist trade, with motorists pausing here before the last thump down Highway 15 to the Geirangerfjord (see p.214). Lom's eighteenth-century heyday is recalled by its **stave church** (mid-May to mid-June & mid-Aug to mid-Sept daily 10am–4pm; mid-June to mid-Aug daily 9am–9pm; 25kr), an enormous structure perched on a grassy knoll above the river. The original church was built here about 1200, but it was remodelled and enlarged after the Reformation, when the spire and transepts were added and the flashy altar and pulpit installed. Its most attractive features are the dinky, shingle-clad roofs, adorned by dragon finials, and the Baroque acanthus vine decoration inside.

Nearby is the town's open-air museum, the **Lom Bygdamuseum Presthaugen** (mid-June to mid-Aug daily 11am–6pm; 20kr), a surprisingly enjoyable collection of old log buildings in a forest setting. Norway teems with this type of museum – stay in the country long enough and the very sight of one will make you want to scream – but Lom's is better than most. It is distinguished by the **Olavsstugu**, a modest hut where St Olav is said to have spent a night, and also by what must be the biggest and ugliest **Storstabburet** (large storehouse) in the country. Museum enthusiasts will also want to visit the **Norsk Fjellmuseum** (Norwegian Mountain Museum; May & Sept Mon–Fri 9am–4pm, Sat & Sun 11am–4pm; June–Aug Mon–Fri 9am–6pm, Sat & Sun 10am–5pm; Oct–April Mon–Fri 9am–4pm; 60kr), a brand new museum which focuses on the Jotunheimen mountains: their fauna and flora, landscapes, farmers and past mountaineers. A **combined ticket** for all the stave church and the two museums costs 70kr and is available at any one of them, as well as the tourist office (see below).

Buses to Lom pull in a few metres west of the main crossroads; most of what you're likely to need is within easy walking distance of here. The church and the open-air museum are across the bridge on the other side of the river, as is the mountain museum, which shares its premises with the **tourist office** (May & Sept Mon–Fri 9am–4pm, Sat & Sun 11am–4pm; early June & early Aug Mon–Fri 9am–6pm, Sat & Sun 10am–5pm; mid-June to mid-Aug Mon–Fri 9am–9pm, Sat & Sun 10am–8pm; Oct–April Mon–Fri 9am–4pm; ☎61 21 29 90). The choicest **accommodation** is in the *Fossheim Hotell* (☎61 21 10 05, fax 61 21 15 10; ③), about 300m east of the crossroads along Highway 15. The main lodge here is neat and smart, with an abundance of pine, and behind, trailing up the wooded hillside, are some delightful little wooden cabins (also ③), some of which are very old and all of which are en suite. The hotel **restaurant** is excellent and reasonably priced. A palatable second-choice hotel is the *Fossberg* (☎61 21 10 73, fax 61 21 16 21; ③), a large, mostly wooden modern place by the crossroads.

Leaving Lom, there are regular **bus** services east to Otta, Lillehammer and Oslo, west for Grotli, Stryn, Hellesylt and Måløy – amongst many fjord destinations. Highway 55 southwest to Sogndal is less well served, by a **local bus** (mid-June to late Aug 2 daily; 3hr 30min).

The Nordfjord and the Jostedalsbreen glacier

Emerge from Highway 5's Fjærland tunnel and you've just journeyed under the **Jostedalsbreen glacier**, which seems somehow to slight its dignity – and environmentally dubious. The highway puts a southerly offshoot of the glacier within easy reach of Fjærland (see p.201) and, more importantly, is the handiest way to get between the Sognefjord and the **Nordfjord**, the next great fjord system to the north.

The inner recesses of the Nordfjord are readily explored along Highway 60, which weaves a tortuous course through a string of unexciting little towns in between the fjord and the glacier. Two mountain roads lead off Highway 60 to different glacial arms, one road branching off at **Olden** for **Briksdalsbreen**, the other at **Loen** for **Kjenndalsbreen**. The first is very popular with tourists, the latter slightly more subdued and therefore probably preferable, but to get a real flavour of the ice fields you should go on a guided **glacier hike**, using **Loen** or **Stryn** as a base. For access to the glacier's eastern side, see the Nigardsbreen (p.205).

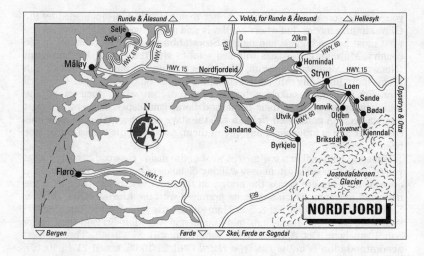

Stryn is an important crossroads where Highway 60 meets Highway 15. From here, it's north to Hellesylt (see p.215), east to Geiranger (see p.216) and west to the Nordfjord itself, with the road dipping and diving along the northern shore of the fjord in between the deep-green reflective waters and severe peaks. It's a handsome enough journey, but the Nordfjord does not have the allure of its more famous neighbours, at least in part because its roadside hamlets lack real appeal. It's 100km from Stryn to the end of Highway 15, where the fishing port of **Måløy** offers several good coastal excursions, not least to the solitary monastic remains of **Selja** island. Long-distance **buses** scuttle along highways 5, 15 and 60, but on minor roads down to the glacier you must rely on intermittent local services.

North from Fjærland to the Jostedalsbreen

Heading north from Fjærland on Highway 5, it's about 30km to the **Kjøsnes** junction, where a bridge marks the start of the country road west along the southern shore of a lake, **Jølstravatnet**. After 12km you reach the **Astruptunet** (June–Aug daily 10am–5pm; Sept Sun 10am–4pm; 50kr), the farmstead home of the artist **Nikolai Astrup** (1880–1928). He mostly painted romanticized rural scenes in bright colours and used soft, flowing forms, but unlike many of his contemporaries he eschewed realism in favour of Neo-impressionism. In that regard, he bridged the gap between his generation of Norwegian painters and the Matisse-inspired artists who followed. The Astruptunet looks pretty much the same as it did during the artist's lifetime, comprising a pretty complex of old timber buildings that includes a sixteenth-century cottage, but a modern gallery housing a selection of Astrup's paintings and woodcuts has replaced the old barn. The Astruptunet is also used for temporary exhibitions, when opening hours can change – call to check (☎57 72 67 82).

Back on Highway 5 at Kjøsnes, it's only a couple of kilometres to the **Skei** crossroads, where you turn north onto the E39 for the twenty-kilometre cruise up the valley to Byrkjelo and the Highway 60 intersection. From the Byrkjelo junction, it's 40km along Highway 60 to **Olden**, where you turn off for the **Briksdalsbreen**, and 7km more to Loen, at the start of the road to the **Kjenndalsbreen**; for more on both of these routes, see p.210.

The Jostedalsbreen

Lurking in the mountains, the **Jostedalsbreen** is a five-hundred-square-kilometre ice plateau that dominates the whole of the inner Nordfjord region and reaches out towards Sognefjord and the Jotunheimen mountains. The glacier stretches irregularly northeast from Highway 5 to Highway 15, with its 24 arms nudging down into the nearby valleys, the clay particles of the meltwater giving the local rivers and lakes their distinctive deep-green colouring. Catching sight of the ice nestling between peaks and ridges can be unnerving: the overwhelming feeling is that it shouldn't really be there. As the poet Norman Nicholson wrote:

> *A malevolent, rock-crystal*
> *Precipitate of lava,*
> *Corroded with acid,*
> *Inch by inch erupting*
> *From volcanoes of cold*

Nicholson's lines are an evocative and accurate description of a phenomenon that, for centuries, presented an impenetrable east–west barrier in Norway, crossed only at certain points by determined farmers and adventurers.

In 1991, the glacier was placed within the protected **Jostedalsbreen Nasjonalpark** in order to co-ordinate its conservation. The main benefit of this for tourists has been the proliferation of worthwhile **guided glacier walks** (June to early Sept only) on its various arms, ranging from two-hour excursions to all-day, fully equipped hikes. Prices start at around 90kr, with a half-day trip about 250kr. A comprehensive leaflet detailing all the various walks is available at local tourist offices and some hostels and hotels – like the *Alexandra* in Loen – and at the national park's three **information centres**. Among the latter, the most readily accessible is the **Norsk Bremuseum** (glacier museum) on the edge of Fjærland (see p.202). The others are the Jostedalsbreen Nasjonalparksenter (mid-May to mid-June daily 9am–4pm, mid-June to mid-Aug daily 9am–6pm, mid-Aug to mid-Sept daily 10am–4pm; ☎57 87 72 00; exhibitions 50kr) in Oppstryn, 20km east of Stryn on Highway 15 – easy to get to by car, but a pain by bus – and the isolated **Breheimsenteret Jostedal**, up a long byroad north of Sogndal, off Highway 55 on the east side of the glacier (see p.205). Each of the three has displays on all things glacial and sells books, souvenirs and local hiking maps.

All three information centres – and most of the tourist offices, hostels and hotels – make bookings for **guided glacier walks**. In principle bookings can be taken up to about 6pm the evening before you want to go, though it's better not to leave it until the last minute. **Equipment** is provided, though you'll need to take good boots, waterproofs, warm clothes, gloves, hat, sunglasses – and your own **food** and **drink**. With a vehicle, you can get within easy striking distance of the designated **starting points** for all the glacier walks. By **bus** it can be tricky, so plan your journey carefully. Several of these places are – or are near – good **vantage points** which allow you to get a good view of the glacier without actually getting onto it. Two of the routes we describe below – to the Briksdalsbreen and the Kjenndalsbreen – begin at such places, and there's a third route on p.205.

GLACIER DANGERS

Glaciers are in constant motion and are potentially very dangerous. Never, under any circumstances, climb a glacier without a guide; never walk beneath a glacier; always heed the instructions at the site.

Though it seems a bit of cheat, you can avoid a long detour off Highway 5 by taking a close peek at a sliver of glacier, Bøyabreen (see p.202), just outside Fjærland.

Olden and the Briksdalsbreen

The hamlet of **Olden** doesn't have much going for it, but it is at the start of the 24-kilometre-long byroad south to **Briksdal**, a scattering of mountain chalets from where it's an easy 45-minute walk to the **Briksdalsbreen**, the most visited arm of the Jostedalsbreen. The path skirts waterfalls and weaves up the river until you finally reach the glacier, surprisingly blue except for streaks of dust and dirt. It's a simple matter to get close to the ice itself as you are only separated from it by a flimsy rope with a small warning sign – be careful. If you don't fancy all of the walk, you can hire a pony and trap at the souvenir shop/café area at the start of the trail, something that will cost you around 175–200kr – but you still have to hike the last bit anyway. Guided glacier walks begin at the café area too. Local **buses** run from Loen/Stryn to Briksdal all year (1–2 daily; 45min/1hr).

Loen and the Kjenndalsbreen

LOEN spreads ribbon-like along the fjord's low-lying, grassy foreshore with snow-capped mountains breathing down its neck. The village is also home to one of Norway's more famous hotels, the *Hotel Alexandra* (☎57 87 50 00, fax 57 87 50 51, *www.alexandra.no*; ⑤, s/r ④), a large and flashy modern block fringed by carefully manicured gardens. The rooms are spacious, infinitely comfortable and furnished in bright modern style; breakfasts are banquet-like. Across the road, the motel-style *Hotel Loenfjord* (☎57 87 57 00, fax 57 87 57 51; ④, s/r ③), owned by the same company as the *Alexandra*, offers less expensive and perfectly adequate rooms.

From Loen, the seventeen-kilometre-long byroad to the **Kjenndalsbreen** begins innocuously enough, gently climbing the river valley and slipping between lush meadows before pressing on beside Lovatnet, a long and slender lake which extends right to the end of the valley. However, after about 10km, the road narrows and gets rougher as it zigzags upwards; the last couple of kilometres – beyond the toll post (30kr) – are quite hairy and should not be attempted after dark. The road peters out at a café and car park, from where it's a rocky twenty-minute walk to a vantage point beside the glacier, whose fissured blue and white folds of ice tumble down the rock face, with a furious white-green river, fed by plummeting meltwater, flowing underneath.

There is a local **bus** from Loen (and Stryn, see opposite) down the first 12km of the valley to **Bødal**, near the **Bødalsbreen** arm of the glacier. The bus is infrequent though (1 daily on schooldays only), and anyway you're better off taking the much more scenic **boat** ride (mid-June to Aug 1 daily, with extra departures during July; 3hr return). Organized by the *Hotel Alexandra*, which issues tickets and takes bookings, the boat trips depart from the **Sande** jetty, 4km up the road from Loen, and head up the lake to a second jetty by the café at the end of the road. The return fare (you come back by bus) is 110kr. **Guided walks** of the Bødalsbreen start at **Bødalssetra**, 5km from Bødal up a bumpy, signposted toll-road and about ten minutes' walk from the car park at the end. From the meeting place to the glacier is an easy 2.5-kilometre stroll.

Stryn and Hornindal

STRYN, just 11km northwest around the fjord from Loen, is the biggest town around here, though with a population of just 1100 that's hardly a major boast. For the most part, it's a humdrum modern sprawl by a long main street, but there is a pleasant pocket of antique timber houses huddled round the old bridge, down by the river just to the south of the main drag – take a few moments to have a look around.

Buses stop beside the river, from where it's a five- to ten-minute walk east to the town centre. The **tourist office**, located in the square just off the main street (June & Aug daily 9am–6pm; July daily 9am–8pm; ☎57 87 23 33), and behind *Johan's Kafeteria*, issues free town maps, has a wide range of local brochures, sells hiking maps and takes bookings for guided walks on the Jostedalsbreen (see p.209). For **accommodation**, look no further than the *Walhalla Gjestgiveri*, Perhusvegen 13 (☎57 87 10 72, fax 57 87 18 94; ①). This provides simple and friendly lodgings plus a tasty breakfast in one of the attractive timber buildings down by the river, about 200m west of the tourist office. Alternatively, the lodge-like **youth hostel** (☎57 87 13 36, fax 57 87 11 06; ①, dorm beds 150kr; June–Aug) is an inconvenient and awkward 1500-metre walk up the hill to the north of the centre – get a map from the tourist office or keep your eyes peeled for the signs on Highway 15. The only reasonable **food** in town is served at *Johan's Kafeteria* on the main street, which has sandwiches, pizzas and cafeteria-style meals.

Heading west out of Stryn, highways 15 and 60 share the same stretch of road until, after 16km, Highway 60 veers north along the shore of **Hornindalsvatn**, at 514m Europe's deepest – and arguably Norway's clearest – lake. After 6km, you reach **HORNINDAL**, a straggly little place distinguished by the **Anders Svor Museum** (June–Aug Mon–Sat 11am–5pm, Sun 1–5pm; 30kr), which occupies a comely Neoclassical structure built in 1953. Hardly a household name today, Svor (1864–1929) was a native of Hornindal who established something of an interna-tional reputation as a sculptor of romantic figures that were once much admired by the bourgeoisie. Clichéd pieces like *Prayer* (Bøn), *Grief* (Sorg) and *A Small Girl* (Lita jente) are typical of his work, though busts of his wife, Brit, and of the polar explor-er Fridtjof Nansen reveal much more originality and talent. Svor's career is typical of his generation too. Like other Norwegian artists, he was keen to escape the back-woods, moving to Kristiania (Oslo) in 1881 and four years later to Copenhagen, the start of an extended exile that only ended after Norway's independence in 1905. The museum exhibits 450 of Svor's works and holds temporary exhibitions; plans to set up a permanent display on local folk music traditions were well under way at time of writing. Beyond Hornindal, Highway 60 zips up the valley to reach, 25km on, the Norangsdal valley and shortly afterwards Hellesylt (see p.215).

Måløy

From Stryn, Highway 15 travels west, trundling over the hills and skimming along the southern edge of Hornindalsvatn before arriving at small-town **Nordfjordeid** after about 50km. Here you can pick up the E39, a good road – despite a complicated route and several time-consuming ferries – that traverses the fjords, leading south to Bergen (290km away), and north to Ålesund (100km). Alternatively, you can push on west for the last leg of the journey to the coast, a 52-kilometre haul along the harsh northern shore of the **Nordfjord**. This finally brings you into the small fishing port of **MÅLØY**, stuck on an island at the fjord's mouth and reached by a massive "singing" bridge: when the wind is in the right direction, the bridge emits an unnervingly high-pitched squeal. Måløy itself hardly sets the pulse racing, but it occupies a grand location on the east shore of the island of **Vågsøy**, whose high, swelling peaks shelter the town from the westerlies that blow in off the Atlantic. For a full blast of the elements drive out of Måløy on the 22km excursion west over Vågsøy to the **Kråkenes lighthouse**, but be warned that the narrow road leading there over the mountains requires nerves of steel. A rather less hair-raising trip is the eleven-kilometre drive along the south shore, through the old fishing station of **Torskangerpollen**, to the unusual **Kannestein rock**, eroded by the sea into the shape of a mushroom and a popular spot for a photo.

Måløy is the terminus of the Nordfjordekspressen bus, which begins in Oslo, shoots up the E6 to Otta and then travels west to Måløy along Highway 15 via Lom and Stryn. **Buses** pull in beside the ferry terminals just to the north of the town centre, where the **tourist office** is on Sjøgata (mid-June to mid-August daily noon–8pm; ☎57 85 08 50). Måløy is a **Hurtigrute** port, with boats departing south at 5.30am for the leisurely three-hour cruise to Florø and the nine-hour journey to Bergen, at 7.30am north to Ålesund and Kristiansund. There's a **Hurtigbåt** service to Florø and Bergen as well, and this clips several hours off the Hurtigrute journey time (1–2 daily; Florø 1hr 15min, 165kr; Bergen 4hr 20min, 495kr one-way). Måløy is short on **accommodation**, but the *Norlandia Måløy Hotell* (☎57 85 18 00, fax 57 85 05 89; ④, s/r ②), a spruce modern chain hotel with a good **restaurant**, will do very nicely; it's on the south side of the centre, five minutes' walk from the tourist office, not far from the bridge.

Around Måløy: Selja

If the weather is good, it's worth considering a day's excursion from Måløy to the remote **islet of Selja**, reached by boat from the village of Selje, 50km from Måløy. The islet is the site of the medieval ruins of the **Selja Kloster**, a monastery built in the tenth century by Benedictine monks and originally named after St Sunniva, allegedly an Irish princess who refused to marry the pagan selected by her father. Royal blood and loyalty to the Catholic faith were prime considerations for beatification – and Sunniva got her saintly reward, but only after spending the rest of her life hidden away in a cave on this lonely island. The most significant part of the surviving ruins is a church tower, but otherwise the dilapidated masonry is rather less impressive than the seashore setting.

From Måløy, you can reach **SELJE** by road along highways 15 and 618, the route taken by a local **bus** (Mon–Fri 7 daily, Sat & Sun 1 daily; 1hr). It is, however, much quicker to get the **Hurtigbåt** (1–2 daily; 20min; 46kr). Once in Selje, you catch a **boat trip** out to the island (late May to late Aug 1–3 daily; 100kr; 2hr) and this includes a guided tour of the ruins; ring the Selje **tourist office** for bookings and sailing schedule (☎57 85 66 06).

Moving on from Måløy

Considering the amount of time it takes to get to Måløy along Highway 15, the last thing you want to do is retrace your steps east. By **bus**, it's well-nigh impossible not to double back, but the **Hurtigrute** offers tempting alternatives in the form of the cruise south from Måløy to Florø (see below) and Bergen (see p.158), or north to Ålesund (see p.221). In either direction, this is a lovely trip with the boat weaving through the islands of the fretted shoreline overseen by severe snow-tipped peaks. A second nautical option to Bergen is the **Hurtigbåt**, which saves time but misses most of the scenery.

Motorists can avoid backtracking too, but the journey south along the coast is a long-winded business and involves a couple of expensive ferry rides. Heading north is a good deal easier, with **Highway 61** threading up the coast and taking in a couple of shorter ferry rides en route to Ålesund, a manageable 120km away. At Dragsund, about halfway, you can detour west along Highway 654, an ambitious thirty-kilometre road whose tunnels and bridges finally lead out to the islet of **Runde**. Just six square kilometres in size, Runde possesses Norway's southernmost bird cliff – the 300-metre **Rundebranden** – where half a million sea birds congregate between late March and August. Common species include puffins, gannets, kittiwakes, fulmars, razorbills and guillemots. Footpaths give easy access to several vantage points overlooking the cliff, or you can take a boat trip round the island from Runde harbour for 100kr (weather permitting, May–Aug 3 daily; 2hr; reservations required on ☎70 08 59 16). If you decide to stay, head for the no-frills **youth hostel** (☎70 08 59 16, fax 70 08 58 70; 100kr dorm beds, ①), 300m from the harbour.

Florø

FLORØ, Norway's westernmost town and birthplace of the Viking chieftain Eric Bloodaxe, certainly doesn't merit the long journey here by road – it's a round trip of 140km along Highway 5, from the E39 – but conveniently it is the nearest stop to Bergen on the Hurtigrute. It scores high on west coast commonalities: it has a blustery island setting, its economy has been boosted by the oil industry, it offers tourists sea-fishing trips and its mostly modern centre is wrapped around the traditional focus of coastal town life, the harbour. The one sight of any note is the **Kystmuseet** (Coastal Museum; mid-June to late Aug Mon–Fri 11am–6pm, Sat & Sun noon–4pm; Sept to mid-June Mon–Fri 10am–3pm, Sun noon–3pm; 25kr), a rambling assortment of old boathouses and dwellings set around two exhibition buildings. These contain a ragbag of local artefacts – tools, kitchen utensils etc – supplemented by a model of an oil platform and a small armada of local wooden boats. The museum is on the south shore of Florø island and the town centre is on the north; it's about 2km between the two.

Buses to Florø terminate by the **ferry dock** from where it's a five- to ten-minute walk east round the harbour to the **tourist office** at Strandgata 30 (mid-June to mid-Aug Mon–Fri 8am–7pm, Sat 10am–5pm, Sun 3–7pm; mid-Aug to mid-June Mon–Fri 8am–3.30pm; ☎57 74 75 05). They have a list of local **accommodation**, with one option being the **youth hostel**, in a smart modern block on Havrenesveien (mid-June to mid-Aug; ☎57 74 06 89, fax 57 74 38 20; ①, no dorm beds), about 1km west of the tourist office; all the rooms here are en suite. Another option is the waterfront *Quality Maritim Hotel*, Hamnegata 7 (☎57 75 75 75, fax 57 75 75 10; ④, s/r ③), a smart chain hotel built in the style of an old warehouse, many of whose eighty-odd rooms have superb views out to sea.

For **food**, head for *Kakebua Konditori* (closed Sun), overlooking the harbour across from the tourist office, where you can eat waffles, cakes and open sandwiches. It's inside a converted nineteenth-century boathouse, and comes complete with life-size models of fisherfolk and a fishing boat. Additionally, the middle of June sees town festivities graced by the world's longest **herring table**, all 400m of it along the main street and groaning under the weight of that famous fish, here pickled or cooked, and the humble boiled potato.

The Geirangerfjord

The **Geirangerfjord** is one of the region's smallest fjords, but also one of its most breathtaking. A convoluted branch of the Storfjord, the Geirangerfjord cuts well inland and is marked by impressive waterfalls, with a village at either end of its snake-like profile – **Hellesylt** in the west and **Geiranger** in the east. Of the two, Hellesylt makes the better base (unless you prefer the tourist crowds of Geiranger), not least because it's close to the start of the wonderful **Norangsdal** valley, where the hamlet of **Øye** is home to one of Norway's finest hotels.

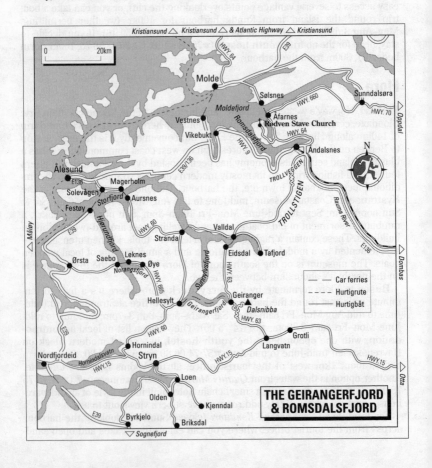

You can reach Geiranger in dramatic style from Åndalsnes to the north via the **Trollstigen** mountain road (see p.219), and a journey along Highway 63 from Highway 15 to the south is similarly exciting. More mundanely, Hellesylt sits right beside Highway 60, though this itself is an especially appealing long-distance route, running north round the inner reaches of the Nordfjord system (see p.207) and finally ending up near Ålesund (see p.221). With regard to public transport, long-distance **buses** heading west along Highway 15 link Otta (see p.124) and Lom (see p.206) with either Grotli and Langvatn (depending on the service), at either of which you can change for the local bus north to Geiranger – but note this connecting service only runs from mid-June to August. The same local service pushes on from Geiranger to Åndalsnes. Hellesylt is on the main Bergen–Ålesund bus route, which passes along Highway 60 through Loen and Stryn; there are several services daily.

Regular **car ferries** (May–Sept 4 daily, extra departures June to late Aug; 1hr 10min; passengers 35kr each way, a car plus driver 110kr) run between Hellesylt and Geiranger (see p.216), turning into the main body of the Geirangerfjord itself about 15min after leaving Hellesylt. It's one of the most celebrated trips in the entire fjord region, the S-shaped waters about 300m deep and fed by a series of plunging waterfalls up to 250m in height. The falls are all named, and the multi-lingual commentary aboard the ferry does its best to ensure that you are familiar with every stream and rivulet. More interesting are the scattered ruins of abandoned farms, built along the fjord's sixteen-kilometre length by fanatically optimistic settlers over the last couple of centuries. The cliffs backing the fjord are almost uniformly sheer, making farming of any description a short-lived and back-breaking occupation – and not much fun for the children either: when they went out to play, they were roped to the nearest boulder to stop them dropping into the fjord.

Hellesylt

In Viking times, **HELLESYLT** was an important and well-protected port. Traders and warriors sallied forth from the village to England, France and Russia, and many old Viking names survive in the area. Nowadays it's primarily a stop-off on tourist itineraries, most visitors staying just long enough to catch the ferry down the fjord to Geiranger. Consequently, by nightfall Hellesylt is quiet and peaceful. For daytime entertainment, there is a tiny **beach** by the ferry quay, the prelude to some very cold swimming. Or you could splash about (as many do) in the waterfall in the village centre.

The **tourist office** is by the jetty (June–Aug daily 9am–5.30pm; ☎70 26 50 52) and so is the turn-of-the-century *Grand Hotel* (☎70 26 51 00, fax 70 26 52 22; ③), whose fancy wooden scrollwork and high-pitched gables have been a local landmark since 1871; however, the interior has been patchily restored. Guests are put up in the modern annexe next door. The hotel's main competitor is the **youth hostel** (☎70 26 51 28; fax 70 26 36 57; ①, dorm beds 100kr; June–Aug), pleasantly set on the hillside above the village and Highway 60 – a 350-metre walk up the signed footpath from the jetty. They have cabins (①), which suit a family of four nicely, and self-catering facilities. Rowing boats can be rented here and from the *Grand*, which also sells fishing licences and rents out fishing equipment. *Hellesylt Camping* (☎70 26 51 88) fills out the shadeless field beside the fjord, about 300m from the quay.

From May through September the frequent **ferry** service along the fjord to Geiranger is in operation, and from mid-June to August there's a paltry **local bus** service to Øye on Mondays through to Fridays.

The Norangsdal valley and Øye

A century ago, pony and trap took cruise-ship tourists from Hellesylt down through the majestic **Norangsdal** valley to what was then the remote hamlet of **ØYE**. By car or bike, it's a simpler journey today – go 5km south on Highway 60 and watch for the turning on the right – but the scene appears not to have changed at all: steep, snow-tipped peaks rise up on either side of a wide valley where a string of farmsteads make the most of what must be pretty lean agricultural pickings. It's a wonderful sight, and at the village of Øye itself, 19km from Highway 60, there's the splendid *Union Hotel* (☎70 06 21 00, fax 70 06 21 16; ④; closed Nov–May), a delightfully restored High Victorian establishment, built in 1891 to accommodate touring aristocrats. Its interior is crammed with period antiques and bygones seemingly hunted down from every corner of the globe by the present owner. Each of the bedrooms is individually decorated in elaborate style and most celebrate the famous people who stayed here, like King Haakon VII and Kaiser Wilhelm II, not to mention the Danish author Karen "*Out Of Africa*" Blixen: enthusiasts might be pleased to see a pair of her lover's boots. It's a great place to spend the night – though you have to turn a blind eye to the occasional period excesses, like the four-posters – and the food is first-rate too. Telephones are banned, which is inducement enough to sit on the terrace and watch the weather fronts sweeping in off the glassy green Norangsfjord, or have a day's fishing – the hotel sells licences and dispenses advice.

The hotel is just outside Øye, which is itself at the eastern tip of the Norangsfjord, but the local ferry leaves from **Leknes**, 8km to the west. This minuscule port occupies a magnificent location at the point where the Norangsfjord meets the **Hjørundfjord**: to the south the mountains bear down on the fjord, to the north the blue-black waters widen out with pyramid-shaped peaks leading off into the distance on either side. Only 40km long, the Hjørundfjord, one of the most visually impressive fjords in the country, takes its name from the days when the Black Death swept Norway, leaving just one person, a woman called Hjørund, alive in this area. The best way to see it is to leave your car at Leknes and take a round trip by **ferry**: there are various destinations along the shore but the easiest option is the return ride to **Saebo** (roughly 1 hourly; 15min each way). The only **bus** down the Norangsdal valley to Øye and Leknes is a summertime service from Hellesylt (mid-June to Aug Mon–Fri 1 daily; 30–45min).

Geiranger

Any approach to **GEIRANGER** is spectacular. Arriving by ferry slowly reveals the little village tucked in a hollow at the eastern end of the fjord, while coming from the Eidsdal ferry dock to the north by road involves thundering along a fearsome set of switchbacks on the Ørneveien, the Eagle's Highway, for a first view of the fjord and the village glinting in the distance. Similarly, the road in from Highway 15 to the south begins unremarkably enough, but soon you're squirming as the road zigzags to arrive in Geiranger from behind. It's a beautiful setting, one of the most magnificent in western Norway, but in the peak season the village is chronically overcrowded with campers and caravanners. Frankly, you'd do better to visit in the shoulder season when the true character of the place is more apparent, the fjord hemmed in by sheer rock walls interspersed with hairline waterfalls, tiny-looking ferries and cruise ships bobbing about on the blue waters below.

Buses to Geiranger stop metres from the waterfront, a stone's throw from the **ferry terminal** and the **tourist office** (May–Sept daily 9am–7pm, Oct–April Mon–Fri 9am–5pm; ☎70 26 30 99), which promotes expensive boat tours of the fjord, though the car ferry is perfectly adequate. There are several **hotels** to choose from, but advance reservations are strongly advised in July and August. Both the large and luxurious *Union Hotel* (☎70 26 30 00, fax 70 26 31 61, *www.union-hotel.no*; ⑤, s/r ④; March to mid-Dec), high up the hillside on the south side of town, and the ultramodern timber-built *Grande Fjord Hotel* (☎70 26 30 90, fax 70 26 31 77; ③; May–Sept), by the shore about 1km north of the centre, have good views and are at a safe distance from the crowds. The *Grande Fjord* also has **cabins** (②) and a **campsite**, which is adjacent to similar *Grande Turisthytter & Camping* (☎70 26 30 68, fax 70 26 31 17). The restaurant of the over-large *Hotel Geiranger*, not far from the ferry dock, is first class.

From mid-June to August, local **buses** run north into Geiranger from either Grotli or Langvatn on Highway 15 – it depends on the service. There are two buses daily, one going straight into Geiranger (50min), the other (2hr) making a dramatic detour up a rough mountain toll-road to the Dalsnibba viewpoint at 1476m, overlooking the Geirangerfjord. This same local bus pushes north out of Geiranger heading for Åndalsnes (see p.218) via the Trollstigen, a journey that takes takes just over three hours. Åndalsnes can also be reached by a number of other routes, including trains from Oslo.

The Romsdalsfjord and around

Easy to reach by bus, train and car, small-town **Åndalsnes** is an ideal base for a visit to the **Romsdalsfjord**, a deep gash in the landscape which stretches west of the town, surrounded by some of the wildest mountains in the whole of the fjord country. If you approach the town from the Geirangerfjord, you'll cross over the mountains south of Åndalsnes via the knuckle-whitening hairpin bends of the **Trollstigen** ("Troll's Ladder"). Travelling here from the southeast, Dombås (see p.131) is where the **E136** and the **Rauma train line** branch west for the thrilling 100-kilometre rattle down through the alpine mountains of the **Romsdal** valley to the Romsdalsfjord – a spectacular journey with engineering to match. Pride of place goes to the **Kylling bru**, an ambitious railway bridge, all of 56m high and 76m long, over the Rauma river, and part of a dramatic hairpin bend that also incorporates a pair of lengthy tunnels. Further down the line (and the E136), after about 90km from Dombås you'll glimpse the tall face of the **Trollveggen** ("troll's wall") to the west – at around 1100m, the highest vertical overhanging mountain wall in Europe. This is a favourite haunt of experienced mountaineers (who, incidentally, didn't conquer it until 1967) and it also attracted cliff-jumping parachutists until several deaths and serious accidents prompted a ban in 1986. Soon afterwards, the train slides down to Åndalsnes, the fjord glistening behind.

The Romsdalsfjord's other prime attraction, and similarly easy to reach by bus or car, is the coastal town of **Ålesund**, whose good-looking centre sports several dozen charming Art Nouveau buildings. Both Åndalsnes and Ålesund possess top-quality **accommodation.**

Åndalsnes

Six hours by train from Oslo, **ÅNDALSNES** is, for many travellers, their first – and sometimes only – contact with the fjord country, a distinction it doesn't really warrant. Despite a wonderful setting between lofty peaks and chill waters, the town itself is unexciting: small (with a population of just 3000), modern and industrial, and sleepy at the best of times. That said, Åndalsnes is an excellent place to orientate yourself at the end of a long journey and everything you're likely to need is near at hand, not least some first-rate accommodation. Åndalsnes also makes an ideal base for further fjord explorations. Within easy reach by ferry, bus and/or car is some wonderful scenery, most famously to be seen from the extraordinary Trollstigen, a mountain road which zigzags south to Valldal; this route is covered below, as is another tempting proposition, the journey west to Ålesund. There's also the matter of **Rødven stave church** (late June to mid-Aug daily 11am–4pm; 30kr), just half an hour's drive away – from Åndalsnes, head east round the Romsdalsfjord and after 22km take the signed turning which covers the final 10km. In an idyllic setting – amid meadows, by a stream and overlooking a slender branch of the fjord – the church dates from around 1300, though its distinctive wooden supports may have been added during the first of several subsequent remodellings in 1712. Every inch a country church, the place's creaky interior holds boxed pews, a painted pulpit and a large medieval crucifix, but it's the bucolic setting which most catches the eye.

Practicalities

Buses all stop outside the **train station**, where you'll also find the **tourist office** (late June to Aug Mon–Sat 10am–7pm, Sun 1–7pm; Sept to mid-June Mon–Fri 10am–3.30pm; ☎71 22 16 22). They provide bus timetables, regional guides and a wide range of local information geared to make you use Åndalsnes as a base. Their free *Dagsturer* (day trips) booklet gives details of all sorts of motoring excursions, and most recommendations include a short hike too. They have details of fishing trips to the fjord (3 daily; 4hr; 250kr), local day-long hikes and guided climbs (from 1400kr), and fixed-rate sightseeing expeditions with Åndalsnes Taxi (☎71 22 15 55), who charge – for example – 400kr for a brief scoot down the Trollstigen. This is, however, hardly a bargain when you consider the special deals offered by local car hire firms. From May to mid-September, Åndalsnes Camping (☎71 22 16 29) charges 550kr for a 24-hour car rental, as does Åndal Bil (☎71 22 22 55), who operate all year. The tourist office has all the latest information on local deals. Local **hiking maps** are sold at *Romsdal Libris*, a couple of minutes' walk from the tourist office in the centre of town.

The tourist office also has a small supply of en-suite **private rooms** (①), which go for around 350kr per double (200kr single), with self-catering facilities and bed linen provided – but note that most are a good walk from the town centre. Alternatively, Åndalsnes has a delightful **youth hostel** (mid-May to mid-Sept; ☎71 22 13 82, fax 71 22 68 35; ①, dorm beds 170kr), a two-kilometre hike west out of town on the E136. To get there, head up the hill out of the centre, turn right onto the E136 at the traffic island at the major road, go past the turning to Dombås, staying on the E136 in the direction of Ålesund; cross the river and it's on the left-

ONWARD FROM ÅNDALSNES

There are special summertime bus and ferry services from Åndalsnes over the Trollstigen to Valldal and Geiranger (mid-June to late Aug 2 daily), with one daily onward connection with the ferry from Geiranger to Hellesylt, the most pleasant destination of the three. The Åndalsnes–Geiranger trip costs 120kr and rail pass holders get a fifty percent discount. Incidentally, from Hellesylt there are buses to Ålesund, though it's more straightforward to take a TogBuss (a train-company-run bus) from Åndalsnes straight to Ålesund (3–4 daily; 2hr 20min). Ålesund is a Hurtigrute port with Bergen-bound ships sailing at 12.45am, northbound 3pm.

Another option is to take a local **bus** (Mon–Sat 5–8 daily, Sun 3 daily; 1hr 20min) to **Molde** (see p.223), a pretty fjord journey involving one short ferry trip from Åfarnes to Sølsnes (43kr car & driver, 17kr passenger; 15min) and a 3km tunnel (50kr toll). Molde itself is a workaday industrial port where you can pick up the bus making the short hop north on the coastal E39 to Kristiansund (4–9 daily; 1hr 35min). Kristiansund has much more to offer than Molde, where you don't want to get stuck – so check bus connections with Åndalsnes tourist office before you set out. However, on reflection, you might decide to go straight to Trondheim (see p.229), five hours by bus from Molde, seven from Ålesund. Molde, Kristiansund and Trondheim are all Hurtigrute ports, a fact which provides yet more possibilities.

Note that rail pass holders get a fifty-percent discount on E39 buses; also be careful to distinguish between Kristiansund and the southern coastal town of Kristiansand: to save confusion, in listings and brochures they are often written as Kristiansund N and Kristiansand S.

hand side. The hostel has a pleasant rural setting and its simple rooms, in a group of modest wooden buildings, are extremely popular, making reservations pretty much essential. The buffet-style breakfast, with its fresh fish, is one of the best hostellers are likely to get in the whole country. Note that the hostel doesn't do evening meals (though there are cooking facilities) and reception is closed from 10am–4pm. Bikes can also be rented here. The other excellent choice, the *Grand Hotel Bellevue*, Åndalsgata 5 (☎71 22 75 00, fax 71 22 60 38; ③), occupies a large whitewashed block with attractive Art Deco touches on a hillock just up from the train station. The rooms on the top floors have great views, well worth the extra 100kr or so you're likely to be asked to pay. The modern *Rauma Hotell*, near the station at Vollan 16 (☎71 22 12 33, fax 71 22 63 13; ③), right in the centre of town, is a bit cheaper, but without much character. Among several local **campsites**, *Åndalsnes Camping og Motell* (☎71 22 16 29, fax 71 22 62 16) has a fine riverside setting about 3km from the town centre – follow the route to the youth hostel but turn first left immediately after the river. It's a well-equipped site with cabins (①) as well as bikes, boats, canoes and cars available for rent.

For **food**, the *Buona Sera* pizzeria, a brief walk from the station up the hill out of town, serves competent Italian food and reasonably tasty steaks, but much better is the snug *Lille Grand Restaurant* in the basement of the *Grand Hotel*, where main courses average around 190kr.

Over the Trollstigen

The alarming heights of the **Trollstigen** or "Troll's Ladder", a trans-mountain route between Åndalsnes and Valldal, are equally compelling in either direction. They are accessible by twice-daily **buses** from mid-June to August, which takes the sweat out of driving – along with scores of other tourists – round eleven hairpins with a maximum gradient of 1:12. Drivers (and cyclists) should be particularly careful in wet weather; and note that the road is generally closed from early October to mid-May – later if the snows have been particularly heavy.

The northern end of the Trollstigen starts gently enough as a turning off the E136 6km southeast of Åndalsnes. It leads up into a valley surrounded by some of the more famous mountain peaks in Norway: to the west, Kongen and Bispen (the "King" and the "Bishop") are the highest. Soon though, the sheer audacity of the route becomes apparent, as the road zigzags across the face of the mountain, halfway up passing directly in front of the tumultuous **Stigfossen Falls** – where the bus stops for photographs. On a clear day the views from here are heart-stopping, the water dropping away 180m under the bridge into the valley.

There is nothing at the top except a bare expanse of mountain and a café – the *Trollstigen Fjellstue* – where the bus makes a stop. From here, it's a five-minute walk to the **Utsikten** (viewing point), where there's a magnificent panorama over the surrounding mountains and valleys. If you're feeling extremely energetic, this is the place to pick up the **Kløvstien**, the original drovers' track over the mountains – abandoned when the road was built – which has been renovated for walkers. It's well signposted all the way back down towards Åndalsnes, crossing the road in four places, and there's a chain to hang on to along the steeper parts. The walk down the Kløvstien takes around four hours, and then there's an easy ninety-minute stroll down the footpath along the Isterdalen valley, which brings you back to Åndalsnes. You can, of course, shorten the walk by starting (or finishing) at Stigfossen. As usual, come properly equipped, watch for sudden weather changes and bear in mind the Trollstigen bus schedules.

Valldal and Tafjord

On the other side of the mountains from Åndalsnes, the Trollstigen slips along the Meierdal on its way to **VALLDAL**, a silent, shadowy village sprawled along the water's edge. If you're marooned, there's a small **youth hostel** (mid-June to Aug; ☎70 25 70 31, fax 70 25 75 11; ①, dorm beds 95kr), 100m from the harbour. However, you'll almost certainly want to press on west along the fjord, either to Linge, 4km on, for the ferry to Eidsdal (every 30min; 10min), or to Liabygda, 12km from Valldal, for the Stranda ferry (every 30min; 15min). Most visitors choose the former service, heading towards Geiranger (see p.216), but if you travel to Stranda you'll find yourself on the scenic Highway 60 midway between Hellesylt (see p.215) and Ålesund (see opposite).

There is another alternative, the fourteen-kilometre fjordside drive east to **TAFJORD**. Don't be too deterred by the power station at the entrance to the village or by the scrawny little harbour with its well-worn café, but stroll up the hill to where a string of old buildings – with thatched roofs, cairn-like chimneys and clapboard walls – show what these fjord villages looked like as late as the 1950s. The only unusual feature is the lack of old housing near the harbour: in 1934, an avalanche several kilometres down the fjord created a tidal wave which washed part of the village away. Should you decide to stay, the village has a couple of campsites, one of which, *Fjordheim Turistsenter* (☎70 25 80 48, fax 70 25 81 33), also provides simple and inexpensive rooms (①).

Ålesund

At the end of the E136, some 120km west of Åndalsnes, the fishing and ferry port of **ÅLESUND** is immediately – and distinctively – different from any other Norwegian town. Neither old clapboard houses nor functional concrete and glass is much in evidence, but instead there's a conglomeration of proud grey and white facades, lavishly decorated and topped with a forest of turrets. There are dragons and human faces, Neoclassical and mock-Gothic facades, decorative flowers and even a pharaoh or two, the whole ensemble set amid the town's several harbours. These architectural eccentricities sprang from disaster: in 1904, a dreadful fire left 10,000 people homeless and the town centre destroyed, but within three years a hectic reconstruction programme saw almost the entire area rebuilt in a bizarre Art Nouveau style which borrowed heavily from the German *Jugendstil* movement. Kaiser Wilhelm II, who used to holiday around Ålesund, footed the bill, and the Norwegian architects, most of whom had learnt their craft abroad, built in a style which ended up an engaging hybrid of folksy local elements and the foreign influences of the time.

Walking down pedestrianized **Kongens gate** reveals most of the architectural highlights, but many of the central streets are equally ornamented. The stylistic intricacies and peccadillos are covered in the verbose *On Foot in Ålesund,* a free leaflet which guides you round town. You can get these at the tourist office (see p.222), where you can also more profitably sign up for one of the **guided walking tours** (mid-June to mid-Aug 3 weekly; 1hr 30min; 50kr). The other obvious

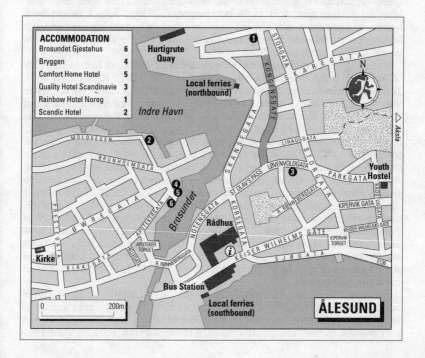

ACCOMMODATION
Brosundet Gjestehus	6
Bryggen	4
Comfort Home Hotel	5
Quality Hotel Scandinavie	3
Rainbow Hotel Noreg	1
Scandic Hotel	2

objective in the town centre is the **park** at the top of Lihauggata. It's a surprise to find monkey puzzle and copper beech trees here, and there's a bust of the town's benefactor, the kaiser, in which – if you're used to images of him as a grizzled older figure in a helmet – he looks disarmingly youthful. The larger statue nearby is of Rollo, a Viking chieftain born and raised in Ålesund, who seized Normandy and became its first duke in 911 – and was an ancestor of William the Conqueror of England. From the park, several hundred steps lead to the top of the **Aksla** hill, where the view out along the coast and its islands is fabulous. Otherwise, Ålesund's lively centre, which drapes around its oldest harbour, the **Brosundet**, makes for a pleasant stroll, and you can watch the ferries and Hurtigbåt coming and going to the islands just offshore.

Ålesund also possesses one of those prestige tourist attractions so beloved of development boards and councillors. It's the **Atlanterhavsparken** (Atlantic Sea-Park; June–Aug daily 10am–8pm, Sept–May Mon–Sat 10am–4pm, Sun 10am–6pm; 75kr), a large-scale recreation of the marine environment including several enormous fish tanks; there's also an outside area with easy footpaths and bathing sites. The Sea-Park is located 3km west of Ålesund on a low-lying headland. From mid-June to August, a local bus heads out there from the town centre (Mon–Fri 4–5 daily).

Practicalities

From north to south, Ålesund's town centre is about 700m wide. The **bus station** is situated on the waterfront, across from the **tourist office** in the Rådhus (June–Aug Mon–Fri 8.30am–7pm, Sat 9am–5pm, Sun 11am–5pm; Sept–May Mon–Fri 8.30am–4pm; ☎70 15 76 00). Southbound local ferries depart from beside the bus station, northbound from the other side of the harbour, and just beyond the northbound ferry terminal is the quay for the **Hurtigrute** (southbound 12.45am, northbound 3pm).

One of Ålesund's real pleasures is the quality of its downtown **hotels**. The pick of the bunch is the *Brosundet Gjestehus*, Apotekergata 5 (☎70 12 10 00, fax 70 12 12 95, *www.brosundet.no*; ③), which occupies an attractively converted waterside warehouse. They have a sauna, washing machines and self-catering facilities, and offer an excellent breakfast. In similar premises, just along the street at no. 1, is the rather more lavish *Comfort Home Hotel Bryggen* (☎70 12 64 00, fax 70 12 11 80; ⑤; s/r ③). Also on the waterfront is the excellent *Scandic Hotel Ålesund*, Molovegen 6 (☎70 12 81 00, fax 70 12 92 10; ⑤, s/r ③), which occupies a brisk, modern block with a bright and cheerful interior – ask for a sea-facing room. Away from the waterfront, in the middle of the town centre, the comfortable *Quality Hotel Scandinavie*, Løvenvoldgata 8 (☎70 12 31 31, fax 70 13 23 70; ④, s/r ②) inhabits a grand old Art Nouveau edifice, unfortunately spoiled by an especially horrid set of automatic front doors. The more mundane *Rainbow Hotel Noreg*, Kongens gate 27 (☎70 12 29 38, fax 70 12 66 60; ④, s/r ③) suffers by comparison with its rivals, but the upper floors of this modern block offer sea views and the rooms are perfectly adequate. There's a small and central **youth hostel** at Parkgata 14 (☎70 11 58 30, fax 70 11 58 59; ①, dorm beds 165kr; May–Sept), at the top of Rådstuggata.

For **food**, the *Sjøbua Fiskerestaurant*, Brunholmgata 1 (☎70 12 71 00; closed Sun), round the corner from the *Comfort Home Hotel Bryggen*, serves wonderful seafood in chic surroundings and even has its own lobster tank. It's expensive but very popular, so reservations are advised. A cheaper if somewhat mundane alternative is *Nilles Pizza* at Kirkegata 1. In sunny weather, everyone flocks to the terrace of the *Metz* café-restaurant, by the Brosundet harbour at Notenesgata 1.

Molde and routes north

A few islands and a couple of fjords to the north of Ålesund is industrial **MOLDE**, which sprawls along the seashore to either side of the tumbling river Moldeelva with a ridge of steep, green hills behind. Despite its modern appearance, Molde is one of the region's older towns, but it was blown to smithereens by the Luftwaffe in 1940, an act of destruction watched by King Håkon from these same hills just weeks before he was forced into exile in England. The new town that grew up in its stead is unremarkable, but it does host a week-long **international jazz festival** of some repute, held annually in the middle of July. Tickets are relatively cheap (100–250kr) and there's a smattering of big names among the homegrown talent. Programme details are widely available across the region and tickets can be purchased either in person or in advance from the Billettkontoret (ticket office; ☎71 20 31 50, fax 71 25 36 35, *www.moldejazz.no*) in Molde Rådhus. Naturally, the big-name concerts are sold out months in advance and accommodation is impossible to find during the festival – but the authorities operate a large official campsite 3km west of the centre for the duration. At other times of the year, you'll not want to hang around and fortunately the **bus station** and the **ferry terminal** are side by side in the centre of town. Nearby is the Rådhus, within which is the **tourist office** (mid-June to Aug Mon–Fri 9am–6pm, Sat 9am–4pm & Sun 10am–3pm; Sept to mid-June Mon–Fri 8.30am–4pm; ☎71 25 71 33).

North to Kristiansund

The **E39** cuts east out of Molde, hugging the Moldefjord before slipping inland to reach, 58km on from Molde, the massive suspension bridge – one of Norway's longest at 623m – which spans the channel between the mainland and the tiny islet of **Bergsøya** (55kr toll). An unlikely road junction, Bergsøya is also the starting point for the five-kilometre-long undersea Freifjord tunnel (60kr toll), at the start of the Highway 70 turning to **Kristiansund** (see p.224), 25km away to the west. If you ignore the Kristiansund turning and keep north along the E39, a floating bridge takes you off Bergsøya for the 170-kilometre-long road and ferry journey to **Trondheim** (see p.229). Alternatively, you can head east along Highway 70 for the 140-kilometre-drive to the E6 junction at **Oppdal** (see p.132), but this journey takes you along the **Sunndalsfjord** and up the remote **Sunndal** valley, the latter often gloomy even in good weather.

A much more enticing route to Kristiansund is along **Highway 64**, which branches north off the E39 just outside Molde. This eighty-kilometre-long road begins by twisting inland, taking in the Kornstadfjord and then the **Atlanterhavsveien** (Atlantic Highway; 40kr toll), a scenic eight-kilometre stretch of road, interspersed with bridges and causeways, that hops from one islet to another along the coast. Note that in terms of **tolls**, taking the Atlanterhavsveien from Molde to Kristiansund will cost you 75kr less than the E39/Highway 70 route.

Nor-Way Busekspress long-distance **buses** travel along the E39 between Ålesund, Molde, Bergsøya (change at the toll station for Kristiansund) and Trondheim once or twice daily; Molde to Trondheim takes a little over five hours. Several local buses connect the Bergsøya toll station with Kristiansund. There is a limited local bus service along the Atlanterhavsveien.

Kristiansund

KRISTIANSUND somehow contrives to look quite dull despite its setting. The town actually straddles three rocky islets, and the enormous natural channel-cum-harbour that they create is one of the finest havens on the west coast. The town was founded in the eighteenth century as a fishing port, and there are a handful of antique clapboard houses along **Fosnagata**, immediately to the north of the main quay – but once again the Luftwaffe polished off most of the old town in 1940. Up the slope to the west of the quay are the few modern streets that now serve as the town centre and nearby too, at the south end of the main har-bourfront, is the modern **klippfiskkjerringa statue** of a woman carrying a fish. The statue recalls the days when cod was laid out along the seashore to dry, pro-ducing the *klippfisk* that was the main source of income in these parts well into the 1950s. Appropriately, the town has a **Norsk klippfiskmuseum** (mid-June to mid-Aug Mon–Sat noon–5pm, Sun 1–4pm; 25kr), housed in an old and well-worn warehouse, the Milnbrygga, east across the harbour. The museum is most pleas-antly reached by small passenger boats, the Sundbåtene (Mon–Fri 6.30am–4pm, Sat 8.30am–1.30pm; 1 hourly), which call at each of the three islets for a flat fare of 10kr per trip. The service was once crucial for getting around Kristiansund, but the three islands are now connected by bridge and the boats are, essentially, an exercise in nostalgia. If you're visiting the *klippfiskmuseum*, you may as well drop by its waterfront warehouse neighbours, the **Hjelkrembrygga** (late June to early Aug Sun 1–4pm; 20kr), which displays old sepia photographs of the locality, and the **Woldbrygga** (same details), whose old boats and rope-making equipment are displayed in a nineteenth-century barrel factory. Of more general interest are the handful of venerable timber houses that make up the **Gamle Byen** (Old Town), situated on the smallest of the three islets, Innlandet – south across the harbour from the main quay. Here too is the distinctive **Lossiusgården**, a large and hand-some house that belonged to an eighteenth-century merchant; unfortunately there's no admission.

Much more popular, however, is the excursion to the minuscule **GRIP**. A low-lying islet that's part of a group 14km offshore, Grip is dotted with brightly paint-ed timber houses and has a much-modified stave church dating from the fifteenth century. The islanders took refuge in the church whenever they were threatened by a storm, as they often were – indeed, when you look at the place, it's amazing that anyone ever lived here at all. There are no permanent residents now, but in the summertime fishermen dock in the sliver of a harbour and there are even some basic guesthouse-style **lodgings** (②). There's a claustrophobia-inducing air about these, and if you're staying when the weather's poor the effect can be quite powerful. From June to late August there's a daily **boat** from Kristiansund to Grip (1 or 2 daily; 140kr return); information on sailing times is available at the tourist office (see below), who will also book you a bed.

Practicalities

Buses to Kristiansund pull in at the north end of the main harbourfront, beside the Nordmørskaia quay. **Hurtigbåt** services leave this same quay for Trondheim, and the boat for Grip departs from here too. A few metres to the east, the **Hurtigrute** coastal steamer docks at Holmakaia (daily departures northbound at 11pm, southbound at 5pm). It takes about five minutes to walk the length of the main harbourfront. About halfway along is the **tourist office** (mid-June to mid-

Aug Mon–Fri 8am–8pm, Sat & Sun 10am–6pm, ; mid-Aug to mid-June Mon–Fri 8am–4pm; ☎71 58 63 80); the Sundbåtene jetty is a very short walk away.

For a **place to stay**, the **youth hostel** (☎71 67 11 04; ➀, dorm beds 135kr; June–Sept) is located at the *Atlanten* **campsite**, signposted off the main road into town, about 1km from the harbourfront. Unfortunately though, the hostel's a depressingly frugal place that's best avoided. Much better (and much pricier) is the modern *First Hotel Grand*, Bernstorffstrand 1 (☎71 67 30 11, fax 71 67 23 70; ➄, s/r ➂), just south of Kaibakken, the short main street linking the south end of the harbour with the main square, Kongens plass. In terms of **restaurants**, the *Smia* stands head and shoulders above its competitors. With superb fish dishes from around 130kr, it's in a cosily converted boat shed metres from the harbour at Fosnagata 30 (☎71 67 11 70). Otherwise, try the *Sjøstjerna*, an inexpensive café-restaurant with seafood specialities located in the pedestrianized area, a short walk up behind the tourist office on Skolegata; the marinated salmon is tasty at 75kr.

travel details

Trains

Bergen to: Finse (4–5 daily; 2hr 15min); Geilo (4–5 daily; 3hr); Myrdal (4–5 daily; 1hr 50min); Oslo (4–5 daily; 6hr 30min); Voss (4–5 daily; 1hr 10min).

Dombås to: Trondheim (3–4 daily; 2hr 30min); Åndalsnes (2 daily; 1hr 30min).

Myrdal to: Flåm (June to late Sept 11–12 daily; Oct–May 2–4 daily; 50min).

Åndalsnes to: Dombås (2 daily; 1hr 30min); Oslo (2 daily; 6hr 30min).

Buses

Balestrand to: Oslo (3 daily; 8hr 15min); Sogndal (2 daily; 1hr 10min).

Bergen to: Dombås (1 daily; 12hr); Grotli (1 daily; 8hr); Haugesund (1–5 daily; 3hr 30min); Hellesylt (1–2 daily; 8hr 15min); Kinsarvik (2 daily; 2hr 40min); Kristiansand (1 daily; 11hr); Loen (3 daily; 6hr 30min); Lofthus (2 daily; 3hr); Nordfjordeid (1–2 daily; 7hr); Norheimsund (3 daily; 2hr); Odda (2–3 daily; 3hr 30min); Oslo (1 daily; 11hr); Skei (3 daily; 5hr); Sogndal (3 daily; 4hr 15min); Stavanger (1–5 daily; 5hr 40min); Stryn (3 daily; 6hr 45min); Trondheim (1 daily; 14hr); Utne (2 daily; 2hr 45min); Voss (4 daily; 1hr 45min); Ålesund (1–2 daily; 10hr).

Fagernes to: Oslo (3 daily; 3hr 20min).

Fjærland to: Oslo (3 daily; 7hr 50min).

Geiranger to: Åndalsnes (mid-June to late Aug 2 daily; 3–4hr).

Kaupanger to: Oslo (3 daily; 6hr 45min).

Kristiansund to: Åndalsnes (2 daily; 3hr); Molde (5 weekly; 2hr); Trondheim (2 daily; 5hr).

Molde to: Kristiansund (5 weekly; 2hr); Trondheim (2 daily; 8hr); Ålesund (4–6 daily; 2hr 15min); Åndalsnes (3–8 daily; 1hr 30min).

Måløy to: Grotli (3 daily; 3hr 20min); Lom (3 daily; 4hr 20min); Nordfjordeid (3 daily; 1hr); Oslo (1 daily; 10hr); Otta (3 daily; 4hr 20min); Stryn (3 daily; 2hr).

Sogndal to: Balestrand (2 daily; 1hr 10min); Bergen (3 daily; 4hr 15min); Fjærland (3 daily; 35min); Kaupanger (2 daily; 20min); Oslo (3 daily; 7hr); Stryn (1–2 daily; 4hr 30min); Voss (3 daily; 3hr).

Stavanger to: Bergen (1–5 daily; 5hr 40min); Haugesund (1–5 daily; 2hr 10min); Kristiansand (2 daily; 4hr 40min).

Stryn to: Bergen (2 daily; 7hr); Hellesylt (1–2 daily; 1hr); Måløy (3 daily; 2hr); Nordfjordeid (1 daily; 2hr); Oslo (1 daily; 8hr 30min); Trondheim (1 daily; 8hr).

Ulvik to: Voss (2–4 daily; 1hr).

Voss to: Bergen (4 daily; 1hr 45min); Gudvangen (4–6 daily; 1hr 10min); Norheimsund (3 daily; 2hr); Odda (1 daily; 2hr 30min); Sogndal (2 daily; 3hr); Ulvik (2–4 daily; 1hr).

Ålesund to: Bergen (1–2 daily; 10hr); Hellesylt (1–2 daily except Sat; 2hr 40min); Kristiansund (5 weekly; 4hr 15min); Molde (4–6 daily; 2hr 15min); Stryn (1–2 daily except Sat; 4hr); Trondheim (1–2 daily; 8hr 10min); Åndalsnes (3–4 daily; 2hr 20min).

Åndalsnes to: Geiranger (mid-June to late Aug 2 daily; 3–4hr); Kristiansund (2 daily; 3hr); Molde (3–7 daily; 1hr 30min); Valldal (June to Aug 2 daily; 2hr); Ålesund (3–4 daily; 2hr 20min).

Boats

A plethora of boats shuttle between the settlements dotting the western fjords. There are two main types of service, **car ferries** and **Hurtigbåt** express passenger boats, and these are supplemented by the **Hurtigrute** coastal steamer. Services are frequent and regular, running many times daily up until about 11pm on some routes. Many shorter crossings are detailed in the text; major routes are given below.

Ferries

Bruravik to: Brimnes (2 hourly; 25mins).

Dragsvik to: Hella (every 30min; 10min); Vangsnes (hourly; 25min).

Fodnes to: Manheller (hourly; 15min).

Geiranger to: Hellesylt (May–Sept 4 daily; Oct–April 2 daily; 1hr 10min).

Gudvangen to: Kaupanger (2 daily; 2hr).

Hella to: Dragsvik (every 30min; 10min); Vangsnes (hourly; 15min).

Kaupanger to: Gudvangen (2 daily; 2hr).

Stavanger to: Tau (hourly; 45min).

Utne to: Kinsarvik (2 hourly; 25min).

Hurtigbåt

Bergen to: Balestrand (1–2 daily; 4hr); Flåm (1–2 daily; 5hr 30min); Florø (1–2 daily; 3hr 30min); Haugesund (2–5 daily; 2hr 40min); Måløy (1–2 daily; 4hr 30min); Selje (1–2 daily; 5hr); Sogndal (1–2 daily; 5hr); Stavanger (2–5 daily; 3hr 50min).

Bergen to: Kinsarvik (1–3 daily; 2hr 20min); Lofthus (1–3 daily; 2hr 35min); Odda (1–3 daily; 3hr 10min), Utne (1–3 daily; 1hr 50min); these routes include some bus travel.

Flåm to: Balestrand (1–2 daily; 1hr 30min); Bergen (1–2 daily; 5hr 15min); Gudvangen (1–3 daily; 2hr); Sogndal (Mon–Sat 1–3 daily; 1hr 10min).

Gudvangen to: Flåm (1–3 daily; 2hr).

Kristiansund to: Trondheim (1–3 daily; 3hr 30min).

Stavanger to: Bergen (2–5 daily; 3hr 50min); Haugesund (2–5 daily; 1hr 15min).

Ålesund to: Molde (Mon–Fri 1 daily; 2hr 15min).

Hurtigrute

Northbound departures: daily from Bergen at 10.30pm; Florø at 4.45am; Måløy at 7.30am; Ålesund at 3pm; Molde at 6.30pm; Kristiansund at 11pm; Trondheim at 12 noon.

Southbound departures: daily from Trondheim at 10am; Kristiansund at 5pm; Molde at 9.15pm; Ålesund at 12.45am; Måløy at 5.30am; Florø at 8am; arrives Bergen, where the service terminates, at 2.30pm.

Bergen–Trondheim journey time is 31hr 30min.

Passenger ferry

Balestrand to: Fjærland (June to mid-Sept 2 daily; 1hr 30min); Hella (June to mid-Sept 2 daily; 15min).

International Ferries

Bergen and to a lesser extent **Stavanger** and **Haugesund** are international ferry ports. For details of sailings see "Basics", p.6.

CHAPTER FOUR

TRONDHEIM TO THE LOFOTENS

The 900-kilometre-long stretch of Norway from Trondheim to the island-studded coast near Narvik marks the transition from the rural south to the blustery north. **Trondheim**, easily the biggest town hereabouts and capital of the fertile – by Norwegian standards – **Trøndelag** province, is readily accessible from Oslo by train, and with its easy-going air and imposing cathedral, remains a highlight of any itinerary. But travel on one of the express trains that thunder further north, and you begin to feel far removed from the capital as you quickly leave the forested south behind. Distances between places grow ever greater, and travelling becomes more of a slog. As Trøndelag gives way to **Nordland** province things get increasingly wild – "Arthurian", thought Evelyn Waugh – and, the scenery apart, there is little of interest between Trondheim and the engaging steel town of **Mo-i-Rana**.

Just north of Mo-i-Rana, on the E6, you cross the **Arctic Circle** – one of the principal targets for many travellers – at a point where the cruel and barren scenery seems strikingly appropriate. On the Arctic Circle, the midnight sun and 24-hour polar night occur once a year, at the summer and winter solstices respectively; the further north from here you go, the longer the period during which you can experience these two phenomena (see box, p.280). Beyond the Arctic Circle, the mountains of the interior lead down to a fretted, craggy coastline and even the towns, the largest of which is the port of **Bodø**, have a feral quality about them. The iron-ore port of **Narvik**, in the far north of Nordland, has perhaps the wildest setting of them all, and was the scene of some of the fiercest fighting between the Allied and Axis forces in World War II. To the west lies the offshore archipelago that makes up the **Vesterålen and Lofoten islands**. In the north of the Vesterålens, between **Harstad** and **Andenes**, the coastline of this island chain is mauled by massive fjords, whereas to the south, the Lofotens are backboned by a mighty and ravishingly beautiful mountain wall. Among a handful of idyllic fishing villages the pick is **Å**, though **Henningsvaer** and **Stamsund** come a close second. Here, as elsewhere on the islands, inexpensive accommodation is available in huts-cum-cabins once used by fishermen and known as *rorbuer* (see p.268).

As for **accommodation** in general, the region has a smattering of strategically located youth hostels, and there are at least a couple of hotels in all the major towns. **Transport** is good, which is just as well given the isolated nature of much of the region. The **Hurtigrute** coastal boat stops at all the major settlements on its route up the Norwegian coast from Bergen to Kirkenes, while the islands are accessed

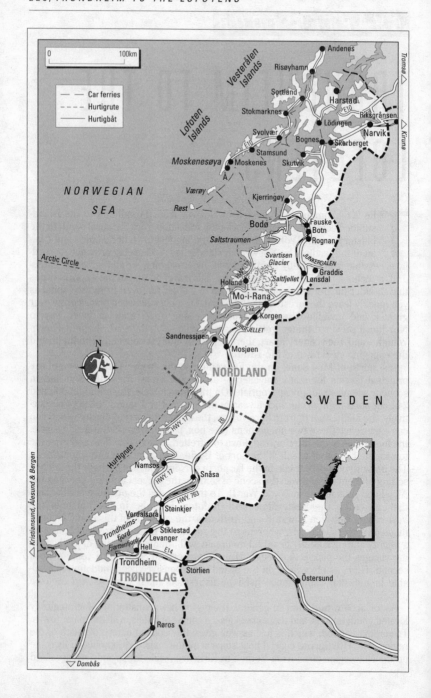

ACCOMMODATION PRICE CODES

The hotels and guesthouses detailed throughout this guide have been graded according to the price categories listed below. Prices given are for the least expensive double room during the high season, although almost every hotel offers seasonal and/or weekend discounts, which can reduce the rate by one or even two grades. Wherever hotels have an official summer rate we've given it (denoted s/r), but bear in mind that many others will provide impromptu summer and weekend discounts. Single rooms, where available, usually cost between 60 and 80 percent of a double. For a more detailed discussion of accommodation see p.37.

① under 500kr	③ 700–900kr	⑤ 1200–1500kr
② 500–700kr	④ 900–1200kr	⑥ over 1500kr

---

by a variety of **ferries** and **express boats**. Sometimes known as the "Arctic Highway", the **E6** is the major road route north along the coast from Trondheim; it's kept in excellent condition, though in summer motor-homes and caravans can make the going very slow. The **train** network reaches as far north as Fauske and nearby Bodø, from both of which **buses** connect with Narvik, itself the terminal of a separate rail line which runs the few kilometres to the border and then south through Sweden. The only real problem is likely to be **time**: it's a day or two's journey from Trondheim to Fauske, and another day from there to Narvik. Unless you've several days to spare, you should think twice before venturing further north: travelling there can be arduous, and in any case it's pointless if done at a hectic pace.

Trondheim

An atmospheric city with much of its antique centre still intact, **TRONDHEIM** was known until the sixteenth century as Nidaros ("mouth of the river Nid"), its importance as a power base underpinned by the excellence of its harbour and its position at the head of a wide and fertile valley. The early Norse parliament, or *Ting*, met here, and the cathedral was a major pilgrimage centre at the end of a route stretching all the way back to Oslo. After a fire destroyed much of the city in 1681, a military engineer from Luxembourg named Caspar de Cicignon rebuilt Trondheim on a gridiron plan, with broad avenues radiating from the centre to act as firebreaks. Cicignon's layout has survived, giving the city centre an airy, elegant air, though most of the buildings date from the commercial boom of the late nineteenth century. With timber warehouses lining the river and doughty stone structures dotting the main streets, the city centre is a suitably dignified and prosperous setting for the cathedral, one of Scandinavia's finest medieval structures.

Trondheim is now Norway's third city, but the pace of life here is slow and easy, and the main sights are best appreciated in leisurely fashion over a couple of days. A genial and eminently likeable place, a visit to Trondheim is also a pleasant way to wave goodbye to city life if you're heading for the wilds of the north.

Arrival, information and city transport

Trondheim is on the E6 highway, 540km from Oslo, a seven- or eight-hour drive. A toll of 20kr is levied in either direction on the E6 near Trondheim, and there's a

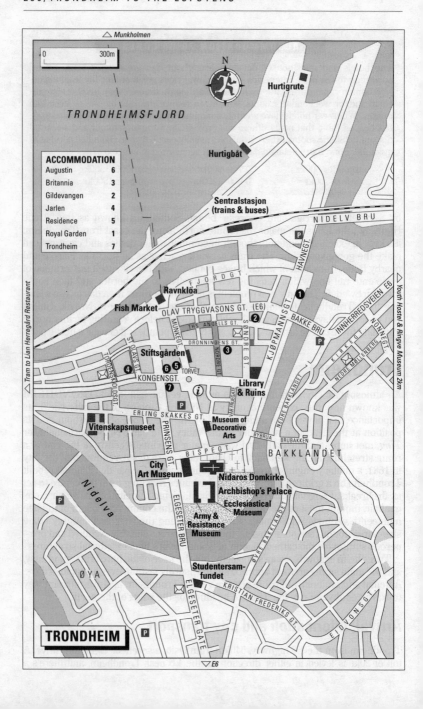

△ *Munkholmen*

0 — 300m

TRONDHEIMSFJORD

Hurtigrute

Hurtigbåt

Sentralstasjon
(trains & buses)

NIDELV BRU

ACCOMMODATION

Augustin	6
Britannia	3
Gildevangen	2
Jarlen	4
Residence	5
Royal Garden	1
Trondheim	7

FJORDGT

Ravnkloa

Fish Market

OLAV TRYGGVASONS GT. (E6)

THS ANGELLS GT.

DRONNINGENS GT.

Stiftsgården

TORVET

KONGENSGT.

Library
& Ruins

ERLING SKAKKES GT.

Vitenskapsmuseet

Museum of
Decorative
Arts

BISPEGT

BAKKLANDET

City
Art Museum

Nidaros Domkirke

Archbishop's Palace

Ecclesiastical
Museum

Army &
Resistance
Museum

ØYA

Studentersam-
fundet

KRISTIAN FREDERIKS GT.

TRONDHEIM

△ Tram to Lian Herregård Restaurant

△ Youth Hostel & Ringve Museum 2km

INNHERREDSVEIEN E6

HAVNEGT

KJØPMANNSGT

BAKKE BRU

SØNDRE GT

NORDRE GT

SOLSIDENS GT

MUNKEGT

NEDRE BAKKLANDET

BYBRUA

BRUBAKKEN

PRINSENS GT.

ELGESETER BRU

ELGESETER GATE

NYDRE BAKKLANDET

EIDSVOLLSGT.

▽ E6

municipal toll of 12kr (Mon–Fri 6am–6pm) to enter the city. On-street **parking** during restricted periods (mostly Mon–Fri 8am–6pm, Sat 10am–1pm) is expensive and hard to find, so head for a car park: try the handy Torvet P-hus, in the centre at Erling Skakkes gate 16, or the marginally cheaper (and slightly less convenient) Bakke P-hus, east across the bridge from the centre at Nedre Bakklandet 60. Rates are around 7kr an hour. At other times, on-street parking is free and spaces are easy to find.

The **Hurtigrute** coastal boat (information on ☎81 03 00 00) docks at the harbour (northbound services from pier 1, quay 1 and southbound from pier 1, quay 2). These twin piers are 600m north of **Sentralstasjon** (☎177), the gleaming bus and train terminal, where the **information kiosk** deals with all transport enquiries. If you're heading for the city centre from the Hurtigrute quay, consider taking a taxi (50kr) as it's a dull twenty-minute walk. The all-year **Kystekspressen passenger express boat** from Kristiansund docks at the Pirterminalen, 300m north of Sentralstasjon.

Trondheim **airport** is 35km northeast of the city at Vaernes, and Flybussen (Mon–Fri & Sun 5am–9pm, Sat 5am–5pm; every 15–30min; 50kr) run to Sentralstasjon, the *SAS Royal Garden Hotel* and the *Britannia Hotel* in the city centre, a 45-minute ride.

From Sentralstasjon, you simply cross the bridge southwards to reach the triangular island on which central Trondheim sits. The **tourist office**, at Munkegata 19 (mid-May to early June & late Aug Mon–Fri 8.30am–6pm, Sat & Sun 10am–4pm; mid- to late June & mid-Aug Mon–Fri 8.30am–8pm, Sat & Sun 10am–6pm; early Aug Mon–Fri 8.30am–10pm, Sat & Sun 10am–8pm; Sept to mid-May Mon–Fri 9am–4pm; ☎73 92 94 00, *www.taas.no*), is right in the centre of town on a corner of the main square, Torvet. They provide the free and very useful *Trondheim Guide* (also available from the information racks at Sentralstasjon) and a wide range of other free tourist literature; they also have a limited supply of private rooms (see p.232), though these are almost entirely out in the suburbs. You can also buy hiking maps and change money here – the latter service is especially handy outside banking hours.

City transport

The best way of exploring the city centre is **on foot** – it only takes about ten minutes to walk from one end to the other – but a convenient alternative is to take advantage of the city's **free bicycle rental**. Brightly coloured municipal bikes are available from racks all over the city centre and are released upon payment of a small deposit (20kr); the money is returned automatically when you slip your bike back into a rack. The bikes are popular, so don't be surprised if you come across a rack that's empty. A map marking the locations of the racks is available from the tourist office. For longer excursions, mountain bikes can be rented from Ila Sikkelsenter, Steinberget 1 (☎73 51 09 40), at about 140kr a day. Otherwise, transport in town is by **buses** and **trams** with flat-fare tickets, from the driver, costing 19kr. If you need to travel outside town, to one of the outlying museums or the campsite, it might be worth buying the unlimited 24-hour public transport ticket, the *dagskort*, which costs 45kr from the driver and is valid on all local buses and trams.

Accommodation

Accommodation is plentiful in Trondheim, with a choice of private rooms, two hostels, and a selection of reasonably priced hotels and guesthouses (*pen-

sjonater). What's more, most of the more appealing places are dotted round the city centre, though the private rooms booked via the tourist office are usually out in the suburbs. These **private rooms** are good value, however, at a fixed rate of 350kr per double per night (250kr single), plus a 30kr booking fee.

Hotels and guesthouses

Best Western Residence, Torvet (☎73 52 83 80, fax 73 52 64 60). Package-tour favourite, with standard double rooms. More expensive than most of its competitors until the summer, when there's a discount of thirty percent. ④, s/r ③.

Britannia, Dronningens gate 5 (☎73 53 53 53, fax 73 51 29 00, *www.britannia.no*). Right in the middle of town, this long-established hotel has a magnificent Art Nouveau breakfast room, complete with a Moorish fountain, Egyptian-style murals and Corinthian columns. The comfortable rooms are heavily discounted in summer. ⑤, s/r ③.

Comfort Hotel Augustin, Kongens gate 26 (☎73 54 70 00, fax 73 55 70 01). Routine chain hotel in a big, old brick building not far from the Torvet. Functional and perfectly adequate rooms. ④, s/r ②.

Pensjonat Jarlen, Kongens gate 40 (☎73 51 32 18, fax 73 52 80 80). Basic rooms at bargain prices, and handy for the sights. ①.

Rainbow Gildevangen, Søndre gate 22b (☎73 51 01 00, fax 73 52 38 98). In a sturdy Romanesque Revival stone building, a couple of minutes' walk northeast of Torvet, this chain hotel offers eighty comfortable, modern rooms at economical prices. ④, s/r ③.

Rainbow Trondheim, Kongens gate 15 (☎73 50 50 50, fax 73 51 60 58). Big and popular chain hotel in a plain and chunky modern block, right in the centre. The bar here is one of the few places where you can get home-made mead (*mjød*), once – as in medieval England – Norway's most popular brew. ④, s/r ③.

Radisson SAS Royal Garden, Kjøpmannsgata 73 (☎73 80 30 00, fax 73 80 30 50). Stylish modern hotel with sweeping architectural lines and wonderfully comfortable beds. Good summer deals make this the one to check out first if you're looking for upmarket lodgings. Banquet-like breakfasts too. ⑥, s/r ③.

Hostels and camping

InterRail Centre, Elgeseter gate 1 (☎73 89 95 38). Take bus #41, #42, #48, #49, #52 or #63 along Prinsens gate and ask for the *Studentersamfundet*: it's the unusual big, red, round building just over the bridge at the south end of Prinsens gate. It takes twenty minutes to walk here from Torvet, half that from the cathedral. Operated by the University's student society, the place offers basic bed-and-breakfast accommodation in a couple of hundred double rooms. Just 105kr per person per night. There's a cheap, all-day café here too, plus the facility to store luggage. Open late June to mid-Aug, 7am–1am daily. ①.

Trondheim Vandrerhjem, Weidemannsvei 41 (☎73 87 44 50, fax 73 87 44 55). A twenty-minute hike east from the centre: cross the Bakke bru, a bridge leading to busy Innherredsveien (the E6), along which you head uphill; turn right into Wessels gate and it's on the left at the fourth crossroads. Bus #63 from Sentralstasjon and Dronningens gate also runs in that direction – ask the driver to let you off as close as possible. This HI hostel, with 20 six-bed and 30 four-bed dorm rooms, and just a couple of double rooms, is very institutional – it looks more like a hospital than somewhere you'd want to spend the night. Open all year except Christmas, New Year and Easter. ①, dorm beds 170kr.

The city centre

The historic centre of Trondheim sits on a small triangle of land bordered by a loop of the River Nid, with the curve of the long and slender **Trondheimsfjord** beyond. **Torvet** is the main city square, a spacious, open area anchored by a statue of Olav Tryggvason, Trondheim's founder (see p.318), perched on a tall stone pillar like some medieval Nelson. The broad avenues that radiate out from here were once flanked by long rows of wooden buildings, which served all the needs of a small town and administrative centre. Most of these older structures are long gone, replaced largely by uninspiring modern buildings, but one notable survivor is the **Stiftsgården**, a fine timber mansion erected in 1774. It is, however, small beer compared with the **cathedral**, an imposing, largely medieval structure that is the city's highlight. The cathedral dominates the southern part of the centre and close by are the much-restored **Archbishop's Palace** and the pick of Trondheim's several museums, the **Museum of Decorative Arts** and the **City Art Museum**. Near here too, on the far side of the old town bridge (the **Bybrua**), is a clutter of old warehouses and timber dwellings that comprises the prettiest and most fashionable part of town, **Bakklandet**, home to the best restaurants and bars.

The cathedral

The goal of Trondheim's pilgrims in times past was the colossal cathedral, **Nidaros Domkirke**, Scandinavia's largest medieval building (May to mid-June & late Aug to mid-Sept Mon–Fri 9am–3pm, Sat 9am–2pm, Sun 1–4pm; late June to late Aug Mon–Fri 9am–6pm, Sat 9am–2pm, Sun 1–4pm; mid-Sept to April Mon–Fri noon–2.30pm, Sat 11.30am–2pm, Sun 1–3pm; 25kr). Gloriously restored following several fires and the upheavals of the Reformation, it remains the focal point of any visit to the city and one of the country's architectural highlights. It's best visited in the early morning, when it's reasonably free of tour groups; conveniently in the cathedral's vicinity, and worth a look, are the much-restored Archbishop's Palace and several art museums.

The cathedral is dedicated to King – later Saint – Olav. Born in 995, **Olav Haraldsson** followed the traditional life of the Viking chieftain from the tender age of 12, "rousing the steel-storm" (as the saga writers described his bloody antics) from Finland to Ireland. He also served as a mercenary to both the duke of Normandy and King Ethelred of England, and it was during this time that he was converted to Christianity. In 1015, he invaded Norway, defeated his enemies and became king, his military success built upon the support of the more prosperous farmers of the Trøndelag, an emergent class of yeomen who were less capricious than the coastal chieftains of Viking fame. However, Olav's zealous imposition of Christianity – he ordered the desecration of pagan sites and the execution of those who refused baptism – alienated many of his followers. The bribes of Olav's rival Knut (Canute), King of England and Denmark, did the rest: Olav's retainers deserted him, and he was forced into exile in 1028. Two years later, he was back in the Trøndelag, but the army he had raised was far too weak to defeat his enemies, and Olav was killed at the battle of **Stiklestad** (see p.241), near Trondheim.

Olav might have lost his kingdom, but the nationwide Church he founded had no intention of losing ground. Needing a local **saint** to consolidate its position, the Church carefully nurtured the myth of Olav, a sanctification apparently assisted by the oppressiveness of the "foreigner" Knut's rule. After the battle of Stiklestad, Olav's body had been spirited away and buried on the banks of the River Nid at what is today Trondheim. There were rumours of miracles in the vicinity of the grave and when the bishop – who had come to investigate these strange goings-on – exhumed the body, he found it undecayed. Olav was declared a saint and his body placed in a silver casket. In 1066 Olav Kyrre, son of Olav's half-brother Harald the Fair-Haired, became King of Norway, and ordered work to begin on a grand church to house the remains in appropriate style. Over the years the church was altered and enlarged to accommodate the growing bands of medieval pilgrims. It achieved cathedral status in 1152, when Trondheim became the seat of an archbishopric whose authority extended as far as Orkney and the Isle of Man. The traditional burial place of Norwegian royalty, the cathedral has also been the scene of every coronation since 1814.

Today's magnificent blue and green-grey soapstone edifice, with its copper-green spire and roof, and a fancy set of gargoyles on the choir, is a true amalgam of architectural styles. The Romanesque transepts, with their heavy hooped windows and dog-tooth decoration, were built by English stonemasons from Lincoln in the twelfth century; and the early Gothic choir, with its pointed arches, flying buttresses and intricate tracery, is clearly influenced by contemporaneous churches in England. The nave was built in the early thirteenth century, also in the early Gothic style, but was destroyed by fire in 1719; the present structure is a painstakingly accurate late nineteenth-century replica.

Inside the cathedral, the half-light hides much of the lofty decorative work, but it is possible to examine the striking early twentieth-century **choir screen**, whose wooden figures are the work of Gustav Vigeland (see p.93). Vigeland was also responsible for the adjacent soapstone **font**, a superb piece of medievalism sporting four bas-reliefs respectively depicting Adam and Eve, John the Baptist baptizing the Christ, the Resurrection and a beguiling Noah and the Ark; Noah peers apprehensively out of his boat, not realizing that the dove, with the tell-tale branch, is up above. The other item of particular interest is a famous fourteenth-century **altar frontal** in a chapel off the ambulatory which is directly behind the high altar. At a time when few Norwegians could read or write, the cult of St Olav had to be promoted visually, and the frontal is the earliest surviving representation of Olav's life and times. In its centre, Olav looks suitably beatific holding his axe and orb; the top left-hand corner shows the dream Olav had before the battle of Stiklestad, of Jesus dropping a ladder down to him from heaven. In the next panel down, Olav and his men are shown at prayer before the battle and, in the bottom right hand corner, Olav meets a sticky end, speared and stabbed by three nasty-looking soldiers. The final panel shows church officials exhuming Olav's uncorrupted body and declaring his sainthood.

At no extra charge, there are English-language **guided tours** of the church during the summer (mid-June to mid-Aug at 11am, 2pm & 4pm; 30min), and you can also take a peek at the assorted Norwegian **crown jewels** (April & May Fri noon–2pm; June to late Aug Mon–Fri 9.30am–12.30pm, Sun 1–4pm; late Aug to Oct Fri noon–2pm; free), kept at the west end of the church. What you won't see is St Olav's silver casket-coffin: this was taken to Denmark and melted down for coinage in 1537. Before you move on, you should certainly climb the cathedral **tower** (late June to late Aug Mon–Fri 9am–6pm, Sat 9am–2pm, Sun 1–4pm; 5kr). From the top, there's a fine view of the city and the forested hills that surround it, with the fjord trailing away in one direction, the river valley in the other.

The Archbishop's Palace

Behind the Domkirke, to the south, lies the heavily restored **Erkebispegården** (Archbishop's Palace). This courtyard complex was originally built in the twelfth century for the third archbishop, Øystein, but two stone-and-brick wings are all that survive of the original quadrangle – the other two were added later. After the archbishops were kicked out during the Reformation, the palace became the residence of the Danish governors. It was subsequently used as the city armoury, and many of the old weapons are now displayed in the **Rustkammeret med Hjemmefrontmuseet** (Army and Resistance Museum; June–Aug Mon–Fri 9am–3pm, Sat & Sun 11am–4pm; Sept–Nov & Feb–May Sat & Sun 11am–4pm; free), which occupies the west wing. The first floor gives the broad details of Norway's involvement in the interminable Dano-Swedish wars that racked Scandinavia from the fifteenth to the nineteenth century. As part of the Danish state, Norway was frequently attacked from the east along the Halden–Oslo corridor, the most memorable incursions being by that most warlike of Swedish kings, Karl XII. Much to the Danish king's surprise, Karl came a cropper in Norway: defeated for the first time and, when he came back for more, shot (possibly by one of his own men) while besieging Fredriksten fortress (see p.110) in 1718. Of more general interest, the second floor describes the German invasion and occupation of World War II, dealing honestly with the sensitive issue of collaboration: you can listen to Vidkun Quisling's broadcast announcing his coup d'état of April 9, 1940. There are also some intriguing displays on the daring antics of the Norwegian Resistance, notably an extraordinary – perhaps harebrained – attempt to sink the battleship *Tirpitz* as it lay moored in an inlet of the Trondheimsfjord in 1942 (see box, p.242). This escapade, like so many others, involved Resistance hero **Leif Larsen**, who worked closely with the Royal Navy organizing covert operations in occupied Norway from their base in the Shetlands. Supplies and personnel were transported across the North Sea by Norwegian fishing boats – a lifeline known, in that classically understated British (and Norwegian) way, as the "Shetland bus"; the book of the same name (see p.337) tells the tale of this remarkable enterprise.

Moving on, the south wing holds a smart **ecclesiastical museum** (early & mid-June Mon–Sat 11am–3pm, Sun noon–4pm; late June to late Aug Mon–Sat 10am–5pm, Sun noon–5pm; Sept to May Tues–Sat 11am–3pm, Sun noon–4pm; 25kr or free with cathedral ticket), largely devoted to a few dozen medieval statues originally retrieved and put away for safekeeping during the nineteenth-century reconstruction of the nave and west facade. Frankly, many of the statues are too battered to be particularly engaging, but they are nicely displayed and several are finely carved. In particular, look out for a life-size sculpture of poor old St Denis, his head in his hands (literally) in accord with the legend that he was beheaded and subsequently spotted carrying his own head to his grave. Downstairs, an assortment of finds unearthed during a lengthy 1990s archeological investigation of the site demonstrates the economic power of the archbishops: they employed all manner of skilled artisans – from glaziers and shoemakers to rope-makers, armourers and silversmiths – and even minted their own coinage.

From the back of the Erkebispegården, you can stroll out onto the grassy lawns beside the **River Nid**. A trio of rusting bastions are reminders of the military defences that once protected this side of town, but it's the setting that appeals. Footpaths snake round to the sturdy old tombs and wildflowers of the **graveyard**, just to the east of the cathedral's main entrance.

The City Art Museum

The **Trondhjems Kunstmuseum**, near the cathedral at Bispegata 7b (June–Aug Mon–Fri & Sun 10am–4pm; Sept–May Tues–Sun noon–4pm; 30kr), is quite small, but features an enjoyable selection of works by Johan Dahl and Thomas Fearnley, the leading figures of nineteenth-century Norwegian landscape painting, as well as the romantic canvases of Hans Gude and his chum Adolph Tidemand. Also displayed is the first overtly political work by a Norwegian artist: *The Strike* was painted in 1877 by the radical Theodor Kittelsen, better known for his illustrations of the folk tales collected by Jorgen Møe and Pieter Asbjørnsen. There's also a diverting selection of Munch's woodcuts, sketches and lithographs here, including several of those disturbing, erotically charged human embodiments of emotions – such as *Lust*, *Fear* and *Jealousy* – that are so characteristic of his oeuvre. Munch's works are not clearly labelled, but an inventory is available free at reception. Most of the permanent collection is removed from view during major temporary exhibitions – even Munch can get the shove.

Museum of Decorative Arts

The delightful **Nordenfjeldske Kunstindustrimuseum** is at Munkegata 5 (Museum of Decorative Arts; early to mid-June Mon–Wed, Fri & Sat 10am–3pm, Thurs 10am–5pm, Sun noon–4pm; late June to late Aug Mon–Sat 10am–5pm, Sun noon–5pm; Sept–May Wed, Fri & Sat 10am–3pm, Thurs 10am–5pm, Sun noon–4pm; 30kr), a couple of minutes' walk north from the cathedral. The museum's collection is too extensive to be shown in its entirety at any one time, so the exhibits are regularly rotated. There's also an ambitious programme of special exhibitions, focusing on contemporary arts, craft and design. Start your visit in the basement, where the historical collection illustrates bourgeois life in Trøndelag from 1500 to 1900 by means of an eclectic assemblage of furniture, faïence, glassware and silver. There are twentieth-century pieces on display here too, notably a fine selection of Art Nouveau. This theme is developed on the first floor where among the temporary exhibitions is a room kitted out by the Belgian designer and architect Henri van de Velde. Unless there's a special exhibition on, the first floor also houses an unusual display of early twentieth-century **tapestries**. Produced in Trondheim, these were based on depictions of medieval folk tales painted by the Norwegian Gerhard Munthe. More modern works can be found on the next floor up, but the highlight there is the room devoted to fourteen tapestries by **Hannah Ryggen**. Born in Malmø in 1894, Ryggen moved to the Trondheim area in the early 1920s and stayed until her death in 1970. Her tapestries are classically naive, the forceful colours and absence of perspective emphasizing the feeling behind them. This is committed art, railing in the 1930s and 1940s against Hitler and Fascism, later moving on to more disparate targets such as the atom bomb and social conformism. But she still made time to celebrate the things she cherished: *Yes, we love this country* (tapestry no. 9) is as evocative a portrayal of her adopted land as you're likely to find.

Bakklandet and the medieval church ruins

It's a couple of minutes' walk east of the cathedral and the Museum of Decorative Arts to the **Bybrua** (Old Town Bridge), an elegant wooden construction with splendid views over Kjøpmannsgata's early eighteenth-century gabled and timbered warehouses, now mostly restaurants and offices. There are more restaurants and several groovy bars at the far end of the bridge in **Bakklandet**, Trondheim's own "left bank", which comprises the brightly painted timber houses of an old neighbourhood.

Crossing back over the Bybrua from Bakklandet, and following the river north along Kjøpmannsgata, you soon come to the **medieval church ruins**, discovered under the **library** at the far end of Kongens gate. A twelfth-century relic of the days when Trondheim had fifteen or more religious buildings, it is thought to have been a chapel dedicated to St Olav, although the evidence for this is a bit shaky. Excavations revealed nearly 500 bodies in the immediate area, which was once the church graveyard, and some skeletons are neatly displayed under glass. Entry is free and the site is accessible during library opening hours (June–Aug Mon–Fri 9am–4pm, Sat 10am–3pm; Sept–May Mon–Thurs 9am–7pm, Fri 9am–4pm, Sat 10am–3pm, Sun noon–4pm). From here, it's just a few minutes' walk west to Torvet.

The Stiftsgården and north to the Ravnkloa

Stretching out along Munkegata just north of Torvet, and a couple of hundred metres from the church ruins, one conspicuous remnant of old timber-town Trondheim survives in the city centre – the **Stiftsgården** (early to mid-June Mon–Sat 10am–3pm, Sun noon–5pm; late June to late Aug Mon–Sat 10am–5pm, Sun noon–5pm; Sept–May open one day monthly – details from the tourist office; guided tours every hour on the hour; 35kr for tour). Built in 1774–78, this good-looking yellow structure is claimed to be the largest wooden building in northern Europe. These days it is an official royal residence, a marked improvement in its fortunes as it was originally built to accommodate the provincial governor. Inside, a long series of period rooms are decorated with fanciful Italianate wall-paintings and furniture in a range of late eighteenth- to early nineteenth-century styles, from Rococo to Biedermeierstil, that reflect the genteel tastes of the early occupants. The anecdotal guided tour brings a smile – but not perhaps 35kr wide.

If sight of Bakklandet's old wooden buildings has whetted your appetite, you'll enjoy the tangle of narrow alleys and pastel-painted clapboard frontages that fills out the sidestreets **north of Kongens gate** and west of Prinsens gate. There's nothing special to look at, but it's a pleasant area for a stroll, after which you can wander over to **Ravnkloa**, the jetty at the north end of Munkegata where the fish market is held – and where ferries leave for Munkholmen (see p.238).

The Museum of Natural History and Archeology

Back at Torvet, it's a five- to ten-minute walk southwest to the university's **Vitenskapsmuseet** at Erling Skakkes gate 47 (Museum of Natural History and Archeology; May to mid-Sept Mon–Fri 10am–5pm, Sat & Sun 11am–5pm; mid-Sept to April Tues–Fri 10am–3pm, Sat & Sun 10am–4pm; 25kr), comprising several collections. At the front, the main building contains an assortment of dusty stuffed animals and a largely incomprehensible ragbag of archeological finds. Don't bother with these, but instead pop into the smaller building on the left, where there's a small but enjoyable **church art** section, with ecclesiastical knick-knacks from pulpits and fonts through to processional crosses and statues of the saints. Even better, in the old *suhmhuset* (hay storehouse), a low, long building at the rear, is a first-rate **historical exhibition** which tracks the development of Trondheim from its foundation in the tenth century to the fire of 1681. Its thoroughly researched, multilingual text is supported by an excellent range of archeological finds, and departs from the predictable "Kings and Queens" tack, investigating everything from sanitary towels and reliquary jars to popular games and attitudes to life and death.

Munkholmen island

Poking up out of the Trondheimsfjord just 2km offshore, the tiny islet of **Munkholmen** is easily reached by boat from the Ravnkloa jetty (late May to early Sept every hour on the hour 10am–6pm; 33kr return). The island has an eventful history. In Viking times it was used as the city's execution ground, and St Olav went to the added trouble of displaying the head of one of his enemies on a pike here, which must have made approaching mariners a tad nervous. In the eleventh century, the Benedictines founded a monastery on the island – hence its name – but it was not one of their more successful ventures: the archbishop received dozens of complaints about, of all things, the amount of noise the monks made, not to mention alleged heavy drinking and womanizing. After the Reformation, the island was converted into a prison, which doubled as a fortress designed to protect the seaward approaches to the city; later still it became a customs house. The longest-serving prisoner was the Danish count Peder Griffenfeld (1635–99), who spent eighteen years cooped up here until his eventual release in 1698. One of the most powerful men in Denmark, Griffenfeld played a leading role in the assumption of absolute power by King Frederick III (see p.322), but was outmanoeuvred and imprisoned by his rivals after the king's death.

Sturdy stone walls encircle almost the entire island, and behind them, sunk in a circular dip, is a set of quaint, almost cottage-like, prison buildings surrounding a cobbled courtyard. There are thirty-minute guided tours of the central part of the **fortress** (late May to early Sept daily 10.30am–5.30pm; 15kr), a cheerful romp through its galleries and corridors. The tour includes a visit to the spacious cell occupied by Griffenfeld, and a glimpse of the gun emplacement the Germans installed during World War II. After the tour you can wander over to the **café**, or scramble along outside the walls and round the rocks beneath to either of a couple of rough, pebbly beaches.

Out from the centre: the Ringve museum

The **Ringve Museum** (late May daily noon–3pm; June to mid-Aug daily 11am–6pm; mid-Aug to mid-Sept daily 11am–3pm; mid-Sept to mid-May occasional guided tours, ring for details on ☎73 92 24 11; 60kr) occupies a delightful eighteenth-century country house and courtyard complex on the hilly Lade peninsula, some 4km northeast of the city centre. Devoted to musical history and to musical instruments from all over the world, the museum is divided into two sections. In the main building, the collection focuses on **antique European instruments** in period settings, with several demonstrations included in a lengthy – and obligatory – guided tour. The second section, in the old barn, contains an **international selection of musical instruments** and offers a self-paced zip through some of the key moments and movements of **musical history**. There are themes like "the invention of the piano" and "pop and rock", not to mention the real humdinger, "the marching band movement in Norway". Immaculately maintained, the surrounding **botanical gardens** make the most of the scenic setting. To get there, take bus #3 or #4 to Lade from near the north end of Munkegata.

Eating and drinking

As befits Norway's third city, Trondheim has a good selection of first-rate **restaurants**, the pick of which are concentrated in Bakklandet and along neighbouring Kjøpmannsgata. Chinese and Italian places are popular, but it's the Norwegian restaurants which offer the most distinctive cuisine, with seafood and Arctic specialities, like char and reindeer, a special treat. The best of Trondheim's **café-bars** are also concentrated in Bakklandet and, as in the rest of urban Norway, these laid-back establishments are the most fashionable places to eat and/or drink, open well into the early hours. The city's busiest **bars** are concentrated right in the centre around the junction of Dronningens gate and Nordre gate. At weekends they're heaving with students, townies and conference delegates, but they are too meat-rackish for many tastes. Finally, the city's mobile **fast-food** stalls are concentrated around Sentralstasjon and along Kongens gate, on either side of Torvet.

Restaurants and café-bars

Benito's Mat og Vinhus, Vår Frue gate 4 (☎73 52 64 22). Offering traditional Italian dishes at reasonable prices, this restaurant is adjacent to the fine *Zia Teresa Pizzeria* (see p.240) and run by the same family.

Bryggen, Øvre Bakklandet 66 (☎73 52 02 30). This is a superb seafood restaurant at the east end of the Bybrua. The daily specials, mostly featuring the catch of the day, are a delight. Main courses average about 180kr.

Chablis, Øvre Bakklandet 62 (☎73 87 42 50). Just metres from the Bybrua, this polished brasserie-restaurant, with its modish furnishings and fittings, serves up excellent food – Norwegian but with a Mediterranean slant. Reasonably priced.

Dromedar, Nedre Bakklandet 3a. A fashionable café-bar with a laid-back atmosphere located a few metres north of the Bybrua. Tasty, filling and inexpensive fare with a wholefood slant.

Havfruen, Kjøpmannsgata 7 (☎73 53 26 26). An excellent fish restaurant near the cathedral – one of the best in town, with prices to match. Try to book in advance. Main courses from 180kr.

Kafé Gåsa, Øvre Bakklandet 58. With its traditional Norwegian decor and clutter of folksy bygones, this intimate café-bar is a charming place. Good Norwegian food and a great terrace in sunny weather.

Lian Herregård, Lianveien 36 (☎72 55 90 77). Up in the forested hills about 10km west of the city centre, this traditional Norwegian restaurant has a terrace bar affording panoramic views over the Trondheimsfjord. Getting there is enjoyable too – catch the Lian tram from St Olavs gate and stay on till you reach the terminus, from where it's a couple of minutes' walk up the hill to the restaurant; note that at weekends the place is often too busy to be much fun. April–September Mon–Fri 11am–6pm, Sat & Sun 11am–4pm; rest of year, telephone for times.

Markens Grøde, Nedre Bakklandet 5 (☎73 53 16 11). The city's main vegetarian restaurant, featuring tasty food at low prices and a friendly atmosphere.

Ni Muser, Bispegata 9. Just along the street from the City Art Museum, this relaxed and fashionable little café-bar serves up tasty snacks and meals from a variety of European cuisines. It's an excellent place, and also has a terrace bar at the back. Prices are low and many customers have an arty/academic look, which is nicely in keeping with the small contemporary art gallery up above. Daily 11am–midnight.

Posepilten, Prinsens gate 32, at Dronningens gate. Easy-going café-bar with a wide-ranging menu – everything from vegetarian specials through to Mexican-style tortillas. Tasty, filling and inexpensive food, and occasional live music too.

New China Garden, Kjøpmannsgata 21 (☎73 51 47 77). Excellent Chinese restaurant specializing in Szechuan dishes at reasonable prices.

Radisson SAS Royal Garden, Kjøpmannsgata 73 (☎73 80 30 00). Despite its riverside setting, the ground-floor café-restaurant of this plush hotel lacks atmosphere, but the all-you-can-eat, self-service buffets are outstanding value at around 75kr. They are available most evenings from about 6pm to 9pm, and the food is very good quality.

Zia Teresa Pizzeria, Vår Frue gate 4 (☎73 52 64 22). East of Torvet, off Kongens gate. Easily the best pizzeria in town, with pizzas from as little as 100kr.

Bars

Bobbys Bar & Snadderi, Søndre gate 22a. Small, intimate bar with a youthful clientele.

Carl Johan Møteplass, Olav Tryggvasons gate 24. Jam-packed at the weekend, this bar is popular with conference delegates and locals in equal measure.

Frakken, Dronningens gate, at the corner with Nordre gate. Bar and nightclub that seems to have most of Trondheim's permed hairdos passing through its doors. Popular generally – and raucous at the weekend.

Underetg, Kjøpmannsgata 7. One floor below the *Havfruen* restaurant, this bar caters for the thirty-somethings and up, and often has live jazz on Friday and Saturday nights.

Listings

Airlines SAS ☎74 80 41 00; Braathens ☎74 84 32 00.

Consulates UK, Sluppenveien 10 (☎73 83 22 00).

Car breakdown NAF ☎73 95 73 95.

Car rental Avis, Kjøpmannsgata 34 (☎73 52 69 15); Budget, Elgeseter gate 21 (☎73 94 10 25) and at the *Royal Garden Hotel*, Kjøpmannsgata 73 (☎73 52 69 20).

DNT Trondhjems Turistforening, at Munkegata 64 (Mon–Fri 9am–4pm; ☎73 92 42 00), is the DNT's local branch, offering advice on the region's hiking trails and huts. They also organize a variety of guided walks and cross-country skiing trips, with activities concentrated in the mountains to the south and east of the city. There are one-day excursions and longer expeditions, to suit different levels of skill and fitness.

Medical emergencies Hospital Casualty Department ☎73 52 25 00; dental emergencies ☎73 50 55 00.

Pharmacy St Olav Vaktapotek, Kjøpmannsgata 65 (☎73 52 66 66). Mon–Sat 8.30am–midnight, Sun 10am–midnight.

Police Kongens gate 87 (☎73 89 90 90).

Post office Main office at Dronningens gate 10 (Mon–Fri 8am–5pm, Sat 9am–1pm).

Taxis Ranks at Torvet, Sentralstasjon, Søndregata and the *Royal Garden Hotel*; or call ☎73 50 50 73 (24hr).

Vinmonopolet A city-centre branch is at Kjøpmannsgata 32.

North from Trondheim: Stiklestad to Fauske

North of Trondheim, it's a long haul up the coast to the next major places of interest: Bodø, the main ferry port for the Lofotens, and the gritty but likeable town of Narvik, respectively 730km and 908km. The easiest way to make the bulk of the trip is by **train**, a rattling good journey with the scenery becoming wilder and bleaker the further north you go – and you'll usually be treated to a blast from the whistle as you cross the Arctic Circle. The train takes nine hours to reach **Fauske**, where the line reaches its northern limit and turns west for the final 65-kilometre dash across to Bodø. At Fauske, there are **bus** connections north to Narvik, a five-hour drive away, but many travellers take an overnight break here – though in fact nearby Bodø makes a far more pleasant stopover.

If you're **driving**, you'll find the E6 – which runs all the way from Trondheim to Narvik and points north – too slow to allow you to cover more than three or four hundred kilometres comfortably in a day. Fortunately, there are several pleasant places to stop, beginning with **Steinkjer** and **Snåsa** in Trøndelag. Steinkjer is a modest little town with a couple of good hotels, Snåsa a relaxed village, again with somewhere good to stay. Further north, in Nordland, the next province up, lies **Mo-i-Rana**, once a grimy steel town, but now attractively remodelled and the obvious starting point for a visit to the **Svartisen glacier**, crowning the coastal peaks close by. The glacier is on the western rim of the **Saltfjellet Nasjonalpark**, a wild and windswept mountain plateau that extends east towards the Swedish border. The E6 and the railway cut through the park, giving ready access, but although this is a popular destination for experienced hikers, it's too fierce an environment for the novice or the lightly equipped.

Stiklestad

Leaving Trondheim, the E6 tunnels and twists its way round the fjord to **HELL**, a busy rail junction, where one line branches north to slice through the dales and hills of Trøndelag, en route to Fauske; the other heads east for the seventy-kilometre-haul to the Swedish frontier, with Østersund beyond. Hell itself has nothing other than its name to recommend it; paradoxically, in Norwegian *hell* means good fortune. Just beyond Hell, the road forks too, with the E6 thumping on north and the E14 heading east. Continuing along the E6, it's about 30km to the **Fættenfjord**, a narrow inlet of the Trondheimsfjord and one-time hideout of the battleship *Tirpitz* (see box, p.242).

After the fjord, the E6 clips past the tedious little towns of **Levanger** and **Verdalsøra**, the latter a centre for the fabrication of offshore oil platforms, and from where it's just 6km inland along Highway 757 to **STIKLESTAD**, probably Norway's most famous village. It was here in 1030 that Olav Haraldsson, later St Olav, was killed in battle, his death now commemorated by the **Stiklestad Nasjonale Kultursenter** (Stiklestad National Culture Centre; June to mid-Aug daily 9am–8pm; mid-Aug to May Mon–Fri 9am–5pm, Sat & Sun 11am–6pm; ☎74 04 42 00, *www.snk.no*), whose assorted museums and open-air amphitheatre are spread out over the pastoral landscape. A descendant of Harald Hårfagri (the Fair-Haired), **Olav Haraldsson** (see p.233) was one of Norway's most important medieval kings, a Viking warrior turned resolute Christian monarch whose misfortune it was to be the enemy of the powerful and shrewd King Knut of England and Denmark. It was Knut's bribes that did for Olav, persuading all but his most loyal supporters to change allegiances – as a Norse poet commented in the cautionary *Hávamál* (the Sayings of Odin), "I have never found a man so generous and hospitable that he would not take a present." Dislodged from the throne, Olav returned from exile in Sweden in 1030, but was defeated and killed here at the Battle of Stiklestad. His role as founder of the Norwegian Church prompted his subsequent canonization, and his cult flourished at Trondheim until the Reformation.

LEIF LARSEN AND THE ATTACK ON THE TIRPITZ

The German battleship *Tirpitz*, commissioned in 1941, spent most of its three-year existence hidden away in the **Fættenfjord** (see p.241), where it was protected by from air attack by the mountains and from a sea attack by a succession of coastal gun emplacements. With the fjord as its base, the *Tirpitz* could sally forth to attack Allied convoys to Russia and as such was a major irritant to the Royal Navy, who dreamt up a remarkable scheme to sink it. The navy had just perfected a submersible craft called the **Chariot**, manned by a crew of two divers and with its own torpedo. The Chariot was just six metres long and driven by electric motors, with the (volunteer) crew sitting astride the submersible to the rear – which must amount to some kind of definition of bravery. The plan was to transport two of these Chariots across from Shetland to Norway in a Norwegian fishing boat and then, just before the first German checkpoint, to attach them to the outside of the boat's hull. The fishing boat would, it was thought, stand a good chance of passing through the German defences when equipped with false papers and a diversionary load of peat. Thereafter, as soon as the boat got within reasonable striking distance, the Chariots could be launched towards the *Tirpitz* and, once they got very close to the ship, their torpedoes would be fired.

The boat selected was the *Arthur*, skippered by the redoubtable **Leif Larsen**, a modest man of extraordinary courage, who, over the course of the war, ran over fifty trips to Norway from the Shetlands. The *Arthur* had a crew of four Norwegian and six British seamen – four to pilot the Chariots and two to help them get into their diving suits. At first the trip went well. As soon as they reached Norway's coastal waters, the crew moved the Chariots from their hiding place in the hold and attached them to the hull. They then fooled the Germans and were allowed into the Trondheimsfjord, but here the weather deteriorated and the Chariots broke loose from the boat, falling to the bottom of the ocean before they could be used. There was, therefore, no choice but to abort the mission, scuttle the *Arthur* and row ashore in the hope that the crew could escape over the mountains to neutral Sweden. They divided into two parties of five, one of which made it without mishap – except for a few lost toes from frostbite – but the other group, led by Larsen, ran into a patrol. In the skirmish that ensued, one of the Englishmen, a certain A.B. Evans, was wounded and had to be left behind; the Germans polished him off.

On September 11, 1944, the *Tirpitz* was caught napping in the Kåfjord (see p.288) by a squadron of bombers which flew in from a Russian airfield to the east, screened by the mountains edging the fjord. The *Tirpitz* was badly damaged in the attack, especially its engines. It managed to limp off to Tromsø, just outside of which it was finally sunk on November 12 by a combined bombing-and-torpedo attack.

The government has spent millions developing the Stiklestad Nasjonale Kultursenter, one of the results being the broad-beamed **Kulturhus**, whose prime attraction is a melodramatic **museum** (60kr) that uses shadowy dioramas and a ghoulish soundtrack to chronicle the events leading up to Olav's death. The dioramas contain few artefacts of note, other than one or two bits of armour and jewellery dating from the period; neither is the text particularly revealing, which is a pity, since something more could have been made of St Olav's position in medieval Christian folklore. One such tale, passed down through the generations, relates how Olav spent the night on a remote farm, only to discover the family praying over a carefully preserved horse's penis. Expressing some irritation – but no surprise – at this pagan ceremony, Olav threw the phallus to the family dog and took the opportunity to explain some of the finer tenets of Christianity to his hosts. There's a second display on St Olav upstairs in the museum, this one focusing on his cult and how it spread across western Europe.

Across from the Kulturhus is a much modified twelfth-century **church**, original to the site and reputedly marking the spot where Olav was stabbed to death. This church used to claim that the stone on which the body was first laid out had been incorporated into its high altar, an assertion that went by the board after the Reformation. Just up the hill from the Kulturhus, a five-minute walk away, is the open-air **amphitheatre**, where the colourful *Olsokspelet* (St Olav's Play), a costume drama, is performed each year as part of the **St Olav Festival**. This is held over several days either side of the anniversary of the battle, July 29, and thousands of Norwegians make the trek here; tickets need to be booked months in advance with the Kultursenter. The amphitheatre also adjoins an **open-air folk museum** containing some thirty seventeenth- to nineteenth-century buildings moved here from the rest of rural Trøndelag.

Stiklestad is difficult to reach without your own transport – in fact, it's more trouble than it's worth, especially as there's nowhere to stay when you get there. A twice-daily train from Trondheim runs to Verdalsøra, 6km away, from where you have to walk, or use one of the taxis that usually wait outside the station. During the St Olav Festival, however, special trains and buses take visitors to the site; details can be obtained from the Trondheim tourist office.

Steinkjer and Snåsa

Back on the E6, it's a further 30km to **STEINKJER**, an unassuming town that sits in the shadow of wooded hills, at the point where the river that gave the place its name empties into the fjord. The Germans bombed the town to bits in 1940 when it was the site of an infantry training camp, and the modern replacement is a tidy, appealing ensemble that fans out from the long main street, Kongens gate. As such, the town is a pleasant spot to rest before the rigours of the journey north. The E6 bypasses Steinkjer town centre, running parallel to – and about 400m to the west of – Kongens gate, with the **train station** in between. Right in the centre of town across from the train station is the *Quality Grand Hotell*, Kongens gate 37 (☎74 16 47 00, fax 74 16 62 87; ④, s/r ③), which manages to seem quite old-fashioned even though it occupies a modern tower block. The rooms on its upper floors have splendid views along the coast, and the hotel restaurant serves tasty Norwegian dishes at reasonable prices. There are several other places to eat nearby, the pick of these being the folksy *Trønderstua*, Kongens gate 33, which sticks to traditional Norwegian fare. The main road also passes the **tourist office** (late June to early Aug Mon–Fri 8am–7pm, Sat 9am–3pm; mid-Aug to mid-June Mon–Fri 8am–4pm; ☎74 16 67 00). There's an all-year municipal **campsite**, *Guldbergaunet Camping* (☎74 16 20 45, fax 74 16 47 35), in the park on the south bank of the river, about 2km inland from the train station.

On the north side of Steinkjer, there's a choice of routes round a long and slender lake, Snåsavatnet. The E6 runs along the north shore, while the more agreeable (and slower) Highway 763 meanders through the farmland and wooded hills to the south. Alternatively, with time and patience, you can leave the E6 just beyond Steinkjer and strike out along the tortuous **Kystriksveien** (the Coastal Route; Highway 17), which threads its way up the west coast. For more detail, see box, p.246.

Staying on the E6 north of Steinkjer, at the far end of the lake you come to **SNÅSA**, a sleepy, scattered hamlet that is a good example of a Trøndelag rural community. Snåsa also possesses a pretty little hilltop church of softly hued grey stone, dating from the Middle Ages and very much in the English style. On the west side of the village – and 6km from the E6 – is the *Snåsa Hotell* (☎74 15 10 57, fax 74 15 16 15; ③, s/r ②), a modern place with somewhat spartan decor but comfortable bedrooms and a lovely setting overlooking the lake; it's a peaceful spot, ideal if you want to rest after a long drive. The hotel also operates a small **campsite** (same numbers; all year) with huts (②) as well as spaces for tents and caravans. There's a restaurant here too, serving mundane but filling Norwegian staples, but note that if you're likely to arrive hungry and late, you should telephone ahead to check it will still be open.

Into Nordland: Mosjøen

Beyond Snåsa, the E6 leaves the wooded valleys of the Trøndelag for the wider, harsher landscapes of **Nordland**. The road bobs across bleak plateaux, scuttles along rangy river valleys and eventually, after 210km, tears down to the town of **MOSJØEN**, first impressions of which are not especially favourable. The setting is handsome enough, with the town centre wedged amid fjord, river and mountain, but prominent here is the aluminium plant, hogging the north side of the centre. Persevere, for Mosjøen was a small-time trading centre long before the factory arrived, and **Sjøgata**, down by the river, is lined by pleasant old timber dwellings, warehouses and shops dating from the early nineteenth century. It's the general flavour that appeals rather than any particular building, in part because the street is still in everyday use. It only takes a few minutes to walk from one end of Sjøgata to the other, and on the way you'll encounter the **Vefsn Museum**, Sjøgata 31b (Mon–Fri 10am–3.30pm, Sat 10am–2pm; 20kr), which has displays on life in old Mosjøen and exhibits the work of contemporary Nordland artists, some of which are very good.

Mosjøen **train station** is beside the E6 on the north side of town, in front of the aluminium plant. From here, it's about 600m to Sjøgata – just follow the signs. The **tourist office** is at the south end of Sjøgata (June–Aug Mon–Fri 8am–6pm, Sat 9am–2.30pm, Sun noon–4pm; Sept–May Mon–Fri 9am–5pm; ☎75 17 61 20). There are several plain, modern **hotels** near the train station, and the pick of these is *Fru Haugans*, metres from the tourist office (☎75 17 04 77, fax 75 17 05 34; ④, s/r ③). There's been an inn here since the eighteenth century and the present version is a well-judged amalgamation of the new and the old. The hotel **restaurant** serves the best dinner in town, mainly Norwegian dishes, and is reasonably priced. Along Sjøgata there are several places to grab a coffee – *Egon*, at no. 1, will do very nicely.

Mo-i-Rana

Beyond Mosjøen, the E6 cuts inland to weave across the mountains of the interior. After 50km, there are panoramic views from the top of **Korgfjellet**, with the high point marked by a motel and a monument honouring those 550 Yugoslav prisoners of war who built this section of the road during World War II. Thereafter, the E6 hairpins down to **Korgen**, sitting pretty beneath the mountains in a bend of a river, before the road slips along the fjord to Mo-i-Rana, 90km from Mosjøen.

THE SVARTISEN GLACIER

Its name literally meaning "Black Ice", the **Svartisen** covers roughly 370 square kilometres of mountain and valley between the E6 and the coast. It's actually divided into two sections – east and west – by the Vesterdal valley, though this cleft is a recent phenomenon: when it was surveyed in 1905, the glacier was one giant block, about 25 percent bigger than it is today; the reasons for this change are still obscure. The highest parts of the glacier are at around 1500m, but its tentacles reach down to about 170m – the lowest-lying glacial arms in Europe. Mo is within easy reach of the glacier: to get there, drive north from Mo on the E6 for about 12km and then take the signed turning to the glacier, a straightforward 23-kilometre drive ending beside the green, glacially fed **Svartisvatnet**. **Boats** (late June to late Aug, hourly, 10am–4pm; 20min each way; 70kr return) shuttle across the lake, but note that the service only begins when the ice has melted: usually this is by late June, but Mo's tourist office (see below) can advise on the prevailing situation. From the boat, the great convoluted folds of the glacier look rather like bluish-white custard, but close up, after a stiff three-hour hike past the rocky detritus left by the retreating ice, the sheer size of the glacier becomes apparent – a mighty grinding and groaning wall of ice edged by a jumble of ice chunks, columns and boulders.

Hugging the end of the Ranafjord, **MO-I-RANA**, or simply "Mo", was a minor port and market town until World War II, after which a large steel plant was built here. The plant dominated proceedings until the 1980s, when there was some economic diversification and the town began to clean itself up: the fjord shore was cleared of its industrial clutter and the E6 re-routed to create the pleasantly spacious, surprisingly leafy, spick-and-span town centre of today. Most of Mo is resolutely modern, but the prettiest building is **Mo kirke**, a good-looking church of 1832 with a high-pitched roof and an onion dome, perched on a hill on the eastern edge of the centre. Enclosed by a mossy stone wall, the well-tended graveyard contains a communal tomb for unidentified Russian prisoners of war and the graves of six Scots Guards killed hereabouts in May 1940. In front of the church is a bust commemorating Thomas van Westen, an eighteenth-century evangelist who spearheaded early attempts to Christianize the Sami (p.292).

Mo-i-Rana is an ideal base for an excursion to the **Svartisen**, Norway's second-largest glacier (see box), but also worth considering are two **underground excursions** – one an easy tour into the **Grønligrotta** (mid-June to mid-Aug daily 10am–7pm; 40min; 60kr), a subterranean limestone cave complete with a river; the other a more arduous pot-holing trip into a network of caves, the **Setergrotta** (mid-June to mid-Aug 2 daily; 2hr; 165kr). Underground equipment is provided at both caves, which are signposted off the road between the E6 and Svartisvatnet. Dates of operation depend upon conditions – ask at Mo tourist office for current information.

Practicalities

Mo's **bus** and **train stations** are close together, down by the fjord on Ole Tobias Olsens gate. The compact town centre lies east of this street, with the foot of the main pedestrianized street, Jernbanegata, opposite the bus station. The **tourist office** is 200m to the south of the bus station, also by the fjord (late June to early

THE COASTAL ROUTE – HIGHWAY 17

Branching off the E6 just beyond Steinkjer (see p.243) is the tortuous **Kystriksveien** (the Coastal Route) or Highway 17, a road which threads its way up the west coast, linking many villages that could formerly only be reached by sea. This is an obscure and remote corner of the country, but apart from the lovely scenery there's little of special appeal, and the seven ferry trips that interrupt the 700-kilometre drive north to Bodø (there are no buses) make it very expensive.

More feasibly, that part of Highway 17 between **Mo-i-Rana** and **Bodø** includes all the scenic highlights, can be negotiated in a day, and saves a packet on ferry fares. To sample this part of the route, drive 37km west from Mo along the E12 for the Highway 17 crossroads, from where it's some 60km north to the **Kilboghamn–Jektvik** ferry (Mon–Sat 6 daily, Sun 3 services; 1hr; driver and car 103kr) and a further 30km to the ferry linking **Ågskardet** with **Forøy** (Mon–Sat 12 daily; 10min; driver and car 39kr). On the first ferry you cross the Arctic Circle, and on the second, after arriving at Forøy, you get a chance to see an arm of the **Svartisen** glacier (see box, p.245), viewed across the slender Holandsfjorden. For an even closer look at the glacier, stop at the information centre in **Holand**, 12km beyond Forøy, and catch the **passenger boat** (late May to early Sept daily 8am–7pm, every 45min to 1hr 30min; 15min; 40kr return) which zips across the fjord to meet a connecting bus; this travels the couple of kilometres up to the Svartisen Turistsenter (☎75 75 00 11), merely 250m from the ice. The Turistsenter has a café, rents cabins (②) and is the base for four-hour guided **glacier walks** (mid-June to mid-Aug only; prior booking is essential). For more on glacier walks see p.209. From Holand, it's 170km on to Bodø (see p.249).

A free **booklet** on the Coastal Route can be obtained at tourist offices throughout the region. Apart from describing every nook and cranny of the road, the booklet contains all of Highway 17's car-ferry timetables.

Aug Mon–Fri 9am–8pm, Sat 10am–4pm, Sun 1–7pm; mid-Aug to mid-June Mon–Fri 9am–4pm; ☎75 13 92 00). They will tell you whether the boat to Svartisen is running and make a reservation on your behalf for either of the underground cave trips detailed on p.245. They also issue free town maps and stock a reasonable range of literature on Nordland, including a free booklet describing the Coastal Route (see box above). There are no buses to the glacier, but **car rental** is available at around 600kr a day from Bilhuset, at the Statoil gas station, Verkstedveien 1 (☎75 12 76 00).

The pick of the town's several **hotels** is the excellently run and very comfortable *Meyergården Hotell*, at the far end of Ole Tobias Olsens gate (☎75 13 40 00, fax 75 13 40 01; ④, s/r ②). Most of the hotel is modern, but the original lodge has survived and is maintained in period style, with stuffed animal heads on the wall and elegant panelled doorways. Mo also has a no-frills **youth hostel** (☎75 15 09 63, fax 75 15 15 30; ①, dorm beds 135kr; mid-May to Aug), which has a pleasant setting on a wooded hillside, 2km south of town just off (and signposted from) the E6. The best **restaurant** is at the *Meyergården Hotell*, with main courses from around 130kr.

The quickest route north from Mo is along the **E6**. This is the route taken by long-distance buses and the train, and has several advantages, not least the scenic journey across the barren wastes of the **Saltfjellet Nasjonalpark**, straddling the Arctic Circle. It is, however, possible to get to Bodø via a scenic detour west along Highway 17, the **Coastal Route** (see box above).

The Arctic Circle Centre

Given its appeal as a travellers' totem, and considering the amount of effort it takes to actually get here, crossing the **Arctic Circle**, about 80km north of Mo, turns out to be a bit of a disappointment. The landscape, uninhabited for the most part, is undeniably bleak, but the gleaming **Polarsirkelsenteret** (Arctic Circle Centre; May & early Sept daily 10am–6pm: early to mid-June & Aug daily 9am–8pm; late June to July daily 8am–10pm) disfigures the scene, a building like a giant lampshade plonked by the roadside and stuffed with every sort of tourist bauble imaginable. Both the bus and the train whizz by, the latter tooting its whistle as it does so, and drivers can of course shoot past too, though the temptation to brave the crowds is strong. Even if you resist the Arctic exhibition (50kr), you'll probably get snared by either the "Polarsirkelen" certificate, or the specially stamped postcards. Outside the centre are poignant reminders of crueller times: a couple of simple stone memorials pay tribute to the Yugoslav and Soviet POWs who laboured under terrible conditions to build the Arctic road – the first road link to Narvik and the precursor of the E6 – for the Germans in World War II.

Saltfjellet Nasjonalpark – Lønsdal and Graddis

The louring mountains in the vicinity of the Arctic Circle Centre are part of the vast **Saltfjellet Nasjonalpark**, a mountain plateau whose spindly pines, stern snow-tipped peaks and rippling moors extend west from the Swedish border to the Svartisen glacier. The E6 and the railway cut inland across this range between Mo-i-Rana and Rognan, providing access to the cairned hiking trails that lattice the mountains. You can also reach the trails from Highway 77, which forks east off the E6 to Sweden down the Junkerdal. The region is the preserve of experienced hikers: the trails are not sufficiently clear to dispense with a compass, weather conditions can be treacherous and, although there's a good network of DNT-affiliated huts, none is staffed, nor do any of them supply provisions. Keys to these huts (most of which are owned by BOT, Bodø's hiking association; see p.249) are available locally, but clearly you have to sort this out with BOT before you set off walking.

Among several possible bases for venturing into the Saltfjellet, **LØNSDAL**, around 110km north of Mo and 20km beyond the Arctic Circle, is the most easily reached either on the E6 or by train from Trondheim/Mo or Bodø (2–3 daily, but some trains only stop at Lønsdal by request; check with the conductor). Not that there's actually much to reach: a one-kilometre-long turning off the E6 leads first to the *Global Hotel Polarsirkelen* (☎75 69 41 22, fax 75 69 41 27; ②), a long wooden building in a sheltered location and with a cosy modern interior, and then to the lonely train station. The hotel has the only **restaurant** for miles around, but the food is good.

From Lønsdal, hiking trails lead off into the Saltfjellet. One of the more manageable options is the four-hour hike east to **GRADDIS**, where there's a **youth hostel** (☎75 69 43 41, fax 75 69 43 88; ①, dorm beds 100kr; mid-June to Aug) in a farmstead on the wooded slopes of the **Junkerdalen**, a remote and rather unwelcoming river valley cut into the Saltfjellet, and therefore itself also a favourite spot from which to explore the plateau. The youth hostel is situated 1500m off Highway 77, about 18km east of the E6 and close to the Swedish border; the route is clearly signposted and there are no buses.

Botn and Fauske

Some 45km north of Lønsdal, the E6 regains the coast at **Rognan**, from where it pushes along the east side of the Saltdalsfjord. About 5km after Rognan, at **BOTN**, keep your eyes peeled for the signposted, one-kilometre-long road up to the **Krigskirkegårder**, truly one of Nordland's most mournful and moving places. Buried here, in a wooded glade high above the fjord, are the Yugoslav prisoners of war and their German captors who died in the district during World War II. The men are interred in two separate **graveyards** – both immaculately maintained, though, unlike the plainer Yugoslav cemetery, the German section is entered by a sturdy granite gateway. Mostly captured Tito partisans, the Yugoslavs died in their hundreds from disease, cold and malnutrition, not to mention torture and random murder, during the construction of the Arctic road to Narvik. In order to avoid the dangerous sailing along the coast, the Germans tried to extend the railway line, which in 1940 terminated at Mosjøen, through here to Bodø and Narvik. This line, the Nordlandsbanen, involved the labour of 13,000 POWs, but the Germans failed to complete it, and it was not until 1962 that the railway reached Bodø.

It's 30km up the E6 from Botn to **FAUSKE**, which, but for a brief stretch of line from Narvik into Sweden further north, marks the northernmost point of the Norwegian rail network. Most northbound travellers spend the night in Fauske rather than making a quick change onto the connecting bus to Narvik, though it's possible to travel west by road or train to Bodø, a much more palatable place to stay.

From Fauske's **train and long-distance bus station**, it's a five- to ten-minute walk down the hill and left at the T-junction to the **local bus station**, **tourist office** (Mon–Fri 9am–5pm, Sat 10am–2pm; ☎75 64 33 03) and 24-hour gas station. It's only a few metres more to the main drag, **Storgata**, which runs parallel to the fjord and doubles as the E6. Here you'll find the handful of shops that passes for a town centre, and you'll also find the better of the town's two **hotels**, the *Fauske*, Storgata 82 (☎75 64 38 33, fax 75 64 57 37; ④, s/r ③), a chunky square block whose interior is made slightly sickly by a surfeit of salmon-coloured streaky marble. Quarried locally, the marble is exported all over the world but is something of an acquired taste. The hotel rooms are comfortable enough, and the big, tasty breakfast is a bargain at 60kr – handy for travellers staying at the spartan **youth hostel** (☎75 64 67 06, fax 75 64 59 95; ①, dorm beds 100kr), which doesn't provide meals. The hostel is about 500m west of the hotel and signposted off Storgata. A third, much more scenic option is the *Lundhøgda* **campsite** (☎75 64 39 66; June–Sept), which occupies a splendid location about 3km west of the town centre, overlooking the mountains and the fjord: head out of town along the E80, the Bodø road, and watch for the campsite sign which will take you down a country lane, ablaze with wild flowers in the summertime and flanked by old timber buildings. The campsite takes caravans, has spaces for tents and also offers huts (①).

Fauske is an important transport hub and one of the departure points – Bodø is another – of the Nord-Norgeekspressen (see p.277), the **express bus** service that carries passengers as far north as Nordkapp (see p.299). The buses leave twice daily from beside Fauske train station, and tickets can be purchased from the driver or beforehand at any bus station. There are left-luggage lockers at the train station and you can pick up information on the region's ferries there. Note that there is a fifty percent discount for InterRail and Scanrail pass holders on the route to Narvik (see p.253), a gorgeous five-hour run past fjords, peaks and snow.

Bodø and around

BODØ, 63km west of Fauske along the E80, is the terminus of the Trondheim train, and can be reached by train or bus from Fauske. Founded in 1816, Bodø struggled to survive in its early years, but was saved from insignificance when the herring fishery became exceptionally productive in the 1860s, a time when the town's harbourfront was crowded with the net-menders, coopers, oilskin-makers and canneries that kept the fleet going. In the early twentieth century, Bodø acquired several industrial plants and became an important regional commercial and administrative centre, but this prosperous town was heavily bombed during World War II, and nowadays there's precious little left of the proud, nineteenth-century buildings that once flanked the waterfront. Nonetheless, Bodø achieves a cheerful modernity, still a bright and breezy place, and within comfortable striking distance of the old trading post of **Kjerringøy**, one of Nordland's most delightful spots. Bodø is also a regular stop on the Hurtigrute coastal service and much the best place from which to hop over to the choicest parts of the **Lofoten Islands** (see p.267).

Arrival, information and accommodation

Bodø's **train station** is at the eastern end of the town centre, in between the waterfront and the long main street, Sjøgata. The southern **Lofotens ferry** (to and from Moskenes, Værøy and Røst) and the **Hurtigrute** use the docks respectively 500m and 700m northeast along the seafront from the train station. The **bus station** is a further 700m west along Sjøgata from the train station, across from the gigantic *Radisson SAS Hotel Bodø*. Beyond the bus station, at the west end of Sjøgata, another dock handles **Hurtigbåt** services for the Lofotens, notably to and from Svolvær and Stokmarknes (see pp.270 & 266). Bodø **airport** is 2km south of the centre; SAS have a ticket office (☎81 00 33 00) there and several authorized agents in the centre – Bennett, Moloveien 20 (☎75 50 60 70), is as good as any. Local buses link the airport with the bus station (Mon–Fri 1–4 hourly, Sat 1–2 hourly, Sun 6 daily), and there's a taxi rank outside the airport.

From the train station, it's just 300m west along Sjøgata to the **tourist office** at Sjøgata 21 (June–Aug Mon–Fri 9am–8.30pm, Sat 10am–4pm & 6–8pm, Sun noon–4pm & 6–8pm; Sept–May Mon–Fri 9am–4pm; ☎75 52 60 00, fax 75 52 21 77, *www.bodoe.com*). The office is good for information on connections to the Lofoten Islands, rents out bikes and also issues an excellent town and district guide. Bodø's local **DNT** branch is Bodø og Omegn Turistforening (**BOT**); for cabin keys and to register, go to Berg Sport, in the town centre at Torvgata 4 (☎75 52 48 90).

There is plenty of **accommodation** in Bodø. The tourist office has a small supply of **private rooms** in the town and its environs, with a fixed tariff of 250–300kr per double, plus a 15kr booking fee (25kr for rooms outside town). Alternatively, the no-frills **youth hostel** is next door to the train station at Sjøgata 55 (☎ & fax 75 52 11 22; ①, dorm beds 140kr) though – apart from the location – it has precious little to commend it. The *Norrøna* is one of several central **hotels**; it's locat-

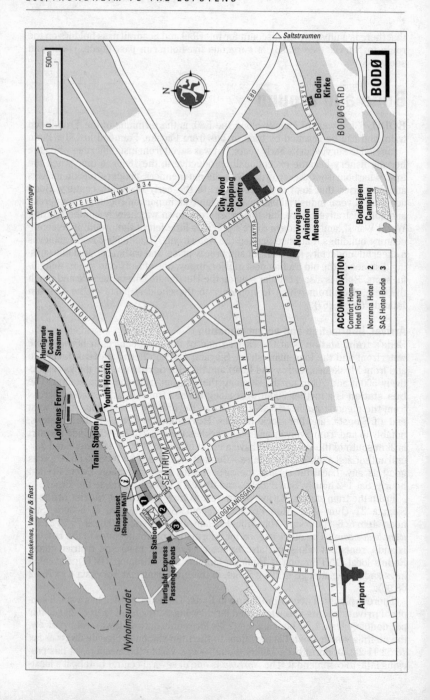

ed in a large modern block at Storgata 4 (☎75 52 55 50, fax 75 52 33 88; ②), close to the bus station. A plusher option is the *Comfort Home Hotel Grand*, nearby at Storgata 3 (☎75 52 00 00, fax 75 52 27 09; ④, s/r ②), whose foyer sports some elegant Art-Deco flourishes. The *Radisson SAS Hotel Bodø*, Storgata 2 (☎75 52 41 00, fax 75 52 74 93; ⑥, s/r ③), is, however, the most appealing place in town, not least because the rooms on the upper floors of this whopping block have great views out to sea. Finally, you can **camp** 3.5km southeast of the centre at *Bodøsjøen Camping* (☎ & fax 75 56 36 80), beside the lake not far from the Bodin kirke – take bus #12 from the bus station. It's open all year and has cabins (②).

The Town

The most popular tourist attraction in Bodø is the **Norsk Luftfartsmuseum** (Norwegian Aviation Museum; June–Aug Mon–Fri 10am–8pm, Sat 10am–5pm, Sun 10am–8pm; Sept–May Tues–Fri 10am–4pm, Thurs 10am–7pm, Sat & Sun 11am–5pm; 70kr), which runs through the general history of Norwegian aviation. It adopts an imaginative approach to the subject, with its own building having been constructed in the shape of a two-bladed propeller: one "blade" houses air force and defence exhibits, the other civilian displays. The spot where the parts meet straddles the ring road and is topped by part of the old Bodø airport control tower. Among the planes to look out for are a Spitfire – a reminder that two RAF squadrons were manned by Norwegians during World War II – and an example of the rare Norwegian-made Hønningstad C-5 Polar seaplane. Bodø was frequently used by the Americans and there's one of their U2 spy planes here. The museum is situated on the ring road, Olav V's gate, about 2km southeast of the town centre, a dreary walk that you can avoid by catching the city transit Sentrumsbussen #801 (Mon–Sat 9am–4pm; every 15min) from the bus station. On the outward journey the bus stops beside the museum, but to pick up the bus for the return leg, you'll have to stroll east along the ring road to the City Nord shopping centre on Gamle Riksvei, a five- to ten-minute walk.

If you have your own transport, consider driving a further 1km south along Gamle Riksvei to the onion-domed **Bodin kirke** (June–Aug daily 10am–7pm; free), a pretty little stone church snugly surrounded by meadows. Dating from the thirteenth century, the church was modified after the Reformation by the addition of a tower and the widening of its windows – dark, gloomy churches were then associated with Catholicism. It is, however, the colourful seventeenth-century fixtures that catch the eye, as well as the lovingly carved Baroque altarboard and pulpit, both painted in the eighteenth century by an itinerant German artist, Gottfried Ezechiel.

Eating and drinking

Bodø is short of good places **to eat** – indeed, if you don't like pizza your choices are extremely limited, though matters may improve when the next phase of the harbour redevelopment is completed. Until then, easily the best bet is the *Pizzakjeller'n*, in the basement of the *Radisson SAS Hotel Bodø*, serving massive pizzas and a wide variety of daily specials from 170kr per main course. Alternatively, the *Neptune Café*, Sjøgata 1, is an unassuming self-service café offering Norwegian standbys from its second-floor premises overlooking the Hurtigbåt terminal. For **drinking**, the *Peacock Pub*, around the corner from the *SAS Hotel Bodø*, has darts and billiards, while the more fashionable *Paviljongen Bar*, at the east end of the Glasshuset, Storgata's shopping precinct, is an amiable spot to nurse a beer.

Out from Bodø:
Kjerringøy, Saltstraumen and the Svartisen glacier

There are three obvious excursions from Bodø: one northeast to the old trading station at **Kjerringøy**, another southeast to the tidal phenomenon known as the **Saltstraumen**, and a third south to the **Svartisen glacier**. The first two can be done by public transport, but are much easier with your own vehicle, while there is an organized tour to the third on a Hurtigbåt. Note, however, that by car, the glacier can also be reached more easily from Mo-i-Rana (see p.245).

Kjerringøy

In summer, there's one local bus a day (65kr day return including Festvåg–Misten ferry) from Bodø bus station to **KJERRINGØY**, 40km north along the coastal Highway 834, where a superbly preserved collection of nineteenth-century timber buildings stands beside a slender, islet-sheltered channel. This was once a **trading post** (late May to late June & early to late Aug daily noon–5pm; late June to late July daily 11am–7.30pm; 40kr), the domain of the Zahl family, who bought fish from the Lofotens' fishermen and supplied them everything from manufactured goods and clothes to farmyard foodstuffs. It was not, however, an equal relationship: the Zahls, who operated a local monopoly until the 1910s, could dictate the price they paid for the fish, and many of the islanders were permanently indebted to them. This social division is still very much in evidence at the trading post, where there's a marked distinction between the guest rooms of the main house and the fishermen's bunk beds in the boat- and cookhouses. Indeed, the family house is remarkably fastidious, with its Italianate busts and embroidered curtains – even the medicine cabinet is well-stocked with formidable Victorian remedies like the bottle of "Sicilian Hair Renewer".

There are enjoyable, hour-long **guided tours** around the main house throughout the summer (late May to late Aug 3–5 times daily; 40kr). They loosely coincide with the bus, and drivers have much more flexibility as Highway 834's Festvåg–Misten car ferry (every half-hour or hour; 10min; passengers 15kr; car and driver day return 42kr) is frequent – combined bus-and-ferry schedule from Bodø tourist office. When you've finished with the tour, you can nose around the reconstructed general store, drop in at the café and stroll the fine sandy beach in front of the complex. It's a peaceful and relaxing spot, and the bus times on Mondays to Fridays make it possible to do a day trip from Bodø. For those who want to **stay** overnight, the old parsonage, *Kjerringøy prestegård*, about 1km north of the trading post along Highway 834 (☎75 50 77 10 or 75 51 11 43; ①), has simple double rooms in the main building and slightly pleasanter ones in the renovated cow-shed next door. If you're using public transport to get back to Bodø to catch a ferry, remember to check the times of the buses from Kjerringøy.

Saltstraumen

Less interesting, but more widely publicized than Kjerringøy, is the maelstrom known as the **Saltstraumen**, 33km southeast of Bodø Highway 17. Here, billions of gallons of water are forced four times daily through a narrow channel that links the inner and outer parts of the fjord. The whirling creamy water is at its most turbulent at high tide, and at its most violent when the moon is new or full – a timetable is available from Bodø tourist office. There's a local **bus** service from

Bodø to the Saltstraumen (Mon–Sat 5–7 daily, Sun 1 daily), but the times rarely coincide with high tides.

Although scores of tourists troop here for every high tide, you can't help but feel they wish they were somewhere else – the scenery is, in Norwegian terms at least, flat and dull, and the view from the bridge which spans the channel unexciting. You can also spend some time at the **Saltstraumen Opplevelsessenter** (Saltstraumen Experience Centre; May daily 10am–6pm; June–Aug daily 10am–10pm; 60kr), housed in two adjoining buildings near the eastern end of the bridge. The centre tells you all you'd ever wanted to know about tidal currents, and then some, and also has several pools where you can take a close look at local marine life.

The Svartisen glacier

Getting to the **Svartisen** glacier (see box, p.245) takes a bit of a sweat, but the most painless way to do it is on a **Hurtigbåt trip** from Bodø. Each trip allows three hours at the glacier, and lasts between six and seven hours in total. Unfortunately these only run from June to August and there are just two or three departures each month – the Bodø tourist office has the times. The trips depart from the express boat quay in Bodø and cost 290kr per person; tickets are purchased on board.

North to Narvik

The 250-kilometre journey north from Fauske to Narvik is spectacularly beautiful, with the E6 rounding the fjords, twisting and tunnelling through the mountains and rushing over high, pine-dusted plateaux. The scenery is the main event and there's rarely anything specific to stop for, with one notable exception: the fascinating old farmstead at **Kjelvik**, where the hardship of rural life in Norway is revealed in idyllic surroundings. At the end of the journey, **Narvik** is an eminently likeable industrial town that witnessed some of the fiercest fighting in Norway during the German invasion of 1940. It's a good place to stop and a useful launching pad for the long haul to the far north or a visit to the Vesterålen or Lofoten islands.

This stretch of the E6 between Fauske and Narvik presents two opportunities to catch a **car ferry** to the Lofotens – one at Skutvik, the other at Bognes. The more southerly of the two is **Skutvik**, 37km to the west of the E6, with ferries to Svolvær in the Vesterålens. At **Bognes**, on the E6, there's a choice of ferries: one sails to Lødingen and the E10 on the Lofotens, while a second hops across the Tysfjorden to **Skarberget** to rejoin the E6 80km west of Narvik. Long-distance **buses** link Bodø, Fauske and Narvik twice daily; the journey from Fauske to Narvik takes five hours.

The E6 north to Kjelvik and Bognes

Beyond Fauske, the E6 scuttles over the hills to the small industrial town of **Straumen** and then threads along the coast to **Sommarset**, an old ferry point where boats crossed the **Leirfjord** until a new stretch of road was built around the fjord in 1986. This new section is an ambitious affair that drills through the mountains with the fjord glistening below. It also passes within 250m of the old farmstead of **KJELVIK**, 58km from Fauske, where a scattering of old wooden buildings, including a cottage, woodshed, forge and mill, nestle in a green, wooded valley – a beautiful spot, but the tenant farmers who worked the land finally gave up the battle in 1967. There was no electricity; no water; the soil was thin; and the only contact with the outside world was by boat: supply vessels would come up the Leirfjord to the Kjelvik jetty, from where it was a steep two-kilometre hike to the farm, 200m above the fjord. There's open access to the farm and wandering around is a delight; you can also follow the old footpath down to the Kjelvik jetty. **Guided tours** of Kjelvik are available (late June to late August daily 11am–6pm; 30kr) and, on the last Saturday of the season, the **Kjelvik festival** sees the old buildings put to their original uses. Griddle-cakes are cooked on the wood stove, and dollops of sour cream and porridge are doled out to visitors.

After Kjelvik, the E6 bores through the mountains to reach, after about 40km, the couple of houses that make up **Kråkmo**, with the lake on one side and the domineering mass of a mighty mountain, Kråkmotind, on the other. This was once a favourite haunt of that crusty reactionary Knut Hamsun (1859–1952), a one-time leading light among Norway's writers, but disgraced by his admiration for Hitler (see p.340).

From Kråkmo, it's 50km more to the turning onto Highway 81 for Skutvik. Highway 81 is only 37km long, but it takes a good hour to drive and gives sight of some dramatic scenery, all craggy shorelines and imposing peaks. About halfway along it passes through the hamlet of **HAMSUND**, site of Knut Hamsun's boyhood home, now the tiny **Hamsun Museum** (summer only; irregular hours; further details on ☎75 77 02 94). At the end of the road, first-come first-served car ferries leave the **Skutvik** jetty for Svolvær (early June to late Aug 8 daily; Sept–May 2–3 daily; 2hr; car & driver 190kr). In summer, arrive two hours before departure to be sure of a space.

Back on the E6, it's a scenic 20km from the Highway 81 turning to **Bognes**, where one ferry heads west to Lødingen on the Lofotens (5–10 daily; 1hr; car and driver 118kr); a second travels to **Skarberget** for the E6 and points north (at least 1 every 90min; 25min; car and driver 62kr). From Skarberget to Narvik is 80km.

Narvik and around

A relatively modern town, **NARVIK** was established less than a century ago as an ice-free port to handle the iron ore brought by train from northern Sweden. It makes no bones about its main function: the **iron-ore docks** are conspicuous, right in the centre of town, the rust-coloured machinery dominating the whole waterfront. Yet, for all the mess, the industrial complex is strangely impressive, its cat's cradle of walkways, conveyor belts, cranes and funnels oddly beguiling.

Narvik's first modern settlers were the navvies who built the nineteenth-century railway line, the **Ofotbanen** (see box, p.256), to the mines in Kiruna, over the border in Sweden – a herculean task commemorated every March by a week of singing, dancing and drinking, when the locals dress up in the costume of the time. The town grew steadily up until World War II, when it was demolished by fierce fighting for control of the harbour and iron-ore supplies. Perhaps inevitably, the rebuilt town centre is rather lacking in appeal, with modern concrete buildings replacing the wooden houses that went before. Nevertheless, try and devote an hour or so to the **Krigsminnemuseum** (War Museum; March to early June,

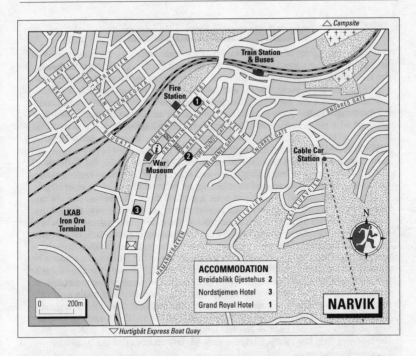

△ *Campsite*

Train Station & Buses

Fire Station ❶

War Museum ❷

Cable Car Station

LKAB Iron Ore Terminal

❸

SNORRES GATE

SNORRES GATE

ACCOMMODATION

Breidablikk Gjestehus 2

Nordstjernen Hotel 3

Grand Royal Hotel 1

NARVIK

0   200m

▽ *Hurtigbåt Express Boat Quay*

late Aug & Sept daily 10am–4pm; early June to late Aug Mon–Sat 10am–10pm, Sun 11am–5pm; 30kr), in the main town square. Run by the Red Cross, the museum documents the wartime German saturation bombing of the town, and the bitter and bloody sea and air battles in which hundreds of foreign servicemen died alongside the local population. It was a complicated campaign, with the German invasion of April 1940 followed by an Allied counterattack spearheaded by the Royal Navy. The Allies actually recaptured Narvik, driving the Germans into the mountains, but were hurriedly evacuated when Hitler launched his invasion of France. The fight for Narvik lasted two months and the German commander wrote of the sea change amongst his Norwegian adversaries, who toughened up to become much more determined soldiers, and skilled ones at that: many were crack shots from their hunting days and all could ski. In the short term, this change of attitude prefigured the formation of the Resistance; in the long term it pretty much put paid to Norway's traditional isolationism. The museum gives a thoroughly moving account of the battle for Narvik and then follows the German occupation of Norway until liberation in 1945. The displays are thoughtfully done, too: one juxtaposes German bullwhips with small toys made by Russian POWs as thanks for food parcels smuggled into the camps by locals, who faced execution if discovered.

There are also **guided tours** of the LKAB mining company's ore-terminal complex (1 daily; 30kr), interesting if only for the opportunity to spend ninety minutes amid such giant, ore-stained contraptions. After its arrival by train, the ore is carried on the various conveyor belts to the quayside, from where some thirty million tons of it are shipped out a year. Ask at the tourist office for details.

THE OFOTBANEN

One of the real treats of a visit to Narvik is the **train ride** into the mountains that back the town and spread east across the Swedish border. Called the **Ofotbanen**, the line passes through some wonderful scenery, slipping between hostile peaks before reaching the rocky, barren and lakelet-studded plateau beyond. A remarkable achievement, the line was completed in 1903 and the navvies endured astounding hardships in the process. Trains from Narvik cross the border – take your passport with you – and arrive (late June to mid-Aug 3 daily; mid-Aug to mid-June 2 daily; 50min one way; 108kr return) at the Swedish settlement of **RIKSGRÄNSEN**, a hiking and skiing centre on the plateau. There's a large and surprisingly plush **hotel** here, the *Riksgränsen* (☎46/98 04 00 80, fax 46/98 04 31 25; ③), where you can buy hiking maps and sports gear as well as renting mountain bikes. You can nose around the place for an hour or three before returning by train to Narvik, or you can hike at least a part of the **Rallarveien**, the old and recently refurbished trail built for the railway construction workers in the last century. This extends west for 15km to Rombaksbotn, a deep and narrow inlet where the navvies once started their haul up the mountains; it also heads deeper into Sweden, to Abisko and Kiruna. A favourite option is to walk from Riksgränsen back towards the coast, picking up the return train at one of the Norwegian stations on the way. The area isn't nearly as remote now that the E10 crosses the mountains to the north of the railway, but the terrain is difficult and weather unpredictable, so hikers will need to be well equipped. There is, in fact, a network of **trails and cabins** strung out in the mountains surrounding the railroad. The cabins are maintained by the DNT affiliate Narvik Turistforening (☎76 94 37 90) and the keys are kept at the fire station back in Narvik. Hiking **maps** are available in Narvik from the Narvik Libris bookshop, Kongens gate 44, just up from the tourist office.

The museum and ore terminal apart, it's best to head for the open country. There's a **cable car** (mid-June to mid-Aug daily noon–1am; 70kr), a stiff fifteen-minute walk up above the town behind the train station, that whisks passengers up the first 700m of the mighty **Fagernesfjellet**. On a clear day the Lofoten Islands are visible from the viewing point at the top of the ride, and this is also a good spot to experience the midnight sun (end of May to mid-July). The cable car stops running in windy conditions; ask at the tourist office before setting out.

Practicalities

Fifteen minutes' walk from one end to the other, Narvik's sloping centre straggles along the main street, Kongens gate, which doubles as the E6. Narvik's public transport system is in a state of flux, but currently the **train station** is at the north end of the town centre and long-distance **buses** also stop outside; the train station has left-luggage lockers. From the station, it's a five- to ten-minute walk along Kongens gate to the **tourist office**, on the main square (early June Mon–Fri 9am–5pm, Sat & Sun 11am–5pm; mid-June to mid-Aug Mon–Fri 9am–7pm, Sat 10am–7pm, Sun noon–7pm; late August daily 11am–5pm; Sept–May Mon–Fri 9am–4pm; ☎76 94 33 09), a couple of doors along from the Krigsminnemuseum. They have the full range of bus and ferry timetables and will make ferry reservations. The dock for the passenger-only **Hurtigbåt** service to Svolvær on the Lofotens is at the south end of the town centre.

As for **accommodation**, you're hardly spoiled for choice, but the pleasant, unassuming *Breidablikk Gjestehus*, Tore Hunds gate 41 (☎76 94 14 18, fax 76 94 57 86; ①), is neat and trim, has views over town and provides a good, hearty breakfast. It's located at the top of the steps at the end of Kinobakken, a side road leading east off Kongens gate, just up from the main town square. Some of the town's **hotels** have seen better days, but the *Grand Royal Hotel*, just up from the tourist office at Kongens gate 64 (☎76 94 15 00, fax 76 94 55 31; ⑤, s/r ③), puts on a show of wood-panelled elegance and has perfectly adequate rooms. Alternatively, there's the much more modest *Nordstjernen Hotell*, just south of the town square at Kongens gate 26 (☎76 94 41 20, fax 76 94 75 06; ②), whose spacious second-floor breakfast room has an uninterrupted view of the iron-ore terminal. The **campsite**, *Narvik Camping* (☎76 94 58 10), is 2km north of the centre on the E6; it's open all year and has cabins (①). There's only one really recommendable **restaurant** in Narvik, *Bjørns Mat og Vinhus*, just over the bridge from the town square at Brugata 3 (☎76 94 42 90). This smart, second-floor place offers an inventive and reasonably priced menu with a Mediterranean slant. The **bar** below is good fun too – again, the best in town.

Moving on from Narvik

There's a choice of several onward routes from Narvik. The Nord-Norgeekspressen **bus** (2–3 daily) makes the four-hour hop north to Tromsø (see p.282) before continuing onto Alta (see p.290) and Nordkapp (see p.299), while another bus service runs direct from Narvik to Alta in ten hours (Mon–Fri & Sun 1 daily). Both trips give sight of some wonderful wild and diverse scenery, from craggy mountains and blue-black fjords to gentle, forested valleys – though it's not perhaps quite as scenic a journey as the E6 from Fauske to Narvik. A third bus service, the Narvik–Lofoten Ekspressen (Mon–Fri & Sun 1 daily) runs west from Narvik to Sortland, Stokmarknes and Svolvær in the Lofoten Islands (see p.267). On all these buses, plus the bus trip south from Narvik to either Fauske (for connecting trains to Trondheim) or Bodø, rail-pass holders get a fifty percent discount.

Narvik's **Hurtigbåt** service operates all year (1 daily Mon–Fri & Sun; 3–4hr; 267kr one-way) to Svolvær. Rail-pass holders get a fifty percent discount. Finally, travellers on the **Ofotbanen** (see box opposite) can stay on the train beyond Riksgrånsen for Kiruna, Uppsala and Stockholm; the ride to Stockholm takes around 18 hours.

The Vesterålen Islands

A raggle-taggle archipelago in the Norwegian Sea, the **VESTERÅLEN ISLANDS**, and their southerly neighbours the Lofotens (see p.267), are like western Norway in miniature: the terrain is hard and unyielding, the sea boisterous and fretful, and the main – often the only – industry is fishing. The weather is temperate but wet, and the islanders' historic isolation has bred a distinctive culture based, in equal measure, on Protestantism, the extended family and respect for the ocean. The islands were first settled by semi-nomadic hunter-agriculturalists some 6000 years ago, and it was they and their Iron-Age successors who chopped down the birch and pine forests that once covered the coasts. It was **boatbuilding** which brought prosperity to the islands: by the seventh century, ocean-going vessels were being built, which enabled the islanders to join in the Viking bonanza. Local clan leaders

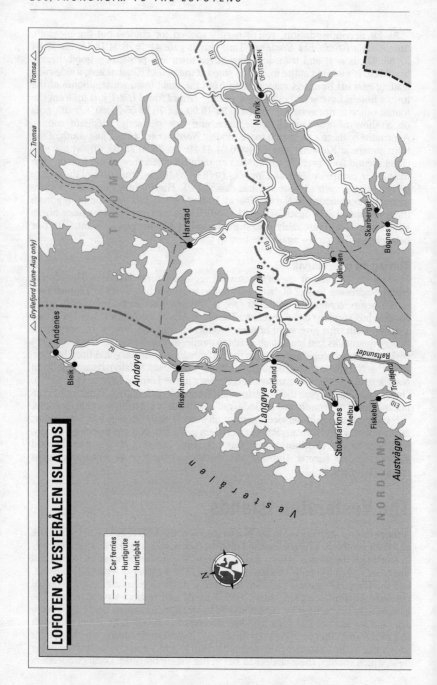

LOFOTEN & VESTERÅLEN ISLANDS

Car ferries
Hurtigrute
Hurtigbåt

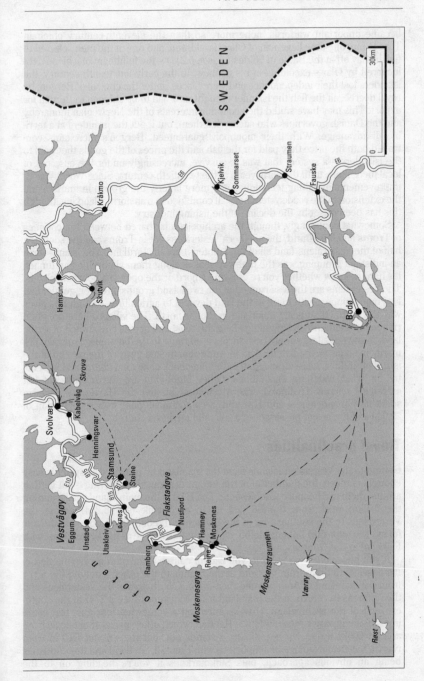

became important warlords, none more so than the eleventh-century chieftain Tore Hund, one-time liegeman of Olav Haraldsson, and one of the men selected to finish Olav off at the Battle of Stiklestad (see p.241) – the fulfilment of a blood debt incurred by Olav's execution of his nephew. In the early fourteenth century, the islanders lost their independence and were placed under the control of Bergen: by royal decree, all the fish the islanders caught now had to be shipped to Bergen for export. This may have suited the economic interests of the Norwegian monarchy and the Danish governors who succeeded them, but it put the islanders at a terrible disadvantage. With their monopoly guaranteed, Bergen's merchants controlled both the price they paid for the fish and the prices of the goods they sold to the islanders – a system that was to survive, increasingly under the auspices of local merchants, until the early years of the twentieth century. Since World War II, improvements in fishing techniques and more latterly the growth in tourism and the extension of the road system have all combined to transform island life, though this has been offset by the decline of the fishing industry.

Somewhat confusingly, though the archipelago is shared between the counties of **Troms** and **Nordland**, the northern Vesterålens are in Troms and the southern half of the Vesterålens (and all of the Lofotens) are in Nordland. The islands form an indistinct grouping – as the highway snakes along them via bridge and tunnel, it's hard to know whether you're crossing a fjord or the open sea between islands. The Vesterålens are the less rugged of the two island groups: greener, gentler and less mountainous, with more of the land devoted to agriculture, though this gives way to vast tracts of peaty moorland in the far north. The villages here are often ribbon-like settlements straggling along the coast and across any stretch of fertile land. Many travellers simply rush through en route to the Lofotens, a mistake primarily in so far as the fishing port of **Andenes**, tucked away at the far end of the island of Andøya, has a strange but enthralling back-of-beyond charm and is a centre for whale-watching expeditions. Other highlights are the magnificent but extremely narrow **Trollfjord**, where cruise ships and the Hurtigrute perform some nifty manoeuvres, and **Harstad**, a comparative giant with a population of 22,000 and the proud possessor of a splendid medieval church.

Travel practicalities

Getting to the Vesterålen Islands from the mainland by **public transport** is easy enough – indeed, the number of permutations is almost bewildering – but getting around them can be more troublesome. The **E10** is the main island road, running the 370km west from the E6 just north of Narvik (see p.254) across the Vesterålens to the southern tip of the Lofotens. The only interruption is the **car ferry** (see opposite) linking Melbu, on the southern edge of the Vesterålens, with Fiskebøl in the Lofotens.

If you have your own **vehicle** you can, of course, come and go as you please. It's possible to drive from one end of the islands to the other, catching the ferry from the mainland to Andenes and then driving south across the Vesterålens and the Lofotens to return to the mainland from Moskenes (see p.274) at the southern end of the archipelago. Drivers intent on a somewhat less epic trip could investigate the **car rental** outlets at Harstad, which offer special short deals from around 500kr a day. No one itinerary stands out, but the E6 and E10 in from Narvik has the advantage of simplicity – with Harstad, Sortland and then Andenes being an obvious approach, plus Stokmarknes if you're heading on to the

Lofotens. Andenes has most to offer as a base thanks to its whale- and bird-watching trips and choice of accommodation.

Car ferries

The main **car ferry** from the mainland to the Vesterålen Islands departs from the jetty at **Bognes**, on the E6 between Fauske and Narvik, and sails to **Lødingen** (6–10 daily; 1hr; car and driver 118kr; passengers 37kr). From Lødingen, it's just 4km to the E10 at a point midway between Harstad and Sortland. A second, but this time seasonal, car ferry runs from remote **Gryllefjord**, 110km west of the E6 well to the north of Narvik, to **Andenes** at the northern tip of the Vesterålens (June–Aug; 3 daily; 2hr; car 230kr, passengers 83kr). Reservations are strongly advised – telephone or fax Andøy Reiseliv in Andenes (☎76 11 56 00, fax 76 11 56 10). A third car ferry links the Lofotens with the Vesterålens about halfway along the E10. This is the **Melbu–Fiskebøl** ferry (every 90min; 25min; 22kr per passenger, 65kr driver and car).

Boats

Hurtigbåt services provide a speedy and economic alternative to the car ferry and Hurtigrute services. One links **Bodø** with **Stokmarknes**, via Svolvaer in the Lofotens (Mon–Fri 1 daily; 5hr 30min; 300kr); another links **Tromsø** with **Harstad** (1–2 daily; 2hr 45min; 350kr). In all cases, advance booking (via the local tourist office) is recommended.

Heading north from Bodø, the **Hurtigrute** threads a scenic route up through the Lofotens to the Vesterålen Islands, where it calls at four places: **Stokmarknes** and **Sortland** in the south, **Risøyhamn** in the north and **Harstad** in the east. None of the four is an especially appealing destination, but workaday Risøyhamn is well on the way to Andenes, while Harstad is a regional centre and transport hub with a fine old church. Cruising southwards from Tromsø, the Hurtigrute follows the same itinerary, but in reverse. Scenically, the one special highlight is the **Raftsundet**, a narrow and imposing sound off which branches the magnificent Trollfjord. The Raftsundet is between Svolvær and Stokmarknes, but note that the Hurtigrute leaves Svolvær at 10pm, and so only during the period of the midnight sun (late May to mid-July) is it possible to see much; in the opposite direction, boats leave Stokmarknes at a much more convenient 3.30pm. This stretch of the journey takes three hours and in summer costs 100kr for passengers, and around 280kr for cars.

The Hurtigrute leaves Bodø for the Lofotens and the Vesterålens at 3pm and departs Tromsø heading south at 1.30am daily. In summer, passenger tickets remain reasonably priced, with the sixteen-hour journey from Bodø to Harstad costing around 590kr, Tromsø to Harstad (6.5hr) 400kr, and there are discounts off-season. The fare for transporting a car from Bodø to Harstad is 360kr, from Tromsø to Harstad 300kr, but on the older vessels, where vehicles have to be hoisted on board, there's a fifty percent surcharge. Advance reservations for cars are essential, but can be made just a few hours beforehand by telephoning the captain – ask down at the harbour or at the port's tourist office for assistance. Special deals, which can reduce costs dramatically, are advertised at local tourist offices.

Buses

A long-distance **bus** leaves **Narvik** once daily to run along the E6 and then the E10 as far as Sortland, where passengers change (after an hour or two's wait) for the onward bus to **Stokmarknes**, the **Melbu–Fiskebøl** ferry and then **Svolvær**. Another long-distance bus runs up the E6 from **Bodø** and **Fauske** to meet the **Bognes–Lødingen** car ferry. At Lødingen, there's a choice of two onward connecting buses: one service continues north to **Harstad**, the other heads west for **Stokmarknes**, the **Melbu–Fiskebøl** ferry and **Svolvær**. As examples of journey times, Narvik–Sortland takes three hours, Bodø–Sortland seven, Bodø–Svolvær ten.

Another very useful service is the **Hvalrutebussen** ("whale bus"), which links Narvik and Tromsø with Andenes, Risøyhamn, Svolvær and, at the southern tip of the Lofotens, Å, and uses the Gryllefjord–Andenes ferry to do it. However the service only operates from June to August, and the route is done in stages: study the timetable carefully to ensure you can get to your destination without an enormous wait. This is straightforward on shorter journeys – like Andenes to Sortland – but at weekends it's mostly the shorter stages that operate.

The most useful of the **local buses** runs from Sortland to Andenes (1–3 daily; 2hr 15min). This bus is one of a number of stages in the much longer Hvalrutebussen service (see above).

Harstad

Readily reached by bus and the Hurtigrute, **HARSTAD**, just 120km from Narvik, is easily the largest town on the Vesterålen Islands. It's home to much of northern Norway's engineering industry, its sprawling docks a tangle of supply ships, repair yards and cold-storage plants spread out along the gentle slopes of the Vågsfjord. This may not sound too enticing, and it's true that Harstad wins few beauty contests. The town does have the odd attraction, and if you're tired of sleepy Norwegian villages, it at least provides a bustling interlude.

The main item of interest, the **Trondenes kirke** (guided tours on the hour every 2hr: early June to mid-Aug Mon 10am–4pm, Tues, Fri & Sun 2–6pm; mid-Aug to late Aug daily at 2.30pm; 20kr; Sept–May, ask for times at the tourist office – see below), occupies a lovely leafy location beside the fjord 3km north of the town centre at the end of the slender Trondenes peninsula. To get there, take the local "Trondenes" **bus** (Mon–Sat 1 hourly; 10min), which leaves the station beside the tourist office and goes past the church; or you can get a taxi at a rank by the bus station. By car, follow Highway 83 north from the centre and watch for the signposted turning on the right. The original wooden church was built at the behest of King Øystein (of *rorbuer* fame – see box, p.268) at the beginning of the twelfth century and had the distinction of being the northernmost church in Christendom for several centuries. The present stone church was erected in the fourteenth century, its thick walls and the scant remains of its surrounding ramparts reflecting its dual function as a church and fortress – for these were troubled, violent times. After the exterior, stern of necessity, the warm and homely interior comes as a surprise. Here, the dainty arches of the rood screen lead into the choir, where each of the three altars is surmounted by a late medieval wooden triptych in bas-relief. Of the trio, the middle triptych is the most charming. Its main panel, depicting the holy family, is fairly predictable, but down below is a curiously cheerful sequence of biblical figures, each of whom wears a turban and sports a big, bushy and exquisitely carved beard.

Back outside, the churchyard is bordered by a dry-stone wall and contains a Soviet memorial to the eight hundred prisoners of war who died hereabouts in

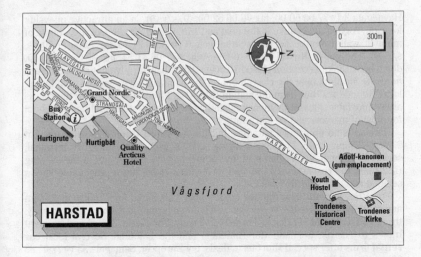

World War II at the hands of the Germans. There's another reminder of the war in the form of the **Adolfkanonen** (Adolf Gun), a massive artillery piece stuck on a hilltop in the middle of the peninsula, to the north of the church. It's inside a military zone, and the obligatory **guided tour** (early June to mid-Aug daily at 11am, 1pm, 3pm & 5pm; mid-Aug to late Aug daily at 1pm; 50kr), which begins at the gate of the compound, 1km up the hillside, stipulates that you have to have your own vehicle to get to the gun, 3km from the gate. Near the church, just south along the fjord, is the **Trondenes Historiske Senter** (Trondenes Historical Centre; June to mid-Aug daily 10am–7pm; mid-Aug to May Sat & Sun 11am–5pm; 30kr), a plush new complex with exhibitions on the history of the locality – dioramas, mood music, incidental Viking artefacts and the like.

Frankly, downtown Harstad doesn't have much going for it, though the comings and goings of the ferry boats are a diversion. In late June, the ten-day **North Norway Arts Festival** (Festspillene i Nord-Norge), featuring concerts, drama and dance, provides a spark of interest (but hotels are full to bursting during the period).

Practicalities

Although Harstad is easy to reach by bus or boat from Sortland, Tromsø and Narvik, it's actually something of a cul-de-sac for car drivers, who have to leave the E10 for the final thirty-kilometre drive north into town along Highway 83. Once you've got there, however, you'll find almost everything you need in the immediate vicinity of the **bus station**. Jetties for **Hurtigbåt** and **Hurtigrute** services are just metres away, and next to the bus station is the **tourist office**, Torvet 8 (early June to mid-Aug Mon–Fri 7.30am–6.30pm, Sat 7.30am–3pm, Sun noon–7pm; mid-Aug to May Mon–Fri 8am–4pm; ☎77 01 89 89), which has a wide selection of tourist literature on the Vesterålens.

As regards **accommodation**, the centre is dotted with modern chain hotels, among which the *Quality Arcticus Hotel* is a short walk from the Torvet at

Havnegata 3 (☎77 06 50 00, fax 76 06 52 00; ⑤, s/r ③), in an attractive quayside location. A good alternative is the neat and trim *Grand Nordic Hotell*, a couple of minutes' walk from the Torvet at Strandgata 9 (☎77 06 21 70, fax 77 06 77 30; ④, s/r ③). The **youth hostel** (June to late Aug; ☎77 06 41 54, fax 77 06 56 33; ①, dorm beds 135kr; reception closed 10.30am–6pm) has the advantage of a pleasant fjordside location, near the church out on the peninsula. It's easy to reach by the local "Trondenes" bus from the station (Mon–Sat 1 hourly; 10min) and the rooms are comfortable, pleasantly furnished and large; however, the building is a school for most of the year and so has a rather cold, institutional feel.

Harstad is no gourmet's paradise, but the *Kaffistova* (Mon–Fri 8am–6pm, Sat 9.30am–2.30pm, Sun 11.30am–4.30pm), across from the Hurtigbåt terminal, serves traditional Norwegian standbys at inexpensive prices, and in the evening *Gallionen*, the restaurant of the *Quality Arcticus Hotel*, has a reasonable line in seafood and offers fjord views too.

From Harstad, the **Hurtigrute** coastal boat sails north for Tromsø at 8.15am and south for points in the Vesterålen and Lofoten Islands at 8.45am. Alternatively, there's a **Hurtigbåt** service to Tromsø (1–2 daily; 2hr 45min; 345kr) and frequent **buses** to Narvik, Sortland (for Andenes) and the Lofotens. Several local **car rental** firms offer special short-term deals: try Europcar, Samagata 33 (☎77 01 86 00), or Statoil Bilutleie, at the Statoil gas station (☎77 04 02 29).

Andenes

Back on the E10 about 30km south of Harstad, it's 60km west along the fjord to the turning for the Lødingen ferry (see p.261) and 40km more to Sortland (see p.266). Just before you reach Sortland, Highway 82 begins its one-hundred-kilometre trek north, snaking along the craggy edges of the island of Hinnøya before crossing the bridge over to humdrum **Risøyhamn**, the only Hurtigrute stop on the most northerly of the Vesterålen Islands, **Andøya**. Beyond Risøyhamn, the scenery is much less dramatic, as the mountains give way to hills in the west and a vast, peaty moor in the east. Highway 82 crosses this moorland, and fine panoramic views of the mountains back on the mainland aside, it's an uneventful journey on to the old fishing port of **ANDENES**. Here, lines of low-slung buildings lead up to the clutter of wooden warehouses and mini-boat repair yards that edge the harbour and its prominent breakwaters. "It is the fish, and that alone, that draws people to Andenes. The place itself has no other temptations," said the writer Poul Alm when he visited in 1944, and although this is too harsh a judgement today, the main emphasis remains firmly nautical. Among Scandinavians at least, Andenes is famous for its "**whale safaris**" (late May to mid-Sept, daily departures at 10.30am, with additional departures at 8.30am, 3.30pm & 5.30pm, subject to demand), three- to six-hour cruises off the coast with a marine biologist on board to point out sperm, killer and minke whales, and dolphins. There's reckoned to be a ninety-per-cent chance of seeing the whales. On the trip, wear warm clothes and be aware that some antiseasickness pills can make some people drowsy. Tickets are around 625kr per person (children 8–16 years, 420kr; 5–8 years, 200kr), the price including lunch. Booking at least a day in advance is strongly advised as the trips are popular, and some are booked up weeks beforehand; the tourist office (see opposite) provides information and takes reservations. The safaris begin with a guided tour of the **Hvalsenter** (Whale Centre; late May to mid-June & mid-Aug to mid-Sept daily 8am–4pm; mid-June to mid-Aug daily 8am–8pm; 20kr), close to the harbour, and actually a rather disappointing way to start. The museum's incidental displays on the life and times of the animal hardly fire the imagination, and neither does the massive, and deliberately dark and gloomy, display of a whale munching its way though a herd of squid.

The other recommended boat trip in Andenes is a cruise round the **bird island of Bleiksøya** (June–Aug 2 daily at 1pm and 3pm; 2 hr; 250kr; bookings through the tourist office), a pyramid-shaped hunk of rock populated by thousands of puffins, kittiwakes, razorbills and, sometimes, white-tailed eagles. Cruises leave from the jetty at **Bleik** (see p.266), an old and picturesque fishing hamlet around 7km southwest of Andenes, with a clear view of the islet; a local bus makes the trip from Andenes to coincide with sailings. The tours cease at the end of August as the birds head south around then.

There are two more noteworthy museums in Andenes. The **Hisnakul** (late May to mid-June & mid-Aug to mid-Sept daily 1–4pm; mid-June to mid-Aug daily noon–6pm; 20kr), in a refurbished timber warehouse near the Whale Centre, is a well-conceived museum-cum-exhibition centre that explores various facets of Andøya life. The centre is short on historical artefacts, plumping instead for imaginative displays such as the two hundred facial casts of local people made in 1994 and an assortment of giant replica bird beaks. There's also a comprehensive explanation of the northern lights (see box, p.280) – Andenes is a particularly good spot to see them – illustrated by first-class photographs and a slide show. The other museum, the **Polarmuseet** (Polar Museum; mid-June to Aug daily 10am–6pm; 25kr), is beside the harbour too, located inside a modest little building with a pretty wooden porch. The interior is mostly dedicated to the Arctic knick-knacks accumulated by a certain Hilmar Nøis, an Andøy man who wintered on Svalbard (see p.308) no less than 38 times. The museum also sells tickets for the guided tour of the adjacent **lighthouse** (same times; 25kr), a forty-metre-high maroon structure built in the 1850s.

Practicalities

Bisecting the town, Andenes' main street, Storgata, is long and straight and ends abruptly at the seafront. From the end of the street, the **bus station** is just a few metres away to the east, and the **tourist office** (late May to mid-Sept daily 8am–8pm; mid-Sept to late May Mon–Fri 8am–4pm; ☎76 11 56 00, fax 76 11 56 10, *www.whalesafari.no*) is located in the Hvalsenter some 300m to the west. They have a comprehensive range of local information and can make reservations for bird-island boat trips, whale safaris and the car ferry to Gryllefjord (a booking fee of 100kr applies to the car ferry). It also has details of local bicycle rental (which costs 100kr per day) and of guided walks in the surrounding district, beginning at 250kr per person for a three- to six-hour hike.

Andenes has a fair sprinkling of inexpensive **accommodation** and several households offer **private rooms** – look out for the signs. But considering how isolated a spot this is, you'd be well advised to make an advance reservation, though if all else fails the tourist office will do their best to help you out. One of the nicer places is the *Sjøgata Gjestehus*, Sjøgata 4 (☎76 14 16 37, fax 76 14 14 53; ②; late May to mid-Sept), which provides simple but inexpensive rooms in a pleasant old timber building just 200m east from the tourist office. Nearby, on the seafront, is the *Lankanholmen Sjøhus* (☎76 14 28 50, fax 76 14 28 55; ②), an unenticing modern complex which includes chalet-style huts, apartments and a very small and very spartan **youth hostel** (same number; ①, dorm beds 125kr;

June–Aug). Andenes has just one **hotel**, the *Norlandia Andrikken*, Storgata 53 (☎76 14 12 22, fax 76 14 19 33; ④, s/r ③), whose main building is a routine modern concrete block with rooms to match, about 900m from the harbour. More positively, the hotel **restaurant** is easily the best place to eat – the Arctic char is superb – and prices are reasonable. For daytime snacks, head for *Jul. Nilsens Bakeri* (Mon–Fri 9am–3pm, Sat 9am–1pm), close to the bus station at Kong Hansgata 1.

Whereas Andenes is likeable, but not particularly pretty, **BLEIK**, just 7km southwest along the coast, is a comely hamlet of picturesque clapboard houses and white picket fences huddling between craggy hills and a long sandy beach. There are several modern rooms here at *Havhusene Bleik* (☎76 14 57 40, fax 76 14 55 51; ②) and a handful of *rorbuer* (③; see box, p.268) too.

Routes out of Andenes are limited. The **car ferry** (June–Aug; 3 daily; 2hr; car 240kr, passengers 83kr; reservation fee 100kr) will get you over to Gryllefjord on the mainland, but this leaves you a good long drive from both Narvik and Tromsø, the nearest worthwhile destinations. Driving south, Highway 82 eventually brings you to the Lofotens. Leaving by **bus**, you can use the Hvalrutebussen service in summer (see p.262), which leaves Andenes once daily to meet the southbound Hurtigrute in Risøyhamn, and there are local services to Sortland throughout the year, though the latter are few and far between at weekends.

Sortland to Melbu

An unappetizing modern sprawl along the shore, **Sortland** is – by virtue of its location near the bridge linking the islands of **Langøya** and **Hinnøya** – something of a transport hub, and bus passengers have to change here for the onward journey south to Stokmarknes and the Lofotens, or to catch the local bus north to Andenes, which originates here. The **tourist office** at Kjøpmannsgata 2 (mid-June to late Aug Mon–Fri 10am–6pm, Sat & Sun 11am–5pm; Sept to mid-June Mon–Fri 10am–5pm; ☎76 12 15 55), a five-minute walk from the bus station in the centre of town, has the customary range of regional information.

The E10 hugs the shoreline for 30km as it pushes southwest from Sortland, before encountering the two bridges that span the straits between Langøya and **STOKMARKNES**, on **Hadseløya**. The longer bridge is equipped with a high frequency sound device that is supposed to stop Langøya's foxes in their tracks, keeping Hadseløya fox-free. Pocket-sized Stokmarknes is itself unremarkable, though its shoreline setting is pleasant enough and you can sample the delights of the **Hurtigrutemuseet** (mid-June to mid-Aug daily 10am–6pm; 25kr), a museum devoted entirely to the history of the Hurtigrute. It's located in the town centre just back from the rangy quayside, where there's a **statue** of Richard With, the skipper responsible for dreaming up the coastal ferry in the 1890s. Indeed, the main reason to stop off in Stokmarknes is to catch the Hurtigrute south to Svolvær, via the Trollfjord. The boat leaves at 3.30pm, sailing down the narrow sound, **Raftsundet**, which separates the harsh, rocky shanks of Hinnøya and Austvågøy. Towards the southern end of the sound, the ship usually makes the short detour to the **Trollfjord**, a majestic tear in the landscape just 2km long. Slowing to a gentle chug, the vessels inch up the narrow gorge, smooth stone towering high above and blocking out the light. At its head, the boats effect a nautical three-point turn and then crawl back to rejoin the main waterway. It's very atmospheric, and the effect is perhaps even more extraordinary when the weather is up. One cautionary note is that when there's thought to be danger of a rock fall in the fjord, the Hurtigrute only pauses at the fjord's mouth before sailing past. Rock falls are most likely to happen in spring; if your main interest in the boat trip is to see the fjord, ask at a tourist office as to conditions before deciding whether to go. The Hurtigrute cruise from Sortland to Svolvær takes three hours and costs 100kr per passenger.

You'll find most facilities in Stokmarknes within a small area, with **buses** pulling in near the harbourfront **tourist office** (mid-June to late Aug Mon–Fri 10am–6pm, Sat 10am–4pm, Sun 11am–4pm; ☎76 15 29 55). They have details of local **accommodation**, though there's not much on offer. The obvious choice is the *Kinnarps Turistsenteret* (☎76 15 29 99, fax 76 15 29 95; ④, s/r ②), a brassy hotel that's plonked on the Børøya islet, about fifteen minutes' walk from the tourist office and at the end of the first of the two Langøya bridges; there are *rorbuer* (③; see box, p.268) run by the hotel round the back too.

The fishing and industrial port of **MELBU**, 15km to the south on the E10, contains the nearest **youth hostel** (☎76 15 71 06, fax 76 15 91 30; ①, dorm beds 130kr), a spartan affair situated 400m from the quay for the **car ferry** to Fiskebøl on the Lofotens (see p.269). Melbu is on the Narvik–Solvær bus route, and the Hvalrutebussen (see p.262) pass through here too.

The Lofoten Islands

A skeletal curve of mountainous rock stretched out across the Norwegian Sea and fringed by stacks and islets, the **LOFOTEN ISLANDS** are the focal point of the northern winter fishing. At the turn of the year, cod migrate from the Barents Sea to spawn here, where the waters are tempered by the Gulf Stream. The season lasts from January to April, but fishing is impossible to ignore at any time of year – it impinges on all aspects of life in the islands. At almost every harbour stand massed ranks of wooden racks used for drying cod for export, burgeoning and odoriferous in winter, empty in summer like so many abandoned climbing frames.

Sharing the same history, but better known and more beautiful than their neighbours the Vesterålens, the Lofoten Islands have everything from sea-bird colonies in the south to beaches and fjords in the north. The boat from Bodø, a popular way to approach, brings you face to face with the islands' most striking feature, the peaks of the **Lofotenveggen** (Lofoten Wall), a 160-kilometre stretch of mountains which, due to the islands' proximity to each other, appears unbroken – a towering set of jagged teeth biting into the skyline and trapping a string of tiny fishing villages tight against the shore. The Lofotens have their own relaxed pace, and are perfect for a simple, uncluttered few days. For somewhere so far north, the weather is exceptionally mild: summer days can be spent sunbathing on the rocks or hiking around the superb coastline; and when it rains, as it frequently does, life focuses on the *rorbuer*, where freshly caught fish are cooked over wood-burning stoves, stories are told and time gently wasted. If that sounds rather contrived, in a sense it is – the way of life here is to some extent preserved like this for tourists. But it's rare to find anyone who isn't less than completely enthralled by it all.

The **E10** weaves a scenic route across the Lofotens, running the 250km from Fiskebøl in the north to Å in the south, linking island to island by bridge and cause-

STAYING IN A RORBU – A FISHERMEN'S SHACK

Right across the Lofotens, **rorbuer** (fishermen's shacks) are rented out to tourists for both overnight stays and longer periods. The first of these were built round the coastline of the island of Austvågøy in the twelfth century, on the orders of King Øystein, so that visiting fishermen, who came here for the winter cod season, could rest easy instead of sleeping under their upturned boats. Traditionally, *rorbuer* were built on the shore, often on poles sticking out of the sea, and usually coloured with a red paint based on cod-liver oil. They consisted of two sections, a sleeping and eating room and a smaller storage area. The name *rorbu* is derived from *ror*, "to row" and *bu*, literally "dwelling". Older islanders still ask "Will you row this winter?", meaning "Will you go fishing this winter?"

At the peak of the fisheries in the 1930s, some 30,000 men were accommodated in *rorbuer*, but from the 1960s the fishing boats have become more comfortable and many fishermen have preferred to sleep aboard. Most of the original *rorbuer* disappeared years ago, and whereas before the 1960s visitors could expect a *rorbu* to be in use as a fisherman's shack, nowadays they are built by the dozen, with the tourist trade specifically in mind. At their best, they are comfortable and cosy seashore cabins, sometimes a well-planned conversion of an original rorbu with bunk beds and wood-fired stoves; at their worst, they are little better than prefabricated hutches in the middle of nowhere. Most have space for between four and six guests and the charge for a hut is in the region of 600kr per night – though some cost as little as 400kr, while others rise to about 1000kr. Similar rates are charged for the islands' **sjøhus** (literally sea-houses), bigger buildings whose format originated in the quayside halls where the catch was processed and the workers slept. Some of the original *sjøhus* have been cleverly converted into attractive apartments with self-catering facilities, many more into dormitory-style accommodation – though the quality again varies enormously. Full lists of *rorbuer* and *sjøhus* are given in the *North Norway Holiday Guide* and the *Lofoten Info-Guide*, free booklets that you can pick up at any local tourist office.

way, and occasionally tunnelling through the mountains. The highway passes through or within a few kilometres of all the islands' main villages, amongst which **Henningsvaer** and **Å** are breathtakingly beautiful, with **Stamsund** only slightly less so. All three make great **bases** for further explorations by boat – and the birdwatching and fishing are particularly popular pastimes while cruising around. There's **mountaineering** too – Austvågøy has the best climbing, and the Lofotens' best climbing school is at Henningsvaer – and **walking**: the islands do not have a well-developed system of huts and hiking trails, but the byroads are quiet and delve into the heart of the landscape. There's more walking and yet more solitude on mountainous **Værøy** and flatter, more agricultural **Røst**, a pair of inhabited islands to the south of Å, reachable by ferry from Moskenes and Bodø.

As regards **accommodation**, the Lofotens have a sprinkling of **hotels**, a handful of which are first-rate (though many are blandly modern), as well as five **youth hostels** and numerous **campsites**, and the local speciality – the *rorbuer* (see box, above).

Travel practicalities

The Lofotens can be reached by car ferry, Hurtigbåt and Hurtigrute, but once you've got there you'll find **public transport** thin on the ground. What local **bus** services there are stick almost exclusively to the **E10**, the islands' only main road. Leave the main highway, however, and you'll mostly have to **walk** – hardly an onerous task in such beautiful surroundings – or sometimes, with a bit of luck, you'll get a ride on a **boat**. There was a time when many islanders would happily offer rides; mass tourism and the construction of the E10 have put paid to that, but the compensation is that the Lofotens now excel in the number and variety of local sea trips offered. Alternatively, **bike rental** is available at the Svolvaer tourist office and at many places you might stay, including some youth hostels.

If you have your own **vehicle**, village-hopping is easy and quick, but it's only when you leave the car and head off into the landscape that the real character of the Lofotens begins to reveal itself; allow time for at least one walk or sea trip. Conversely, if you don't have a vehicle and want to reach the islands' remoter spots, it's worth considering renting a car, an inexpensive option if a few people share the cost. There are local **car rental** outlets at Svolvaer and Stamsund and special short-term deals can bring costs down to around 500kr a day.

Car ferries

From the mainland to the **Lofotens**, the principal **car ferry** service connects tiny Skutvik, 40km west of the E6 midway between Fauske and Narvik, with Svolvær (early June to late Aug 8 daily; Sept–May 2–3 daily; 2hr; 55kr per passenger, 190kr per car and driver). Queues are common and it's a first-come first-served ferry, so arrive about two hours before departure to make sure of a place. A second car ferry service links **Bodø** with the southern peripheries of the Lofotens (1–2 sailings daily). Leaving Bodø, the boat usually calls first at the tiny port of **Moskenes**, just a few kilometres from the end of the E10, before sailing on to one or both of the small islands of **Røst** and **Værøy**. The trip from Bodø to Moskenes takes four and a quarter hours; allow a further two hours to Værøy and four from Moskenes to Røst. The fare from Bodø to Moskenes is 112kr for passengers, 405kr for a car and driver. Advance reservations can be made through Bodø tourist office for a fee of 100kr; otherwise drivers should arrive at least two hours before departure to make sure of a place. If you're driving to the Lofotens on the **E10**, which branches off the E6 north of Narvik, you'll use a third car ferry linking **Melbu** on the Vesterålen Islands with **Fiskebøl** on the Lofotens (every 90min; 25min; 22kr per passenger, 65kr car and driver).

Boats

Hurtigbåt passenger express boats provide a speedy and economic alternative to the car ferry and Hurtigrute services. One links **Bodø** with **Svolvaer** (Mon–Fri & Sun 1 daily; 4hr; about 220kr); another links **Narvik** with **Svolvaer** (Mon–Fri & Sun 1 daily; 4hr; 255kr per person). For Hurtigbåt services to the Vesterålen Islands see p.261. In all cases, advance booking (via the local tourist office) is recommended.

The **Hurtigrute** leaves **Bodø** at 3pm daily for two ports in the Lofotens, **Stamsund** and **Svolvær**, of which Stamsund is preferable, especially for a short stay. Thereafter the Hurtigrute nudges through the **Raftsundet**, the narrow channel that gives access to the Trollfjord (see p.266). From June to September tickets from Bodø cost 253kr to Stamsund and 271kr to Svolvær, less off-season. Transporting a car from Bodø to Stamsund costs 280kr, and 300kr to Svolvær, but on the older vessels, where vehicles have to be hoisted on board, there's a fifty-percent surcharge. Advance reservations for cars are essential, but can be made just a few hours beforehand by telephoning the captain – ask down at the harbour or at the port's tourist office for assistance. Look out for special deals, which can reduce costs dramatically; these are advertised at local tourist offices.

Buses

There are two long-distance **bus** services from the mainland to the Lofotens. One is from **Fauske** to **Svolvær** (1 daily except Sat; 10hr 15min; one-way 379kr) via the Bognes–Lødingen and Melbu–Fiskebøl ferries; you can also start the journey at **Bodø**. The other service is from **Narvik** to **Svolvær** (1 daily except Sat; 8hr; 321kr) via the Melbu–Fiskebøl ferry.

On the Lofotens, there are **local buses** Monday through Friday, at least a couple of times daily, between most of the larger villages, but there are often no services at all on Sunday, sometimes Saturday too. One useful service travels the E10 linking Å, Leknes and Svolvær (Mon–Sat 1–2 daily). It's a component part of the much longer **Hvalrutebussen** service (see p.262) linking Å, Svolvær and Andenes with Narvik and Tromsø on the mainland and incorporating a journey on the Gryllefjord–Andenes ferry. To avoid getting stuck, make sure you pick up a bus and ferry **timetable** from any island tourist office or bus station.

Planes

Flights leave Bodø for the **Lofotens** airports – or rather airstrips – at Svolvær and Leknes twice or three times daily, and there's a once-daily service to Røst and Værøy. Note that the Leknes airport is miles from anywhere you might want to visit, and the onward taxi will cost a bomb. The carrier is Widerøe, an SAS partner, and tickets can be purchased at any travel agent or at the *Radisson SAS Hotel Bodø*. Stand-by, youth and excursion fares make flying to the islands a surprisingly economic option, with return fares starting at about 600kr.

Svolvær

By and large, **SVOLVÆR**, on the east coast of **Austvågøy**, the largest of the Lofotens, is a disappointing introduction to the islands. The Lofotens' administrative and transport centre, it has all the bustle but little of the charm of the other fishing towns, though it does have more accommodation than its neighbours. Better still, its surroundings are delightful, and can be visited on two local boat trips. Every day several **cruises** (return trip 3hr; 220kr; buy tickets on board) leave Svolvær for the **Trollfjord**, an impossibly narrow, two-kilometre-long stretch of water (see p.266). Alternatively, consider visiting the islet of **Skrova**, a fine spot, ideal for a quiet stroll, and easy to reach on the Svolvær–Skutvik ferry, which sails a couple of times a day in both directions (Mon–Sat). The ride to Skrova from Svolvaer takes just thirty minutes and costs about 25kr each way. Svolvær also boasts one of the archipelago's most famous **climbs**, the haul up to the top of the forty-metre-high Svolværgeita ("Svolvær goat"), a stone column perched on a hill behind the town. The column has two pinnacles – the horns of the "goat" – which daring-daft mountaineers jump between.

Practicalities

Ferries to Svolvær dock on the edge of town, about ten minutes' walk – or a brief taxi ride – from the town centre. The **bus station** is a few metres from the busy **tourist office** (late May to mid-June Mon–Fri 9am–4pm, Sat 10am–2pm; mid- to late June Mon–Fri 9am–4pm & 5–7.30pm, Sat 10am–2pm, Sun 4–7pm; late June to mid-Aug Mon–Sat 9am–4pm & 5–8pm, Sun 10am–9.30pm; mid-Aug to late Aug Mon–Fri 9am–7pm, Sat 10am–2pm; Sept to mid-May Mon–Fri 8am–4pm; ☎76 07 30 00, fax 76 07 30 01), beside the main town square by the harbour. They have maps, accommodation lists and details of local public transport. They will reserve accommodation anywhere in the Lofotens (for a 35kr booking fee) and can reserve ferry tickets for a fee of 125kr. Svolvær is a good place to **rent a car**, with both Avis and Budget, among others, offering some economic short-term deals from around 500kr per day.

As for **accommodation**, the enjoyable, wooden *Svolvær sjøhuscamping*, by the seashore at the foot of Parkgata (☎ & fax 76 07 03 36; ①), is a snug fishing house, and the price includes use of the showers and well-equipped kitchen. To get there from the square, turn right up the hill along Vestfjordgata and it's to the right, past the library. Alternatively, the *Hotel Havly* (☎76 07 03 44, fax 76 07 07 95; ③), centrally located behind the bus station, occupies a plain modern tower block and has simple, adequate rooms, while the *Norlandia Royal Hotel* (☎76 07 12 00, fax 76 07 08 50; ④), a few metres up from the main square at the end of Torggata, is similar but a good bit plusher. Pride of place, however, goes to the gleaming and popular *Rica Hotel Svolvær* (☎76 07 22 22, fax 76 07 20 01; ③, s/r ②), whose various buildings, in the style of the traditional *sjøhus*, occupy a prime harbourside location. For **food**, the self-service café of the *Rimi* superstore, just up from the harbour, provides Norwegian standbys at inexpensive prices, but for something to really savour, head for the *Rica Hotel Svolvær*, which has a first-rate restaurant and bar.

Kabelvåg

KABELVÅG's pretty wooden centre, draped around the shore of a narrow and knobbly inlet, is immediately more appealing than that of Svolvær, 6km east along the coast. The most important village on the Lofotens from Viking times until the early years of the twentieth century, Kabelvåg was the centre of the fishery and home to the islands' first *rorbuer*, built in 1120, and the first inn, which dates from 1792. The late nineteenth-century **Vågan kirke**, a big and breezy timber church beside the E10 on the eastern edge of the village, is a reminder of those busier times, its hangar-like interior built to accommodate a congregation of over a thousand. The village holds other attractions too. Near the cove, about 1500m west of the centre in the neighbourhood of Storvågan, is the **Lofotmuseet** (Lofoten Museum; early to mid-June & mid- to late Aug daily 9am–6pm; mid-June to mid-Aug daily 9am–9pm; Sept–May Mon–Fri 9am–3pm; 35kr). It traces the history of the islands' fisheries and displays the definitive collection of fishing equipment and other cultural paraphernalia. Nearby, the **Galleri Espolin** (early to mid-June daily 10am–6pm; mid-June to mid-Aug daily 10am–8pm; mid-Aug to Oct & mid-Feb to May Sun–Fri 11am–3pm; 35kr) features the paintings and sketches of Kaare Espolin Johnson, a minor but locally renowned Norwegian artist of romantic inclination.

On weekdays there's an hourly **bus** service from Svolvær to Kabelvåg, but only a couple of buses a day on Saturdays and Sundays. Buses drop you near the centre of the village, where there are pleasant **rooms** at the *Kabelvåg Hotel* (☎76 07 88 00, fax 76 07 80 03; ②), in an old timber building near the harbour – along with the *Præstenbrygga* **restaurant**, where you should head for a meal or a drink.

Kabelvåg also has a **youth hostel** (☎76 07 81 03, fax 76 07 81 17; ①, dorm beds 130kr; mid-June to mid-Aug), in the school building east of the centre across the harbour, and 500m from the E10.

Henningsvær

Heading southwest from Kabelvag, it's 11km on the E10 to the seven-kilometre-long turning for **HENNINGSVÆR**, the most beguiling of headland villages, a cobweb of cramped and twisting lanes lined with brightly painted wooden houses. These frame a tiny inlet that literally cuts the place in half, forming a sheltered, picture-postcard harbour that's only partly disturbed by busloads of package tourists.

For all the tourist bustle, however, the village is well worth an overnight **stay**. The smartest hotel is the quayside *Henningsvær Bryggehotell* (☎76 07 47 50, fax 76 07 47 30; ④), an attractive modern building in traditional style right on the waterfront, but the more economical choice is the *sjøhus* of *Den Siste Viking* (☎76 07 49 11, fax 76 07 46 46; ①), unadorned accommodation that's right in the centre and doubles as the home of the Lofotens' best **mountaineering school**, Nord Norsk Klatreskole (same number). The school operates a wide range of all-inclusive climbing holidays, catering to various degrees of fitness and experience. Prices vary greatly depending on the trip, but a three-day, one-climb-a-day holiday costs in the region of 3000kr per person, with equipment provided. Their prospectus is only printed in Norwegian, but they'll gladly discuss the various options with you in English if you drop by.

Also worthwhile are **fishing trips**, a morning or afternoon's exhilarating excursion for around 250kr, booked down at the harbour, or you could visit the **Karl Erik Harr Gallery** (March daily noon–3pm; late May to early June & late Aug daily 10am–6pm; mid-June to mid-Aug daily 9am–9pm; 45kr), which exhibits (and sells) the work of this contemporary artist, as well as a small selection of early nineteenth-century Lofoten paintings and photographs. For **food**, the *Bryggehotell* has a first-rate, if pricey, restaurant and the café-bar at *Lars Larsen's Rorbuer* features that commonest of all traditional island dishes, dried salted cod.

Vestvågøy: Stamsund and around

It's the next large island to the southwest of Austvågoy, **Vestvågøy**, that captivates many travellers to the Lofotens. This is due in no small part to the laid-back charm of **STAMSUND**, whose older buildings are strung along the rocky, indented seashore in an amiable jumble of crusty port buildings, wooden houses and *rorbuer*. This is the first port at which the Hurtigrute coastal boat docks on its way north from Bodø, and is much the best place to stay on the island. Getting there by bus from Austvågøy is reasonably easy too, with several buses making the trip daily, though you do have to change at **Leknes**, the administrative centre of Vestvågøy and site of the airport, 16km away to the west. By car, the quickest way to Stamsund is to turn south off the E10 down along Highway 815, a scenic forty-kilometre-long coastal drive.

The village **tourist office** is situated just 200m from the ferry dock (mid-June to mid-Aug daily 6–9.30pm; ☎76 08 97 92). However you may well get as much, if not more, information at the friendly **youth hostel** (Jan to mid-Oct & late Dec;

CHRIS COE

Bryggen at dusk, Bergen

TRIP/W. JACOBS

Bergen

CHRIS COE

Fish market, Bergen

Josteldalsbreen glacier

Fjærlandfjord

Hardangerfjord

Stabbur, Østerbø

Nidaros Cathedral, Trondheim

TRIP/N. PRICE

Svalbard

GREG EVANS

PHIL LEE

Sami elder

Viking carving, Urnes stave church

☎76 08 93 34, fax 76 08 97 39; ①, dorm beds 80kr). This is made up of several *ror-buer* and a *sjøhus* perched over a pin-sized bonny bay, about 1km down the road from the port and 200m from the nearest bus stop – ask to be let off. The hostel has a washing machine and tumble-drier, and rents bikes (85kr a day); its warden is also the best source of information on just about everything to do with Vestvågøy, from fishing through to hiking and cycling. The fishing is in fact first-class: the hostel rents out rowing boats and lines to take out on the (usually still) water, or you can head off on an organized fishing trip for just 150kr. Afterwards you can cook your catch on the wood-burning stoves and eat alfresco on the verandah overlooking the bay. Unsurprisingly, many travellers return time and again.

Even when the hostel is full, the warden will usually fit you in somewhere, but in the unlikely event you're turned away, push on along the coast to **STEINE**, 3km beyond the ferry harbour. At this hamlet, where an offshore archipelago of islets confettis the coastline, the comfortable *Steine Rorbuer* (☎ & fax 76 08 92 83; ①) are to be found snuggling up to the seashore.

The west coast of Vestvågøy

Admirers of wild scenery should consider heading out to the island's blustery **west coast**. It's accessed by a series of turnings off the E10 as the road slices across Vestvågøy's drab central valley. Beginning in Stamsund, the first part of the excursion is the hilly sixteen-kilometre trip to the E10 at **Leknes**, a commercial centre with an airport near the highway. Don't stop, but instead keep going for another 3km to the first signposted byroad, which leads the 10km west to **Utakleiv**, perched on the edge of a wide bay and surrounded by austere cliffs. There's more stern scenery at the end of the next turning off the E10, this time at **Unstad**, which is reached along a narrow road that winds up into the hills and tunnels through to the village. But it's the third (and bumpy) side road that leads to the prettiest spot, **Eggum**, a huddle of houses dwarfed by the mountains behind and with a whopping pebble beach in front. The views are fabulous. Without a car, these places are difficult to reach: cyclists will face stiff gradients and often strong winds and, although the bus service along the E10 itself is good, there are no regular buses off it to the west coast.

South to Reine

By any standards the next two islands of the archipelago, **Flakstadøya** and **Moskenesøya**, are extraordinarily beautiful. As the Lofotens taper towards their southerly conclusion, the rearing peaks of the Lofotenveggen crimp a sea-shredded coastline studded with fishing villages. The E10 travels along almost all of this dramatic shoreline, west of Leknes even tunnelling under the sound separating Vestvågøy from Flakstadøya (toll 65kr to use the tunnel). About 20km from Leknes, on Flakstadøya itself, an even more improbable byroad somehow wiggles the 6km through the mountains to **NUSFJORD**, an extravagantly picturesque fishing village in a tight and forbidding cove. Unlike many fishermen's huts else-where in the Lofotens, which were erected in response to tourist demand rather than that of the fishing fleet, the ones here are the genuine nineteenth-century article, and the general store, with its wooden floors and antique appearance, fits in nicely too. Inevitably, it's tourism that largely supports the local economy, and the village is on the day-trippers' itinerary, but it's still a beguiling place, with

accommodation available in more than thirty comfortably refurbished *rorbuer*. The one-bedroom versions hold two to four people (②), the two-bedroom ones have space for five (②). There's also a **bar-restaurant** here. Advance reservations with *Nusfjord Rorbuer* (☎76 09 30 20, fax 76 09 33 78) are advised.

Back on the E10, it's a further 5km to the **Flakstad kirke**, a distinctive onion-domed, red timber church built out of driftwood in 1780. The building announces the beginning of **Ramberg**, the island's administrative centre – if that's what you can call the smattering of services (garage, supermarket and suchlike) straggling the sandy beach in the shadow of the mountains.

Pressing on south from Ramberg, over the first of several narrow bridges, you're soon on **Moskenesøya**, where the road squirms across the mouth of the Kirkefjord, hopping from islet to islet to link the fishing villages of **Hamnøy**, on the north side of the inlet, with **REINE** to the south. Reine is an odd little place, a scattering of wooden houses almost overwhelmed by its magnificent surroundings; it's also the departure point for many **boat trips**. These include midnight sun cruises (late May to mid-July 1 weekly; 5hr; 390kr), coastal voyages (June to mid-Aug 1 weekly; 4hr; 290kr), fishing expeditions and excursions to the Moskenstraumen (see below). For information about these trips, ask at the Moskenes tourist office (see opposite) or at local accommodation establishments. Reine has several *rorbuer* complexes, the neatest of which is *Reine Rorbuer* (☎76 09 22 22 or 76 09 22 25; ②) in the older part of town, at the end of the short promontory just off the E10.

Moskenes and Å

From Reine, it's a couple of kilometres to **MOSKENES**, the port midway between Bodø and the southernmost bird islands of Værøy and Røst – not that there's much here, just a handful of houses dotted round a horseshoe-shaped bay. There is, however, a **tourist office** (early June Mon–Fri 10am–5pm; mid-June to mid-Aug daily 10am–7pm; ☎76 09 15 99) by the jetty, and a basic **campsite** (June–Aug; ☎76 09 13 44; ①) up a gravel track a five-minute walk away.

Six kilometres further south the road ends abruptly at the tersely named Å, one of the Lofotens' most delightful villages, its huddle of old buildings rambling along a foreshore that's wedged in tight between the grey-green mountains and the surging sea. Unusually, so much of the nineteenth-century village has survived that a good portion of Å has been incorporated into the **Norsk Fiskevaersmuseum** (Norwegian Fishing Village Museum; late June to late Aug daily 10am–6pm; Sept to mid-June Mon–Fri 10am–3.30pm; 40kr), an engaging attempt to recreate life here at the end of the nineteenth century. There are over twenty buildings to examine, including the houses of the two traders who dominated things hereabouts and the fishermen who did their bidding. According to the census of 1900, Å had 91 inhabitants, of whom 10 were traders and their relatives, 18 servants, and 63 were fishermen and their families. It was a rigidly hierarchical society underpinned by terms and conditions akin to serfdom. The fishermen did not own any land and had to pay for the ground on which their houses stood, by means of unpaid work on the merchant's farmland during the summer harvest. No wonder Norwegians emigrated in their thousands. The museum has a series of displays which detail every aspect of village life – and very well presented it is too. Afterwards, you can extend your knowledge of all things fishy by visiting the **Tørrfiskmuseum** (Stockfish Museum; early to mid-June Mon–Fri

11am–4pm; late June to late Aug daily 11am–5pm; 35kr) – stockfish being the air-dried fish that was the staple diet of most Norwegians well into the twentieth century.

As at nearby Reine (see opposite), several **boat trips** are on offer here in Å. There are day-long fishing expeditions (Mon–Sat June–Aug 1 daily; 3hr; 260kr) and, weather and tides permitting, regular cruises (June to mid-Aug 1 weekly; 4hr; 390kr) to the **Moskenstraumen** – the maelstrom described by Edgar Allen Poe in his short story *A Descent into the Maelstrom*.

> *Even while I gazed, this current acquired a monstrous velocity. Each moment added to its speed – to its headlong impetuosity. In five minutes the whole sea... was lashed into ungovernable fury... Here the vast bed of the waters seamed and scarred into a thousand conflicting channels, burst suddenly into frenzied convulsion – heaving, boiling, hissing...*

There are other places to see similar phenomena in Norway – the Saltstraumen near Bodø (see p.252) is perhaps more accessible – but the Moskenstraumen is the original.

A local **bus** runs along the length of the E10 from Leknes to Å once or twice daily from late June to late August, less frequently the rest of the year. Times do not, however, usually coincide with sailings to and from Moskenes. Consequently, if you're heading from the Moskenes ferry port to Å, you'll either have to walk – it's an easy 6km – or take a taxi.

All the **accommodation** in Å is run by one family, who own the **youth hostel** (①, dorm beds 125kr); the assortment of smart *rorbuer* (①–②), surrounding the dock; and the adjacent *sjøhus*, which offers very comfortable and equally smart, hotel-standard rooms (②). The same family also run the **bar** and the only **restaurant**, where the seafood is very good. Bookings for all these on ☎76 09 11 21, fax 76 09 12 82.

Værøy and Røst

Dangling from the main island chain, **Værøy** and **Røst** are the most southerly of the Lofotens, and the most time-consuming to reach. Indeed, unless you're careful, the irregular ferry schedules can leave you stranded on either for several days, though the gist of the timetable is that **car ferries** either run from Bodø to Moskenes once a day and then vary their route to Værøy and/or Røst – or less frequently sail there direct from Bodø. The fare from Bodø to Værøy is 103kr per person, 370kr for a car; Bodø to Røst 124kr, 450kr; between Værøy and Røst it's 55kr and 188kr. From Bodø, there is one daily **flight** to Røst and another to Værøy, with standby, summer and youth discount fares making a flight a reasonably economic proposition, especially if booked at least fourteen days in advance; SAS in Bodø or elsewhere will advise.

If you do make it here, Værøy and Røst are internationally famous for their **bird colonies**, the crags hosting an incredible number of puffins, eiders and the rare sea eagles, as well as cormorants, kittiwakes, guillemots and more recent immigrants like the fulmar and gannet. There are lots of **bird trips** to choose from, and for a decent length (say three-hour) excursion you can reckon on paying between 250kr and 350kr. The weather here is uncommonly mild throughout the year, hiking trails are ubiquitous, and the occasional beach glorious and deserted.

Værøy

Of the two islands, **VAERØY**, just 8km long, is the more visually appealing, comprising a slender, lightly populated, grassy-green coastal strip which ends suddenly in the steep, bare mountains that backbone the island.Værøy's few kilometres of roads primarily connect the farmsteads of the plain, but one squeezes through a narrow pass to wobble along a portion of the coast to the airport. The island is, however, best explored on foot, either along the steep (and sometimes dangerous) footpaths of the mountains, or on the much easier and clearer hiking trail which slips down the west coast before crossing a neck of land on its way to **Måstad**. Abandoned in the 1950s, the inhabitants of this isolated village varied their fishy diet by catching puffins from the neighbouring sea cliffs, a hard and difficult task in which they were assisted by specially bred dogs known locally, appropriately enough, as puffin dogs.

Ferries dock at the southeast tip of the island, about 200m from the **tourist office** (mid-June to mid-Aug Mon–Fri 10am–2pm, ☎76 09 52 10), which can advise on boat tours and **accommodation** – though you would be foolhardy not to arrange this beforehand: the options are limited to a **guesthouse** at the old vicarage, the *Gamle Prestegård* (May–Sept; ☎76 09 54 11, fax 76 09 54 84; ②); and a **youth hostel** (mid-May to mid-Sept; ☎76 09 53 52, fax 76 09 57 01; ①, dorm beds 85kr), comprising some refurbished *rorbuer,* some of which can be rented at any time of the year. Both of these establishments are some 4km from the jetty. The well-equipped hostel also offers bicycle and boat rental and runs boat trips to the island's **bird cliffs**, which occupy the southwest corner of the island and are much too steep and slippery to approach on foot.

Røst

Even smaller than its neighbour, **RØST** is also immediately different, its smattering of lonely farmsteads dotted over a pancake-flat landscape interrupted by dozens of tiny lakes. The **airport** is on the edge of the island, a little more than 1km northwest of the main village, which is itself 2.5km north of the **ferry port**. Again, the **tourist office** (mid-June to mid-Aug Mon–Fri noon–3pm, Sat hours vary to coincide with the arrival of the boat; ☎76 09 64 11, fax 76 09 62 84) is close to the jetty, and the island has a **youth hostel** (May–Aug; ☎76 09 60 00, fax 76 09 61 09; ①, dorm beds 105kr), about 1km away from the quay. The hostel organizes **boat trips** to the jagged islets that rise high above the ocean to the southwest of Røst, their steep cliffs sheltering the seabird colonies.

travel details

Trains

Narvik to: Riksgrånsen (2–3 daily; 50min); Stockholm (1 daily; 18hr).

Trondheim to: Bodø (2–3 daily; 10hr); Dombås (3–4 daily; 2hr 30min); Fauske (2–3 daily; 9hr 20min); Mo-i-Rana (2–3 daily; 7hr); Oslo (3–4 daily; 7hr); Otta (3 daily; 3hr); Røros (1–2 daily; 2hr 30min); Steinkjer (2–3 daily; 1hr 20min); Stockholm (2 daily; 12hr).

Buses

Bodø to: Fauske (3 daily; 1hr 10min); Harstad (1 daily; 8hr); Narvik (2 daily; 7hr); Sortland (1–2 daily; 7hr); Svolvær (1 daily; 10hr 20min).

Fauske to: Bodø (2–3 daily; 1hr 10min); Harstad (1 daily; 6hr 30min); Narvik (2 daily; 5hr 30min); Sortland (1–2 daily; 6hr); Svolvær (1 daily; 8hr 30min).

Harstad to: Fauske (1 daily; 6hr 30min).

Narvik to: Alta (1 daily; 14hr); Bodø (2 daily; 7hr); Fauske (2 daily; 5hr 30min); Sortland (1 daily; 3hr 40min); Svolvær (1 daily; 7hr 30min); Tromsø (1–2 daily; 4hr 40min).

Sortland to: Andenes (1–3 daily; 2hr 15min).

Svolvær to: Å (Mon–Fri 1–2 daily; 3hr 20min).

Trondheim to: Bergen (2 daily; 14hr); Kristiansund (2–3 daily; 5hr); Otta (2 daily; 4hr); Stryn (2 daily; 7hr 20min); Ålesund (2–3 daily; 8hr).

Nord-Norgeekspressen

The Nord-Norgeekspressen (North Norway Express Bus) complements the railway system. It runs north from Bodø and Fauske to the Nordkapp in four segments: Bodø–Narvik via Fauske (2 daily; 7hr); Narvik–Tromsø (1–2 daily; 4hr 40min); Tromsø–Alta (1 daily; 6hr 30min); and

Alta–Nordkapp (Mon–Fri & Sun 1–2 daily; 6hr). If you have the stamina, you can change from one bus to the next at every stop on the main Nord-Norgeekspressen route except Tromsø, where you have to stay the night. See also "Travel Details" in the North Norway chapter.

Car ferries

Bodø to: Moskenes (1–3 daily; 4hr 15min); Røst (3–4 weekly; 8hr); Værøy (3–4 weekly; 7hr).

Bognes to: Lødingen (5–10 daily; 1hr).

Fiskebol to: Melbu (11–13 daily; 25min).

Skarberget to: Bognes (11–14 daily; 25min).

Svolvær to: Skutvik (early June to late Aug 7–8 daily; Sept–May 2–3 daily; 2hr).

Hurtigbåt

Bodø to: Svolvær (Mon–Fri & Sun 1 daily; 5hr 30min).

Harstad to: Tromsø (1–2 daily; 2hr 45min).

Narvik to: Svolvær (Mon–Fri & Sun 1 daily; 4hr).

Trondheim to: Kristiansund (1–3 daily; 3hr 30min).

Hurtigrute

Northbound departures: daily from Trondheim at noon; Bodø at 3pm; Stamsund at 7.30pm; Svolvær at 10pm; Stokmarknes at 1am; Sortland at 3am & Harstad at 8.15am.

Southbound departures: daily from Harstad at 8.45am; Sortland at 1.15pm; Stokmarknes at 3.30pm; Svolvær at 7.30pm; Stamsund at 9.30pm; Bodø at 4am & Trondheim at 10am.

Journey time Trondheim–Harstad 43hr, Trondheim–Tromsø 51hr.

CHAPTER FIVE

NORTH NORWAY

aedeker, writing a hundred years ago about Norway's remote **northern provinces** of Troms and Finnmark, observed that they can "hardly be recommended for the ordinary tourist" – a comment which isn't too wide of the mark even today. These are enticing lands, no question, the natural environment they offer stunning in its extremes, with the midnight sun and polar night (see box, p.280) emphasizing the strangeness of the terrain; but the travelling can be hard, the specific sights widely separated and, when you reach them, subtle in their appeal.

Troms' intricate, fretted coastline has influenced its history since the days when powerful Viking lords operated a trading empire from its islands. Indeed, over half the population still lives offshore in dozens of tiny fishing villages, but the place to aim for is **Tromsø**, the so-called "Capital of the North" and a lively university town where, in 1940, King Håkon and his government proclaimed a "Free Norway" before fleeing into exile. Beyond Tromsø, the long trek north begins in earnest as you enter **Finnmark**, a vast wilderness covering 48,000 square kilometres, but home to just two percent of the Norwegian population. Much of the land was laid waste during World War II, the combined effect of the Russian advance and the retreating German army's scorched-earth policy, and it's now possible to drive for hours without coming across a building more than fifty years old. The first obvious target in Finnmark is **Alta**, a sprawling settlement and important crossroads that is famous for its prehistoric rock carvings. From here, most visitors head straight for the steely cliffs of **Nordkapp** (the North Cape), Europe's northernmost point, sometimes with a detour to the likeable port of **Hammerfest**, and leave it at that; but some doggedly press on to **Kirkenes**, the last town before the Russian border, where you feel as if you're about to drop off the end of the world. From Alta, the other main alternative is to travel inland across the eerily endless scrubland of the **Finnmarksvidda**, where winter tem-

---

ACCOMMODATION PRICE CODES

The hotels and guesthouses detailed throughout this guide have been graded according to the price categories listed below. Prices given are for the least expensive double room during the high season, although almost every hotel offers seasonal and/or weekend discounts, which can reduce the rate by one or even two grades. Wherever hotels have an official summer rate we've given it (denoted s/r), but bear in mind that many others will provide impromptu summer and weekend discounts. Single rooms, where available, usually cost between 60 and 80 percent of a double. For a more detailed discussion of accommodation see p.37.

① under 500kr	③ 700–900kr	⑤ 1200–1500kr
② 500–700kr	④ 900–1200kr	⑥ over 1500kr

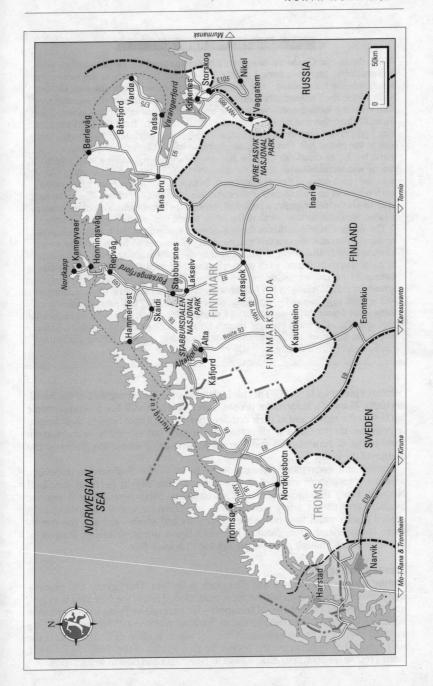

ARCTIC PHENOMENA

Within the **Arctic Circle**, an imaginary line drawn round the earth at latitude 66.5 degrees north, there is a period around midsummer during which the sun never makes it below the horizon, even at midnight – hence the **midnight sun**. On the Arctic Circle itself, this only happens on one night of the year – at the summer solstice – but the further north you go, the greater the number of nights affected: in Bodø, it's from the first week of June to early July; in Alta, from the third week in May to the end of July; in Hammerfest, mid-May to late July; and in Nordkapp early May to the end of July. Obviously, the midnight sun is best experienced on a clear night, but fog or cloud can turn the sun into a glowing, red ball – a spectacle that can be wonderful but also strangely disconcerting. All the region's tourist offices have the exact dates of the midnight sun, though note that these are calculated at sea level; climb up a hill and you can extend the dates by a day or two. The converse of all this is the **polar night**, a period of constant darkness either side of the winter solstice; again the further north of the Arctic Circle you are, the longer this lasts.

The Arctic Circle also marks the typical southern limit of the **northern lights**, or Aurora Borealis, though this extraordinary phenomenon has been seen as far south as latitude 40 degrees north. Caused by the bombardment of the atmosphere by electrons, carried away from the sun by the solar wind, the northern lights take various forms and are highly mobile – either flickering in one spot or travelling across the sky. At relatively low latitudes hereabouts, the aurora is tilted at an angle and is often coloured red – the sagas tell of Vikings being half scared to death by them – but nearer the pole, they hang like gigantic luminous curtains, often tinted greenish blue. Naturally enough, there's no predicting when the northern lights will occur, but in wintertime they are not uncommon – and on a clear night they can be simply awe-inspiring.

peratures plummet to -25°C. This high plateau is the last stronghold of the **Sami**, northern Norway's indigenous people, many of whom still live a semi-nomadic life tied to the movement of their reindeer herds. You'll spot Sami in their brightly coloured traditional gear all across the region, but especially in the remote Sami towns of **Kautokeino** and **Karasjok**, strange, disconsolate places in the middle of the plain.

Finally, and even more adventurously, there is the **Svalbard** archipelago, whose icy mountains rise out of the Arctic Ocean 640km north of mainland Norway. Once the exclusive haunt of trappers, fishermen and coal miners, Svalbard now makes a tidy income from adventure tourism – everything from guided glacier walks to snowmobile excursions and whale-watching. You can fly there independently from most of Norway's larger towns, including Tromsø, at bearable prices, though most people opt for a package tour.

Travel practicalities
Public transport in Troms and Finnmark is by **bus**, **Hurtigrute** and **plane** – there are no trains. For all but the most truncated of tours, the best idea is to pick and mix these different forms of transport – for example by flying from Tromsø to Kirkenes and then taking the Hurtigrute back, or vice versa. What you should try to avoid is endless doubling-back on the E6, which is often difficult as this is the only road to run right across the region. To give an idea of the distances involved, from Tromsø it's 300km to Alta, 500km to Nordkapp and 800km to Kirkenes.

The principal long-distance **bus** is the Nord-Norgeekspressen, which links Tromsø with Nordkapp, via Alta and Honningsvåg (late June to mid-Aug 1 daily except Sat; 14hr). During the same period, this key service is supplemented by an early morning service (Mon–Fri) from Alta to Nordkapp; there's also a bus from Tromsø to Alta (April to late Oct 1 daily except Sat). Alta is also where you pick up the bus to Karasjok and Kirkenes (March–Dec 4–5 weekly), with an additional service (March–Dec 1 daily Mon–Fri & Sun) as far as Karasjok. North of Alta, all the buses use the E6 and pass through Skaidi, where you change for Hammerfest. There is also a bus linking Hammerfest with Karasjok and Kirkenes (March–Dec 1 daily Mon–Fri & Sun). Bus **timetables** are available at most tourist offices and bus stations. On the longer rides, it's a good idea to buy tickets in advance.

The main **highways** are all well-maintained, but **drivers** will find the going a little slow as there's some pretty tough terrain to negotiate. You can cover 250–300km in a day without any problem, but try for much more and it all becomes rather wearisome. Be warned also that in July and August the E6 north of Alta can get congested with caravans and motor homes on their way to Nordkapp. You can avoid the crush by starting early or, for that matter, by driving overnight – an eerie experience when it's bright sunlight in the wee hours of the morning. In **winter**, driving conditions can be appalling and, although the Norwegians make a spirited effort to keep the E6 open, they don't always succeed. If you're not used to driving in these sort of conditions, don't start here – especially during the polar night. If you intend to use the region's **minor roads**, be prepared for the worst and certainly take food and drink, warm clothes and, if possible, a mobile phone (which some car rental firms can supply). Keep an eye on the fuel indicator too, as petrol stations are confined to the larger settlements and they are often 100–200km apart. Car repairs can take time since workshops are scarce and parts often have to be ordered from the south.

Much more leisurely is the **Hurtigrute**, which takes the best part of two days to cross the huge fjords between Tromsø and Kirkenes. En route, it calls at eleven ports, mostly remote fishing villages but also Hammerfest and Honningsvåg, where (northbound only) it pauses for a couple of hours so that special buses can cart passengers off to Nordkapp and back. One especially appealing option, though this has more to do with comfort than speed, is to combine **car and boat** travel. Special deals on the Hurtigrute can make this surprisingly affordable and tourist offices at the Hurtigrute's ports of call will make bookings. Incidentally, you may well find that using the same rented vehicle throughout – taking it on the Hurtigrute where necessary, and only returning it when you get back to the place where you rented it – is cheaper than the cost of a one-way rental: one-way, car drop-off charges cost anything up to 3500kr.

With regard to **air travel**, the region has several **airports** including those at Tromsø, Hammerfest, Honningsvåg and Kirkenes. Summer discounts and special offers make flying an economic possibility – ask for details at any SAS or Braathens office. Both these airlines also fly to Svalbard.

As for **accommodation**, all the major settlements have at least a couple of hotels and the main roads are sprinkled with campsites. If you have a tent and a well-insulated sleeping bag, you can, in theory, bed down more or less where you like, but the hostility of the climate and the ferocity of the mosquitoes, which breed in marshy areas of the Finnmarksvidda, make most people think (at least) twice. There are youth hostels at Tromsø, Alta, Lakselv and Kirkenes.

Tromsø

TROMSØ has been called, rather preposterously, the "Paris of the North", and though even the tourist office doesn't make any pretence to such grandiose titles today, the city is without question the effective capital of northern Norway. Easily the region's most populous town, it has credentials that go back to the Middle Ages – there's been a church here since the thirteenth century, and seafarers were using its sheltered harbour long before. Tromsø received its municipal charter in 1794, when it was primarily a fishing port and trading station, and flourished in the middle of the nineteenth century when its seamen ventured north to Svalbard to reap rich rewards hunting Arctic foxes, polar bears and, most profitable of all, seals. Subsequently, Tromsø became famous as the jumping-off point for a string of Arctic expeditions, its celebrity status assured when the explorer Roald Amundsen flew from here to his death somewhere on the Arctic ice cap in 1928. Since those heady days, Tromsø has grown into an urbane and likeable small city with a population of 58,000 employed in a wide range of industries and at the university. It's become an important port too, for although the city is some 360km north of the Arctic Circle, its climate is moderated by the Gulf Stream, which sweeps up the Norwegian coast and keeps its harbour ice-free. Give or take the odd museum, Tromsø is short on specific sights, but its amiable atmosphere and fine mountain-and-fjord setting more than compensate. It also possesses a clutch of good restaurants, some lively bars and several enjoyable hotels.

Arrival, information and orientation

At the northern end of the E8, 73km from the E6 and 250km north of Narvik (see p.254), Tromsø's compact centre slopes up from the waterfront on the hilly island of Tromsøya. The island is connected to the mainland by bridge and tunnel. The **Hurtigrute** docks in the town centre at the foot of Kirkegata, while **Hurtigbåt** services arrive at the quay about 150m to the south. Long-distance **buses** arrive at and leave from the parking lot, a few metres away. On the other side of Tromsøya is the **airport**, 5km west of the centre, from where Flybussen (daily 6am–11pm 4–5 hourly; 35kr) run into the city, stopping at the *Radisson SAS Hotel* on Sjøgata and at several other central hotels; the taxi fare for the corresponding journey is 70kr.

Tromsø's **tourist office**, Storgata 61 (June to mid-Aug Mon–Fri 8.30am–6pm, Sat & Sun 10am–5pm; mid-Aug to May Mon–Fri 8.30am–4pm; ☎77 61 00 00), is a couple of minutes' walk straight up Kirkegata from where the long-distance buses stop. They issue free town maps, have a small supply of private rooms (see p.284) and supply oodles of local information, including details of bus and boat sightseeing trips out among neighbouring islands. An eight-hour excursion, which gives you plenty of time to savour the scenery, costs around 350kr. Tickets for most trips can be purchased here at the tourist office, which also sells a one-day **tourist ticket** (50kr, valid 24hr from when it's first used) offering unlimited city bus travel, though most places of interest can easily be reached on foot.

The town centre is small enough to make **orientation** easy: Storgata is the main street and north–south axis. It's interrupted by Stortorget, the main square. The busiest part of the town centre spreads south of the square as far as Kirkegata and east to the harbourfront. It only takes five minutes to walk from

TROMSØ

Airport & Youth Hostel

Ishavskatedralen (Arctic Cathedral), Cable Car & E8

Polar Museum

Domkirke

★ Buses

Hurtigrute Quay

Hurtigbåt Quay

Art Museum of North Norway

Mack Brewery

ACCOMMODATION

Kongsbakken Gjestehus	2
Radisson SAS Hotel Tromsø	5
Rainbow Polar Hotell	6
Rica Ishavshotel Tromsø	4
Skipperhuset Pensjonat	1
Comfort Home Hotel With	3

0   200 m

▽ Polaria (100m), Tromsø Museum (2.5km) & Art Museum

one side of the centre to the other, but for the outlying attractions you can either catch a local bus, or **rent a bike** from Sportshuset, Storgata 87 (Mon–Fri 9am–7pm, Sat 10am–4pm; ☎77 66 11 00). There is a **taxi** rank on Stortorget and another by the Domkirke.

Accommodation

Tromsø has a good supply of modern, central **hotels**, though admittedly the majority occupy chunky concrete high-rises. Less expensive are the town's **guesthouses** (*pensjonater*) and the **youth hostel**. The tourist office has a small list of **private rooms** at around 300kr per double per night (200kr single), but most are stuck out in the suburbs.

Hotels

Comfort Home Hotel With, Sjøgata 35 (☎77 68 70 00, fax 77 68 96 16). Pleasantly situated down by the harbourfront, this likeable hotel has a nautical air and brisk modern bedrooms. ⑤, s/r ③.

Radisson SAS Hotel Tromsø, Sjøgata 7 (☎77 60 00 00, fax 77 68 54 74). This plush, downtown high-rise offers smart and comfortable modern rooms, and ultra efficient service. ④, s/r ③.

Rainbow Polar, Grønnegata 45 (☎77 68 64 80, fax 77 68 91 36). Small, modern rooms decorated in typical chain-hotel style, but summer and weekend discounts make this place a real bargain; central location too. ③, s/r ②.

Rica Ishavshotel Tromsø, Fr. Langes gate 2 (☎77 66 64 00, fax 77 66 64 44). Perched on the harbourfront, this imaginatively designed hotel is partly built in the style of a ship, complete with a sort of crow's nest bar. Lovely rooms and unbeatable views of the waterfront. Best place in town. ⑤, s/r ③.

Guesthouses, hostels and camping

Kongsbakken Gjestehus, Skolegata 24 (☎77 68 22 08, fax 77 68 80 44). This guesthouse has wide views over the city from the hillside behind the town centre. Seventeen simple rooms. Worth booking ahead in summer. ①.

Skipperhuset Pensjonat, Storgata 112 (☎77 68 16 60, fax 77 65 62 92). North of Stortorget, by Bispegata, this guesthouse is a long-standing favourite with budget travellers, and has good, cheap rooms. Occupies a large and old timber town house. Rooms with showers (②), and without (①); four-bedded rooms too.

Tromsdalen Camping, Elvestrandvegen (☎77 63 80 37, fax 77 63 85 24). The nearest campsite to the city centre, 1500m from the Ishavskatedralen, is on the mainland side of the bridge, by a river and near a football field. Several city buses go near there – ask at the bus station. Cabins available; open all year.

Tromsø Vandrerhjem, Gitta Jønsons vei 4, Elverhøy (☎ & fax 77 68 53 19), about 2km west of the centre. This barracks-like HI hostel is a basic affair and can be noisy. No food is available, but there's a store close by and self-catering facilities. Reception closed 11am–5pm. A couple of city buses go near there – ask at the bus station – or else it's a stiff thirty-minute walk. Open late June to late Aug. ①, dorm beds 100kr.

The City

One of Tromsø's most distinctive buildings is its **Domkirke** (June–Aug Tues–Sun noon–4pm; free). Erected on Storgata in 1861, the cathedral bears witness to the prosperity of the town's nineteenth-century merchants, who became rich on the back of the barter trade with Russia. They part-funded the church's construction, the result being the large and handsome structure of today, its imposing spire poking high into the sky. From the church, it's a gentle five-minute stroll north past the shops of Storgata to the main square, **Stortorget**, site of a daily open-air **market** selling flowers and knick-knacks. The square nudges down to the waterfront, where fresh fish and prawns are sold direct from inshore fishing boats throughout the summer. Follow the harbour round to the north and you're in the heart of old Tromsø: the raised ground close to the water's edge was the centre of the medieval settlement and it was here that the locals built the first fortifications. Nothing now remains of the medieval town, but you can discern the shape of a later, eighteenth-century fort in the modest knoll at the end of Skansegata.

Close by, in an old wooden waterfront warehouse, is the city's most enjoyable museum, the **Polarmuseum i Tromsø** (Polar Museum; daily: mid-May to mid-June 11am–6pm; mid-June to Aug 11am–8pm; Sept to mid-May 10am–3pm; 30kr). The museum begins with a rather unappetizing series of displays on trapping in the Arctic, but beyond is an outstanding section on Svalbard, which includes archeological finds recently retrieved from an eighteenth-century Russian trapping station there. Most of the finds come from graves in which the artefacts were preserved by the permafrost. Among many items, there are combs, leather boots, parts of a sledge, slippers and even – just to prove illicit smoking is not a recent phenomenon – a clay pipe from a period when the Russian company in charge of affairs did not allow trappers to smoke. Two other sections on the first floor focus on seal hunting, an important part of the local economy until the 1950s. Upstairs, on the second floor, a further section is devoted to the polar explorer **Roald Amundsen** (1872–1928), who spent thirty years searching out the secrets of the Arctic and Antarctic. In 1901, he purchased a sealer, the *Gjøa*, here in Tromsø and then spent three years sailing and charting the Northwest Passage. The *Gjøa* was the first vessel to complete this extraordinary voyage; today, the ship is exhibited in Oslo (see p.89). In 1910, Amundsen set out in a new ship, the *Fram* – also on display in Oslo (see p.89) – for the Antarctic, or more specifically the South Pole. On December 14, 1911, Amundsen and four of his crew became the first men to reach the South Pole, famously just ahead of their British rival Captain Scott. The museum exhibits all sorts of oddments used by Amundsen and his men – from long johns and pipes through to boots and ice picks – but it's the photos that steal the show, providing a fascinating insight into the way the expeditions were organized and the hardships endured. Judging from the heroic poses, Amundsen clearly liked having his picture taken and maintained an amazing set of eyebrows to prove his derring-do. Finally, there's another extensive section on Amundsen's contemporary **Fridtjof Nansen** (1861–1930), a polar explorer of similar renown who, in his later years, became a leading figure in international famine relief. In 1895, Nansen and his colleague Hjalmar Johansen made an abortive effort to reach the North Pole by dog sledge after their ship – also named the *Fram* – got packed in by the ice. It took them fifteen months to get back to safety, a journey of such epic proportions that tales of it captivated all of contemporary Norway.

The Art Museum of Northern Norway and Polaria

On the other side of the city centre, the eminently profitable Mack brewery, at the corner of Storgata and Musegata, proudly boasts that it is the northernmost brewery in the world – and dreams up all sorts of bottle labels adorned with ice and polar bears to emphasize the point. Just up Musegata, the **Nordnorsk Kunstmuseum** (Art Museum of Northern Norway; Tues–Sun 11am–5pm; free) occupies the second and third floors of a large and attractive late nineteenth-century building. It's not a large collection, but it is well-presented and contains examples of the work of many Norwegian painters, from lesser-known figures like Axel Revold and Christian Krohg to the likes of Munch (see p.91), a few of whose works are displayed. There are also several romantic peasant scenes by Adolph Tidemand and a couple of ingenious landscapes by both the talented Thomas Fearnley and Johan Dahl. The permanent collection is enhanced by frequent loans from the National Gallery in Oslo (see p.79) and by a lively programme of temporary exhibitions. Down below, on the first floor and in the basement, is the **Tromsø Kunstforening** (Art Society; Tues–Sun 11am–5pm; 20kr), whose temporary exhibitions of Norwegian contemporary art are often the work of Nordland artists.

Doubling back down Musegata, it's a couple of hundred metres south along Storgata to **Polaria** (daily: May–Aug 10am–7pm; Sept–April noon–5pm; 70kr), a lavish new complex which deals with all things Arctic, including an aquarium filled with Arctic species, a 180-degree cinema showing a film on Svalbard, and exhibitions on polar explorations.

South of the centre: the Tromsø Museum

About 3km from the centre, near the southern tip of Tromsøya, is the **Tromsø Museum** (June–Aug daily 8am–8pm; Sept–May Mon–Fri 8.30am–3.30pm, Sat noon–3pm, Sun 11am–4pm; 20kr), whose varied collections feature nature and the sciences downstairs, and culture and history above. Pride of place goes to the medieval religious carvings, naive but evocative pieces retrieved from various Nordland churches. There's also an enjoyable section on the Sami which features displays on every aspect of Sami life – from dwellings, tools and equipment through to traditional costume and hunting techniques. To get to the museum, take bus #28 from the centre (Mon–Sat every 30min, Sun hourly).

East of the centre: the Arctic Cathedral and the cable car

Over the spindly Tromsø bridge, on the other side of the water in the suburb of Tromsdalen, is the desperately modern **Ishavskatedralen** (Arctic Cathedral; May & mid-Aug to mid-Sept daily 4–6pm; June to mid-Aug Mon–Sat 10am–8pm, Sun 1–8pm; 15kr), completed in 1965. Its strikingly white, glacier-like appearance is achieved by means of eleven immense triangular concrete sections, representing the eleven Apostles left after the betrayal. The entire east wall is formed by a huge stained-glass window, one of the largest in Europe. The organ is highly unusual, built to represent a ship when viewed from beneath – recalling the tradition, still seen in many a Norwegian church, of suspending a ship from the roof as a good-luck talisman for the seafarers among the congregation. Among several bus services, #28 (Mon–Sat every 30min, Sun every hour) comes this way – but it's only a few minutes' walk.

From the Ishavskatedralen, it's a fifteen-minute walk – or a short ride on bus #28 – to the city's **cable-car** terminus. From the top (421m), the views of the city and its surroundings are extensive, and at the *Fjellstua* restaurant (☎77 63 86 55) you can treat yourself to a meal with a panoramic backdrop. There are regular daily cable-car departures from April to September (10am–5pm) and also an evening schedule from late May to late August (5pm–1am); return tickets are 60kr. Note that services are suspended during bad weather.

Eating, drinking and entertainment

Tromsø has a reasonably good range of places to **eat and drink** – certainly it's as well served as any comparable Norwegian city. Its cafés and restaurants are concentrated in the vicinity of the tourist office on Storgata, while most of the livelier bars, many of which sell the local brew, Mack, are handily located in the centre too.

The **Kulturhuset**, Grønnegata 87 (☎77 64 18 88), is the main venue for cultural events of all kinds, and the main **cinema**, Fokus, is close by at Grønnegata 94 (☎77 68 07 29). The tourist office has details of performances.

Restaurants and cafés

Brankos, Storgata 57 (☎77 68 26 73). Slovenian restaurant with good food and folksy decor. Reasonably priced. Open Mon–Sat evenings.

Paletten, Storgata 51. This café-bar maintains an arty reputation by hosting occasional exhibitions. Tasty Norwegian lunches (meatballs, smorgasbord) for 49kr.

Sagatun Café, Richard Withs plass 2. Reasonably priced self-service cafeteria on the first floor of the *Saga Hotell*. Mon–Fri 7am–6pm; Sat 9am–4pm; Sun noon–6pm.

Sjømatrestauranten Arctandria, Strandtorget 1 (☎77 61 01 01). Easily the best food in town, either in the upstairs restaurant, where main courses start at around 190kr, or downstairs in the café-bar at about twenty percent less. The range of fish in the restaurant is quite superb, with the emphasis on Arctic species, and there's also reindeer and seal. The café-bar has a tad less variety, but that's not to quibble.

Store Norske Fiskekompani, Storgata 73 (☎77 68 76 00). Smart restaurant offering a superb range of seafood. Main courses around 190kr.

Bars

Blå Rock Café, Strandgata 14. Raucous R&B bar with CD jukebox and weekend discos.

Meieriet Café & Stor pub, Grønnegata 37. Lively, youthful spot near the Kulturhus.

Skipsbroen, inside the *Rica Ishavshotel*. Overlooking the waterfront, this smart little bar occupies part of the hotel's slender tower.

Teaterkafeen, in the Kulturhus, Grønnegata 87, on the corner of Stortorget. This arts-centre establishment stays open until 1am most days for trendy drinking and snacks.

Tromsø Jernbanestasjon, Strandgata 33. Done up in the style of a railway carrriage, this appealing bar attracts a wide-ranging clientele and has a good variety of ales.

Ølhallen Pub, Storgata 4. Solid, some would say staid, brewery pub, adjoining the Mack brewery, whose various brews are its speciality. Mon–Fri 9am–5pm; Sat 9am–1pm.

Listings

Banks Sparebanken, Fr. Langes gate 19; K-BANK, Grønnegata 80.

Car rental Europcar, Alkeveien 5 and at the airport (☎77 67 56 00); Avis, Vestregata 16 (☎77 61 58 50).

Cruises to Svalbard Troms Fylkes Dampskibsselskap, down on the harbourfront (☎77 64 82 00, fax 77 64 82 40) offer week-long, all-inclusive cruises from Tromsø to the west coast of Svalbard (late June to late Aug; from 7000kr per person).

DNT Troms Turlag, Grønnegata 32 (☎77 68 51 75).

Left luggage Lockers inside the *Venteromskafé*, beside the Hurtigbåt quay (mid-July to Aug Mon–Fri 6.30am–11.45pm, Sat 10am–11.45pm, Sun noon–midnight; Sept to mid-July Mon–Fri 6.30am–11.45pm, Sat 10am–3pm, Sun noon–midnight; 15kr per day).

Maps Centrum Libris, Sjøgata 31.

Pharmacy Svaneapoteket, Fr. Langes gate 9 (☎77 60 14 80).

Post office Main office at Strandgata 41 (Mon–Fri 8.30am–5pm, Sat 10am–2pm).

Travel agents Bennett Reisebyrå, Roald Amundsensplass 1 (☎77 62 15 00).

Vinmonopolet Off-licence at Storgata 33.

Into Finnmark: from Tromsø to Alta

Beyond Tromsø, the vast sweep of the northern landscape slowly unfolds, with silent fjords cutting deep into the coastline beneath ice-tipped peaks which themselves fade into the high plateau of the interior. This forbidding, elemental terrain is interrupted by the occasional valley where those few souls hardy enough to make a living in these parts struggle on – often by dairy farming. A particular problem for them, curiously enough, is the abundance of Siberian garlic (*Allium sibiricum*): the cows love the stuff, but if they eat a lot of it, the milk tastes of onions. In summer, cut grass is dried everywhere, stretched over wooden poles that form long lines on the hillsides, like so much washing hung out to dry.

Slipping along the valleys and traversing the mountains in between, the **E8** and then the E6 follow the coast pretty much all the way to Alta, some 410km – and about nine hours' drive – to the north. Drivers can save around 120km (although not necessarily time and certainly not money) by turning off the E8 25km south of Tromsø onto **Highway 91**. This cuts across the peninsula and then uses two **car ferries** to rejoin the E6 at Olderdalen, some 220km south of Alta. The first ferry is Breivikeidet–Svendsby (Mon–Fri 6am–8pm, Sat 8am–8pm, Sun 10am–9pm; every 1–2hr; 25min; 55kr car and driver); the second Lyngseidet–Olderdalen (Mon–Fri 7am–7pm, Sat 9am–7pm, Sun 11am–9pm; every 1–2hr; 40min; 85kr car and driver). This is the route used by most long-distance buses. Whichever route you choose, you enter **Finnmark** around 60km short of a tiny village that bears the name **KÅFJORD**. Situated beside the E6, its nineteenth-century church (now restored) was built by the English company who operated the area's copper mines until they were abandoned as uneconomic in the 1870s. The Kåfjord itself is an arm of the Altafjord, and was used as an Arctic hideaway for the *Tirpitz* and other German battleships during World War II to protect them from the British. From here, it's just 20km further east to Alta.

It's also possible to head here by public transport from Tromsø. From April to late October, the Nord-Norgeekspressen **bus** departs Tromsø for Alta and Nordkapp once daily except on Saturday. The journey times are seven hours and fourteen hours respectively. There's an additional once-daily service to Alta and another, early in the morning (Mon–Fri), from Alta to Nordkapp. Buses also head east from Alta along the E6 to Kirkenes. To reach Hammerfest by bus, change at Skaidi (see p.300), on the E6. The **Hurtigrute** leaves Tromsø at 6.30pm, taking eleven hours to reach Hammerfest (see p.295).

Alta

Despite the long haul to get here, first impressions of **ALTA** are not encouraging. With a population of just 16,000, the town strings along the E6 for several kilome-

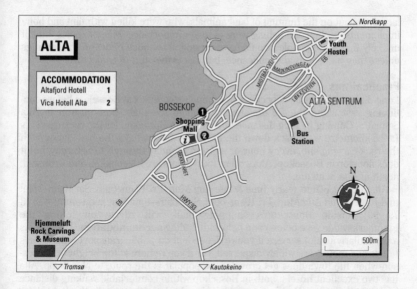

tres, comprising a series of unenticing settlements. The ugliest part is **Alta Sentrum**, now muddled by a platoon of soulless concrete blocks. Alta was interesting once – for a couple of centuries not Norwegian at all but Finnish and Sami, and host to an ancient and much-visited Sami fair. World War II polished off the fair and destroyed all the old wooden buildings that once clustered together in Alta's **Bossekop** district, where Dutch whalers settled in the seventeenth century.

For all that, Alta does have one remarkable feature, the most extensive area of **prehistoric rock carvings** in northern Europe. This UNESCO World Heritage site, the **Helleristningene i Hjemmeluft** (Rock Carvings in Hjemmeluft; mid-June to mid-Aug daily 8am–11pm; early June and late Aug daily 8am–8pm; Sept daily 9am–6pm; Oct–April Mon–Fri 9am–3pm, Sat & Sun 11am–4pm; 40kr), is located beside the E6, 2.5km before Bossekop as you approach Alta from the southwest. A visit begins at the **museum**, which provides a wealth of background information, comparing the carvings, for example, with others found around the world. It also offers a history of the Alta area, particularly the salmon-fishing industry, and documents the conflicts around the development of the nearby hydroelectric power station, which involved flooding land used by the local Sami community. The rock carvings themselves extend down the hill from the museum to the fjordside. A clear and easy-to-follow footpath and boardwalk circumnavigate the site, taking in all the carvings in about an hour. On the trail, there are thirteen vantage points offering close-up views of the carvings, recognizable though highly stylized representations of boats, animals and people picked out in red pigment (the colours have been retouched by researchers). They make up an extraordinarily complex tableau, whose minor variations – there are four identifiable bands – in subject matter and design indicate successive historical periods. The carvings were executed, it's estimated, between 6000 and 2500 years ago, and are indisputably impressive: clear, stylish, and touching in their simplicity. They provide an insight into a prehistoric culture that was essentially settled and largely reliant on the hunting of land animals, who were killed with flint and bone implements; sealing and fishing were of lesser importance. Many experts think it unlikely that these peoples would have expended so much effort on the carvings unless they had spiritual significance, but this is the stuff of conjecture.

Practicalities

Long-distance buses usually call at the shopping complex at Bossekop before continuing east along the E6 for another 2km to the main **bus station** in Alta Sentrum. Coming by long-distance bus, get off in Bossekop for the rock carvings (a 2.5-kilometre walk back down the E6); a **local bus** links the bus station with the rock-carving site, every hour or so from Monday through to Saturday, but it does not stop in Bossekop. Alta's other focal points are Elvebakken and Kronstad, north of Alta Sentrum.

Alta **tourist office** (early June & late Aug Mon–Fri 10am–5pm, Sat 10am–3pm; mid-June to mid-Aug Mon–Fri 10am–6pm, Sat 10am–4pm, Sun noon–4pm; ☎78 43 79 99), inside Bossekop's shopping mall, will advise on hiking the Finnmarksvidda (see below) and help with finding **accommodation**. The latter is a particularly useful service if you're dependent on public transport – the town's hotels and motels are widely dispersed – or if you're here at the height of the season when the town does get crowded, so popular is the route to Nordkapp. Alta has two excellent **hotels**, both in Bossekop within comfortable walking distance of the tourist office. The first, a couple of hundred metres away, is the *Vica Hotell Alta* (☎78 43 47 11, fax 78 43 42 99; ④, s/r ③), a small, cosy hotel decorated in the style of a mountain lodge, with lots of pine panelling. Alternatively, the *Altafjord Hotell* (☎78 43 70 11, fax 78 43 70 13; ④), a five- to ten-minute walk away to the west, down by the fjord, offers three sorts of rooms – run-of-the-mill in the main building, cottage-style down by the fjord (the best choice) and in turf-roofed buildings, a spick-and-span version of the traditional-style house. Less costly by far is the **youth hostel**, in a plain chalet about 700m north of Alta Sentrum at Midtbakkveien 52 (☎ & fax 78 43 44 09; ①, dorm beds 120kr; mid-June to mid-Aug). To get there from Alta Sentrum, walk east up the E6 to the next roundabout, where you turn left and then first left again – a fifteen-minute stroll. Food isn't available, but there are self-catering facilities. There are also several **campsites** in the vicinity of Alta, the nearest and best-equipped being the four-star *Kronstad Camping* (☎78 43 03 60, fax 78 43 11 55), an all-year site with cabins beside the E6 at the east end of town, some 5km from Alta Sentrum.

Easily the best **restaurant** in town is at the *Vica Hotell Alta*, where they specialize in regional delicacies – cloudberries, reindeer and the like. Prices are very reasonable and traditional Sami dishes are often on the menu too.

The Finnmarksvidda

Venture far inland from Alta and you enter the **Finnmarksvidda**, a vast mountain plateau which spreads southeast beyond the Finnish border. Rivers, lakes and marshes lattice the region, but there's barely a tree, let alone a mountain, to break the contours of a landscape whose wide skies and faraway horizons are eerily beautiful. Distances are hard to gauge – a dot of a storm can soon be upon you, breaking with alarming ferocity – and the air is crystal-clear, giving a whitish lustre to the sunshine. A couple of roads cross this expanse, but for the most part it remains the preserve of the few thousand semi-nomadic **Sami** who make up the majority of the local population. Many still wear traditional dress, a brightly coloured affair of red bonnets and blue jerkins or dresses, all trimmed with red, white and yellow embroidery. You'll see permutations on this traditional costume all over Finnmark, but especially at roadside souvenir stalls and, on Sundays, outside Sami churches.

Setting aside the slow encroachments of the tourist industry, lifestyles on the Finnmarksvidda have remained remarkably constant for centuries. The main occupations are reindeer-herding, supplemented by hunting and fishing, and the pattern of Sami life is mostly still dictated by the animals. During the winter, the reindeer graze the flat plains and shallow valleys of the interior, migrating towards the coast in early May as the snow begins to melt – hard to believe, but it can reach 30°C here in summer. By October, both people and reindeer are journeying back from their temporary summer quarters. The long, dark winter is spent in preparation for the great **Easter festivals**, when weddings and baptisms are celebrated in **Karasjok** and **Kautokeino**, the region's two principal settlements. This is without question the best time to be here – in themselves, neither Karasjok nor Kautokeino is especially appealing – when the inhabitants celebrate the end of the polar night and the arrival of spring. There are folk-music concerts, church services and traditional sports, including the famed reindeer races. Details of these Easter festivals are available at any Finnmark tourist office, or you can telephone or, even better, fax the Kautokeino (☎78 48 48 00, fax 78 48 58 90) and Karasjok (☎78 46 80 00, fax 78 46 62 12) festival offices. Summer visits, on the other hand, can be disappointing, since most families and their reindeer are at coastal pastures in the north and there is precious little activity.

From Alta, the only direct route into the Finnmarksvidda is south along Highway 93 to Kautokeino, a distance of 130km. Highway 93 presses on south into Finland, while Highway 92 branches off and leads the 130km east to Karasjok, where you can rejoin the E6 (but well beyond the turning to Nordkapp). **Bus** services across the Finnmarksvidda are no more than adequate: there is one bus a day, except on Sundays, from Alta to Kautokeino, and a twice-daily service (except Sat), along the E6 from Alta to Karasjok. A further service links Karasjok with Hammerfest once or twice daily except on Saturdays, but there are no buses between Karasjok and Kautokeino.

The best time to **hike** in the Finnmarksvidda is in August and early September – after the peak mosquito season and before the weather turns cold. For the most part the plateau vegetation is scrub and open birch forest, which makes the going fairly easy, though the many marshes, rivers and lakes often impede progress. There are a handful of clearly demarcated hiking trails and a smattering of appropriately sited but unstaffed huts; for detailed information, ask at Alta tourist office.

Kautokeino

It's a three-hour bus ride from Alta, deep into the Finnmarksvidda, to **KAU-TOKEINO** (Guovdageaidnu), the principal winter camp of the Norwegian Sami and the site of a huge reindeer market in spring and autumn. Nonetheless, it's still a desultory, desolate-looking place that straggles along the banks of the Kautokeinoelva, though one that has become something of a tourist draw on account of the jewellers who have moved here from the south. Every summer, these jewellers line the long main street with souvenir booths, attracting Finnish

THE SAMI

The northernmost reaches of Norway, Sweden and Finland, and the Kola peninsula of northwest Russia, are collectively known as **Lapland**. Traditionally, the indigenous population were called "Lapps", though in recent years this name has fallen out of favour and been replaced by the term **Sami**, although the change is by no means universal. The new name comes from the Sami word *sámpi* meaning both the land and its people, now numbering around 70,000 scattered across the region. Among the oldest peoples in Europe, the Sami are probably descended from prehistoric clans who migrated here from the east by way of the Baltic. Their three distinct languages, each of which breaks down into a number of markedly different regional dialects, are closely related to Finnish and to Estonian. There are, however, many common features, including a superabundance of words and phrases to express variations in snow and ice conditions. In this chapter, we give the Sami names of settlements in brackets after the Norwegian versions.

Originally, the Sami were a semi-nomadic people, living in small communities (*siidas*), each of which had a degree of control over the surrounding hunting grounds. They mixed hunting, fishing and trapping, preying on all the edible creatures of the north, but it was the wild reindeer that supplied most of their needs. This lifestyle changed in the sixteenth century when the Sami switched over to reindeer herding, with communities following the seasonal movements of the animals. What little contact the early Sami had with other Scandinavians was almost always to their disadvantage – as early as the ninth century, a Norse chieftain by the name of Ottar boasted to the English king Alfred the Great of his success in imposing a fur, feather and hide tax on his Sami neighbours.

These early depredations were, however, nothing compared with the dislocation of Sami culture that followed the efforts of Sweden, Russia and Norway to control and colonize Sami land. It took the best part of two hundred years for the competing nations to agree their northern frontiers – the last treaty, between Norway and Russia, was signed in 1826 – and meanwhile hundreds of farmers had settled in "Lapland", to the consternation of its indigenous population. Meanwhile, in the manner of many colonized peoples, Norway's Sami had accepted the religion of their colonizers, succumbing to the missionary endeavours of Pietist Protestants in the early eighteenth century. Predictably, the missionaries frowned upon the Sami's traditional shamanism, although the more progressive among them sup-

day-trippers like flies. Their wares are not tourist tat, however, and a visit to **Juhl's Silver Gallery** (daily June to early Aug 8.30am–10pm; mid-Aug to May 9am–6pm; ☎78 48 61 89, fax 78 48 69 66) is a must. Located just 3km south from the handful of buildings that passes for the town centre – follow the signs – this smart complex of workshops and showrooms makes and sells exquisitely beautiful, high-quality silver work, supplemented by a much broader range of quality craftwork influenced by traditional Sami design.

Back in the town centre, near the river, the small **Kautokeino Bygdetun Museum** (Kautokeino Parish Museum; mid-June to mid-Aug Mon–Sat 9am–7pm, Sun noon–7pm; 20kr) features a history of the town inside and a number of draughty-looking Sami dwellings outside. You'll spot the same little turf huts and skin tents (known as *lavvu*) all over Finnmark – often housing souvenir stalls. Not far away, across the river to the south of the tourist office along the main drag, stands the modern **Kautokeino kirke** (late June to mid-Aug daily 10am–8pm;

ported the use of Sami languages and even translated hundreds of works. Things got even worse for the Sami in Norway towards the end of the nineteenth century, when the government, influenced by the Social Darwinism of the day, embarked on an aggressive policy of "**Norwegianization**". New laws banned the use of indigenous languages in schools, and only allowed Sami to buy land if they could speak Norwegian. It was only in the 1950s that these policies were abandoned and slowly replaced by a more considerate, progressive approach.

More recently, the Sami were dealt yet another grievous blow by the **Chernobyl nuclear disaster** of 1986. This contaminated not only the lichen that feeds the reindeer in winter, but also the game, fish, berries and fungi that supplement the Sami diet. Contamination of the reindeer meat meant the collapse of the export market, and promises of compensation by the various national governments only appeared late in the day. Furthermore, the cash failed to address the fact that this wasn't just an economic disaster for the Sami, but a threat to their traditional culture based around reindeer herding. Partly because of the necessarily reduced role of reindeer, other expressions of Sami **culture** have expanded. Traditional arts and crafts are now widely available in all of Scandinavia's major cities and the first of several Sami films, *Veiviseren (The Pathfinder)*, was released to critical acclaim in 1987. Sami music (*joik*) has also been given a hearing by world-music and jazz buffs. Although their provenance is uncertain, the rhythmic song-poems that constitute *joik* were probably devised to soothe anxious reindeer; the words are subordinated to the unaccompanied singing and at times are replaced altogether by meaningless, sung syllables.

Since the international anti-colonial struggles of the 1960s, the Norwegians have been obliged to re-evaluate their relationship with the Sami. In 1988, the country's constitution was amended by the addition of an article that read: "It is the responsibility of the authorities of the state to create conditions enabling the Sami people to preserve and develop its language, culture and way of life". The following year a Sami Parliament, the **Sameting**, was opened in Karasjok. Certain deep-seated problems do remain and, as with other aboriginal peoples marooned in industrialized countries, there have been heated debates about land and mineral rights and the future of the Sami as a people, above and beyond one country's international borders. Neither is it clear quite how the Norwegian Sami will adjust to having something akin to dual status – as an indigenous people of the region and citizens of a particular country – but at least Oslo is asking the right questions.

free), a delightful wooden building whose interior is decorated in bright, typically Sami colours – also to be seen when the Sami turn up here in their Sunday best. Also worth a quick look is the **Kautokeino Kulturhuset** (Cultural Centre), on the north side of town. Winner of various architectural awards, the building houses the only Sami theatre in Norway.

Practicalities

Doubling as Highway 93, Kautokeino's main street is 1500m long, and most of its facilities, including the **bus stop**, are clustered near the **tourist office** (early June to July daily 9am–7pm; early Aug to mid-Aug 9am–4pm; mid- to late Aug 10am–4pm; ☎78 48 65 00), which marks what is effectively the town centre. The tourist office provides town maps and has details of local events and activities, from fishing and hiking through to "Sami adventures" (late June to mid-Aug; 4hr; 300kr per person) – these typically include a boat trip and a visit to a *lavvu* where you can sample traditional Sami food and listen to *joik*. The main local tour organizer is Cávso Safari (☎78 48 75 88, fax 78 48 76 39).

The only **hotel** as such is the modest and modern *Norlandia Kautokeino* (☎78 48 62 05, fax 78 48 67 01; ④, s/r ③), on the north side of town just off Highway 93. There are also a couple of **campsites** near the river on the southern edge of town, primarily *Kautokeino Camping og Motell* (☎78 48 54 00, fax 78 48 78 00), with cabins (①) and a few frugal motel rooms (②). The *Norlandia Kautokeino* has a competent **restaurant**.

Karasjok

The only other settlement of any size on the Finnmarksvidda is **KARASJOK** (Kárásjohka), Norway's Sami capital, which straddles the E6 on the main route from Finland to Nordkapp and consequently sees plenty of tourists. Spread across a wooded river valley, it has none of the desolation of Kautokeino, but it still conspires to be fairly mundane, despite the siting of the Sami parliament and library here, and the opening of several ethnic-jewellery and fine-art shops. The busiest place in town is the **Samelandssenteret tourist office**, beside the E6 and Highway 92 crossroads (late June to early Aug Mon–Sat 9am–6pm, Sun 10am–6pm; mid-Aug to mid-June Mon–Fri 9am–4pm, Sat 10am–2pm; ☎78 46 69 00, fax 78 46 67 35), in what amounts to the town centre. The tourist office incorporates a café and a Sami souvenir shop, replete with authentic arts and crafts. During the summer, there are also displays of various traditional Sami skills in the grounds around the centre – the usual sort of stuff with the obligatory reindeer brought along as decoration. From here, it's a short walk north along the Nordkapp road to the right turn leading along Museumsgata to **De Samiske Samlinger** (Sami Museum; April to early June & mid-Aug to Oct Mon–Fri 9am–3pm, Sat & Sun 10am–3pm; early June to mid-Aug Mon–Sat 9am–6pm, Sun 10am–6pm; Nov–March Mon–Fri 9am–3pm, Sat & Sun noon–3pm; 25kr). This attempts an overview of Sami culture and history, with outdoor exhibits comprising an assortment of old dwellings that illustrate, more than any other aspect, the frugality of Sami life. Inside, a large, clearly presented collection of incidental bygones includes a colourful sample of folkloric Sami costumes. You may also want to take a peek at the **Gamle kirke**, on the opposite side of the river to the town centre and the only building left standing here at the end of World War II. Of simple design, it dates from 1807, making it easily the oldest surviving church in Finnmark.

A couple of kilometres east of the tourist office, on the road to Kirkenes, the **Samisk Kunstnersenter** (Sami Artists' Centre; June to mid-Aug Mon–Fri 10am–3pm, Sat & Sun 11am–3pm; mid-Aug to May closed Sun; ☎78 46 68 98, fax 78 46 70 62) showcases the work of contemporary Sami artists; but don't expect folksy paintings – Sami artists are a diverse bunch and as likely to be influenced by post-modernism as reindeer-herding.

However diverting these sights may be, you'll only get a feel for the Finnmarksvidda if you venture out of town. The tourist office has the details of local **guided tours**: options include dog-sledging, a visit to a Sami camp, a boat trip on the Karasjokka river, cross-country skiing and even gold-panning. The region's most popular long-distance **hike** is the five-day haul across the heart of the Finnmarksvidda, from Karasjok to Alta via a string of strategically located huts; ask at Alta's tourist office (see p.290) for details.

Practicalities

There are only two **buses** a day to Karasjok along the E6 from Alta and Kirkenes, and a couple more from Hammerfest, but nothing at all on Saturdays. Schedules mean that it's usually possible to spend a couple of hours here before moving on, which is quite enough to see the sights, but not nearly long enough to get the real flavour of the place. Buses to Karasjok pull in at the **bus station**, on Storgata. From here, it's a signposted five- to ten-minute walk west to the **tourist office**, beside the E6/Highway 92 crossroads. They issue free town maps, provide a full list of local accommodation and have details of all the guided tours on offer.

The best **hotel** in town is the *Rica Hotel Karasjok* (☎78 46 74 00, fax 78 46 68 02; ④, s/r ③), a breezy modern establishment a short stroll north of the tourist office along the E6. More modest and less expensive accommodation is provided by the unassuming *Annes Overnatting og Motell* (☎78 46 64 32; ②), east of the tourist office along the E6 towards Kirkenes, and by *Karasjok Camping*, a ten-minute walk west from the tourist office on the Alta road (☎78 46 61 35, fax 78 46 66 97), which has cabins (②) as well as spaces for tents. For **food**, the *Rica Hotel Karasjok* has the unusual *Gammen* restaurant, a wooden turf-covered hut where Sami-style meals can be eaten around an open fire. It's good fun, and a chance to find out whether reindeer meat – inevitably the staple ingredient, with a gamey flavour – is to your liking.

Moving on from Karasjok, it is 130km west to Kautokeino; 240km north to Nordkapp; 220km northwest to Hammerfest and 320km east to Kirkenes.

Hammerfest

HAMMERFEST, some 150km north from Alta, is, as its tourist office takes great pains to point out, the world's northernmost town. It was also, they add, the first town in Europe to have electric street-lighting. Hardly fascinating facts, but both give a glimpse of the pride that the locals take in making the most of what is, indisputably, an inhospitable location. Indeed, it's a wonder the town has survived at all: a hurricane flattened the place in 1856; it was burnt to the ground in 1890; and the retreating Germans mauled it at the end of World War II. Yet, instead of being abandoned, Hammerfest was stubbornly rebuilt for a third time. Nor is it the grim industrial town you might expect from the proximity of the offshore oil wells, but a bright, cheerful port that drapes around a horseshoe-shaped harbour sheltered from the elements by a steep rocky hill. The occasional dignified wooden building recalls the town's nineteenth-century heyday as the centre of the *Pomor* trade in which Norwegian fish were traded for Russian flour by the boat-load. But don't get too carried away: Bill Bryson, in *Neither Here Nor There*, hit the nail on the head with his description of Hammerfest as "an agreeable enough town in a thank-you-God-for-not-making-me-live-here sort of way". Neither is the town's main employer, the harbourfront fish-processing plant, the stuff of Arctic romance.

The Town

Running parallel to the waterfront, **Strandgata**, the town's principal street, is a busy, 500-metre-long run of supermarkets, clothes and souvenir shops, partly inspired by the town's role as a stop-off for cruise ships on the way to Nordkapp.

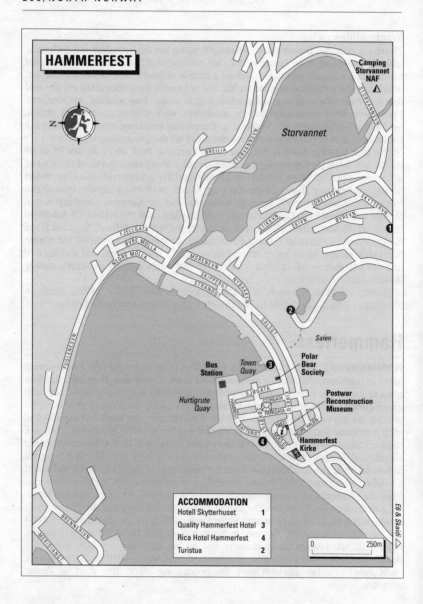

HAMMERFEST

Camping
Storvannet
NAF

Storvannet

BREILIA

STORVANNSVN

IDRETTSVN

SKYTTERVN

SLIKKVN

SKIVN

ØVREVN

1

FJELLGATA

ØVRE MOLLA

NEDRE MOLLA

MORENEVN

SKIPPERGT

NYBAKKEN

STRANDGT

SALSGT

2

Salen

Bus
Station

*Town
Quay*

3

Polar
Bear
Society

*Hurtigrute
Quay*

SJØGATA

HAMNEG

STORGATA

KIRKEG

PARKGATA

BATTERIET

SØRØYGT

NEDRE HAUEN

INFO

Postwar
Reconstruction
Museum

4

Hammerfest
Kirke

FUGLENESVN

BRENNELIVN

MERIDIANGT

E6 & Skaidi

ACCOMMODATION

Hotell Skytterhuset	1
Quality Hammerfest Hotel	3
Rica Hotel Hammerfest	4
Turistua	2

0   250m

However, most of the activity takes place on the **main quay**, off Sjøgata, with tourists emerging from the liners to beetle around the harbourfront, eating shellfish from the stalls along the wharf or buying souvenirs in the small, summertime Sami market. The Hurtigrute spends a couple of hours here too, arriving at 5.30am on its way north, 11.45am heading south.

Beyond that, it's the general atmosphere of the place that appeals rather than any specific sight, though the tiny town centre does muster a couple of attractions, beginning with the **Isbjørnklubben** (The Royal and Ancient Polar Bear Society; June–Aug Mon–Fri 8am–7pm, Sat & Sun 10am–5pm; Sept–May daily 11.45am–1pm; free), up from the quay in the basement of the town hall. The society's pint-sized museum – full of stuffed specimens of the animal- and seal-skin-covered furniture – tells the story of Hammerfest as a trapping centre and its own dubious history as an organization that hunted and trapped polar bears, eagles and arctic foxes. They'll try and cajole you into supporting the organization by becoming a member – honestly, you can live without forking out 150kr for the certificate. A good deal better is the purpose-built **Gjenreisningsmuseet** (Museum of Postwar Reconstruction; mid-June to mid-Aug daily 8am–7pm, mid-Aug to mid-June Mon–Fri 9am–5pm; 40kr plus 20kr for English guide-book as labelling is only in Norwegian), a five-minute walk west of the main quay up Kirkegata. This begins with a fascinating section on the hardships endured by the inhabitants of Finnmark during the German retreat, in the face of the advancing Russians, in late 1944. The Germans ordered a general evacuation and then applied a scorched-earth policy, which left almost all of the region's towns and villages in ruins. Just in case any of his soldiers got the wrong idea, Hitler's orders stipulated that "Compassion for the population is out of place". Refugees in their own country, the Norwegians found shelter wherever they could and several thousand hid out in caves until May 1945, though many died from cold and malnutrition. Subsequent sections of the museum deal with postwar reconstruction, giving a sharply critical account of the central government bureaucracy initially put in charge. Under the weight of complaints, it was disbanded in 1948, and control being passed back to the municipalities. Interestingly, the left-wing Labour Party, who co-ordinated the reconstruction programme, adopted an almost evangelical stance, crusading against dirtiness, inequality and drunkenness in equal measure.

For something a little more energetic, take the **footpath** that zigzags up **Salen**, the hill behind town. It takes about fifteen minutes to reach the plateau at the top, from where there are panoramic views out across the town and over to the nearby islands in good weather; as a further incentive, there's a good café-restaurant, the *Turistua* (see p.298). The footpath begins a couple of minutes' walk from the main quay on Salsgata, one block south of Strandgata.

Practicalities

Hammerfest is situated on the island of **Kvaløya**, which is linked to the mainland by bridge. Buses pull into the **bus station** at the foot of Sjøgata and the **Hurtigrute** docks at the adjacent quay, as does the **Hurtigbåt** from Honningsvåg (early June to mid-Aug 1 daily; 2hr). From this dock, it's a couple of hundred metres to the main quay halfway up Sjøgata.

The **tourist office** (mid-June to mid-Aug Mon–Fri 9am–7pm, Sat & Sun 10am–5pm; mid-Aug to mid-June Mon–Fri 9am–4pm, Sat & Sun 10am–3pm; ☎78 41 21 85) is a short walk west of the main quay. To get there, walk down Sørøygata and you'll spot it on the left, or pop in after you've visited the Gjenreisningsmuseet – it's just round the back. They issue free town maps and have details of local excursions, easily the most popular of which is the boat-and-bus trip to Nordkapp (early June to mid-Aug 1 daily; 9hr; 815kr return). The excursion comprises a

Hurtigbåt boat ride to and from Honningsvåg, where a connecting bus ferries passengers to and from Nordkapp. The tourist office does not change money, but the **post office**, nearby on Parkgata, does (Mon–Fri 8.30am–5pm, Sat 10am–2pm).

Hammerfest's half-dozen **hotels** include the enjoyable *Quality Hammerfest Hotel*, Strandgata 2 (☎78 42 96 00, fax 78 42 96 60; ④, s/r ③). This occupies a prime spot, metres from the main quay and, although it's housed in a routine modern block, the cosy interior has a pleasant, slightly old-fashioned air, the rooms equipped with chunky wooden fittings that pre-date the chipboard craze of the 1960s. Equally appealing is the *Rica Hotel Hammerfest*, Sørøygata 15 (☎78 41 13 33, fax 78 41 13 11; ④, s/r ③), an attractive modern place with sea views that sits on a grassy knoll a couple of minutes' walk west of the main quay. More unusual is the *Turistua* (☎78 41 46 11, fax 78 41 45 55; ④; mid-May to Aug), a modern, all-timber one-storey complex on top of the Salen hill behind town. Built in the style of a mountain lodge, but with fancy Viking-style carving and turf roofs, the *Turistua* offers extremely comfortable, spick-and-span bedrooms, and there are great views over town from the café-restaurant. To get there by car, head east from the main quay along Strandgata and, after about 400m, watch for the signposted 2.5-kilometre-long turning on the right. This leads round a lake, Storvannet, which lies at the bottom of a steep-sided valley dotted with the houses of Hammerfest's one and only suburb. The road then climbs up the east side of Salen to approach *Turistua* from the rear. On the way up, you'll pass the tiny lakeshore *Storvannet Camping NAF* (☎78 41 10 10; June–Aug), with tent spaces and a few four-bed cabins (①), and then the unenticing *Hotell Skytterhuset*, Skytterveien 24 (☎78 41 15 11, fax 78 41 19 26; ③), in a large prefabricated block up on the hillside. Unless you're particularly energetic, you'll not want to walk to any of these places from the centre – either take a taxi or a local bus (infrequent) from the bus station.

For **food**, the *Rica Hotel Hammerfest* possesses the best **restaurant** in town, with sea views and seafood; main courses start from around 190kr. There are more views from the self-service *Turistua* café-restaurant, which serves up traditional Norwegian standbys at reasonable rates. More economical still is *Løkkes*, across from the Hurtigrute quay on Hamnegata, a well-tended, family-run café providing tasty meals. The liveliest **bar** in town is *Kaikanten*, Sjøgata 19.

Moving on from Hammerfest

Except on Saturdays, there's a once- or twice-daily **bus** from Hammerfest to Karasjok and Kirkenes. This passes through Skaidi, on the E6, where you change for the Nord-Norgeekspressen service to Honningsvåg and Nordkapp (late June to mid-Aug 1–2 Mon–Fri & Sun). Note, however, that not all the buses make the connection, so be sure to check at Hammerfest bus station before you set out. The other main bus service links Hammerfest with Alta, again once or twice daily except on Saturday. The **Hurtigrute** departs Hammerfest heading south at 1.15pm and takes ten-and-a-half hours to reach its next major port of call, Tromsø (around 540kr one way, cars around 320kr). Sailing north, the Hurtigrute departs at 7.45am and reaches Honningsvåg at 5pm (308kr, 300kr), where it stops for two hours, enough for special connecting buses to make the return trip to Nordkapp. From early June to mid-August, a **Hurtigbåt** leaves Hammerfest for Honningsvåg once daily; the journey time is two hours and the one-way fare 300kr. Again, connecting buses take passengers on to Nordkapp. Finally, Hammerfest has several **car rental** companies offering attractive short-term deals from around 600kr a day: try Hammerfest Bilsenter, Seilmakerveien 1 (☎78 41 40 66), or ask at the bus station, where the regional bus company, FFR (☎78 41 71 66), is an agent for Hertz. If, however, Nordkapp is your goal, comparable deals are available at Honningsvåg, 160km from Hammerfest.

Nordkapp

At the northern tip of Norway, the treeless and windswept island of **Magerøya** is mainly of interest to travellers as the location of the **Nordkapp** (North Cape), generally regarded as Europe's northernmost point – though in fact it isn't: that distinction belongs to the neighbouring headland of **Knivskjellodden**. Somehow, everyone seems to have conspired to ignore this simple latitudinal fact and now, while Nordkapp has become one of the most popular tourist destinations in the country, there isn't even a road to Knivskjellodden. Neither has the development of the Nordkapp as a tourist spot been without its critics, who argue that the large and lavish visitor centre – **Nordkapphallen** – is crass and grossly overpriced; their opponents simply point to the huge number of people who visit. Whatever, it's hard to imagine making the long trip to Magerøya without at least dropping by Nordkapp, and the island has other charms too, notably a bleak, rugged beauty that's readily seen from the E69 as it threads across the mountainous interior from Honningsvåg, on the south coast, to Nordkapp, a distance of 34km.

The obvious base for a visit to Nordkapp is the island's main settlement, **Honningsvåg**, a middling fishing village with a clutch of chain hotels. More appealing, however, is the tiny hamlet of **Kamøyvaer**, nestling beside a narrow fjord just off the E69 between Honningsvåg and Nordkapp, and with a couple of family-run guesthouses. Bear in mind also that Nordkapp is within easy striking distance of other places back on the mainland – certainly the picturesque fishing-station-cum-hotel at **Repvåg**, and maybe even Hammerfest (see p.295) and Alta (see p.288), respectively 180km and 211km away.

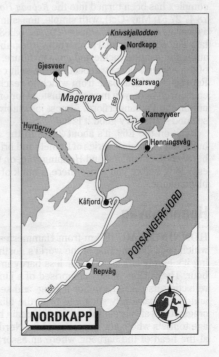

Arriving from Tromsø, Alta and Skaidi, the Nord-Norgeekspressen **bus** stops at both Honningsvåg and Nordkapp twice daily between Monday and Friday and once on Sunday, but only between late June and mid-August. The schedule is such that on weekdays, you can take the first bus to Nordkapp, spend a couple of hours there and then catch the second bus back. On

Saturdays, and at other times of the year, the best way of reaching Nordkapp is to rent a **car** or get a **taxi** in Honningsvåg, where special Nordkapp deals are commonplace. In winter, roughly from mid-October to mid-May, the road to Nordkapp is closed by snow, but the (fanatically) determined can get there on a guided **excursion by snowmobile**. You can also reach Honningsvåg (but not Nordkapp) by boat: there is a seasonal **Hurtigbåt** service from Hammerfest (see p.298) and the **Hurtigrute** arrives at either 5pm (northbound) or 6.45am (southbound) daily. In both cases, the boats are met by special buses, which cart passengers off to Nordkapp and back.

North from Skaidi to Repvåg and Magerøya island

At the **Skaidi** crossroads near Hammerfest, the E6 veers east to clip across a bleak plateau that brings it, in 23km, to the turning for Nordkapp. This road, the **E69**, scuttles north along the shore of the **Porsangerfjord**, a deep and wide inlet flanked by bare, low-lying hills whose stone has been fractured and made flaky by the biting cold of winter. Here and there, the shore is interrupted by massive monoliths, but for the most part the scenery is unusually tame and the shoreline accommodates a string of fishermens' houses – plus the wooden racks used to air-dry their catch. After 48km, the E69 zips past the byroad to **REPVÅG**, an old timber fishing station on a promontory just 2km off the main highway. A rare and particularly picturesque survivor from prewar days, the buildings here are painted red in the traditional manner and perch on stilts on the water's edge. The whole complex has been turned into the *Repvåg Hotell og Rorbusenter* (☎78 47 54 40, fax 78 47 27 51; May–Oct), with simple, unassuming rooms (③) in the main building, as well as a cluster of *rorbuer* (②); see p.268. It's a charming place to stay – solitary and scenic in equal proportions, the public areas of the hotel decked out with authentic nautical tackle and cosy furniture. Neither is tourism the only concern of the owners, as is evidenced by the split cod nailed to the outside walls to dry. Repvåg is an ideal base from which to reach the Nordkapp, though once you're ensconced here, you may settle instead for one of the hotel's boat and fishing trips out on the Porsangerfjord. Almost inevitably, the hotel **restaurant** specializes in seafood – and very good it is too.

Back on the E69, it's about 25km to the ambitious – and amazingly costly to build and maintain – series of tunnels and bridges (110kr toll) that span the straits between the mainland and Honningsvåg, on the island of **Magerøya**, which you'll espy long before you arrive there, a hunk of brown rock looking like an inverted blancmange.

Honningsvåg

HONNINGSVÅG, 160km from Hammerfest, is officially classified as a village, which robs it of the title of the world's northernmost town – hard luck considering it's barely any smaller nor less hardy in the face of adversity than its neighbour. The village, mostly comprised of a jumble of well-worn modern buildings, reflecting its role as a minor fishing- and sea-port, straggles along the seashore and is comparatively sheltered from the blizzards of winter by the surrounding crags. It has also accumulated several chain hotels catering primarily for the package tourists who come here, bound for Nordkapp. Honningsvåg is at its prettiest at the head of the harbour, where an assortment of timber warehouses, dating back to the days when the village was entirely reliant on fish, make an attractive ensemble. With wide eaves to protect against the snow, and draped with fishing nets and tackle, these good-looking buildings on crusty timber stilts jut out into the water, each with its own jetty where fishing smacks are roped in tight against the wind.

Practicalities

The village is strung out along its main drag, Storgata, for about one kilometre. Buses from the mainland, including the long-distance Nord-Norgeekspressen, pull into the **bus station** at the west end of Storgata. **Hurtigbåt** and **Hurtigrute** services dock at the adjacent jetty and are met by special Nordkapp excursion buses. The **tourist office** is here too (Mon–Fri 8.30am–4pm; ☎78 47 25 99).

All of Honningsvåg's **hotels** are along or near Storgata. Walking east from the bus station, it's a few metres to the first, the *Rica Hotel Honningsvåg* (☎78 47 23 33, fax 78 47 33 79; ④, s/r ③; mid-May to Aug), a routine modern block with nearly two hundred modern rooms. Its sister hotel, the all-year *Rica Bryggen* (☎78 47 28 88, fax 78 47 27 24; ④, s/r ③), occupies a similar but slightly smarter concrete high-rise about 500m to the east, down at the head of the harbour. Again, the rooms are bright, modern and comfortable, but hardly inspiring. More appealing is the adjacent *Best Western Honningsvåg Brygge Hotel* (☎78 47 64 60, fax 78 47 64 65; ④, s/r ③), a tasteful and intelligent conversion of a set of wooden warehouses perched on one of the old jetties. The rooms here are smart and cosy – and advance reservations are strongly advised. There is cheaper accommodation at *NAF Nordkapp Camping* (☎78 47 33 77, fax 78 47 11 77; May–Sept), a complex comprising a **campsite** (①) and **cabins** (②), located about 8km from Honningsvåg on the road to Nordkapp – and just 50m from the bus stop. Right next door is the sprawling, chalet-style *Rica Hotel Nordkapp* (☎78 47 33 88, fax 78 47 32 33; ④, s/r ③). For **food**, the *Best Western Honningsvåg Brygge* boasts the best **restaurant** by far – *Sjøhuset*, where the seafood is delicious, with main courses from 170kr; it's closed Mondays and Sunday evenings out of season.

Moving on, there are several ways to reach Nordkapp from Honningsvåg. The cheapest option is the bus (late June to mid-Aug Mon–Fri 2 daily, Sun 1 daily; 45min; 54kr each way), but if there's a group of you car rental can be a reasonably inexpensive option too. FFR, the local bus company, act as agents for Hertz and offer four-hour deals from around 600kr; enquire at the bus station. The taxi fare to Nordkapp, including an hour's waiting time after you get there, is 700kr return (one-way 400kr, and journeys after 10pm 800kr return); contact Nordkapp Taxisentral (☎78 47 22 34). In **winter**, North Cape Adventures (☎78 47 52 48) organize snowmobile trips to Nordkapp from the hamlet of Skarsvåg, 24km north of Honningsvåg; they also arrange transport from Honningsvåg to Skarsvåg. To stand a chance of seeing the northern lights, try to go when the weather's clear.

North from Honningsvåg to Nordkapp

The E69 winds out of Honningsvåg, staying close to the shore to reach, 9km on and just after the *Rica Hotel Nordkapp* (see above), the turning for **KAMØY-VAER**, a pretty little village tucked in tight between the sea and the hills just 2km from the main road. Here, right on the jetty, the old timber fishing station has been converted into the charming *Havstua* (☎78 47 51 50, fax 78 47 51 91; ②; mid-

May to mid-Sept), with twenty simple but smart and extraordinarily cosy rooms in a delightful spot. A few metres away, just back from the jetty, is the *Árran Nordkapp Gjestehus* (☎78 47 51 29, fax 78 47 51 56; ②; late May to Aug), not quite as appealing perhaps, but still a pleasant, family-run guesthouse in a brightly painted and well-tended home. The food at the *Havstua* is first-rate – but note that it's advisable to book dinner in advance.

Beyond the Kamøyvaer turning, the E69 twists a solitary course up through the hills to cross the high-tundra plateau, the mountains stretching away on either side. It's a fine run, with snow and ice lingering well into the summer and impressive views over the treeless and elemental Arctic terrain. From June to October this is pastureland for herds of reindeer, which graze right up to the road, paying little heed to the occasional vehicle unless they get very close. The Sami, who bring them here by boat, combine herding with souvenir selling, setting up camp at the roadside in full costume to peddle clothes, jewellery and antler sets, which some motorists are daft enough to attach to the front of their vehicles. About 29km from Honningsvåg, the E69 passes the start of the **hiking trail** that leads to the actual tip of Europe, the headland of **Knivskjellodden**, stretching about 1500m further north than its famous neighbour. The hike takes between two and three hours each way, but the terrain is too difficult and the climate too unpredictable for the inexperienced or poorly equipped hiker.

Nordkapp

Many visitors, when they finally reach the **Nordkapp**, feel desperately disappointed – it is, after all, only a cliff and, at 307m, it isn't even all that high. But for others there's something about this greyish-black hunk of slate, stuck at the end of a bare, wind-battered promontory, that exhilarates the senses. Some such feeling must have inspired the prehistoric Sami to establish a sacrificial site here, and the Nordkapp certainly stirred the romantic notions of earlier generations of tourists, often inspiring them to metaphysical ruminations. In 1802, the Italian naturalist Giuseppe Acerbi, author of *Travels through Sweden, Finland and Lapland*, exclaimed, "The northern sun, creeping at midnight along the horizon, and the immeasurable ocean in apparent contact with the skies, form the grand outlines in the sublime picture presented to the astonished spectator." Quite – though the seventeenth-century traveller Francesco Negri wasn't far behind: "Here, where the world comes to an end, my curiosity does as well, and now I can return home content."

Flights of fancy apart, North Cape was named by the English explorer Richard Chancellor in 1553, as he drifted along the Norwegian coast in an attempt to find the Northeast Passage from the Atlantic to the Pacific. He failed, but managed to reach the White Sea, from where he and his crew travelled overland to Moscow, thereby opening a new, northern trade route to Russia. The account of his exploits, published in the geographer Richard Hakluyt's *Navigations*, brought them to the attention of seamen across Europe, but it was to be another three hundred years before the Northeast Passage was finally negotiated by the Swede Nils Nordenskjøld in 1879. In the meantime, just a trickle of visitors ventured to the Nordkapp. Among them, in 1795, was the exiled Louis Philippe of Orleans (subsequently king of France), but it was the visit of the Norwegian king Oscar II in 1873 that opened the tourist floodgates.

Nowadays the lavish **Nordkapphallen** (North Cape Hall; daily: early April to late May & early Sept to early Oct 2–5pm; late May to early June noon–1am; early

June to early Aug 9am–2am; early Aug to late Aug 9am–midnight; late Aug to early Sept noon–5pm; 175kr including parking; ☎78 47 68 60), hewn out of the rock of the Cape, entertains thousands of visitors. Fronted by a statue of King Oscar II, the main building contains a restaurant, cafés, souvenir shops, a post office – where you get your letters specially stamped – and a cinema showing – you guessed it – films about the cape. There's a viewing area too, but there's not much to see except the sea – and, weather permitting, the midnight sun from May 11 to July 31. Having made it here, you can join the Royal North Cape Club at the information desk for a 150kr lifetime membership fee. Gluttons for financial punishment can stay here in **Suite 71° 10' 21"** – as in Nordkapp's latitude. At the top of the building's one and only tower, the suite offers a 270-degree view through its enormous windows and is a favourite with honeymooners, though quite why this should be considered a romantic spot is hard to discern. If it's booked in advance, the suite costs 3500kr per night, but the price tumbles to 1900kr if it's rented on spec.

A **tunnel** runs from the main building to the cliff face. It's flanked by a couple of little side-chambers, one of which is a chapel, where you can get married, and by a series of displays detailing past events and visitors, including the unlikely appearance of the King of Siam in 1907, who was so ill that he had to be carried up here on a stretcher. At the far end, the cavernous **Grotten Bar** offers caviar and champagne, long views out to sea through the massive glass wall and (of all things) a mock bird cliff. Alternatively, to escape the hurly-burly, you may decide to walk out onto the surrounding headland, though this is too bleak a spot to be much fun.

East to Kirkenes

East of Nordkapp the landscape is more of the same: a relentless expanse of barren plateaux and ocean. Occasionally the monotony is relieved by the sight of a determined village commanding sweeping views over the fjords that slice into the mainland, but generally there is little for the eyes of a tourist. Nor is there much to do in what are predominantly fishing and industrial settlements, and there are few tangible attractions beyond the sheer impossibility of the chill wilderness.

The **E6** weaves a circuitous course across this vast territory, travelling close to the Finnish border for much of its length. The only obvious target is the Sami centre of **Karasjok** (see p.294), 240km from Nordkapp, 220km from Hammerfest, and easily the region's most interesting town. Frankly, there's not much reason to push on further east unless you're intent on picking up the **Hurtigrute** as it bobs along the remote and spectacular shores of the Barents Sea. Among its several ports of call, the nearest to Karasjok is **Kirkenes**, a town that comes close to epitomizing remoteness, 320km to the east near the Russian frontier. Kirkenes is actually the northern terminus of the Hurtigrute, from where it begins its long journey back to Bergen. Taking the boat also means that you can avoid the long haul back the way you came – and by the time you reach Kirkenes you'll probably be heartily sick of the E6. The other shortcut is to **fly** to (or from) Kirkenes. SAS operates regular flights there from several Norwegian cities including Alta, Oslo and Tromsø.

Accommodation in this part of Norway is very thin on the ground, being confined to a handful of the larger communities. Campsites are more frequent and usually have cabins for rent, but they are mostly stuck in the middle of nowhere. Remarkably, the Norwegians keep the E6 open all year, though driving in the long polar darkness (late Nov to late Jan) is much too precarious for most. The main long-distance **bus** service links Alta with Kirkenes, via Skaidi (where you can change for Hammerfest, see p.295) and Karasjok, running three or four times weekly from March to December, and taking eleven hours to do it.

East from Nordkapp on the E6

Beyond the junction of the E69 Nordkapp road, the **E6** bangs along the western shore of the **Porsangerfjord**, a wide inlet that slowly shelves up into the sticky marshes and mud flats at its head. After about 45km, the road reaches the hamlet of **STABBURSNES**, which is home to the small but enjoyable **Stabbursnes Naturhus og Museum** (Stabbursnes Nature House and Museum; early June & mid- to late Aug daily 10am–5pm; mid-June to early Aug daily 9am–8pm; Sept–May Tues & Thurs noon–3pm, Wed noon–6pm; 25kr), which provides an overview of the region's flora and fauna. There are diagrams of the elaborate heat-exchanger in the reindeer's nose that helps stop the animal from freezing to death in winter, and blow-ups of the warble fly which torments it in summer. There are also examples of traditional Sami handicrafts and a good section on Finnmark's topography, examining, for example, how and why some of the region's rivers are slow and sluggish, whilst others have cut deep gashes in the landscape. The museum is on the eastern periphery of – and acts as an information centre for – the **Stabbursdalen Nasjonalpark**, a wedge-edged chunk of land that contains the world's most northerly pine forest covering the slopes of the Stabbursdalen river valley, which runs down from the Finnmarksvidda plateau to the Porsangerfjord. The lower end of the valley is broad and marshy, but beyond lie precipitous canyons and chasms – challenging terrain, with a couple of marked hiking trails. If that sounds too much like hard work, opt instead for the easy 2.8-kilometre stroll east from the museum along the thick gravel banks of the Stabbursdalen river where it trickles into the Porsangerfjord. It's an eerily chill landscape and there's a good chance of spotting several species of wetland bird in spring and summer: ducks, geese and waders like the lapwing, the curlew and the arctic knot are common. Indeed, these salt marshes and mud flats are such an important resting and feeding area for migratory wetland birds that they have been protected as the Stabbursnes **nature reserve**.

From Stabbursnes, it's about 15km south to **Lakselv**, a fishing port at the head of the Porsangerfjord, and another 70km to Karasjok (see p.294), the best place to spend the night. Pushing on, the E6 weaves its way northeast along the Finnish border to reach, 180km from Karasjok, **TANA BRU**, a Sami settlement around the suspension bridge over the River Tana, one of Europe's best salmon rivers, which sweeps down to the Tanafjord and the Barents Sea. Beyond the village, the E6 follows the southern shore of the **Varangerfjord**, a bleak, weather-beaten run, all colour and vegetation being confined to the opposite coastline with its scattered farms and painted fishing boats. As the road swings inland, it's something of a relief to arrive in Kirkenes (see p.306).

East from Nordkapp by Hurtigrute

Beyond Nordkapp, the **Hurtigrute** steers a fine route round the top of the country, nudging its way between tiny islets and craggy bluffs, and stopping at a series of remote fishing villages. Amongst them the prettiest is probably **Berlevåg**, which sits amid a landscape of eerie greenish-grey rock, splashes of colour in a land otherwise stripped by the elements.

From Berlevåg, it's five hours more to **VARDØ**, Norway's most easterly town, built on an island a couple of kilometres from the mainland, to which it's connected by an underwater tunnel. Like every other town in Finnmark, Vardø was savaged in World War II and subsequently rebuilt. Its present population is just 3000, and its main attraction, located about 500m to the west of the Hurtigrute quay, is the **Vardøhus Festning** (Vardø fortress; daily 8am–10pm; 10kr), a star-shaped fortress built in the 1730s at the behest of Christian VI. When this singularly unprepossessing monarch toured Finnmark he was greeted, according to one of his courtiers, with "expressions of abject flattery in atrocious verse." He had the fortress built to guard the northeastern approaches to the country, but it has never seen active service and its bastions and ramparts have survived pretty much intact. Scrambling around them is good fun, and Vardø's one and only **tree**, a rowan sheltering inside the fortress, is a reminder of what's missing from the flat and barren landscape outside. In fact, Vardø is the only Norwegian town within the arctic climatic zone, hardly much consolation when you can see your breath on a bright but perishingly cold June afternoon. Within the fortress walls, there is also a small **museum** (mid-June to mid-Aug Mon–Fri 9am–6pm, Sat & Sun 10.30am–6pm; mid-Aug to mid-June Mon–Fri 9am–3pm; 20kr), which contains a beam from an earlier medieval stronghold, signed by a succession of Norwegian kings. These far northern areas were long regarded by the church as the realm of the devil, and in the seventeenth century Vardø became the site of Norway's largest witch hunt. Over eighty women were burned alive here between 1621 and 1680, most meeting their deaths at the spot marked by a stake in the fortress grounds.

A short boat trip away from Vardø is Norway's most easterly point, the islet of **Hornøya**, a rocky **bird reserve** where thousands of sea birds nest every summer. To arrange excursions, contact either the **tourist office** (mid-June to Aug; ☎78 98 82 70), beside the fortress, or Vardø port authorities on the quayside.

Heading for Kirkenes, the **Hurtigrute** reaches Vardø at 5.15am and leaves just thirty minutes later; and southbound it docks here at 5pm and departs at 6pm – quite enough time to make it to the fortress and back. You can also stay the night and the best bet is the neat and trim *Vardo Hotell* (☎78 98 77 61, fax 78 98 83 97; ④, s/r ③), close to the Hurtigrute quay at Kaigata 8. Vardø is at the end of the E75, 76km from Vadsø (see below) and 125km from the E6. The only **bus** here is a local service from Vadsø (March–Dec 1–2 daily; 1hr 30min).

Vadsø and the Varangerfjord

VADSØ, a little under four hours by Hurtigrute (northbound only) from Vardø and 50km east of the E6, used to be purely Finnish-speaking, and even now half the population of 6000 claims Finnish origin. Its main claim to fame is as the administrative centre of Finnmark, which – to be blunt – isn't much to get excited about. Russian bombers and German soldiers between them destroyed almost all the old town during World War II; the result is the mundane modern town centre of today. There's really no reason to get off the boat, but there are a couple of minor sights to see if you do, beginning with the **Innvandrermonumentet** (the Immigration Monument), bang in the centre of town, which commemorates the many Finns who migrated here in the nineteenth century. Nearby, the

Esbensengården, an old patrician mansion dating from 1840, forms part of the municipal **museum** (late June to Aug Mon–Fri 9am–5.30pm, Sat & Sun 10am–2pm; Sept–May Mon–Fri 10am–2pm; 20kr), which focuses on the Finnish immigrants too.

After Vadsø, the Hurtigrute takes a couple of hours to cross the deep blue waters of the **Varangerfjord** on the last stage of its journey to Kirkenes. There's snow on the mainland here even in July, which makes for a picturesque chug across the fjord, the odd fishing boat the only sign of life.

Kirkenes and the Russian border

During World War II the mining town and ice-free port of **KIRKENES** suffered more bomb attacks than any other place in Europe apart from Malta. What was left was torched by the German army retreating in the face of liberating Soviet soldiers, who found 3500 local people hiding in the nearby iron-ore mines. The mines finally closed in 1996, threatening the future of the 6000-strong community, which is desperately trying to kindle trade with Russia to keep itself afloat.

Kirkenes is almost entirely modern, with long rows of uniform houses spreading out along the Barents Sea. If that sounds dull, it's not to slight the town, which makes the most of its inhospitable surroundings with some pleasant public gardens, lakes and residential areas – it's just that it seems an awful long way to come for not very much. That said, once you've finally got here it seems churlish to leave quickly, and it's certainly worth searching out the **Saviomuseet**, housed in the old library at Kongensgate 10b, about 300m south of the tourist office (Savio Museum; late June to late Aug daily 10am–6pm; Sept to mid-June Mon–Fri 10am–4pm; 20kr). This small museum displays the work of the local Sami artist, John Savio (1902–38), whose life was brief and tragic – orphaned at the age of three, he was ill from childhood and died in poverty aged 36, of tuberculosis. This lends poignancy to his woodcuts and paintings, which evoke a mood of loneliness through their depictions of the Sami way of life and the overbearing power of nature. The museum also hosts travelling contemporary art exhibitions, some of which are very good indeed. The other museum of note, the **Grenselandmuseet** (Grenseland Museum; daily: mid-June to mid-Aug 10am–6pm; mid-Aug to mid-June 10am–3pm; 30kr), is about 800m south of the tourist office, at the end of Solheimsveien beside one of the town's lakes. This mainly deals with the history of the region and its people, and includes a detailed account of the events of World War II, illustrated by some fascinating old photos.

Practicalities

Kirkenes is the northern terminus of the **Hurtigrute**, which arrives here at 11.15am and departs for Bergen at 1.45pm. It uses the quay just over 1km east of the town centre; a local bus shuttles between the two. Kirkenes **airport** is 13km west of town; there is a local bus to the centre but it's not a frequent service, so you may well have to take a taxi. Long-distance and local buses share the same **bus station** in the town centre at the west end of Kirkegata. From here, it's after 300m southeast to the **tourist office** (mid-June to late Aug Mon–Fri 8.30am–6pm, Sat & Sun 10am–6pm; Sept to mid-June Mon–Fri 8.30am–4pm; ☎78 99 25 44, fax 78 99 25 25), next to the *Rica Arctic Hotel*. They issue free town maps, have lots of ideas as to how to while away time here and provide general information about excursions to Russia.

CROSSING INTO RUSSIA

From Kirkenes, it's just 16km southeast along the E105 to **Storskog**, Norway's only official border crossing-point with Russia. You can take photographs of the frontier, provided you don't snap any Russian personnel or military installations – which rather limits the options as there's little else to see. This crossing is used by around 90,000 people a year, but it's not open for casual day-trippers; in any case, the only convenient settlement nearby is the ugly Russian mining town of **Nikel**, around 40km to the south, from where you can – extraordinarily enough – travel by train all the way to Vladivostok. Several Kirkenes travel agents organize day and weekend tours into Russia, the most worthwhile of which are those to the Arctic port of **Murmansk**. These trips include the price of a visa, and must therefore be booked at least ten days ahead; if you want to go at less notice, you will be charged more for an express visa service. Among the town's travel agents, Bennet BTI, in the centre at Dr. Wessels gate 15 (☎78 99 28 60), is as good as any. They have details of one-day excursions to Murmansk both by bus (around 900kr per person) and Hurtigbåt (1200kr). For longer trips, you can try to sort out a visa direct with the Russian embassy at home, or here at the Russisk Konsulat, Arbeidergata 6 (☎78 99 37 37). Otherwise, you'll have to be content with the reflection that if you have made it to Kirkenes and the border, you are further east than Istanbul and as far north as Alaska.

The town's best **hotel** is the *Rica Arctic*, a smart modern block in the centre at Kongensgate 1 (☎78 99 29 29, fax 78 99 11 59; ④, s/r ③). The similarly modern *Rica Hotel Kirkenes* occupies a glum-looking three-storey block about 700m south of the tourist office at Pasvikveien 63 (☎78 99 14 91, fax 78 99 13 56; ④, s/r ②). Inexpensive accommodation is provided at the **youth hostel** (☎ & fax 78 99 88 11; ①, dorm beds 130kr; late June to late Aug), in a plain prefabricated chalet some 6km out of town on the E6 in Hesseng; beds need to be booked in advance. Much more handy is *Barbara's Bed & Breakfast*, with just two cosy rooms and about 500m east of the tourist office at Henrik Lunds gate 13 (☎78 99 32 07; ①).

Around Kirkenes: Øvre Pasvik Nasjonalpark

Hidden away some 120km south of Kirkenes, where the borders of Norway, Finland and Russia intersect, is the ten-by-nine-kilometre parcel of wilderness that comprises the **Øvre Pasvik Nasjonalpark**, a western offshoot of the Siberian taiga. The park's sub-arctic pine forest covers a series of low-lying hills that make up about half the total area, and below lie swamps, marshes and lakes. Wolverines and bears live in the forest, and there are also traces of the prehistoric Komsa culture, notably the vague remains of pit-traps beside a lake, Ødevatn. The Kirkenes tourist office has details of guided tours, but you really have to be an expert wilderness hiker-cum-survivalist to delve into the park under your own steam. The absence of natural landmarks makes it easy to get lost, especially as there are no marked footpaths, nor any map that can be relied upon. If you're undeterred, and have your own vehicle (there's no public transport), then drive south from Kirkenes for about 100km along Highway 885 through the pine forests of the Pasvik River valley as far as **Vaggatem**. Turn off the main road here and follow the rough forest road south to a lake, Sortbrysttjern, from where a footpath takes you into the park at another lake, Ellenvatn. If you want to **stay**, the only option is Vaggatem's *Øvre Pasvik Café and Camping* (☎ & fax 78 99 55 30), which also has six cabins to rent (①).

Svalbard

The **Svalbard archipelago** is one of the most inhospitable places on earth. Six hundred and forty kilometres north of the Norwegian mainland (and just 1300km from the North Pole), two-thirds of its surface is covered by glaciers, the soil frozen to a depth of up to 500m. The archipelago was probably discovered in the twelfth century by Icelandic seamen, though it lay ignored until 1596 when the Dutch explorer Willem Barents named the main island, **Spitsbergen**, after its needle-like mountains. However, apart from a smattering of determined adventurers – from seventeenth-century whalers to eighteenth-century monks – few people ever lived here until, in 1899, rich coal deposits were discovered, the geo-

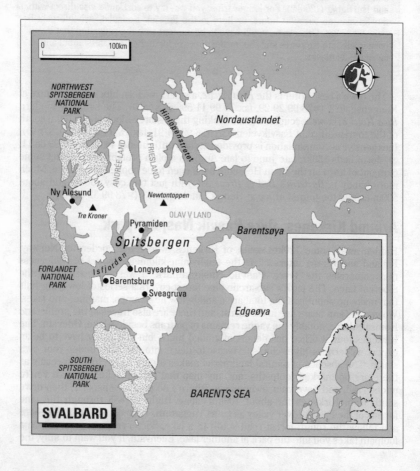

logical residue of a prehistoric tropical forest. The first coal mine was opened by an American seven years later and passed into Norwegian hands in 1916. Meanwhile, other countries, particularly Russia and Sweden, were getting into the coal-mining act, and when, in 1920, Norway's sovereignty was ratified by international treaty, it was on condition that those other countries who were operating mines could continue to do so. It was also agreed that the islands would be a demilitarized zone, which made them, incidentally, sitting ducks for a German squadron, which arrived here to bombard the Norwegian coal mines in World War II.

Despite the hardships, there are convincing reasons to make a trip to this oddly fertile land, covering around 63,000 square kilometres. Between late April and late August there's continuous daylight; the snow has virtually all melted by July, leaving the valleys covered in flowers; and there's an abundance of wildlife – over a hundred species of migratory birds, arctic foxes, polar bears and reindeer on land; and seals, walruses and even whales offshore. In winter, it's a different story: the polar night, during which the sun never rises above the horizon, lasts from late October to mid-February; and the record low temperature is a staggering -46°C – not counting the wind-chill factor.

Practicalities

The simplest way to reach Svalbard is to **fly** to the archipelago's airport at Longyearbyen on Spitsbergen. Braathens operates services there from a variety of Norwegian cities, including Oslo, Bergen, Trondheim, Tromsø, Alta and – nearest of all – Hammerfest, on average four or five times weekly. SAS also flies to Longyearbyen, but only from Oslo via Tromsø. The Tromsø–Longyearbyen flight takes an hour and forty minutes and a standard fare with Braathens is 2630kr return, though special deals are commonplace and reduce this to around 1500kr. However, before you book your flight, you'll need to reserve accommodation in Longyearbyen (see p.310) and – unless you're happy to be stuck in your lodgings – you'd be well-advised to book on any of the guided excursions that take your fancy too. There's a wide range on offer, from hiking and climbing through to kayaking, snowmobiling, glacier walking, helicopter rides, Zodiac boat trips, wildlife "safaris" and ice caving. In the first instance, further information is available from Info-Svalbard, Postboks 323, N-9170 Longyearbyen (☎79 02 23 03, fax 79 02 10 20, *www.svalbard.com/info*). A very good travel and tour agency is Svalbard Polar Travel, Postboks 540, N-9170 Longyearbyen (☎79 02 34 00, fax 79 02 34 01, *www.svalbard-polar.com*). You can, of course, take pot luck when you get there, but be warned that wilderness excursions are often fully booked weeks in advance.

Otherwise, there are **adventure cruises** to Svalbard (involving polar-bear spotting and the like). An all-inclusive, week-long boat trip from Tromsø costs in the region of 7000kr, whereas a three-day flight, excursion and accommodation deal from Tromsø to Longyearbyen will be in the region of 4500kr; contact the Tromsø tourist office (see p.282) for further details. It's also possible to go on a tour from Britain: Arctic Experience (see "Basics", p.7, for address and details) runs an excellent range of all-in camping and hiking tours to the archipelago in July and August; prices vary with the itinerary and length of stay, but a ten-day trip costs around £2000.

Finally, if you are determined to strike out into the wilderness **independently**, you first have to seek permission from, and log your itinerary with, the governor's office, Sysselmannen på Svalbard, in Longyearbyen (☎79 02 31 00) – and they will certainly expect you to carry a gun (because of the polar bears). Note also that there are no road connections between any of Svalbard's settlements, though there are about 45km of road around Longyearbyen. The only public transport, apart from the airport bus, is a pricey air service from Longyearbyen to minuscule Ny Ålesund.

Spitsbergen

The main island of the Svalbard archipelago, **Spitsbergen**, is the only one that is permanently inhabited; its three Norwegian and two Russian settlements have a total population of around 3000. With just over 1000 inhabitants, the only Norwegian settlement of any size is **LONGYEARBYEN**, which huddles on the narrow coastal plain below the mountains and beside the Isfjorden, roughly in the middle of the island. It was founded in 1906, when John M. Longyear, an American mine owner, established the Arctic Coal Company here, the first to begin mining on the archipelago. Longyearbyen is now well equipped with services, including shops, cafés, a cinema, post office, bank, swimming pool, several tour companies, a campsite, a couple of guest houses and three hotels – but note that advance reservations are essential for all accommodation.

There are **four other settlements** on Spitsbergen – two Norwegian and two Russian. The former consist of Ny Ålesund (20 inhabitants) to the northwest of Longyearbyen and Sveagruva (20) to the southeast; the latter are Barentsburg (950) and Pyramiden (650) to the west and north respectively. However, there are no road connections. If you do make it to the Russian settlements, you'll find they accept Norwegian kroner.

Longyearbyen practicalities

The **airport** is 5km west of town and both Braathens (☎79 02 19 22) and SAS (☎79 02 16 50) have offices there. An airport bus, the Flybussen (March–Sept; 35kr), runs from the airport into town, or you can take a taxi (60kr). Longyearbyen straggles inland from the Isfjorden for a couple of kilometres. The few buildings that pass for the town centre is where you'll find the all-year **Info-Svalbard tourist office** (☎79 02 23 03). This is equipped with a full range of leaflets on the archipelago and has information on a wide range of trips – from dog-sledging and ice-caving to snowmobile excursions and glacier walks.

In terms of **accommodation**, the unassuming *Svalbard Kro & Hotell* (☎79 02 24 50; fax 79 02 10 05; ④; March–Sept) is right in the centre near the tourist office. They also run *Nybyen Gjestehus* (☎79 02 24 50; fax 79 02 10 05; ③; mid-Feb to Sept), which offers simple but adequate rooms in refurbished miners' quarters from the 1940s; this is located almost 2km from the tourist office on the southern edge of town. The plushest hotel is the surprisingly swish, modern and central *Svalbard Polar Hotel* (☎79 02 35 00, fax 79 02 35 01; ⑤). Another option is the spick-and-span *Funken Hotell* (☎79 02 24 50, fax 79 02 10 05; ④), up the hill about 1km south of the tourist office. Finally, *Longyearbyen Camping* (☎79 02 24 50, fax 79 02 10 05; late June to Aug) charges just 65kr per person per night. Obviously, you must come fully equipped to survive what can be, at any time of the year, a cruel climate.

The *Svalbard Polar Hotel* boasts the best **restaurant** in town, but it is expensive. Other, cheaper choices include the straightforward *Café Busen*, near the tourist office, and, across the river at the southern edge of town, the *Huset – Longyearbyen Grill og Restaurant* (☎79 02 25 00), which specializes in Arctic dishes and is attached to a bar and the cinema. For **drinking**, the liveliest hangout is the *Funken Bar*, part of the hotel from which it takes its name.

travel details

Buses

Alta to: Hammerfest (1–2 daily except Sat; 3hr); Honningsvåg (late June to mid-Aug 1–2 daily except Sat; 5hr); Karasjok (1 daily except Sat & Sun; 5hr); Kautokeino (1–2 daily except Sat; 2hr 30min); Kirkenes (1 daily except Sat & Sun; 9hr 45min); Skaidi (1–2 daily except Sat; 1hr 40min); Tromsø (April to late Oct 1–2 daily; 7hr).

Hammerfest to: Alta (1–2 daily except Sat; 3hr); Skaidi (1–2 daily except Sat; 1hr 15min).

Honningsvåg to: Alta (late June to mid-Aug 1–2 daily except Sat; 5hr); Lakselv (March to late Oct 1–3 daily except Sat; 4hr); Nordkapp (late June to mid-Aug 2 daily except Sat; 50min).

Karasjok to: Hammerfest (1 daily except Sat; 2hr 30min); Kirkenes (1 daily except Sun; 5hr 30min).

Kautokeino to: Alta (1–2 daily except Sat; 2hr 30min).

Kirkenes to: Alta (5 weekly; 11hr); Hammerfest (1 daily except Sun; 12hr 30min); Karasjok (1 daily except Sun; 5hr 30min); Vadsø (1–2 daily; 3hr 30min).

Lakselv to: Alta (1–2 daily except Sat; 3hr 30min); Hammerfest (1–2 daily except Sat; 3hr); Honningsvåg (March to late Oct 1–3 daily except Sat; 4hr); Kirkenes (1–2 daily except Sat; 7hr).

Skaidi to: Hammerfest (1–2 daily except Sat; 1hr 15min).

Tromsø to: Alta (April to late Oct 1–2 daily; 7hr); Narvik (2 daily; 7hr); Nordkapp (late June to mid-Aug 1 daily except Sat; 14hr); Skaidi (late June to mid-Aug 1 daily except Sat; 9hr).

Vadsø to: Vardo (1 daily; 1hr 30min).

Nord-Norgeekspressen

The Nord-Norgeekspressen (North Norway Express Bus) runs between Nordkapp and Bodø via Alta, Tromsø, Narvik and Fauske, with a change of vehicle in Alta, Tromsø and Narvik. Heading south from Nordkapp for Bodø, you'll need to stay overnight in Tromsø. See also "Travel Details" in the Trondheim to the Lofotens chapter.

Hurtigrute

Northbound departures: from Tromsø at 6.30pm; Hammerfest at 7.45am; Honningsvåg at 5pm; Båtsfjord at 2.30am; Vardø at 5.45am; Vadsø at 9.30am; terminates at Kirkenes at 11.15am. Tromsø–Kirkenes journey time is 41hr.

Southbound departures: from Kirkenes at 1.45pm; Vardø at 6pm; (no Tromsø-bound stop at Vadsø); Båtsfjord at 9.15pm; Honningsvåg at 6.45am; Hammerfest at 1.15pm; Tromsø at 1.30am.

Hurtigbåt

Hammerfest to: Honningsvåg (early June to early Aug 1 daily; 3hr).

Tromsø to: Harstad (1 daily; 2hr 30min).

HISTORY

Despite its low profile these days, Norway has a fascinating history. Explorers and conquerors of northern Europe and its islands, its people roamed the Atlantic as far as the North American mainland. Though at first an independent state, from the fourteenth century Norway came under the sway of first Denmark and then Sweden. Independent again from 1905, Norway was propelled into World War II by the Nazi invasion of 1940, an act of aggression that transformed the Norwegians' attitude to the outside world. Gone was the old insular neutrality, replaced by a liberal internationalism exemplified by Norway's leading role in the environmental movement.

EARLY CIVILIZATIONS

The earliest signs of human habitation in Norway date from the end of the last Ice Age, around 10,000 BC. In Finnmark – the far north of the territory – the **Komsa** culture was reliant upon seal-fishing, whereas the peoples of the **Fosna** culture, further south near present-day Kristiansund, hunted seals and reindeer. Both these societies were essentially static, dependent upon flint and bone implements. At Alta, the Komsa people left behind hundreds of **rock carvings and drawings**, naturalistic representations of their way of life dating from the seventh to the third millennia BC.

As the edges of the icecap retreated from the western coastline, so new migrants slowly filtered north. These new peoples, of the **Nøstvet-økser** culture, were also hunters and fishers, but they were able to manufacture stone axes, examples of which were first unearthed at Nøstvet, near Oslo. Beginning around 2700 BC, immigrants from the east, principally the semi-nomadic **Boat Axe** and **Battle-Axe peoples** – so named because of the distinctive shape of their stone weapons/tools – introduced animal husbandry and agriculture. The new arrivals did not, however, overwhelm their predecessors; the two groups coexisted, each picking up hints from the other – a reflection of the harsh infertility of the land.

These late Stone Age cultures flourished at a time when other, more southerly countries were already using metal. Norway was poor and had little to trade, but the Danes and Swedes exchanged amber for copper and tin from the bronze-making countries of central Europe. A fraction of the imported bronze subsequently passed into Norway, mostly to the Battle-Axe people, who appear to have had a comparatively prosperous aristocracy. This was the beginning of the Norwegian **Bronze Age** (1500–500 BC), which also saw a change in burial customs. In the Stone Age, the Battle-Axe peoples had dug shallow earth graves, but these were now supplanted by **burial mounds** enclosing coffins in which supplies were placed in readiness for the afterlife. Building the mounds must have involved a substantial amount of effort, suggesting the existence of powerful chieftains who could organise the work, and who may also have been priests. Rock carvings became prevalent in southern Norway during this period too – images of men ploughing with oxen, riding horses, carrying arms and using boats to navigate the coastal water passages – workaday scenes supplemented by drawings of religious or symbolic significance. In general terms, however, the Bronze Age was characterized more by the development of agriculture than by the use of metal, and stone implements remained the norm.

Around 500 BC Norway was affected by two adverse changes: the climate deteriorated, and trade relations with the Mediterranean were disrupted by the westward movement of the Celts across central Europe. The former encouraged the development of settled, communal farming in an attempt to improve winter shelter and storage, with each clan resident in a large stone, turf and timber dwelling; the latter cut the supply of tin and copper and subsequently isolated Norway from the early **Iron Age**. The country's isolation continued through much of the **Classical period**. The Greek geographer Pytheas of Marseilles, who went far enough north to note the short summer nights, probably visited southern Norway, but the regions beyond remained the subject of vague speculation. Pliny the Elder mentions "Nerigon" as the great island south of the legendary "Ultima Thule", the outermost region of the earth, while Tacitus, in his *Germania*, demonstrated knowledge only of the Danes and Swedes.

The expansion of the Roman Empire in the first and second centuries AD revived Norway's trading links with the Mediterranean. Evidence of these renewed contacts is provided across Scandinavia by **runes**, carved inscriptions dating from around 200 AD, whose 24-letter alphabet – the *futhark* – was clearly influenced by Greek and Latin capitals. Initially, runes were seen as having magical powers – to gain their knowledge, the god Odin hung for nine nights on *Yggdrasill*, the tree of life, with a spear in his side (see p.331) – but gradually their usage became more prosaic. Of the eight hundred or so rocks bearing runic inscriptions across southern Norway, most commemorate events and individuals: mothers and fathers, sons and slain comrades.

The renewal of trade with the Mediterranean also spread the use of **iron**. Norway's agriculture was transformed by the use of iron tools, and the pace of change accelerated in the fifth century AD, when the Norwegians learnt how to smelt the brown iron ore, limonite, that lay in their bogs and lakes – hence its common name, **bog-iron**. Clearing the forests with iron axes was relatively easy and, with more land available, the pattern of settlement became less concentrated. Family homesteads leapfrogged up the valleys, and a class of wealthy farmers emerged, their prosperity based on fields and flocks. Above them in the pecking order were local **chieftains**, the nature of whose authority varied considerably. Inland, the chieftains' power was based on landed wealth and constrained by feudal responsibilities, whereas the coastal lords, who had often accumulated influence from trade, piracy, and military prowess, were less encumbered. Like the farmers, these

seafarers had also benefited from the iron axe, which made boat-building much easier. An early seventh-century ship found at Kvalsund, near Hammerfest, was eighteen metres long, its skilfully crafted oak hull equipped with a high prow and stern, prefiguring the vessels of the Vikings.

By the middle of the eighth century, Norway had become a country of small, independent **kingships**, its geography impeding the development of any central authority. In the event, it was the **Yngling** chieftains of southeast Norway who attempted to assert some sort of wider control. Their first leaders are listed in the **Ynglinga Tal**, a paean compiled by the Norwegian *skald* (court poet) Thjodolf in the ninth century. According to Thjodolf, early royal life had its ups and downs: king Domaldi was sacrificed to ensure the fertility of his land; Dag was killed by an accidental blow from a pitchfork; and Fjolnir got up in the night to take a leak, fell into a vat of mead and drowned.

THE VIKINGS

Overpopulation, clan discord and the lure of commerce all contributed to the sudden explosion that launched the **Vikings** (from the Norse word *vik*, meaning creek, and -*ing*, frequenter of), upon an unsuspecting Europe in the ninth century. The patterns of attack and eventual settlement were dictated by the geographical position of the various Scandinavian countries. The Swedish Vikings turned eastwards, the Danes headed south and southwest, while the Norwegians sailed west, their longships landing on the Hebrides, Shetland, Orkney, the Scottish mainland and western Ireland. The Pictish population were not able to offer much resistance and the islands were quickly overrun, becoming, together with the Isle of Man, the nucleus of a new Norse kingdom which provided a base for further attacks on Scotland and Ireland.

The Norwegians founded Dublin in 836, and from Ireland turned their attention eastward to northern Britain. Elsewhere, Norwegian Vikings settled the Faroe Islands and Iceland, and even raided as far south as Moorish Spain, attacking Seville in 844. The raiders soon became settlers, sometimes colonizing the entire area – as in Iceland and the Faroes – but mostly intermingling with the local population. The speed of their assimilation is, in fact, one of the Vikings' most striking features: William the Conqueror

(1027–87) was the epitome of the Norman baron, yet he was also the descendant of Rollo, the Viking warrior whose army had overrun Normandy just a century before.

The whole of Norway felt the stimulating effects of the Viking expeditions. The economy was boosted by the spoils of war, the standard of living rose, and the population grew in physical stature as health and nutrition improved. Farmland was no longer in such short supply; cereal and dairy farming were extended into new areas in eastern Norway; new vegetables, such as cabbages and turnips, were introduced from Britain; and farming methods were improved by overseas contact – the Celts, for instance, taught the Norwegians how to thresh grain with flails.

The Vikings also rigorously exploited the hunting and fishing clans that roamed the far north of Norway. Detailed information on Finnmark in the late ninth century comes from a surprising source: a Norwegian chieftain named **Ottar** who dwelt, so he claimed, "northernmost of all Norsemen", and who visited Alfred the Great's court in about 890. Ottar regaled Alfred with tales of his native land, which the king promptly incorporated within his translation of a fifth-century Latin text, the *History of the World* by Paulus Orosius. Ottar, who boasted that he owed political allegiance to no one, had a few cows, sheep and pigs and a tiny slice of arable land, which he ploughed with horses, but his real wealth came from other sources. Fishing, whaling and walrus hunting provided both food for his retinue and exportable commodities. He also possessed a herd of six hundred tame reindeer – plus six decoy animals used to snare wild reindeer – and extracted a heavy tribute from the Sami (see box, pp.292–293), payable in furs and hides.

The Vikings' brand of **paganism** (see p.331), with its wayward, unscrupulous deities, underpinned their inclination to vendettas and clan warfare. Nevertheless, institutions slowly developed which helped regulate the blood-letting. Western Norway adopted the Germanic *wergeld* system of cash-for-injury compensation; every free man was entitled to attend the local *Ting* or parliament, while a regional *Lagting* made laws and settled disputes. Justice was class-based, however, with society divided into three main categories: the lord, the freeman, and the thrall or slave, who was worth about eight cows. The Vikings were industrious slavers, opening slave markets wherever they went, sending thousands to work on their land back home and supplying the needs of other buyers.

Viking **decorative art** was also pan-Scandinavian, with the most distinguished work being the elaborate and often grotesque animal motifs that adorned their ships, sledges, buildings and furniture. This craftsmanship is seen at its best in the **ship burials** of Oseberg and Gokstad, both on display in Oslo's Viking Ships Museum (p.88). The Oseberg ship is thought to be the burial ship of Åse, wife of the early ninth-century Yngling king, Gudrød Storlatnes. She was also the mother of Halfdan the Black, whose body had a very different fate from her own – it was chopped up, and the bits were buried across his kingdom to ensure the fertility of the land.

NORWAY'S FIRST KINGS

It was from the Ynglings of Vestfold that Norway's first widely recognized king, **Harald Hårfagri** (Fair-Hair), claimed descent. Shortly before 900 (the exact date is unclear), Harald won a decisive victory at Hafrsfjord (near modern Stavanger), which gave him control of the coastal region as far north as Trøndelag. It sparked an exodus of minor rulers, most of whom left to settle in Iceland. The thirteenth-century *Laxdaela Saga* records the departure of one such family, the Ketils of Romsdal, who would not be "forced to become Harald's vassals or be denied compensation for fallen kinsmen". Harald's long rule was based on personal pledges of fealty; with the notable exception of the regional *Lagtings*, there were no institutions to sustain it, and when he died his kingdom broke up into its component parts. Harald did, however, leave a less tangible but extremely important legacy: from now on every ambitious chieftain was not content to be a local lord, but strove to be ruler of a kingdom stretching from the Trøndelag to Vestfold.

Harald's son, **Erik Bloodaxe**, struggled to hold his father's kingdom together, but was outmanoeuvred by his youngest brother, **Håkon the Good**, who secured the allegiance of the major chieftains before returning home from England where he had been raised (and Christianized) at the court of King Athelstan of Wessex. Erik fled to Northumbria to become king of Viking York. Initially, Håkon was well-received, and, although his attempts to introduce Christianity failed, he did carry out a number of far-ranging reforms. He established a common legal code for the whole of Vestfold and Trøndelag, and also introduced the system of *Leidangr*, the division of the coastal districts into areas, each of which was responsible for maintaining and manning a warship.

However, Håkon's rule was punctuated by struggles against Erik's heirs. With the backing of the Danish king Harald Bluetooth, they defeated and killed Håkon in battle in 960. Håkon's kingdom then passed to one of Erik's sons, **Harald Greycloak Eriksson**. This forceful man set about extending his territories with gusto. Indeed, he was, in Bluetooth's opinion, much too successful; keen to keep Norway within his sphere of influence, the Dane slaughtered Greycloak on the battlefield in 970 and replaced him with a Danish appointee, **Håkon Sigurdsson**, the last genuine heathen to rule Norway. But again Bluetooth seems to have got more than he bargained for. Sigurdsson based himself in Trøndelag, a decent distance from his overlord, and it's believed he soon refused to recognize Danish suzerainty: certainly the Christian Bluetooth would not have sanctioned Sigurdsson's restitution of pagan sacred sites.

In 995 **Olav Tryggvason**, another Viking chieftain who had been baptized in England, sailed to Norway to challenge Sigurdsson, who was conveniently dispatched by one of his own servants before the fighting started. Olav quickly asserted control over the Trøndelag and parts of southern and western Norway. He founded Nidaros (now Trondheim), from where he launched a sustained and brutal campaign against the pagan Tronds, which secured him the adulation of later saga writers. Despite his evangelical zeal, Olav's religious beliefs are something of an enigma: he had pagan magicians in his personal retinue, and was so good at predicting the future from bird bones that he was called *Craccaben* (Crowbone). Olav's real problem remained the enmity of the Danish-controlled southeastern regions of Norway, and of Bluetooth's son Svein Forkbeard, who regarded Norway as his rightful inheritance. In alliance with the Swedish king, Svein defeated Olav at a sea battle in the Skagerrak in 1000, and Norway was divided up among the victors.

MORE SETTLEMENTS ABROAD

Meanwhile, Norwegian settlers were laying the foundations of independent Norse communities in the Faroes and Iceland, where they established a parliament, the *Alting*, in 930. The Norwegian Vikings went on to make further discoveries: Erik the Red, exiled from Norway and then banished from Iceland for three years for murder, set out in 985 with 25 ships, fourteen of which arrived in **Greenland**. The new colony prospered, and by the start of the eleventh century there were about three thousand settlers. This created a shortage of good farmland, making another push west inevitable. The two **Vinland sagas** (see p.338) provide the only surviving account of these further explorations, recounting the exploits of Leif Eriksson the Lucky, who founded a colony he called Vinland on the shores of **North America** around 1000 AD.

Norse settlers continued to secure resources from the Vinland region for the next few decades, until they were driven out by the native population. The Viking site discovered at L'Anse aux Meadows in Newfoundland may have been either Vinland itself or the result of one of these foragings. The Greenland colonists carried on collecting timber from Labrador up until the fourteenth century, when the climate is known to have cooled and deteriorated, making the sea trip too dangerous. Attacks by the Inuit and the difficulties of maintaining trading links with Norway then took their toll on the main Greenland colonies. All contact with the outside world was lost in around 1410, and the last of the half-starved, disease-ridden survivors died out towards the end of the fifteenth century, just as Christopher Columbus was eyeing up his "New World".

THE ARRIVAL OF CHRISTIANITY

Olav Haraldsson sailed for Norway from England in 1015, taking advantage of the problems caused by the death of the Danish king, Svein Forkbeard. Svein's son and successor Knut – King Canute of England – was preoccupied with other problems and wasn't able to muster much support from his Norwegian earls, so Olav soon gained recognition as king of much of Norway. Significantly, although Olav was an experienced Viking, he arrived by merchant ship with just a hundred men, a clear sign of the

passing of the Viking heyday. Across Europe, the emergence of feudal states had curtailed the Viking freebooters, and within Norway power was shifting from the old warrior aristocracy to the yeoman-farmers of the interior. Their support, while it lasted, underpinned Olav's success.
. For twelve years Olav ruled in peace, founding Norway's first national government. His authority was based on the regional *Tings* – consultative and broadly democratic bodies which administered local law – and on his willingness to deliver justice without fear or favour. The king's most enduring achievement, however, was to make Norway **Christian**. Olav had been converted during his days as a Viking, and vigorously imposed his new faith on his countrymen. Wherever necessary he executed persistent heathens and destroyed their sacred places. The dominant position of the new religion was ensured by the foundation of the Norwegian church, whose first priests were consecrated in Bremen.

It was foreign policy rather than pagan enmity that brought about Olav's downfall. In scheming with the Swedish king against Knut, who had now consolidated his position as king of Denmark and England, Olav provoked a Danish invasion, whose course was smoothed by massive bribes to Norwegian chieftains and landowners. The chieftains, who had suffered at the hands of Olav, not unexpectedly helped Knut, and even the yeomen failed to rally to Olav's cause – possibly alienated by his imperious ways. In 1028, Olav was forced to flee, first to Sweden and then to Russia, while Knut's young son Svein and his mother, the English Queen Aelfgifu, took the Norwegian crown. Two years later, Olav made a sensational return at the head of a scratch army, only to be defeated and killed by an alliance of wealthy landowners and chieftains at **Stiklestad**, the first major Norwegian land battle.

The petty chieftains and yeomen-farmers who had opposed Olav soon fell out with their new king: Svein had no intention of relaxing the royal grip and his rule was at least as arbitrary as that of his predecessor. Their subsequent rebellion seems also to have had nationalistic undertones – many Norwegians had no wish to be ruled by a Dane. Svein fled the country, and Olav's old enemies popped over to Sweden to bring back Olav's young son, **Magnus**, who became king in 1035.

The chastening experience of Svein's short rule transformed the popular memory of Olav. With surprising speed, he came to be regarded as an heroic champion, and there was talk of miracles brought about by the dead king's body. The Norwegian church, looking for a local saint to enhance its position, fostered the legends and had Olav canonized. The remains of **St Olav** were then reinterred ceremoniously at Nidaros, today's Trondheim, where the miracles increased in scope, hastening the conversion of what remained of heathen Norway.

HARALD HARDRÅDA

On Magnus' death in 1047, **Harald Hardråda** (Olav's half-brother) became king, and soon consolidated his grip on the whole of Norway from the Trøndelag to the Oslofjord. Hardråda was the last of the Viking heroes. A giant of a man, reputedly almost seven feet tall with a sweeping moustache and eccentric eyebrows, Hardråda had fought alongside Olav at Stiklestad. After the battle, he and his men had fled east, fighting as mercenaries in Russia and ultimately Byzantium, where Hardråda was appointed the commander of the Varangians, the Norse bodyguard of the Byzantine Emperor.

Back in Norway, Harald dominated the country by force of arms for over twenty years, earning the soubriquet "Hardråda" (the Hard) for his ruthless treatment of his enemies, many of whom he made "kiss the thin lips of the axe" as the saga writers put it. Neither was Hardråda satisfied with being king of just Norway. At first he tried to batter Denmark into submission through regular raiding, but the stratagem failed and he finally made peace with the Danish king, Svein, in 1064.

When the death of Edward the Confessor presented Harald with an opportunity to press his claim to the English throne, he sailed on England, landing near York with a massive fleet in 1066. Just outside the city, at Stamford Bridge, his army was surprised by Harold Godwinson, the new Saxon king of England. It was a battle of crucial importance, and one that gave rise to all sorts of legends, penned by both Norse and English writers. The two kings are supposed to have eyed each other up like prize-fighters, with Hardråda proclaiming his rival "a small king that, but one that stood well in his stirrups", and Harold promising the Norwegian "seven feet of English ground, or as much more as he is taller than other men". Hardråda was defeated and killed, and the threat of a Norwegian conquest of England had – though no one realized it at the time – gone forever. (The victory did not, however, do much for Godwinson, whose weakened army trudged back south to be defeated by William of Normandy at the Battle of Hastings.)

MEDIEVAL CONSOLIDATION

Harald's son, **Olav Kyrre** (the Peaceful) – who had been spared his life after Stamford Bridge on the promise never to attack England again – went on to reign as king of Norway for the next 25 years. Peace engendered economic prosperity, and treaties with Denmark ensured Norwegian independence. Three native bishoprics were established, and cathedrals built at Nidaros, Bergen and Oslo. It's from this period, too, that Norway's surviving **stave churches** date: wooden structures resembling an upturned keel, they were lavishly decorated with dragon heads and scenes from Norse mythology, proof that the traditions of the pagan world were slow to disappear. (For more on stave churches see p.137.)

The first decades of the twelfth century witnessed the further consolidation of Norway's position as an independent power, despite internal disorder as the descendants of Olav Kyrre competed for influence. Civil war ceased only when **Håkon IV** took the throne in 1240, ushering in what is often called "The Period of Greatness". Secure at home, Hakon strengthened the Norwegian hold on the Faroe and Shetland islands, and in 1262 both Iceland and Greenland accepted Norwegian sovereignty. When his claim to the Hebrides was disputed by Alexander III of Scotland, Håkon assembled an intimidatory fleet, but died in 1263 in the Orkneys. Three years later the Hebrides and the Isle of Man (always the weakest links in the Norwegian empire) were sold to the Scottish crown by Håkon's successor, **Magnus the Lawmender** (1238–80).

Under Magnus, Norway prospered. Law and order were maintained, trade flourished and, in striking contrast to the days of Hardråda, the king's court even followed a code of etiquette compiled in what became known as the *Konungs skuggsja* or "King's Mirror". Neither was the power of the monarchy threatened by feudal barons as elsewhere in thirteenth-centu-

ry Europe. Given Norway's difficult geography, farms were too scattered to be incorporated within a feudal system. As a consequence, the nobility had little surplus wealth to build castles and were drawn into the centralized administration of the state, a process that only happened several centuries later in the rest of western Europe. Norwegian **Gothic art** reached its full maturity in this period, as construction began on the nave at Nidaros Cathedral and on Håkon's Hall in Bergen.

Magnus was succeeded by his sons, first the undistinguished Erik and then **Håkon V** (1270–1319), the last of medieval Norway's talented kings. Håkon continued the policy of his predecessors, making further improvements to central government and asserting royal control of Finnmark through the construction of a fortress at Vardø. His achievements, however, were soon to be swept away along with the independence of Norway itself.

LOSS OF SOVEREIGNTY

Norway's independence was threatened from two quarters. With strongholds in Bergen and Oslo, the **Hanseatic League** and its merchants had steadily increased their influence, exerting a monopoly on imports and controlling inland trade. The power of their international trading links was felt in Norway as the royal household grew increasingly dependent on the taxes the merchants paid. The second threat was **dynastic**. When Håkon died in 1319 he left no male heir and was succeeded by his grandson, the three-year-old son of a Swedish duke. The boy, Magnus Eriksson, was elected Swedish king two months later, marking the virtual end of Norway as an independent country until 1905.

Magnus assumed full power over both countries in 1332, but his reign was a difficult one. When the Norwegian nobility rebelled he agreed that the monarchy should again be split: his three-year-old son, Håkon, would become Norwegian king when he came of age, while the Swedes agreed to elect his eldest son Erik to the Swedish throne. It was then, in 1349, that the **Black Death** struck, spreading quickly along the coast and up the valleys, killing almost two-thirds of the Norwegian population. It was a catastrophe of huge proportions, its effects compounded by the way the country's agriculture was structured. Animal husbandry was easily the most important part of

Norwegian farming, and harvesting and drying winter fodder was labour-intensive. Without sufficient fodder, the animals died in their hundreds and famine conditions prevailed for several generations.

Many farms were abandoned and, deprived of their rents, the petty chieftains who had once dominated rural Norway were almost entirely swept away as a class. The vacuum was filled by royal officials, the *syslemenn*, each of whom exercised control over a large chunk of territory on behalf of a Royal Council. The collapse of local governance was compounded by dynastic toing and froing. In 1380, Håkon died and Norway passed into Danish control with Olav, the son of Håkon and the Danish princess Margaret, becoming ruler of the two kingdoms. It was a union that was to last 400 years.

THE KALMAR UNION

Despite Olav's early death in 1387, the resourceful Margaret persevered with the union. Proclaimed regent by both the Danish and (what remained of the) Norwegian nobility, she engineered a treaty with the Swedish nobles that not only recognized her as regent of Sweden but also agreed to accept any king she should nominate. Her chosen heir, **Erik of Pomerania**, was foisted on the Norwegians in 1389. When he reached the age of majority in 1397, Margaret organized a grand coronation with Erik crowned king of all three countries at Kalmar in Sweden – hence the **Kalmar Union**.

After Margaret's death in 1412, all power was concentrated in Denmark. In Norway, foreigners were preferred in both state and church, and the country became impoverished through paying for Erik's various wars. Incompetent and brutal in equal measure, Erik managed to get himself deposed in all three countries at the same time, ending his days as a Baltic pirate.

UNION WITH DENMARK

In 1439, Sweden left the union, and in 1450, a Danish count, Christian of Oldenburg, was crowned king of Norway and Denmark. Thereafter, Norway simply ceased to take any meaningful part in Scandinavian affairs. Successive monarchs continued to appoint foreigners to important positions, appropriating Norwegian funds for Danish purposes and even mortgaging Orkney and Shetland in 1469 to the

Scots. Literature languished as the **Old Norse** language was displaced as the official tongue by Danish – and indeed Old Norse soon came to be regarded as the language of the ignorant and inconsequential. Only the Norwegian church retained any power.

It looked briefly as if Norway might break the Danish stranglehold. In 1501–2, a Swedish-Norwegian nobleman, **Knut Alvsson**, crossed the border and soon overran southern Norway as far as Bergen. But he was resisted by the Danish heir to the throne (later Christian II) and treacherously murdered as he sued for peace.

Christian II imposed a crash programme of "Danicization" on the Norwegians and mercilessly hunted down his opponents, but his attempts to dominate the Swedes led to his forced abdication in 1523. The leaders of the Norwegian opposition rallied under the archbishop of Nidaros, Olav Engelbrektsson, but their attempt to gain terms from the new king Frederik I failed. The Danish civil war that followed the death of Frederik resulted in the victory of the Protestant Christian III and the loss of Norway's last independent national institution, the Catholic Church. In 1536 Christian declared that Norway should cease to be a separate country and that the Lutheran faith should be established there. Though slow to take root among the Norwegian peasantry, **Lutheranism** served as a powerful instrument in establishing Danish influence. The Bible, catechism and hymnal were all in Danish, the bishops were all Danes and, after 1537, so were all the most important provincial governors in Norway. Christian even carted the silver casket that had contained the bones of St Olav back to Copenhagen, where he melted it down into coins.

In many respects, Norway became simply a source of raw materials – fish, timber and iron ore – whose proceeds lined the royal purse. Naturally enough, the Swedes coveted these materials too, the upshot being a long and inconclusive war (1563–70) which saw much of Norway ravaged by competing bands of mercenaries. Ironically, the Swedish attempt to capture Norway induced a change of attitude in Copenhagen: keen to keep their subjects happy, a degree of decentralization became the order of the day, and the Danes appointed a Governor-General (*Stattholder*) to administer justice in accordance with traditional Norwegian law.

The **Reformation** in Norway was very much an instrument of Danish colonization rather than a reflection of widespread intellectual ferment: the urban apprentices and craftsmen who fired the movement elsewhere in Europe simply didn't exist in significant numbers in rustic Norway. Neither did the **Renaissance** make much impact: the first printing press wasn't established until 1643, and the reading public remained minuscule, though the country produced a surprising number of humanist writers. Indeed, the only real expression of the Renaissance spirit was imported by **Christian IV** (1588–1648). Among the Danish kings of the period, he proved the most sympathetic to Norway. He visited the country often, improving the quality of its administration and founding new towns – including Kongsberg, Kristiansand and Christiania (later Oslo) – whose buildings were laid out on a spacious gridiron plan.

At last the Norwegian economy began to pick up. The population grew, trade increased and, benefiting from the decline of the Hanseatic League, a native bourgeoisie began to take control of certain parts of the economy, most notably the herring industry. But Norwegian cultural self-esteem remained at a low ebb: the country's merchants spoke Danish, mimicked Danish manners and read Danish literature. What's more, Norway was a constant bone of contention between Sweden and Denmark, the result being a long series of wars in which its more easterly provinces were regularly battered by the competing armies.

The year 1660 marked a turning point in the constitutional arrangements governing Norway. For centuries, the Danish Council of State had had the power to elect the monarch and impose limitations on his or her rule. Now, a powerful alliance of merchants and clergy swept these powers away to make **Frederik III** absolute ruler. This was, however, not a reactionary coup, but an attempt to limit the power of the conservative-minded nobility. In addition, the development of a centralized state machine would, many calculated, provide all sorts of job opportunities to the low-born but adept. Norway was incorporated into the administrative structure of Denmark with royal authority delegated to the *Stattholder*, who governed through what soon became a veritable army of professional bureaucrats.

There were positive advantages for Norway: the country acquired better defences, simpler taxes, a separate High Court and further doses of Norwegian law, but once again power was exercised almost exclusively by Danes. These functionaries were allowed to charge for their services, and there was no fixed tariff – a swindler's charter for which the peasantry paid heavily. So much so, in fact, that one of the *Stattholders*, **Ulrik Gyldenløve**, launched a vigorous campaign against corruption, his efforts rewarded by a far-reaching series of reforming edicts promulgated in 1684.

THE EIGHTEENTH AND EARLY NINETEENTH CENTURIES

The **absolute monarchy** established by Frederik III soon came to concern itself with every aspect of Norwegian life. The ranks and duties of a host of minor officials were carefully delineated, religious observances tightly regulated and restrictions were imposed on everything from begging and dress through to the food and drink that could be consumed at weddings and funerals. This extraordinary superstructure placed a leaden hand on imagination and invention. Neither was it impartial: there were some benefits for the country's farmers and fishermen, but by and large the system worked in favour of the middle class. The merchants of every small town were allocated exclusive rights to trade in a particular area and competition between towns was forbidden. These local monopolies placed the peasantry at a dreadful disadvantage, nowhere more iniquitously than in the Lofotens, where fishermen not only had to buy supplies and equipment at the price set by the merchant, but had to sell their fish at the price set by him too.

The Dano-Norwegian functionaries who controlled Norway also set the **cultural** agenda, patronizing an insipid and imitative art and literature. The writings of **Petter Dass** stand out from the dross, however – heartfelt verses and descriptions of life in the Nordland where he worked as a pastor. There were liberal, vaguely nationalist stirrings too, in the foundation of the Norwegian Society in Copenhagen twelve years later.

More adventurously, there was renewed missionary interest in Norway's old colony of Greenland. Part of it was down to an eccentric ethnic obsession – the clergyman concerned, a certain Hans Egede, was looking for Inuit with Viking features – but Bergen's merchants footed the bill on condition he built them a fur-trading station over there. In the event, it was a poor investment – the trading monopoly was given to a Dane. There was also missionary work in Finnmark, where a determined effort was made to convert the Sami (see box, pp.292–293). This was a very different undertaking from Egede's, and one that reflected the changing temperament of the Lutheran church of Norway, which had been reinvigorated by **pietist** clergymen. One of their number, Thomas von Westen, learnt the Sami language and led an extraordinarily successful mission to the far north. He was certainly a good deal more popular than many of his fellow pietists down south who persuaded Christian VI (1730–46) to impose draconian penalties for such crimes as not observing the Sabbath or not going to church regularly.

In the meantime, there were more wars between Denmark and Sweden. In 1700, **Frederik IV** (1699–1730) made the rash decision to attack the Swedes at the time when their king, Karl XII, was generally reckoned to be one of Europe's most brilliant military strategists. Predictably, the Danes were defeated and only the intervention of the British saved Copenhagen from falling into Swedish hands. Undeterred, Frederik tried again, and this time Karl retaliated by launching a full-scale invasion of Norway. The Swedes rapidly occupied southern Norway, but then, much to everyone's amazement, things began to go wrong. The Norwegians successfully held out in the Akershus fortress in Christiania (Oslo) and added injury to insult by holding on to Halden too. A naval commander, **Peter Tordenskiold**, became a national hero in Norway when he caught the Swedish fleet napping and ripped it to pieces off Strømstad. Karl was forced to retreat, but returned with a new army two years later. He promptly besieged the fortress at Halden for a second time, but while he was touring his troops someone shot him in the head – whether it was one of his own soldiers or a Norwegian has been the subject of heated debate ever since. Whatever the truth, Karl's death enabled the protagonists to agree the **Peace of Frederiksborg** (1720), which ended hostilities for the rest of the eighteenth century.

Peace favoured the growth of trade, but although Norway's economy prospered it was hampered by the increasing **centralization** of the Dano-Norwegian state. Regulations pushed more and more trade through Copenhagen, to the irritation of the majority of Norwegian merchants who were accustomed to trading direct with their customers. Increasingly, they wanted the same privileges as the Danes, and especially, given the chronic shortage of capital and credit, their own national bank. In the 1760s, Copenhagen did a dramatic U-turn, abolishing monopolies, removing trade barriers and even permitting a free press – and the Norwegian economy bloomed. Nonetheless, the bulk of the population remained impoverished and prey to famine whenever the harvest was poor. The number of landless agricultural labourers rose dramatically, partly because more prosperous farmers were buying up large slices of land, and for the first time Norway had something akin to a proletariat.

Despite this, Norway was one of the few European countries little affected by the French Revolution. Instead of political action, there was a **religious revival**, with Hans Nielson Hauge emerging as an evangelical leader. The movement's characteristic hostility to officialdom caused concern, and Hauge was imprisoned, but in reality it posed little threat to the status quo. The end result was rather the foundation of a fundamentalist movement that is still a force to be reckoned with in parts of west Norway.

THE END OF UNION WITH DENMARK

Denmark-Norway had remained neutral throughout the Seven Years' War (1756–63) between England and France, and renewed that neutrality in 1792, during the period leading up to the **Napoleonic Wars**. The prewar years were good for Norway: overseas trade, especially with England, flourished, and demand for Norwegian timber, iron and cargo-space heralded a period of unparalleled prosperity. However, when Napoleon implemented a trade blockade – the Continental System – against Britain, he roped in the Danes. As a result, the British fleet bombarded Copenhagen in 1807 and forced the surrender of the entire Dano-Norwegian fleet. Denmark, in retaliation, declared war on England and Sweden. The move was disastrous for the Norwegian economy, which had suffered bad harvests in 1807 and 1808, and the English blockade of its seaports ruined trade and led to starvation.

By 1811 it was obvious that the Danes had backed the wrong side in the war, and the idea of an equal union with Sweden, which had supported Britain, became increasingly attractive to many Norwegians. By attaching their coat-tails to the victors, they hoped to restore the commercially vital trade with England. They also thought that the new Swedish king would be able to deal with the Danes if it came to a fight – just as the Swedes had themselves calculated when they appointed him in 1810. The man concerned, Karl XIV Johan, was, curiously enough, none other than Jean-Baptiste Bernadotte, formerly one of Napoleon's marshals. With perfect timing, he had helped the British defeat Napoleon at Leipzig in 1813. His reward came in the **Treaty of Kiel** the following year, when the great powers instructed the Danes to cede to Sweden all rights in Norway (although they did keep the dependencies of Iceland, Greenland and the Faroes). Four hundred years of union had ended.

UNION WITH SWEDEN 1814–1905

The high-handed transfer of Norway from Denmark to Sweden did nothing to assuage the growing demands for greater independence. Furthermore, the Danish Crown Prince Christian Frederik roamed Norway stirring up fears of Swedish intentions. The prince and his supporters convened a Constituent Assembly, which met at Eidsvoll in April 1814 and produced a **constitution**. Issued on May 17, 1814 (still a national holiday), this declared Norway to be a "free, independent and indivisible realm" with Christian Frederik as its king. Not surprisingly, Karl Johan would have none of this and, with the support of the great powers, he invaded Norway. Completely outgunned, Christian Frederik barely mounted any resistance. In exchange for Swedish promises to recognize the Norwegian constitution and the *Storting* (parliament), he abdicated as soon as he had signed a peace treaty – the so-called **Convention of Moss** – in August 1814.

The ensuing period was marred by struggles between the *Storting* and **Karl XIV Johan** over the nature of the union. Although the constitution emphasized Norway's independence, Johan had a suspensive veto over the *Storting's* actions; the post of *Stattholder* in Norway could be held by a Swede; and foreign and diplomatic matters concerning Norway remained entirely

in Swedish hands. Despite this, Karl Johan proved popular in Norway, and during his reign the country enjoyed a fair amount of independence. From 1836 all the highest offices in Norway were filled exclusively by Norwegians and democratic local councils were established, in part due to the rise of the peasant farmers as a political force.

The gradual increase in prosperity had important **cultural implications**. The layout and buildings of modern Oslo – the Royal Palace, Karl Johans gate, the university – date from this period. Johan Christian Dahl, the most distinguished Scandinavian landscape painter of his day, was instrumental in the moves to establish the National Gallery in Oslo in 1836, while others began to champion all things Norwegian. One result was a massive six-volume topographical survey of the country by a certain Jens Kraft. Furthermore, the poet, prose writer and propagandist Henrik Wergeland proclaimed the ideals of the Romantic movement, decrying the civil servant culture that had dominated Norway for so long in favour of the more sincere qualities of the peasant farmer. The **temperance movement** sought to bring Norwegian peasantry up to these lofty ideals, and was instrumental in initiating laws to prohibit the use of small stills, once found on every farm; the movement acquired government patronage in 1844. By the mid-nineteenth century, consumption of spirits had dropped drastically and coffee rivalled beer as the national drink.

However, under both Oscar I (1844–59) and Karl XV (1859–72) it was **pan-Scandinavianism** that ruled the intellectual roost. This belief in the natural solidarity of Denmark, Norway and Sweden was espoused by the leading artists of the period, including Henrik Ibsen and Bjørnstjerne Bjørnson. Oscar, a liberal monarch, found himself in some sympathy with the prevailing views, and in 1848 promised aid to Denmark when their troops were forced to withdraw from Schleswig-Holstein in the face of a Prussian advance. Though there was little enthusiasm anywhere for an actual engagement, the gesture was seen as a victory for pan-Scandinavianism. Not so in 1864, though, when Austria and Prussia declared war on Denmark. Karl wanted to help, but Swedish public opinion and the Norwegian *Storting* were unenthusiastic about the prospect, and pan-Scandinavianism died a toothless death. The loudest cries of treachery came from **Henrik Ibsen**, whose poetic drama, *Brand*, was a spirited indictment of Norwegian perfidy.

Economic growth continued. By 1880 Norway had the world's third-largest merchant navy (after the USA and Britain), and whaling expanded with the Norwegian invention of the harpoon. Considerable overpopulation in rural areas at this time was solved to some degree by widespread **emigration** to North America: in 1910 a US census recorded 800,000 of its inhabitants as either first- or second-generation Norwegian.

CULTURE IN THE SECOND HALF OF THE NINETEENTH CENTURY

Culturally, this was a fruitful time for Norway, with the rediscovery of the **Norwegian language** and its folklore by a number of academics. They formed the nucleus of the National Romantic movement, which did much to restore the country's cultural self-respect. Following on were famous authors like Alexander Kielland, who wrote most of his works between 1880 and 1891, and Knut Hamsun, epitomized by his 1890 novel, *Hunger*. As for music, **Edvard Grieg** (1843–1907) was inspired by old Norwegian folk melodies, and two of his most famous suites were composed for Ibsen's *Peer Gynt*. Grieg was at the centre of Oslo musical life between 1866 and 1874, his debut concert as a conductor being the first to consist entirely of works by Norwegian composers. The artist **Edvard Munch** was also active during this period, completing many of his major works in the 1880s and 1890s, while the internationally acclaimed dramatist **Henrik Ibsen** returned to Oslo in 1891 after a prolonged self-imposed exile.

THE RUN-UP TO INDEPENDENCE

Norway's domestic politics changed with the rise to power in the 1850s of **Johan Sverdrup**. Realizing that independence would only come about if the *Storting* assumed real executive power, his new Reform Society won their first success when a bill was passed to allow annual sessions of parliament. That the *Storting* was increasingly determined to rule emerged in the later struggle over whether the king's ministers should be answerable to parliament. Sverdrup's efforts ensured that a bill was passed to that

effect in 1872 and again in 1874 and 1877. Each time, the then king **Oscar II** (who reigned from 1872 until 1907) used his suspensive veto until, in 1880, the bill was passed for the third time in an unchanged form. Thereafter, the *Storting* no longer required royal assent but Oscar still claimed an absolute veto on constitutional matters.

Sverdrup rallied Norwegian support and the 1882 *Storting* elections gave the Venstre (Left) Party a formidable majority. In 1884, the party impeached the supporters of the king's veto, as well as the prime minister. Sverdrup headed a new ministry which was to take its authority from the *Storting*, not the crown – in effect a straight transition to full parliamentary government.

The Venstre Party scored another huge parliamentary majority in 1885. However, the party split over rows concerning the foreign policy of the two countries (solely in Swedish hands since 1814). The year 1891 saw victory for a Radical Left Party under Johannes Steen, which demanded a separate foreign ministry for Norway. Initial demands were for a separate Norwegian consular service, reasonable enough given the extent of the country's merchant shipping interests. But the king refused to agree and the matter was referred to a Union Committee, which sat inconclusively until Steen assumed power again in 1898 with a new majority government. That year, the Flag Law to remove the Union sign from the Norwegian mercantile marine flag became operational, and further attempts at compromise failed. To their credit, Oscar and his prime minister took the crisis calmly and refused to sanction the use of force – an option preferred by the Swedish right.

When the *Storting* finally voted to establish a separate Norwegian consular service in 1905, Oscar again refused to sanction the move. The government resigned, claiming that as the king no longer exercised his constitutional functions the union should be dissolved. A plebiscite in August 1905 returned an overwhelming vote in favour of the **dissolution of the union**, which was duly confirmed by the Treaty of Karlstad. A second plebiscite determined that independent Norway should be a **monarchy** rather than a republic and, in November 1905, Prince Karl of Denmark (Edward VII's son-in-law) was elected to the throne as **Håkon VII**.

EARLY INDEPENDENCE: 1905–39

Norway's independence came at a time of further economic advance, engendered by the introduction of hydroelectric power. Social reforms also saw funds being made available for unemployment relief and accident insurance schemes, and the passage of a Factory Act governing safety in the workplace. An extension to the franchise gave the vote to all men over 25 and, in 1913, to women too. The education system was reorganized, and substantial sums were spent on defence. This prewar period also saw the emergence of a strong trade union movement and of a Labour Party committed to revolutionary change.

Since 1814 Norway had had little to do with European affairs, and at the outbreak of **World War I** it declared itself strictly neutral. Its sympathy, though, lay largely with the Western Allies, and the Norwegian economy boomed as its ships and timber were in great demand. By 1916, however, Norway had begun to feel the pinch as German submarine action hit both enemy and neutral shipping, and by the end of the war Norway had lost half its chartered tonnage and 2000 crew. The Norwegian economy also suffered after the USA entered the war because the Americans imposed strict trade restrictions in their attempt to prevent supplies getting to Germany, and rationing had to be introduced across Norway. Indeed, the price of neutrality was high: there was a rise in state expenditure, a soaring cost of living and, at the end of the war, no seat at the conference table. In spite of its losses, Norway got no share of confiscated German shipping, although it was partly compensated by gaining sovereignty of Spitsbergen and its coal deposits – the first extension of the Norwegian frontiers for 500 years.

In 1920 Norway entered the new League of Nations. Later that decade, the decline in world trade led to decreased demand for Norway's shipping. Bank failure and currency fluctuation were rife, and, as unemployment and industrial strife increased, a burgeoning Norwegian **Labour Party** took advantage. With the franchise extended and the introduction of larger constituencies, it had a chance to win seats outside the large towns for the first time. At the 1927 election the Labour Party, together with the Social Democrats from whom they'd split, were the biggest grouping in the *Storting*.

However they had no overall majority and because many feared their revolutionary rhetoric, they were manoeuvred out of office after only fourteen days. Trade disputes and lockouts continued and troops had to be used to protect scabs.

During the war, **Prohibition** had been introduced as a temporary measure and a referendum of 1919 showed a clear majority in favour of its continuation. But the ban did little to quell – and even exacerbated – drunkenness, and it was abandoned in 1932, replaced by the government monopoly on the sale of wines and spirits that remains in force today. The 1933 election gave the Labour Party more seats than ever. Having shed its revolutionary image, a campaigning, reformist Labour Party benefited from the growing popular conviction that state control and a centrally planned economy were the only answer to Norway's economic problems. In 1935 the Labour Party, in alliance with the Agrarian Party, took power – an unlikely combination since the Agrarians were profoundly nationalist in outlook, so much so that their defence spokesman had been the rabid anti-Semite **Vidkun Quisling**. Frustrated by the democratic process, Quisling had left the Agrarians in 1933 to found *Nasjonal Samling* (National Unification), a fascist movement which proposed, among other things, that both Hitler and Mussolini should be nominated for the Nobel Peace Prize. Quisling had good contacts with Nazi Germany but little support in Norway – local elections in 1937 reduced his local representation to a mere seven, and party membership fell to 1500.

The Labour government presided over an improving economy. By 1938 industrial production was 75 percent higher than it had been in 1914; unemployment had dropped as expenditure on roads, railways and public works increased. Social welfare reforms were implemented and trade union membership increased. When war broke out in 1939, Norway was lacking only one thing – adequate defence. A vigorous member of the League of Nations, the country had pursued disarmament- and peace-oriented policies since the end of World War I and was determined to remain neutral.

WORLD WAR II

In early 1940, despite the threat posed by Hitler, the Norwegians were preoccupied with Allied mine-laying off the Norwegian coast – part of their attempt to prevent Swedish iron ore being shipped from Narvik to Germany. Indeed, such was Norwegian naivety that they made a formal protest to Britain on the day of the German invasion. Caught napping, the Norwegian army offered little initial resistance and the south and central regions of the country were quickly overrun, the Germans declaring that they were there to protect Norway from the British. King Håkon and the *Storting* were forced into a hasty evacuation of Oslo and headed north to Elverum, evading capture by just a couple of hours. Here, at the government's temporary headquarters, the executive was granted full powers to take whatever decisions were necessary in the interests of Norway – a mandate which later formed the basis of the Norwegian government-in-exile in Britain.

The Germans contacted the king and his government in Elverum, demanding, amongst other things, that Quisling be accepted as prime minister as a condition of surrender. Though their situation was desperate, the Norwegians rejected this outright and instead chose resistance. The ensuing campaign lasted for two months and, although the Norwegians fought determinedly with the help of a few British regulars, they were no match for the German army. In June both king and government fled to Britain from Tromsø in northern Norway. The country was rapidly brought under Nazi control, Hitler sending Josef Terboven to take full charge of Norwegian affairs.

The fascist NS was declared the only legal party in Norway and the media, civil servants and teachers were brought under party control. As **civil resistance** grew, a state of emergency was declared: two trade union leaders were shot, arrests increased and a concentration camp was set up outside Oslo. In February 1942 Quisling was installed as "Minister President" of Norway, but it was soon clear that his government didn't have the support of the Norwegian people. The church refused to cooperate, schoolteachers protested and trade union members and officials resigned en masse. In response, deportations increased, death sentences were announced and a compulsory labour scheme was introduced.

Military resistance escalated. A military organization (MILORG) was established as a branch of the armed forces under the control of the High Command in London. By May 1941 it had enlisted 20,000 men (32,000 by 1944) in clandestine groups all over the country. Arms and instructors came from Britain, radio stations were set up and a continuous flow of intelligence about Nazi movements sent back. Sabotage operations were legion, the most notable being the destruction of the heavy-water plant at **Rjukan**, foiling a German attempt to produce an atomic bomb. Reprisals against the resistance were severe, but only a comparative handful of Norwegians actively collaborated with the enemy.

The **government-in-exile** in London continued to represent free Norway to the world, mobilizing support on behalf of the Allies. Most of the Norwegian merchant fleet was abroad when the Nazis invaded, and by 1943 the Norwegian navy had seventy ships helping the Allied convoys. With the German position deteriorating, neutral Sweden adopted a more sympathetic policy to its Norwegian neighbours, allowing the creation of thinly-disguised training grounds for resistance fighters. These camps also served to produce the police detachments that were to secure law and order after liberation.

When the Allies landed in Normandy in June 1944, overt action against the Nazis in Norway by the resistance was discouraged, since the Allies couldn't safeguard against reprisals. By late October, the Russians had crossed the border in the far north. The Germans, forced to retreat, burned everything in their path and drove the local population into hiding. To prevent the Germans reinforcing their beleaguered Finnmark battalions, the resistance planned a campaign of mass railway sabotage, stopping three-quarters of the troop movements overnight. As their control of Norway crumbled, the Germans finally **surrendered** on May 7, 1945. King Håkon returned to Norway on June 7, five years to the day since he'd left for exile.

Terboven committed suicide and the NS collaborators were rounded up. A caretaker government took office, staffed by resistance leaders, and was replaced in October 1945 by a majority **Labour government**. The Communists won eleven seats, reflecting the efforts of Communist saboteurs in the war and the prestige that the Soviet Union enjoyed in Norway after liberation. Quisling was shot, along with 24 other high-ranking traitors, and thousands of collaborators were punished.

POSTWAR RECONSTRUCTION

At the end of the war, Norway was on its knees: the far north – Finnmark – had been laid waste, half the mercantile fleet lost, and production was at a standstill. Recovery, though, fostered by a sense of national unity, was quick; it took only three years for GNP to return to its prewar level. Norway's part in the war had increased her prestige in the world. The country became one of the founding members of the United Nations in 1945, and the first UN Secretary-General, Tryggve Lie, was Norwegian Foreign Minister. With the failure of discussions to promote a Scandinavian defence union, the *Storting* also voted to enter NATO in 1949.

Domestically, there was general agreement about the form that social reconstruction should take. In 1948, the *Storting* virtually unanimously passed the laws that introduced the Welfare State. The 1949 election saw the government returned with a larger majority and Labour governments continued to be elected throughout the following decade. As national prosperity increased, society became ever more egalitarian, levelling up rather than down. Subsidies were paid to the agricultural and fishing industries, wages increased, and a comprehensive social security system helped to eradicate poverty. The state ran the important mining industry, was the largest shareholder in the hydroelectric company and built an enormous steel works at Mo-i-Rana to help develop the economy of the devastated northern counties. Rationing ended in 1952 and, as the demand for higher-level education grew, new universities were created for Bergen, Trondheim and Tromsø.

THE END OF THE POSTWAR CONSENSUS

The political consensus began to fragment in the early 1960s. Following constitutional changes in the 1950s concerning rural constituencies, there was a realignment in centre politics, the outmoded Agrarian Party becoming the **Centre Party**. Defence squabbles within the Labour Party led to the formation of the **Socialist People's Party** (SF), which wanted Norway out of NATO and sought a renunciation of nuclear weapons. The Labour Party's 1961 declaration that no nuclear weapons would be stationed in Norway except under an immediate threat of war did not placate the SF, who unexpectedly took two seats at the election that year. Holding the balance of power, the SF voted with the Labour Party until 1963, when it helped bring down the government over mismanagement of state industries. A replacement coalition collapsed after only one month, but the writing was on the wall. Rising prices, dissatisfaction with high taxation and a continuing housing shortage meant that the 1965 election put a **non-socialist coalition** in power for the first time in twenty years.

Under the leadership of **Per Borten** of the Centre Party, the coalition's programme was unambitious. However, living standards continued to rise and although the 1969 election saw a marked increase in Labour Party support, the coalition hung on to power. Also that year, **oil and gas** were discovered beneath the North Sea and, as the vast extent of the reserves became obvious, so it became clear that the Norwegians were to enjoy a magnificent bonanza – one which was destined to pay about 25 percent of the government's annual bills.

Meanwhile, Norway's politicians, who had applied twice previously for membership of the **European Economic Community** (EEC) – in 1962 and 1967 – believed that de Gaulle's fall in France presented a good opportunity for a third application, which was made in 1970. There was great concern, though, about the effect of membership on Norwegian agriculture and fisheries, and in 1971 Per Borten was forced to resign following his indiscreet handling of the negotiations. The Labour Party, the majority of its representatives in favour of EEC membership, formed a minority administration, but when the 1972 referendum narrowly voted "No" to joining the EEC, the government resigned.

With the 1973 election producing another minority Labour government, the uncertain pattern of the previous ten years continued. Even the postwar consensus on **Norwegian security policy** broke down on various issues – the question of a northern European nuclear-free zone, the stocking of Allied material in Norway – although there remained strong agreement for continued NATO membership.

In 1983, the Christian Democrats and the Centre Party joined together in a non-socialist coalition, which lasted only two years. It was replaced in 1986 by a minority Labour administration, led by **Dr Gro Harlem Brundtland**,

Norway's first woman prime minister. She made sweeping changes to the way the country was run, introducing seven women into her eighteen-member cabinet, but her government was beset by problems for the three years of its life: tumbling oil prices led to a recession, unemployment rose (though only to four percent) and there was widespread dissatisfaction with Labour's high taxation policies.

At the **general election** in September 1989, Labour lost eight seats and was forced out of office – the worst result that the party had suffered since 1930. More surprising was the success of the extremist parties on both political wings – the anti-NATO Left Socialist Party and the right-wing, anti-immigrant Progress Party both scored spectacular results, winning almost a quarter of the votes cast, and increasing their representation in the *Storting* many times over. This deprived the Conservative Party (one of whose leaders, bizarrely, was Gro Harlem Brundtland's husband) of the majority it might have expected, the result being yet another shaky minority administration – this time a **centre-right coalition** between the Conservatives, the Centre Party and the Christian Democrats, led by Jan Syse.

The new government immediately faced problems familiar to the last Labour administration. In particular, there was continuing conflict over joining the **European Community**, a policy still supported by many in the Norwegian establishment but flatly rejected by the Centre Party. It was this, in part, that signalled the end of the coalition, for after just over a year in office, the Centre Party withdrew its support and forced the downfall of Syse. In October 1990, Gro Harlem Brundtland was put back in power at the head of a **minority Labour administration**, remaining in office till her re-election for a fourth minority term in 1993. The 1993 elections saw a revival in Labour Party fortunes and, to the relief of the majority, the collapse of the Progress Party vote. However, it was also an untidy, confusing affair where the main issue, membership of the EU, cut across the traditional left-versus-right divide.

PRESENT-DAY NORWAY

Following the 1993 election, the country tumbled into a long and fiercely conducted campaign over **membership of the EU**. Brundtland and her main political opponents wanted in, but despite the near-unanimity of the political class, the Norwegians narrowly rejected the EU in a referendum on November 28, 1994. It was a close call (52.5 percent versus 47.5 percent), but campaigning by farmers and fishermen, who were unhappy with what they saw as the economic consequences of joining, and by women's groups and environmentalists, who felt that Norway's high standards of social care and "green" policies would suffer, managed to swing opinion against the EU. Unlike the Labour government of 1972, the Brundtland administration soldiered on afterwards, wisely soothing ruffled feathers by promising to shelve the whole EU membership issue until at least 2000.

The 1997 election saw a move to the right, the main beneficiaries being the Christian Democratic Party and the ultra-conservative Progress Party. In itself, this was not enough to remove the Labour-led coalition from office – indeed Labour remained comfortably the largest party – but the right was dealt a trump card by the new Labour leader, **Thorbjørn Jagland**. During the campaign he had promised that the Labour Party would step down from office if it failed to elicit less than the 36.9% of the vote it had secured in 1993. Much to the chagrin of his colleagues, Jagland's political chickens came home to roost when Labour only received 35% of the vote – and the old coalition had to go, leaving power in the hands of an unwieldy right-of-centre, minority coalition. Bargaining with its rivals from a position of parliamentary weakness, the new government has found it difficult to cut a clear path – or at least one very different from its predecessor. That said, it has managed to antagonize the women's movement through some of its social legislation, whose none-too-hidden subtext seems to them to read "A woman's place is in the home."

Environmental issues have attracted much heated debate too, most notably the threat of **acid rain** to the Norwegian countryside. Norway is one of the highest net recipients of sulphurous waste products in the world (many of these from the UK) and records acid pollution levels comparable to the most heavily polluted industrial regions of Europe. The country plays an active role in international campaigning against acid rain, part of a sustained attempt to raise the profile of environmental issues worldwide. This is backed up domestically by increasingly stringent anti-pollution laws. **Road build-**

ing is also becoming very controversial. The long-standing rural isolation of parts of the country led to the postwar aspiration to connect all of the country's villages to the road system. Give or take the occasional hamlet, this has now been achieved and a second phase is underway, involving the upgrading of roads. Wherever this makes conditions safer, the popular consensus for it survives, but there is increasing opposition to the prestige projects so favoured by status-seeking politicians. In part, this change in attitude has been influenced by events abroad, especially the anti-road campaigns in the UK.

Norwegians will not be shifted when it comes to **whaling and sealing**, continuing to stand firmly by industries that they've pursued for decades. This is inexplicable to many Western Europeans, who point to Norway's eminently liberal approach to most other matters, but the Norwegians see things very differently: why, many of them ask, is the culling of seals and mink seen in a different light from the mass slaughter of farmed animals?

In the longer term, quite what Norway will make of its splendid isolation from the EU is unclear. The situation is mitigated by Norway's membership of the European Economic Agreement (**EEA**), the free trade deal of January 1994 to which the EU is also party. Whatever happens, and whether or not there is another EU referendum, it's hard to imagine that the Norwegians will suffer any permanent economic harm. They have, after all, a superabundance of natural resources and arguably the most educated workforce in the world.

This isn't to say the country doesn't collectively fret – a modest increase in the amount of drug addiction and street crime has produced much soul-searching, the belief being that an advanced and progressive social policy should be able to eliminate such barbarisms. This characteristically thoughtful approach is very much to Norway's credit, as is its refusal to be satisfied with a residual level of unemployment (about 6–7 percent) that is the envy of other Western governments.

LEGENDS AND FOLKLORE

Norway has an exceptionally rich body of historical legend and folk tradition, and one that plays an important part in the national consciousness. Most famous are the **sagas**, mainly written in Iceland between the twelfth and fourteenth centuries, and which constitute a vast collection of part-historical, part-fictionalized stories covering several centuries of Norse history. Thanks to the survival of one of these sagas, the *Poetic Edda* (see opposite), our knowledge of **Norse mythology** is far from conjectural. Much that was not recorded there survived in the oral tradition, to be revived from the 1830s onwards by the artists and writers of the National Romantic movement. Some set about collecting the **folk tales** and legends of the rural regions. The difficulties they experienced in rendering the Norwegian dialects into written form – there was no written Norwegian language per se – fuelled the language movement, and sent the academic Ivar Aasen roaming the countryside to assemble the material from which he formulated *Landsmål* (see p.350).

SAGAS

The Norwegian Vikings settled in Iceland in the ninth century, and throughout the medieval period the Icelanders had a deep attachment to, and interest in, their original homeland. The result was a body of work that is one of the richest sources of European medieval literature. That so much of it has survived is due to Iceland's isolation; most Norwegian sources disappeared centuries ago.

All the **sagas** feature real people and tell of events which are usually known to have happened, but the plots are embroidered to suit the tales' heroic style. They reveal much about a Norse culture in which arguments between individuals might spring from comparatively trivial disputes over horses or sheep, but due to a strict code of honour and revenge, every insult, whether real or imagined, had to be avenged, and personal disputes soon turned into clan vendettas. Plots are complex, the dialogue laconic, and the pared-down prose omits unnecessary detail. New characters are often introduced by means of tedious genealogies, neces-

sary to explain the motivation behind their later actions (though the more adept translations render these explanations as footnotes). Personality is only revealed through speech, facial expressions and general demeanour, or the comments and gossip of others.

The earliest Icelandic work, the **Elder** or **Poetic Edda** (various English editions are available), comprises 34 lays dating from as early as the eighth century. It gives insights into early Norse culture and pagan cosmogony and belief; it's not to be confused with the **Younger** or **Prose Edda** (an English edition is published by the University of California Press), written centuries later by the most distinguished of the saga writers, Snorri Sturluson.

Also noteworthy are *The Vinland Saga, Njal's Saga* and the *Laxdaela Saga*, tales of ninth- and tenth-century Icelandic derring-do; and *Harald's Saga*, a rattling good yarn celebrating the life and times of King Harald Hardråda. English translations by Magnus Magnusson and Hermann Palsson of all the above are published by Penguin.

NORSE MYTHOLOGY

The Vikings shared a common **pagan faith,** whose polytheistic tenets were upheld across all of Scandinavia. The deities were worshipped at a thousand village shrines, usually by means of sacrifices in which animals, weapons, boats and other artefacts, even humans, were given to the gods. There was very little theology to sanctify these rituals; instead the principal gods – Odin, Thor and Frey – were surrounded by mythical tales attributing to them a bewildering variety of strengths, weaknesses and powers.

ODIN AND FRIGGA

The god of war, wisdom, poetry and magic, **Odin** was untrustworthy, violent and wise in equal measure. The most powerful of the twelve Viking deities, the Aesir, who lived at Asgard, he was also lord of the **Valkyries**, women warrior-servants who tended his needs while he held court at **Valhalla**, the hall of dead heroes. As with many of the other pagan gods, he had the power to change into any form he desired. Odin's wife, **Frigga**, was the goddess protecting the home and the family.

At the beginning of time, it was Odin who made heaven and earth from the body of the giant Ymir, and created man from an ash tree, woman from an alder. However, **Yggdrasil**, the tree of life which supported the whole universe, was beyond his control; the Vikings believed that eventually the tree would die and both gods and mortals would perish in the **Ragnarok**, the twilight of the gods. Among the Anglo-Saxons, the equivalent of Odin was Woden, hence the origin of the word "Wednesday".

THOR

One of Odin's sons, **Thor** appears to have been the most worshipped of the Norse gods. A giant with superhuman strength, he was the short-tempered god of thunder, fire and lightning. He regularly fought with the evil Frost Giants in Jotunheim (see p.128), his favourite weapon being the hammer, Mjolnir, which the trolls (see opposite) had fashioned for him. His chariot was drawn by two goats – Cracktooth and Gaptooth – who could be killed and eaten at night, but would be fully recovered the next morning, providing none of their bones were broken. It's from Thor that we get "Thursday".

LOKI

A negative force, **Loki** personified cunning and trickery. His treachery turned the other deities against him, and he was chained up beneath a serpent that dripped venom onto his face. His wife, **Sigyn**, remained loyal and held a bowl over his head to catch the venom, but when the bowl was full she had to turn away to empty it, and in those moments his squirmings would cause earthquakes.

FREY

The god of fertility, **Frey**'s pride and joy was Skidbladnir, a ship that was large enough to carry all the gods, but could still be folded up and put into his bag. He often lived with the elves (see opposite) in Elfheim.

FREYA

Freya was the goddess of love, healing and fertility. "Friday" was named after her.

HEL

The goddess of the dead, **Hel** lived on their brains and bone marrow. She presided over "Hel", where those who died of illness or old age went, living a miserable existence under the roots of Yggdrasil, the tree of life.

THE NORNS

Representing the past, the present and the future, the **Norns** were the three goddesses of fate, casting lots over the cradle of every new-born child.

FOLK TALES AND LEGENDS

Norway's extensive oral folklore was first written down in the early nineteenth century, most famously by **Peter Christen Asbjørnsen** and **Jørgen Moe**, whose compilations first started appearing in 1842; these became immensely popular and ran to many editions. Despite all the nationalist kerfuffle about the Norwegianness of the tales, many of them were in fact far from unique to Norway. But while they shared many characteristics – and had the same roots – as folk tales across the whole of northern Europe, they were populated by stock characters who were recognizably Norwegian – the king, for example, was always pictured as a wealthy Norwegian farmer.

There are three types of Norwegian **folk tale**: **comical tales**; **animal yarns**, in which the beasts concerned – most frequently the wolf, fox and bear – talk and behave like human beings; and most common of all, **magical stories** populated by a host of supernatural creatures. The folk tale is always written matter-of-factly, no matter how fantastic the events it retells. In this respect it has much in common with the **folk legend**, though the latter purports to be factual. Norwegian legends "explain" scores of unusual natural phenomenon – the location of boulders, holes in cliffs etc – and are populated by a cast of supernatural beings, again broadly familiar across northern Europe.

The assorted **supernatural creatures** of folk tale and legend hark back to the pagan myths of the pre-Christian era, but whereas the Vikings held them of secondary importance to their gods, in Norwegian folk tales they take centre stage. In post-Christian Norwegian folk tradition, these creatures were regarded as the descendants of children that Eve hid from God. When they were discovered by him, they were assigned particular realms in which to dwell, but their illicit wanderings were legion. Towards the end of the nineteenth century, book illustrations by **Erik Werenskiold** and **Theodor Kittelsen** (see p.80) effectively defined what the various supernatural creatures looked like in the Norwegian public's imagination.

As mythologized in Norway, the creatures of the folk tales possess a confusing range of virtues and vices. Here's a brief guide to some of the more important.

GIANTS

Enormous in size and strength, the **giants** of Norwegian folklore were reputed to be rather stupid and capable both of kindly actions and great cruelty towards humans. They usually had a human appearance, but some were monsters with many heads. They were fond of carrying parts of the landscape from one place to another, dropping boulders and even islands as they went. According to the Eddic cosmogony, the first giant, Ymir, was killed by Odin and the world made from his body – his blood formed the sea, his bones the mountains etc. Ymir was the ancestor of the evil Frost Giants, who lived in Jotunheim, and who regularly fought with Thor.

TROLLS

Spirits of the underground, **trolls** were ambivalent figures, able both to hinder and help humans – and were arguably a folkloric expression of the id. The first trolls were depicted as giants, but later versions were small, strong, misshapen and of pale countenance from living in darkness; sunlight would turn them into stone. They worked in metals and wood and were fabulous craftsmen. They made Odin's spear and Thor's hammer, though Thor's inclination to throw the weapon at them made them hate noise; as late as the eighteenth century, Norwegian villagers would ring church bells for hours on end to drive them away. If the trolls were forced to make something for a human, they would put a secret curse on it; this would render it dangerous to the owner. Some trolls had a penchant for stealing children and others carried off women to be their wives.

ELVES

Akin to fairies, **elves** were usually divided between good-hearted but mischievous white elves, and nasty black elves, who brought injury and sickness. Both lived underground in a world, Elfheim, that echoed that of humans –

with farms, animals and the like – but made excursions into the glades and groves of the forests. At night, the white elves liked singing and dancing to the accompaniment of the harp. They were normally invisible, though you could spot their dancing places wherever the grass grew more luxuriantly in circular patterns than elsewhere. The black elves were also invisible, a good job considering they were extremely ugly and had long, filthy noses. If struck by a sunbeam, they would turn to stone. Both types of elf were prone to entice humans into their kingdom, usually for a short period – but sometimes forever.

WIGHTS

In pre-Christian times, the Vikings believed their lands populated with invisible guardian spirits, the **wights** (*vetter*), who needed to be treated with respect. One result was that when a longship was approaching the shore, the fearsome figurehead at its prow was removed so as not to frighten the *vetter* away. Bad luck would follow if a *vetter* left the locality.

DRAUGEN

Personifying all those who have died at sea, the **draugen** was a ghostly apparition who appeared as a headless fisherman in oilskins. He sailed the seas in half a boat and wailed when someone was about to drown. Other water spirits included the malicious river sprite, the **nixie**, who could assume different forms to lure the unsuspecting to a watery grave. There were also the shy and benign **mermaids** and **mermen**, half-fish and half-human, who dived into the water whenever they spied a human. However they also liked to dress up as humans to go to market.

WITCHES

As with **witches** across the rest of Europe, the Scandinavian version was an old woman who had made a pact with the Devil, swapping her soul in return for special powers. The witch could inflict injury and illness especially if she had something that the victim had touched or owned – anything from a lock of hair to an item of clothing. She could disguise herself as an animal, and had familiars – usually insects or cats – which assisted her in foul deeds. Most witches travelled through the air on broomsticks, but some rode on wolves bridled with snakes.

FLORA
AND FAUNA

There are significant differences in climate between the west coast of Norway, warmed by the Gulf Stream, and the interior, but these variations are of much less significance for the country's flora than altitude and latitude. With regard to its fauna, wild animals survive in significant numbers in the more inaccessible regions, but have been hunted extensively elsewhere. Norway's west coast remains well populated by seabirds.

FLORA

Much of the Norwegian landscape is dominated by vast **forests of spruce**, though they are a fairly recent feature: the original forest cover was mainly of pine, birch and oak, and only in the last two thousand years has spruce spread across the whole of southeast and central Norway. That said, a rich variety of **deciduous trees** – notably oak, ash, lime, hazel, rowan, elm and maple – still flourish in a wide belt along the south coast, up through the fjord country and as far north as Trondheim, but only at relatively low altitudes. For their part, **conifers** thin out at around 900m above sea level in the south, 450m in Finnmark, to be replaced by a birch zone where there are also aspen and mountain ash. These deciduous trees contrive to ripen their seeds despite a short, cool summer, and can consequently be found almost as far north as the Nordkapp (North Cape) – as can the most robust of the conifers, the pine. Some 200m higher up, the birch fizzle out to be replaced by willow and dwarf birch,

while above the timber line are bare mountain peaks and huge plateaux, the latter usually dotted with hundreds of lakes.

Norway accommodates in the region of 2000 plant species, but few of them are native. The most sought-after are the **berrying** species that grow wild all over Norway, mainly cranberries, blueberries and yellow **cloudberries**. Common in the country's peat bogs, and now also extensively cultivated, the cloudberry is a small herbaceous bramble whose fruits have a tangy flavour that is much prized in Norway. In drier situations and on the mountain plateaux, **lichens** – the favourite food of the reindeer – predominate, while in all but the thickest of spruce forests, the ground is thickly carpeted with **mosses** and **heathers**.

Everywhere, spring brings vivid **wild flowers**, splashes of brilliant colour at their most intense on the west coast where a wide range of mountain plants are nourished by the wet conditions and a geology that varies from limestone to acidic granites. Most of these species can also be found in the Alps, but there are several rarities, notably the **alpine clematis** (*Clematis alpina*) found in the Gudbrandsdalen valley, hundreds of miles from its normal homes in eastern Finland and the Carpathian Mountains. Another, larger group comprises about thirty **Canadian mountain plants**, found in Europe only in the Dovre and Jotunheim mountains; quite how they come to be there has long baffled botanists.

The mildness of the west coast winter has allowed certain species to prosper beyond their usual northerly latitudes. Among species that can tolerate very little frost or snow are the star hyacinth (*Scilla verna*) and the purple heather (*Erica purpurea*), while a short distance inland come varieties that can withstand only short icy spells, including the foxglove (*Digitalis purpurea*) and the holly (*Ilex aquifolium*). In the southeastern part of the country, where the winters are harder and the summers hotter, the conditions support species that can lie dormant under the snow for several months a year – for example the blue anemone (*Anemone hepatica*) and the aconite (*Aconitum septentrionale*).

In the far north, certain Siberian species have migrated west down the rivers and along the coasts to the fjords of Finnmark and Troms. The most significant is the **Siberian garlic** (*Allium sibiricum*), which grows in such abundance that farmers have to make sure their cows don't eat too much of it or else the milk becomes onion-flavoured. Other Siberian species to look out for are the fringed pink (*Dianthus superbus*) and a large, lily-like plant, the sneezewort (*Veratrum album*).

FAUNA

The larger Arctic **predators** of Norway, principally the lynx, wolf, wolverine and bear, are virtually extinct, and where they have survived they are mainly confined to the more inaccessible regions of the north. To a degree this has been caused by the timber industry, which has logged out great chunks of forest. The smaller predators – the fox, the Arctic fox, the otter, the badger and the marten – have fared rather better and remain comparatively common.

In the 1930s, the **beaver** had been reduced to just 500 animals in southern Norway. A total ban on hunting has, however, led to a dramatic increase in their numbers, and the beaver has begun to recolonize its old hunting grounds right across Scandinavia. The **elk** has benefited from the rolling back of the forests, grazing the newly treeless areas and breeding in sufficient numbers to allow an annual cull of 40,000 animals; the red deer of the west coast is flourishing too. Otherwise, the Norwegians possess about two million sheep and around 200,000 domesticated **reindeer**, most of whom are herded by the Sami (see box, pp.292–293). The last wild reindeer in Europe, some 15,000 beasts, wander the Hardangervidda and its adjacent mountain areas.

Among Norway's rodents, the most interesting is the **lemming**, whose numbers vary over a four-year cycle. In the first three to four years there is a gradual increase, which is followed, in the course of a few months, by a sudden fall. The cause of these variations is not known, though theories are plentiful. In addition to this four-year fluctuation, the lemming population goes through a violent explosion every eleven to twelve years. Competition for food is so ferocious that many animals start to range over wide areas. In these so-called **lemming years** the mountains and surrounding areas teem with countless thousands of lemmings, and hundreds swarm to their deaths by falling off cliff edges and the like. In lemming years, predators and birds of prey have an abundant source of food and frequently give birth to twice as many young as normal – not surprising considering the lemmings are extremely easy to catch. More inexplicably, the snowy owl leaves its polar habitat in lemming years, flying south to join in the feast: quite how they know when to turn up is a mystery. The Vikings were particularly fascinated by lemmings, believing that they dropped from the sky during thunderstorms.

With the exception of the raven, the partridge and the grouse, all the **mountain birds** of Norway are **migratory**, reflecting the harshness of winter conditions. Most fly back and forth from the Mediterranean and Africa, but some winter down on the coast. Woodland species include the wood grouse, the black grouse, several different sorts of owl, woodpeckers and birds of prey, while the country's lakes and marshes are inhabited by cranes, swans, grebes, geese, ducks and many waders. Most dramatic of all are the coastal nesting cliffs, where millions of **seabirds**, such as kittiwakes, guillemots, puffins, cormorants and gulls, congregate. What you won't see is the great auk, a flightless, 50cm-high bird resembling a penguin that once nested in its millions along the Atlantic seaboard but is now extinct: the last Norwegian great auk was killed in the eighteenth century and the last one of all was shot near Iceland a century later.

The waters off Norway once teemed with **seals** and **whales**, but indiscriminate hunting has drastically reduced their numbers, prompting several late-in-the-day conservation measures. The commonest species of **fish** – cod, haddock, coalfish and halibut – have been over-exploited too, and whereas there were once gigantic shoals of them right along the coast up to the Arctic Sea, they are now much less common. The cod, like several other species, live far out in the Barents Sea, only coming to the coast to spawn, their favourite destination being the waters round the Lofoten Islands.

The only fish along Norway's coast that can survive in both salt and fresh water is the **salmon**, which grows to maturity in the sea and only swims up-river to spawn and later to die. In the following spring the young salmon return to the sea on the spring flood. Trout and char populate the rivers and lakes of western Norway, living on a diet of crustacea which tints their meat pink, like the salmon. Eastern Norway and Finnmark are the domain of **whitefish**, so called because they feed on plant remains, insects and animals, which keep their flesh white. In prehistoric times, these species migrated here from the east via what was then the freshwater Baltic; the most important of them are the perch, powan, pike and grayling.

BOOKS

Books in English on Norway, and for that matter on Scandinavia as a whole, are surprisingly scant: few travellers have written well (or indeed at all) about the region over the years, and historical works tend to concentrate almost exclusively on the Vikings. That said, Norwegian literature is increasingly appearing in translation – notably the Icelandic sagas and selected modern novelists – and it's always worth looking out for a turn-of-the-century *Baedeker's Norway and Sweden*, if only for the phrasebook, from which you can learn the Norwegian for "Do you want to cheat me?", "When does the washerwoman come?" and "We must tie ourselves together with rope to cross this glacier."

Several Scandinavian publishing houses carry a reasonable range of English titles. They include Grøndahl og Dreyers Forlahg, Fred Olsengate 5, PO Box 1153 Sentrum, N-0107 Oslo (☎22 98 56 00); and the Scandinavian University Press, Kolstadgt 1, PO Box 2959, Tøyen, N-0608 Oslo (☎22 57 54 00, fax 22 57 53 53, *www.scup.no*). In the UK, Norvik Press is an excellent source of old and new Scandinavian writing: for their catalogue write to the University of East Anglia, Norwich NR4 7TJ (☎01603/593356, fax 250599, *www.uea.ac.uk/llt/norvik_press*). Their American partners are Dufour Editions, PO Box 449, Chester Springs, Pennsylvania 19425, USA (☎610/458 5005, fax 458 7103).

Most of the books listed below are paperbacks and in print – those that are out of print (o/p) should be easy to track down in secondhand bookshops. Where there are separate UK and US publishers, they are stated in that order and separated by a semicolon; if neither country is mentioned, the book is published by the same company in both. If the book is published outside the UK and US, its city of publication is given.

TRAVEL AND GENERAL

Ranulph Fiennes, *Ice Fall in Norway* (o/p). A jaunt on the Jostedalsbreen glacier with Fiennes and his pals in 1970, long before he got famous. A quick and enjoyable read, though the occasional sexist comment may make you wince.

Thor Heyerdahl, *The Kon-Tiki Expedition* (Flamingo; Washington Square Press). You may want to read this after visiting Oslo's Kon-Tiki Museum (p.89). The intrepid Heyerdahl's accounts of his expeditions aroused huge interest when they were first published, and remain ripping yarns though surprisingly few people care to read them today. You may also want to track down *The Ra Expeditions* and *The Tigris Expedition*, both currently out of print.

Luce Hinsch (et al), *Monuments and Sites: Norway – A Cultural Heritage* (Scandinavian University Press, Oslo). Coffee-table volume with parallel French and English text, exploring the architectural byways of the country in great detail. For the specialist.

Christoph Ransmayr, *The Terrors of Ice and Darkness* (Grove-Atlantic, US). Clever mingling of fact and fiction as the book's main character follows the route of the Austro-Hungarian Arctic expedition in 1873. A story of obsession and, ultimately, madness.

Mark Kurlansky, *Cod: A Biography of the Fish that Changed the World* (Vintage; Penguin). This wonderful book tracks the life and times of the cod and the generations of fishermen who have lived off it. There are sections on over-fishing and the fish's breeding habits, and recipes are provided. Norwegians figure frequently – cod was their staple diet for centuries.

Roy Owen, *Norwegian Railways – from Stephenson to High-Speed* (Balholm Press, UK). In-depth study of the Norwegian railway system, with chapters on everything from passenger rolling stock to the individual lines and signalling.

Constance Roos, *Walking in Norway* (Cicerone, UK). This well-researched and informative guide outlines hiking routes in almost every part of Norway, with useful sections on conditions in the mountains and equipment. It's easily the best of its type on the market, though the descriptions of some of the hiking routes lack detail.

Leif Ryvarden, *Lofoten and Vesterålen* (NOR-TRA Books, Oslo). Available through the Norwegian Tourist Board, this travel book describes every part of the archipelago, which it explores by way of eight suggested routes. The pieces on the history, geology, climate, flora and fauna of the islands are especially useful.

Elizabeth Su-Dale, *Culture Shock, Norway: A Guide to Customs & Etiquette* (Kuperard; Graphic Arts Center Publications). Everything you'd ever wanted to know about the Norwegians and their way of life, and then some. Extremely useful if you're planning a long stay, though the book is a tad conventional in outlook.

Erling Welle-Strand, *Motoring in Norway* (NORTRA Books, Oslo). Available through the Norwegian Tourist Board, this 1997 book details every sight of conceivable interest on almost any part of the Norwegian road system. Also by the same author is *Mountain Hiking in Norway* (NOR-TRA Books, Oslo), a good general introduction to the subject with helpful suggestions for routes.

Mary Wollstonecraft, *Letters written during a Short Residence in Sweden, Norway and Denmark* (Bison & Open Gate; University of Nebraska Press). For reasons that have never been entirely clear, Wollstonecraft, the author of *A Vindication of the Rights of Women*, and mother of Mary Shelley, travelled Scandinavia for several months in 1795. Her letters home represent a real historical curiosity, though her trenchant comments on Norway often get side-lined by her intense melancholia.

HISTORY AND MYTHOLOGY

Peter Christen Asbjørnsen and Jørgen Moe, *Norwegian Folk Tales* (Grøndahl og Dreyers Forlahg, Oslo). Of all the many books on Norwegian folk tales, this is the edition you want – the illustrations by Erik Werenskiold and Theodor Kittelsen are superb. Heinemann (UK) publish this edition too.

Johannes Brøndsted, *The Vikings* (o/p). Extremely readable account with valuable sections on social and cultural life, art, religious beliefs and customs.

Martin Conway, *No Man's Land* (Damms Antikvariat, Oslo). Superb and vastly entertaining account of the history of Spitsbergen (Svalbard) from 1596 to modern times. Full of intriguing detail – when he was 14, Admiral Nelson was almost killed by a polar bear which he set out to hunt on the ice at night.

Fredrik Dahl, *Quisling: A Study in Treachery* (Cambridge University Press). A comprehensive biography of the world's most famous traitor, Vidkun Quisling – the man presented in all his unpleasant fullness.

Rolf Danielsen (et al), *Norway: A History from the Vikings to Our Own Times* (Scandinavian University Press, Oslo). Thoughtful and well-presented account investigating the social and economic development of Norway – a modern and well-judged book that avoids the "kings and queens" approach to its subject.

H.R. Ellis Davidson, *The Gods and Myths of Northern Europe* (Penguin; Viking). A handy, first-rate companion to the sagas, this "who's who" of Norse mythology includes some useful reviews of the more obscure gods. Displaces the classical deities and their world as the most relevant mythological framework for northern and western European culture.

T.K. Derry, *A History Of Scandinavia* (University of Minnesota Press, US). Thorough account of the history of the region, but rather better as a reference source than a read. First published in 1980.

John Haywood, *The Penguin Historical Atlas of the Vikings* (Penguin; Viking). Accessible and attractive sequence of maps charting the development and expansion of the Vikings as explorers, settlers, traders and mercenaries.

David Howarth, *The Shetland Bus* (The Shetland Times Ltd, UK). Entertaining and fascinating in equal measure, this excellent 1951 book, by one of the British naval officers involved, details the clandestine wartime missions that plied between the Shetlands and occupied Norway.

Gwyn Jones, *A History of the Vikings* (Oxford University Press). Superbly crafted, erudite account of the Vikings with excellent sections on every aspect of their history and culture. The same author wrote *Scandinavian Legends and Folk Tales* (o/p), an excellent and enjoyable analysis of its subject.

Ivar Libaek (et al), *A History of Norway* (Grøndahl og Dreyers Forlahg, Oslo). The most accessible and certainly the best illustrated history of Norway. An enjoyable read, but too bulky to take with you.

F. Donald Logan, *The Vikings in History* (Routledge). Scholarly re-examination of the Vikings' impact on medieval Europe; indispensable for the Viking fan.

Magnus Magnusson and Hermann Palsson (translators), *The Vinland Sagas: The Norse Discovery of America* (Penguin; Viking). These two sagas tell of the Vikings' settlement of Greenland and of the "discovery" of North America in the tenth century. The introduction is a particularly interesting analysis of the two outposts.

Alan Palmer, *Bernadotte* (o/p). Biography of Napoleon's marshal, later King Karl Johan of Norway and Sweden, a fascinating figure whom this lively and comprehensive book presents to good effect.

Ronald Popperwell, *Norway* (o/p). Published in 1972, this first-rate and enjoyable history is well-considered and concisely written, and remains perhaps the best book on the subject. Sections provide extremely useful insights into everything from the theatre to prohibition.

Else Roesdahl, *The Vikings* (Penguin). A lucid account of the 300-year reign of Scandinavia's most famous cultural ambassadors, and the traces that they've left throughout northern Europe.

Alexander R. Rumble (et al), *The Reign of Cnut* (Leicester University Press, UK). Often overlooked, King Cnut (aka Canute) ruled a vast swathe of northern Europe – including England and Norway – at the beginning of the eleventh century. This academic book has several interesting chapters on aspects of his reign – for example military developments and his influence on names of people and places in England.

P.H. Sawyer, *Kings and Vikings* (Routledge). Traces the origins of Viking activity, assesses its effects on the rest of Europe and on Scandinavia itself, and follows the Vikings' gradual transformation from bands of pagan raiders into settled, Christian societies.

Kathleen Stokker, *Folklore Fights the Nazis: Humor in Occupied Norway 1940–1945* (University of Wisconsin, US). A book that can't help but make you laugh, and one that also provides a real insight into Norwegian society and its subtle mores. The only problem is that Stokker adopts an encyclopedic approach, which means you have to plough through the poor jokes to get to the good ones.

Raymond Strait, *Queen of Ice, Queen of Shadows: The Unsuspected Life of Sonja Henie* (Scarborough House). In-depth biography of the ice-skating gold medallist, film star and conspicuous consumer, whose art collection was bequeathed to the Oslo museum that bears her name (see p.94).

Snorri Sturluson, *Egil's Saga, Laxdaela Saga, Njal's Saga*, and *King Harald's Saga* (all Penguin; Viking). Icelandic sagas (see p.331), written in the early years of the thirteenth century, and which tell of ninth- and tenth-century derring-do. There's clan warfare in the Laxdaela and Njal sagas, more bloodthirstiness in Egil's, and a bit more biography in King Harald's, penned to celebrate one of the last and most ferocious Viking chieftains – Harald Hardråda (see p.319). Amongst those who worked on these English translations was the UK TV celebrity Magnus Magnusson, who has been a leading light in the effort to popularize the sagas. See also the *Vinland Sagas*, above.

Eilert Sundt, *Sexual Customs in Rural Norway: A Nineteenth-Century Study* (Iowa State University Press, US). First published in 1857, the product of a research trip by a pioneer sociologist, this book doesn't have much sex, but does have lots about rural life – a hard existence if ever there was one. Interesting sections on diet, clothes and associated manners and mores.

ARCHITECTURE AND THE VISUAL ARTS

Marie Bang, *Johan Christian Dahl* (Scandinavian University Press; OUP). Authoritative and lavishly illustrated book on Norway's leading nineteenth-century landscape painter.

Gunnar Bugge, *Stave Churches in Norway* (Grøndahl og Dreyers Forlahg, Oslo). The most complete book on the subject, providing a brief account of every surviving stave church of significance in the country. For the specialist.

Einar Haugen and **Camilla Cai**, *Ole Bull: Norway's Romantic Musician and Cosmopolitan Patriot* (University of Wisconsin Press, US). A neglected figure, Ole Bull, the nineteenth-century virtuoso violinist and utopian socialist, deserves better – and this biography delves into every facet of his eventful career.

J.P. Hodin, *Edvard Munch* (Thames & Hudson). The best available general introduction to Munch's life and work, with much interesting historical detail.

Neil Kent, *The Triumph of Light and Nature: Nordic Art 1740–1940* (Acta Universitatis Upsaliensis, Uppsala). Beautifully illustrated critical chronicle of Scandinavian art during its most influential periods. Highly recommended, but hard to get hold of.

Robert Layton, *Grieg* (Omnibus Press, UK). Clear, concise and attractively illustrated book on Norway's greatest composer. Essential reading if you want to get to grips with the man and his times.

Ole Henrik Moe, *Song of Norway: Norwegian Landscape Painting from 1814 to the Present* (Grøndahl og Dreyers Forlahg, Oslo). Don't be put off by the cumbersome title: this is an excellent introduction to its subject with first-class illustrations and informative text.

Marion Nelson (et al), *Norwegian Folk Art: The Migration of a Tradition* (Abbeville). Lavishly illustrated book discussing the whole range of folk art, from wood carvings through to bedspreads and traditional dress. It's particularly strong on the influence of Norwegian folk art in the US, but the text sometimes lacks focus.

LITERARY FICTION AND BIOGRAPHY

Kjell Askildsen, *A Sudden Liberating Thought* (Norvik, UK). Short stories, in the Kafkaesque tradition, from one of Norway's most uncompromisingly modernist writers. We have printed the title story on pp.344–345.

Jens Bjørneboe, *The Sharks* (Norvik; Dufour). Set at the end of the last century, this is a thrilling tale of shipwreck and mutiny by a well-known Norwegian writer, who had an enviable reputation for challenging authoritarianism of any description. Also recommended is his darker trilogy – *Moment of Freedom, The Powderhouse*

and *The Silence* (all Norvik; Dufour) – exploring the nature of cruelty and injustice.

Johan Bojer, *The Emigrants* (Greenwood; Minnesota Historical Society). One of the leading Norwegian novelists of his day, Bojer (1872–1959) wrote extensively about the hardships of rural life. *The Emigrants*, the only one of his books currently in print in English, deals with a group of young Norwegians who emigrate to North Dakota in the 1880s – and the difficulties they experience. In Norway, Bojer is better-known for *Last of the Vikings* (o/p), a heartrending tale of the fishermen from the tiny village of Rissa in Nordland, who are forced to row out to the Lofoten fishery every winter simply to earn enough money to live. It was first published in 1921.

Camilla Collett, *The District Governor's Daughters* (Norvik; Dufour). Published in 1854, this heartfelt demand for the emotional and intellectual emancipation of women is set within a bourgeois Norwegian milieu. The central character, Sophie, struggles against her conditioning and the expectations of those around her. An important early feminist novel.

Knut Faldbakken, *The Sleeping Prince* (o/p). Shades of *The Lonely Passion of Miss Judith Hearne* in this story of a middle-aged spinster's fantasies as she awaits her sleeping prince – an absorbing and spirited novel by one of Norway's better writers.

Robert Ferguson, *Enigma: the Life of Knut Hamsun* (o/p). Detailed and well-considered biography by an author who also produced *Ibsen*, an in-depth biography of the playwright (Hutchinson, UK).

Jostein Gaarder, *Sophie's World* (Phoenix; Berldey). Hugely popular novel that deserves all the praise heaped upon it – it's beautifully and gently written, with puffs of whimsy all the way through. It bears comparison with Hawking's *A Brief History of Time*, though the subject matter here is philosophy, and there's an engaging mystery story tucked in here too. Also try *Through A Glass Darkly* (Phoenix, UK).

Janet Garton & Henning Sehmsdorf (eds), *New Norwegian Plays* (Norvik Press; Dufour). Four plays written between 1979 and 1983, including work by the feminist writer Bjørg Vik and a Brechtian analysis of Europe in the nuclear age by Edvard Hoem.

Knut Hamsun, *Hunger* (Rebel; Penguin). Norway's leading literary light in the 1920s and early 1930s, Knut Hamsun (1859–1952) was a writer of international acclaim until he disgraced himself by supporting Hitler – for which many Norwegians never forgave him. Recently there has been a resurgence of interest in the author, including the making of a biographical film, *Hamsun*, starring Max von Sydow. Of Hamsun's many novels, it was *Hunger* (1890) that made his name, a trip into the psyche of an alienated and angst-ridden young writer, which shocked contemporary readers. The book was to have a seminal influence on the development of the modern novel. In the latter part of his career Hamsun began advocating a return to the soil and basic rural values. He won the Nobel Prize for Literature for one of his works from this period, *Growth of the Soil* (Souvenir; Random House), but you have to be pretty determined to plough through its metaphysical claptrap.

William Heinesen, *The Black Cauldron* (Dedalus Press; Hippocrene). It would be churlish to omit the Faroese William Heinesen, whose evocative novels delve into the subtleties of Faroese life – and hence also shed light on the related culture of western Norway. This particular book, arguably his best, is rigorously modernistic in approach and style – an intriguing, challenging read, with the circling forces of Faroese society set against the British occupation of the Faroes in World War II.

Sigbjørn Holmebakk, *The Carriage Stone* (Dufour, US). Evil and innocence, suffering and redemption, with death ever-present in the background, make this a serious and powerful novel. These themes are explored through the character of Eilif Grotteland, a Lutheran priest who loses his faith and resigns his ministry.

Henrik Ibsen, *The Complete Major Prose Plays* (Putnam; New American Library). The key international figure of Norwegian literature, Ibsen (see p.147) was a social dramatist, keen to portray contemporary society, in all its forms and with all its hypocrisies, through his characters. Comparatively few of his plays are ever performed in Britain or the US, apart perhaps from *A Doll's House* and *Hedda Gabler*. All his major plays are contained in this inexpensive volume. For a critical appraisal, try James McFarlane's *Ibsen and Meaning* (Norvik Press; Dufour) and see Robert Ferguson on p.339.

Bjorn Larsson, *Long John Silver* (Harvill, UK). This chunky novel, by a Swedish veteran sailor with an extensive knowledge of eighteenth-century British sea lore, uses his specialist knowledge to great effect – a charming twist on Stevenson's original.

Jonas Lie, *The Seer* (Forest Books; Dufour). The celebrated nineteenth-century Norwegian writer – who spent over thirty years living abroad – is represented here by his first great success, the novella *The Seer*, and eight other short stories.

Sigbjørn Obstfelder, *A Priest's Diary* (Norvik Press; Dufour). The last, uncompleted work of a highly regarded Norwegian poet who died of consumption in 1900, aged 33. A moody, intense piece of prose-poetry, it is just a segment of an ambitious project that Obstfelder intended to be his life's major undertaking.

Cora Sandel, *Alberta and Freedom* (Ohio University Press, US); *Alberta Alone* (Ohio University Press, US), *Alberta and Jacob* (The Women's Press; Ohio University Press). The *Alberta* trilogy follows the struggle of a young woman to prove herself in a hostile environment. With its depth of insight and contemporary detail, it ranks as a major work of twentieth-century Norwegian literature.

Amalie Skram, *Under Observation* (Women in Translation, UK). Confined to a mental hospital against her will, Skram (1846–1905) had a terrible time at the hands of her tyrannical male doctor, and based this chunky novel on her experiences. Skram was one of the first women writers in Norway and a pioneer feminist.

Sigrid Undset, *Kristin Lavransdatter: The Bridal Wreath* (Vintage, US)/*The Wreath*, (Penguin, UK), *The Cross* (Vintage), *Gunnar's Daughter* (Penguin, US) and *The Wife* (Penguin). The prolific Undset, one of the country's leading literary lights, can certainly churn it out. This historical series – arguably encapsulating her best work – is set in medieval Scandinavia and has all the excitement of a pulp thriller, along with subtle plots and deft characterisations. Try also her much praised , also set in medieval times.

Herbjørg Wassmo, *Dina's Book: A Novel* (Black Swan; Arcade). Set in rural northern Norway in the middle of the nineteenth century, this strange but engaging tale has a plot centred on a powerful but tormented heroine. See opposite for an extract.

NORWEGIAN LITERATURE

It was **Jostein Gaarder**'s *Sophie's World* that brought Norwegian literature to a worldwide audience in the 1990s, though in fact the Norwegians have been mining a deep, if somewhat idiosyncratic, literary seam since the middle of the nineteenth century. From Ibsen onwards, the country's authors and playwrights have been deeply influenced by Norway's unyielding geography and stern pietism, their preoccupations often focused on anxiety and alienation. **Herbjørg Wassmo** and **Kjell Askildsen**, represented here by one story apiece, are two of Norway's finest contemporary writers.

HERBJØRG WASSMO

Two volumes of poetry marked Herbjørg Wassmo's writing debut in 1976, at the age of 34. She soon turned to prose though, and achieved her greatest recognition with two series of novels about contrasting women. Dina, the female protagonist of *Dina's bok* (Dina's Book, 1989) and *Lykkens sønn* (The Son of Fortune, 1992), is wilful to the point of ruthlessness: she eliminates her husband and, while the funeral is in progress elsewhere, takes a new lover. Yet beneath her toughness is a deep sense of betrayal: rejected as a child by her father after she accidentally caused her mother's death, Dina has grown up expecting anyone she trusts to betray her. Set in the mid-nineteenth century, the Dina stories have as their backdrop a rural community in Wassmo's native northern Norway. The extract we have chosen from *Dina's Book* comes from the beginning of the novel.

DINA'S BOOK

The eyes of the Lord preserve knowledge, and he overthroweth the words of the transgressor.

Proverbs 22:12

Dina had to take her husband, Jacob, who had gangrene in one foot, to the doctor on the other side of the mountain. November. She was the only one who could handle the wild yearling, which was the fastest horse. And they needed to drive fast. On a rough, icy road.

Jacob's foot already stank. The smell had filled the house for a long time. The cook smelled it even in the pantry. An uneasy atmosphere pervaded every room. A feeling of anxiety.

No one at Reinsnes said anything about the smell of Jacob's foot before he left. Nor did they mention it after Blackie returned to the estate with empty shafts.

But aside from that, people talked. With disbelief and horror. On the neighbouring farms. In the parlours at Strandsted and along the sound. At the pastor's home. Quietly and confidentially.

About Dina, the young wife at Reinsnes, the only daughter of Sheriff Holm. She was like a horse-crazy boy. Even after she got married. Now she had suffered such a sad fate.

They told the story again and again. She had driven so fast that the snow crackled and spurted under the runners. Like a witch. Nevertheless, Jacob Gronelv did not get to the doctor's. Now he no longer existed. Friendly, generous Jacob, who never refused a request for help. Mother Karen's son, who came to Reinsnes when he was quite young.

Dead! No one could understand how such a terrible thing could have happened. That boats capsized, or people disappeared at sea, had to be accepted. But this was the devil's work. First getting gangrene in a fractured leg. Then dying on a sleigh that plunged into the rapids!

Dina had lost the power of speech, and old Mother Karen wept. Jacob's son from his first marriage wandered, fatherless, around Copenhagen, and Blackie could not stand the sight of sleighs.

The authorities came to the estate to conduct an inquiry into the events that had occurred up to the moment of death. Everything must be stated specifically and nothing hidden, they said.

Dina's father, the sheriff, brought two witnesses and a book for recording the proceedings. He said emphatically that he was there as one of the authorities, not as a father.

Mother Karen found it difficult to see a difference. But she did not say so.

No one brought Dina down from the second floor. Since she was so big and strong, they took no chance that she might resist and make a painful scene. They did not try to force her to come downstairs. Instead it was decided the authorities would go up to her large bedroom.

Extra chairs had been placed in the room.

And the curtains on the canopy bed were thoroughly dusted. Heavy gold fabric patterned with rows of rich red flowers. Bought in Hamburg. Sewn for Dina and Jacob's wedding.

Oline and Mother Karen had tried to take the young wife in hand so she would not look completely unpresentable. Oline gave her herb tea with thick cream and plenty of sugar. It was her cure for all ills, from the scurvy to childlessness. Mother Karen assisted with praise, hair brushing, and cautious concern.

The servant girls did as they were told, while looking around with frightened glances.

The words stuck. Dina opened her mouth and formed them. But their sound was in another world. The authorities tried many different approaches.

The sheriff tried using a deep, dispassionate voice, peering into Dina's light-grey eyes. He could just as well have looked through a glass of water.

The witnesses also tried. Seated and standing. With both compassionate and commanding voices.

Finally, Dina laid her head of black, unruly hair on her arms. And she let out sounds that could have come from a half-strangled dog.

Feeling ashamed, the authorities withdrew to the downstairs rooms. In order to reach agreement about what had happened. How things had looked at the place in question. How the young woman had acted.

They decided that the whole matter was a tragedy for the community and the entire district. That Dina Grønelv was beside herself with grief. That she was not culpable and had lost her speech from the shock.

They decided that she had been racing to take her husband to the doctor. That she had taken the curve near the bridge too fast, or that the wild horse had bolted at the edge of the cliff and the shaft fastenings had pulled loose. Both of them.

This was neatly recorded in the official documents.

They did not find the body, at first. People said it had washed out to sea. But did not understand how. For the sea was nearly seven miles away through a rough, shallow riverbed. The rocks there would stop a dead body, which could do nothing itself to reach the sea.

To Mother Karen's despair, they gradually gave up the search.

A month later, an old pauper came to the estate and insisted that the body lay in Veslekulpen, a small backwater some distance below the rapids. Jacob lay crooked around a rock. Stiff as a rod. Battered and bloated, the old fellow said.

He proved to be right.

The water level had evidently subsided when the autumn rains ended. And one clear day in early December, the unfortunate body of Jacob Grønelv appeared. Right before the eyes of the old pauper, who was on his way across the mountain.

Afterward, people said the pauper was clairvoyant. And, in fact, always had been. This is why he had a quiet old age. Nobody wanted to quarrel with a clairvoyant. Even if he was a pauper.

Dina sat in her bedroom, the largest room on the second floor. With the curtains drawn. At first she did not even go to the stable to see her horse.

They left her in peace.

Mother Karen stopped crying, simply because she no longer had time for that. She had assumed the duties that the master and his wife had neglected. Both were dead, each in his or her own way.

Dina sat at the walnut table, staring. No one knew what else she did. Because she confided in no one. The sheets of music that had been piled around the bed were now stuffed away in the clothes closet. Her long dresses swept over them in the draught when she opened the door.

The shadows were deep in the bedroom. A cello stood in one corner, gathering dust. It had remained untouched since the day Jacob was carried from the house and laid on the sleigh.

The solid canopy bed with sumptuous bed curtains occupied much of the room. It was so high that one could lie on the pillows and look out through the windows at the sound. Or one could look at oneself in the large mirror with a black lacquered frame that could be tilted to different angles.

The big round stove roared all day. Behind a triple-panelled folding screen with an embroidered motif of beautiful Leda and the swan in an erotic embrace. Wings and arms. And Leda's long, blond hair spread virtuously over her lap.

A servant girl, Thea, brought wood four times a day. Even so, the supply barely lasted through the night.

No one knew when Dina slept, or if she slept. She paced back and forth in heavy shoes with metal-tipped heels, day and night. From wall to wall. Keeping the whole house awake.

Thea could report that the large family Bible, which Dina had inherited from her mother, always lay open.

Now and then the young wife laughed softly. It was an unpleasant sound. Thea did not know whether her mistress was laughing about the holy text or if she was thinking about something else.

Sometimes she angrily slammed together the thin-as-silk pages and threw the book away like the entrails from a dead fish.

Jacob was not buried until seven days after he was found. In the middle of December. There were so many arrangements to be made. So many people had to be notified. Relatives, friends, and prominent people had to be invited to the funeral. The weather stayed cold, so the battered and swollen corpse could easily remain in the barn during that time. Digging the grave, however, required the use of sledge-hammers and pickaxes.

The moon peered through the barn's tiny windows and observed Jacob's fate with its golden eye. Made no distinction between living and dead. Decorated the barn floor in silver and white. And nearby lay the hay, offering warmth and nourishment, smelling fragrantly of summer and splendour.

One morning before dawn, they dressed for the funeral. The boats were ready. Silence lay over the house like a strange piety. The moon was shining. No one waited for daylight at that time of year.

Dina leaned against the windowsill, as if steeling herself, when they entered her room to help her dress in the black clothes that had been sewn for the funeral. She had refused to try them on.

She seemed to be standing there sensing each muscle and each thought. The sombre, teary-eyed women did not see a single movement in her body.

Still, they did not give up at once. She had to change her clothes. She had to be part of the funeral procession. Anything else was unthinkable. But finally, they did think that thought. For with her guttural, animal-like sounds, she convinced everyone that she was not ready to be the widow at a funeral. At least not this particular day.

Terrified, the women fled the room. One after another. Mother Karen was the last to leave.

She gave excuses and soothing explanations. To the aunts, the wives, the other women, and, not least of all, to Dina's father, the sheriff.

He was the hardest to convince. Bellowing loudly, he burst into Dina's room without knocking. Shook her and commanded her, slapped her cheeks with fatherly firmness while his words swarmed around her like angry bees.

Mother Karen had to intervene. The few who stood by kept their eyes lowered.

Then Dina let out the bestial sounds again. While she flailed her arms and tore her hair. The room was charged with something they did not understand. There was an aura of madness and power surrounding the young, half-dressed woman with dishevelled hair and crazed eyes.

Her screams reminded the sheriff of an event he carried with him always. Day and night. In his dreams and in his daily tasks. An event that still, after thirteen years, could make him wander restlessly around the estate. Looking for someone, or something, that could unburden him of his thoughts and feelings.

The people in the room thought Dina Grønelv had a harsh father. But on the other hand, it was not right that such a young woman refused to do what was expected of her.

She tired them out. People decided she was too sick to attend her husband's funeral. Mother Karen explained, loudly and clearly, to everyone she met:

'Dina is so distraught and ill she can't stand on her feet. She does nothing but weep. And the terrible thing is, she's not able to speak.'

First came the muffled shouts from the people who were going in the boats. Then came the scraping of wood against iron as the coffin was loaded onto the longboat with its juniper decorations and its weeping, black-clad women. Then the sounds and voices stiffened over the water like a thin crusting of beach ice. And disappeared between the sea and the mountains. Afterward, silence settled over the estate as though this were the true funeral procession. The house held its breath. Merely let out a small sigh among the rafters now and then. A sad, pitiful final honour to Jacob.

The pink waxed-paper carnations fluttered amid the pine and juniper boughs across the sound in a light breeze. There was no point in travelling quickly with such a burden. Death and its detached supporting cast took their time. It was not Blackie who pulled them. And it was not

Dina who set the pace. The coffin was heavy. Those who bore it felt the weight. This was the only way to the church with such a burden.

Now five pairs of oars creaked in the oar-locks. The sail flapped idly against the mast, refusing to unfurl. There was no sun. Grey clouds drifted across the sky. The raw air gradually became still.

The boats followed one another. A triumphal procession for Jacob Grønelv. Masts and oars pointed toward ocean and heaven. The ribbons on the wreaths fluttered restlessly. They had only a short time to be seen.

Mother Karen was a yellowed rag. Edged with lace, it is true.

The servant girls were wet balls of wool in the wind.

The men rowed, sweating behind their beards and moustaches. Rowing in rhythm.

At Reinsnes everything was prepared. The sandwiches were arranged on large platters. On the cellar floor and on shelves in the large entry were pewter plates filled with cakes and covered by cloths.

Under Oline's exacting supervision, the glasses had been rubbed to a glistening shine. Now the cups and glasses were arranged neatly in rows on the tables and in the pantry, protected by white linen towels bearing the monograms of Ingeborg Grønelv and Dina Grønelv. They had to use the linen belonging to both of Jacob's wives today.

Many guests were expected after the burial.

Dina stoked the fire like a madwoman, although there was not even frost on the windows. Her face, which had been grey that morning, began slowly to regain its colour.

She paced restlessly back and forth across the floor with a little smile on her lips. When the clock struck, she raised her head like an animal listening for enemies.

Translated by Nadia Christensen; reprinted by permission of Norvik Press.

KJELL ASKILDSEN

Born in Mandal in southern Norway in 1929, **Kjell Askildsen** came to literary prominence in the 1950s, when his Kafkaesque accounts of alienated individuals created quite a stir. Subsequent stories adopted a more political tone and although his output has hardly been prolific

– in forty years he has published just five short novels and five slim collections of short stories – by the 1970s, he was widely regarded as one of Scandinavia's finest writers. In recent years, Askildsen has chosen to express himself through the monologues of old men, whose ordinary, everyday struggles hold loneliness and despair at bay, though these are themselves just manifestations of the abyss – the metaphysical nothingness of existence. These are not, however, dreary, self-indulgent monologues, for each is underpinned by a steel-like spirit of endurance and illuminated with sharp flashes of dry humour. Nor are they devoid of human values, such as justice, human dignity, and common decency, upheld in spite of the cool knowledge of life's futility and the quirky frailty of old age. *A Sudden Liberating Thought* was published in 1987.

A SUDDEN LIBERATING THOUGHT

I live in a basement; it's due to the fact that my life has been going downhill, in every sense of the word.

My room has only one window, and only its upper portion is above the sidewalk; this causes me to see the outside world from below. It's not a very big world, but it often feels big enough.

I can only see the legs and the lower part of the body of those who walk by on the sidewalk on my side of the street, but after living here for four years I mostly know to whom they belong. This is because there's little traffic; I live far up a dead end street.

I am a taciturn person, but sometimes I talk to myself. The things I say then have to be said, it seems to me.

One day, having just seen the lower part of the landlord's wife pass by as I stood by the window, I felt suddenly so lonely that I decided to go out.

I put on my shoes and coat and stuck my reading glasses in my coat pocket, just in case. Then I left. The advantage of living in a basement is that you walk up when you are rested and down when you come home tired. That's the only advantage, I guess.

It was a warm summer day. I went to the park beside the abandoned firehouse, where I can usually sit undisturbed. But I had scarcely sat down when some old fellow my own age came along and sat down beside me, though there were plenty of vacant benches. I had gone out because I felt lonely, to be sure, but not to talk;

just for a change. I was becoming more and more nervous that he would say something, and I even thought of getting up and leaving, but where was I to go, this being the place I'd set my mind on. But he remained silent, and that struck me as being so sympathetic that I felt quite well-disposed toward him. I even tried to look at him, without attracting his attention, of course. But he noticed it, because he said, 'You will excuse me for saying so, but I sat down here because I thought I wouldn't be disturbed. I can move if you wish, no trouble.'

'Sit,' I said, somewhat bewildered. Naturally, I didn't make any further attempt to observe him, he had my deepest respect. Naturally too, even more so, I did not speak to him. I felt something strange inside me, something not-lonely, simply a kind of well-being.

He sat there for about half an hour; then he got up, with a bit of difficulty, turned to me and said, 'Thanks. Goodbye.'

'Goodbye.'

He left, taking remarkably long steps and flailing his arms, as though sleep-walking.

The following day at the same time, or a little earlier, I went again to the park. After all the thoughts and speculations he had evoked in me, it seemed somehow the natural thing to do; it was hardly a free choice, whatever that may be.

He came. I saw him from afar and recognized him by his gait. That day too there were vacant benches, and I was curious to know whether he would choose to sit with me. I looked in another direction naturally, pretending I hadn't even seen him, and when he sat down I made as though I didn't notice him. He didn't seem to take any notice of me either; it was a somewhat unusual situation – a sort of unplanned non-meeting. I must admit I felt uncertain whether or not I wanted him to say something, and after half an hour or so I felt just as uncertain whether to leave first or wait till he had gone. Actually, it wasn't an unpleasant uncertainty – I could go on sitting there in any case. But suddenly it occurred to me for some reason or other that he had gotten an edge on me, and then my decision came easily. I stood up, looked at him for the first time and said, 'Goodbye.'

'Goodbye,' he answered, looking me straight in the eye. One couldn't find fault with his glance in any way.

I left. As I was walking away, I couldn't help wondering how he would characterize my gait,

and suddenly I felt my body jam up and my steps turn stiff and awkward. I was annoyed, no use denying it.

That evening as I stood beneath the window looking out – there wasn't very much to see – I thought that if he came the following day I would say something. I even figured out what I was going to say, how I would introduce what might turn out to be a conversation. I would wait a quarter of an hour and then I would say, without looking at him, 'It's about time we start talking.' No more, just that. Then he could answer or not answer, and if he didn't answer I would get up and say, 'In the future I would prefer that you sit on another bench.'

I also came up with many other things that evening, things I would say if a conversation should develop, but I rejected most of them as uninteresting and too commonplace.

The following morning I was excited and uncertain, even wondering whether I shouldn't stay home. I resolutely pushed aside the decision of the evening before; if I did go, I certainly wouldn't say anything.

I went, and he came. I didn't look his way. Suddenly it occurred to me how odd it was that he always came less than five minutes after I myself had turned up – as if he had been standing somewhere nearby and seen me coming. Sure, I thought, of course he lives in one of those buildings beside the firehouse, he can see me from one of the windows.

There was no time to speculate any further on this, for he suddenly began talking. I have to admit that what he said made me feel pretty uneasy.

'Excuse me,' he said, 'but if you don't mind, perhaps it's about time we start talking.'

I didn't answer right away; then I said, 'Perhaps. If there's something to say.'

'You aren't sure there's anything to say?'

'I'm probably older than you.'

'That's not impossible.'

I didn't say any more. I felt a disagreeable uneasiness, on account of the peculiar exchange of roles that had taken place. He was the one who had started the conversation, and very nearly with my own words, and it fell to me to answer as I had imagined he might answer. It was as if I could just as well be him and he just as well be me. It was disagreeable. I wanted to leave. But having, so to speak, been forced to identify with him, I found it difficult to hurt or even offend him.

A minute may have gone by before he said, 'I'm eighty-three.'

'Then I was right.'

Another minute passed.

'Do you play chess?' he asked.

'A long time ago.'

'Almost nobody plays chess any more. All those I've played chess with have died.'

'It's been at least fifteen years,' I said.

'The most recent one died last winter. No great loss actually, he didn't have his wits about him any more. I would always beat him after less than twenty moves. But he did get a certain pleasure from it, presumably the last pleasure that remained to him. Maybe you knew him.'

'No,' I said quickly, 'I didn't know him.'

'How can you be so... Well, that's your business.'

He was certainly right about that and I felt like saying so, but gave him credit for not completing his question.

Then I saw him turn his face to look at me. He sat like this for quite a while. It was anything but pleasant, so I got my eyeglasses from my coat pocket and put them on. Everything in front of me – trees, houses, benches – disappeared in a fog.

'You're nearsighted?' he said after a while.

'No,' I said, 'quite the contrary.'

'I mean – you need glasses to see what's far away.'

'No, quite the contrary. It's the things nearby I have problems with.'

'I see.'

I didn't say any more. When I noticed that he turned his face away again, I removed my glasses and put them back in my pocket. He said nothing more either, so when I thought a suitable amount of time had passed, I got up and said courteously, 'Thanks for the chat. So long.'

'So long.'

I walked away with firmer steps that day, but when I got home and had calmed down, I started again making hasty plans for my next meeting with him. Pacing the floor, I came up with many absurdities, a subtlety or two as well; I wasn't above triumphing over him a bit, but that was simply because I looked upon him as my equal, in spite of everything.

I didn't sleep well that night. When I was still young enough to believe that the future could offer surprises, it often happened that I slept poorly, but that was long ago, before it became clear to me, I mean absolutely clear, that the day you die it doesn't matter whether you've had a good or a miserable life. So the fact that I slept poorly that night both surprised and upset me. Nor had I eaten anything that could've caused it, only a couple of boiled potatoes and a tin of sardines; I had slept soundly on that many times before.

The following day he didn't come until almost a quarter of an hour had gone by. I had started giving up hope – it was an unaccustomed feeling: having a hope to give up. But then he came.

'Good morning,' he said.

'Good morning.'

Then we said nothing more for a while. I knew very well what I would say if the pause grew too long, but I preferred that he talk first, and he did.

'Your wife ... is she still alive?'

'No, she isn't, it's been a long time, I've mostly forgotten her. And yours?'

'Two years ago. Today.'

'Oh. Then it is a day of mourning of sorts.'

'Well, yes. You can't help feeling the loss, of course. But I don't celebrate it by visiting her grave, if that's what you mean. Graves are a damn nuisance. Beg pardon. I didn't choose my words very well.'

I didn't answer.

'Beg pardon,' he said, 'if I've hurt your feelings, I didn't mean it that way.'

'You haven't.'

'Good. For all I knew you might even be religious. I had a sister who believed in eternal life. What conceit!'

I was again struck by the fact that he actually sat there speaking my lines, and for a moment I was foolish enough to think that it was nothing but my imagination, that he didn't even exist, that in reality I sat there talking to myself. And it was probably this piece of folly that made me ask a completely unpremeditated question, 'Who are you really?'

Fortunately he didn't answer immediately, so I managed to edge away somewhat from a rather awkward situation.

'Don't misunderstand me. I wasn't really speaking to you. It was simply that I came to think of something.'

I noticed how he turned his face to look at me, but this time I didn't take out my glasses. I said, 'Besides, I would rather not leave the impression that I am in the habit of asking about things to which there are no answers.'

Afterward we sat in silence. It wasn't a restful silence; I would have preferred to leave. In a couple of minutes, I thought – if he hasn't said anything in two minutes I'll leave. And I began to count the seconds in my mind. He didn't say anything, and I got up, to the second. He also got up, the very same moment.

'Thanks for the chat,' I said.

'The same to you. Too bad you won't play chess.'

'I don't think you would enjoy it very much. Besides, your partners seem to be in the habit of dying.'

'Yes indeed,' he said, suddenly seeming absent-minded.

'So long,' I said.

'So long.'

That day I was more tired than usual when I got home; I had to lie down a few moments. After a while I said aloud, 'I'm old. And life is very long.'

When I woke up the next morning it was raining. To say I was disappointed would be putting it mildly. But as the day wore on and the rain didn't let up, I realized I would go to the park no matter what. I wouldn't be able not to. It wasn't important to me that he should show up as well, that wasn't the point. It was only that, if he came, I wanted to – had to – be there. As I found myself sitting on that wet bench in the rain, I even hoped he wouldn't come. There was an element of exposure, of indecency, in sitting so completely alone in a rain-soaked park.

But he came all right – didn't I know it! By contrast with me, he wore a black raincoat that reached almost to the ground. He sat down.

'You defy the weather,' he said.

It was obviously meant just as an observation, but because of what I had been thinking immediately before he turned up, it seemed to me somewhat tactless, so I didn't answer. I noticed I had become ill-humoured and that I regretted having come. Besides, I was starting to get wet and my coat felt heavy, it seemed almost ludicrous to go on sitting there, so I said, 'I just went out for some fresh air, but then I got tired. I'm an old man.'

And to forestall any speculations on his part, I added, 'Old habit, you know.'

He didn't say anything, which struck me, quite absurdly, as being provocative. And what he said finally, after a long pause, didn't make me feel any more well-disposed toward him.

'You don't like people very much, do you, or am I mistaken?'

'Like people?' I answered. 'What do you mean?'

'Well, you know, it's only the sort of thing one says. I didn't mean to be intrusive.'

'Of course I don't like people. And of course I like people. If you asked me if I liked cats or goats, or butterflies for that matter, but people. Besides, I hardly know anybody.'

I regretted my last remark at once, but luckily that was not what he latched on to.

'That was quite something,' he said. 'Goats and butterflies!'

I could hear him smiling. I had to admit I had been unduly dismissive, so I said, 'If you want a general answer to a general question, I do like both goats and butterflies more unconditionally than I like people.'

'Thanks, I got the point long ago. I'll remember to be more precise the next time I presume to ask you something.'

He said this in a friendly way, and it is no exaggeration to say that I felt sorry, even though my being difficult was simply due to my low spirits. And because I felt sorry, I said something I at once felt sorry having said, 'Beg pardon, but words are almost the only things still left to me. Beg pardon.'

'By all means. It was my fault. I ought to have considered who you are.'

My heart sank – did he know who I was? Did he come here every day because he knew who I was? I couldn't help feeling both uneasy and insecure, so much so that I acted almost automatically, sticking my hand into my coat pocket in search of my glasses.

'What do you mean?' I said. 'Do you know me?'

'Yes. If that's the right word. We have met before. I didn't realize it when I first sat down on this bench. It gradually dawned on me that I'd seen you before, I just wasn't able to place you, not till yesterday. It was something you said, and suddenly I knew what my connection with you was. You don't remember me, do you?'

I stood up.

'No.'

I looked straight at him. I was quite unaware of ever having seen him.

'I am... I was your judge.'

'You, you –"

I couldn't think of anything more to say.

'Sit down, please.'

'I'm wet. Indeed! You were… so it was you. Indeed! Well, goodbye, I have to go.'

I left. It wasn't a dignified exit, but I was upset, and I walked faster than I'd done in many years. When I got home I had barely the strength to rid myself of my soaked overcoat before tumbling into bed. I had violent palpitations, and I was firmly determined never to set foot in the park again.

But after a few moments, when my pulse functioned normally again, my thoughts began to do so as well. I accepted my reaction: something hidden had emerged into the light again and I'd been caught off guard, that was all. There was no mystery about it.

I got up from the bed. It gives me a certain satisfaction to state that I was my old self once more, completely. I planted myself underneath the window and said aloud, 'He shall see me again.'

The following day the nice weather was back, which was a relief, and my coat was practically dry. I went to the park at the usual time; he wasn't going to notice anything irregular about me, or imagine he'd got an edge on me.

But when I approached the bench he was already there, so he was the one who was behaving irregularly.

'Good morning,' he said.

'Good morning,' I answered, taking my seat, and so as to take the bull by the horns I added at once, 'I thought you might not show up today.'

'Bravo,' he said. 'Zero for you.'

That was an answer I couldn't find fault with. He was, indeed my equal.

'Did you often feel guilty?' I asked.

'I don't understand.'

'As a judge, did you often feel guilty? After all, it was your profession to assign to others the required amount of guilt.'

'It was my profession to define the law on the basis of other people's assessment of guilt.'

'Are you trying to excuse yourself? It isn't necessary.'

'I didn't feel guilty. On the other hand, I often felt at the mercy of the law's rigidity. As in your own case.'

'Yes. Because you're not superstitious, after all.'

He gave me a quick glance.

'What do you mean by that?' he said.

'It is only superstitious people who think it is a doctor's business to prolong the suffering of those who are doomed.'

'Aha, I understand. But aren't you afraid that legalization of euthanasia could be misused?'

'Of course it couldn't be misused. For then euthanasia would no longer be euthanasia but murder.'

He didn't answer; I cast a sidelong glance at him: he had a sullen, impassive expression. That was okay by me, though I didn't know whether his sullenness was due to what I had said, or whether he simply looked like that habitually; it was hard to tell, since I had practically never looked at him. Now I felt like making up for lost time and inspecting him thoroughly, and so I did, openly, turning my face and staring at his profile. It was the least I could permit myself in the presence of the man who had sentenced me to prison for several years. I even fished out my glasses and placed them on my nose. It wasn't at all necessary, I could see him clearly without, but I felt a sudden desire to provoke him. It was so unlike me to stare directly at a person that I felt alien to myself for a moment; it was a strange and not at all disagreeable sensation. And the fact that I committed this one breach of my usual behaviour turned out to be surprisingly infectious. For the first time in many years, I laughed; it must have sounded quite ugly. Anyway, without looking at me, he said in a brusque tone, 'I don't care what you're laughing at, but it doesn't sound like you're enjoying yourself. And that's a pity. For in other respects you are a sensible person.'

I immediately felt mollified, as well as a little ashamed, and I withdrew my eyes from his angry profile, saying, 'You're right. It wasn't much of a laugh.'

More than that I didn't want to give him.

We sat in silence. I thought about my wretched life and grew melancholy. I visualized the judge's home, with good chairs and big bookshelves.

'You probably have a housekeeper?' I said.

'Yes. Why do you ask about that?'

'I'm merely trying to imagine the existence of a retired judge.'

'Oh, it's nothing to brag about. You know, the inactivity, all those idle days.'

'Yes, time refuses to pass.'

'And it's the only thing that's left.'

'Time that gets to feel too slow, full of illness to boot perhaps, which slows it even more – then it's over. And when the moment finally comes, we think: what a meaningless life.'

'Well, meaningless – '

'Meaningless.'

He didn't answer. Neither of us said another word. After awhile I got up, however lonely I felt; I didn't want to share my depression with him.

'Goodbye,' I said.

'Goodbye, doctor.'

Depression breeds sentimentality, and the word 'doctor,' spoken without a tinge of irony, sent a warm wave through me. I turned abruptly and hurried off. And right there and then, before I was out of the park, I knew I wanted to die. I wasn't surprised; at most I was surprised that I wasn't. All at once both my depression and my sentimentality seemed to have vanished. I slowed my pace, feeling an inward calm that called for slowness.

When I got home, still feeling a lucid calm inside me, I took out writing paper and an envelope. On the envelope I wrote: 'To the judge who sentenced me.' Then I sat down at the little table where I usually eat and began to write this story.

Today I went to the park for the last time. I was in a strange, almost audacious mood, due perhaps to the unaccustomed joy I had felt in putting my previous meetings with the judge into words or, more likely, to the fact that I hadn't wavered in my decision, not for a moment.

Today, too, he was sitting there when I came. I thought he looked troubled. I greeted him more amicably than usual, it came quite naturally to me. He gave me a quick glance, as if to ascertain whether I really meant it.

'Well,' he said, 'you're having one of your better days today?'

'I'm having my good day, yes. And you?'

'Reasonably good, thanks. So you don't believe any more that life is meaningless?'

'Oh yes, completely.'

'Hmm. I wouldn't be able to live with such a realization.'

'You're forgetting the instinct of self-preservation, aren't you? It's very tenacious and has been the bane of many a rational decision.'

He didn't answer. I hadn't intended to sit there long, so after a brief pause I said, 'We won't be seeing each other any more. Today I've come to say goodbye.'

'Is that so? What a pity. Are you going away?'

'Yes.'

'And you won't be back?'

'No.'

'Hmm. Really. I hope you won't think me too familiar when I tell you I'll miss our meetings.'

'Nice of you to say so.'

'Time will drag even more.'

'There are lonely men sitting on many other benches.'

'Oh, you don't understand what I mean. May I ask where you're going?'

Some have maintained that he who knows he's going to die within twenty-four hours feels free to do whatever he wants. It isn't true; one is, even then, incapable of acting contrary to one's nature, one's self. To be sure, giving him an open and honest answer wouldn't have been to behave contrary to my nature, but I had decided in advance not to reveal my destination to him, seeing no reason why I should upset him – he was, in spite of everything, the only person who would be bereaved by my passing, if I may say so. But what should I answer?

'You will be informed,' I said at last.

I noticed he was taken aback, but he didn't say anything. Instead he put his hand in his inside pocket and took out his wallet. After looking around in it for a moment, he held out his card to me.

'Thanks,' I said, putting it in my coat pocket. I felt I should go. I got up. He too got up. He held out his hand. I took it.

'Take care,' he said.

'Thanks, you too. Goodbye.'

'Goodbye.'

I left. I had a feeling he didn't sit down again, but I didn't turn around to check. I walked calmly homeward, thinking about nothing in particular. Something inside me was smiling. After reaching the basement I stood awhile underneath the window and looked out at the empty street, before sitting down at the table to finish this story. I'm going to put the judge's card on top of the envelope.

It's done. In a moment I'll fold the sheets and place them in the envelope. And now, just before it's going to happen, as I am about to undertake the only definitive act a human being is capable of executing, there is one thought that overshadows all the others: Why didn't I do this long ago?

Translated by Sverre Lyngstad;
reprinted by permission of Norvik Press.

A BRIEF GUIDE TO NORWEGIAN

There are two official Norwegian languages: **Riksmål** or **Bokmål** (book language), a modification of the old Dano-Norwegian tongue left over from the days of Danish dominance; and **Landsmål** or **Nynorsk**, which was codified during the nineteenth-century upsurge of Norwegian nationalism and is based on rural dialects of Old Norse provenance. Roughly eighty percent of schoolchildren have *Bokmål* as their primary language, and the remaining twenty percent are *Nynorsk* speakers, concentrated in the fjord country of the west coast and the mountain districts of central Norway. Despite the best efforts of the government, *Nynorsk* is in decline – in 1944 fully one-third of the population used it. As the more common of the two languages, *Bokmål* is what we use here.

You don't really need to know any Norwegian to get by in Norway. Almost everyone speaks some English, and in any case many words are not too far removed from their English equivalents; there's also plenty of English (or American) on billboards, the TV and at the cinema. Mastering "hello" or "thank you" will, however, be greatly appreciated, while if you speak either Danish or Swedish you should have few problems being understood. Incidentally, Norwegians find Danish easier to read than Swedish, but orally it's the other way round.

BASIC PHRASES

do you speak English?	*snakker du engelsk?*	excuse me	*unnskyld*
yes	*ja*	good morning	*god morgen*
no	*nei*	good afternoon	*god dag*
do you understand?	*forstår du?*	good night	*god natt*
I don't understand	*jeg forstår ikke*	goodbye	*adjø*
I understand	*jeg forstår*	today	*i dag*
please	*vær så god* (is near enough, though actually there's no direct equivalent).	tomorrow	*i morgen*
		day after tomorrow	*i overmorgen*
		in the morning	*om morgenen*
thank you (very much)	*takk* (*tusen takk*)	in the afternoon	*om ettermiddagen*
you're welcome	*vær så god*	in the evening	*om kvelden*

SOME SIGNS

entrance	*inngang*	cycle path	*sykkelsti*
exit	*utgang*	no smoking	*røyking forbudt*
gentlemen	*herrer/menn*	no camping	*camping forbudt*
ladies	*damer/kvinner*	no trespassing	*uvedkommende forbudt*
open	*åpen*	no entry	*ingen adgang*
closed	*stengt*	pull/push	*trekk/trykk*
arrival	*ankomst*	departure	*avgang*
police	*politi*	parking fees	*avgift*
hospital	*sykehus*		

QUESTIONS AND DIRECTIONS

where? (where is/are?)	*hvor?* (*hvor er?*)	can you direct me to . . . ?	*kan de vise meg veien til . . . ?*
when?	*når?*	it is/there is	*det er* (*er det?*)
what?	*hva?*	(is it/is there)	
how much/many?	*hvor mye/hvor mange?*	what time is it?	*hvor mange er klokken?*
why?	*hvorfor?*	big/small	*stor/liten*
which?	*hvilket?*		
what's that called in Norwegian?	*hva kaller man det på norsk?*		

Phrasebooks are thin on the ground, but Berlitz's Norwegian–English mini-dictionary has a useful grammar section and a menu reader, while Routledge's more comprehensive (and much heavier) *Norwegian Dictionary* has much the same. As for learning the language, there are tapes and books in the *Teach Yourself Norwegian* course, by Margaretha Danbolt Simons.

PRONUNCIATION

Pronunciation can be tricky. A **vowel** is usually long when it's the final syllable or followed by only one consonant; followed by two it's generally short. Unfamiliar ones are:

ae before an r, as in b**a**d; otherwise as in s**ay**

ø as in f**u**r but without pronouncing the r

å usually as in s**aw**

øy between the **ø** sound and b**oy**

ei as in s**ay**

Consonants are pronounced as in English except:

c, q, w, z found only in foreign words and pronounced as in the original language

g before i, y or ei, as in **y**et; otherwise hard

hv as in **v**iew

j, gj, hj, lj as in **y**et

rs almost always as in **sh**ut

k before i, y or j, like the Scottish lo**ch**; otherwise hard

sj, sk before i, y, ø or øy, as in **sh**ut

cheap/expensive	*billig/dyrt*	near here?	*i nærheten?*
early/late	*tidlig/sent*	how do I get to . . . ?	*hvordan kommer jeg til . . . ?*
hot/cold	*varm/kald*		
near/far	*i nærheten/langt borte*	how far is it to . . . ?	*hvor langt er det til . . . ?*
good/bad	*god/dårlig*	ticket	*billett*
vacant/occupied	*ledig/opptatt*	single/return	*en vei/tur-retur*
a little/a lot	*litt/mye*	can you give me a lift to . . . ?	*kan jeg få sitte på til . . . ?*
more/less	*mer/mindre*		
can we camp here?	*kan vi campe her?*	left/right	*venstre/høyre*
is there a youth hostel	*er det et vandrerhjem*	go straight ahead	*kjør rett frem*

NUMBERS

0	*null*	9	*ni*	18	*atten*	70	*sytti*
1	*en*	10	*ti*	19	*nitten*	80	*åtti*
2	*to*	11	*elleve*	20	*tjue*	90	*nitti*
3	*tre*	12	*tolv*	21	*tjueen*	100	*hundre*
4	*fire*	13	*tretten*	22	*tjueto*	101	*hundreogen*
5	*fem*	14	*fjorten*	30	*tretti*	200	*to hundre*
6	*seks*	15	*femten*	40	*førti*	1000	*tusen*
7	*sju*	16	*seksten*	50	*femti*		
8	*åtte*	17	*sytten*	60	*seksti*		

DAYS AND MONTHS

Sunday	*søndag*	January	*januar*	August	*august*
Monday	*mandag*	February	*februar*	September	*september*
Tuesday	*tirsdag*	March	*mars*	October	*oktober*
Wednesday	*onsdag*	April	*april*	November	*november*
Thursday	*torsdag*	May	*mai*	December	*desember*
Friday	*fredag*	June	*juni*		
Saturday	*lørdag*	July	*juli*		

(Note: days and months are never capitalized)

GLOSSARY

Apotek Chemist.

Bakke Hill.

Bokhandel Bookshop.

Bre Glacier.

Bro/bru Bridge.

Brygge Quay or wharf.

Dal Valley/dale.

DNT (Den Norske Turistforening) Nationwide hiking organisation whose local affiliates maintain hiking paths across almost all of the country.

Domkirke Cathedral.

Drosje Taxi.

E.kr AD.

Elv/bekk River/stream.

Ferje/ferge Ferry.

Fjell/berg Mountain.

Flybussen Airport bus (literally "plane bus").

F.kr BC.

Foss Waterfall.

Gågate Urban pedestrianised area.

Gate (gt.) Street.

Gamle byen Literally "Old Town"; used wherever the old part of town has remained distinct from the rest (eg Fredrikstad, p.108). Also spelt as one word.

Hav Ocean.

Havn Harbour.

Hurtigbåt Passenger express boat; usually a catamaran.

Hurtigrute Literally "quick route", but now familiar to tourists as the name of the boat service along the west coast from Bergen to Kirkenes.

Hytte Cottage, cabin.

Innsjø Lake.

Jernbanestasjon Railway station.

Kirke/kjerke Church.

Kfum/kfuk Norwegian YMCA/YWCA.

Klokken/kl. O'clock.

Klippfisk Salted fish, usually cod.

Moderasjon Discount or price reduction.

Moms or mva Sales tax – applied to almost all consumables.

Museet Museum.

NAF Nationwide Norwegian automobile association. Membership covers rescue and repair.

NORTRA Government agency, partly privatized, responsible for producing much tourist literature and a series of books on various aspects of Norway – from fishing through to motoring.

Rabatt Discount or price reduction.

Rådhus Town hall.

Rorbu Originally a simple wooden cabin built near the fishing grounds for incoming (ie non-local) fishermen. Many cabins are now used as tourist accommodation.

Sami Formerly called Lapps, the Sami inhabit the northern reaches of Norway, Finland and Sweden – Lapland.

Sentrum City or town centre.

Sjø Sea.

Sjøhus Harbourside building where the catch was sorted, salted, filleted and iced. Many are now redundant and some have been turned into tourist accommodation.

Skog Forest.

Slott Castle, palace.

Stavkirke Stave church.

Storting Parliament.

Tilbud Special offer.

Torget Main town square, often home to an outdoor market; sometimes spelt Torvet.

Vandrerhjem Youth hostel.

Vann/vatn Water or lake.

Vei/veg/vn. Road.

Øy/øya Islet.

ART AND ARCHITECTURAL TERMS

Ambulatory Covered passage around the outer edge of the choir in the chancel of a church.

Art Deco Geometrical style of art and architecture popular in the 1930s.

Art Nouveau Style of art, architecture and design based on highly stylized vegetal forms.

Popular in the early part of the twentieth century.

Baroque The art and architecture of the Counter-Reformation, dating from around 1600 onwards, and distinguished by extreme ornateness, exuberance and complex but harmonious spatial arrangement of interiors.

Classical Architectural style incorporating Greek and Roman elements – pillars, domes, colonnades etc – at its height in the seventeenth century and revived, as Neoclassical, in the nineteenth century.

Fresco Wall painting – made durable through applying paint to wet plaster.

Gothic Architectural style of the thirteenth to sixteenth centuries, characterized by pointed arches, rib vaulting, flying buttresses and a general emphasis on vertical lines.

Misericord Ledge on choir stall on which occupant can be supported while standing; often carved with secular subjects (bottoms were not thought worthy of religious ones).

Nave Main body of a church.

Neoclassical Architectural style derived from Greek and Roman elements – pillars, domes, colonnades, etc – popular in Norway throughout the nineteenth century.

Renaissance Movement in art and architecture developed in fifteenth-century Italy.

Rococo Highly florid, light and graceful eighteenth-century style of architecture, painting and interior design, forming the last phase of Baroque.

Rood screen Decorative screen separating the nave from the chancel.

Romanesque Early medieval architecture distinguished by squat forms, rounded arches and naive sculpture.

Stucco Marble-based plaster used to embellish ceilings, etc.

Transept Arms of a cross-shaped church, placed at ninety degrees to nave and chancel.

Triptych Carved or painted work on three panels. Often used as an altarpiece.

Vault An arched ceiling or roof.

INDEX

In Norwegian, the letters Æ, Ø and Å are considered to come at the end of the alphabet, after Z; entries in this index are arranged accordingly.

Stay in touch with us!

ROUGH*NEWS* **is Rough Guides' free newsletter. In four issues a year we give you news, travel issues, music reviews, readers' letters and the latest dispatches from authors on the road.**

I would like to receive ROUGH*NEWS*: please put me on your free mailing list.

NAME . . . .

ADDRESS . . . .

Please clip or photocopy and send to: Rough Guides, 62–70 Shorts Gardens, London WC2H 9AB, England or Rough Guides, 375 Hudson Street, New York, NY 10014, USA.

IF KNOWLEDGE IS POWER,
THIS ROUGH GUIDE IS A POCKET-SIZED
BATTERING RAM

£6.00
US$9.95

Written in plain English, with no hint of jargon, the Rough Guide to the Internet will make you an Internet guru in the shortest possible time. It cuts through the hype and makes all others look like nerdy textbooks

AT ALL BOOKSTORES • DISTRIBUTED BY PENGUIN

www.roughguides.com

Check out our Web site for unrivalled travel information on the Internet.
Plan ahead by accessing the full text of our major titles, make travel reservations and keep up to date with the latest news in the Traveller's Journal or by subscribing to our free newsletter ROUGH*NEWS* · packed with stories from Rough Guide writers.

ROUGH GUIDES: Travel

Amsterdam
Andalucia
Australia

Austria
Bali & Lombok
Barcelona
Belgium &
  Luxembourg
Belize
Berlin
Brazil
Britain
Brittany &
  Normandy
Bulgaria
California
Canada
Central America
Chile
China
Corfu & the
  Ionian Islands
Corsica
Costa Rica
Crete
Cyprus
Czech & Slovak
  Republics
Dodecanese &
  the East Aegean

Dominican
  Republic
Egypt
England
Europe
Florida
France
French Hotels &
  Restaurants
  1999
Germany
Goa
Greece
Greek Islands
Guatemala
Hawaii
Holland
Hong Kong &
  Macau
Hungary
India
Indonesia
Ireland
Israel & the
  Palestinian
  Territories
Italy
Jamaica
Japan
Jordan
Kenya

Laos
London
Los Angeles
Malaysia,
  Singapore &
  Brunei
Mallorca &
  Menorca
Maya World
Mexico
Morocco
Moscow
Nepal
New England
New York
New Zealand
Norway
Pacific
  Northwest
Paris
Peru
Poland
Portugal
Prague
Provence & the
  Côte d'Azur
The Pyrenees
Rhodes & the
  Dodecanese
Romania
St Petersburg

San Francisco
Sardinia
Scandinavia
Scotland
Scottish
  highlands and
  Islands
Sicily
Singapore
South Africa
South India
Southwest USA
Spain
Sweden
Syria

Thailand
Trinidad &
  Tobago
Tunisia
Turkey
Tuscany &
  Umbria
USA
Venice
Vienna
Vietnam
Wales
Washington DC
West Africa
Zimbabwe &
  Botswana

AVAILABLE AT ALL GOOD BOOKSHOPS

ROUGH GUIDES: Mini Guides, Travel Specials and Phrasebooks

MINI GUIDES

Antigua
Bangkok
Barbados
Big Island of
  Hawaii
Boston
Brussels
Budapest

Dublin
Edinburgh
Florence
Honolulu
Jerusalem
Lisbon
London
  Restaurants
Madrid
Maui
Melbourne
New Orleans
Seattle
St Lucia

Sydney
Tokyo
Toronto

TRAVEL SPECIALS

First-Time Asia
First-Time
  Europe
Women Travel

PHRASEBOOKS

Czech
Dutch

Egyptian Arabic
European
French
German
Greek
Hindi & Urdu
Hungarian
Indonesian
Italian
Japanese

Mandarin
  Chinese
Mexican
  Spanish
Polish
Portuguese
Russian
Spanish
Swahili
Thai
Turkish
Vietnamese

AVAILABLE AT ALL GOOD BOOKSHOPS

ROUGH GUIDES:
Reference and Music CDs

REFERENCE

Classical Music
Classical:
  100 Essential CDs
Drum'n'bass
House Music
Jazz
Music USA

Opera
Opera:
  100 Essential CDs
Reggae
Reggae:
  100 Essential CDs
Rock
Rock:
  100 Essential CDs
Techno
World Music
World Music:
  100 Essential CDs
English Football
European Football

Internet
Millennium

ROUGH GUIDE MUSIC CDs

Music of the
  Andes
Australian
  Aboriginal
Brazilian Music
Cajun & Zydeco

Classic Jazz
Music of
  Colombia
Cuban Music
Eastern Europe

Music of Egypt
English Roots
  Music
Flamenco
India & Pakistan
Irish Music
Music of Japan
Kenya & Tanzania
Native American
North African
Music of Portugal

Reggae
Salsa
Scottish Music
South African
  Music
Music of Spain
Tango
Tex-Mex
West African
  Music
World Music
World Music Vol 2
Music of
  Zimbabwe

AVAILABLE AT ALL GOOD BOOKSHOPS

Discover the music of Scandinavia

THE ROUGH GUIDE

Artists include:

Värttina (Sweden)

Wimme (Samiland)

JPP (Finland)

Sorten Muld
(Denmark)

Hedningarna
(Sweden)

Knut Reiersrud
(Norway)

Sample the rich fiddle tradition of Sweden, the bold experimentation of Finnish musicians and Lapland's Sami joik together with tracks reflecting the cultural diversity of Norway, Iceland, Greenland and Denmark. A fascinating overview of the thriving musics springing from Nordic roots.

Other available Rough Guide music CDs and cassettes include: Irish Folk, English Roots, Eastern Europe, Gypsies, Salsa Dance, Tango, Brazil, Cuba, Africa, South Africa, Zimbabwe and many more!

The Rough Guide CDs (and cassettes) are available worldwide through selected record and book shops.

You can also order direct from World Music Network
(£9.99 per CD and £6.99 per cassette + £1.95 p&p per order)

To place an order or to receive a free catalogue with details of over 40 Rough Guide CDs contact:

WORLD · MUSIC · NETWORK

6 Abbeville Mews, 88 Clapham Park Road, London SW4 7BX
tel: 020 7498 5252 • fax: 020 7498 5353
email: post@worldmusic.net • website: www.worldmusic.net

STANFORDS
MAPS
CHARTS
BOOKS

Est.1852

World Travel starts at Stanfords

Maps, Travel Guides, Atlases, Charts
Mountaineering Maps and Books, Travel Writing
Travel Accessories, Globes & Instruments

Stanfords
12-14 Long Acre
Covent Garden
London
WC2E 9LP

Stanfords
at Campus Travel
52 Grosvenor Gardens
London
SW1W 0AG

Stanfords
at British Airways
156 Regent Street
London
W1R 5TA

Stanfords in Bristol
29 Corn Street
Bristol
BS1 1HT

International Mail Order Service
Tel: 0171 836 1321 **Fax**: 0171 836 0189

The World's Finest Map and Travel Bookshops

Net Savings @Hostelling International

Don't leave your booking to chance

If you can't afford to gamble... don't!

HOSTELLING INTERNATIONAL

netsavings@hostellinginternational.org.uk

the perfect getaway vehicle

low-price holiday car rental.

rent a car from holiday autos and you'll give yourself real freedom to explore your holiday destination. with great-value, fully-inclusive rates in over 4,000 locations worldwide, wherever you're escaping to, we're there to make sure you get excellent prices and superb service.

what's more, you can book now with complete confidence. our £5 undercut* ensures that you are guaranteed the best value for money in holiday destinations right around the globe.

drive away with a great deal, call holiday autos now on **0990 300 400** and quote ref RG.

holiday autos miles ahead

*in the unlikely event that you should see a cheaper like for like pre-paid rental rate offered by any other independent uk car rental company before or after booking but prior to departure, holiday autos will undercut that price by a full £5. we truly believe we cannot be beaten on price.